£12.00

3775. 109

SM402

ENGLISH PLACE-NAME SOCIETY

The English Place-Name Society was founded in 1924 to carry out the survey of English place-names and to issue annual volumes to members who subscribe to the work of the Society. The Society has issued the following volumes:

The volumes for the following counties are in preparation: *Berkshire, Cheshire* (Part 5), *Dorset, Kent, Leicestershire & Rutland, Lincolnshire, the City of London, Shropshire, Staffordshire.*

All communications with regard to the Society and membership should be addressed to:

THE HON. SECRETARY, English Place-Name Society, University College, Gower Street, London W.C.1.

ENGLISH PLACE-NAME SOCIETY. VOLUME XLVII
FOR 1969–70

GENERAL EDITOR
K. CAMERON

THE PLACE-NAMES OF
CHESHIRE

PART IV

ENGLISH PLACE-NAME SOCIETY. VOLUME XLVII

THE PLACE-NAMES OF CHESHIRE

By
J. McN. DODGSON

PART IV
THE PLACE-NAMES OF
BROXTON HUNDRED AND
WIRRAL HUNDRED

CAMBRIDGE
AT THE UNIVERSITY PRESS
1972

Published by the Syndics of the Cambridge University Press

Bentley House, 200 Euston Road, London NW1 2DB

American Branch: 32 East 57th Street, New York, N.Y.10022

© English Place-Name Society 1972

Library of Congress Catalogue Card Number: 77–96085

ISBN: 0 521 08247 1

Printed in Great Britain
at the University Printing House, Cambridge
(Brooke Crutchley, University Printer)

The collection from unpublished documents of material for the Cheshire volumes has been greatly assisted by grants received from the British Academy

CONTENTS

PREFACE

THIS IS the penultimate volume of *The Place-Names of Cheshire*. Part V will contain the place-names of the City of Chester and its suburbs, the general Introduction to the whole work, and the usual apparatus of indexes. In Part IV, as in the previous Parts, there are a number of references to matters which will be dealt with in Part V, and these are listed in the Index of Cross-references. I apologise again, for that system of publication which causes the apparatus of the work to appear last of all, and I am grateful for the patience of those who use these books and who await the many explanations which have been deferred to the final Part.

I owe an apology, also, to Professor John Kousgård Sørensen for the mishandling of his name in numerous instances where I have acknowledged his help. Mutual friends advise me (he being, of course, too modest to object) that in his own country he is referred to as J. Kousgård Sørensen. I hope that in the interest of economy he will overlook my abbreviation of his name to 'Sørensen' and 'J. K. Sørensen' in my references, and forgive 'J. M. Dodgson' for this breach of etiquette.

JOHN McNEAL DODGSON

University College London
St Hilary's Day 1971

ADDENDA AND CORRIGENDA

Notes and material supplied by the following correspondents are indicated by initials.

A.R.   Mr Alexander Rumble, Research Assistant to the Society
R.N.D. Mr R. N. Dore
B.D.   Professor Bruce Dickins
K.J.   Professor Kenneth Jackson

VOL. XLIV

THE PLACE-NAMES OF CHESHIRE, PART I

p. xxvii. Add '*CroR* Rental of Crown Rents, co. Chester, National Library of Wales MS. 9089 D.'.

p. xxxix. Add '*Shrews* The Cartulary of Shrewsbury Abbey, National Library of Wales MS. 7851 D (l13, with additions from 14 and 15).'

p. xliii. Add 'o *more*'.

p. 7. For WIRRALL read WIRRAL.

p. 21, s.n. R. DEE. The Welsh form of the r.n. is used for the name of the city in *Cestria quem Kambri Deverdoeu dicunt* 1189 Gir VI 139. (B.D.)

pp. 21–2, s.n. R. DEE. See also addendum to 4 56–7 s.n. STRETTON.

p. 38, s.n. R. WEAVER. Add '*aqua de Wyure* 1321 *StRO*'. (A.R.)

p. 39, s.v. ROAD-NAMES, III. Add '*le Blakestrete* 1343 *Chol* (in Capenhurst), v. 4 202.'.

pp. 40–1, s.v. VII. See now addendum to 4 56–7 s.n. STRETTON.

p. 42, s.v. VIII. See now addendum to 4 56–7 s.n. STRETTON.

pp. 43–4, s.v. X. See now addendum to 4 56–7 s.n. STRETTON.

p. 53, s.n. *Hardgreue*. See addendum to 4 228 s.n. HARGRAVE.

p. 83, s.n. *Harewode*. See addendum to 4 228 s.n. HARGRAVE.

p. 101, s.n. HAREBARROW. See addendum to 4 228 s.n. HARGRAVE.

p. 114, l. 7. Add '*Mac(k)sfield* 1660 *StRO*'. (A.R.)

p. 138, s.n. HARROP. See addendum to 4 228 s.n. HARGRAVE.

p. 138, s.n. SALTERSFORD. Add '*Sawtersfield* 1660 *CroR*'. (A.R.)

p. 164, s.n. WINCLE. For '[winklə]' read '['winkəl]', and cf. 2 vii.

p. 207, s.n. WORTH. Add '*Wr'th* 1281 (1578) *ChRR* (p)'. (R.N.D., A.R.).

p. 244, l. 14. For '250 *supra*' read '250 *infra*'.

p. 256, s.n. BOSDEN. Add '*Bosed'n* (lit. *Boled'n*) 1281 (1578) *ChRR* (p)'. (R.N.D., A.R.)

p. 278, FIELD-NAMES, (*b*), s.n. *Rasseboth*'. Add '*v.* 4 xiv (addendum to 2 25 s.n. Ross Mill in Hale) for another instance of rasse.'.

p. 314, s.n. HAREWOOD LODGE. See addendum to 4 228 s.n. HARGRAVE.

VOL. XLV

THE PLACE-NAMES OF CHESHIRE, PART II

p. 12, s.n. BAGULEY. Add '*Baggel'g'* 1281 (1578) *ChRR* (p)'. (R.N.D., A.R.)

p. 17, s.n. CARRINGTON. B.D. observes that the pers.n. *Kari* is found in ON as well as ODan. See addendum to 4 147 s.n. *Caryngfeld*.

p. 24, s.n. OLLERBARROW. Delete 'lost,'. R.N.D. observes that the house still exists among the shops in the main shopping street of Hale. Until recently a sub-police-station, it is now a W.V.S. centre. It is a 'listed' building and there is no doubt of its identity. Sheaf[3] 32 is misleading, and refers only to the demolition of the outbuildings of Ollerbarrow early this century when it ceased to be a farm.

p. 25, s.n. ROSS MILL. R.N.D. draws attention to the following forms, A.R. has verified the *ChRR* reading; *molendinum meum de Rasse* 1281 (1578) *ChRR* (PRO, Chester 2, 238, m5v; the form is omitted from the calendar in DKR xxxix 190; the document is indifferently reported by J. P. Earwaker *Local Gleanings* xi (May 1880)), *Rass Mill* 19 Balshaw *Stranger's Guide to Altrincham*. These spellings indicate that this p.n., and probably also the associated Ross Mill Mdw, Ross Flatts, 2 12, contains the el. rasse, which may now be more confidently supposed in *Rasseboth'* etc., in Dukinfield (1 278, where it is discussed).

p. 27, para (*b*). Add '*le Crossidhock*' 1281 (1578) *ChRR* (a boundary-mark, 'oak-tree marked with a cross', from ME *crossed* (not recorded in this sense until 1494 NED) and āc);' and '*le Holghebrock*' 1281 (1578) *ChRR* ('brook at a hollow', *v.* holh, brōc);'.

p. 27, para. (*b*), s.n. *Shurley*. Add '*Schyrlgsyche, Schirlgsyche* 1281 (1578) *ChRR* (PRO, Chester 2, 238, m5v, probably a bad copy for *Schyrl'gsyche* etc.; Earwaker, *Local Gleanings* xi (May 1880), reads *Styrlgsyche* erroneously), 'the watercourse at *Schirl'g*', *v.* sīc.'. (R.N.D., A.R.)

p. 28, s.n. RINGWAY. Add '*Ringeye* 1281 (1578) *ChRR* (PRO, Chester 2, 238, m5v), *Ringeie* 1281 (1578) Local Gleanings (J. P. Earwaker, *Local Gleanings relating to Lancashire and Cheshire*, xi (May 1880); a translation of *ChRR* loc. cit.). The imparking of the woods of Hale lying in Ringway is referred to in this record.'. (R.N.D., A.R.)

p. 30, s.n. DAVENPORT GREEN. Hamo de Massy, lord of Dunham, granted land in Hale and Ringway formerly held by Robert de le Heth, to Jurdan son of Peter de *Dauenepord*' 1281 (1578) *ChRR* (PRO, Chester 2, 238, m5v). (R.N.D., A.R.)

p. 50, s.n. *Harlagh*. See addendum to 4 228 s.n. HARGRAVE.

p. 57, l. 17. Add '*Rosthesthorn* 16 *Harl*. 2061'.

p. 73, s.n. KNUTSFORD. Add '*Knitsford* 1660 *CroR*'. (A.R.)

p. 94, para. (*b*), l. 6. For 'an elder' read 'wild plum'.

p. 94, para. (*b*), l. 8. For 'Sørenson' read 'Sørensen'.

p. 101, s.n. ARLEY. See addendum to 4 228 s.n. HARGRAVE.

p. 148, s.n. DARESBURY. Add '[ˈdɛːrzbəri] older local [ˈdɑːrzbri]'. l. 2. For *-byre* read *-byr(e)*.

p. 173, s.n. NORTON PRIORY, l. 5. Add '*Norton nuper prioratus* 1660 *CroR*,'. Note also part of the buildings, *Fitton house in Norton Priorie* 1660 *CroR*, from the surname *Fitton*.

p. 176, s.n. RUNCORN. Add '*Rancorn* 1660 *CroR*'. (A.R.)

p. 178, s.n. MILLBROW. Add '*Rancorn Mill* 1660 *CroR*'. (A.R.)

pp. 195–6, s.n. CONDATE. See addendum to 4 56–7 s.n. STRETTON.

p. 196, l. 18. For '(King Street 1 43), Iter x,' read '(King Street, 1 43 (Route X)),'.

p. 208, s.n. SHIPBROOK. Add '*Shippebroke* 1351 *StRO*'. (A.R.)

p. 238, s.n. HARBUTT'S FIELD. Add 'The various routes and p.ns. from AntIt are further discussed 4 xiv (addendum to 4 56–7 s.n. STRETTON).'.

p. 241, l. 2. After 'ib,' add '*Mideluuychus* 1153–81 (1346) (m15) *Shrews*,'. l. 5. After '*-wiche*' add ', *-Witch*'.

p. 262, s.n. WARMINGHAM. Add '*Wormingeham* 1290 *StRO*'. (A.R.)

p. 263, s.n. MILL HO. Cf. *molend' in Wormingeham* 1290 *StRO* (D 593, A, 1, 18, 8). (A.R.).

p. 301, s.n. DAVENPORT. Add '*Dauenepord*' 1281 (1578) *ChRR* (p)'. (R.N.D., A.R.).

p. 308, s.n. SCHOLAR GREEN. Add *Schelagh*' 1366 (m15) (p), *Scolehull* 1397 (m15) (p), *Scolehall*' 1420 (m15), all from *Harl*. 2061.

p. 319, s.n. *Harewodehacrus*. See addendum to **4** 228 s.n. HARGRAVE.
p. 326, col. 1, l. 4. For '*Codingeheye*' read '*Codingeheye*'.
col. 1, l. 8. For '*C*raplow' read '*C*raplow'.

VOL. XLVI

THE PLACE-NAMES OF CHESHIRE, PART III

p. 29, s.n. MAYOWSE. For 'Childer Thornton 325' read 'Thornton Hough 326'.
p. 30, s.n. NANTWICH. Add '*salina...de Wichio* m12 *StRO, in Wichia* l12 *StRO, in Wicho Maubench* m12 *StRO, in predicto Wiko* l13 *StRO*'. (A.R.)
p. 34, s.n. WOOD ST. Add '*in alto Wodestret*(*e*) c.1297, 1321 *StRO, alterum Wodestrete* 1321 *ib*, 'the high-, the other Wood St.'.'. (A.R.).
p. 38, l. 15. After '1548 Pat', insert '*the Lead Wallings in Nantwich* 1660 *CroR*,'. (A.R.)
p. 38, l. 20. Note that William de Chetelton mentions *salinam meam de Wichio... iuxta fossam prope illam de Worulestona* ('my salt-house in the Wich...next to the ditch near the salt-house of Worleston') m12 *StRO* (D593, A, 1, 28, 1). (A.R.)
p. 79, s.n. SALTERSICH. Add '*Salteresiche, Saltaressiche* l13 *StRO*'. (A.R.)
p. 82, s.n. AUDLEM. Add '*Audelima* m12 *StRO* (p)'. (A.R.)
p. 130, s.n. AUSTERSON. Add '*elfstaneston*' m12 *StRO* (p)'. (A.R.)
p. 151, s.n. WORLESTON. Add '*Worulestona* m12 *StRO*'. (A.R.)
p. 169, s.n. STOCKERLANE, l. 4. Add '*Stokhall iuxta Darnall* 1442 *StRO*'. (A.R.)
pp. 169–70, s.n. POOLHEAD. Add '*piscaria in Darnall pole* 1442 *StRO*'. (A.R.)
p. 210, s.n. *Harlescloh*. See addendum to **4** 228 s.n. HARGRAVE.
p. 211, s.n. HAREWOOD HILL. See addendum to **4** 228 s.n. HARGRAVE.
pp. 221–2, s.n. FRODSHAM. Add '*Frodeshall* 1660 *CroR*'. (A.R.)
p. 224, s.n. MILL BANK. Add '*Frodeshall Mill* 1660 *CroR*'. (A.R.)
p. 244, l. 3, s.n. The Hurst. Add '*Hurst* l13–e14 (m15) *Harl.* 2061, f. 24*r*'.
p. 277, l. 5. Add '*Kelshall* 1366 (m15) *Harl.* 2061 (p)'.
p. 320, l. 9 from foot, s.n. TIRESFORD. For 'l13 (n.d.) Sheaf' read 'l13–e14 (m15) *Harl.* 2061'.
p. 325, s.v. CHILDER THORNTON. Delete '29,'.
p. 326. Before 'THREAPWOOD' insert 'THORNTON HOUGH, 29: **4**'.

VOL. XLVII

THE PLACE-NAMES OF CHESHIRE, PART IV

p. 3, s.n. Harrow Flan. Add '(*v.* 262 *infra*)'.
p. 4, s.n. BICKERTON FM. Add '*v.* 262 *infra*'.
p. 5, ll. 5–8. Some authorities think Smith's explanation nonsense, but it is worth its place in the Society's volumes because it is a feasible figurative interpretation which happily invites the place-name student to the contemplation of folk-lore and etymology at the same time as it offers occasion for experiment and exercise in the field.
p. 8, s.n. HETHERSON GREEN. The first el. might be an OE pers.n. *Hǽðhere*. (B.D.)
p. 12, s.n. Bourth. *Bourth* is not a likely anglicization of Welsh *y berth*, which would have produced English *berth*.
p. 16, s.n. THE KOPJE. B.D. observes that the spelling *Kopje* would be due to the Boer War 1899–1902. The name is that of a coppice in the park of Bolesworth Castle. It appears in the 6″ O.S., 1912 Edition, Sheet LIV. N.E.
p. 19, s.n. Scutch Fd. 'Either 'a field covered with couch-grass' or 'a field on which flax or hemp is scutched'.' (B.D.)

p. 20, s.n. *Huclou*; p. 27, s.n. *Hocloue*. Alternatively, cf. Hucklow Db 131, from an OE pers.n. *Hucca*, and Huxley 101 *infra*.

p. 20, s.n. *Tikehall*. Add 'Cf. Tickhill YW 1 52.'

p. 27, s.n. *Hocloue*. See addendum to p. 20, s.n. *Hucloue*.

pp. 28–9, s.n. CUDDINGTON. B.D. concurs with Dr von Feilitzen upon OE *Cud(d)a*. OE *Cydda* should be withdrawn.

p. 37, s.n. MACEFEN. K.J. observes that Welsh *ffin* has [iː], a high front long vowel, and in *maes ffin* or *maes y ffin* it bears the main stress. The English form *Macefen* ['meisfen] requires the original Welsh [iː] to be shortened and lowered by English speakers in what became the unstressed syllable of an anglicized borrowed name, since otherwise one would expect the form *Macefine* with [ai].

p. 39, s.n. MALPAS. The Lat. forms ll. 6–8 are in ablative case after *de* in surnames, etc. The nominative form of the p.n. is exemplified by *Malus Passus* 1189 Gir, etc.

p. 42, s.n. Gams Hillock. Davy Gam esquire was killed at Agincourt, *Henry V* IV viii. (B.D.)

p. 50, s.n. *Dyotesmor*. B.D. observes the modern surname *Dyott*.

p. 55, s.n. *Mabotesmedewe*. B.D. notes the modern surname *Mabbott*.

p. 55, s.n. *Stotefilismedue*. B.D. suggests the meaning 'bullock' for stot (cf. ON *stútr* 'bullock').

p. 55, s.n. HORTON. Add '[ˈhɔːrtən]'.

pp. 56–7, s.n. STRETTON; and in other references to AntIt and to the place-names CONDATE, BOVIUM, MEDIOLANUM at 1 40–41 (Route VII), 42 (Route VIII), 43–4 (Route X), 2 196, 238, 3 302. The treatment of the AntIt material in parts 1–4 of *The Place-Names of Cheshire* has been overtaken by an important study (also based upon better textual apparatus), 'The British Section of The Antonine Itinerary' by A. L. F. Rivet, with an appendix on the place-names by Kenneth Jackson, in *Britannia* 1 (1970) 34–82, which arrives in time to be at once a relief and an embarrassment.

The Ch parts of the British section of AntIt, following Mr Rivet's text, are as follows. Iter II: *Mamucio* (Manchester) – xviii Roman miles (actually 20) – *Condate* (2 195–6, in Witton near Northwich) – xx – *Deva leg xx Vic* (Chester) – x – *Bovio* (?Holt in Denbighshire) – xx (actually 15) – *Mediolano* (Whitchurch Sa). The errors of distance are due to aberrations of milestone-placing (Rivet, pp. 38–9) and to palaeographic confusion of numerals x and v. The identification of *Bovio* with Holt is not certain (Rivet, p. 43 n. 29) because Holt is not on the direct line of Roman road Chester–Stretton–Malpas. Rivet refers to W. F. Grimes, *Y Cymmrodor* XLI (1930) 6–8 on this question. Iter X: *Mamucio* (Manchester) – xviii Roman miles (actually 20) – *Condate* – xviiii (actually 24) – *Mediolano*. Rivet assumes a route *via* Middlewich (Harbutt's Field 2 238). Iter XI, Chester to Caernarvon, is only in modern Cheshire for a short distance (Rivet, pp. 54–5).

The p.ns. in the Ch section of AntIt are discussed by Professor Jackson, in the appendix to Mr Rivet's article at the pages cited.

Bovio (Rivet p. 69), a derivative of Brit *boṷ- 'cow', with -ịo- derivational suffix. (Ch 4 57 treats *Bovio* as the ablative of *Bovium* a place-name formed from the gen.pl. of Lat. *bovis*.)

Condate (Rivet p. 71), Brit. *Condatis* or neut. *Condati*, from *com '(together) with', da- reduced grade of either IE *dō- 'give' or IE *dhē- 'put', and verbal-adjective suffix -ti(s); 'The Confluence'. The French p.ns. *Condé*, *Condat* and *Condes* are of the same origin. (Cf. Ch 2 195–6).

Deva (Rivet, p. 72), the name given to Chester, is the name of R. Dee, Brit. *Dēṷā 'The Goddess'. (Cf. Ch 1 21–2, 3 xiii.)

Mamucio (Rivet, p. 76; corrupt text reads *Mamcunio*), contains Brit. *mammā 'breast; round, breast-like hill'.

Mediolano (Rivet, p. 77, 'a familiar Gallo-Brittonic p.n., Milan being the best known'), from Brit. **medi̯o*- 'middle, midst', and *lāno- probably 'plain, level ground' (cf. Lat. *plānus*), meaning 'The Central Plain'. (Cf. Ch 4 57).

p. 58, s.n. TILSTON. Add '[ˈtilstən] older local [ˈtilssn̩]'.

p. 75, l. 3. This Survey accepts Stenton's identification of *æt Fearndune* 924 ASC with Farndon Ch. The identification with Faringdon Brk should be withdrawn from the next edition of DEPN.

pp. 86–7, s.n. Plocks. Upon the observation that the sense of *plocc 'log, lump of wood' (s.v. *plock* NED) appears to be restricted to certain southern counties, K.J. points out that Irish *pluc* 'lump, club', which seems to be a loan-word from English, and which is evidently as old as the tenth or eleventh century at least, is not likely to have been borrowed from Southern English but more likely from Midland English and possibly *via* Chester.

p. 88, l. 5. *Pechmundis*- is probably a scribal error for *Pedmundis*-. l. 8. An OE pers.n. *Pēodmund is possible. (B.D.)

p. 103, s.n. Filkins. Add 'Cf. Filkins Lane 125 *infra*.'. (B.D.)

p. 104, s.n. EGG BRIDGE. There is a rare English surname *Egg*. (B.D.)

p. 105, s.n. HARGRAVE. See addendum *infra* to 4 228 s.n. HARGRAVE.

p. 108, s.n. CHRISTLETON. The origin is taken to be OE *(*æt*) *cristenan tūne* '(at) the Christian enclosure or farm', or *(æt) *cristena tūne* '(at) the Christians' enclosure or farm', from OE cristen as adj., 'Christian', in dat.sg., or as sb., 'a Christian', in gen.pl., with common substitution *r–n* > *r–l*, *r–r*. The derivation from OE cristel-mæl 'a cross' given in DEPN and EPN 1 122 requires the complete elision of the -mæl- component. The complete absence of -mel-, -mal- spellings distinguishes Christleton Ch from the other instances of p.ns. in OE cristel-mæl (cyrstel-mæl, cristen-mæl, cristesmæl) cited by EPN 1 122. The elision of the -mæl- component is not well evidenced, for Ekwall's suggestion DEPN 107 that the first el. of Chrishall Ess could be a reduced form of cristel-mæl, rather than the more obvious OE *Crist* 'Christ', is unnecessary, cf. EPN 1 122 s.v. Crist, Ess 521 (with addenda Wa xlix).

p. 110, s.n. Hargreaves Hill. See addendum *infra* to 4 228 s.n. HARGRAVE.

p. 115, s.n. Horn Nips. B.D. also has noted an apparent similarity with OE *horngēap* (Beowulf 82). I withdrew from the draft a remark upon this, since the significance of such an allusion could not be discerned at this place.

p. 132, s.n. ASH HAY LANE. Add '*Asheheyes* 1593–1607 *CorpMisc*'.

p. 133, para. (*a*). Add the following from 1593–1607 *CorpMisc* (Hurleston Rental); s.n. Heath Fd, '*Heathfeild*'; s.n. Horse Hay, '*Horsehey*'; s.n. Intake, '*Intacke*'; s.n. Moor Fd, '*the Moore, Picton Towne More, the Moore Bridges*'; s.n. Sheep Cote Hays, '*Sheepcote Hey*'; s.n. Sinders, '*Synders, the Sinders* (v. synder)'; s.n. Sleaks, 'The Hurleston Rental 1593–1607 accounts for *meadowing in* (*the*) *Stakes, Staks meadowinge*. There is some confusion of *l* and *t* in the MSS. The el. might be staca 'a stake'.'; s.n. Within Hay, '*Wythenfeild*'.

p. 133. After para. (*a*) add as para. (*b*) the following forms from 1593–1607 *CorpMisc* (Hurleston Rental); *Blackfeld* (v. blæc); *Cowhey, the Cow Hey* (v. (ge)hæg); *the Eyes* (drainage ditches in *Picton Moor*, perhaps from ēa, but probably from ēg 'island, a water-meadow' in a transferred sense 'ditch surrounding an ēg'); *the Longe Crofte(s)*; *Marled Croft*; *Myddlehey*; *the Nyrour Buttes* ('nearer'); *Plankneys Hey*; (*the*) *Stakes, meadowing in the Stakes, Staks meadowinge* (perhaps the same as Sleaks *supra*, since *l* and *t* are liable to be confused in the MSS. The el. might be either slicu or staca 'a stake'); *Tompsons Croftes, Tompsonsheyes* (widow *Tompson*, tenant); *the Thatch Hey, Thatchhey* (v. þæcc, (ge)hæg; a place liable to flood, where reeds were grown for thatch); *Wayefeilde* (v. weg); *Wheathey*.

p. 135, s.n. PLEMSTALL. Add '*Plempstowe* 1596 *CorpMisc*'.

p. 139, s.n. CHAPELHOUSE FM. Add '*Wirvin Chappell* 1593–1607 *CorpMisc*'.

p. 139, para. (*a*). Add the following from 1593–1607 *CorpMisc* (Hurleston Rental); s.n. Brook Dale, '*Brocke Dale*'; s.n. Bunbury Mdw, '*Bunburyes Meadowe*'; s.n. Crosshays, '*Crosses three feildes, Crosses Meadowe, -Moorehey, -Longe Feild & -Gorsty Hill*'; s.n. East & West, '*East and West*'; s.n. Gorse Hill, '*Gorstye Hills, Gorstyhill(s), Gorsty Hill*'; s.n. Gorsty Fd, '*Gorstycrofte*'; s.n. Heath, '*Wirvin Heath*'; s.n. Long Green, 'Cf. (*the*) *Lower Greene, -Greine, Harrgreine, v.* lower, hēarra'.

p. 140, first para., s.n. Long Mdw, add 'Cf. *Longe Feld* 1593–1607 *CorpMisc*'; from the same source, s.n. Moor(s), Moor Hay, add '*Moorehey, the Moore, Wervin Moore Bridge, the Moore Bridges, Wirvin Moore (Dytches), the Eye(s) at Wirvin Moore.* The 'eyes' were drainage ditches, ēg in a transferred sense.'; s.n. Ox Pasture, add '*Oxe Hey*'; s.n. Pocket, add '*Bunburyes Pockettes* (from the surname *Bunbury*)'; s.n. Rushy Mdw, add '*Rushe Meadowe*'; s.n. Stanlas, add '*Standall Hey*'; s.n. Swartins, add '*Swartinges* (lit. *Swarl-*)'; s.n. White Fd, add '*White Feld*'; s.n, Withy Hay, add '*Wythenhey*'.

p. 140, para. (*b*). Add the following from 1593–1607 *CorpMisc* (Hurleston Rental), *Dunscrofte, Rugh Heyes* (*v.* rūh), *Sparke Meadowe* (*v.* spearca), *Wheate Crofte.*

p. 145, para. (*b*), s.n. Glaseors Hey. K.J. notes that the *Glaseour* family lived at Lea Hall 175 *infra* in the latter part of the seventeenth century.

p. 146, s.n. FLOOKERSBROOK. K.J. reports a spelling *Flottersbrooke* 17, source not specified.

p. 146, s.n. FOLLY HO. A 'wyndymilne' and a 'horse milne' are accounted for in the Hurleston Rental 1593–1607 (*CorpMisc* C/Ch 436).

p. 147, s.n. Mainwaring Heys. Add 'Cf. the tenant George *Manwaringe* 1593–1607 *CorpMisc*'.

p. 147, s.n. *Caryngfeld*, cf. **2** 17, s.n. CARRINGTON. B.D. observes that the pers.n. *Kari* is found in ON as well as ODan.

pp. 155–6, s.n. CASTLE HILL. Cf. Orm² II 857. B.D. draws attention to an earlier allusion, *custodia de Pulford* l12(16) cited by F. M. Stenton, *The First Century of English Feudalism* (2nd ed., 1961), 211, from a deed (M.M. 1/3/1) in the Lincs. Archives Office. The term *custodia* here indicates guardianship of a castle, from which it is to be supposed that the castle of Pulford already existed.

p. 157, s.n. BALDERTON. Add '[ˈbɔːldərtən] older local [ˈbɔːðərtən]'. Add 'Cf. Balderton Nt 209.'.

p. 158, l. 4. After 'days.' add 'Cf. Clayley 90 *supra*.'.

p. 160, s.n. CLAVERTON. The DB spelling *Claventone* (f. 268b) contains *n* probably by an original misreading of ꞇ (*r*). Another DB mistake was observed under Worleston **3** 151.

p. 168, second para., s.n. *Gobbinshire*. The surname *Gobbin* appears among the tenants in the Hurleston Rental 1593–1607 (*CorpMisc* C/Ch 436).

p. 179, l. 6, s.n. Horsestone. B.D. suggests that this may refer to a 'horse-stone', i.e. a mounting block.

p. 179, para. (*b*), s.n. *Edeuenetisgraue*. Perhaps a misreading for *Edeneuetis-*, from the Welsh pers.n. *Ednyfed*. (B.D.)

p. 179, para. (*b*), s.n. *Gruggeworth*. B.D. suggests the Welsh nickname *Gryg*, e.g. the Welsh poet Rhys Gryg, d. 1234.

p. 182, s.n. MOOR LANE. Add '*Stooke Moore* 1598 *CorpMisc*'.

p. 192, s.n. MOUNT MANISTY. Perhaps *Manisty* was the surname of an engineer. (B.D.)

p. 194, l. 3 from foot; p. 196, para. (*b*), l. 3. In view of the date K.J. prefers the MWelsh form *Hywel*.

p. 196, para. (*b*), l. 3. See addendum to **4** 194, l. 3 from foot.

p. 198, s.n. ELLESMERE PORT. Add '[ˈelzmiːr] older local [ˈelzmər]'. The name of the port is taken from the canal, which is named after Ellesmere Sa.

p. 199, l. 2 from foot, s.n. Pullingers. B.D. notes an English surname *Pullinger*.

p. 209, s.n. PLUMHOUSES. The first el. could be a surname *Plumb*. (B.D.)

p. 214, para. (*b*), l. 5. *Gronw* is a contracted form of *Goronwy*.

p. 217, s.n. Little Delight. Add '(*v.* 337 *infra*)'.

p. 228, s.n. HARGRAVE. This p.n. could also be derived from hara 'a hare', like Hargrave **4** 105. Cf. addendum to Harrop **1** 138 at **3** xiv. The vexed question of whether hara 'a hare' or hār² 'hoar, grey' is to be cited as first el. in p.ns. in *Har(e)*-, especially those which do not show ME *hore*- spellings, is controlled by various factors, (i) the co-incidence of form *Har(e)*- resulting from the eME shortening of OE *hār*- in cpds., (ii) the co-incidence of *Har(e)*- p.ns. with boundary locations (*v.* **4** 228 for the semantics, EPN **1** 234 for instances), (iii) the habitat of the hare, an animal more usually associated with field and heath than with woodland. This last consideration ought to be taken into account in all instances of *Har(e)*- p.ns. whose second el. is a woodland term, e.g. with bearu, Harebarrow **1** 101; with græfe, *Har(d)greue* **1** 53, Hargrave **4** 105, 228, Hargeaves Hill **4** 110; with wudu, *Harewode* **1** 83, *Harewodehacrus* **2** 319, Harewood Hill **3** 211, Harewood Lodge **1** 314. Names in lēah may be added (although the meaning of this el. is ambiguous between 'woodland' and 'clearing' and does not clearly indicate the oecological context), Arley **2** 101 (with *Harlagh* **2** 50), *Harlescloh* **3** 210. The 'boundary' factor affects Harebarrow **1** 101 (on an estate and township boundary), Hargrave **4** 105 (on a township boundary, the boundary of Broxton and Eddisbury Hundreds, adjacent to R. Gowy which appears to have been an ancient frontier extending from Tarvin **3** 281 to Macefen **4** 37, *v.* LCHS CXIX 32), Hargrave **4** 228 (on a parish boundary adjacent to Raby **4** 228, on the boundary of the Norse enclave in Wirral, *v.* Sagabook XIV 309–10), and Arley, *Harlagh* **2** 101, 50 (near a township boundary, on the boundary of the DB Hundreds of *Bochelau* and *Tunendune*). It would be advisable to leave the identification of the first el. in such p.ns. an open question between hār² and hara, but derivation from hār² might be preferred in *Har(e)*- p.ns. whose second el. is a woodland term and which lie near a boundary.

p. 234, s.n. Hurt Hey. B.D. suggests *hurt* 'whortleberry'.

p. 235, ll. 13–14 from foot. These spellings are unreliable. *Liscarie* probably represents *Liscard*; *Lyscarye, Lyscurye* probably represent *-carþe, -curþe*.

p. 244, s.nn. *Hondeponnesfeld, Lylleponne*. B.D. suggests the sense 'salt-pan'.

p. 250, s.n. POULTON. The form *Poulton Lancelyn* is still in use, e.g. as the address of the author Mr R. Lancelyn Green.

p. 253, s.n. Yolk of Egg. Add '(*v.* 337 *infra*)'.

p. 253, para. (*b*), s.n. *Hertesflore*. If archaeological, this p.n. could suggest a Roman mosaic floor with a hunting scene; if figurative, flōr may here allude to the stamping-ground of the rutting stag, etc.

p. 256, l. 9, s.n. Hell Hole. Add '(*v.* 336 *infra*);'.

p. 261, l. 3, s.n. North and South. Add '(*v.* 337 *infra*)'.

p. 267, ll. 3–6. Upon reflection, K.J. observes that the mention of OIrish *Dagan* is unnecessary. *Dagan* with [aȝ] cannot be the same as *Tegan* with [eg].

p. 285, s.n. Croft Mellon. K.J. notes that there is no such word in Welsh as *croch* 'hollow'.

p. 286, s.n. *Johnson's Hallond*. Johnson Mdw is a f.n. in Newtom cum Larton, *TA* 289, omitted from p. 302, para. (*a*). Johnsons Hey (Brow) are f.ns. in West Kirby, *TA* 225, omitted from p. 296, l. 1.

p. 290, para. (*a*), s.n. Mulses Hey. Add '(This may contain a form of the p.n. Meols, *v.* 297 *infra*)'.

p. 292, s.n. Bithells Cower. *Cower* is a mis-written form for *Cover* 'a covert'. *Bithell* is a surname (Welsh *ab Ithel*). (B.D.)

p. 295. To the *TA* forms in para. (*a*) add 'Johnsons Hey (Brow) (*v. Johnson's Hallond* 286 *supra*);'.

p. 298, l. 2. Add 'Another -*u*- spelling of the p.n. Meols (cf. 297, l. 6 from foot), may appear in Mulses Hey 290 *supra*.'.

p. 300, s.n. ARNOLD'S EYE. The final el. could be ON **eyrr** 'a sandbank', as in the name Point of Air in Fl and Isle of Man.

p. 302, para. (*a*). Add 'Johnson Mdw (*v. Johnson's Hallond* 286 *supra*);'. Some of the f.ns. in this list may belong to Grange township, see 4 290, l. 9.

p. 307, l. 7, s.n. North and South. Add '(*v.* 337 *infra*);'.

p. 307, para. (*b*), s.n. *Vluyngreuefeld*. B.D. suggests the OE fem.pers.n. *Wulfwynn*.

p. 312, s.n. Thwaite Lane. The term ME *thwayt* is here applied to clearings newly made in 1337, which indicates that ON þveit was a living el. here 1337–57.

p. 322, l. 11. The initial *M-* of *Massie* would be transferred to the unstressed final syllable of Saughall, i.e. ['sɔːgə 'masi] > ['sɔːgəm 'masi] > ['sɔːgəm ('masi)]; but there is evidence of interchange of -*am* and -*all* in unstressed position in spellings of Frodsham 3 221 (see addenda *supra*).

p. 328, para. (*b*), ll. 9–10; p. 334, l. 11 from foot. For 'Poulton (Fd)' read 'Poulton, Poolton Fd'.

p. 334, l. 11 from foot. See addendum *supra* to 4 328, para. (*b*), ll. 9–10.

VI. BROXTON HUNDRED

Broxton Hundred

Atiscros Hund' 1086 DB

Dudestan Hund' 1086 DB, *hundred' de Dudestan* 1217–29 (1580) Sheaf, *hundred' de Duddeston* 1217–29 Tab, *hundred of Dudestan* 1499 (19) Orm[2] II 633, *hundredum de Duistan* 1499 Sheaf[3] 30 (6558, from the same document as prec.)

Brex(is) 1260 Court, *Hundr' de Le Brex'* 1293 Indict, *hundred' de Brexin* c.1296 Court, and spellings as for Broxton 12 *infra*

'Æti's cross', from the OE pers.n. *Æti* and **cros**, at Croes Ati in Flintshire, *v.* NCPN 233. 'Dudd's stone', from the OE pers.n. *Dud(d)* and **stān**, meeting-place unknown, but cf. foll. The hundred is now called after Broxton 12 *infra*, but there is no record of a hundred-meeting at Broxton, and it looks as if the meeting was at *Golborne Hundred* 88 *infra* (perhaps *Dudestan*) save that the barony of Malpas kept its own hundred-court at Malpas, *v.* 39 *infra*. Broxton Hundred contains *Dudestan* Hundred less its detached parts now included in Eddisbury Hundred (Rushton, Over, Little Budworth, Alpraham, *Alretone* and *Opetone* 3 291, 170, 184, 300, 211, 161 and Thornton le Moors 3 258), and less its members Bettisfield, *Burwardestone* and Worthenbury now included in Flintshire, and with the addition of Picton, Upton, Guilden Sutton, Mickle Trafford & Wervin 132, 142, 126, 133, 137 *infra*, from *Wilaveston* (Wirral) Hundred, and Newton by Chester 145 *infra* from Chester Hundred, and Marlston cum Lache, Claverton and Dodleston 162, 160, 156 *infra*, from *Atiscros* Hundred. The following are lost places in the hundred of *Dudestan*.

Burwardestone 1086 DB f. 264, 'the farm or enclosure belonging to the guardian of a stronghold', or 'Burgweard's farm', from **burh-weard** or the OE pers.n. *Burgweard*, and **tūn**, cf. Burwardsley 93 *infra*. Tait 121 n.94 observes that *Burwardestone*, which contained a salt house (cf. Lower & Higher Wych 51 *infra*), probably comprised Iscoyd in Flintshire (containing Lower Wych), and Stockton, Wychough & Wigland (containing Higher Wych) 46, 53, 50 *infra*.

CALVINTONE 1086 DB f. 265, 'bare enclosure', or 'farm at a bare place', from cal(e)wan, wk.gen. or dat.sg. of calu, 'bare', perhaps used as a substantive, with tūn. It is listed in DB with Poulton 153 *infra*, *v.* Tait 143 n.117, n.118. The name is not Carden (53 *infra*) as suggested by Brownbill, LCHS NS xv 102.

Broxton Hundred comprises that part of Cheshire between R. Dee to the west, and R. Gowy and the Peckforton Hills to the east. A few townships lie west of R. Dee, and a few south-east of the hills. It is bounded by R. Gowy and Eddisbury and Nantwich Hundreds to the east, by Shropshire and the detached part of Flintshire to the south, by R. Dee and Denbighshire and Flintshire to the west, by Chester and Wirral Hundred to the north. In the southern part of the hundred the land rises abruptly to 600'–700' in a sandstone escarpment which runs south-west from Beeston 3 302 *supra* to Edge and Overton 31, 45 *infra*. To the south-east of this escarpment, a few townships of the hundred lie on the glacial drift overlying the Upper Triassic strata, and belong to the Weaver basin. The head-streams of R. Weaver are in Bulkeley, Bickerton 17, 4 *infra* and Peckforton 3 311. Away from the foot of the escarpment a low ridge of Bunter sandstone with glacial clays, of 100' elevation, runs north-west as far as the rift-valley which joins the Dee and Gowy estuaries north and north-east of Chester.

UNIDENTIFIED PLACE-NAMES IN BROXTON HUNDRED. *Ashton* 1313 ChRR (*v.* æsc, tūn); *Boclond* 1260 Court (p) ('land granted by charter', *v.* bōc-land); *Cyssley* 1419 Orm² II 710; *Doddelegh* 1321 Chol (from the OE pers.n. *Dodda* and lēah); *Holsiche* 1539 Plea, 1564 ChRR, -*suche* 1545 Plea, 1554, 1565 ChRR ('watercourse in a hollow', *v.* hol², sīc); *Huldiches* (cf. *Hilditche's Gutter* 336 *infra*); *Lascheford* 1405 Chol ('ford at a boggy stream', *v.* læc(c), ford); *le Podemor* 1331 Tab (p), *Podmore* 15 Rich ('toad marsh', *v.* pode, mōr¹); *Sondell* (*cuttlake*) 1450 Chol ('(dug watercourse at) sand-hill', *v.* sand, hyll, cut, lacu); *le Schawhouses* 1353 Indict ('houses at a wood', *v.* sc(e)aga, hūs); *Sheppenhall* 1633 Chol; *Strethul* c.1200 *ib* (p) ('hill at a paved road', *v.* strǣt, hyll); *Sudbury*, -*buri* 1354 *ib* (p) ('south manor', *v.* sūð, burh); *Wyrlone* or -*loue* c.1290 Chol A13 (p) (from wīr 'bog-myrtle', and lane 'a lane', or hlāw 'a mound, a hill').

i. Malpas

The ecclesiastical parish of Malpas contained the townships 1. Agden, 2. Bickerton, 3. Bickley, 4. Bradley, 5. Broxton, 6. Bulkeley, 7. Chidlow, 8. Cholmondeley, 9. Chorlton, 10. Cuddington, 11. Duckington, 12. Edge, 13. Egerton, 14. Hampton, 15. Larkton, 16. Macefen, 17. Malpas, 18. Newton by Malpas, 19. Oldcastle, 20. Overton, 21. Stockton, 22. Tushingham cum Grindley, 23. Wigland, 24. Wychough.

1. AGDEN (Ho & HALL) (118–510440)

Agetun 1208–29 (1580) Sheaf, *-ton* 1328 Pat, 1329 Plea, 1348 *Eyre*, 1431 ChRR

Aggeton c.1347 AD, 1351 Plea *et freq* to 1598 ChRR, *Aggetton* 1343 ChGaol (p)

Agton 1368 ChCal (p), 1448 ChRR, 1523 ib *et freq* to 1668–71 Sheaf, *Aggton* 1516 Orm[2]

Agdon 1508 ChRR (lit. *Aydon*), 1520 Plea *et freq* to 1724 NotCestr, *Aggdon* 1561 ChRR

Agden 1559 ChRR, (*-House, -Hall*) 1831 Bry, *Agden or Agton* 1668–71 Sheaf.

'Aggi's farm', from tūn and the ODan pers.n. *Aggi* (Fellows Jensen 1), as stated in Barnes[1] 226. The pers.n. also appears in *Aggesahe* 10 *infra*. Cf. Agden 2 42.

BROOK HO, named from Grindley Brook 47 *infra*, *v.* brōc. GRINDLEY BROOK BRIDGE No. 1, *Crinsley Bridge* 1690, 1775 Sheaf, cf. Grindley (Brook Bridge) 47 *infra*, *v.* brycg. HILL FM, cf. *Hill Field* 1838 *TA*, *v.* hyll. MILL COTTAGES, cf. *Mill Bank* 1838 *ib*, *v.* myln, banke. SANDHOLES, cf. *Sand Hole Field* 1838 *ib*, *v.* sand, hol[1].

FIELD-NAMES

The principal forms are 1838 *TA* 5.

(*a*) Black Fd; Bottoms (*v.* botm); Cockshoot Fd (*v.* cocc-scyte); Eight Butts (*v.* eahta, butte); Fearney Bank; Harrow Flan; Hatchfield (*v.* hæc(c)); Heath Piece; Hunters Fd; Jacks Pasture; Kiln Pits; Leech Croft; Marl Fd; Milking Bank (*v.* milking); Nettles (*v.* netele); Olley Fd (*v.* alor); Park (*v.* park); Rabbit Bank; Rens Park (*v.* wrenna, park); Round Bank (*v.* rond); Slang (*v.* slang); Three Shires (the boundaries of Ch and Sa meet Fl here, *v.* þrēo, scir[1]).

2. BICKERTON (HALL) (109–510530)

Bicretone 1086 DB
Bikertun, -ton 1180–1220 *Chol et freq* with variant spellings *Bi-,
Byker-, -ir-, -yr-, -ur-, Bykker-, -tone* to 1724 NotCestr, *Bickerton*
1350 Chamb (p), 1399 ChRR, 1513 *ChEx et freq, the Nerre
Bykerton* 1450 *Chol, the hall of Bykerton* 1466 AD, *Fur Bickerton*
?1640 Sheaf[1] 3 108
Clifbikerton 1281 Plea, 1282 Court, *-bykirton* 1303 *Chol
Becurton* 1306–26 *Chol* (p), *Bekur-* 1464 *ib, Bekertone* 1326 *ib* (p),
-ton 1498, 1519, 1524 *ib, Bekir-* 1456 ChRR, *Bekyr-* 1514 *Chol
Birkerton* 1480 ChRR (p)
Bri(c)kerton 1724 NotCestr

'The bee-keepers' farm', from bīcere and tūn, with hall. The
affixes are ME nerre 'nearer', OE fyrr (ME *fur(re)*) 'farther', and
clif 'a cliff', from Bickerton Hill *infra*. Bickerton is a mile or so from
Bickley, *v.* 7 *infra*, cf. Bickley Brook 8 *infra*.

BICKERTON FM, *The Arrows* 1831 Bry.   BICKERTON HILL (109–
500528), 1668–71 Sheaf, 1831 Bry, *the Cliffe* l13 (1637) Rich, *le Clif*
1303 *Chol, the Mickelcliffe* 1305 (1637) Rich, *Butterton Hill* 1690
Sheaf, *Bickerton's Hill* 1838 *TA*, from clif 'a cliff, a steep slope'
and hyll 'a hill', with micel 'great', cf. *Clifbikerton* (etc., under
Bickerton) *supra*, Rawhead *infra*.   COOMB DALE, *v.* cumb, dæl[1].
DEAN'S LANE, *Dean's Meadow* 1838 *TA*.   DROPPINGSTONE WELL,
v. 94 *infra*.   GALLANTRY BANK, 1842 OS, *Gallows or Gallantry
Bank* 1831 Bry, *Gallatree-, Gallowtree Bank(e)* ?1640 Sheaf[1] 3 108,
Gallow Hill 1690 Sheaf, 'gallows-tree hill', the site of a gibbet,
Sheaf[1] 3 107, *v.* galg-trēow, banke, galga, hyll.   GOLDFORD FM &
LANE, *v.* golde, ford.   HILL FM, HILLSIDE, named from Bickerton
Hill *supra*.   HOUGH COTTAGE, *The Hough* 1838 *TA, v.* hōh.
LITTLE HEATH.   LONG LANE.   MAD ALLEN'S HOLE, discussed
Sheaf[1] 3 pp. 27, 65, 69, 73. The name is taken from a man hired by a
local landlord to impersonate a hermit in an artificial cave here. The
'hermit' is also popularly associated with Harthill Coombs 92
infra, and a local name *Allenscome's Cave* was invented, which
associated the Coombs with Mad Allen's Hole (Sheaf, *loc. cit.*, 65, 69).
MAIDEN CASTLE (109–497528), 1819 Orm[2], *the Maiden Tower* 1710
Sheaf[3] 39 (8394), an iron-age hill-fort, *v.* Varley 69, *v.* mægden,
castel(l), a common fortification-name, 'unused, untaken castle-

(-site)', *v*. Cu 255–6. Local folklore offers the usual explanation that this place was defended by stratagem by the women of the district against Welsh raiders while the English men were away. Smith (WRY 4 71) suggests this type of p.n., used of derelict fortifications, often Iron-Age hill-forts and the like, means 'old fortification offering a privacy where maidens may indulge their fancy'. MUSKET'S HOLE, *Musket Hole* 1842 OS, *Muskett Dale, Muskett's Field* 1838 *TA*, from hol[1] 'a hollow', dæl[1] 'a valley', with either the surname *Muskett* or ME *muskit, muskett* 'male sparrow-hawk'. THE POOL. QUARRY HO. RAW HEAD (109–508548), 1819 Orm[2], the northern summit of Bickerton Hill, *v*. hrēaw (*hraw*-), hēafod, cf. 'the naked summit of Raw Head' Orm[2] II 644. RAW-HEAD FM, *Goat House* 1842 OS, cf. prec., *v*. gāt. SALTER'S LANE, 1842 *ib*, *v*. saltere, lane. This and foll. are part of a salt-way from Nantwich to Farndon, *v*. 1 48 (Route XXV). SANDY LANE, cf. prec. TOWER WOOD. TOWNSEND FM. YEWTREE FM, *The Cottages* 1831 Bry.

FIELD-NAMES

The undated forms are 1838 *TA* 48. Of the others, 13, 1281–2, 1302[2], 1302–3, 1305, 1306[2], 1315 are (1637) Orm[2], 1250–70, 1250–1300, 1302, 1303, 1305[2], 1306, 1315[2] (1637) Rich, 14 (17), 1668–71, 1926 Sheaf, 1351 *Eyre*, 1421 ChRR, 1422 Plea, 1466 AD, 1842 OS, 1860 White, and the rest *Chol*.

(*a*) Big & Little Barns; Big Hays (*v*. (ge)hæg); Bird's Hill (1860. White 186 reports archæology here); Black Heath Fd (*v*. blæc, hǣð); Burnthouse Well 1842 (*v*. brende[2], hūs); Clay Bank; Colts Foot Fd (probably named after the plant); Cow Hay (*v*. (ge)hæg); Cross Croft & Fd, Cross Lane Fd (*v*. cros); Crow Foot Mdw; Dale (*v*. dæl[1]); Twenty Demath (*v*. day-math); Drumbo Fd (dial. *drumble* 'a wooded dingle', cf. dumbel); Each Man's Fd (*Eych(e)mans* 1646, 1648, presumably common land, or land in multiple ownership, 'everybody's field', from ME *eilcman*, OE *ǣlc mann*, *v*. NED s.v. *each* c); Big & Little Fearnalls (*the fearney knowle* 14 (17), 'ferny hill', *v*. fearnig, cnoll); Flatts; Forrin(g)s; Furacres (*v*. fyrr, æcer); Hall Fd; Hemp Yard (*v*. hemp-yard); Hob Fd; Intake (*v*. inntak); Lambeth; Leasow (*v*. lǣs); Marsh; Mill Fd (*le Mulnefyld* 1420, 1421, 1422, cf. *the mylnedych, Milnhurst, Bickerton Milne* 1250–70, *the Milnestede* 1250–1300, *Milnehurst* 1281–2, *the-* 1302, 1302–3, 1303, *the ould milne of Bickerton* 1306, *Milnehurst a brook where a milne has been* 1668–71, *v*. myln, feld, dīc, hyrst, mylne-stede, ald); Moor Bank & Fd (cf. *le mor* 1303[2], *v*. mōr[1]); Pickhoo (*v*. pichel); Pingo (*v*. pingel); Piper's Flat; Ridden, Ridding (*the Riddeng* 14 (17), *le longe Ruding, le Ruding iuxta villam* 1303[2], *le Olderuding* 1337, *v*. ryding); Roach Croft; Ronks Moor; Royall Moore 1715 (*Ruylsmore*

1306, *Ruylesmor* 1397, *-more* 1450, *Royles more* 14 (17), *Rullesmore* 1524, '(marsh at) rye-clearing', from ryge and lēah, with mōr[1]); Rush Hill; Sand Hills (cf. *the sand ales* 14 (17), *v.* sand, halh (nom. pl. halas), hyll); Shrugs (*v.* shrogge 'a bush, brushwood'); Southage; Spark Croft, Spark Green Mdw (*Spar Green* 1842, *v.* spearca, grēne[2]); Stinking Croft; Thoroughly; Town Mdw (*v.* toun); Trooper's Alley 1926 (a local name for a ledge on Bickerton Hill); Windmill Fd; Withen Mdw, Within's Mdw & Yard (*v.* wiðegn, geard); Yewkins Croft.

(b) *Birchencliffe* 1306 (*v.* bircen[2], clif); *Blacksiche* 1250–70 (*v.* blæc, sīc); *Chyterishalyth* c.1303 (probably 'nook with a sewer', *v.* scitere, halh); meadow called *Colemans* 1604, *-Colemans Wythens* 1627 (from the surname *Coleman* and wiðegn); *the four Acres* 1466 (*v.* fēower, æcer); *the Fox Feld(e)s or blak earthes* 14 (17) (*v.* fox, feld, blæc, eorðe); *the hanging oake* 1250–70 (1637) (*v.* hangende, āc); *Hakelegh* 1250–1300, 13, 1302[2], 1305, 1305[2], *Haukleigh* 1250–1300, *Hauke-* 1315, 1315[2], *Hawkleigh* 1306, 1306[2] ('hawk glade', *v.* hafoc, lēah); *le Hewygwey* c.1303 (*v.* weg); *Hindsmere dale* 14 (17) ('(valley at) the hind's pool', from hind and mere[1], with dæl[1]); *Hugynslonde of Larketon* 1450 ('the selion of Hugin of Larkton', from the ME pers.n. *Hugin* (diminutive of *Hugh*) and land); *the lang sich yeard* 14 (17) ('(enclosure at) the long watercourse', *v.* lang, sīc, geard); *the lid yeat* 14 (17) (*v.* hlid-geat); *Rocfallen Ach* c.1200 (probably 'ash-tree felled by a fall of rock' or 'fallen from a rock', from æsc with rokke and the pa.part of ME *fallen* (OE *feallan*) 'to fall'); *le Rochilake* c.1303 ('rocky stream', *v.* rochi, lacu); *le siche* 1337 (*v.* sīc); *Walchmonstreete, Walesmonsweye* (*v.* 1 48 (Route XXV)); *le Wodeh(o)uslone* 1337, cf. *boscus de Bikerton* c.1200, *the wood houses of Bickerton* 1250–1300 ('(lane to) houses in a wood', *v.* wudu, hūs, lane); *put sub Yvine Ach* c.1200 ('pit under an ivy-grown ash-tree', *v.* pytt, īfegn, æsc).

3. BICKLEY (HALL, MILL & TOWN) (109–5348) ['bikli]

Bichelei 1086 DB, *Bikeleg'* e13 *AddCh et freq* with variant spellings *Byke-, Bikke-, Bykke-, Byky-, Biky-, Bicke-, Bycke-, -legh, -ley(e), -lee* to 1579 Chol

Bicklegh 1272–1307 EatonB *et freq* with variant spellings *-ley* (from 1414 ChRR), *Bik-, Byck-, Byk-, Bic-, -ley(e), -legh;* Bickley Hall 1683 Chol, *-Mill* & *-Town* 1831 Bry, *-Hall Farm* 1839 TA, *-Wind Mill* 1842 OS

Bekelegh 1329 Chol, *-ly* 1374 *ib*, *-lay* 1386 *ib* (p), *-ley* 1400, 1463, 1487 *ib*, *Beckeley* 1536 ChRR

Bykeslegh 1400 ChRR (p)

Bicklem c.1536 Leland

Buckley 1724 NotCestr

'Glade of the bees'-nests or beehives', from bīc and lēah, with hall, myln, toun. The first el. of this p.n. is debatable. Ekwall

(DEPN *Bickenhall* to *Bicton*) takes the OE pers.n. *Bic(c)a* as the first el. in a numerous series of p.ns, but, under *Bickleigh, Bickley*, he admits the possibility that not all these p.ns. contain the pers.n. To accept the pers.n. derivation in *all* of them would suppose *Bic(c)a* a very widely used pers.n. indeed (cf. the equally suspect *Billa* in *Bilborough, Billing*, etc., DEPN). Smith, EPN s.v. bīc, proposes that an OE word *bīc is to be reckoned with, and that this word is the stem of OE bīcere, bēocere 'a bee-keeper' and is the origin of ME, ModEdial. *bike* 'a nest of wild bees, a bees'-nest, a beehive'. NED records *bike* from a.1300. Early instances appear in Ch deeds, of manorial appurtenances and rights 'in hauec, in *Bihic*, in Thac, in Tol, . . .' 1257 *AddCh* 51376 at Tilston, 'in *beking* et in cropping . . .' 1278 *AddCh* 50709 at Church Minshull, 'in hauekis, in *Bykis*, in Tak', in Tol, . . .' 1320–25 *AddCh* 50490 at Churton by Farndon.

The etymology of this OE *bīc given in EPN 1 34–5 is dismissed by Ekwall (NoB (1957) 143 and Studies[3] 82) and Löfvenberg (ESt XLIII 40), cf. JEPN 1 12. Ekwall, Studies[3] 82 notes the rejected suggestion in NED s.v. *bike*, that ME *bike* might arise from an OE *bēoc a contracted form of an OE *bēo-wīc (*v.* bēo, wīc, cf. Bewick NbDu 19, YE 59), rejected because such an origin is expected to produce spellings *beke, *beek. As Ekwall points out, this objection is not fatal. He notes ME *sīk* 'sick' from OE *sēoc*, and *beke* c.1450 MED for *bike*. There are *Beke-* spellings for 1329 for Bickley Ch, and *AddCh* 50709 contains *beking* 1278. If the form *bike* is a northern dial. form, then the original OE base might have been an Angl. OE *bīo-wīc. The loss of -*w*- in such a formation would lead to hiatus between *i* and *ī* or a long *īi* diphthong (resulting from *bī(e-w)īc), either of which could explain the spelling *bihic* 1257 *AddCh* 51376. Again, if, as suggested in EPN 1 35, the word bīcere, bēocere 'a bee-keeper' is formed with the agent-noun suffix -ere[3], the stem word would be an OE *bīc, *bēoc. Such variants would also explain the *i* and *e* spellings in Bickley; further, they could have served as the stems for wk. masc. formations *bīca, *bēoca with the same meaning as *bīcere, *bēocere.

Despite the impossibility, at this stage, of providing a certain etymology for OE *bīc (> ME *bike*) 'a bees'-nest', the word is a formal possibility, and its occurrence in the p.n. Bickley Ch is made more likely by the proximity of this place to Bickerton 4 *supra* which contains bīcere, bēocere. A similar association of *bike-* and *bikere-* is seen again in Bickley Wo 53. This persuades me to see in Bickley and Bickerton allusions to bee-keeping and honey-gathering in this part of Ch (perhaps the reason for the Welsh translation of the p.n. Beeston 3 302–3 into *y Fêl Allt* 'the honey rock'). However, Dr von Feilitzen advises me that he would prefer Ekwall's explanation (Studies[3] 81–2, DEPN), OE *bica, *bice 'a woodpecker'. The topography of Bickley does not invite the adoption of the alternative sense suggested by Ekwall in discussion of the p.n. Purbeck Do, a figurative use of OE *bica 'a pecker, a bill, a beak, a promontory' also noted by Löfvenberg ESt XLIII 40 (cf. JEPN 1 12).

The p.n. Bickley Ch is to be derived from either the OE pers.n. *Bic(c)a*, or OE *bica, *bice 'a woodpecker', or OE *bīca gen.pl. of *bīc (the word lying behind ME *bike*) 'a bees'-nest, a beehive'. I follow the late Professor Smith in preferring the latter, but I cannot dismiss the others.

BICKLEY BROOK (> Bar Mere *infra* > Steer Brook 1 35), 1831 Bry, *aqua de Bikerton* c.1200 Chol, *Coisly Brook* 1700 *ib*, *v.* brōc, cf. Bickerton 4 *supra*, Quoisley 3 106.

BICKLEY MOSS, *mora de Bykeley* 1394 Chol, *Bykley Heth* 1524 *ib*, *Bykleye Heath* 1537 *ib*, *Byckeley Mosse* 1554 *ib*, *Bykley Hethe* c.1650 *ib*, *Bickley Mosse* 1668–71 Sheaf, *the Moores* 1695 Chol, *The Moore* 1699, *the Moors in Bickley* 1709 *ib*, *v.* mōr[1], hǣð, mos, cf. Moss Wood *infra*.

BICKLEYWOOD (109–520479), *the (prince's) wood of Bik(k)elegh, -ley* 1357 BPR, *-Bykelegh* 1357 ChRR, 1358 AD, *Bickley Wood* 1640 Chol, *(-Farm)* 1839 TA, *The Woods* 1699 Chol, *The Wood* 1831 Bry, cf. *the wood peece* c.1543 Chol, *-peice* 1683 *ib*, *-Peace* 1699 *ib*, *Wood Field* 1699 *ib*, *v.* wudu, pece.

HETHERSON GREEN (FM) & HALL (109–528498)

> *Hetheston* 1506, 1507, 1536 Plea, 1508, 1536 ChRR, (*-alias Helaston*) 1540 Chol, (*Helaston alias-*) 1567 *ib*
> *Hetherston* 1509, 1536 Orm[2], 1570 (17) Sheaf, *Hetherson* 1567, 1599 Chol, *-Green* 1842 OS, *Etherson* 1579 Chol, *Heatherson* 1661 *ib*, *Hatherstone Green* 1831 Bry
> *Heyston* 1536 Plea, ChRR, Orm[2] II 602
> *Helaston* 1540 Chol, *Heleston alias Heylaston, Helaston* 1567 *ib*

Ederson 1591 Sheaf, *Hederson Greene* 1667 *Chol*, *-Green* 1671
Sheaf, *Hedderson-*, *Hoddersons-*, *Hoderson-* 1700 *Chol*, *Header-
son-* 1705 *ib*
Hethehousey Grene c.1650 *Chol*
Headerton Greene 1705 *Chol*
Edwardson Green 1860 White
This name is insoluble with the material available, *v.* grēne[2] 'a
green'. The first component may be a p.n. in tūn and an el. in
gen.sg. inflexion, since it exhibits the usual -*ston* > -*son* development.

No MAN'S HEATH (109–515480), *Nomonheth* 1483 ChRR, *-e* 1483
Orm[2], *No Mans Heath* 1671 Sheaf, *Noemans-* 1705 *Chol*, *Nomans-*
1716, 1828 *ib*, 'no man's heath, heath nobody owns', cf. No Man's
Land Sx 77, Wo 191, *v.* nān mann, hǣð.

HIGHER SNAB (109–545485), (*le*) *Snabbe* 1506 *Chol*, Plea, 1508 ChRR,
1515 *MinAcct*, *Snab* 1668–71 Sheaf, *The-* 1694 *Chol*, *the Snabb* 1819
Orm[2], *Higher Snabb* 1842 OS, cf. Lower Snab 3 110, perhaps snæp
'a boggy piece of land', since the place is near Bickley Moss *supra*,
but Professor Löfvenberg observes that the el. snabbe appears to
suit the forms, and although snabbe in the sense 'a steep place, a
projecting part of a hill, a rugged point' will not fit the topography
of this place, the word may, in this instance, refer to a peninsula or
projecting tongue of dry ground pointing into a bog. This would
suit both the spellings and the locality.

WILLEY FM & MOOR (109–5346)

Wildeleg(h) 1300 Plea, (*-in Bykylegh*) 1332 *Chol*, (*mora de-*) *-ley*
1394 *ib*
Wilbelmor 1348 *Chol*
Willey 1488 ChRR (p), *Willey* (*More*) 1581, 1636 *Chol*, *-Moor(e)*
1621, 1622 *ib*, *Willey or Willey More* 1671 Sheaf, *Willymoor*
1838 *TA*, *Willey Farm* 1842 OS, *Wylley* 1557 *Chol*, *Wiley Farm*
1831 Bry, cf. *Willey Meadowes* 1693 *Chol*
Welley more 1571 *Dav*
Willowmore 1690 Sheaf
Willamore 1700 Sheaf

'Wild clearing', from wilde 'waste, uncultivated, wild', and lēah,
with mōr[1].

BANK HO, *v.* banke.   BARHILL FALL, *the Barrel Fall* 1819 Orm², named from a subsidence in land belonging to Barhill Fm 48 *infra*, in 1657, Orm² II 647, *v.* (ge)fall, cf. foll.   BAR MERE (BRIDGE & HO), *Boremere* 1397 *Chol*, *le mere* 1487 *ib*, *Barmeer* 1700 *ib*, *-mere* 1819 Orm², 'wild-boar lake', *v.* bār², mere¹. The latter form is influenced by Welsh bar¹ (PrWelsh barr) in Barhill, cf. prec. BICKLEY BROOK COTTAGES, cf. Bickley Brook *supra*.   BICKLEY FIELD (109–526472), *-Feild* 1703 *Chol*, the site of the discovery in 1812 of the Malpas Diploma, Sheaf¹ 2 321, Orm² II 648. This land is named from its lying in Bickley but belonging to Barhill Fm in Tushingham 48 *infra*.   BICKLEY OLD SCHOOL, *The School* 1831 Bry, *Bickley School* 1842 OS, *v.* scōl.   BIRCH PITS, 1842 *ib*, 'pits growing with birch-trees', probably old marlpits, *v.* birce, pytt. BRET'S MERE, *Bret(t)s-* 1831 Bry, 1842 OS, probably from the surname *Brett* and mere¹, cf. *Hugh Bratts Old Feilde* 1700 *Chol*. CROSS LANES COTTAGES & FM, *v.* cros.   GORSTYHILL COTTAGE, *v.* gorstig.   GROTSWORTH LANE   MOSS FM, *v.* Bickley Moss *supra*.   MOSS WOOD, *v.* 23 *infra*.   PIPEHOUSE FM, *The Pipe* 1831 Bry, *Pipe House* 1842 OS, *v.* pīpe 'a conduit'.   QUOISLEY BRIDGE, cf. Quoisley 3 106.   RED HALL, 1842 OS, *v.* rēad. SUNNYSIDE.   YEWTREE FM, *-House* 1831 Bry.

FIELD-NAMES

Of the forms, 1250–1300, 1303 are (1637) Rich, 1255–61 Plea, 1259 Court, 1358 AD, 1831 Bry, and the rest *Chol*.

(a) Barn Craft 1700; Bench Fd 1699 (*v.* benc); Bottom Close 1700; Broad Fd 1699 (cf. *Brade Medowe* 1536, *v.* brād); Broome Fd 1700, Broomey Feild 1703 (*v.* brōm, brōmig); Burly Feild 1700 (*v. Burley* 22 *infra*); Christich 1700; Collyes 1697 (*the-* 1659, *v.* colig); Coomorl Medow 1700; Crabtree Heath 1700; Crimes 1703 (*v.* cryme, cf. *le Crymbe* 2 171); Five-, Three Days Math 1699 (*v.* day-math); Dovehouse Fd 1699; Green Croft; Han Hill 1703; Harry Croft 1700; Old Hopyard 1699 (*v.* hoppe, geard); The Lane 1700; Little Croft 1700; Lomford land 1700; Long Croft 1700; Middlefield 1700; Mill Fd 1699; Moorgate 1693 (*v.* mōr¹, gata 'an allotment of pasture'); Old Fd, -Feild(e) (Lane) 1700 (*v.* ald, feld); the Orchard 1699; Ridding 1700 (cf. *the Litle Ridding* 1674, *v.* ryding); the Three Ruxells 1700; Stable Mdw 1699; Steels Mdw 1695; Tanners Me(a)dow 1700; Wellchmans Croft 1700 ('Welshman's croft', *v.* wels(c)hman); Well Fd 1700; Windmill Moss 1831; Woody Croft 1700.

(b) *Aggesale Wood* 1255–61 Plea (DKR xxvi 36, for foll.), *boscus nomine Aggesahe* 1259 (from sc(e)aga 'a wood, a copse', with the same ODan pers.n. *Aggi* as in Agden 3 *supra*); *Birthels Lane* c.1650 (from **lane** and *The Birtles* 22 *infra*); *The Black Croft* 1674 (*v.* **blæc**, **croft**); *Cleycroft* 1487 (*v.* **clæg**, **croft**); *Hawkeserte, Haykesyorde* 1250–1300, *Hawkiserte* 1303, *haye del Hawkesherd* 1337, *Haukeserd* 1358 ('the hawk's gap or cleft', *v.* **hafoc-scerde**, cf. *The Hawkesyord* 1 166); *Heafeld miln poole* 1653 ('(mill-pool at) the high field', *v.* **hēah**, **feld**, **myln**, **pōl**[1]); *Killonhowse* 1487 (*v.* **cyln**, **hūs**); *Turnyng Hurst* 1536, *Turning Hurst* (*Moor & Meadow Moore*) 1588 (perhaps 'winding wood', from eModE *turning* pres.part., and **hyrst**, with **mǣd**, **mōr**[1]); *Willey Purse in Willey Moor* 1622 (probably from **purs**, but perhaps a *purse-net* (dial.) in which ducks were trapped, cf. Willey Moor *supra*).

4. BRADLEY (BRIDGE, BROOK, FM & GREEN) (109–510460)

Bradeleg' 1259 Court *et freq* with variant spellings *-legh, -lewe, -ley(e), -leigh* to *Bradeley* 1724 NotCestr, *Bradelegh iuxta (le) Malpas* 1369 Chol, 1370 Plea, *Bradeley Grene* 1569 Orm[2]
Braddeleye 1373 Pat (p), *-ley* 1507 Plea
Bradley near Malepase 1476 ChRR, *Bradley* 1445 *ib et freq*, (*-alias Bradlegh*) 1528 Plea, (*-iuxta Agden*) 1588 ChRR, (*-alias Welsh Bradley*) 1668–71 Sheaf, *Bradleigh near Malpas* 1569 ChRR, *Bradley Green* 1816 Orm[2], *Bradley Brook (House), Bradley Hall* 1831 Bry, *Bradley Bridge* 1842 OS

'Broad glade', from **brād** and **lēah**, with **grēne**[2], **brōc**, **hall**, **brycg**. Bradley is in Malpas parish, and near Agden 3 *supra*. The affix *Welsh-* (*v.* **Welisc**) alludes to this place's proximity to Wales and distinguishes it from Bradley 3 228. It seems likely that there was a Welsh interest here in the thirteenth century, cf. *Madoc de Bradeleg'* 1260 Court 24, and there may have been a notable Welsh influence in the population in the seventeenth. The brook joins Wych Brook 1 39.

FOX COVERT, cf. *Fox Holes* 1838 *TA*. HILLSIDE. HOUGH BRIDGE [huf], *Off Bridge* 1831 Bry, cf. *the Hough Headlands* 1838 *TA*, named from Hough Fm 40 *infra*, *v.* **brycg**, **hēafod-land**. STAG HALL, 1831 Bry, cf. *Stagfielde* 1537 Chol, *v.* **stagga** 'a stag'. TOP FM, cf. *Top Croft & Field* 1838 *TA*, *v.* **top**.

FIELD-NAMES

The undated forms are 1838 *TA* 65. Of the others 13 is AD, 1357–8 Orm[2], 1668–71 Sheaf, and the rest *Chol*.

(a) Bache (*Bach* 1668–71, *v.* bæce[1]); Little Barn Goff (perhaps ModEdial. *goaf* (ME *golfe*) 'a bay in a barn, a hay-rick'; although NED records this as an EAngl word, it must have had a wider distribution, for it appears as "The Gulfs", the local name for a part of Kendal We giving name to Gulfs Rd in that town); Black Fd; Bottoms (*v.* botm); Bourth (perhaps from Welsh porth (masc.) 'gateway', with an anglicised form with voiced initial consonant. Welsh *y borth*, from *porth* (fem.), would mean 'the harbour' which is impossible here. Professor Richards suggests an anglicisation of Welsh *y berth* 'the hedge', from Welsh *perth* (fem.)); Brook Bank; Broomy Flat (*v.* brōmig, flat); Cappers Loon (*v.* land); Cats Croft (*v.* catt); Chidlow Fd (cf. Chidlow 20 *infra*); Clapgate Fd (*v.* clapgate); Clem Park (*v.* Clemley 3 47); Cranberry Bank (*v.* cranberry); Crooked Redding (*v.* croked, ryding); Day Bank (*v.* dey); Doles (*v.* dāl); Flat Fd; Goose Lane 1777 (*v.* gōs); Hanmers Fd (from the surname *Hanmer*, a notable Sa family); Hopley Fd; Horse Pasture; House Fd; Hunt Moor (*Hunt More* 1537); Intake (*v.* inntak); Keys Croft; Long Fd (*Longefyelde* 1560, *v.* lang, feld); Marl Bank; Mill Fd (cf. 'a water-mill in *Bradelegh*' 1357–8, *v.* myln); Moor Croft (*v.* mōr[1]); Moss Fd (*v.* mos); Motterheads Mdw (probably from the surname *Mottershead*, cf. 1 203–4); New Hays (*v.* (ge)hæg); Overton Fd (*v.* uferra, tūn); Penfold Fd (*v.* pynd-fald); Princes Acre 1777 (*the Prynce Acre* 1537); Puresables Yard; Rebels Green; Reddish Moor (perhaps a 'rye eddish', from ryge and edisc, but more likely a p.n. like Reddish La 30, 'reed ditch', from hrēod and dīc, with mōr[1]); Ridding (*v.* ryding); Rough (*v.* rūh); Sand Hole Fd (*v.* sand, hol[1]); Six and Eight Pence (either a rent or a purchase, *v.* 337 *infra*); Tom Fd, Town Fd (*v.* toun); White Fd; Yate Fd (*v.* geat).

(b) *Castelwode* 13 ('wood at, or belonging to, a castle', *v.* castel(l), wudu. There were castles at Malpas, Oldcastle and Shocklach 40, 44, 64 *infra*); *Caulande Riddinge* 1560 (perhaps '(cleared land at) the cabbage-patch', *v.* cāl, land, ryding; but *u* may represent *f* or *v* and the first el. could be calf 'a calf'); *Cokeseys londe* 1637 (from the surname *Cokesay*, cf. Cooksey Wo 312, and land); *the High Lane* 1560 (*v.* hēah, lane); *Killcroft* 1560 (*v.* cyln, croft); *Leuildeslewe* (lit. *Len-*) 13 (AD C5655, '*Lēofhild's* clearing or wood', a ME formation, from an OE fem. pers.n. *Lēofhild* (Feilitzen 312) and lēah); *Parkyns Crofte* 1554, *Parkins Close* 1560 (from the ME pers.n. *Perkin* and croft, clos); *le Stanshurste* 1453 (Chol C2, endorsed *The Glancers* 17 (? for *Stancers*), 'the wood at the stone', *v.* stān (gen.sg. stānes), hyrst); *Urian Rydding* 1537 ('Urian's cleared-land', from the ME and ModE pers.n. *Urian* (< Welsh *Urien*) and ryding).

5. BROXTON (109–4854) ['brɔkstən, 'brɔksn̩]

Brosse 1086 DB

Brexis 1163–81, 1272–1307 *JRC* (p), 1260 Court, 1283 Cl (p), 1284 Ipm, c.1295 *Chol*, 1307–27 *Orm*[2], c.1358 ChRR (p), *Brecsis* c.1220 Bark (p), *Brexes* c.1220 *Chol, Clif, JRC, Bun* all (p)

Brex' 1216–72 *AddCh*, 1260, 1281 (p), 1282 (p), 1287 (p) Court, 1265–84 (1640) Chest (p), 1270–95 *ChFor* (p) (Barnes[1]), 1272–4, 1274 *JRC* (p), 1285, 1290 Ipm, 1290, 1303 (p), 1305 (p) *Chol*, 1306 ChF, 1307 Plea, *Le Brex'* 1293 *Indict*

Brexin 1216–72 *AddCh* (p), 1260 (p), 1282 (p), c.1296 Court, 1287 (p), c.1310 Chest, 1288 Plea (p), c.1290 *Chol*, *Brexun* 1272 *ib* (p), 1328 ChRR (p), *Brexen* 1278 Whall (p), c.1295 *Chol*, 1317 City (p), *Brexyn* 1285 *Chol*, *Brexon* c.1290 (p), c.1303 (p), c.1310, c.1330 (p) *ib*, 13 AD (p), 1331 *Blun* (p), 1357 *Tourn* (p), 1387 ArlB, 1439 Orm[2], *Brexone* 14 *Sotheby* (p), *Brex'n* 1307 *Eyre*, *Brexene* 1310 ChRR

Brexens 1219 *BW* (p), *Brexins* 1291 Tax, *Brexnus* c.1300 *Chol* (p), e14 *AddCh*

Broxun 1259 Court (p), c.1290 (p), c.1310, 1325, c.1340 *Chol*, 1345 *Eyre*, 1400 Pat, 1417 AD, *Broxon'* 1300–20 *AddCh* (p), 1307 *Chol* (p), 1308 (1565) ChRR, 1313 Plea *et freq* to 1565 ChRR, *le Broxon* 1395 ChRR (p), 1410 ib (p), *Broxin* 1308 Plea, *Broxen* 1311 ib (p), 1355 BPR, 1363 Orm[2], *Brox'n* 1320 *Chol*, 1344 *ChGaol*

Brocton 1260–61 Orm[2]

Broxton 1284–7 Tab, 1383 Pat, 1418 ChRR *et freq*, *Broxston* 1428 *Chol*, 1465 ChRR

Broxne 1287 Court (p), 1318 *Chol* (p)

Brexne 14 *Sotheby* (p)

Broxsun 1310 *Chol*, *Broxson* 1344 *ChGaol* (Barnes[1]), 1622, 1660 Sheaf, *Broxsen* 1622 ib

Bruxon 1312 (1637) Rich (p)

Broxem 1313 Orm[2]

Breccon 1317 City (p)

Brexiun 1325 *Chol* (p)

Braxton 1417 Sheaf

Broxom' 1460 *Outl*

Boxton 1535 Plea, 1690 Sheaf

The *-ton* form of this p.n. is not historical, it is the product of an inversion of the *-ston* > *-son* development observed in Austerson 3 130, Snelson 1 93. Ekwall (DEPN and ES 64 219) derives this p.n. from OE *burȝæsn, *burȝæns 'a burial place' (cf. EPN s.v., and Burwains La 85, Brainshaugh Nb (DEPN), Bornesses NRY 283, 325), postulating a variant *borȝæsn which he then develops, from its dat.sg.fem. form *borʒsne, *borhsne, with metathesis and svarab-hakti vowel > *borəhsne, *borohsne, *bərohsne > *brocsne, and > *bor-ehsne, *bərehsne > *brecsne. This process does not account for the forms Brexis, -es, Brecsis and Brexens, -ins, Brexnus, which Ekwall does not note. It is, therefore, possible that Broxton contains some other stem, but since this el. has not been identified, Ekwall's etymology must stand until an equally ingenious explanation is found.

An alternative solution is perhaps suggested by the following observations. First, the forms suggest plural inflexions similar to those noted in Studies³ 29–34; -is, -es representing ME nom.pl. -es (< OE -as), perhaps replacing an OE nom.pl. in -e if DB Brosse is accurate; -un, -on, -in, -yn, -en, -em, -om, -ne representing an OE dat.pl. form in -um; and -ens, -ins, -nus representing a ME nom.pl. -(e)s added to Brexen, the reduced dat.pl. form taken as nom.sg. It should be noted that Broxton was two manors DB, and still has two halls, and that a similar circumstance at Caldy 282 infra has in-fluenced the syntax of the p.n. It seems that Brexens could mean 'the two places called Brexen'. Second, the same unidentified el. may lie behind another difficult p.n., Bursledon Ha, with hyll and dūn (both 'a hill' – Broxton is in hilly country, the missing element may be a hill-name, cf. Brown Knowl infra, Peckforton Hills 3 312). The early forms of Bursledon recorded by Mr J. E. B. Gover and Professor Ekwall are Brixendona c.1170, Brixenden 12, Bursedona 1208, Norbursedone 13, Burxedun' 1218, Brexheldene 1228, Bercildon 1245, Bursindene 1248, Bursyngdon 1288, Burstlesden 14. Ekwall (Studies³ 23 and DEPN) derives this p.n. from an OE *Beorhtsiginga-dūn ('the hill of the people of Beorhtsige') in order to explain the -x- spelling. But this is rather forced. The basis of Bursledon could be an OE form *brihs- identical with the OE *breohs- in Broxton. The hill-name context might suggest an old p.n. or even a folk-name upon Brit *brigā, late Brit *breʒa, Welsh bre 'a hill' (Barnes¹ 239), but the -ʒ- value of late Brit g in this word would hardly produce the [χ] implied by OE -h-, unless this were another analogy with the -k-form in Pembroke (from penn and broʒ, cf. LHEB 458, R. Duckow 1 22, xxi. There is a f.n. Broxes 1841 TA 153 in Dutton (2 114), which might be analogous, but it is not recorded early.

BOLESWORTH CASTLE & HILL FM (109–493557) [ˈboulzwəþ]

Boylthiswrth 1281 *AddCh* (p)
Bowliswrth' l13 *Chol* (p), *Bowlesworth* 1308 (1565) ChRR, *Boules-
worth* 1306 ChF, 1307 Plea *et freq* ib, *Chol*, ChRR to 1348 *Eyre*,
1572 ChRR
Bolesworth 1461 Sheaf, (*-Castle*) 1819 Orm², (*-Hill*) 1831 Bry,
Bolles- 1517, 1520 ChEx, 1539 Plea, 1546 Orm², *-worthe* 1539
(1564) ChRR, 1583 Orm², *Bolsworth* 1668–71 Sheaf
Bawlesworth (*hill*) 1465 *Chol*
Boldisworth 1541 *Chol*

The earliest form probably represents *Boythlisworth* with metathesis of *-thl-*. The p.n. would be OE *Bōðles worð* 'curtilage of a
house', from bōðl and worð (cf. bōðl-tūn), with castel(l) and hyll.
The castle is a well-done eighteenth-century extravagance, *v.* Orm²
II 678.

BANKHEAD (FM), *Barnhill Bank, Pages Farm* 1842 OS, cf. *Pages
Field* 1839 *TA*, *v.* banke, hēafod. *Page* is a surname. Cf. foll.
BARNHILL (FM, HO & WOOD), *Varne hill* 1690 Sheaf, *Barn-Hill*
1750, 1779 ib, *Barnhill* (the hamlet), *Barn Hill* (the farm), *Boles-
worth Wood* 1831 Bry, *v.* bere-ærn, hyll, cf. prec. and Bolesworth
supra.   BROWN KNOWL, 1842 OS, *Broxton Hill & Brow Knowl
Plantation* 1831 Bry, cf. *Hill Croft, Field & Wood* 1839 *TA*, *v.*
brūn¹, cnoll, hyll. Cf. Broxton *supra*, Peckforton Hills 3 312.
BROXTON BRIDGE, *v.* brycg.   BROXTON LOWER- & OLD HALL,
OLD HALL FM, *Higher- & Lower House* 1668–71 Sheaf, *The Higher-
& The Lower Hall* 1819 Orm², *Broxton Hall* 1831 Bry (Old Hall
6″), *Lower Broxton* 1842 OS (Lower Hall 6″), cf. Sheaf³ 39 (8394).
BROXTON WOOD, 1831 Bry, *Broxon Wood* 1323 AD, *Lee Cliff Wood*
1842 OS, *v.* lēah, clif, wudu.   COAL PIT (a wood), cf. *Coal Pit
Field* 1839 *TA*, *v.* col¹, pytt.   COOMBS WELL, cf. Harthill Coombs
92 *infra*, *The Coombes* 1842 OS, *The Comb* 1831 Bry, *Cumbes, The
Coombs Wood* 1839 *TA*, and *aqua vocat' Cowmbesbroke* 1465 *Chol*,
v. cumb 'a valley', brōc, wella 'a spring'.   THE DRUMBO, *-Drumba*
1839 *TA*, dial. *drumble* 'a wooded ravine', cf. dumbel.   FOX HO,
perhaps *Foxmore House* 1668–71 Sheaf, *v.* fox, mōr¹.   FULLER'S
MOOR, 1842 OS, *-More* 1668–71 Sheaf, 'fuller's marsh', *v.* fullere,
mōr¹.   GLEGG'S HALL, *Clegs Hill* 1831 Bry, from the surname
Glegg and hall.   HARTHILL POOL, *v.* 92 *infra*.   HOLYWELL
FM, *Holiwell* 1429 Sheaf, 1609 *Chol*, *Holly-* 1635 ib, *Holli-* 1750 Sheaf,

Holy- 1842 OS, *Halliwell House* 1668–71 Sheaf, named from Holy Well 72 *infra*, and beside Holywell Brook 1 29.   IVY FM.

KING JAMES'S HILL, *King James' Hill* 1831 Bry, probably connected in popular tradition with the tale of 'Higgledy-Piggledy Malpas Scot' and the divided rectory of Malpas.   THE KOPJE, *v.* copis, the dialect form *coppy* in a Dutch disguise.   LOWER FM. MEADOW BANK, 1839 *TA.*   THE MOUNT, *Mount Pleasant* 1842 OS.   OAKBANK FM, *Dark Lane Farm* 1831 Bry, cf. *Darke Lane* 1668–71 Sheaf, *Dark Lane* 1842 OS, *v.* deorc, lane, āc, banke. OAK FM, *Okes* 1269–70 Orm², *Oakes-House* 1702 *AddCh*, *Oaks* 1668–71 Sheaf, *The Oaks* 1819 Orm², *v.* āc.   OLD HALL FM, *v.* Broxton Old Hall *supra.*   PADGELANE COTTAGES & FM, cf. *Pads Croft & Field* 1839 *TA*, from dial. *pad* 'a path' (*v.* pæð), lane, cf. Padgbury 2 298.   SALTER'S LANE, *Salters Lane* 1842 OS, *v.* saltere, lane, cf. *Welshman's Street* 1 48 (Route XXV).   SMALL BROXTON FM, from ModE *small* 'little'.   SMITH'S PENTREY or SMITHFIELD (lost), 1819 Orm² II 676, 'Smith's, or the smith's, village and field', *v.* pentref, feld.   STABLE BANK, *v.* stable, banke. STONE PARLOUR, *le Stonehouse* 1522 *Chol. v.* stān, hūs, parlur. WALKER'S WOOD, 1842 OS.

FIELD-NAMES

The undated forms are 1839 *TA* 78. Of the others 1307–27 is Orm², 1349 *Eyre*, 1483, 1521 *Chol*, 1668–71 Sheaf, 1831 Bry.

(a) Bache (*v.* bæce[1]); Best Mdw; Bookley Fd, Buckley Fd (perhaps belonging to Bulkeley 17 *infra*); Bottoms (*v.* botm); Bromielow ('broomy hill', *v.* brōmig, hlāw); Broomhill (*v.* brōm, hyll); Buckley Fd (*v.* Bookley Fd *supra*); Bursley Mdw (cf. Burwardsley 93 *infra*); Circular (from its shape); Clemley (cf. Clemley 3 47); Cliff Hill (*v.* clif); Col Hall; Coney Graves (*v.* coningre); Danglemore; Deal Fd; French Wheat Piece (*v.* French wheat); Frizmore; Genesis Croft; Gorse Hovel Mdw (*v.* gorst, hovel); Grigg (*v.* grig², Welsh *grug*); Hall Moor (*le Hall More* 1521, *v.* hall, mōr[1]); Harthill Fd & Mdw (cf. Harthill 92 *infra*); Hob Fd (cf. *Hobcliffe* 1307–27, probably 'goblin's cliff', *v.* hob, clif); Hoo Fd (*v.* hōh); Hooks (*v.* hōc); Hurst (*v.* hyrst); The Lay (dial. *ley* 'a pasture', *v.* lēah); Liners Heath 1668–71 (*lynaltesheth* 1349 (PRO Chester 17, 3, m.45) perhaps for -*alces*-, thus 'heath at flax-corner', from līn and halc, with hǣð); Marl Yard (*v.* geard); Masquerade (*freq*); The Moors; Nant Mdw (Welsh nant 'a wood'); Old Fd; Old Woman's Croft; Ox Leasow (*v.* lǣs); Rands (*v.* rand, cf. *Swolnebuttes* 27 *infra*); Ravens Croft; Red Looms (*v.* rēad, loom); Big Ridding (*great Ryddyng* 1521, *v.* ryding); The Ridges; Rock Fd (*v.* roke); The Rough; Salt Marsh (*v.* salt, mersc); Sheepcote Fd (*v.* scēp, cot);

Shoulder of Mutton (*v.* 337 *infra*); Long Slang (*v.* slang); Smooth Hayes (*v.* smēðe, (ge)hæg); Spark Fd (*v.* spearca); Tegg Yard (*le Tegge yorth* 1483, 'teg's enclosure or fold', *v.* tegga, geard); Well Fd; Wetwood (*v.* wēt, wudu); White Banks (*v.* hwīt, banke); Windmill Fd (1831 Bry).

6. BULKELEY (109-5354) ['bukli, 'bulkli]

Bulceleia 1170 Facs (p), *Bulkeleh, Bulkileia* 1180–1220 *Chol* (p) *et freq* with variant spellings *Bulk-* (to 1656 Orm[2]), *Bulki-* (to 1374 AD), *Bulky-* (to 1459 ChRR), *Bulc(k)-, -le(h), -ley(e), -leg(h), -l(ee), -ly, -lei(e), -lg(h), -leigh(e), -leghe, -leia; Bulkelewe* 1272–1327 *JRC* (p), *Bulkilethe* 1300 *Dav* (p)

Bwlkeleh 12 Rich (p), *Boulkeleg'* c.1240 *Chol* (p), *Boolkeley* 1578 *ib* *Bolkilegh* c.1230 *Chol* (p), *-leg* 1325 *ib*, *Bolky-* 1307–27 *ib*, *-legh* 1303 EatonB, 1332 *Chol*, *Bolkele* 1241 Lib (p), *-ley* 1279 *CoLegh*, *-leye* 1309 Sheaf (p), *-legh* 1330 *Chol* (p)

Bulkyllg' 1302 *Chol*, *Bulkylley* 1307–27 Orm[2] (p)

Buckley 1308–27 MidCh (p), *-legh* 1316 ib (p) *et freq* with variant spellings *-ley, -legh, -lie, Bucley(e), Bukle(y)* to 1783 *Chol*

Bulkerleigh 1302 (1637) Rich

Bokelegh 1322 ChRR, *-ley* 1577, 1578 *Chol*

Bulkeileigh 1334, 1336 MidCh (p), *Bulkeyley* 1540 AD (p)

Bukylegh 1337 *Eyre* (p), *Bucky-* 1397 ChRR (p), *Buckeley* 1521 AD, 1593 *Chol*, *Bukeley* 1578 *ib*

Boukelly 1578 *Chol*

'Bullocks' clearing', *v.* bulluc, lēah. For the *-i-* spellings, cf. Botterley 3 142.

HADLEY (lost), *Hadley Hurst* 1302 (17) *Chol*, *Hadlehurst* 1302 (1637) Rich, *Hadleghhurst* 1315 *Chol*, *Hadelegh* 1316 *ib* (p), *Hadleigh* 1314 (1637) Orm[2], *Longe Hadley* 1602 *Chol*, *the two Hadleys* 1705 *ib*, *the lesser Hadley* 1731 *ib*, *Little- & Long Hadley* 1839 *TA* (Grid Ref. 109-527530), *Hadley, Long & Near Hadleys* 1838 *TA* 162 (34 *infra*, Grid Ref. 109-527528), 'clearing overgrown with heather', *v.* hǣð, lēah, hyrst 'a wooded hill'.

BULKELEY HALL, *Hall of Buckley* 1648 *Chol*, *aula de Bulkyley* 1429 Orm[2], cf. *the hall of bukley dyd staund in bokeley hey, the place ys known to this dey & called the hall yordes* 1578 *Chol*, *-the Hall Yardes* 1593 *ib*, *-Yards* 1629 *Vern*, also foll., Manorhouse Fm *infra*, and *le Hall feld* 1421 Orm[2], *Hall Field* 1839 *TA*, *Hall Meadow* 1700

Chol, *v*. hall, geard, feld, mǣd. BULKELEYHAY, *Bukely-, Bokeley Hey* 1577, 1578 *Chol, Buckeley-* 1593 *ib, Buckley Hey* 1629 *Vern, -Heyes, -Hayes* 1694 *Chol*, 'the fenced-in enclosure', *v*. (ge)hæg, cf. prec. and Bulkeley *supra*. BULKELEY HILL, *Bukle Hill wher the hedde of Wyver river is* c.1536 Leland, *Bulkley Hill* Eliz I *Surv, Bulkley Hill* 1668–71 Sheaf, *Bulckley Hill* 1743 *Chol, v*. hyll, cf. Peckforton Hills 3 312, Bulkeley *supra*, R. Weaver 1 38. BULKE-LEY MILLS, *molendinum de Bulkylegh* 1308, 1315 *Chol, Buckley Milnes* 1783 *ib, Bulkley Mille* 1668–71 Sheaf, cf. *le Mulnehurst* 1302 (17) *Chol, le milnebrok* c.1320 *ib*, *the Mill Hole* 1690 *ib, Mill Field* 1796 *ib, Mill Hole & Meadow* 1839 *TA, v*. myln, hyrst, brōc, hol[1], feld. The *Mill Hole* was a water meadow in a hollow near the mill. CHOLMONDLEY LANE, *v*. lane, cf. Cholmondeley 21 *infra*. COM-MON FM, cf. *Common Land & Lot* 1839 *TA, v*. commun, hlot, land. GREENLANE COTTAGE, *v*. grēne[1], lane. MANORHOUSE FM, *Old Hall* 1831 Bry, *v*. ald, hall, maner, cf. Bulkeley Hall *supra*. WAL-NUT-TREE FM. YEWTREE COTTAGE, FM & HO.

FIELD-NAMES

The undated forms are 1839 *TA* 106. Of the others 1250–1300 (1637), 1262 (1637), 1302 (1637), 1315 (1637)[2] are Rich, 1304 *Dav*, 1314 (1637), 1315 (1637), 1429 Orm[2], 1629 *Vern*, 1668–71, 1884 Sheaf, 1831 Bry, and the rest *Chol*.

(a) Abrahams Croft 1731 (1700, *Abraham Croft* 1593, *Abrams Crofts* 1629, from the ME pers.n. *Abraham*); Ash Beach ('valley with ash-trees in it', *v*. æsc, bece[1]); Ash Hole ('ash-tree hollow', *v*. æsc, hol[1]); Asp Fd 1731 (1705, *v*. æspe); Bank Acre, Banks Mdw (cf. *Bank Craft* 1700, *v*. banke, croft); Barker's Croft (cf. *the two Barkers feildes* 1606, *barkehowse fyld* 1525, *v*. bark-howse, barkere); Barley Fd (*lee Barlefyld* 1525, 'the barley field', *v*. le, bærlic, feld); Barn Fd (1790, cf. *Barn(e) Croft* 1705, 1731); Barrel Fd (cf. Barhill 48 *infra*); Beach (*v*. bece[1]); Bean Croft (1796); Bottoms (*v*. botm); Bowling Croft (perhaps *croftum Willelmi Bolding* c.1320, but probably a place where bowls was played); Broadhay 1705 (*v*. brād, (ge)hæg); Brook Fd (1705, *v*. brōc); Bulkeley Fd (cf. *Bulkilgh' Croft* 1304, *v*. croft, cf. Bulkeley *supra*, Town Fd *infra*); Chapel Fd & Ho (cf. *Chapel Lane* 1831, *v*. chapel); Civils Mdw (*the Seavils Meadow* 1700, *Sevill's Meadow* 1796); Clay Acres & Flatt (*the Clay Acre* 1790, cf. *Clay croft* 1705, *v*. clæg, æcer, flat, croft); Clemley (cf. Clemley 3 47); Coat Wd (*v*. cot); Cock Pit (*v*. cockpit); Colly Croft (*v*. colig); Further- & Near Friday (*v*. Frigedæg); Gate Acre, Mdw & Wd (*v*. gata 'a pasture'); Grannum's Croft 1796 ('gran-dame's croft', probably dower land); Green Fd (1550, *v*. grēne[1]); Hales Mdw 1790; Heath Fd (*lee Hythfyld* 1525, cf. *Bulkeleigh heth* 1262 (1637), *bruerium de Bulkyllg'* 1302, *bruerium inter le Walschemonnisstrete et villa de*

Pecforton c.1320, *Bulkley Heath* 1668–71, *v.* hǣð, feld, cf. *Welshman's Street* 1 48 (Route XXV), Pecforton 3 311); Hough (*le Hogh* 1315, *lee-* 1525, *le Hoxh* 1320, *the Great Hough* 1606, *v.* le, hōh, grēat); The Kings Parlour 1884 (Sheaf[1] 3, p. 162, the local name for a view-point on a crag of Bulkeley Hill, *v.* cyning, parlur); Know(l) (*le Knowle* 1302 (17), *dura terra de le Chnol* 1320, *Knowle Field* 1796, cf. *Held infra, v.* cnoll); The Luck; Marl Fd; Marsh; Middle Fd (cf. *the Middel Croft* 1640, *v.* middel); Narrow Croft 1796; New Fd (1790); The Paddock 1790; Little Park (cf. *the Parks* 1606, *Park Field* 1790, *v.* park); Patch Croft 1736 (*v.* pacche); Penny Croft (*v.* peni(n)g); Pinfold Croft (*v.* pynd-fald); Road Fd; Rushy Piece (*Russy Peice* 1700, *Rushy-* 1731, *-Peece* 1705); Scutch Fd; Smithy Croft (cf. *the Smithie Cottage* 1657, *v.* smiðð e); Spark Mdw (*v.* spearca); Sty Fd (*la Sty* 1304, *v.* stigu); (Back- & Middle-) Town Fd (*the two Town Fields* 1550, *-Towne Feilds* 1640, *the Big-*, *the Little Town Field* 1736, *Town Croft* 1790, *-Field* 1796, *v.* toun, cf. Bulkeley Fd *supra*); Two Butts (cf. *Butts* 1796, *Wardy's Buttes* 1550, *v.* butte. *Wardys* is gen.sg. of the surname *Ward*); Wheat Fd 1705; Big- & Far Wd, Wood Croft (cf. *the Woodfields*, *the Great- & -Little Wood* 1629, *v.* wudu).

(*b*) *Alde Rene*, *-Rhene*, *-Rehne* c.1220, *-Rene* 1315 ('the old boundary strip', *v.* ald, rein); (*H*)*Atfordislegh* 1315, *Atfordes-* 1316 ('(glade at) the heath ford', from hǣð and ford, with lēah); *the Barhasse feild* 1593 (this was near the site of old Bulkeley Hall, and may be from barras 'a barrier', cf. *barrace* NED); *Bircheneleg* 1320 (*v.* bircen[2], lēah); *Blakelache* 1320 ('black boggy stream', *v.* blæc, læc(c)); *the branned crofts* 1550, *-brunt-* 1577 (*v.* brende[2]); *Breeches Cloughes* 1629 ('dells where land has been broken in', *v.* brēc, clōh); *Brounesbruche* 1347 ('intake belonging to one Brown', from bryce and the ME pers.n. or surname *Broun* (<OE *Brūn*)); *Bulkeley Lane* 1593, 1597 (*v.* lane); *le Calreheye* 1302, cf. *the calves croft* 1550 (*v.* calf (gen.pl. calfra), (ge)hæg, croft); *Candelanesgreues* 1320, *Kandelannes grene* 1360, (cf. 'land formerly held by *Candelan*' c.1310, from the ME (OFr) pers.n. and surname *Gandel(e)yn*, *Candelayn* (<Romance *Wantelin*, OG *Wandel-*, *Wandilo*, *v.* Forssner 246, Bardsley s.n. *Candlin*) and grǣfe 'a wood'); *Cat(e) Acre* 1580, *the Catacre* 1606 (*v.* catte, æcer); *le Clives* c.1320 (*v.* clif; *le cloke* 1320 (perhaps 'the dell', from clōh, but Professor Löfvenberg notes that the form is probably an instance of ME *cloke* 'a claw' in some transferred topographical sense); *Darle hurst* 1302 (17) ('(wooded-hill at) the deer wood', from dēor and lēah with hyrst); *the Dingowe* 1606 ('the dell', *v.* dingle); *Farleyhelde* c.1230, *Farnelegh-* c.1310, *Farnilegh-* 1327, *Franlegh Held* 1338 ('(hill-side at) the ferny clearing', from fearn(ig) and lēah with helde); *torrens qui vocatur Gladi(h)aue-*, *Cladiaue Rinle* 1220, c.1220, *Gladiaue-* 1315 ('(runnel at) the cheerful enclosure', from glæd[1] and (ge)hæg, haga, with rynel); *le Grene* 1429 (*v.* grēne[2]); *Grene Mening Wei*, *-Wey* c.1220, *-Meing-* 1315 (from the adj. grēne[1] 'green, grass-grown', and a road-name which also occurs at *Menihincwey* c.1220, in Minshull Vernon, 2 250, *v.* weg 'a way, a road'. The Bulkeley example was a way marking an estate boundary (*Chol* D, 32, 33, 35, 46), and the Minshull Vernon road may have coincided with one (*AddCh* 50681). This suggests major highways,

cf. 1 47 (Route XXII), *Welshman's Street* 1 48 (Route XXV). The word *mening* could be an *-ing*-suffix derivative of (ge)mǣne 'held in common, shared'; but with the form *menihinc* it would indicate derivation from OE *menigeo, menigu* 'a multitude, a crowd' with *-ing*[1] noun-suffix or *-ing-*[4] connective particle. The forms are too early for *meinie* (1290 NED) 'a crowd, a troop, a multitude'. Such a road-name would mean 'way used by the multitude, road along which crowds pass'); *Heghhurstesmor* 1332 ('(marsh at) the high wood-hill', from hēah and hyrst, with mōr[1]); *le Held* 1302 (17), *-Held(e)* 1320, 1324, 1372, *the Heldeknol* 1315 (1637)[1], *-Holde-* 1315 (1637)[2], *Heldelone* 1360 ('the slope, the declivity', v. helde, cnoll, lane, cf. Know(l), *Farleyhelde supra*); *le hoke* 1310 (v. hōc cf. *Huclou infra*); *Holyn Hourst* 1578, *Holine-* 1593 ('holly wood-hill', v. holegn, hyrst); *(le) Holkebroc* c.1320, 1320 ('brook in a hollow', v. holc(e), brōc); *Huclou* c.1320 ('mound or hill at a hook or bend', v. hūc, hlāw, cf. *le hoke supra* and *Hocloue* 27 *infra*); a piece of land called *Keneuardis* 1308 (from the OE pers.n. *Cyneweard*); *mora* 1320, *the moore Crofte* 1606 (v. mōr[1], croft); *Oateslowe* 1347 ('Odo's hill', from the ME (OG) pers.n. *Odo, Ote(s)* (cf. Bardsley, Reaney, s.n. *Oat, Oade*) and hlāw); *strata vocata Pecfortonlowen* 1413 (v. lane, cf. Pecforton 3 311); *le Pullondes* 1347 ('selions near a pool', v. pull, land); *Ridley Forde* 1314 (1637), *Ridlegh Forde* c.1320 (v. ford, cf. 3 314); *le Rugges* 1347 ('the ridges', v. hrycg); *the Salehurst* 1302 (1637) ('the willow wood', v. salh, hyrst); *Saltersway* (v. 1 48, (Route XXV)); *Thurse Hole* 1429 ('giant's or demon's hole', v. þyrs, hol[1]); *Tikehull* c.1320 ('Tica's hill', from the OE pers.n. *Tica* and hyll); *Walshmonstreet* (v. 1 48 (Route XXV)); *le Weylond* 1315 ('selion near a road', v. weg, land).

7. CHIDLOW (HALL) (109–5045)

> *Chiddelowe* 1282 Court, 1313 Orm[2], *Chydde-* 1551 Chol, *Chide-, Chyde-* 1328 ib et freq to 1592 ChRR
> *Chedelowe* l13 Chol, 1359 Eyre (p), *Ched(e)-* 1498 Sheaf
> *Childelowe* 1358 JRC (Barnes[1] 247), 1446, 1460 ChRR, 1474 Orm[2]
> *Chidlowe* 1396 ChRR, *Chyd-* 1406 ib (p), *Chidlow* 1509 ib, (*-Farm*) 1831 Bry, (*-Hall*) 1842 OS, *Chidlaw* 1640 Chol
> *Shidlow* 1515 MinAcct

'Cidda's mound', from the OE pers.n. *Cidda* (cf. Problems 100, DEPN s.n. *Chiddingfold*) and hlāw, cf. Ivy Ho *infra*, and *Chidlow Hill* 1841 TA, v. hyll.

DODD'S LANE, cf. *Dods Croft* 1841 TA, probably from the surname *Dodd*.   IVY HO, 1842 OS, *Chidlow Hall* 1831 Bry, v. hall, cf. Chidlow Hall *supra*.

FIELD-NAMES

The undated forms are 1841 *TA* 104, 1329[1] is AD, 1329[2] *AddCh.*

(*a*) Aston Fd (*v.* æsc, tūn); Hemp Fd (*v.* hænep); Hodge Hill (*v.* hocg, hyll, cf. *Hodg Croft* 1 158); Milking Bank (*v.* milking); Red Gough ('the red one', from rēad reduplicating Welsh coch 'red').

(*b*) *le Espenfeld* 1329[1], *-Espene-* 1329[2] ('field growing with aspens', *v.* æspen, feld).

8. CHOLMONDELEY (109–5451) ['tʃɔumli, 'tʃʌmli]

Calmundelei 1086 DB, *Chalmundeley* 1447 Chol (p), *-mund(e)-* 1475 *ib*, *Challemondeley* 1536 ChRR, Plea

Chelmundeleia 1180–1220 Chol (p) *et freq* with variant spellings *Chele-, Cel-, -m(u)nd(e)-, -munda-, -l(egh), -le(h), -l'gh, -leg(he), -ll', -ley* to 1369 Chol, *Chelmond(e)l'* 1298 *ib*, *-mondeley* 1400 *ib*

Cholmonlegh 1209 Tab, *-ley* 1454, 1472 ChRR (p), 1504 Pat (p), *-munly* 1393 Chol, *-ley* 1427 *ib*

Cholemundel' 1217–29 (1580) Sheaf, *Cholmundeleg'* c.1240 Chol *et freq* with variant spellings *Cho(l)-, Col-, -mund(e)-* (to 1610 Speed), *-mond(e)-* (from 1314 ChRR), *-mud(d)e-, -mod-, -l(e)g(h), -l(eighe), -ley(e), -le, -logh, -ly(e)*; *Cholmendeley* 1447 Chol, *-mandley* 1657 *ib*

Cholmundes-, -is-, -le(ia), -leg' e13 Chol, AddCh, *-esleye* 1225–49 Chest (p), *-legh* 1348 ChRR (p), *Scholumdesley* 13 Whall (p), *Scholmundisl'* 1310 Chol, *Cholmondeslegh* 1347 Sheaf, 1361 BPR (p)

Chelmnlegh 1310 Chol, *Chelmunleye* 1321 *ib* (p), *-ley* 1400 *ib*, *-monley* 1392 Pat (p)

Chelmundesleg' 1349 Rich, *-legh* 1389 *Dav* (p)

Cholnondelegh 1364 AD (p)

Chalumley 1394, 1400 Pat (p)

Cholmeley 1397 Pat (p), 1417 AD (p) *et freq* with variant spellings *Cholm(y)-, -lye, -leighe* to 1724 NotCestr

Chelmeley 1398 Pat, ChRR (p), 1400 Chol, *Chelmley* 1694 ChetOS VIII

Chalmesley 1403 Pat (p)

Jolmonney 1404 Chol (p)

Chomley c.1420 Sheaf, 1470 Chol, 1537 ChRR, 1558–79 ChancP (p), *Chomeley* 1554 *Dow* (p)

Cholmidley 1553 Pat (p)

Choulmondeley 1574 *Dow*
Chumondleigh 1640 Sheaf

'Cēolmund's wood or clearing', from the OE pers.n. *Cēolmund*
and lēah, cf. Cholmondeston 3 136, Chulmleigh D 377.

THE BIRTLES (lost, 109–552498, a wood), 1689 *Chol, boscus de
Bir(i)chlis* e13 *AddCh, -Birchelis* 1305 *Chol, -es, -Brichles, le Byrchel'*
1310 *ib, boscus de Birchel'* 1323, 1339 *ib, -Birthel'* 1330 *ib, le Birteles*
1362 *ib, Brichull* 1334 *Chol* (p), woods of *Birtle* 1517 AD, cf. *Birthels
Lane* c.1650 *Chol* (11 *supra*), 'the little birch-trees', *v.* bircel, cf.
Birtles 1 72.

BURLEY (lost)

> *Burlegh* c.1240 *Chol* (an assart), *-leg'* 1285, 1328 (p) *ib*, (molen-
> dinum de-) c.1290, (stagnum de-) *-l'g* c.1290 *ib*
> *Burhel'* c.1290 *Chol, Burghelegh* 1318 *ib* (p), *Burghlegh* 1359 *ib* (p)
> *Borruueleg'* c.1290 *Chol, Borrueleg'* 1325 *ib* (p), *Borulegh* 1331,
> 1332 *ib* (p), 1340 *Eyre* (p), *Borewelegh* 1316 *Chol* (p), *Boroley*
> 1413 *ib* (p), *Borowley* 1425 *ib* (p)
> *Burwelegh'* 1322, 1331 *Chol* (p), *Burroley* 1410 *ib* (p)
> *The four Burley Fields* 1670 *Chol*, the *Burley Field* (in four parts)
> 1734 *ib*, cf. *Burly Feild* 1700 *ib* 10 *supra*.

'Glade at a fortified place', *v.* burh, lēah. The first el. is in the
gen.sg. form, burge, which also appears in *Burhemare* c.1240,
Borowomer' 1343 *Chol* (A2, A67), a boundary of *Burley, v.* burge,
(ge)mǣre.

CROXTON GREEN, 1831 Bry, *Croxton'* 1310–30 *Chol, -Greene* 1668–71
Sheaf, *Croxon Green* 1704, 1728 *Chol, Croxen-* 1727 *ib*, probably
analogous with Croxton 2 236 *supra*, from the pers.n. OE *Crōc*
(from ON *Krókr* or ODan *Krōk*) and tūn, with grēne[2]. The place
gives rise to a surname, cf. Ralph Croxton of *Croxton Green* 1570
Orm[2] II 144.

BANKHOUSE FM, cf. *Bank House* 1786 *Chol*, 1842 OS, *The Banke,
Banky Peece* 1670 *Chol, Bank's Croft* 1734 *ib, v.* banke, hūs, pece.
The surname *Banks* appears in eighteenth-century leases in Cholmondeley.   CASTLE FM, *Castle Inn* 1831 Bry, named from Cholmondeley Castle *infra*.   CASTLE HILL, perhaps as prec., but cf. *le*

Castelhull infra. CHAPEL MERE, *Chapel Mare* 1668-71 Sheaf, *Chapell Meare* 1671 ib, *The Chapel Mear* 1738 *Chol*, a lake, *v.* mere[1], named from *Cholmondeley Chapel* 1842 OS, *capella de Chelmundelegh* c.1295 *Chol, Cholmondley Chappell* 1599 *ib, Cholmley-* 1724 NotCestr, cf. *a chapel of woode* c.1536 Leland. This lake, or Moss Mere *infra*, was *Acmare* e13 AddCh, *Ocmer* 1298 *Chol, Hocmer'* 1336 *ib, aqua de Okmere* 1394 *ib, Okemere* 1397 *ib*, cf. (*Little*) *Acmarehurst* e13 AddCh, *Hocmer'hurst* 1322 *Chol, Okemeres-* 1359 *ib*, 'oak mere', *v.* āc, mere[1], hyrst. CHOLMONDELEY BRIDGE, *v.* brycg. CHOLMONDELEY CASTLE, *the newly erected Mansion House called Cholmondeley Castle* 1787 *Chol*, like Peckforton Castle 3 312 and Bolesworth Castle 14 *supra*, an eighteenth-century extravagance, *v.* castel(l), cf. Old Hall *infra*. CHOLMONDELEY MERES, 1842 OS, *les Meres* 1363 *MinAcct, the Two Meers* 1787 *Chol*, collectively *Park Mere* 1831 Bry, severally *Chomley Meare, Ockley Mere* 1668-71, cf. *Hoppley Meare Meadow* 1653 *Chol, Hopley-* 1687 *ib, Hopley Meadow* 1689 *ib, v.* mere[1], park. *Ockley* is 'oak wood', *v.* āc, lēah. *Hopley* is 'grass-hopper glade' or 'glade at a hollow', from hoppa or hop[1], with lēah, cf. Hopleys Croft 42 *infra*. CHOLMONDELEY PARK, 1842 OS, *New Park* 1670 *Chol, -e* 1700 *ib, v.* nīwe, park, cf. Park Fm *infra*. CORONATION WOOD. DOWSE GREEN, 1717 *Chol, -Greene* 1730 *ib, Douse Greene* 1668-71 Sheaf, *Dousd Greene, Dousd Fields* 1670 *Chol, the three Dowse Feilds, -Fields* 1699, 1717, 1730 *ib*, 'pleasant green', from douce 'sweet, pleasant', and grēne[2], with feld. FIELDS FM, *v.* feld. GARDEN COVERT. HIGGINSFIELD HO, *Higginsfeilds* 1694 *Chol, -Field* 1831 Bry, *Higens Fields* 1750 *Chol, Higgens Feld* 1842 OS, from feld and the ME pers.n. *Higgin* or the surname *Higgins*. LONG WALK COTTAGES, *v.* walk 'a place for walking'. MARL PIECE (a wood), cf. *Marle Field, Marld Croft, Old-, Farther- & Hither Marle Field* 1670 *Chol, v.* marle, marled, croft, ald. MOSS MERE & WOOD, *Cholmondeley Roughs* 1831 Bry, *Bickley Moss Plantation, Moss Mere* 1842 OS, cf. *mosseta de Cholmundelegh'* 1348 *Chol, Cholmundeley Moss* 1517 AD, *Cholmondeley Moss* 1705 *Chol, Mosse Croft, the Moore, Litle Moore, the Three Moores* 1670 *ib*, also Chapel Mere *supra*, Bickley Moss 10 *supra, v.* mos, mere[1], mōr[1], rūh. NEVILL'S WOOD. OLD HALL (lost), 1831 Bry, *le Hawl* 1285 *Chol, Cholmeley Haul* c.1536 Leland, *Cholomondeley Hall* 1643 Sheaf, *Cholmley Hall* 1694 *Chol, v.* ald, hall. This ancient residence was superseded by the 'castle' built on another site. PARK FM, PARKSIDE COTTAGES & FM,

Parkside Farm 1786 *Chol, Old Park Farm* 1831 Bry (twice), *Park Farm & Side* 1842 OS, cf. *the old park* 1699 *Chol, the old Park Pale* 1711 *ib, the Old Pale* 1747 *ib, Pale Meadow* 1734, 1761 *ib, v.* park, sīde, ald, pale. The new park is at Cholmondeley Park *supra.* SCHOOL FM, *v.* scōl. SICILYOAK FM, *Cecilly Oak* 1842 OS, *Common Farm & Lane* 1831 Bry, *v.* commun. The later name appears to be a popular form of 'sessile oak'.   WANNER HILL FM (lost), 1786 *Chol, Warrant Hill* 1668–71 Sheaf, 1738 *Chol, (the) Warren Hill* 1670, 1718 *ib, the house at the Warren Hill, The Warrant House* 1753 *ib,* 'rabbit-warren hill', *v.* wareine, hyll, cf. Warrans House Fd 3 300.   WEAVER COTTAGE & FM, near the head-stream of R. Weaver.   WOODEND COTTAGE, *v.* wudu, ende[1].

FIELD-NAMES

The undated forms are 1670 *Chol* A205. Of the others e13 is *AddCh,* 1272–1307, 1316[2] Orm[2], 1304 Chamb, 1325[2], 1400, 1407, 1409, 1412, 1421 ChRR, 1422 Plea, 1482 Rich, 1668–71, 1919 Sheaf, 1831 Bry, 1842 OS, and the rest *Chol.*

(*a*) Aldersey (cf. Aldersey 82 *infra*); Bach Meadow(e) 1684, 1699, (*Beach (Meadow), Beach or Beane Croft* 1670, *v.* bæce[1], cf. Beane Croft *infra*); Backside; Barn(e) Croft, Fd, Yard 1734 (*Barnecroft, Barneyarde* 1670, cf. *le Berneflat* 1456, *v.* bere-ærn, croft, geard, flat); Bartlams Fd 1738 (*Bartloms Field* 1670); Beane Croft, Beane Yarde (*v.* bēan, croft, geard, cf. Bach Meadow(e) *supra*); The Bear Fd 1717, 1730; Bebington's Ground 1729 (1670, cf. Peter & William *Bebynton* of *Cholmeley* 1492 *Chol,* from Bebington 245 *infra, v.* grund); Bigfield; Black-Brook Croft 1730 (*Black Brook Field & Meadow* 1670, *Blackbrook Croft* 1717, *v.* blæc, brōc); Black Croft; Blackfield 1699 (*Blake Feild* 1684, *le Blakefeld* 1355, cf. *the Blake Flattes* 1451, 1452, *v.* blæc, feld, flat); Blackhouse Croft; Breretons Croft 1730 (1670. The *Brereton* family held part of the Malpas barony); Brick Kill Coppy (*v.* bryke-kyl, copis); Bridge Fd; The Brynn 1787 (*-e* 1734, *Brynn* 1670, 'the hill', *v.* bryn(n)); Broad Fd; Brook Leasow (*v.* lǣs); The Broome (*v.* brōm); Broomy Croft 1699 (1670, *v.* brōmig); Buckley Platt (*v.* plat[2], cf. Bulkeley 17 *supra*); Butteycroft (*v.* butty); Cadiell Mdw 1747 (*le litle Caldeleg'* 1315, *Caldelegh* 1317, 1320, *Cadily Meadow* 1670, *-ley-* 1711, *The Kedel(e)y Meadow* 1691, 1726, 'cold clearing', *v.* cald, lēah, mǣd); Calve(r)s Croft 1734 (*Caluer Croft* 1670, *v.* calf, croft); The Caudlands Croft 1730 (*-Caudlandes Craft* 1691, *-Caudland Croft* 1726, 'cold selions', *v.* cald, land, croft); Churtons Ground 1730 (1670, *v.* grund. *Churton* is probably a surname from Churton 70 *infra*); Clay Croft & Fd; Clover Croft 1738; Cockshutt Croft (*le Cokshotefyld* 1456, *v.* cocc-scyte, feld); Colleys 1700 (*v.* colig); Cook's Craft 1700 (*Cooks Croft* 1670, *v.* croft, pytt. *Cook* is a surname); Cooks Pitt 1735 (cf. Cookspit 3 143); Cow Fd; Crab Hill Mdw 1735; Cross Flat 1787 (*v.* cros); Long Crow (*Big &-* 1787, *v.* crew); Croues

Mosse 1668–71 (*Crouemos* c.1230 (p), *le-* 1341, *Crouuemosse iuxta Bykurton* 1420 (lit. *Cronne-*, Orm[2] ii 640 reads *Croune-*), *Crouuemosse* 1421, 1422 (ChRR, Plea, lit. *Croune-*), cf. *Locronemosfeld* 1363, *Cronemossefeld* 1366, 'crow's marsh' or 'crane's marsh', the forms being uncertain, *v.* **crāwe, cron, mos, feld**); Curtisfield; Dairy House Fm 1787 (*Darie Croft* 1670, *v.* **deierie**); Dans Fd 1787; Two-, Three-, Four-, Five-, Six-, Ten-, Eighteen- & Thirty Dayes Math 1670, 1734, 1738 (*v.* **day-math**); Deans Fd; Dodes Ground, Dods Wd & Yarde (*Dodds Woode* 1598, a wood belonging to Hugh *Dodd*, *v.* **grund, wudu, geard**); Dog Kennel Croft 1738 (*-Coppy* 1670, *v.* **kenel, copis**); Duffa's Mdw (*v.* **dovehouse**); Edgerow Croft 1800 (*Edgrue Croft* 1670, *Edgreu* 1738, *v.* **hecg-rǣw**); Neare Fart Peece; Faugh Croft (*v.* **falh**); The Filance Flatt 1699 (*The Filances Flat* 1695, *v.* **filand(s)**); Fishpond Fd 1800 (*Fish Pan Field* 1738, *v.* **fisc, ponde** (OE **pand*, see Löfvenberg 158, EPN 2 69)); Furley Fd; Big & Little Gaily 1776 (*Galymoore* 1670, *Gally-* 1734, *v.* **gagel, -ig**[3], **mōr**[1]); Glade Fd; Gors(t)ycroft (*v.* **gorstig**); Greasy Lees (*le Gresedeleg* 1315, *-legh* 1317, 1320, 'grazed clearing', from the ME pa.part. gresede, grasede 'having been grazed' (OE *grasian* 'to graze, to pasture') and **lēah**); Greenfield; Grestons Heath 1670, 1738 (*le Graystainshez* c.1290, 'heath at grey stones', from **grǣg**[1] and **stān**, with **hǣð**, cf. Greyleston 34 *infra*); Guild Hay 1787; Hackers Hill 1842 (*Heccarst Hill* 1670, *Hackers Hill* 1734, *Harcot(t)s Hill* 1786, cf. *Accar's or Aker's Croft* 1919, *Harcourts Croft* 1670, *Harcotts Croft* 1741, and cf. *Harecourt Heth* 1482, *v.* **hyll, croft, hǣð**. The *Harcourt* family held land here c.1300, 1305 *Chol*); Hakes Moss 1787 (*le Haukesmos* 1310, *v.* **hafoc, mos**); Hands Croft; The Hatch Fd 1768 (*v.* **hæc(c)**); Hatilifield 1754 (*v.* **hǣðiht, lēah**); the Four Haughs 1738 (*le Halgh* 1362, *Great* & *Little Haugh* 1670, cf. *the Haughlanes* 1730, and *de(l) Halgh* 1349 (p), 1354 (p), *v.* **halh, leyne**); Hawkins Mosses 1730 (1717, *Hawkins Moss(e)* 1670, 1699, *v.* **mos**); Hawk Lane 1831 (*v.* **halc**); Hempbutt & -yard (*v.* **hænep, butte, hemp-yard**); Hill Fd, Great & Little Hill (*le Hulfeld* 1362, *Hulle* 1484, *v.* **hyll, feld**); Holly-bush Croft; the Holme 1684 (*v.* **holmr**); the Horse Moor 1787; The Husbandman's Ho 1738 (*v.* **inntak**); Jack Croft (two crofts called *Jakcroftes* 1451, 1452, 'little crofts', *v.* **jack**); The Kedeley Mdw 1730 (*v.* **Cadiell Mdw** *supra*); Kennerl(e)y Mdw 1700, 1734 (cf. *Kenelly Green* 1670, *v.* **grēne**[2]); Kiln Croft, Kill Moore (cf. *le Kylneflat(t)* 1456, *v.* **cyln, flat, mōr**[1], **croft**); Knowle Banke (*v.* **cnoll, banke**); Lane Croft 1670 (*v.* **leyne**); Long Butts 1691 (*v.* **butte**); Meer Fm 1787 (cf. *the Meare* 1705, *v.* **mere**[1], cf. Cholmondeley-, Chapel- & Moss Mere *supra*); Midle Fd (*the Midell Felde* 1451, 1452, *v.* **middel, feld**); Milking Yarde 1670 (*v.* **milking, geard**); Mill Fd (*v.* Windmill Fd *infra*); Naggs Pasture (*v.* **nagge**); Nettlewood 1710 (*v.* **netel(e), wudu**); Oatfield; Old Fd (*le Oldefeld* 1362, *v.* **ald, feld**); Ollar Croft, Ollery Croft (cf. *le Croffte de Holre* 1285, *v.* **alor, croft**); Orchard Croft & Coppy (*v.* **copis**); Ouercrofte (*v.* **uferra**); Oxfield; Par Fd 1787 (*Parrcroft* 1670, *Par Croft* 1734); Pease Croft, Eddish & Fd (*v.* **pise, edisc**); Pick Fds 1787; Pingo 1776 (cf. *Pingo's Greaue* 1670, *v.* **pingot, grǣfe**); Pittfield; Plumb Croft 1787 (*the Plombtree Crafts* 1691, *the Plumbtree Croft* 1726, 1730, *v.* **plūme, trēow**); The Higher Pool 1738 (*Lower* & *Over Poole Meadow* 1670, *v.* **pōl**[1]); The Privy-, -Privie Croft 1754, 1768; Rabitt Bank

1738 (*v.* rabbit); Radcocks Greene 1668–71 (from a surname *Radcock* and grēne[2]); Red Croft; Ridley Fd (cf. Ridley 3 313); Rough Fd; The Ruly 1738 (*Roulowe(hull)* 1362, *Rowlow* 1397, *Rooly Garden, Galymoore Rooly* 1670, 'rough mound', *v.* rūh, hlāw, hyll, gardin, cf. Gaily *supra*); Rushey Fd 1734 (*v.* riscig); Rye Flatt (*le Ruyflatt* 1362, *v.* ryge, flat); The Sake Fds 1796 (*Farther-, Hither- & Litle Sake Field* 1670); Middle Seat Fd 1787 (*Middle Seat* 1670); Shondes Bankes 1657 (*v.* banke); Lower Shoot (*v.* scēat); Silver Fd 1735; The Slack 1734 (*v.* slakki); The Slang 1700 (*v.* slang); Square Croft & Fd 1730, 1734 (-*Field* 1691, *v.* square); Tack Croft 1734 (cf. *the hither Take Field* 1687, probably a shortened form of 'intake', *v.* inntak); The Temple Fd 1787 (probably from some ornamental park building); Tomblissons Green 1700 (*Tumbleson Greene* 1668–71, from the surname *Tomlinson* and grēne[2]); Town Fd 1730, Town Moore 1769 (*Town Moore* 1659, *Towne Meadow* 1670, *v.* toun); (The) Wall Fd & Croft 1734 (*Wallcroft* 1670, *the Wallfeild* 1691, cf. *the Wall Bank & Meadows* 1702, *v.* wælla); Well Croft, Fd & Mdw (cf. *Well Moore* 1734, cf. prec.); Windmill-, Mill Fd (*le Mulnefeld* 1362, cf. *molendinum de Chelmundelegh* 1320, *molendinum ventriticum* 1348, *le Molyn de Eue* 1397, *Cholmondeley Mills* 1686, *water mill & windmill at Cholmondeley* 1709, and *le Mulnewey* 1362, *la Mulnebrok* 1355, *le-* 1362, *v.* myln, wind-mylne, feld, weg, brōc); The Woodhey Croft 1768 (cf. *boscus de Cholmundisleg* e13, *le Wodefyld* 1456, *the Wood Heath* 1638, *v.* wudu, feld, hǣð, (ge)hæg); The Woolery Croft 1754 (-*Wollerey-* 1738, -*Wellery-* 1753, probably 'owlery', i.e. 'covered with alders', *v.* alor); Wett Moore (*v.* wēt, mōr[1]); Wheat Croft (cf. *Wheat Field* 1734, *v.* hwǣte); White Moore (*v.* hwīt, mōr[1]); the Litle Yard 1691 (*v.* lȳtel, geard).

(b) *Achel'g* c.1290, *Acheleg'* 1325 ('ash-wood', *v.* æsc, lēah); *Anichefleg'* c.1240 (*Chol* A 2, unintelligible); *Annotesfeld* 1332, *Annotescroft* 1339, 1355, 1362 ('Annot's field', from the ME fem. pers.n. *Annot(e)* (diminutive of *Ann*, a pet-form of *Annes* < *Agnes*) and feld, croft; probably the same land as *croftum Agnete filie Hugonis* 1325 *Chol* A 39, 'the croft of Agnes Hugh's daughter', which suggests that the Cholmondeley pedigree in Orm[2] II 637 omits a daughter of Hugh de Cholmondeley II contemporary with Agnes daughter of Kenric de Cholmondeley); *via de Bikeleg'* c.13 (cf. Bickley 6 *supra*); *le Brodeheth* 1317 (*v.* brād, hǣð); *le Brodemedue* 1326 (*v.* brād, mǣd); *le Brochurst* 1310 ('brook wood', *v.* brōc, hyrst, but possibly 'badger hill', *v.* brocc); *Burhemare* (*v.* Burley *supra*); *le Castellhull* 1362 ('hill suitable for a castle', *v.* castel(l), hyll. This was adjacent to *Roulowe* (The Ruly *supra*), cf. Castle Hill *supra*. The Ruly and *le Castelhull* may have been tumuli); *le Clyff* 1414 (*v.* clif); *le Crossitake* c. 1290 ('intake at a cross', *v.* cros, inntak); *Darleg'hurst* 1310 ('(wooded-hill at) the deer glade', *v.* dēor, lēah, hyrst); *le Euesingreue* 1323, 1326, *le Heuesingreue* 1324 ('pollarded wood', *v.* efesung, grǣfe); *Farintislee Siche* e.13 (*v.* lēah, sīc. The first el. may be the ME (OFr) pers.n. *Fer(r)ant*, cf. Reaney s.n. *Farrand*); *le Fyflond* 1355 ('five selions', *v.* fīf, land); *le Gleshousfeld* 1311, 1325 ('field at a glass-works', *v.* glas-hous, feld, and *Glasshouse* 3 244); *le Grenesiche* 1310, *le Grensiche*, -*Greneseche* 1316 (*v.* grēne[1], sīc); *le Hauedbuttesende* 1310 ('the end of the head-land', *v.* hēafod-butte, ende[1]); *Heghurstesmor* 1317, 1320, 1332, (*lega de) Heghurst* 1362 ('(marsh at) the high wooded-hill', from hēah and hyrst, with mōr[1]); *Henriesfeld* 1362 ('Henry's field', from the ME (OFr) pers.n. Henri and feld); *Herteplowe* 1305, 1362 ('place where the hart plays', *v.* heorot, plaga); *Hocloue* 1336 ('mound at a hook of land or a promontory', *v.* hōc, hlāw, cf. *Huclou* 20 *supra*); *Hondecroft* 1362 ('hound's croft', or 'Honde's croft', from hund or the ME pers.n. *Honde* and croft); *le Konctingalere* c.1290 (final el. alor 'alder-tree'); *the litell hey* 1451, 1452, *le lytull haye* 1456 (*v.* lȳtel, (ge)hæg); *le Longe Flatt* 1362 (*v.* lang, flat); *le Longetrenche* 1362 (*v.* lang, trenche); *le Lonnkake* 1326 (unintelligible. The final el. may be āc 'an oak'); *le Marcerescroft* 1362 (*v.* croft. *Marcere* would be either OE *mearcere* 'one who makes a mark', recorded in the sense 'a scribe, a notary', OE **mearcere* 'one who keeps or lives at a boundary-mark' (cf. mearc), or, as Dr von Feilitzen observes, the OG pers.n. *Marcher* (cf. *Marcere* the name of a moneyer in 9 and 10, Forssner 286)); *Meyleres leghe* 1323, 1325, *Meyleresteghle* 1326, *Meylerestele* 1362 ('Meilyr's clearing and stile', from the Welsh pers.n. *Meilyr*, with lēah, stīgel, cf. *Hugo filius Meylor'* 1331, *Hugo Mayler de Cholm'delegh* 1387 *Chol* A 45, A 103); *le Meredyche* 1397 ('boundary ditch', *v.* (ge)mǣre, dīc); *le Neuebuging* 1338 ('the new building', *v.* nīwe, bigging); *le Quistansnelesleg'* 1285, *Wistanishale* c.1290, *Quistanesbroc* 1325 ('Wīgstān Snell's wood' and 'Wīgstān's corner and brook', from the OE pers.n. *Wīgstān* and lēah, halh, brōc, with the surname *Snell*, cf. OE *snell* 'smart, bold, active'); *le Rene* 1310 (*v.* rein); *le Scoridhoc* 1310 ('notched oak', *v.* scored, āc); *le Shagh'* 1362 (*v.* sc(e)aga); *le Swolnebuttes* 1362 (described as 'a place of land between two *rands* (*v.* rand) in the field called *le Halgh* (cf. The Haughs *supra*)', perhaps 'swallowed selions', from butte and the ME pa.part. *swolȝen* from *swelȝen* 'to swallow, to overwhelm', alluding to land reverted to an uncultivated condition and overgrown with weeds, etc.); *le Watyrladebroc* c.1290, *le vaterlodebroc* c.1290, 1325, *le Waterlode broc* 1328, 1332 ('the conduit brook', *v.* wæter, (ge)lād, brōc); *Weghthull* 1272–1307 (*v.* wiht 'a bend', hyll); *le lydiate de Workesloue* 1334, *Workeslowehache* 1362 (from hlid-geat 'a swing-gate', and hæc(c) 'a wicket-gate', with a p.n. recorded only as a local surname *Wirkislawe* c.1290, -*lowe* 1298, *Wirkes*- 1304, *Wircuslowe* 1314, -*lawe* 1316[2], *Wyrkeslowe* 1325[2], 1409, *Workeslowe* 1315, 1400, -*lou(w)e* 1334, 1355, 1359, *Workesley* 1412, from an OE pers.n. *Weorc* or *Wirc* (as in Wirksworth Db, etc., cf. Db 414) and hlāw 'a mound, a hill'); *Wistanishale* (*v.* *Quistans*-, *supra*); *Wolfotesrudyng* 1355 ('Wulfgēat's cleared-land', from the OE pers.n. *Wulfgēat* and ryding); *le Yardroue* 1325 ('rough ground near an enclosure', *v.* geard, rūh).

9. CHORLTON (COTTAGE, (OLD) HALL, LANE & LODGE) (109–4648)

Cherl(e)ton 1283 Cl, Ipm, 1284 CRC, and nine examples to 1378 AD (p), 1528 (1592) Orm[2] (p)

Chorleton 1284 Ch, 1290 Ipm *et freq* with variant spellings *Chorlle*-, *Schorle*- to 1588 ChRR, *Chorltone* 1289 Court, -*ton* 1330 Cl (p), 1648 ChRR *et freq*, (*Chorleton iuxta Cudynton*) 1329 Plea,

(-*Malpas*) 1350 ib, *Chorlton Hall* 1819 Orm², *Chorlton Cottage, House & Lodge* 1831 Bry
Chorlynton 1386 *Chol*
Charleton 1396 ChRR, 1656 Orm², *Charlton* 1635 *Chol*
Chorleston 1430 ChRR
Chalton 1727 Sheaf
Chatton 1769 *Chol*
'Peasants' farm', *v.* ceorl (gen.pl. ceorla), tūn.

FIELD-NAMES

The undated forms are 1838 *TA* 112.

(a) Bottomless Pit Fd (*v.* botm-les, pytt); Big & Little Broom (*v.* brōm); Cross Fd (*v.* cros); Higher & Lower Crunn (Welsh crwn 'round'); Goose Taddow; Griggy Fd (*v.* grig² (Welsh *grug*, Pr Welsh **grŭg*) 'heath, heather'); Heys (*v.* (ge)hæg); Kettles Croft (*v.* keddle-dock); Little Hill; Milking Bank (*v.* milking); Pinfold Fd (*v.* pynd-fald); Pootles ('small enclosures', *v.* pightel); Red Croft; Rye Fd (*v.* ryge); Sand Hole Fd (*v.* sand, hol¹); Stone Pit Fd (*v.* stān, pytt); Teir Main (Welsh, 'narrow land', *v.* tir, main); Ten Main (Welsh, 'small farm or holding', *v.* tyddyn, main); Ten Shilling Fd (*v.* scilling); Town Fd; Underhill (*v.* under, hyll); Whole Grass.

10. CUDDINGTON (GREEN & HALL) (109–4546)

Cuntitone 1086 DB
Kydinton 1284 Ch, -*yn*- 1350 *Eyre*, *Kydd*-, (-*iuxta Malpas*) 1475 *Chol*, *Kiddinton* 1577 Saxton, *Kiding*- 1484 Orm², (-*alias Cudington*) 1582 *Chol*, *Kyddyngton* 1542 Plea, -*ing*- 1551 Pat, -*inge*- 1580 Orm², *Cydding*- 1635 *Chol*, *Kidding*- 1560 ib and 8 examples to 1727 Sheaf, 1838 *TA*, 1860 White
Cudin(g)ton 1288 Court *et freq* with variant spellings -*yn*- (1288 Orm² to 1508 ChRR), -*yng*- (1360 BPR to 1567 ChRR), *Cudding*- (from 1355 Plea (p)), *Cuddyn*- (1362 ChRR), *Kudynt*- (1368 *Chol*), *Kudyn*- (1497 *Chol*), *Cudington iuxta Malpas* 1288 Court, *Cudynton iuxta Tilstan* 1357 *Tourn*, *Cuddington alias Kiddington* 1640 Orm², *Cuddington Green & Hall* 1831 Bry
Codington 1289 Court (p), -*yng*- 1523 ChRR, *Codding*- 1631 *Chol*, *Codinton* c.1303 ib (p), -*tone* 1320 ib
Kedynton 1432, 1454 *AddCh*
Kuyddington 1620 Orm²

Perhaps 'farm called after Cydda', from the OE pers.n. *Cydda* and -ingtūn, but Dr von Feilitzen rightly prefers the OE pers.n. *Cud(d)a* indicated by the *-u-* and *-o-* forms, explaining the *-i-* forms as evidence of the occasional change *-u- > -i-* before dentals seen in Didcot Brk (DEPN), Diddington Hu (BdHu 254), Dinnington YW 1 146. Cf. Tilston, Malpas 58, 38 *infra*.

THE BANK, 1842 OS, *Bank House* 1831 Bry, *v.* banke. BARN WELL, *v.* bere-ærn, wella. BROOKSIDE. BROUGHTON GORSE, *v.* gorst, cf. Broughton, in Worthenbury, Fl. CARDING FIELDS. CHERRYHILL, 1831 Bry. CRABTREE FM, *Crab Tree House* 1831 ib *v.* crabbe, trēow. CUDDINGTON HEATH, *Cudyngton Hethe* 1532 *Chol, Kiddington Heath Lands* 1692 *ib*, cf. Heath Fm *infra*, *v.* hǣð. CUDDINGTON MILL, 1831 Bry, *a Watur Milne in Kudynton* 1497 *Chol*, cf. Millhouse *infra*, *v.* myln. THE DINGLE, *v.* dingle. FIELD'S FM. HEATH FM, cf. Cuddington Heath *supra*. THE MOUNT, *Mount Pleasant* 1831 Bry. THE PITS, PITS FM, *v.* pytt. TINKWOOD, 1842 OS, cf. *Tinkwood Fd* 1838 *TA*, 'an acre of land called *Tincoyd*' 1320 *Chol*. The final el. is Welsh coed 'a wood', cf. wudu. On the face of it, the name looks like the familiar Welsh *Ty'n y Coed*, 'the little holding by the wood', with *tyddyn*, 'a small holding', having loss of intervocal *ð* and contraction. It is uncertain however whether this loss and contraction could have taken place so early; though the fact that *Ty'n y Coed* and *Ty'n y Caeau* ('the little holding in the fields') are among the commonest p.ns. in Wales might be taken to suggest that it may be quite old. An alternative and perhaps preferable explanation would be that *Tincoyd* 1320 is *tŷ yn y coed*, 'the house in the wood', with *tŷ* 'house'.

FIELD-NAMES

The undated forms are 1838 *TA* 139. Of the others, 1300–20, 1310 are *AddCh*, 1831 Bry, and the rest *Chol*.

(*a*) Addlands (*v.* hēafod-land); Antikeys; Argoedd (Welsh, 'near the wood', *v.* ar, coed); Bellent; Black Flat (*v.* blæc, flat); Blains Fd; Blethums Croft (probably 'Blethyn's croft', from the Welsh pers.n. *Bleddyn*, cf. *Blethens Croft* 43 *infra*); Booth Vane; Branders (*le brunned house* 1532, *v.* brende[2], hūs); Brook Fd (*le Brokfeld* 1310, cf. *ductus de Cudynton* 1300–20, *v.* brōc, feld); Big & Little Broom (*the greate Broome* 1650, *v.* brōm); Calf Kit Mdw (*v.* calf-kid); Cocktus; Cumbers, Cumbers Bank & Brook (*v.* cumber, banke, brōc); Furlong (*v.* furlang); Goblin; Gravener(s) Acre (from the Ch surname *Grosvenor* and æcer); Hauve (perhaps ModEdial hauve 'turning to the left', cf. gee, *v.* EDD); Hogs Croft (*v.* hogg); Little Jets; Big Litter; Marly Newearth (*v.* marle, -ig[3], nīwe, eorðe); Masters; Mauld Yard (*v.*

molde, geard); Milking Bank (v. milking); Oate Hey 1684 (v. āte, (ge)hæg); Oldcastle Fd (v. Oldcastle 44 *infra*); Pear Tree Croft & Fd (*the Peartree Hey* 1684, cf. *Pear Tree Farm* 1831, v. peru, trēow); Pickoo (v. pichel); Pin Maker; Poor Fd (v. pouer(e)); Roylands Mdw (v. rye-land); Skenna; Souchall; Suchans; Under Hill (v. under, hyll); Up the Field; Walk Fd (v. walk); Way Fd (v. weg); Whitening Yard; Whole Grass; Will Mdw (v. wella); Within Fd (v. wīðegn).

(b) *Chorlleton' Wey* 1300–20 (v. weg, cf. Chorlton 27 *supra*); *le Forde* 1310 (v. ford); *Hawoterthely* 1320 ('(clearing at) Hawot's ploughland', from a ME pers.n. *Hawot*, diminutive of *Hawe*, and erð, with lēah); *Le Lawe* 1310 (v. hlāw).

11. DUCKINGTON (WOOD) (109–4952)

> *Dochintone* 1086 DB, *Docinton* c.1290 *Chol*, *Dokinton*, *-yn-* 1290
> *ib*, Ipm *et freq* to 1552 *Dav*, *Dokington* 1288 Court (p), *-yng*
> 1427 ChRR, *Dokenton* 1549 ib, *Dockington* 1656 Orm[2], *Dogynton*
> 1441 ChRR
> *Ducintona* 1216–72 AddCh, *Dukinton'* 1216–72 ib, *-yn-* 1426 *Chol*,
> *Duckenton* 14 (17) Sheaf, *Duckington* 1430 EatonB, 1539 ArlB,
> 1724 NotCestr, (*-Barn*, *-Hill* & *-Wood*) 1831 Bry
> *Tuckington* 1727 Sheaf

'Farm called after Ducc(a)', from an OE pers.n. *Ducc(a)* (discussed under Ducklington O 317, Duxford C 92–3) and -ingtūn.

BANK FM, v. banke.   THE HEIR'S WOOD, v. eyr.   HETHER WOOD, v. hæddre.   LOWER FM, v. lower.   PINFOLD, v. pyndfald.   RANDALL'S ROUGH, v. rūh.

FIELD-NAMES

The undated forms are 1838 *TA* 149. Of the others, c.1290, 1632 are *Chol*, 14 (17) Sheaf, 1552 *Dav*.

(a) Beachen (perhaps analogous with Beachin 86 *infra*, from an OE *bēcen, either as a sb. 'place where beeches grow', from bēce[2], -en[1], or as an adj. 'growing with beeches', from bēce[2], -en[2]); Bottoms (v. botm); Cross Fd (v. cros); Duckington Common (cf. *bruerium de Dokinton* c.1290, v. hæð, commun); Big & Little Dunnows; Farlong Fd (v. furlang); Griston Fd; Hadland Fd (v. hēafod-land); Hall Fd (v. hall); Islands; Judd Bank; Lady's Acre (v. hlǣfdige); The Moors (v. mōr[1]); Ox Hay Mdw (v. oxa, (ge)hæg); Pingo (v. pingot); Rough (v. rūh); Spoostitch (v. spōn, stycce, cf. Spoon Studge 3 302); The Worst That Ever Was Seen (v. 337 *infra*); Town Fd; Wood Fd.

(b) *Caldewalle*(*croft*) c.1290 ('(croft at) the cold spring', from **cald** and **wælla**, with **croft**); *via ecclesie* c.1290 ('church-way', *v.* **cirice, weg**); *le Dale* c.1290, *Duckenton Slade* 14 (17) ('the valley', *v.* **dæl**[1], **slæd**); *Maynwaringes Erthes* 1552, *Mannerings Earth* 1632 ('ploughlands belonging to the *Mainwaring* family', *v.* **erð**).

12. EDGE (GREEN, HO, LANE *&* SCAR) *&* LITTLE EDGE (lost) (109–4850)

Eghe 1086 DB (twice)

Egge c.1170 *Chol et freq* to 1577 ChRR, *Parva-* c.1190 *Chol*, *Magna-* c.1303 *ib*, *Great-* 1311 Ipm, *Little-* 1353 BPR, *Mangna-* 1369 *Chol*, *Mikel-* 1426 *ib*, *le Egge* 1472 ChRR, *the-* 1558–1603 *Surv, le Egge Grene* 1476 *Chol*

Hegge 1272 *Chol* (p), 1426 Sheaf

Magna-Egges 1312 Plea

Great Edge 1401 ChRR, *Edge* 1406 *ib et freq*, *Easte Edge* 1642 Sheaf, *Little Edge, Edge Green* 1831 Bry, *le Edge* 1460 *Chol*, *Edgge* 1558 Orm[2], *Great- & Little-* 1577 *ib*

Magna Ege 1422 Plea, *Ege* 1458 *Chol*, 1587 ChRR, 1635 Sheaf

Hege 1513, 1514 *Chol*

Egy 1554 Pat

'The edge', from **ecg**, with **grēne**[2] 'a green', **lane**, and **sker** (cf. dial. *scar*) 'a rocky cliff, a scar'. The place is named from Edge Scar (109–478503). Little Edge is shown by Bryant at 109–472513 near Grange Fm *infra, v.* **micel, lȳtel, parva, magna,** and **ēast**.

BEECH HOUSE FM, *le Bech*(*e*) c.1327 *Chol, Eggebeche in Mangna Egge* 1369 *ib*, 'the valley-stream', *v.* **bece**[1]. BRYNCAEWANNEDD, *Brown Walled* 1838 *TA*, *-Wallet* 1842 OS, named in Welsh 'the hill of the field of the moors' or 'moor-fields hill', from **bryn(n)** and **cae**, with **gweunydd**, pl. of **gwaun** 'a moor, a hill-pasture', and in English 'brown wallet', *v.* **brūn**[1], **walet** 'a wallet', presumably from the shape of a field here. DAIRY FM, 1831 Bry, *v.* **deierie**. DYER'S FM, *Yew Tree House* 1831 Bry, cf. *Dyers Meadow* 1838 *TA*, from the surname *Dyer*. EDGE HALL, *the halle of Egge* 1524 *Chol*, *the Hall of Edge or the Lower Hall of Edge* 1595 Sheaf, 1626 Orm[2], *v.* **hall, lower**, cf. foll. HIGHER HALL, 1831 Bry, *the Higher Hall of Edge* 1604 Sheaf, cf. prec., *v.* **higher**. EDGE MILL, 1831 Bry, cf. *molendina de Egge* c.1310 *Chol, novum & vetus molendinum* c.1314, *a water mill in Great Edge called Standishe Mylne* 1558 Orm[2], *two water mills Standish Mylnes* 1626 *ib*, *v.* myln, nīwe, ald. *Standish(e)* may be a surname *Standish*, or from stān with dīc or edisc. GAM'S WOOD, 1831 Bry, *Gains Wood* 1842 OS, from the Welsh nickname *Gam* 'crooked, bent' and wudu, cf. Gam's Hillock 42 *infra*. GATEHOUSE FM, *v.* gate-hous. GRANGE FM, cf. *Little Edge supra*. HALL LANE, cf. Edge Hall *supra*. HAMPTONBY, a residence near the boundary of Hampton 34 *infra*. HEATHFIELD, cf. *Heath Field* 1838 *TA*, *the higher-* & *the lower Heth(e)* 1551 *Chol*, *the little Heaths* 1719 *ib*, *v.* hǣð, feld. THE HEIR'S WOOD, *v.* eyr. KIDNALL HO, *Kidnal* 1842 OS, *v.* Kidnall 45 *infra*. LOWCROSS MILL FM, *Low Cross Mill* 1831 Bry, cf. Lowcross 59 *infra*, *v.* myln. MANOR HO. MATES LANE, cf. Richard *Mate* 1860 White. PARK COTTAGES, cf. *Park Field* 1838 *TA*, *v.* park. RIDLEY'S COVERT, *The Ridleys* 1838 *ib*, perhaps from a surname, cf. Ridley 3 313. ROUND HO, 1831 Bry, *v.* rond. SCAR LANE, cf. Edge Scar *supra*, *v.* lane. SIMMONDS GREEN, *Simonds Green* 1831 Bry, from grēne[2] and the surname *Simmond(s)*. WITNEY LANE (FM), cf. *Big Whitney, Whitney Bank* & *Meadow* 1838 *TA*, perhaps the origin of the surname *Whiteneie* 1299 Plea, *Whyteney* 1393 Plea, *Whitney* 1412 ChRR, *Whiteney* 1414 ib, *Whitnay* 1417 ib, 'white enclosure', *v.* hwīt (obl. hwītan), (ge)hæg. LOWER WOOD, *Bath Rough* 1831 Bry, *v.* bæð, rūh, cf. foll. UPPER WOOD, *Edge Wood* 1831 Bry, *v.* wudu, cf. prec.

FIELD-NAMES

The undated forms are 1838 *TA* 160. Of the others 1576 is Orm[2], 1642 Sheaf, 1819 Orm[2], 1831 Bry, and the rest *Chol*.

(a) The Beachins, Far & Near Beachin (*v.* bēcen); Black Croft; Far-, Middle- & Near Blakeney (*Blakinhull* c.1308 (*Chol* C 15, endorsed *Blakenhull* 17), *Blakenul* 1328, *lytull Blakenyll* 1476, 'black hill', *v.* blæc (obl. blacan), hyll); The Bowling; Broad Croft; Broom Fd (*v.* brōm); Brown Heath; Big & Little Burrows Heath (*Borrowes Heaths* 1728, *v.* borow, hǣð); Church Acre; Cow Hayes (*le Cowhey* 1476, *v.* cū, (ge)hæg); Dee Bank (*v.* dey); Draw Croft; Long Eddish (*v.* edisc); Ferney Bank; The Gates Heath (*v.* gata); Gorsty Banks (*v.* gorstig); Green End Fd ('field at the end of the green', *v.* grēne[2], ende[1], cf. Edge Green *supra*); Hall Hayes (*le Halleheye* 1392, *le hall hay* 1470, *the Hall Hey* 1472, *-Heys* 1819, *v.* hall, (ge)hæg); The Hall Loon (*v.* hall, land); Harratt Fd (*v.* heriot); Hepperston Fd; Hob Fd (*Hobfeld* 1476, 1533, *Hobbe felde* 1512, *v.* hob); The Houghlands (*v.* hōh, land); The Irons (*v.* hyrne, cf. Heronbridge 336 *infra*); Isabel Fd & Bank; Kettles Fd (*v.* keddle-dock); Kitchen Fd; Leg of Mutton Fd (*v.* 336

infra); Long Hill Bank (*v.* lang, hyll); Marl Fd (*the litull- & the mikel Marletfeld* 1450, *v.* marle, marled, feld); Meadow Furlong; Milking Bank (*v.* milking); Big- & Little Moor; Mud Fd (*v.* mudde); New Heys (*v.* (ge)hæg); The Nine Butts (*v.* nigon, butte); The Old Fd; Orchard Piece; Oven Fd (*v.* ofen); Penny Ridding (*v.* peni(n)g, ryding); The Quarry; Red Flat; The Ridding (*v.* ryding); Rosset; Round Bank; Shoulder of Mutton Fd (*v.* 337 *infra*); The Slang (*v.* slang); Snig Mdw ('eel meadow', *v.* snygge); Speeds Acre; Stone Stile Fd (*v.* stān, stigel); Terrick; Thirsty Fd (*v.* þurstig); Tilston Wood Fd (cf. *Tilston Lane* 1831, cf. Tilston 58 *infra*); Triangle Fd; Watering Pit; Way Fd (*v.* weg); White Croft (*v.* hwīt); Wilkridden.

(b) *the Dene* 1450 (*v.* denu); *aqua de Egge* 1346 (*v.* wæter); (*le*)*Forde* 1409 (p), 1417 (p) (*v.* ford); *the Hall Yordes* 1450 (*v.* hall, geard); *Heusters Croftes* 1462 (from the ME occupational name *heuster(e)* 'dyer' and croft); *le Hoole Landes* 1546, *le Hoolelands* 1551, *the Holoones* 1617 ('selions in a hollow', *v.* hol², land); *le greue vocat' Hursted* 1546, 1551 (from hyrst and stede or hēafod, with græfe); *Johnsons Heth* 1551 (held by William *Johnson, v.* hǣð, cf. foll. and Heathfield *supra*); *Larkton Heathes* 1638 (*v.* hǣð, cf. prec. and Larkton 36 *infra*); *The Longe Croft* 1450 (*v.* lang, croft); *The Solers Shepfeld* 1450 (*v.* scēp, feld); *le Townefeld* 1546 (*v.* toun, feld); *Troutfield* 1576.

13. EGERTON (BANK, GREEN & HALL) (109–5251) [ˈedʒər-, ˈedʒətən, ˈedʒərtn̩]

> *Eggirton* e13 *AddCh* (p), c.1300 *Chol* (p), *Egirthon* 1272–1307
> *AddCh* (p), *Hegirton* 1295 *Vern* (p), *Egirton* 1314 *Chol* (p), 1324 *ib*
> (p), *Egyrtone* 1333 *Dav* (p), *-ton* 1354 *Chol*
> *Eggerton* 1259 Plea *et freq* to 1591 AD (p), with variant spelling
> *Heggerton* 1312 *Chol* (p); *Egerton* 1282 Court (p) *et freq* with
> variant spellings *-don* 1283 Cl (p), *-tun* 1429 AD (p); *Hegertona*
> 1295 (17) Sheaf, *Egerton Green* 1750 *Chol*, *Egerton Bank &
> Hall* 1831 Bry
> *Edgerton* c.1582 AD (p)

From tūn 'an enclosure, a farmstead', with banke, grēne², hall. The first el. is probably a pers.n. but the form is obscure. It could be the OE pers.n. *Ecgheard* or *Ecghere* (cf. DEPN), uninflected, or the gen.sg. *Ecgware* of the OE fem. pers.n. *Ecgwaru*. However, Dr von Feilitzen may well be right in taking Egerton as analogous with Tibberton Wo 170 (*Tidbrihtincgtun* > DB *Tidberton*), i.e. as a reduced form of an -ingtūn p.n. upon the pers.n. *Ecghere*, *v.* -ing-⁴.

YEWTREE FM.

FIELD-NAMES

The undated forms are 1838 *TA* 162. Of the others, 1250–5 is Orm², 13 AD, 1352 BPR, 1634, 1657 *Chol*.

(*a*) Ball Fd; Barn Fd (*the Barne Feild* 1657, *v.* bere-ærn); Barns Grove; Buckley Fd (cf. Bulkeley 17 *supra*); Chapel Mdw (cf. 'the chapel of our Lady in the town of Eggerton' 1352, *v.* chapel(e)); Church Hough (*v.* cirice, hōh); Crooked Croft (*v.* croked); Seven Demath (*v.* day-math); Ebber Fd; Eighteen Butts (*v.* butte); Greyleston Heath (cf. Grestons Heath 25 *supra*); Hadley, Long- & Near Hadleys (*v. Hadley* 17 *supra*); The Kennant, Kennant Fd & Mdw (Welsh ceunant 'brook in a hollow, a dingle'); Lapinger Mdw ('lapwing meadow', *v.* hlēapewince (cf. dial. *lappinch*) 'a lapwing'); Long Butts (*v.* butte); Muck Fd (*v.* muk); Nook Fd; Persey Bank & Mdw; Peticoat Fd; Pit Kettle Fd (*v.* pytt, keddle-dock); Purse (*v.* purs); Long Ramer, Ramer Fd & Mdw; Ridding (*v.* ryding); The Rowley (*v.* rūh, lēah); Sandhills (*Sandhull* 1250–5, *v.* sand, hyll); Twacken; Wall Fd (*v.* wælla); White Flatts (*the Whit Flat* 1634, *v.* hwīt, flat); Whitemeadow.

(*b*) *Redmorisfeld* 13 ('(field at) red moor', *v.* rēad, mōr¹, -es², feld); *le Waylond* 13 ('selion on a path', *v.* weg, land).

14. HAMPTON (CROFT, GRANGE, GREEN, HALL, HEATH, HO, OLD HALL & POST) (109–5049)

> *Hantone* 1086 DB, *Hanton* 1259 Court, H3 *AddCh*, c.1310 *ib* (p), 1368 *Chol*, 1665 Sheaf, (*-iuxta Eggerton*) 1420 *Chol*
>
> *Hampton* 1260 Court *et freq*, (*-iuxta Eggerton*) 1422 Plea, *-tona* 1283 Cl (p), *manerium de Hampton*, *Hampton Wood* 1466 AD, *Hampton Heth* 1476 *Chol*, *-Grene* 1523 Sheaf, *-Heath* 1582 *Chol*, *-Post* 1656 Orm², *-Cover*, *-Green*, *-Heath* & *-Lower Hall* 1831 Bry, *-Meadow* & *-Wood* 1838 *TA*
>
> *Hamton* 1306, 1348 *Chol*

'High farm or enclosure', from hēah (wk.dat. hēan) and tūn, with croft, grange, grēne², hall, hǣð, hūs, post & wudu. Hampton Heath gives name to *Heathes Yoardes* 1636 *Chol*, *Little Heath* 1722 *ib*, *Heath Field* 1838 *TA*, *v.* geard, lȳtel. Hampton Post (109–507497) is 'so called of an old tree standing in the road of Chester way, from Whitchurch, and reckoned for a mark for Passengers travelling that way and another way, which there crosseth that and leadeth from Malpas into the other part of Cheshire', 1656 Orm² II 590.

ASHTONS-CROSS (109–502555), *Ashton Crosse* 1705 *Chol*, *-Cross* 1842 OS, *Stone House* 1831 Bry, cf. *Ashton's Croft Field* 1838 *TA*, *v.*

cros 'a cross', stān, hūs. The place is a cross-roads on the old Whit-church-Chester road, cf. Hampton Post *supra*. *Ashton* is either a surname, or a p.n. 'ash-tree enclosure or farm', *v.* æsc, tūn.

BOBBERHILL (109–515486), 1831 Bry, *v.* hyll. 1″ OS puts *Robberhill*, the name used by the inhabitants, but the current register of elec-tors has *Bobberhill* and a particular of sale dated 1925 (CRO DDX 256/5) uses this form (ex. inf. Mr Redwood). The p.n. may be associated with the surname *Bobenhull*, *Bobenill* 1288 Court 104, 122, 'Bob(b)a's hill', from the OE pers.n. *Bob(b)a* and hyll. BROOMY BANK, *Broomy Bank Farm* 1831 Bry, *v.* brōmig, banke. COMMON FM, near No Man's Heath 9 *supra*, *v.* commun. LOWER HOUSE FM, *v.* lower.   MANOR HO, 1831 Bry, *Hampton* 1842 OS.   MIDDLE HO, *v.* middel.

FIELD-NAMES

The undated forms are 1838 *TA* 185. Of the others 1250–5 is Orm[2], 1397, 1524, 1596 *Chol*, 1466 AD, 1523 Sheaf, 1842 OS.

(*a*) Air Bank; Bennett's Fd (*Benettesheye* 1397, *Benettes Filde* 1466, *-Feld & Medowe* 1524, 'Benet's enclosure, field & meadow', from the ME pers.n. *Benet* (*Benedict*) and (ge)hæg, feld, mǣd); Brandhurst Fd & Mdw (*le Brynderith Lane, the Brynderith* 1523, from branderith, brandreth 'a brazier, a grate, a grating, a frame-work' and lane); Bristle Gorse (*Bristull Crofte* 1466, perhaps '(croft at) land-slip hill', from (ge)byrst[1] and hyll, with croft); Chaise Lane Mdw; Church Hill (*v.* cirice, hyll); Clemley Park (cf. Clemley 3 47); Cockshut (*Cokeshote Filde* 1466, *v.* cocc-scyte); Cote Fd (*v.* cot); Deanshaw (*Danshawe Filde* 1466, 'valley wood', *v.* denu, sc(e)aga); Goffs Heath 1842 (from the surname *Goff* and hǣð); Gorse Heath Croft (*v.* gorst); The Hall Moor 1737 (*-More* 1466, 1524, *v.* hall, mōr[1]); Kitchen Fd (*v.* cycene); Knowle Bank (*v.* cnoll, banke); Marl Fd (cf. *Marleruse Filde* 1466, 'marler's field', *v.* marle, marlere, feld); Nook Fd (*v.* nōk); Old Fd (*v.* ald); Piece Nook (*v.* pece, nōk); Pinfold Mdw (*v.* pynd-fald); Post Fd (*v.* Hampton Post *supra*); Pudwell (*Pudwall Filde* 1466, 'toad well', *v.* pode, wælla); Long Slang (*v.* slang); Spout Bank (*v.* spoute); Sweet Fd; Windmill Fd.

(*b*) *Cromburley More* 1466 ('(glade at) the crooked earthwork', *v.* crumb, burh, lēah, with mōr[1]); *Deacons Crofte* 1596; *rivulum de Hanton* 1250–5; *the Hurstyate* 1523 ('gate at a wooded hill', *v.* hyrst, geat); *the Milne Filde* 1466 (*v.* myln); *Pament Lane* 1596 (*v.* pavement, lane); *the Shawe* 1466 (*v.* sc(e)aga); *Three Acres alias Cornefild* 1523 (*v.* þrēo, æcer, corn[1], feld); *White Medowes* 1466 (*v.* hwīt, mǣd).

15. LARKTON (HALL & HILL) (109–5051)

Lavorchedone 1086 DB

Lau-, Laverketon, -tun 1180 *Chol* (p) *et freq ib, ChFor, AddCh,*
Plea, Court, Sheaf, Orm[2] to 1320

Loverketon 1259 Court (p)

Larketon 13 AD (p) *et freq* with variant spellings *Larke-* (to 1537
ChRR), *Lark-* (from c.1290 *Chol*), *Larck(e)-, Larc-; Larkton
Hill & Farm* 1831 Bry

Lerketon 1320 *Chol*

Larton 1492 *Chol,* and 8 examples *ib,* Sheaf, ChRR, Orm[2] to 1819
ib, (-*alias Larckton*) 1711 *Chol,* (-*Larkton*) 1819 Orm[2], *Lare-*
1524 *Chol,* 1530 Plea, *Larton Hill* 1842 *TA*

Larkden 1508 Orm[2]

'Lark hill', from lāferce and dūn (the second el. replaced by tūn
'a farmstead, a village' and denu 'a valley'), with hall, hyll. Cf.
Dean's Lane *infra.* The hill is the southern end of Peckforton Hills
3 312 *supra.*

DEAN'S LANE, cf. *le Dene* 1306 *Chol, The Deanes* 1637, 1693 *ib,*
Deans Field e19 *ib,* 'the valley, fields at the valley', *v.* denu, lane.

FIELD-NAMES

The undated forms are e19 *Chol* C193. Of the others, 1831 is Bry, 1842
TAMap 106, 1842[2] OS, and the rest *Chol.*

(a) Ankins Gorse (*Hankins Gorse* 1692, 1815, from the surname *Hankin*
and gorst); Barnfield (*Barne-* 1692, *v.* bere-ærn); the Clover Fd 1737
(*Clovergrass Field* 1705, *v.* clǽfre); Coney Groves (*Cunny Green Field* 1692,
1705, *v.* coningre); Crabtree Fd (1692, *v.* crabbe, trēow); Crickets Croft
(*Cricketts-* 1705, -*Crofts* 1692); The Cuttings 1729 (*v.* cutting); The (Two)
Days Math (Mdw) 1737 (*v.* day-math); Flash Fd (1692, *v.* flasshe); Gorsy
Fd; Graston Fd (*Great-* & *Little Sheep Field* 1705, *v.* scēp); Gritcha Fds
1692 (perhaps 'great shaw', *v.* grēat, sc(e)aga); Hankins Gorse (*v.* Ankins
Gorse *supra*); Hawthorns Cottage 1815; Big- & Little Heath (*Larton
Heath, Little Heath* 1705, cf. *Larton Common* 1842, *v.* hǣð, commun); High
Fd (1692); Hill Croft (cf. Larkton Hill *supra*); Larton Bank (1692, -*Banke*
1705, *v.* banke); Long Fd 1737 (*v.* lang, feld); Lower Mdw 1737; Far Moor
(*v.* mōr[1]); Nuncio Fd; Park (*New Coppy* 1705, *v.* nīwe, copis, park); Riddings (*v.* ryding); Ridley Broome 1705 (1692, *v.* brōm); Round Fd (*v.*
rond); Royall Moore 1715 (*v.* 5 *supra*); Big & Little Sand Hill(s) (*Grett
& Litull Sandhill* 1524, *Big & Little Sandil* 1737, *v.* sand, hyll); Sellars
1705; Sheep Fd (*v.* Graston *supra*); Street Fd (1692, *v.* strǣt. The road is

109–507520 to 501505, Bickerton to Ashtons-Cross); Thunder Bolt Fd (*Thunderbag Field* 1692, 1705); Well Fd (1737, *v.* wella); Wilkins Plat (*v.* plat²); Withins Mead (*v.* wiðegn, mǣd); the Yard 1692 (cf. *le overyordes* 1469, *v.* uferra, geard).

(*b*) *Ayneswode* 1497 ('Hayne's wood', from an OE pers.n. *Ægen*, or a ME pers.n. *Hayne* (cf. OG *Hageno*, Reaney s.n. *Hain*), and wudu); *le Brodefeld* 1469 (*v.* brād, feld); *Colletfyldus* 1497 ('Collet's fields', from the ME pers.n. or surname *Colet*, diminutive of *Nicholas*, and feld); *le croft* 1306 (*v.* croft); *le Heyeyord* 1339 ('hay enclosure', *v.* hēg, geard); *le Lake* 1339 ('the water-course', *v.* lacu); *Seynt John Feld* 1524 ('St John's field', perhaps associated with St John's church, Chester, 337 *infra*); *the Smalemor* 1397 ('narrow marsh', *v.* smæl, mōr¹).

16. MACEFEN (109–5147), MAESFEN (a house, 109–520468) ['meisfen]

> *Masefen* 1170 *Facs et freq* with variant spelling *-ffen* (1546 *Chol*) to 1727 Sheaf, (*-alias Masewen*) 1615 *ChCert*, (*-or Macefen, Masewin*) 1671 Sheaf, (*-Hall*) 1882 Orm², *le Masefen* 1260 Court (24, *Ken' du Masefen* (p))
>
> *Masefin* 1180–1220 *Chol* (p)
>
> *Massefen* e13 *AddCh* (p), 1216–72 *ib* (p), 1528 Plea, ChRR
>
> *Masefon* 1348 *Chol*
>
> *Mazefen* 1362 (1618) *ChCert*, 1519 Orm²
>
> *Masfen* 1421 AD, 1431 *Chol*, 1445 ChRR, 1451 *ib* (p), 1528, 1531 *Chol*, 1663 Sheaf
>
> *Macefen* 1424 *Chol*, 1476, 1487 *ib*, 1490 ChRR (p), 1506 (p), 1509 ib, 1520 Plea, 1819 Orm², *-ven* 1524 *Chol*
>
> *Maisfen* 1428 Orm²
>
> *Maesfen* 1440 Hesk (p), 1692 *Chol*, 1819, 1882 Orm²
>
> *Mesefen* 1469 *Chol* (p)
>
> *Macfen* 1487 *Chol*
>
> *Macepen* 1523 ChRR
>
> *Macefwen* 1564 *Chol*
>
> *Masewen* 1615 *ChCert*, *-win* 1671 Sheaf
>
> *Mansen* 1724 NotCestr
>
> *Macefin* 1769 *Chol*

Macefen is Welsh *maes y ffin* 'the boundary field' or 'open land near a boundary' from Welsh maes 'a plain, a field' and ffin 'a boundary'.

WI-, WYVERCOT (lost), c.1300 *Chol* J. This lost place in Macefen is apparently the same as *Wyuercote* 1298 Court 150, Orm² II 254 (lit.

Wyner-), 1290 Plea (DKR xxvi 41, lit. *Wyner-*), *Wyvercote* 1290 Ipm
II 463, *Wever-* 1290 ib 459, a place in the St Pierre family's share of
the Malpas barony. The published forms are referred by Ekwall
(DEPN) to a place *Weavercote* which he associates with the r.n.
Weaver together with Weaver and Weaverham 3 163, 205. *Weavercote* has not been found, and the form is not recorded. Macefen is
not near the R. Weaver. The p.n. is from **cot** 'a cottage, a hut' and
the ON pers.n. *Viðfari* (Feilitzen 406).

BIRCH HOUSE (lost), 1741 *Chol*, 1690 Sheaf, *v.* birce, hūs.   MILL-
MOOR FM, 1831 Bry, *le myll mor*' (and the site of a mill) 1487, *le
millmore* 1488, *le myll morr*' 1505, *Milln Mo(o)re Mill(n)* 1741 all
Chol, 'marsh near a mill', *v.* myln, mōr[1].

FIELD-NAMES

The undated forms are 1838 *TA* 248. Of the others, 1347 is *Dav*, 1401
Sheaf, 1408 ChRR, 1831 Bry, and the rest *Chol*.

(a) Ash Fd; Bank; Black Croft; Bottom (*v.* botm); Brine Pit Fd (*v.* brīne,
pytt); Broomy Fd, Heys & Ley (*v.* brōmig, (ge)hæg, lēah); Common;
Three Demaths (*v.* day-math); Gorrey Hill Croft & Ho; Heifer Moor;
Hemp Yard (*v.* hemp-yard); Hill Fd; Hough Stone (*v.* hōh, stān); Macefen
Fds (*Macefen Field & Meadow* 1741); Marl Fd; Milking Bank (*v.* milking);
Mill Fd; Narrow Fd (*v.* nearu); New Fd; New Leasow (*v.* lǣs); Old Fd;
Old Road; Orchard Fd; Oven Croft (*v.* ofen); Rough Mdw; Seven Butts
(*v.* butte); Town Fd; Way Fd (*v.* weg); White Patch.

(b) *le Callerheye* 1348 ('the calves' enclosure', *v.* calf (gen.pl. calfra),
(ge)hæg); *Cressewallebrok*' 1348 ('(brook at) cress well', *v.* cresse, wælla,
brōc); *mossetum Johannis de Foxecotes* 1348 (cf. *Foxcote* 1339 (p), 1393 (p),
1401 (p), 1408 (p), *Foxcotus* 1347 (p), 'fox's den', *v.* fox, cot); *Herdewike
saye, -wyke-, Herdewykesawe* c.1300, *Herdewykeschawe* 1308 ('copse at the
herdsmen's buildings', *v.* heorde-wīc, sc(e)aga); *Lartons grounde alias
Lartons Feldes* 1551 (*v.* Larkton 36 *supra*); *Le Ouerefeld* c.1300 (*v.* uferra,
feld); *le Peselond* 1348 ('selion where peas grow', *v.* pise, land); *Wynnys
gronde* 1511, 1546 ('Wynn's ground', from the surname *Wynn* and grund).

17. MALPAS (109–4847) ['mælpəs, 'mɔ:lpəs], older local ['mɔ:pəs]

Depenbech 1086 DB, *Depen-, Depinbache* 1344 *ChGaol* (Barnes[1]
291), 'a burgage (& curtilage) in *Depinbeche* in (the township of)
Malpas' 1346 *Chol* C 301, 411, '(in) villa de *Malpas* siue (in
villa de) *Depenbach(e)*' 1469, 1473 *ib* C 391, 427, 343, *Depen-
bache* 1523 Sheaf[3] 10

Malpas 1121–9 (1285), 1150 Chest (p), 1208–10 Dieul, 1225 VR
  (p), 1260 Court (p), 1285 *Chol et freq* with variant spellings
  -phase, -pace, -paas, -pass(e), -pase; le Malpas 1319 ChRR to
  1488 *MinAcct, the-* 1466 AD (p), 1474, 1519 *Chol, Malpas
  alias Castell-, -Castle Malpas* 1527, 1528 Plea, 1592 ChRR
(de) Malopassu c.1170 *Chol* (p) *et freq* with variant forms *Molopassu,
  Malopas', Malapassu, Malum Passu, Malopassa, Malupassu* to
  1386 ChRR, *del Malo Passu* 1352 ib (p); *v.* Addenda
Maupas 1208–29 Dieul, 1229–33 Chest (p), 1257 Pat *et freq* with
  variant spellings *-pass(e)* to 1653 Sheaf, *le Maupas* 1295 Ipm,
  Mawpas alias Malpas 1536 ChRR
Malepes c.1220 Sheaf (p), *-pas* 1260 Orm² (p), 1327 Cl *et freq*
  with variant spellings *-pace, -passe, -pase* to 1619 Sheaf, *le
  Malepas* 1370 *Chol*, 1379 Orm², *le Malepace* 1384 *AddCh*
Melpas 1525 ChRR
Mallepasse 1548 Pat

'The difficult passage', *v.* **mal²**, pas, cf. Castle Hill *infra*. The
name also occurs at Malpas (Mon.) *v.* NCPN 239, DEPN s.v. The
French name (and its Latin form *Malus Passus*) superseded the OE
name, 'at the deep valley with a stream in it', from **dēop** (wk.dat.
dēopan) and bece¹, bæce¹. *Depenbech* alludes to the valley and stream
of Bradley Brook at Hough Bridge & Fm *infra*, on the true alignment of the Roman road (*v.* Stretton 56 *infra*) between Malpas
High Street and Whitchurch Sa. The traverse in the hollow at
Hough must have become progressively difficult, whence the p.n.
Malpas, for the line of road has been diverted to take Bradley
Bridge (109–499460) and only resumes the direct Roman alignment
at 118–517435 in Agden township. It may well be that the ancient
nucleus of Malpas was towards Hough Fm and Bradley Brook, that
Depenbech ought to be identified with Hough, and that the medieval
town-site was created by the castle. The route along this Roman road
and the proximity of the Welsh frontier would account for the
medieval importance of Malpas, which was the seat of one of the
barons of the earldom of Chester, with a castle and a toll-passage,
and a jurisdiction known as MALPAS HUNDRED, cf. Castle Hill *infra*,
and *curia de Malo Passu* 1290 Ipm, *the barony of-, baronia de-,
baron(es) de(l)-, -Malpas, -Malopassu* 1317 InqAqd, 1347, 1367
BPR, 1421 ChRR, *the hundred of-, hundred' de-, -Malpas, -Malopassu*
1328 Pat, 1329 Plea, 1354, 1360 BPR, 1431 ChRR, *v.* **baronie,**

hundred, cf. 1 *supra*, *Halton Hundred* 2 2. The extent of the hundred appears to be that of the barony, and is described in Orm[2] II 592.

STREET-NAMES

CHURCH ST., 1813 *Chol*, named from Malpas parish church, *v.* cirice; HIGH ST., *alta strata* 1341 *ib*, *v.* hēah, cf. 'Malpas, a little Sonday market having iii streates' c.1536 Leland v 30. The High St is on the line of a Roman Rd *v.* Malpas *supra*; OLDHALL ST., named from *the Hall of Malpas* 1655 *Chol*, *Old Hall* 1724 NotCestr, *Malpas Hall* 1777 *Chol*, cf. 'His (Sir Randle Brereton's) fair place is at the very end of *the south streate*' c.1536 Leland v 30, *v.* sūð, ald, hall; WELL ST., named from TOWN WELL, *Town Well*, *Well Lane* 1831 Bry, *fons de Malo Passu* 1352 *Chol*, cf. *Well Way Lake* 1841 *TA*, *le Walleway* 1404 *Chol*, *v.* toun, wella, wælla, lane, weg, lacu.

CASTLE HILL, 1841 *TA*, *Malpas Hill* 1831 Bry, the site of the castle of Malpas, cf. *the castle of-*, *castellum de-*, *castrum del-*, *-Malpas*, *-Malo Passu* etc. 1327 Pat *et freq* to 1488 MinAcct, *Malpas alias Castell-*, *-Castle Malpas* 1527, 1528 Plea, 1592 ChRR, cf. Malpas *supra*, *v.* castel(1), hyll.

EBNAL (FM & GRANGE) (109–495485 and 502483) ['ebnəl]

> *Ebenhale* 1216–72 AddCh (p), *Ebben-* 1342 Eyre (p), *Ebenaleheth* 1346 *Chol*
> *Hebbinale* 1272 *Chol* (p)
> *Ebenhall* 1416 Sheaf
> *Ebnale* 1416 ChRR, 1422 Plea
> *Ebnall* 1421 ChRR *et freq* to 1695 *Chol*, (*Lower*) *Ebnall Greene*, *Ebnall Hill* 1582 *ib*, *Higher & Lower Ebnal* 1831 Bry, *Ebnal* 1842 OS

'Ebba's nook', from the OE pers.n. *Ebba* and halh (dat.sg. hale), with grēne[2], hǣð, hyll, higher, lower.

HOUGH BRIDGE (109–497457), HOUGH FM (109–495460) [hʌf], *The Hough* 1842 OS, *le Halgh* 1300 Plea (p) *et freq* with variant spelling *-Halghe* to 1569 ChRR, *le Halx* 1352 *Chol*, *le Halxgh* 1369 *ib*, *Haughe* 1554 *ib*, 'the hollow, the nook', *v.* halh. The farm lies in a valley running down to Bradley Brook, *v.* Malpas *supra*.

BAWBROOK, 1842 OS, named from a watercourse here, *Balle Broke* 1554 *Chol*, perhaps 'brook under a hill', from ball and brōc, since the place is under the hill at Cross o' th' Hill *infra*, cf. *Baugh Field*

1841 *TA*, *Ballefeld* 1472 *Chol*, *Ball-* 1524 *ib*, *-fyelde* 1560 *ib*. BRADLEY BRIDGE, cf. Malpas *supra*, *v.* brycg, Bradley 11 *supra*. BROSELAKE, *Well House* 1831 Bry, cf. Well St. *supra*, *v.* wella, hūs. The modern name is unintelligible. CHORLTON LANE 1882 Orm², *v.* lane, cf. Chorlton 27 *supra*. CROSS O' TH' HILL, *Crosse Hill* 1619 *Chol*, *Cross-* 1777 *ib*, 1831 Bry, *Crossal Hill* 1842 OS, *Coffir Hill* 1690 Sheaf, 'hill with a cross on it' and 'the cross on the hill', *v.* cros, hyll. THE FIELDS, cf. *The Field* 1841 *TA*, *v.* feld. GOODMOOR ROUGH, *Goodmore* 1583 *Chol*, *Good Moor* (*Rough*) 1841 *TA*, *v.* gōd², mōr¹, rūh. GRAMMAR FIELD, *Grammers Field &* *Moor* 1777 *Chol*, *Grammar Field*, *Moor & Wood* 1841 *TA*, probably part of the endowment of the grammar school founded in Malpas in 1527, *v.* Orm² II 618. HOLLOW WOOD, *Hawley Wood* 1831 Bry, *v.* holh, lēah, wudu. LEADGATE, *Lidyate* 1413 *Chol* (p), *Lydyate* 1501 *Dow*, *the Lydgate* 1779 *Chol*, *Lidgate* 1831 Bry, cf. *Lidiate Croft* 1692 *Chol*, *Lid-*, *Ludgate Croft & Field* 1841 *TA*, 'swing-gate', from hlid-geat, with croft and feld. LEES FM, *le Lees* 1472 *Chol*, *Malpas Leyes* 1543 *ib*, *Lees Tenement* 1783 *ib*, *The Leys* 1842 OS, *v.* lǣs. THE MOSS, MOSS FM & HO, *Sputyll mosse* 1472 *Chol*, *Moss near Malpas* 1727 Sheaf, *The Moss* 1831 Bry, *Hermitage Moss* 1842 OS, *v.* mos. The reason for the later name is unknown, cf. ermitage. The earliest name may be from spoute 'a spring' and hyll. OAT HILL, *the-* 1777, *Hothul(l)* 1321, *Hotul* 1322, *the Oathile* 1777 all *Chol*, cf. Roman Tee *infra*. This is probably a ME p.n. 'hot hill', *v.* hāt (ME *hot(e)*) 'hot' and hyll, alluding to warm ground, probably on account of a sheltered and sunny situation. The first el. has been replaced by āte 'oats', the second by hygel 'a hillock', in *Oathile* 1777. PRESTON HALL, 1831 Bry, *v.* prēost, tūn. WHITEGATE FM, *White Gate Field* 1841 *TA*, *White Gate* 1842 OS, *v.* hwīt, geat.

FIELD-NAMES

The undated forms are 1841 *TA* 249. Of the others, 1209–28 is AD, 1347², 1352, 1461 ChRR, 1347¹, 1466 *Dav*, 1359, 1430 *Eyre*, 1360¹, 1530 Plea, 1671 Sheaf, 1831 Bry, and the rest *Chol*.

(a) (Two-, Four-, etc.) Acre(s) (cf. *the Forty Acres* 1778, *v.* æcer); Ankers Fds 1737 (cf. The Moss *supra*); Bake House Fd (cf. *Bakers Field* 1778, *v.* bæc-hūs); Barkas (*le Barkhousyord* 1404, 'tan-house yard', *v.* bark-howse, geard); Bottoms (*v.* botm); Bradley Fd (cf. Bradley 11 *supra*); Brewers Croft (*Brewers Field* 1692, *Brewhouse Croft* 1737, *v.* brew-hous, brewere);

Briery Fd (*v.* brērig); Broad Hay 1708 (*v.* brād, (ge)hæg); Brookest (*Brock-hurst* 1636, 1699, 'badger wood', *v.* brocc, hyrst); Broom (*v.* brōm); Cams Hillock (*v.* Gams- *infra*); Chancilors Fd (cf. *the Chancellors Peice* 1694, *v.* pece. This may be named from Thomas Egerton (of Ridley 3 313), Lord Chancellor of England c.1598); Cholmondeley Fd & Mdw (1778, cf. Cholmondeley 21 *supra*); Church Croft; Clay Hole (cf. *Clay Hole Tenement* 1778, *v.* clæg, hol¹); Clomley (cf. Clemley 3 47); The Close (*le Clos* 1324, 1330, *v.* clos); Coat Fd (*v.* cot); Cock Fight, Cock Pit Croft (*v.* cock-fight, cockpit); Coids Croft 1777 (perhaps from Welsh coed 'a wood'); Conney Fd (*Corney Field* 1777, *v.* coni); Crab Tree Fd (1777, *v.* crabbe, trēow); The Cuttinge 1694 (*Cuttinges* 1582, 'pieces of land cut off a larger field', *v.* cutting); Dallinger(s), Dallengers; Dee Bank (*v.* dey, banke); Delune (*v.* dey, land, dial. *loon*); Diars Yate 1635 (*v.* geat); Duns Flat & Hill (*Dunse Field* 1537, from *dunce* (NED) 'a dunce', flat, hyll); Earliest Croft; Edish (*v.* edisc); Evans-, Evins Fd; The Flat (*v.* flat); Gams Hillock (cf. Gams Wood 32 *supra*, Cams Hillock *supra*, from the Welsh nickname *Gam* from *cam* 'crooked, bent', *v.* hylloc. A certain Welsh gentleman called Dafydd Gam was at Agincourt); Gorsty Fd & Leasowe (cf. *Gorstie Croft* 1582, *v.* gorstig, feld, croft, lǣs); Greene Croft 1694 (*v.* grēne¹); Green Lane Fd, Green Way (Lane) Croft (*the Green Way Croft* 1777, *v.* grēne¹, weg); (Lower) Hampton Hay (*le Hampton Heys-*, *-Hay(e)s vel (siue) Hampton Medoos*, *-Medoes* 1488, 1494, *Hamptonshey* 1500, *Hampton Haye* 1520, 1523, 1525, *Hantonhey* 1530, *v.* (ge)hæg, mǣd, cf. Hampton 14 *supra*); Harbour Fd (*v.* here-beorg); The Hatchfeild 1711 (*v.* hæc(c)); Heys Barn 1831 (*v.* (ge)hæg); Higher Fd (cf. *le Nethir feld* 1321, *altus campus*, *le Nethirfeild* 1346, *superiores campi*, *le Netherfild* 1466, *Ouerfeld* 1472, *the higher- & the nether field* 1529, *High Field* 1777, *v.* neoðera, hēah, uferra); Hooleys Bank (*v.* banke); Hopleys Croft (cf. *Hopleys Townfield* 1779, from the surname Hopley, cf. *Hoppelegh* 1352 (p), *Hopley* 1461 (p), 'grass-hopper clearing', *v.* hoppa, lēah, cf. Townfield *infra*); Big Hustans; Intake (*v.* inntak); Key Fd (*Kayefelde* 1524, *Keys Fyeld* 1554, perhaps 'hedge field', from Welsh cae 'a hedge' with an anglicised gen.sg. (-es²), and feld, but Professor Löfvenberg suggests that the first el. may be cǣg 'a stone'); The Kiln (*v.* cyln); Lane Farm 1831 (named from Tilston Lane 59 *infra*); Lay Head (*v.* lēah, hēafod); Leech Hill(s) (*v.* lece); Top Malpas, Malpas Fd (*Malpas Croft & Fielde* 1543, *Malpas Field* 1599, cf. Town Fd *infra*); Marl Fd (*v.* marle); Masty Lane Croft; Miccle Croft (*v.* micel); Mill Fds (*Milne Field where several milnes were lately erected, part called Windy Milne Bancke* 1659, *Big- & Little Mill Field* 1777, *v.* myln, feld, wind-mylne, banke, cf. Windmill Fd *infra*); the Myrie Croft 1711 (*v.* myry); New Heys (*v.* (ge)hæg); Old Fd; Oldcastle Fd (cf. Oldcastle 44 *infra*); Oven Croft 1777 (*v.* ofen); Painters' Croft 1813; (Little) Park (*Big Park, Two Lower Parks* 1796, *v.* park); Peartree Fd (*Pear Tree Croft* 1796); Peas Bank & Mdw (*Peas's Meadow* 1777, *Peer's-* 1783, perhaps from the ME pers.n. *Piers* (*Peter*)); Pentre Fd (Welsh pentref 'village, homestead'); Pin Fold (*v.* pynd-fald); Plott (*v.* plot); Poor Fd (*v.* pouer(e)); Quis Croft (*v.* quist); Quillet (*v.* quillet(t)); Rough (*v.* rūh); Sanders Butt 1779 (*v.* butte); Sand Hole Fd (*v.* sand, hol¹); Shell Croft (*the-* 1777); Shrug(s) (*v.* shrogge);

Slang (v. slang); Sleape 1683 ('slippery, muddy place', v. slǣp); Sparrow Meare 1671; Stile Fd (cf. *le Steygullond* 1404, 'selion at a stile', v. stigel, land); Stone Pit Fd(s) (*Stone Pitt Feild* 1694, v. stān, pytt); Sweet Fd (v. swēte); German- & Roman Tee (cf. *the Oathile or Roman T* 1777, cf. Oat Hill *supra*. The f.ns. are from the shape of the fields); Tentry Fd 1777 (*the Teyntre Filde* 1503, v. tentour); (Big- & Little) Town Fd (cf. *the lower Town Field* 1640, and Malpas Field, Hopleys Croft *supra*); Under Hill (v. under, hyll); The Unlocks Croft 1796; Wall Stone; Warvin Lake 1777 (from lacu 'a watercourse', Warvin seems similar to Wervin 137 *infra*); Water Field Croft; White Fd; Wigland Croft 1640 (cf. Wigland 50 *infra*); Windmill Fd (cf. Mill Fds *supra*); Withins (v. wīðegn).

(b) *Blethens Croft* 1582 (from the Welsh pers.n. *Bleddyn* and croft); *Bolehustede* 1346 ('site of a house of logs', v. bola, hūs, stede); *boscus de Chathul, Nant Chathul* 1333 ('(wood and valley at) the wood hill', from Brit cēto- 'a wood' and OE hyll 'a hill', with prefixed Welsh nant 'a valley'); *Cokonshul* 1321 (final el. hyll, first el. probably a mis-written form *cokous-*, gen.sg. of ME cuccu 'a cuckoo', possibly a pers. by-name, cf. Reaney s.n. *Cuckow*); *Creswall Hill* 1524, 1560 ('cress spring or stream', from cresse and wælla, with hyll); *Durpitt Croft* 1582 ('deer-trap', v. dēor, pytt); *Flax Mareleput* 1472 ('marl-pit at a place where flax grows', v. fleax, marle-pytt); *le Hadinges* 1341 (perhaps an early instance of ModE *heading* in the sense 'a bank, a dam' (1662 NED)); *Hamptoneswey* 1321 (v. weg, cf. Hampton 34 *supra*); *le Malpas heth* 1320, *le Hethyleye* 1321, *le Heht* 1395 (v. hǣð, hǣðig, lēah); *Hyntwike Yate* 1495 (a road-name, '(gateway at or to) the hamlet or work-buildings at a road', from hynt and wīc, with geat. The road may be the Roman road, cf. Malpas *supra*); *le Holxheway* 1347 ('road in a hollow, sunken road', v. holh, weg. This may be the road past Hough Fm *supra*); *Jankyn Ridyngis* 1481 ('Jankin's cleared-lands', from the ME pers.n. *Jankin* and ryding); *le Knol(les)* 1341, *le Knolles, -us* 1347[2] (p), 1347[1] (p), 1348 (p), *le Cnolles* 1354 (p), *Knolles* 1359 (p) (v. cnoll); *Lytlemore* 1321, *le lytyll more* 1472 (v. lȳtel, mōr[1]); *Pykfeld* 1472 (v. pīc[1], feld); *Pilatenhalewh* 1209–28, *-hale* 1360[1] (p), *Pylatenhale, -on-* 1360[2] ('nook growing with pill-oats', v. pil-āte, halh); *le Prestisfeld* 1326, *-es-* 1339, *-us-* 1356, *-filde* 1475 ('the priest's field', v. prēost, feld); *Rippon Feldes* 1481, *Ripton* 1583; *le Rymoreshall* 1457 (a messuage, v. hall. A family surnamed *le Rymour* lived at Malpas c.1332–1360 Chol C 254, 340, 409); *le Sondy-*, *-Sondihul(l)* 1341 (v. sandig, hyll); *le Stonery Ford* 1450 ('ford at a stony place', v. stanry, ford); *Wade Hadlond* 1472 (v. hēafod-land. *Wade* is either the ME pers.n. *Wade* (OE *Wada*) or (ge)wæd 'a ford'); *Warde ys lond* 1495 ('Ward's selion', from the ME pers.n. or surname *Ward(e)* and land. The form is an example of the transition from ME gen.sg. *-es, -ys* to the possessive-pronoun formula *-his-*); *Way Croft* 1582 (cf. *le Weilond* 1341, v. weg, land, croft).

18. NEWTON BY MALPAS, NEWTON HALL (109–465455)

Neuton 13 AD, c.1280 *Chol* (p) *et freq* to 1518 Plea, AD, (*-iuxta Malpas*) 1288 Court, (*-Cudynton*) 1315 Plea, (*-(H)oldecastel*) 1329, 1333 AD, (*-nigh-*, *nygh Malpas*)1518 ib

Newton (*near Malpas*) 1370 (19) Orm², *Newton* 1417 AD *et freq*, (*-by Oldcastle*) 1500 Orm², (*-iuxta Oldecastell*) 1532 *Chol*, *Newton Hall* 1831 Bry

'The new farm', from nīwe and tūn, with hall.

DOG LANE, *v.* dogga, lane, cf. *infra.*

FIELD-NAMES

The undated forms are 1838 *TA* 290.

(*a*) Broad Hays (*v.* (ge)hæg); Gorstey Gardens (*v.* gorstig, gardin); Long Heys (*v.* (ge)hæg); Milking Bank Fd (*v.* milking); Old Grass Mdw; Old Heys (*v.* (ge)hæg); Pinfold Fd (*v.* pynd-fald); Slangs (*v.* slang); Town Fd; Well Fd.

19. OLDCASTLE (FM, HEATH & WELL) (118–4644)

Oldcastil 13 AD, *Holde-* 1260 Court, *Oldecastell* 1289 ib *et freq* with variant spellings *Holde-*, *Old(e)-*, *-castel(l)*, *-castele* to 1567 ChRR, *le-* 1345 *Eyre* (p), 1362 Orm², *Oldcastle* 1356 ChRR *et freq*, *Olde Castell* 1560 *Chol*, *Old Castle* 1656 Orm²

Le Veu Chastel 1284 Ch, *-Castell* 1284 CRC

'The old (i.e. the former) castle', from ald and castel(l) with hǣð and wella. The site of an old castle is at CASTLE HILL (118–466442), 1838 *TA*, cf. Orm² II 666.

THE GREAVES, GREAVES WOODS, *Greues* 1259 Court (p), *Greves* 1539 Plea, *-ys* 1546 Orm², *Graves Farm* 1831 Bry, *Greaves* 1842 OS, 'the groves', *v.* grǣfe.

DOG LANE (FM), *Ploughley Farm* 1831 Bry, cf. Dog Lane *supra.* HOLLY BANK.   OLDCASTLE MILL, 1842 OS, 'a water-mill in Old-castle' 1357 Orm², *Oldecastelemulne* 1362 ib, *Alports Mill* 1831 Bry, *v.* myln. *Alport* was the surname of the manorial lords of Overton 45 *infra.*   PARADISE BROOK (lost), 1831 ib, *v.* I 32.   TOPWOOD, *v.* top.   WELL ROUGH, *Wych Rough* 1831 ib, *Woodhouse Rough* 1842 OS, *v.* rūh, cf. Oldcastle Well *supra*, Wood Ho *infra*, Lower

Wych 51 *infra*.   WOOD HO, 1831 Bry, 'house at a wood', cf.
boscus de-, wood of Oldcastil 13 AD *et freq* with spellings as for Oldcastle to 1333 AD, *Oldecastellwode* 1484 *Chol, v.* wudu, hūs.

FIELD-NAMES

The undated forms are 1838 *TA* 305.

(*a*) Backstone Fd (*v.* bæc-stān); Booths Doles (*v.* bōth, dāl); Bottoms (*v.*
botm); Britches Fd (*v.* brēc); Little Cae Maur (Welsh, 'big field', *v.* cae,
mawr); Charlton Fd (cf. Chorlton 27 *supra*); Combermere (cf. Combermere
3 93); Doles (*v.* dāl); Glead Fd; Gradder; Hayes (*v.* (ge)hæg); Henfaes,
-fas (Welsh, 'old field', *v.* hen, maes); Island (*v.* ēg-land); Kiddington Fd
(*v.* Cuddington 28 *supra*); Kiln Fd (*v.* cyln); Malpas Lane 1831 (cf.
Malpas 38 *supra*); Marl Fd; Old Marl (*v.* marle); Ox Pasture; Pinfold Fd
(*v.* pynd-fald); Red Fd (*v.* rēad); Big- & Little Rostler; Slang (*v.* slang);
Steens Croft; Big Vron (Welsh, *v.* bron(n) 'a hill-side'); Great Wern
(Welsh, *v.* gwern 'a swamp, place where alders grow'); Whare Fd (*v.* wer,
wær 'a weir'); Wheat Eddish (*v.* hwǣte, edisc); Whythin Fd (*v.* wiðegn).

(*b*) *Windyates* 1260 Court ('windy gaps', *v.* wind-geat. The location
is not known. The name is that of a *vivarium* or game-preserve held with
Oldcastle and Shocklach in the barony of Malpas, cf. Court 34. It may have
been in the Peckforton Hills towards Broxton, to the north of Malpas
parish.)

20. OVERTON (FM, HALL & HEATH) (109–4748)

Ovretone 1086 DB

Overton 1288 *Chol et freq*, (*-iuxta Malpas*) 1457 *ib, le Overton*
   1354 *ib, Overton vulgo Ourton* 1671 Sheaf, *Overton Hall &*
   -Heath (*Farm*) 1831 Bry

Ourton 1329 ChRR (p), 1671 Sheaf, *Horton* 1394 ChRR, 1404,
   1413 ib, *Orton* 1490 *Chol*, 1551 Pat, 1656 Orm², (*-alias Overton*)
   1666 *Chol*

'Farm at a hill', from ofer² and tūn, with hall and hǣð, cf. Overton
Scar *infra*.

THE BEECHES, *Malpas Hill* 1831 Bry, *v.* bēce², cf. Malpas 38
supra.   CHARITY HOUSE FM, *v.* charity.   GIPSY'S HOLE, a cave
in Overton Scar, the site of a gipsy camp, White 197, *v.* hol¹.
KIDNALL (HILL), *Kidnall* 1831 Bry, *Kidnal* (*Hill*) 1842 OS; no
evidence is available about this p.n.   SCAR FM, OVERTON SCAR,
Overton Scar, The Scar(r) 1819 Orm², 1831 Bry, 1832 *TA, v.* sker
(cf. dial. *scar*), a rock cliff forming the southern extremity of the

central ridge of uplands, whence the p.n. Overton *supra, v. 2 supra.*
WHITEWOOD LANE, *v.* hwīt, wudu.

FIELD-NAMES

The principal forms are 1832 *TA* 312. Of the others, 1208–29 is (1580)
Sheaf, 1657 *Chol*, 1831 Bry.

(*a*) Black Pool (*v.* pōl[1]); Broomhill (*v.* brōm, hyll); Clay Croft (cf. *Great-
& Little Clayfield* 1657, *v.* clæg); Day Loom ('dairy selion', *v.* dey, loom);
Foxs Cross; Hall Ground; Hatch Fd (*v.* hæc(c)); Marl Fd; Muddy Mdw;
Outlet (*v.* outlet); Overton Lodge 1831; Big Park (*v.* park); The Riddings
(*v.* ryding); Rock Fd (*v.* roke); Rye Bank (*v.* ryge); Tilston Lane 1831
(cf. Tilston 59 *infra*); White Fd; Wold House Croft (probably 'wood
house', *v.* wudu, hūs).

(*b*) *molendinum de Overton* 1208–29 (*v.* myln).

21. STOCKTON (HALL & DINGLE) (109–4745)

Stocton 1288 Court (p) *et freq* with variant spellings *-tone, Stok-*
(1304 Chamb (p) to 1536 ChRR) to 1588 ChRR, *Stockton*
(*Heath*) 1671 Sheaf, *Stockton Hall* 1831 Bry
Stocston c.1308 *Chol* (p)

'Enclosure or farmstead at a dairy hamlet', from stoc and tūn,
with hæð, hall and dingle. The heath adjoined Oldcastle Heath, and
is the location of *Old Castle Smithy* 1831 Bry, 1860 White, *v.* smiððe,
cf. Oldcastle 44 *supra*.

FIELD-NAMES

The undated forms are 1837 *TA* 370, and 1842 OS.

(*a*) Bank; Boroughs Croft (*v.* burg 'a burrow'); Brown Banks (*v.* brūn[1]);
Cockshut Fd (*v.* cocc-scyte); Griggy Fd (*v.* grig[2], Welsh grug); Ox Hay
(*v.* (ge)hæg); Rostler; Shenton Rough (cf. *Stockton Rough* 1842, *v.* rūh.
Shenton is a surname); Water Head Bank ('hillside at the source of a stream',
from wæter and hēafod, with banke); Well Moor (*v.* wella, mōr[1]).

22. TUSHINGHAM CUM GRINDLEY (109–5246), 1741 *Chol*, *Tussyn-*
cham et Grenley 1473 *ib*, *v.* Grindley, Tushingham *infra*.

GRINDLEY (BROOK (BRIDGE No. 2)) (118–520435) [ˈgrindli]

> Grenleg' 1230 Chol (p), 1260 Court (p), -legh 1308 Ipm (p),
> -ley(e) 1314 Chol, -le(e) 1330 ib, 1338 Cl, Grenelegh 1317 Orm[2],
> -lee 1417 Chol, Grenley Broke 1534 ib
> Grynleye 1299 Ipm (p)
> Grynesley 1530 Sheaf
> Gryndley 1543 Orm[2], Grindley 1799 Chol, -Brooke 1665 Sheaf

'Green wood or clearing', from grēne[1] and lēah, with brōc. The stream, le Brock 1334 Chol, becomes Wych Brook 1 39, and gives name to GRINDLEYBROOK hamlet and the bridge, cf. 3 supra.

TUSHINGHAM HALL & Ho (109–529450 & 118–526449) [ˈtuʃiŋəm]
> Tusigeham 1086 DB
> Tussinhgham 1260 Court (p)
> Tussingham 1288 Court (p), Chol et freq with variant spelling
> -yng- to 1724 NotCestr, (the hall of) Tusshyngham 1543 Chol,
> Tushinghame 1632 ib, -ham 1633 ib, (-Hall) 1831 Bry
> Tussincham 1272–1307 Orm[2], 1317 Chol et freq with variant spelling
> -yn- to 1545 Orm[2], -ynsham 1472 ChRR (p), aula de Tussincham
> 1314 Orm[2]
> Tussinham 1311 Plea
> Tussigham 1314 Chol
> Tussigcham 1315, 1316, 1330 Chol, Tussicham 1316, 1332 ib
> Tussingcham 1315, 1316 Chol, 1318 Eyre, 1330, 1332, 1334, 1393
> Chol, 1601 Orm[2], -yng- 1492 Chol
> Tussingeham 1383 Chol, -ynge- 1392 ib, Plea, 1394 Chol
> Tussyncam 1416 ChRR

Ekwall (DEPN) explains this p.n. as 'the village of Tūnsige's people', from an OE pers.n. Tūnsige and -ingahām (v. -ingas, hām). The -incham, -ingcham spellings indicate that this p.n. is analogous with Altrincham 2 7, i.e. hām and an -ing[2] formation. The absence of Tuns- spellings, and the similar form of Tussemos infra, Tussemore 55 infra, indicate that the first el. of Tushingham is an -ing formation upon the same word as appears as first el. in these other p.ns., i.e. the original of ME *tuss(h)e 'a tuft' (cf. tush 1570 NED sb 2 'a tuft', tusk 1530 NED sb 2, tussock 1550 NED 'a tussock'), probably an OE *tusce 'a tuft'. Tussing- would mean 'a place where tufts of grass or rushes, etc., grow; a tufty place', v. -ing[1], ing[2].

BARHILL FM, *Barellesgreue* 1394 *Chol* (C 877, perhaps *-grene*), *Barrel* 1397 Orm², *Barell* 1403 ib, 1417 *Chol*, (*le-*) 1488 *ib*, *Barrell* 1633, 1661 *ib*, *the Barrel Farm* 1819 Orm², *Barhull* 1513 *ChEx* (p), *-hill* (*Tenement*) 1780 *Chol*, *The Barhill* 1831 Bry, *Barehill* 1632 *Chol*, *Barchill* 1632 *ib*, *Barrehill* 1668 *ib*, *Barrhill* 1709 *ib*, probably 'hill called *Barr*', from Welsh *bar*¹ (Pr Welsh **barr**) 'a top, a summit' and hyll, with græfe or grēne². Part of this estate lay in Bickley, *v.* Barhill Fall 10 *supra*. This p.n. has affected the name of Bar Mere 10 *supra*. The farm is at 109–525467.

BELLOW HILL (FM) (118–525443), BELL O' TH' HILL (109–523454). These names are confused. The material is *Belle Hill* c.1610 Sheaf¹, 2, p. 361, *Belley* and *Grenley or Bellyhill* 1671 Sheaf³ 48 (9795) *Bellowhill* 1675 ib 29 (6353), 1690 ib 5 (883), *The Signe of the Bel*, *The Bell Inn* 1675 ib, *The Bell* 1831 Bry, *The Bell, -Ball*, (cf. *Bell-*, *Ball Field*) 1838 *TA*, *Bell o' th' Hill* 1842 OS. It is supposed by local historians (Sheaf, loc. cit.) that the p.n. *Bellow Hill* is a back-formation from the name of the inn '*The Bell*' on the Hill. It appears as likely that the inn-name was suggested by the hill-name, which could be derived from belg 'a rounded hill' (*Belly-*), and belle 'a bell', which was itself used figuratively in hill-names. *Bellow* probably contains belle and hlāw or hōh. Bell o' th' Hill might have been the site of *le Castelward infra*, and a motte-and-bailey mound may lie behind the names.

ST CHAD'S CHAPEL, *Saynt Cedde Chapell* 1519 *Chol*, *Chadde Chappell* 1621 *ib*, *Chad Chapel* 1636 Orm², 1715 *Corp*, 1831 Bry, *Chadwich Chapel* 1656 Orm², *Chappell of St. Chad* 1724 NotCestr, 'St Cedd's chapel'. *Chadwich* is presumably 'Cedd's hamlet', *v.* wīc. There appears to have been a chapel here since the fourteenth century, cf. *Chapel Croft, Field & Lane, Chantry Meadow* 1838 *TA*, *le Chapelfeld* 1349, 1354 *Chol*, *le Chapellfyld* 1492 *ib*, *-feild* 1492 Orm², *the Chappelmeadow* 1727 *Chol*, fields adjoining the chapel. *v.* chapel(e). chaunterie. Cf. Hollywell Ridding *infra*.

COOKS LANE. GORSTYHILL COTTAGE, cf. *Gorse Cote Field*, *Gorsty Field* 1838 *TA*, *v.* gorst, gorstig, hyll, cot. HIGH ASH, 1842 OS, *-Farm* 1831 Bry, *v.* hēah, æsc. HILLTOP FM, near Bell o' th' Hill *supra*, *v.* hyll, topp. LAND OF CANAAN, 1838 *TA*, 1842 OS. LLOYD'S TENEMENT, *v.* tenement. MOOREND TENE-

MENT, MOORHEAD COTTAGE & FM, MOORSIDE FM, named from Willeymoor *infra*, *v.* mōr[1], ende[1], hēafod, sīde, tenement. PEARL FM, cf. *Purl Field & Meadow* 1838 *TA*, *v.* pyrl(e) 'a bubbling stream'. SANDHOLE FM, cf. *Sandfield* 1838 *ib*, *v.* sand, hol[1], feld. THROSTLES NEST, *v.* þrostle, nest. TILEYARD COTTAGE, cf. *Tile Yard Field* 1838 *ib*, *v.* tile-yard. WATLING BANK, probably named after the Roman road 'Watling Street'. WILLEYMOOR (LANE), *v.* Willey Moor 9 *supra*. WOBBS PLANTATION & WELL, *v.* cwabbe 'a marsh, a bog'. YEWTREE FM.

FIELD-NAMES

The undated forms are 1838 *TA* 404. Of the others, 1314 is Orm[2], 1328 ChRR, 1362 (1618) *ChCert*, 1529 *ChEx*, 1620 Sheaf, 1831 Bry, and the rest *Chol*.

(*a*) The Acre; Bank Fd; Barren Fd; Bow Croft; Brookall Croft; Broom Fd (*v.* brōm); Brow Fd (*v.* brū); Butty Piece (*v.* butty); Castle Houses 1831 (lost buildings at 109–534463, perhaps named from some architectural feature. The situation, marsh-land, is against association with *le Castelward infra*); Cock Pit Fd (*v.* cockpit); Dadles Fd; Drovers Fd; Endless; Flash Mdw (*v.* flasshe); Flax Boughs (cf. *le Flaxpoll* 1348, *le Flaxeyorde* 1492, *v.* fleax, pōl[1], geard); Fowls's Fd; Gate Fd (*v.* gata); Gravelly Bank (*v.* gravel(l), banke); Green Hayes (*v.* grēne[1], (ge)hæg); Grindleston Fd 1727 (*v.* grindel-stān, cf. Whetstone Fd *infra*); Hall Bank & Moor (*v.* hall, banke, mōr[1]); Hill Fd; Hollywell Ridding (*the Holy Well* 1620, a well near St Chad's Chapel *supra*, *v.* hālig, wella, ryding); Kiln Fd (*v.* cyln); Lower Heath (*the Lower Heaths* 1733, *v.* hǣð); Marl Croft & Fd (*v.* marle); Milestone Fd (*v.* mīl-stān); Missick ('boggy ground', *v.* mizzick); New Purchase (*v.* 337 *infra*); Pickhill, Pingle (*v.* pichel, pingel); Ranmoor Fd (cf. *Ranneslake* 1362 (1618), 'raven's stream', *v.* hræfn, lacu, mōr[1]). The reference is to a toll-passage at this place, presumably the same as 'a fourth part of Tussyncham ferry' 1483–4 Orm[2] II 625); Ridding (*v.* ryding); Road Piece (*v.* rād); Seven Pound Fd; Spur Moor (cf. *Sporewei* 1315, *le Sporewey* 1325, 'pathway', *v.* spor, weg, mōr[1]); Town Fd (*le Tounfeld* 1354, *the great Townfeild* 1656, *v.* toun); Wargreaves (perhaps 'poorer, worse, less valuable woods', from werre and grǣfe, *v.* Wargraves 242 *infra*); Well Bank, Fd & Mdw (cf. *Wallecroft* 1394, *v.* wælla, croft); Whetstone Fd (*v.* hwet-stān, cf. Grindleston Field *supra*); Whore Stone Croft 1777 ((*le*) *hor*(*e*)*ston*(*es*)*feld* 1354, 1377, 1394, 1492, '(croft and field at) the old grey stone', from hār[2] and stān, with feld, croft); Windmill Fd; Wood Fd.

(*b*) *Adlemore* 1295 ('filthy marsh', *v.* adela, mōr[1]); *le Atenalgh* 1354 ('oaten nook', *v.* āte, halh); *le Bachebrok* 1377 (*v.* bæce[1], brōc); *le Berecrofte* 1490 ('barley croft', *v.* bere, croft); *Browesheye* 1394 ('enclosure at a brow', *v.* bru, -es[2], (ge)hæg); *le Castelward* 1314 ('the castle ward', from castel and ME warde 'the circuit of the walls of a castle'. The reference is to 'an assart between the castle ward and the hall of Tussincham', Orm[2] II 657); *le Cokshetefeld* 1354 ('field at a cock-shoot', *v.* cocc-scyte, feld); *Davyesmedwe* 1376 ('Davy's meadow', from the ME pers.n. *Davy* and mæd); *Dyotesmor* 1314[2] ('Dyot's marsh', from the ME fem. pers.n. *Dyot(a)* (diminutive of *Dye*, for *Dionisia*) and mōr[1]); *le Eleronlond* 1394 ('selion growing with alders', *v.* elren, land); *Grenelond* 1314[2] ('green selion', *v.* grēne[1], land); *Grenleyeruding*, 1314[2], 1326 (*v.* ryding, cf. Grindley *supra*); *Grenley Wey* 1314[2], *-leye-* 1326, *Grenlewey* 1330, 1332 ('way to, or at, Grindley', *v.* weg, cf. Grindley *supra*); *le Hauedlond* 1364 (*v.* hēafod-land); *le Haynryddyng* 1490 ('enclosure of cleared-land', *v.* hegn, ryding); *Henlowe* 1377, 1394, *le Henlowe* 1492 ('hen-hill', *v.* henn, hlāw, perhaps a hill frequented by wood-hens); *le Heye* 1295 (*v.* (ge)hæg); *Hobbemede* 1394, *le Hobe Medowe* 1490 ('tussocky meadow', *v.* hobb(e), mæd); *le Lyes* 1490 ('the clearings', *v.* lēah); *le Lyttlemor* 1348 (*v.* lȳtel, mōr[1]); *Madocuswalle* 1334 ('Madoc's spring', from the Welsh pers.n. *Madog* and wælla); *Medwesfeld* 1376, *le Meduefeld* 1377 (*v.* mæd, feld); *le parrokes* 1348 (*v.* pearroc); *le Spryng* 1496, *Sprynge* 1529 (*v.* spring 'a young wood'); *Talretheragh* 1348 (Welsh, 'Rhydderch's end or head-land', from the Welsh pers.n. *Rhydderch* and tâl 'end, head' perhaps here 'a hill, the end of a hill'); *Thurwardeslegh feld* 1377, *Thorouardesle*, *Thoroweardesle* 1394 (a field in Bickley and Tushingham, *v. Chol* C 870–877, and perhaps the same as *Porowald* (lit. *Yoro-*) 1328 ChRR (DKR XXXVI 166), from the ON pers.n. *Porvarðr* (Fellows Jensen 317) and lēah); *Tussemos* 1314[2], 1326 (from mos 'a bog', and the el. tuss(h)e discussed under Tushingham *supra*, cf. *Tussemore* 55 *infra*); *le Quitemorbrok* 1315, 1332, *le Quitemorsbroc* 1325, *le Quitemor* 1330 ('(brook at) the white marsh', from hwīt and mōr[1], with brōc); *Wignesbruge* 1376 (from brycg 'a bridge, a causeway', with the ME pers.n. *Wighen*, *Wigein*, *Wygan* (< OBret *Uuicon*, *Guegon*), *v.* Reaney s.n. *Wigan*); *Wlethereslond* 1354 (perhaps 'Gwledyr's land', from the rare Welsh pers.n. *Gwledyr* and land).

23. WIGLAND (HALL) (118–4944)

Wiggelaunde 1208–29 AD, *-lond* 1271 Plea (p) *et freq* with variant spellings *Wig(g)e-*, *Wyg(g)e-*, *-lond(e)* to 1442 ChRR (p)

Wygllond c.1300 Chol (p), *Wigland* 1305 (1637) Rich, *et freq* with variant spellings *Wyg-*, *-lond(e)*, *-land(e); Whigland* 1685 Chol, *Wigland* (*Cottage & Farm*) 1831 Bry

Wegelond 1301 (p), c.1310 (p), c.1325 Chol

Wyggwolond 1313 Chamb (p)

Wygglynde 1442 ChRR (p)

Wiklond 1443 ChRR

Wyghland 1533 Chol

'Wicga's land', from the OE pers.n. *Wicga* and land. Cf. Wigmoor 55 *infra*.

HIGHER WYCH (118–496435) & LOWER WYCH (in Iscoyd Fl, 118–485443) [witʃ]

Fulewic 1096–1101 (1150), 1150 Chest, *Fullewich* 1096–1101 (1280) ib, *Fulwich* 1295 Ipm *et freq* with variant spellings, *-wich(e)*, *-wicus*, *-wych(e)*, *-wicke*, *Fo(u)l-*, *Foule-*, *Fowle-*, *Foylle-* to 1626 Orm², *Le Fulwich* 1295 Ipm, *Fulwich Superior & Inferior* 1299 Plea, *Nether(e)-* & *Over(e)folwich*, *-wych* 1328 Pat, 1329 Plea, *Les Fulwiche* 1409 Orm², *Foulewiche in com. Flynt* 1473–4 Morris 59, *Foulewiche alias Dritwyche* 1482 Chol, *W(h)ichehagh' alias Fulwiche* 1508 ChRR, 1515 *MinAcct*

Upper Wych 1208–29 AD, *le Overe Wych* c.1305 Chol, *le Ouerwiche* 1388 Tab, *Layerwyche* 1526 Plea, *(the) Over-*, *-Loour-*, *-Layher-*, *-Lagher-*, *-w(h)iche*, *-wich(e)* 1528 ib, Orm², ChRR, Chol, *Lougherwyche* 1530 Sheaf, *Nederwiche* 1535 Orm², *Nether-* 1559 ChRR, *Upper & Lower Wych Salt Works* 1831 Bry

Wyz Maupas 1257 Pat, *the wiches hard by le Malpas* 1357 BPR, *villa de Wyche* 1472 Chol, *the Wychhouse* 1555 Sheaf, *the Wiche* 1882 Orm² II 664

Dritwyche 1482 Chol (*Foulewiche alias-*), *Dirtwich* 1485 ChRR *et freq* with variant spellings *Dyrthe-* (1489 ChRR), *Dyrt(e)-* (1529 Plea, c.1536 Leland), *Dirte-* (1555 Sheaf), *Durt-* (1599 AD), *Dert-* (c.1536 Leland), *Drit(e)-* (1486 *MinAcct*), *Dryt-* (1537 ChRR), *Dret-* (1486 *MinAcct*), *Drayte-* (1530 Sheaf), *Droyt(e)-* (1530 Chol, 1555 Sheaf), *Droit-* (1551 Pat to 1668 Chol), *-wich(e)*, *-wych(e)*, *-which(e)*, *-wch* to (*Upper & Lower-*) 1882 Orm², *Foulewich alias Dretwiche* 1486 *MinAcct*, *Drytwiche alias Fulwyche alias Wichehagh* 1537 ChRR, *Netherdretwyche* 1524 Sheaf, *the Hygher-*, *-Heygher-*, *-Lower-*, *-Logher-*, *-Drayte-*, *-Droyte-*, *-whiche*, *-wyche* 1530 Chol, Sheaf, *Overdroytwich(e)* 1556 ib, *Upper Durtwich* 1665 Chol, *Higher & Lower Dirtwich* 1842 OS, *the twoo Drayte Wiches* 1530 Sheaf, *Droywich* 1555 ib

'The higher and lower factories', 'the dirty works', from wīc and fūl, drit, with uferra, neoðera, higher, upper, lower, superior, inferior, and feld, mǣd, hūs and hall. These were salt-wiches, cf. 'two Wichehouses otherwise named Saltehouses in the townes of Ouerwiche and Lagherwiche in Iscoyde' 1528 Chol H 80 (cf. Orm² II 618, 663, DKR xxx 143), and 'six saltcottes and six tofts in Drytwiche alias Fulwyche alias Wichehagh' 1537 ChRR (DKR xxxix 150), *v.* wych(e)-hous(e), salt-hūs, salt-cote. They were part of the barony of Malpas 39 *supra*, lying in Wigland, Wychough (cf. 53 *infra*) and Iscoyd Fl, and anciently within, or appurtenant to, the lost DB manor of *Burwardestone* 1 *supra*. Cf. Droitwich Wo 285.

BANK FM, 1831 Bry.   FIELDS HO, *v.* feld.   MOUNT PLEASANT. SCHOLAR'S WOOD, *Hunters Moor* 1831 ib, 1838 *TA*.   TAYLOR'S ROUGH, *v.* rūh.   WELLMEADOW WOOD, cf. *Well Field* (*Meadow*), *Well Rough* 1838 *TA*, *v.* wella.

FIELD-NAMES

The undated forms are 1838 *TA* 430. Of the others, 1516 is Orm[2], 1831 Bry, and the rest *Chol*.

(a) Ben Rhaye; Brook Croft; Chidlow Hayes (cf. *Wigland Crofte alias Chydlowe Crofte* 1579, *v.* croft, (ge)hæg, cf. Chidlow 20 *supra*); Cou Leasow (*v.* cū, lǣs); Dead Megs (*v.* meg); Dole Croft (*v.* dāl); The Flatches (*v.* flasshe); The Green; Hill Fd; Horse Moor (*v.* hors, mōr[1]); Irish Bottoms (*v.* botm); Long Fd (*le lone ville de Wygelond* 1317, *v.* lang, feld); Mals Haven (*the Masawavin* 1568, unintelligible); Maltkin (cf. *Malt House* 1831, *v.* malte-kylne, mealt-hūs); Meadow; Mill Banks, Fd & Mdw (cf. 'one mill in Wiglande' 1516, 'a water mill with the mill-dam in Wiglande' 1594, *v.* myln); The Moors; Moss Fd; Oven Croft (*v.* ofen); Pingo (*v.* pingot); Rough; Round Bank; Sidlands ('wide selions', *v.* sīd, land); Sour Dock Fd (*v.* sūr, docce); Spring Bank (1831); Tentry Fd (*v.* tentour); Watering Pit Croft; Wood Fd.

(b) *le Blake Hereye* 1312 (perhaps 'black, or dark, pasture or herdsmen's shed', from blæc 'black', and ON erg 'a shieling, a summer pasture'); *Bolders Feld* 1475, *le Boldersfilde* 1478; *the Brenthrege* 1568 ('burnt ridge', *v.* brende[2], hrycg); *Breretons Fild* 1589, *-Fields* 1594, *Brereton-* 1657 (the Brereton family were lords of part of Malpas barony); *þe grete broke* 1470 (cf. *magnum et parvum rivulum* 1478, *v.* grēat, brōc); *Canaridings* 1657 (*v.* ryding); *le Chirnelond* 1312; *Coltesbache* 1272, *þe-* 1470, *le-* 1478, *Cottes Back* 1475 ('the colt's valley', *v.* colt, bæce[1]); *le Foxyorthes* 1478 (*v.* fox, eorðe); *þe Gorstye Hey & Bonke* 1470, *le Gorstebanke* 1478 (*v.* gorst(ig), banke, (ge)hæg); *le Hampton Grounde* 1478 (*v.* grund, cf. Hampton 34 *supra*); *le Helde Tounesfeld* 1312 ('the town-field on a hillside', *v.* helde, toun, feld); *le Holwemedewe* c.1305 ('meadow in a hollow', *v.* holh, mǣd); *Kenanescroft* 1317 ('Cynan's croft', from the Welsh pers.n. *Cynan* and croft); *Neuboldesfeld* l13 ('field at the new house', from nīwe, and bold, with feld); *le Horchardeshue* 1312 (last el. unintelligible, *v.* orceard); *le Outelone* 1328 (*v.* ūt, lane).

24. WYCHOUGH (109–4845) ['witʃʌf]

Wychalewh' 1208–29 AD

Wychehalgh' 1347 *Eyre et freq* with variant spellings *Wich(e)-,*
Wych(e)-, -(h)algh(e), -halge, -allgh, -aulgh to *Wichalgh* 1842 OS

Wychelhalgh 1460 ChRR

Wichehagh alias Fulwiche 1508 ChRR, *Drytwiche alias Fulwyche
alias Wichehagh* 1537 ib, *Whichehagh' alias Fulwiche* 1515
MinAcct, Wichehaugh 1559 ChRR, *Wyche-Haugh* 1654 Orm²,
Wych- 1642 Sheaf

Wichough 1663 Sheaf, *Wychough* 1724 NotCestr, 1831 Bry,
Whichough 1727 Sheaf, 1769 *Chol*

'Valley at a wīc', *v.* wīc, halh. The wīc is Lower Wych *infra*.

CAE DÛ WOOD, *Cadey Wood* 1831 Bry, *Big & Little Cae Dû* 1839
TA, 'black field', *v.* cae, du.   HILL FM, 1831 Bry.   HOW-
CROFTS, *Wains Rough* 1831 ib, *Waen Slough* 1842 OS, perhaps 'bog
in a meadow', from Welsh gwaun (spelt gwaen) and slōh.   MANOR
FM, *Wyche Farm* 1831 Bry, *Wichalgh* 1842 OS, *v.* wīc, cf. foll. and
Wychough *supra*.   LOWER WYCH, *Foulewiche in com. Flynt*
1473–4 Morris 59, mostly in Iscoyd Fl, *v.* 51 *supra*.

FIELD-NAMES

The undated forms are 1839 *TA* 452.

(a) Bottoms (*v.* botm); Drakes Mdw; Foxes Folly; Gassuck; Green Fd;
Kiln Croft (*v.* cyln); Lower Moor (cf. *Lower Rough* 1831 Bry); Milking
Bank (*v.* milking); Mill Mdw; Ox Pasture; Stockton Fd (cf. Stockton 46
supra); Wich Fd (*v.* wic, cf. Lower Wych *supra*).

ii. Tilston

The ecclesiastical parish of Tilston contained the townships 1. Carden,
2. Horton, 3. Stretton, 4. Tilston. Cf. Grafton 61 *infra*.

1. HIGHER & LOWER CARDEN (109–4653), CARDEN BANK, CLIFF,
(LOWER) HALL, HALL FM, LODGE, MARSH & DEER PARK ['ka:rdən]

Kauerthin 1230 CoLegh, *Kawrdin* 1230–40 Orm² (p), *Caworthin*
1300 Plea (p), *Cawardyn* 1302 Chamb (p) *et freq* with variant
spellings *Ka-, Ca-, -werth-, -uerd-, -w(e)rd-, -wryth-, -worth-,*

-word-, -ward-, -warth-, -wyrth-, -wurth-, -(e)n, -yn(e), -in to
Cawarden 1724 NotCestr, *Cauwarthyn* 1324 *Chol* (p), *Carwarden* 1775 Sheaf

Kaurdin m13 Orm[2] (p), *-yn* 1320 *Chol, Caurdyn* 1363 Orm[2] *et freq*
to 1475 ChRR, *Caurthyn* c.1300 *Chol* (p) *et freq* with variant
spellings *-yne, -in, -on* to 1458 Orm[2], *Caur(e)den* 1463, 1466
ChRR *et freq* to 1530 Plea, *Cawreden* 1471 *Chol* (p), *le Ouere*
Caurthyn 1307–27 *AddCh, le Nether-* 1313 *ib, Nether- & Over*
Caurden 1530 Plea

Superior Cauthrin 1272–1307 *AddCh*

Gaurthyn c.1340–50 AD (p)

Caerden 1462 Plea, 1489 ChRR, *Cairden* 1489 Earw

Cuorden 1476 *Chol*

Cardeyn 1511 Orm[2], *-dyn* 1517 Plea, (*Nether- & Overe-*) *Carden*
1527 Orm[2], *Carden alias Cawarden* 1601 ib, *Carden Hall &*
Greene 1668–71 Sheaf, *Carden Cliff* 1819 Orm[2], (*Lower*) *Carden,*
Carden Farm, Marsh & Park 1831 Bry, *Cardin* 1700 Sheaf

'Enclosure at a rock', from carr and worðign, with uferra, neoðera,
superior, higher, lower, and hall, clif, grēne[2], banke, loge, mersc and
park. Carden Green is at Lower Carden. The rock from which the
place is named appears in the two 'scars' on the west side of Carden
Cliff hill. The development of the modern form is similar to that of
Hawarden Fl.

THE BIRCHES, 1840 *TA, v.* birce.   BOWLING ALLEY HO, 1842 OS.
CARDEN BROOK (> Coddington Brook 86 *infra*), *Bartonebrok* 1312
AddCh, the Brooke 1577 *Chol,* cf. *Stretton Brook* 1671 Sheaf, a
hamlet at Brook Hill Field 58 *infra, v.* brōc, cf. Barton 68 *infra,*
Brook Meadow 69 *infra.*   CLIFF BANK, 1831 Bry, *v.* clif, banke,
cf. Carden Cliff *supra.*   FRENCH BANK, *v.* French wheat.   GOLBORNE'S WOOD, 1840 *TA, Golburn Wood* 1842 OS, from the surname
from Golborne 88 *infra* and wudu.   HOOK'S BROOK & ROUGH,
Hawks 1840 *TA,* from hōc, halc 'a hook of land', alluding to the
land in the bend of Hook's Brook at 109–467523. The brook joins
Carden Brook *supra.*   MOOR GORSE, *Carden Moor Covert* 1840
ib, Carden Moor 1842 OS, *v.* mōr[1], gorst.   ROUND HILL, *v.*
rond.   STONE HO, 1831 Bry.   WINDMILL FM.

FIELD-NAMES

The undated forms are 1840 *TA* 93. Of the others, 1178–90 is *Bun*, 1588 *Chol*, and the rest *AddCh*.

(a) Carden Wd (*-Wood(e)* 1588, v. wudu); Cordiwell Mdw (*Caldewalle-medwe* 1272–1307, v. cald, wælla, mæd); Cow Leys (v. læs); Cross Fd (v. cros); Crumps; Dale Fd (v. dæl[1]); Everson; Farthings (v. fēorðung); Little Hoose (v. hol[1]); Horn Close; Kilkens; Kiln Fd; Loofas; Marl Fd (cf. *Marle Croft(e)* 1588, v. marle); Pentre Fd (*le Pentref* 1307–27, v. pentref); Quillet (v. quillet(t)); Radish; Sandfield; Sitch (v. sīc); Sough (v. sogh); Slang (v. slang); Town Fd; Wigmoor (*Wigemora* 1178–90 (p), *Wiggemor* 1310, *Wygemor*, *Wyggemorsiche iuxta Bartonebrok* 1312, *Wigmore*, *Uigmore* 1588, 'Wicga's marsh', from the OE pers.n. *Wicga* (cf. Wigland 50 *supra*) and mōr[1], sīc, though the first el. could be wigga. Cf. Barton 68 *infra*, Carden Brook *supra*.)

(b) *Alstanescroft* 1312 ('Alstān's croft', from croft and the pers.n. *Alstān* (<OE *Ælfstān*, *Æðelstān*) discussed by Feilitzen 152, cf. Austerson 3 130); *vadum de Barton* 1307–27 ('ford leading to Barton', v. ford, cf. Barton 68 *infra*. This may have been near Clutton Ford Bridge 72 *infra*); *le Brechis de Caurthyn* c.1300, *Caurthynesbruches* c.1312 ('the breakings-in of land', v. brēc, bryce); *le Bulgh'* 1312 (v. Welsh bwlch 'a pass, a gap'); *Dovehouse Flatt* 1588 (v. flat); *Le Fereweokwey* 1312 *AddCh* 51385 (a road, v. weg. The rest is unintelligible); *Hoggerudyng* 1312 ('hogs' clearing', v. hogg, ryding); *Mabotesmedewe* 1313 ('Mabot's meadow', from the ME fem. pers.n. *Mabot* (diminutive of *Mab*, for *Mabilia*) and mæd); *Pasture Fi(e)lde* 1588; *Caurthynes schawe* c.1300 (v. sc(e)aga); *Stotefilismedue* 1307–27 (('meadow at) the ox field', v. stot, feld, -es[2], mæd); *Tussemore* 1307–27, *-mor* 1313 ('tussocky marsh', from mōr[1] and the ME word *tuss(h)e 'a tuft', discussed under Tushingham 47 *supra*, cf. *Tussemos* 50 *supra*); *Tuffinge Meadowe*, *Tuftinge Meadow* 1588 ('tufty meadow', v. tuffe, tufte, -ing[1], mæd).

2. HORTON (FM, GREEN & HALL) (109–4549), *Horton* c.1240 AD *et freq* with variant spelling *-tone*; (*-iuxta Tylstan*) 1315 Plea, (*-iuxta Malpas*) 1321 *Chol*, (*-near Shoklace*) 1355 Plea, *Horton Green & Hall* 1831 Bry, 'dirty farm', from horu and tūn, with grēne[2] and hall. The township is near Malpas, Shocklach and Tilston 38 *supra*, 63, 58 *infra*, and is so distinguished from Horton 3 188, 275.

CHURCH CROFT, 1838 *TA*, v. cirice, croft.   HORTON HO, *Parkers Farm* 1831 Bry.   MEADOWS FM, *The Meadows* 1831 ib, v. mæd.

FIELD-NAMES

The undated forms are 1838 *TA* 208. Of the others, 1314–15 is Orm[2], c.1330 *Chol*, 1558–1603 *Surv*, and 1831 Bry.

(a) Ankers Croft (v. ancra); Breadley Croft; Bridge Fd; Bringley Mdw; Broad Fd; Brook Croft (cf. *Horton Broke* 1558–1603, v. brōc); Cae William ('William's field', from Welsh cae and the English pers.n. *William*); Cows Hays (v. (ge)hæg); Dods Moor Croft (from mōr[1] and croft, with the surname *Dod*); Evans Fd (from the Welsh pers.n. *Evan*); Flats; The Gates (v. gata); Horton Wd; Kiln Fd (v. cyln); Knowl Fd (v. cnoll); The Laughuns (perhaps for 'lawns' or 'loons', v. launde, land. The -gh- would be an orthographic convention for a diphthongized long vowel, as in Soughuns *infra* or the English form of the surname *Vaughan* (vɔːn, vɔːən) from Welsh *Fychan* from *bychan* 'little', cf. Dale Vaughan in Shocklach Oviatt 67 *infra*); The Lea (v. lēah); Maer Croft (v. mere[2] 'a mare'); Maidens Mdw (v. mægden); Marl Yards (v. geard); The Massey; Moiles Fd; New Bridge 1831 (at 109–448496); Old Fd (*le Aldefeld* c.1330, v. ald, feld); Pingo (v. pingot); Quillet (v. quillet(t)); Long- & Short Ridding(s) (v. ryding); Seakes; Slang (v. slang); Soughuns (perhaps 'sounds, soonds', i.e. 'the sands', from sand, -gh- indicating a diphthongized long vowel as in Laughuns *supra*, but cf. Soughan's 65 *infra*); Ten Shilling Croft (v. scilling, cf. 337 *infra*); (Horton) Town Fd (*Horton* (*Laugher*) *Towne Fylde* 1558–1603); Two Butts (v. butte); Wall Fd (v. wælla); Werny David (Welsh, either *gwerni Dafydd* 'David's marshes', or *gwern y defaid* 'sheep marsh', from gwern and defaid (pl. of dafad 'a sheep') or the pers.n. *Dafydd*, cf. Gwern y ddavid in Shocklach Oviatt 67 *infra*); Windmill Hill; Within Mdw (v. wīðigen); Withy Bridge Fd (v. wīðig, brēc).

(b) *Aldritchescroft* c.1330 ('Æðelrīc's croft', from the OE pers.n. *Æðelrīc* (Feilitzen 151), but cf. *Alrīc* (Feilitzen 150), and croft); *Benileg'broc* c.1330 ('(brook at) the glade where berries grow', from begen and lēah with brōc); *Birchissahe* c.1330 ('birchen shaw, a wood of birches', v. bircen[2], sc(e)aga); *le blokelond* c.1330 ('the bleak, or bare land or selion', v. blāc, land); *Edeshal(x)h* c.1330 ('Ēad's nook', from an OE pers.n. *Ēad*, as in Eddisbury 3 213, and halh); *le Shagh* 1315 (p) (v. sc(e)aga).

3. STRETTON (HALL, LOWER HALL, HALL FM & MILL) (109–4452)

Stretton 12 Tab, *Stretun* 1260 Orm[2] (p), *Stretton* 1282 Court *et freq, passim*, (*-iuxta Tilston*) 1287 Plea, (*-Barton*) 1289 Court, (*-Horton*) 1357 *Tourn*, (*-on the Hill*) 1514 Orm[2], (*-iuxta Crue*) 1546 (1574) *ChCert, molendinum de Stretton* 1345 Eyre, *Stretton Hall* 1724 NotCestr, *-Mill* 1831 Bry

Stratton 1492 Plea (Barnes[1] 311), cf. John de *Stratton* 1361, 1362 BPR III 411, 447

'Farm or enclosure by a Roman road', from strǣt and tūn, with hall and myln. The Roman road from which Stretton is named would be Iter II of the Antonine Itinerary, Chester (*Deva Legio xx Victrix*) – ten Roman miles – *Bouium* – twenty – *Mediolanum* – twelve – *Rutunium* – eleven – Wroxeter (*Vrioconium*). *Bouium* (*Bouio* 4 (8)

AntIt, 'place of the oxen', Lat *bovis*, gen.pl. *bovium*) was probably at Holt (Denbighshire) or Farndon 73 *infra*. Cf. Beeston DEPN & 3 302. *Mediolanum* (*Media-*, *Mediolano* 4 (8) AntIt, *Mediolano* 7 RavGeog, 'mid-plain', *v. Archæologia* XCIII (40) was somewhere near Whitchurch Sa, according to *Archæologia loc. cit.* Whitchurch is nineteen or twenty miles from Chester *via* Farndon or Holt, and ten or eleven miles from Farndon. It has to be taken that the twenty Roman miles shown by AntIt between *Bouium* and *Mediolanum* is either an error of *xx* for *x*, or a sum of the two ten-mile legs of the route Chester-*Bouium*-*Mediolanum*. Whitchurch is about twenty-four miles from *Condate* (2 195) either by King Street (1 43, Route X) and *Salinis* (*v.* 2 238), or by a direct route across Eddisbury hundred and through Tarporley (*v. Petevinnisty* 1 42–3, Route IX), and the distance of nineteen Roman miles given by Iter X of AntIt between *Condate* and *Mediolanum* is probably an error, *xviiii* written for *xxiiii*. Whitchurch is about twenty-three Roman miles from Wroxeter, the distance given by AntIt as between *Mediolanum* and *Viroconium*, and so the readings twenty Roman miles from *Bouium* and nineteen from *Condate* would give no cross-bearing, intolerable for a nodal point important in both AntIt and RavGeog, cf. 3 238. Associated with the *Mediolanum*-Chester road, not identified but perhaps in Ch, is *Sandonio* 7 RavGeog, a place either between *Mediolanum* and Chester, or on a western branch-road from *Mediolanum*, *v. Archæologia* XCIII 8–9 and 45. The *Mediolanum*-Chester road exists or has been found at 109–495463 to 457515 and 407655 to 418595. I.D. Margary, *Roman Roads in Britain* 2 31, has attempted to trace the intervening part. Ekwall (DEPN) was misled by the error of Court 76 which reads *Strecton* for the *Stretton* of *Plea* (PRO, Chester 29/3/m1), cf. *Mottershead* 1 203. *v.* Addenda.

MILL COPPICE, *v.* myln, copis, cf. Stretton Mill *supra*. MRS. LECHE'S GORSE, *v.* gorst. TOM IRON'S ROUGH, *Tom Irons Rough* 1831 Bry, *Tom Irons* 1842 OS, *Tom Highan's Wood*, *Highans* 1840 TA, cf. *Tom Higgins Wood* 1831 Bry. This odd p.n. is probably 'corners of land belonging to the town', from toun and hyrne, with rūh and wudu, cf. Heronbridge 336 *infra* and Town Fd 3 22. The spelling *Highans* for *Irons* has been misconstrued (typical of Bryant) as a form of the surname *Higgin(s)*. THE WETREINS, WETREINS FM, GORSE, GREEN & LANE, the *Wethernes* 1558–1603 *Surv*, *Wetreams Green* 1767 ChRR, *Wetreans Green* 1831 Bry, *Wetrains-*

1842 OS, 'the wet boundary-selions, *v.* wēt, rein, gorst, grēne[2], lane.

FIELD-NAMES

The undated forms are 1840 *TA* 375. The others are 1671 Sheaf, 1831 Bry.

(*a*) Booth Mdw (*v.* bōth); Brook Hill Fd (cf. *Stretton Brook* 1671, a hamlet of Stretton (Sheaf[3] 48 (9775)) presumably near Stretton Mill, *v.* Carden Brook 54 *supra*); Caldecot (cf. Caldecott 62 *infra*); Chain Fd; Earthings, Yetherings ('ploughed lands', *v.* erðing, cf. yrðing); Fold Fd (*v.* fald); Quarter Fd Mdw (*v.* quarter); Reans (*v.* rein, cf. Wetreins *supra*); Redgate Fd (cf. *Red Gate* 1831, a part of the Stretton to Malpas road (the Roman road discussed under Stretton *supra*) at 109–450521 to 452520, from rēad 'red' and gata 'a road', cf. Tilston Ford 59 *infra*); Slang (*v.* slang); Stubbs (*v.* stubb); Wheat Eddish (*v.* hwǣte, edisc); Yetherings (*v.* Earthings *supra*).

4. TILSTON (COURT, GREEN & LODGE) (109–4651)

Tilleston 1086 DB, *Ty-*, *Tilleston* 1291 Tax

Tilestan 1217–72 AddCh, *Ty-* 1260 Court (p), c.1345 *Chol*

Tilstan 1217–72 AddCh, 1257 *ib et freq* with variant spelling *Tylstan* to 1662 *Chol*, *Tilstan near Caurthyn* 1459 Plea

Tileston c.1250 Sheaf, *Ty-* 1260 Court (p)

Tilston 1287 Plea (Court 76 reads *-en*), 1290 Ipm *et freq* with variant spelling *Tylston* to 1767 ChRR, *Tilston Green* 1558–79 ChancP, 1831 Bry, *-Hall* 1724 NotCestr

Tilton 1297 CRV

Tyldeston' 1436 *Chol*, 1536 Plea, ChRR, *Ti-* 1508 ib, 1530 Orm[2], 1537 ChRR, *Tildestone* 1508 ib, *Tildyston* 1536 ib

Taleston 1550 MinAcct, *Talleston alias-* 1561 Pat

Telston 1558–1603 *Surv*

'Tilli's or Til(l)a's stone', from the OE pers.ns. *Tilli* or *Til(l)a* and stān, with grēne[2], hall, court, and loge. The place is on the line of a Roman road, cf. Tilston Lane *infra*, and the stone might have been a milestone or some similar feature.

ISLE FM (109–459517) [ˈaiəl, ˈail]

Yhevill 1290 Ipm, *Yevel* 1370 Plea, 1632 Orm[2], *Yevelie, Yeverleye, Yevell* 1561 Tab

Yehull 1335 ChRR (p), 1337 *AddCh*

Yoile 1470 *Chol*, 1491 Sheaf, 1559, 17, 1671 ib, *Yoyle* 1491 ib, 1632 ib, Orm[2], (*the-*) 1607 Sheaf, *Yoyll* 1491 ib, *Yoyell* 1527

(1592) ChRR, 1528 Plea, 1530 ib, 1632 Orm², *Yoyoll* 1528 Plea,
1632 Orm²
Yovle 1506 Sheaf
The Yeyll 1570 Sheaf, *The Yiel, -Yeil* 1693 ib
Yowley by Mallpas 1580 Sheaf, *Hall of Yowley* 1610 ib
Ylough 1610 Sheaf
Yoleiw 1610 Sheaf
Yewlowe, Hall of Yelow 1613 Sheaf
The Yeoile or Isle Farm 1662 Chol
the Hile 1676 Sheaf
Isle Farm 1662 *Chol, Isle* 1722 Sheaf
The Ilie 1746 Sheaf

'Yew-tree hill', from īw and hyll, with hall and ferme. Final hyll
in unstressed position has been confused with lēah. The identification of these forms is worked out in Sheaf³ 31 (7144–5, 7165).

LOWCROSS HILL & FM, cf. LOWCROSS MILL FM 32 *supra*

(assartum quoddam iuxta) *Crucem Louce* 1216–72 *AddCh*
Loukecros 1217–72, 1300–20 *AddCh*
Lowecros 1347 *Eyre, Lowcrosse* 1541 *Chol*, 1543 Plea, 1550 Sheaf,
1615 ChRR, *Lowe-* 1544 Plea, 1586 *Chol, Lowcross Brook* 1671
Sheaf (a hamlet), *-Farm & Smithy* 1831 Bry, *-Hill* 1842 OS
Locrosse 1470 *Chol, -(house)* 1640 Orm²
Locrusts Hall 1558–79 ChancP

A p.n. in cros 'a cross', with brōc, ferme, hyll, hall, smiððe,
myln. The first el, which has been confused with lágr 'low', appears
to be the ME pers.n. *Luke* (Lat *Lucas*), cf. Reaney 206 s.n. *Luke.*
The forms *Louce, Louke* would represent the anglicised gen.sg. of
Lucas. The smithy was at 109–467505.

TILSTON LANE (lost, 109–463510 to 472500), 1831 Bry, *le Strete*
1257 *AddCh, strata* 1307–27 ib, *alta strata que ducit de Malo Passu
versus Cestr'* e14 ib, v. strǣt, lane, cf. 1 42 (Route VIII).

THE CROFT.   FLAGS COTTAGES.   HOBB HILL, 1831 Bry, *Hobhill
Croft & House* 1662 *Chol, Hob Hill* 1840 *TA*, from hob 'a hobgoblin'
and hyll.   LITTLEHILL, 1840 *TA*, v. lȳtel, hyll.   LONG LANE
(FM).   TILSTON FORD BRIDGE (109–454519) & LITTLE TILSTON
BRIDGE (109–455517), *Stretton or Tilston Bridges* 1831 Bry, cf. *The*

Fords 1840 *TA*, *le Redeforde* 1325 *AddCh*, *the Two Fords Meadow*, *the Littleford Meadow* 1662 *Chol*, *Tilston Ford* 1671 Sheaf (a hamlet), *v*. ford, twā, lȳtel. There are several fords in the village. Tilston Ford Bridge is on the Roman road near *Red Gate* 58 *supra*. It may be the location of *le Redeford* 'red ford' or reedy ford', from rēad or hrēod, and the p.ns. may be associated.   YEW TREE FM.

FIELD-NAMES

The undated forms are 1840 *TA* 394. Of the others, c.1250 is Sheaf, c.1345, 1406, 1586, 1662 *Chol*, 1354 (19), 1625 Orm[2], 1552 *Dav*, 1558–1603 *Surv*, 1831 Bry, and the rest *AddCh*.

(*a*) Acre; Adams Croft (*Adamiscroft* 1322, 'Adam's croft', from the ME pers.n. *Adam* and croft); Ashton Fd; Barn Field Croft (cf. *Barne Croft* 1662); Brook Fd (cf. *Furthest-*, *Great- & Middle Brooke Croft* 1662, *v*. brōc); Brown Knowl (*v*. brūn[1], cnoll); Cockshut Fd (*v*. cocc-scyte); Cow Hay Lane, Cow Hey (*the Cowe Hye* 1558–1603, *v*. (ge)hæg); The Cravenage; Cribbs 1831 (*v*. crib); Cross Fd (*the Crosse Fylde Egge* 1558–1603, *le Crosse Feld* 1586, *v*. cros, feld, ecg, cf. Lowcross *supra*); Drakeneys; Elbows Croft (*v*. elbowe); Finsdale (*Fendesdale* 1325, 'Devil's hollow', *v*. fēond, dæl[1]); Five Butts (*v*. butte); Flag Fd (*v*. flagge); Hamperloon (*Le Hamfurlong* 1312, 'the home furlong', *v*. hām (cf. home), furlang); Hill Fd (cf. *Hill Croft* 1662); Hopeless Fd (*v*. 336 *infra*); Hovel Fd (*v*. hovel); Knowls (*v*. cnoll); Little Mdw (1662); Long Fd (*The Longe Fylde* 1558–1603, *v*. feld); Marl Fd (*v*. marle); Mill Fd (-*Feild* 1662, cf. Lowcross Mill Fm 59 *supra* and *vetus- & medium molendinum de Tilstan* 1216–72, *duo molendina-*, *vetus-*, *superior-* 1216–72, 1257, *le Oueremilne* 1322, *le Middilmulne* 1325, *Tylston Mill* 1354 (19), *molendinum aquaticum de Tylston* 1406, *v*. myln, ald, uferra, middel, superior); New Fd (cf. *The Newe Close* 1558–1603, *v*. nīwe, clos); Nunbrooks (*Nonbrok*, *Nunbrek* 1558–1603); Nutsen; Owlerey Fd (*v*. alor); Park (cf. *Great & Little Park Croft* 1662, *v*. park); Rich Banks; Riddings (cf. *Le Lee Ruding* 1312, *v*. lēah, ryding); Shackles Croft; Shoulder of Mutton (*v*. 337 *infra*); Sid Fd (Professor Löfvenberg observes that the first el. may reflect OE **sydde* 'mud, slough', cf. Löfvenberg 179, YW 7 255); Sullage; Tilston Wd(s) (*Tylston Woodde* 1552, *v*. wudu); Town Fd; Wheat Butts (cf. *Wheate Croft* 1662, *v*. hwǣte); The Worst I Ever Came In (*v*. 337 *infra*).

(*b*) *le Cleyes*, *Clayes* 1625 (*v*. clǣg); *le Crokedehallond*, *le Woghhallond* 1307–27 ('crooked head-land', *v*. croked, wōh, hēafod-land); *Dokebrok(e)* 1307–27, 1322 ('duck brook', *v*. dūce, brōc); *Ennyons Croft* 1552 ('Eynon's croft', from the Welsh pers.n. *Eynon* (*Enniawn*, *Ennion*) and croft); *The Fullies* 1662 (perhaps 'foul clearings' from fūl and lēah); *le Heyston* 1216–72 ('heath enclosure', *v*. hǣs, tūn); *Holchewei* c.1345 ('hollow way', *v*. holh, weg); *le Hon(g)gyngelond* 1322 ('selion on a hill', *v*. hangende, land); *Hop Croft* 1662 (*v*. hoppe); *Kilne Croft* 1662 (*v*. cyln); *le Lowe* 1216–72, 1307–27 ('the mound, the hill', *v*. hlāw); *Lysecroft* 1322 (perhaps 'lice croft', *v*.

lūs, croft); *le Olereneshaght* 1307–27 ('alder wood', *v.* alren, sceagiht. Unless this is a scribal error for *-shaghe*, the form *-shaght* must be an instance of the adj. in *-sceagiht* being used elliptically as a noun, i.e. for *le Olereneshaght-croft*, *-feld*, etc.); *le Ryland Crought* 1558–1603 (*v.* rye-land, croft); *Smalbroke* 1325, *Smale Broc* c.1345 ('narrow stream', *v.* smæl, brōc); *Wfedes Halg'* c.1250, *Huferdis-*, *Hufedes Halg'*, *Hodeshalych* 1216–72 ('Wulfheard's nook', from the OE pers.n. *Wulfheard* and halh); *le Woghhallond* (*v. Crokedehallond supra*).

iii. Grafton

Grafton was an extra-parochial liberty, a township of Tilston parish since 1841, a distinct hamlet in Tilston parish in 1724. The origin of this extra-parochial status is not clear. It may be that Grafton is the place in the manor of Tilston in dispute at DB f.264 (Tait 123) 'Of the land of this manor the bishop of Chester claims half a hide, but the county does not bear him out that it belongs to his bishopric'. If this were so, there would be some reason for the special parochial status, the place being taken as in some degree a peculiar of the diocese. But this would suppose that the constitution of the ecclesiastical parish of Tilston took cognizance of a manorial structure which existed prior to, but was specifically set aside by, the Domesday survey, and it is not known how far such a supposition can be extended.

GRAFTON (HALL) (109–4451), *Grafton* 1319 (p), 1320 ChRR *et freq, passim, -Hall* 1724 NotCestr, 'farm at a grove', *v.* grāf, tūn. The form *Grafton by Dutton* 1769 *Chol* C 753 is inexplicable.

CASTLE TOWN LANE (lost), 1831 Bry, named from Castletown 64 *infra*, which is partly included in Grafton in *Castletown Farm* 1845 *TA* 179. TILSTON FORD BRIDGE, *v.* 59 *supra*.

iv. Threapwood

An extra-parochial liberty partly in Ch and partly in Fl.

LOWER & UPPER THREAPWOOD (109–4445, 118–4444) [ˈþriːpwud] *Threpewood* 1548 Pat, *Threpwoode* 1550 *MinAcct, Threapwood* 1751 Sheaf, *Lower & Upper Threape Wood* 1842 OS, 'disputed wood', *v.* þrēap, wudu, cf. Wo 219. Threapwood is probably so named from the fact that it was in neither Ch nor Fl, yet in both. Sheaf[3] 32 (7232) and Hanmer 143–5, report that in 1773 *Threap Wood or Common*, of about three hundred acres, was reputed to be in no county, parish,

town or hamlet; no land tax or rates were payable, the sheriffs of
Cheshire and Flintshire had no jurisdiction there, nor had the Justices
of the Peace, and apparently no civil court could deal with cases
arising within the area. The name recurs at 3 89, 96, and the analogous prēap-hyrst appears in Threaphurst 1 287, 288, *Threphurstisclok*
1 66, and possibly in Threeper's Drumble 3 54.

FRONTIER HO. Threapwood was indeed a frontier town!   THE
HOLY LAND, 1831 Bry, perhaps alluding to the blissful circumstances
described under Threapwood *supra*.   MILL HO, named from an
old windmill, *Bevans Mill* 1831 ib, *v.* myln.   PARADISE BROOK,
1831 ib, *v.* 1 32.   SARN BRIDGE, 1831 ib, named from Sarn Fl, *v.*
brycg. *Sarn* is Welsh sarn 'a road, a causeway'.

v. Shocklach

The parish of Shocklach contained the townships 1. Caldecott, 2. Church
Shocklach, 3. Shocklach Oviatt.

1. CALDECOTT (GREEN & HALL) (109–4351) [ˈkɔːdi-, ˈkɔːdkət]

> *Caldecote* 1086 DB, 13 *Vern et freq* with variant spellings *-kote,
> -cot', -cott; Caldecote iuxta Shokelache* 1317 AddCh, *Caldecate*
> 1370 Plea, *Caldocode* 1385 AD, *Caldecott Green & Farm* 1831
> Bry
> *Calecot* c.1208 Dieul, 1308–29 Whall (p)
> *Caldecotes* 1344 ChGaol
> *Calkote* 1354 Chamb, *-cote* 1507 AD, *-cot* 1464 *Outl*, 1505 ChRR
> *et freq* with variant spellings *-cott(e), Call-* to 1727 Sheaf,
> *Calcote Green* 1668–71 ib
> *Caldcott* 1615 ChCert
> *Coale Coates* 1665 Sheaf

'Cold huts, cheerless shelters', from cald and cot, with grēne[2] and
hall. This is a common type of English p.n. which also occurs several
times in Denmark and Normandy. Professor Sørensen refers to K.
Hald, *Vore Stednavne* (2nd ed., 1965) 159–60 where it is thought
that the p.n. was brought to these countries from England by Danish
vikings, alluding to temporary huts and dwellings, cold because they
could not be heated, cf. the common type *Coldharbour*.

THE BEACH, 1842 OS, *le Beche* 1319 AD, *the Beach in Calcot* 1591 Sheaf, *the Batche* 1624 ib, 'the valley with a stream', v. **bece¹**, **bæce¹**, cf. Castletown 64 *infra*.

CASTLETOWN ROUGH, v. 64 *infra*.

FIELD-NAMES

The undated forms are 1839 *TA* 353. The others are AD.

(*a*) Barrow (*v.* bearu); Boat Mdw (*v.* bōt); Cru(i)n (probably Welsh crwnn 'round'); Crux; Domley Bank; Heys (*v.* (ge)hæg); Kettle Barns; March; Marl Yard (*v.* marle, geard); Pose; Slangs (*v.* slang); Tinkers Pit (*v.* tink(l)ere, pytt); Twenty Pound Mdw; Wind Moorhill.

(*b*) *Byrchenehalflond* 1321 ('half-selion growing with birches', *v.* bircen², half, land); *Braderfitlond* 14 (*v.* brād (comp. brādra), fit, land); *le Cammek* 1321 ('the bend', Welsh cameg 'arch, arc, bend, a bent thing'); *Dackalesmerebuttes* 14 (*v.* mere¹, butte. The first el. is obscure, perhaps a pers.n., but Professor Löfvenberg thinks *Dackales*- may be the gen. of an OE cpd. p.n. **Dāchalh*, from OE **dāc* 'a jackdaw' (cf. DEPN s.n. Kigbeare D) and halh 'a nook'); *Dunnesgrene* 14 ('Dunn's green', from the OE, ME pers.n. *Dun(n)*, and grēne²); *le Grenewey* 1321 ('the green way', *v.* grēne¹, weg); *Hauetbuttes* 1321 (*v.* heved-butte); *Leewyth'mes* 14 (perhaps 'withens at a clearing', from lēah and wiðegn); *Wad(e)med* 1360, *Wademedo* c.1400 ('ford meadow', *v.* (ge)wæd, mǣd).

2. CHURCH SHOCKLACH (109–4350) [ˈʃɔklatʃ]

> *Chircheshokelache* 1313 Orm², thereafter with spellings as for Shocklach *infra* and *Chirche*- (to 1518 AD), *Churche*- (from 1518 Plea), *Church*- (from 1523 ChRR), *Chirchescheschokelach* 1380 AD, *Schyrcheschokeche* 1385 ib
> *Shok(e)lache iuxta Horton* 1506 Plea, 1508 ChRR

'The township of Shocklach in which the church stands', *v.* cirice, cf. Shocklach *infra*, St Edith's Church *infra*. This township adjoins Horton 55 *supra*.

SHOCKLACH, CHURCH- & -OVIATT [ˈʃɔklatʃ, ˈouvjət]

> *Socheliche* 1086 DB, *Soke*- c.1220 Chol
> *So(c)hel'* 1208–29 (1580) Sheaf
> *Sokeleche* 1209–29 Chol, *Sockleg'* 1260 Court (p)
> *Sokelach(e)* 13 AD (p), *Sochlac'* 1281 CRV (p), *Sockelache* 1327 Misc, *Soklache* 1421 Orm²

Shokelach c.1240 AD with variant spellings *Shok(e)-*, *Sc(h)ok(e)-*, *S(c)hock-*, *Sshoke-*, *Shokke-*, *Shoc(h)-*, *-lach(e)*, *-lace*, *-lack*, *-latch*, *Shocklach* (from 1429 Orm²)

Soglache 1281 CRV (p), *Sogh-* 1324 AD, *Soghlach* 1362 (1618) ChCert

Choglache 1281 CRV (p), *Schoghelach* 1287 Court (p), *-lache* 1350 Pat (p), *Schoglache* 1309 Orm² (p), *Schog(h)-*, *Schohlache* 1309 Plea, *Shogelache* 1328 ChRR (p), *Schoȝlache* 1340 Chol, *Shogh-lache* 1356 Orm²

Shoclech 1284 Ch, *Schokleche* (lit. *-keche*) 1385 AD, *Shokleche* 1530 Chol, *Shocklech* 1579 Sheaf, *Shok-* 1663 ib

Shoclegh 1284 CRC, *Shok-* 1527 ChCert

Chokelache 1293 Court, *-lake* c.1415 Sheaf (p)

Schoklage 1319 AD, Chol, *Shok-* 1349 Pat (p) *et freq* with variant spellings *S(c)hok(e)-*, *Sho(u)gh-*, *Shock(e)-*, *Shokc-*, *-lag(e)*, *-ladge* to 1629 Orm²

Schokolach' 1331 Chol

Schekelache 1339 Chol, *Scechelach* 1̸14 AD

Sogkelage 1355 BPR

Shokylach 1389 Pat

Shoklege 1̸14 AD, *Shoke-* 1505 (1523) ChRR, *Shockledg* 1̸14 AD, *-ledge* 1587 Chol, 1746 Sheaf, *Shocke-* 1560 Chol, *Shockleg'* 1428 ib

Shocklaiche 1445 Orm²

Choklage 1528 Chol

Stokeslache 1535 Orm²

Sholache 1535 VE

Shokliche 1536 Plea, *Shockliche* 1536 Orm², *Shocklich* 1635 Sheaf, *Shocklidge* 1565, 1700 ib

Shuclage 1541 Chol

Shaklache 1550 MinAcct, 1560 Sheaf

Chakelace (lit. *-late*) 1560 Sheaf

Sehockelach 1567 ChRR

'Boggy stream haunted by an evil spirit', *v.* **scucca**, **læc(c)**, **lece**. Cf. Church Shocklach *supra*, Shocklach Oviatt 66 *infra*.

CASTLETOWN (BRIDGE & ROUGH) (109–434508), *castrum de-*, *castle of Shokelach*, etc. 1290 Ipm, 1327 Misc, 1366 Chol, 1401 Orm², 1488 MinAcct, 1499 Orm², *Shocklache Castle* 1401 Sheaf, *Castleton*

Shoglach c.1360 ib, *Castilton* (*Soghlach*) 1362 (1618) *ChCert*, *Castel-ton* 1529 *ChEx*, (*the*) *Castletowne* 1624, 1671 Sheaf, *-town* 1709 *Chol*, *Castil Shokelache* 1362 (1618) *ChCert*, cf. *Castle Field Hill* 1839 *TA*, *Castle Mound* 1842 OS, 'hamlet at a castle', from **castel(l)** and **toun**, with **brycg** and **rūh**. The site of this castle was mostly obliterated by builders in 1927 (Sheaf[3] 24 (5551)). It commanded the crossing of a small, deep valley (cf. The Beach 63 *supra*), *passagium* 1208–29 (1580) Sheaf, *passagium vocatum Tholyhate* 1290 Ipm, *passagium apud Castleton Shoglach in loco vocato le Tolyate* c.1360 Sheaf, 1362 (1618) *ChCert*, 'the toll-gate', v. **toll, geat**, cf. ModE **toll-gate** (1773, NED).

St Edith's Church, *le Church* 1344 ChRR (p), *chapel of Shokelache* 1352 BPR, *church of-* 1377–99 AD, *l'eglise de Shokelach* 1380 ib, *capella Sancte Edithe* 1535 VE, *St Tedith Chappell* 1607 Sheaf, *Church Shocklach* 1831 Bry, *Shocklach Chapel* 1842 OS, v. **cirice, chapel**. The dedication is to *Ēadgȳð*, abbess of Wilton, d. 984, daughter of King Edgar.

Grafton Gorse, cf. Grafton 61 *supra*.   Lane-End, 1842 OS, *Lane End Farms* 1831 Bry.   Lordsfields, *Lords Field* 1839 *TA*, *The Lords Fields* 1842 OS, v. **hlāford, feld**.   Lower Hall (109–421501), on the west bank of R. Dee, which has turned away from the old course which forms the county and parish boundary west of this house.   Manor Ho.   Moore Fm.   Par Green (Hall), *Par Green* 1831 Bry, *Park Green* (*Farm*) 1860 White, v. **pearr, grēne**[2].   Pinfold Fm, v. **pynd-fald**.   The Soughan's, Sough-an's Fm, *Sufferns* 1831 Bry, *Saughans* 1839 *TA*, *Soughfin* 1842 OS, perhaps 'secluded corners of land at a bog', from **sogh** and **hyrne**, whence [ˈsʌfənz], but cf. Soughuns 56 *supra*.

FIELD-NAMES

The undated forms are 1839 *TA* 353. Of the others, c.1240, 1322–3 are AD, 1342 ChRR, 1394 Orm[2], 1530 Sheaf, 1831 Bry, the rest *Chol*.

(a) Cae Kendrick (Welsh, 'Kendrick's field', from **cae** and the Welsh pers.n. *Cynwrig*, ME *Kenwrec*, ModE *Kendrick*); Clomley Park (cf. Clemley 3 47); Colts Croft; Cross Fd (1778, *the Crosse Fielde* 1544, v. **cros**. There is an ancient stone cross near St Edith's Church *supra*); The Eyces, The Eyes ('the water-meadows', v. **ēg**. One of the forms is a duplicate plural); Harrow Down; Hitchens (this may be *Hitchings*, 'a place fenced with hurdles', *v.* hicce, -ing[1], but the surname Hitchen is possible, cf. Hitchen's Fm 67 *infra*); Key Fd (*v.* cae); New Bridge 1831 (*v.* 56 *supra*); New Fd 1778 (cf. *the Newe Haye* 1561, *New Hay(e)s* 1699, 1718, and foll., *v.* nīwe, (ge)hæg); Old Fd (1637, *the Olde Felde* 1561, *v.* ald, cf. prec.); Parlour Croft (*v.* parlur); The Peggs; Puccow (*v.* pūca 'an elf'); Sherrifs Fd (*v.* scīr-(ge)rēfa); Square Croft 1778 (*Squire Croft* 1743); Tropen; Wade Mdw (*v.* (ge)wæd); Welch Mdw (*v.* Welisc); Windmill Hill; Little Wyle 1772 (1743); Long Yews.

(*b*) *Bonileg* c.1240, *Bunlee Wood* 1322–3, *Bunlegh'* 1340 ('Buna's clearing or wood', or 'reedy glade', from the OE pers.n. *Buna* or bune and lēah, with wudu); *The Orchard Croft* 1561; *Pentratha* 1394 (Orm² II 687, possibly a place in Wales, perhaps 'Adda's village', from pentref and the Welsh pers.n. *Adda*, i.e. *Adam*); *the Whayne* 1561 (perhaps a lengthened form of winn[1], wynn 'a pasture', cf. *Comberwheyn* I 211); *le Wode* 1342 (p) (*v.* wudu).

3. SHOCKLACH OVIATT (109–4348) [ˈʃɔklatʃ ˈouvjət]

> *Shoghlache Ovyet* 1309 Plea, thereafter with spellings as for Shocklach 63 *supra*, and variant forms of the suffix *Ov-, Ouyet, Oviet(e)* (1309 Plea, 1316 AD to 1570 ChRR), *Ov-, Ouyot(t)* (14, 1341 AD to 1535 Orm²), *Ovyotes* (1362 (1618) ChCert), *Owiot* (1379 *Chol*), *Oviat(t), Ov-, Ouyate, Ovyat(t), Ouiate* (from 1429 Orm²), *Oveat* (1528 ib)
>
> *Ovyot Shokelach* 1389 Pat
> *Schokelachoyt* 1392 AD
> *Shoglagehelt* 1397 Pat
> *Schokleg' Hocwate* 1428 *Chol*
> *Shoklache Gwyat(t)* 1527 (1592) ChRR, 1528 Plea
> *Shoklache Eweat* 1528 Plea
> *Shoklache Eveatt* 1528 Plea
> *Shokelache Evoyt* 1536 ChRR
> *Shochlach Ovett* 1716 Sheaf

Probably 'Ūfegēat's part of Shocklach', from the OE pers.n. *Ūfegēat* (*v.* Feilitzen 420 n.1), but possibly 'Wulfgēat's part ...', from the OE pers.n. *Wulfgēat* (*v.* Feilitzen 342, 419). Dr. von Feilitzen prefers *Ūfegēat* for this p.n. There is no indication of the particular man who gave his name to this place, but the names *Vluiet* (< *Wulfgēat*) and *Vuiet* (< *Ūfegēat*, but possibly *Wulfgēat*) appear among the TRE tenants of Ch in DB, and he may have been one of these. Cf. *Onyoteshay* 3 140, *Wolfotesrudyng* 27 *supra*, and *Adam son of Ouyt* 1288 Court 233, *William filius Ovieth-, -Ouieti Gheri* H3, 1236 *AddCh* 43899, 43903.

DOGKENNEL COVERT & FM, *Dog Kennel* 1842 OS, cf. *Dog Kennel Croft* 1839 *TA*. FISH FM, *The Fish* 1831 Bry, a public house. FLENNEN'S BROOK BRIDGE, cf. Flennen's Brook 1 24. HITCHEN'S FM, *Hichins Milkings* 1831 Bry, *Hitchen* 1842 OS. The first component is probably the surname *Hitchen*, but it could be from hiche 'a hurdle' and -ing[1], cf. *Quickhyken infra*. The final component is *milking* (NED) 'the act of milking', denoting a place where cows were milked, or where milch-cows were specially pastured, as in the frequent f.n. *Milking Bank*, v. milking. LANE-END, 1842 OS, *Lane End Farms* 1831 Bry. NEWHOUSE FM. THE PURSER, -*Farm* 1831 ib, *Pyrshalgh, Purshaw* 1625 Sheaf, *Pursall*, -*ell* 1671 ib, cf. *Great Pursa, Little Pursey, Pursa Field* 1839 *TA*, v. pyrige, sc(e)aga. THE ROUGH. SHOCKLACH GREEN & HALL, *The Hall of Shocklach* 1623 Sheaf, *Shocklach Hall* 1724 NotCestr, *Shocklach Greene* 1625 Sheaf, -*Green* 1839 *TA*, cf. *Little Green* 1831 Bry, v. grēne[2], hall. TOP HO.

FIELD-NAMES

The undated forms are 1839 *TA* 353. Of the others 13, 1293, 14, 1316 are AD, 1356 Orm[2], 1831 Bry, and the rest *Chol*.

(a) Acre Gutter (v. æcer, goter); The Butts (v. butte); Cae Coed, Car Coed (*Kay Koyd* 1637, *Kaye Coyde* 1561, *Kycoyd* 1699, 1718, *Kai Quide* 1772, Welsh, 'field or enclosure at a wood', v. cae, coed); Cae Ddu (Mawr) (Welsh, 'big black field', v. cae, du, mawr. The spelling *Ddu* is unexpected after the masc. *cae*. This document was probably written by an Englishman); Cae Ithel, -Robin, etc., (from cae and the pers.n. *Ithel, Robin*, etc.); Cobby Mdws 1831; Dale Vaughan (*le Dole Vechan* 1528, -*Vehan* 1550, -*Vaughan* 1778, *Doolevaughan* 1551, 1556, *The Doll Voughan* 1637, *Dolvaughan* 1699, 1718, Welsh, 'the little meadow', from dôl 'a meadow' and bychan (fem. bechan) 'little'); Eller Bank (v. ellern, banke); Ffynnog; Gwern y ddavid (Welsh, cf. *Dauiesacr' de Ridlegh' in Weisfordesmor* 1331 (cf. Westford Moor *infra*), *Croftdeuet* 1331, *Rydleys Feldes* 1539, *Weyryloth Dauid* 1552, 'David de Ridley's ploughland, croft, fields and marsh-land', from gwern, gweirglodd, æcer, croft, and the ME pers.n. *David* (Welsh *Dafydd*) and the surname from Ridley 3 313, cf. Werny David in Horton 56 *supra*); Gwern Wen (Welsh, 'white marsh', v. gwern, gwen); Maes Lidiat (Welsh, 'swing-gate field', v. maes, llidia(r)t, cf. hlid-geat); Mask Hill; Mill Fd & Pasture (cf. *molendinum aquaticum* 1383, v. myln); The Rushes (v. risc); Wern Hill (v. gwern, hyll); Westford Moor (*Weys-, Weisfordesmor* 1316, *Wesfordismor* 14, *Weyesfordesmor* 1318, *Weis-* 1331, *Qwern' Waysford* 1379, 'marsh at a ford on a road-way', from weg and ford, with mōr[1], gwern).

(b) le Chyrche-, -Chirche Eyes 1318 ('the church meadows', v. cirice, ēg); Caytanguistul 1396 (Welsh, 'Tangwystl's field', from the Welsh fem.

pers.n. *Tangwystl* and **cae**); *in crofto popte* 1316; *Quickhyken* 1561 (perhaps 'quick-set enclosures', *v.* **cwic**, **hiche**, -ing[1], cf. Hitchen's *supra*; but Professor Löfvenberg thinks the form is a mis-spelling of ModE *quicken* 'mountain ash' or 'couch-grass', cf. **cwicen**); *Sokelachismor* 13, *Chokelachemore* 1293, *le moor* 1331, *Shoghlachemore* 1356, cf. *Shokelage mor'* in com. de *Flynt* 1445, *Guernshoklege, Guersholege* 1362, *Gwerneshockelage* 1562 ('the marsh of Shocklach', from OE **mōr**[1], Welsh **gwern**. The location is The Wern Fl, 109–416474, 418486.)

vi. Farndon

The ecclesiastical parish of Farndon contained the townships 1. Barton, 2. Churton by Farndon, 3. Clutton, 4. Crewe, 5. Farndon (now a c.p. including part of Crewe *supra*). It seems obvious that Aldford 76 *infra* was originally the moiety of the manor of Farndon held by earl Edwin TRE and Hugh Bigot 1086, and it is supposed that the parish of Aldford represents this, whilst the other moiety, which belonged to the bishop of Chester (i.e. Coventry and Lichfield) TRE and 1086, retained the original name and remained as Farndon parish. The separation of the Aldford moiety into a distinct parish probably followed the development of Aldford, with its castle guarding a crossing of the Dee, into the capital of the extensive fee of Aldford early in the twelfth century, at which date the bisection of Churton 70, 81 *infra*, by a parish boundary on the line of the manorial boundary, would take place. Cf. Tait 183 n.176, Orm[2] II 754.

1. Barton (109–4454)

 Berton' 13 *AddCh*, 1318 Orm[2] (p), 1560 *Chol*
 Barton' 13 *AddCh*, c.1240 AD *et freq* with variant spellings -*tun* 1287 Chest (p), -*toun* c.1300 *Chol* (p), -*tton* 1308 *ib* (p), *Barton iuxta Codyngton* 1302 ChF, -*iuxta Stretton* 1514 *Chol*, -*on the Hill* 1597 Sheaf, -*vpon the Hyll* 1598 *Chol*

'Barley farm', *v.* **ber(e)tūn**, **bærtūn**. Barton stands on the end of a spur rising 50 feet above the general level (*v.* **hyll**, cf. The Hill *infra*), and adjoins Coddington 85 *infra*, Stretton 56 *supra*, and gives name to Carden Brook 54 *supra*.

Barton Lodge. Barton Plantation, cf. *Barton Gorse* 1831 Bry. Clutton Ford Bridge, *v.* 72 *infra*. Morrislake Bridge & Cottage, *Morris Lake Bridge* 1842 OS, 'bridge over a marsh watercourse', from **mareis** (cf. dial. *marish*) or *moorish* adj. (NED) 'boggy, swampy', and **lacu**, with **brycg**.

FIELD-NAMES

The undated forms are 1840 *TA* 41. Of the others 13 is *AddCh*, 1643 Orm[2] III 431, 1664 Sheaf, 1831 Bry, and the rest *Chol*.

(a) Barton Gorse 1831 (*v.* gorst); The Birches (1664, *v.* birce); Birches Mdw (*the Birch Meadow* 1697, 1741, *v.* birce); Brook Mdw (cf. *Brocforlong* 14, *Broke Feld* 1547, *the Broockefilde* l16, *Brokefyld, -fielde* 1600, *Brokefyld Meadowe* 1600, *The Brook Field* 1697, 1741, *v.* brōc, furlang, feld, mǣd, cf. Carden Brook 54 *supra*); Caldecots Croft (cf. Caldecott 62 *supra*); Close (*v.* clos); Crabtree Fd (cf. *the Crabtree Lounde* l16, *v.* crabbe, trēow, land); Crooked Croft 1741 (1697, *v.* croked); Drayton Butts (*the Dreton Buttes* 1543, *Dreytton Buttes* 1547, (*The*) *Dretton Buttes* 1577, 1578, *Drayton Buttes* 1600, 'selions at a "Drayton", or belonging to one *Drayton*', from dræg and tūn, or the surname *Drayton*, with butte); Gatley (1576, *Gatel(e)y* 1577, l16, 'goats' clearing', *v.* gāt, lēah); Gorsty Feild (*v.* gorstig); Highans, Highan's Fd (cf. Iron Fd *infra*); The Hill (*v.* hyll, cf. Barton *supra*); Hooseleys (*the Two Owsleys* 1697, 1741, 'blackbird glades', *v.* ōsle, lēah); Iron Fd, Highans, Highan's Fd (*Iron(e)filde* l16, *The Hyron Fi(e)ld(e)* 1576, 1599, 1600, *Hiron Fylde* 1600, *The Highon Field* 1664, *The Hiron* 1697, 1741, 'field at a corner', *v.* hyrne, feld, cf. Heronbridge 336 *infra*); Kiln Croft (*the Kylne Croft* 1553, *the Kyll Crofte* 1577, *the Killcrofte* 1578, l16, *the Greate-, the Lytle Kylne Crofte* 1600, *v.* cyln, croft); Knolls (*v.* cnoll); Little Fd (1697, -*Filde* l16, *Litle-, Lytlefielde, -fylde* 1600, *v.* lȳtel, feld); Long Croft (*the-* 1697); The Marsh, Marsh Mdw (*le Mersshe* 1542, cf. *the Harremarshe, the Lode Marshe, Crokettes Marshes* 1576, *the Grostie-, -Grostye Marshe, the Harrowe Marshe, the Lower Marshe* 1577, 1578, *Higher- & Lower Marsh* 1600, *v.* mersc, hēarra, (ge)lād, gorstig, lower. *Crokett* is the surname of Thomas *Crokket* 1461 *Chol*, cf. Stubbs, *Crocket(t)es Meadowe infra*); The New Close 1741 (l16, *le Newe Closse* 1543, *v.* clos); New Hays (*the Newe Hey* 1599, *v.* (ge)hæg); Pingo (*v.* pingel); Quarter Field Mdw (*le Qwarter Feld'* 1514, (*the*) *Quarterfield* (*Meadowe*) 1599, *the Warfor Filde* c.1543, *v.* quarter); Snail Pits (*Snelles Put, Snelles Puttes Furlunc* 13, *Snails Pitt* 1697, 1741, 'Snell's pit', from the OE pers.n. or ME surname *Snell* and pytt, with furlang); Stoney Foot Mdw ('meadow at stony ford', from stānig and ford, with mǣd, cf. *Stanerford* 73 *infra*); Stubbs (*le Stubbes* 1514, *the-* 1543, 1600, *Crockett Stubbes* 1577, 1578, *v.* stubb, cf. The Marsh *supra*); Swellings; Town Fd (*the Townefilde* l16, *-Fieldes* 1577); Well Fd (cf. *le Walle Buttis* e14, *le Wallebuttes* 1322, *the Well Closse* 1577, *The Well Croft* 1578, (*the*) *Wall(e)crofte* l16, *the* (*Great- & Lytle-*) *Wall Croft* 1600, 'selions, close and croft at a well', *v.* wella, wælla, butte, clos, croft).

(b) *Alde Halg'* 13 ('old nook', *v.* ald, halh); *Barton Cross* 1643 (*v.* cros); *Barton Laon* 1542, *Farne Lane alias Barton Lane* 1578 (*v.* lane, cf. Barton *supra*, Farndon 73 *infra*); *The Body Lounde, The ii Boddie Landes* l16; *Breretons Meadowe* 1599 (from mǣd and the surname *Brereton*); *Brademed(e)we* c.1300, e14, 1322 (*v.* brād, mǣd); *le Bruchus* l13, *le Breches* e14, *Bruches* 14 ('the broken-in lands', *v.* bryce, brēc); *Crocket(t)es Meadowe* 1576, l16, *Crockettes Me(a)dowe by the Brooke* 1577, 1578 (cf. The Marsh

supra, v. mǣd); *Farne Lane* (cf. *Barton Laon supra*); *Fitton's Croft, Field &*
Meadow 1664 (named from the *Fitton* family of Carden); *the Har & Loer*
Flatt c.1543, *the Harre-, the Higher- & the Lower Flatt(e)* l16 (*v.* flat);
the Greve Loounde l16 ('selion at a grove', *v.* grǣfe, land); *the Hall Filde*
c.1543 (*v.* hall, feld); *Hyllway Medowe* 1547 ('(meadow at) the road over a
hill', from hyll and weg, with mǣd); *Holenden* 14 (p) ('hollow valley',
v. hol², denu); *Honeg'weland* 14; *Hulewale-, Hullewalle Furlunc, Hulwal(l)es*
Sti 13 ('(furlong and path at) the well near a hovel', from hulu and wælla,
with furlang, stīg); *le Hullond* l13 ('selion on a hill', *v.* hyll, land); *the Kill*
Greve Lounde l16 ('selion at kiln-wood', *v.* cyln, grǣfe, land); *the Lytle*
Meadowe 1599 (*v.* lȳtel, mǣd); *apud Longe Londes Henden* 13 (*v.* lang, land,
ende¹); *the Marled Hallant* 1543, *-Hallonds, -Hallandes* 1576, l16, cf. *the*
Marled Field 1599 (*v.* marled, hēafod-land, feld); *Mere Furlunc* 13 ('furlong
near a pool', *v.* mere¹, furlang); *the Mylne Croft* 1564, *the Milne Fielde* 1599
(*v.* myln, croft, feld); *Negtmereslond* 13 ('the Nightmare's selion', *v.* niht-
mare, land, cf. *Nahtmarefurlong* 87 *infra*); *the New Acre* 1553 (*v.* nīwe,
æcer); *le Olde Crofte* 1542 (*v.* ald, croft); *the Parke* 1543, 1599 (*v.* park);
hauetland Patricii de Barton 14 ('Patric de Barton's headland', *v.* hēafod-
land); *the Pinfold* 1600 (*v.* pynd-fald); *Poulhewet* 14 ('place, near a pool,
where trees are hewn', *v.* pōl¹, hīewet); *Russhemore Lound* 1543 ('(selion at)
the rush marsh', from risc and mōr¹, with land); *the Short(e) Lo(u)nde*
1576, l16 (*v.* sc(e)ort, land); *Stretton Lane* 1600 (*v.* lane, cf. Stretton 56
supra); *Weperston'* l13 (perhaps 'Weeper's farm or enclosure', from tūn
and a ME pers. by-name *Wepere* 'the weeper, a man who weeps', cf.
weeper (c.1380) NED); *Vestemar Felde* 1543, *Westmore Fild* 1576, (*the*)
Westemorefilde l16 ('west-marsh field', from west and mōr¹, with feld);
Wlfegrene, Wlfletegrene (or *-greue*) l13 ('Wulfflǣd's green or grove', from
the OE fem. pers.n. *Wulfflǣd* and grēne² or grǣfe).

2. CHURTON BY FARNDON (109–417563), 1723 Sheaf, *Farne in*
dimidia Churton 1663 ib, the half of Churton which lies in Farndon
parish, cf. Churton by Aldford 81 *infra*. The village of Churton
infra is divided by the parish boundary, *v.* 68 *supra*

CHURTON (109–418565) [ˈtʃərtən]

> *Churton* c.1170 Chol (p), 1316 City (p), 1468 Plea *et freq*
> *Chirton* c.1190 Chol (p), e13 (17) Dieul, 1260 Court (p), 1290 Ipm
> *et freq* to 1535 VE, *-tone* 1309 ChRR
> *Chyrton* 1300–20 AddCh, 1305 ChF (p), 14 AddCh, 1414 ChRR
> *Cherton* m13 (17) Sheaf, 1300–20 AddCh, 1454 ib
> *Chorton* 1698 Sheaf

DEPN and EPN propose 'church enclosure', from cirice and tūn,
by analogy with Cheriton D, Ha, K, So, Chirton Nb, W. The form
Chyrchton c.1334 VR in DEPN refers to a place in Over parish, cf.

Church Hill 3 171. There is no record of a church at Churton. The place may have been named from some British establishment, but Farndon 73 *infra* was a manor held by the bishop of Chester (i.e. Coventry & Lichfeld) in 1086 and 1066, supporting two priests, so Churton may be named from some connection with Farndon parish church. However, Churton could be 'farm or enclosure at a hill or mound', a Welsh-English hybrid derived from OE **cyrc* a metathesised form of OE **crȳc* < PrWelsh *crūg*, *v.* cruc[1], tūn, cf. *Church Leys* 3 90.

DENTON (lost), 1319, 1329, *campus de Denton'* 1216–30, 14, 1321, *Dentonfeld* 1307–27, *-tone-* 14, all *AddCh* 50415–50509, 'farm or enclosure in a valley', from denu and tūn, with feld. This lost place is described in *AddCh* 50438–9 in which *Blakegre(ue)feld, le Wythynnes, le Stokkyfeld, Elenesgorstes* and *Yldremor, infra,* are *in diversis locis de Denton.*

BOWLING ALLEY PLANTATION. CHURTON HALL, 1724 NotCestr, *v.* hall. CRABTREE COTTAGE, *v.* crabbe, trēow. HOB LANE, 'boggart's lane', *v.* hob, lane. KNOWL LANE, *v.* cnoll. SIBBERSFIELD HALL, 1860 White, *Sivesfields Farm* 1831 Bry, *Sivvers Fields* 1842 OS, cf. *Sibboths Fields* 1663 Sheaf[3] 30 (7618), probably 'Sibota's fields', from the ME fem. pers.n. *Sibota* (from *Sibilla*), cf. Forssner 225.

FIELD-NAMES

The undated forms are 1663 Sheaf[3] 30 (6718). Of the others 1494 is Sheaf, and the rest *AddCh*. The material from 1663 Sheaf, may belong to either part of Churton or to King's Marsh or Aldford 75, 77 *infra*.

(*a*) Almer Mdw (cf. Almere in Allington, Denbighshire, NCPN 194); the Arbor Crofte (*v.* here-beorg); Fitchfield (*v.* ficche); Gorse Marshes (*v.* gorst, mersc); the Hankies Marshes (from the surname *Hankey* and mersc); Hay Lane (*v.* (ge)hæg, lane); Meare Crofte ('boundary croft', *v.* (ge)mǣre); the Wallcrofte (*v.* wælla, croft); Yardleys Crofts.

(*b*) *le Blakegrefeld, -greuefeld* 1307–27, *le Blacgreuefeld* 1325 ('(field at) the black grove', from blæc and grǣfe, with feld); *le Bothum* 14 ('the bottomland', *v.* boðm); *Cheteland* 1494 ('escheated land', *v.* cheet-land); *Elenesgorstes* 1307–27, 14 ('Elene's gorse-land', from the ME fem. pers.n. *Elene* and gorst); *le Fynken* 1326; *Frydyescroft* 1319 (*v.* Frigedæg, croft); *le Hauedlond* 14, cf. *le Muclehauedlond iuxta Stanlach* 14, *Mucylhauetlond iuxta Sanlage* 1321 ('the (big) head-land', *v.* hēafod-land, mycel); *le Lowecroft* 14 ('croft at a mound', *v.* hlāw, croft); *Madokesfeld* 14 ('Madoc's field', from the Welsh pers.n. *Madog* and feld); *le Mersh'* 14, *le Mershfeld*

1306–26, -*feeld* 1320–5 (*v.* mersc, feld); *Meregreue* 14 ('boundary wood', *v.* (ge)mǣre, grǣfe); *le Portwey* 14 ('way to a market town', *v* port-weg. This is probably the Aldford–Farndon road, part of the way from Chester to Malpas, *v.* 1 42 (Route VIII); *Quotkey Yollen* 1494 (Welsh, 'Iolyn's (hedged-)field', from coetgae 'a quickset hedge, land enclosed by a hedge, a field, a close, an enclosure, a park', and the Welsh pers.n. *Iolyn*, cf. *Gruffyd ap Yollyn* 1494, 'Griffith son of Iolyn'); *le Romstanes* 1326 ('stones at an open space', *v.* rūm, stān); *le Rughlond'* 14 (*v.* rūh, land); *le Shorte-buttes* 14 (*v.* sc(e)ort, butte); *Stanlache* c.1300–20, (*le hul de*) *Stanlach* 14, *Sanlage* 1321 ('stony bog-stream', *v.* stān, læc(c)); *le Stokkyfeld* 1307–27 ('field with tree-stumps in it', *v.* stocc, -ig³, feld); *le Sychefeld* 14 ('field at a watercourse', *v.* sīc, feld); *le Wallelond* 14 ('selion at a well', *v.* wælla, land); *le Wytefeld* 1300–20, -*white*- 1326, -*Whyte*- 1337 (*v.* hwīt, feld); *le Wythynnes, Chirton' Wythynnes* 1307–27, *le Wythynes* 1325 (*v.* wiðegn); *Yldremor* 1307–27, *Yildremore, Yildermor* 1307–27, 14 ('elder-tree marsh', from mōr¹, and ME hilder (c.1325 NED)).

3. CLUTTON (HILL) (109–464544)

   Clutone 1086 DB, *Clutton* 1275 Ipm *et freq*, (-*in hundred de Broxon*) 1485 ChRR, (-*iuxta Codynton*) 1534 Plea, (*Higher*) *Clutton* 1819 Orm², *Clutton Hill* 1840 *TA*
   Clotton m13 Orm², 1465 ChRR (p)
   Clucton 1337 Plea

'Farm at a hill', from clūd and tūn, with hyll, higher. It adjoins Coddington 85 *infra*.

BROXTON BRIDGE, *v.* brycg, cf. Broxton 12 *supra*. CLUTTON FORD BRIDGE, *v.* ford, brycg, cf. 55 *supra*. HOLY WELL (109–473552), 1831 Bry, *Halliwell, Hallywell in Chowley* 1668–71 Sheaf, cf. Holywell Brook 1 29 & Holywell Fm 15 *supra*, 'holy well', *v.* hālig, wella. LOWER FM. PARKERS HILL, *v.* hyll. SHAW-GREEN PIT (FM), *Shawe* 1429 Orm², *Shaw Green in Higher Clutton* 1819 ib, *Shaw Green Pit* 1842 OS, *Shay*- 1831 Bry, 'pit at wood-green', from sc(e)aga and grēne², with pytt.

FIELD-NAMES

The undated forms are 1840 *TA* 125. Of the others c.1320, 1322 are *AddCh*, 1331 ChRR, 1338 Orm², 1533 *Chol*.

(*a*) Bald Reading (*v.* balled(e), ryding); Bents (*v.* beonet); The Bottoms (*v.* botm); Cat Tail Fd (*v.* catt, tægl); Clay Fd (*le Clayfelde* 1533, *v.* clæg, feld); Cliff Fd (*v.* clif); Cock Bank (*v.* cocc², banke); Fox Glove; Hazel

Groves (cf. *Heselyngreue* 1322, 'hazel wood', *v.* hæslen, grǣfe); Holmes Hall; The Moor (*v.* mōr¹); Night Walk (*Knyght Wall* 1533, 'boys' well', *v.* cniht, wælla); Nook (*v.* nōk); Ox Moor (*v.* mōr¹); Pentry Fd (*v.* pentref); Pingo (*v.* pingel); (Long) Slang (*v.* slang); Soils; The Span (*v.* spann¹); Sudmore (probably 'south marsh', *v.* sūð, mōr¹); Town Fd; Wargloss (perhaps Welsh gweirglodd 'a meadow'); Way Fd (*v.* weg); Well Fd; Willmore Hill (*v.* hyll. *Willmore* may be 'marsh at a spring' or 'wild marsh', from wella or wilde, with mōr¹).

(*b*) *Baggeplok* c.1320 ('badger's plot', or 'bag-shaped plot', *v.* bagga, plocc); *le Cruymbes* 1338 (p) (*v.* cryme, cf. *le Crymbe* 2 171); *le Halle* 1331 (p) (*v.* hall); *Stanerford* c.1320 ('ford at a stony place', *v.* stǣner, ford, cf. Stoney Foot 69 *supra*).

4. CREWE (HALL), CREWE HILL (a residence) (109–4252) [kruː]
   Creuhalle 1086 DB
   Cryu 1096–1101 (1280), 1150 Chest
   Cruwe 1188–91 Chest, e13 ib, 1333 AD, (-*by Farundun*) c.1340 ib
   Crue 13 Dieul, 1257 (17) Chest (p), c.1294 *ChFor et freq* to 1609
       Chol, (-*iuxta Farndon*) 1505 ChRR, 1507 AD, (-*Malpas*) 1517
       ChRR, 1527 *ChCert*
   Cruue c.1294 *ChFor*, *Crwe* c.1310 Chest, 1350 Plea, 1433 ChRR,
       (-*by Farondon*) 1412 AD
   Eure 1318 Pat (p), 1386 ib, ChRR, Orm²
   Creu 1324 ChRR, 1474 ib (p), *Crewe* 1326 ib (p) *et freq* with
       variant spelling *Crew*; (-*by Farnedon*) 1429 AD, (-*Caldecote*)
       1451 ib
   Crwue 1471 ChRR (p)

'Hall at a weir or fish-trap', *v.* cryw, hall. Crewe Hall is *Manor House* 1831 Bry, *Crew* 1842 OS, and Crewe Hill, so named 1831 Bry, is *Crew Hall* 1842 OS (*v.* hall, hyll). The hamlet of Crewe (109–423532) was *Crewe Nook* 1831 Bry, -*Hook* 1842 OS, lying in the north-east corner of the township, *v.* nōk, hōc. *Crewe Barn* 1831 Bry was at 109–423526, *v.* bere-ærn. Cf. Crewe, Crewood 3 9, 195. The fish-trap or weir would be in R. Dee.

CREWE GORSE, *v.* gorst.

5. FARNDON (109–4154) [ˈfaːrndən]
   (*æt*) *Fearndune* 924 (11) ASC (C), -*dun* c.1118 FW (s.a. 924),
       c.1130 SD (s.a. 924)

(*æt*) *Farndune* 924 (11) ASC (D), *Farndun* 1333 AD, *Farndon* 1245
   Pat (p) *et freq* with variant spellings *Farne-* (1369 AD to 1619
   Cre), *-doun* (1321 *AddCh*), *-den* (1644 Sheaf)
Ferentone 1086 DB
Ferendon 1152 MRA, *Ferend'* 13 *AddCh*
Farendun 1194–8 Chest, *Pharendon* e13 *Bun* (p), *Farrendon'* 1216–
   30 *AddCh*, *Farendon* 1245 Cl (p) *et freq* with variant spellings
   -in-, *-un-*, *-on-*, *-dun* to 1529 ChRR, *Farrunden* 1560 Sheaf
Fardon 1277 Misc, 1360 AD, 1507 ib, *Fardoun* 1352 BPR
Farnton 1321 *AddCh*, 1524 Plea, 1656 Orm[2], *Farneton* 1553 Pat,
   (*Farnedon alias-*) 1579 Orm[2]
Faryngdon 1385 ChRR (p)
Faryngton 1391 (p), 1398 ChRR (p), 1507 AD (p), 1508 Pat,
   Farynton 1404 ChRR (p)
Ferneton 1546 Dugd, *Fernton* 1577 Sheaf
Farne 1575 Sheaf, 1600 Cre, 1663, 1671, 1680 Sheaf, *Farn* 1643
   Orm[2], 1698 *Assem*

'Fern hill', *v.* fearn, dūn. Stenton (*Anglo-Saxon England*, (second
edn.) 334–5, and *The Athenæum* 7th October 1905) identifies Farndon
with the *F(e)arndun* at which Edward the Elder died in 924. He
cites William of Malmesbury (who was following reliable authority,
cf. ASE 335 n.1, 315 n.1) for the fact that the last campaign of Edward the Elder (Alfred's son) was mounted against an alliance of
Mercians and Welshmen. On this campaign, he quelled a revolt of
the men of Chester, re-garrisoned the town, and died a few days
later. In ASC (C) and (D) the place of his death is given as 'at
F(e)arndune in Mercia'. In FW and SD the place is described as a
royal town. In DB, Farndon was two manors, one held by the bishop
of Chester, the other by the earl of Chester, *v.* 68 *supra*, Aldford
76 *infra*, which suggests that an Anglo-Saxon royal manor had been
divided under the Norman earldom. Ekwall (DEPN) follows Earle
& Plummer (*Two of the Saxon Chronicles* II 381) and identifies the
place with Faringdon Brk. The origin of this tradition appears to be
Higden VI, v, 'Rex Edwardus obiit apud *Farnedoun* (*Farundun*,
Fernedon, *Farndoun*, cf. *Faryngdoun* Trev, *Farndon* Higd Anon) xii
milliaribus ab Oxonia ad occidentem distantem'. Higden was a monk
of Chester, and if any tradition of Edward's dying at Farndon had
been known in his day, he might have been expected to report it.
It has to be supposed that the fact was forgotten by his day, and that

he identified *F(e)arndun* as best he might. Certainly, Stenton's identification removes the need to consider how the king reached a death-bed in Berkshire a few days after quelling a revolt in Chester. Since Farndon originally included Aldford, the king might, in fact, have died at Aldford.

DENAMERE (109–399558), cf. *Denemey* 14 *AddCh*, 1320, m14 *ib*, a tract of water-meadow beside R. Dee. The final el. may be ēg 'an island, a water-meadow'.

FARNDON OR HOLT BRIDGE, *Holt Bridge* c.1536 Leland, *Farndon Bridge* 1831 Bry, v. brycg, cf. Holt in Denbighshire, NCPN 203. SIBBERSFIELD COTTAGES & LANE, v. 71 *supra*. TOWNFIELD LANE, *the Town-Field* 1750 Sheaf, v. toun, feld. TWITCH HOOKS LANE (local), 1909 Sheaf[3] 7 (1403), *The Twitch Hooks* 1881, 1884 ib, named from a windlass fixed at the top of a steep lane to help wagons up from the R. Dee, presumably fitted with ropes carrying hooks for 'twitching', i.e. tugging, vehicles.

FIELD-NAMES

Of the forms c.1294 is *ChFor*, 1305, 1575, 1644, 1658 Sheaf, 1307–27, 14, m14 *AddCh*, 1333, 1397 AD, 1535 VE, 1631 Orm².

(b) *Alsies Smethe* 1333, *Alsyessmethes* 14 ('Alsige's smithy', from the pers.n. *Alsige* (< OE *Ælfsige*, *Æðelsige*, v. Feilitzen 151) and smiðõe); *þe Commonwood* 1658 (v. commun, wudu); *la graunge* 1397 (v. grange); *Farndon Hay* 1631 (v. (ge)hæg); *bruera* 1305 (v. hǣð); *þe Hill* 1658 (v. hyll); *the Loar House* 1644 (v. lower, hūs); *the Park* 1575 (v. park); *Routlothefeld* 1333 ('(field at) the red hollow', from rauðr and laut, with feld); *Ruddeneymor* 1307–27, *Ruddereyes-* 14, *Ruddeney* 14, m14, *Roddeney* 1333 ('(marsh at) Rudda's water-meadow', from the OE pers.n. *Rudda* and ēg, with mōr¹); *capella Sancte Helene* 1535 ('St Helen's chapel'); *Shortemoresmedue* 14 ('(meadow at) the short marsh', from sc(e)ort and mōr¹, with mǣd); *Teynerudyng'* 14 (perhaps 'tithed clearing', from tēonde and ryding); *Wythylegh* 1307–27 ('willow glade', v. wïðig, lēah).

vii. King's Marsh

KING'S MARSH, KINGSLEE, MARSH HOUSE & LANE (109–4354)

Vruemers 1208–29 Dieul

Ouermershe c.1294 *ChFor et freq* with variant spellings *Oure-*,

Over(e)-, Houre-, -merhs(e), -mersh(e), -merssh(e), -mersch to 1599
ChRR, *-marssh* 1359 Chamb, *-marsh* 1386 ChRR, *-marshe* 1418
ib, *Over Marshe alias Kings Leyes alias Langs Marshe* 1632 Orm[2]
Overmermersch 1348 Chamb
Overmestrch 1351 Chamb
Orvermersshe 1430 ChRR
Kings Leyes 1632 Orm[2], *King's Lee* 1882 ib
King's Marsh 1727 Sheaf, *Kings Marsh Farm & Road* 1831 Bry
Marsh House 1842 OS

'Marsh on a hill', *v.* ofer[2], mersc. The later names, 'king's marsh'
and 'clearing(s) or meadow-land' from cyning, mersc and læs or
lēah, arise from the fact that King's Marsh was an extra-parochial
liberty of the earldom of Chester, hence of the Crown, where
visitors to the county seeking the earl's protection or coming to his
aid in time of war, might pitch tents or booths for a year and a day,
v. Orm[2] II 753.

EDGERLEY LANE, cf. Edgerley 81 *infra*.   LODGE FM.   ROW-
LEYHILL, *Rowley Hill* 1831 Bry, *Ruley Hill* 1842 OS, '(hill at) the
rough clearing', from rūh and lēah with hyll.   THE ROYALTY, *v.*
roialte.   THE STARLING'S WOOD.

FIELD-NAMES

The undated forms are 1847 *TA* 223. See also 71 *supra*.

(*a*) Barton Marsh (cf. Barton 68 *supra*); Bindsberry; Breeze Marsh
('gadfly marsh', *v.* brēosa, mersc); Chaw Cut Fd; Crewe Fd (cf. Crewe 73
supra); Big & Little Damage Fd (*the two Deminges* 1663 Sheaf (lit. *Demi'ges*),
v. demming 'a dam'); Edgerley Marsh (cf. Edgerley 81 *infra*); Filkins
Hey; Lady's Hey(s) (*v.* hlǣfdige, (ge)hæg); Marl Fd (cf. *the Marld Flatt*
1663, *v.* marled, flat); The Picklings; Rake Hey ('enclosure near a path',
v. rake, (ge)hæg); Sinsberry; Taw Marsh; Ten Pound Marsh; White Fd;
Withe Marsh (*v.* wiððe, mersc).

viii. Aldford

The ecclesiastical parish of Aldford contained 1. Aldford, 2. Buerton (now
a c.p. containing part of Bruera 122 *infra*, cf. Saighton), 3. Churton by
Aldford, 4. Edgerley. This parish represents a division of the original manor
of Farndon, *v.* 68, 74 *supra*.

1. ALDFORD (109–4159) [ˈɔːldfəd, ˈɔːdfəd]

Ferentone 1086 DB f.266b
Aldefordia 1153 Dugd, c.1170 Dieul, *-ford* 1154–60 (1330) Ch,
  Ald(e)ford c.1200 Dieul, Whall, 13 Chest *et freq* with variant
  spellings *Alde-* (to 1561 ChRR), *-forde, -forda, -forthe; le
  Aldeford* 1430 Sheaf, *Aldford alias Odford* 1724 NotCestr
vetus vadum c.1195 Luciani
Audeford 1208–15 (1499) ChQW, 1254 Pat, 1260 Court (p), 1499
  ChQW, *Audford* 1620 Sheaf, 1656 Orm²
Aldreford 1290 Cl, *Alderford* 1290 Ipm, *-forde* 1498 ChRR
Elleford 1314 ChRR, *Elford* 1351 BPR *et freq* with variant spellings
  E(l)le-, -ford(e) to 1515 *Chol*, ChRR
Adleford 1400 ChRR
Aldford 1493 (1558) ChRR, 1521 Orm², 1558 ChRR and five times
  with variant spelling *-fforde* to 1586 ib
Hadford 1535 VE
Odford 1663, 1672, 1698, 1719 Sheaf, 1694 Mere, (*Aldford alias-*)
  1724 NotCestr
Oldford 1666 Sheaf

'The old ford', *v.* ald, ford, cf. Farndon 68, 73 *supra*. The
Chester–Malpas Roman road (1 42 (Route VIII)) crossed R. Dee at
Ettoneford near Iron Bridge *infra*, and the site of Aldford castle,
commanding this line of road and the Iron Bridge crossing (cf. Blobb
Hill, Hales Fd *infra*), suggests that it would be this old ford which
gave name to the village. The adj. *old*, i.e. 'former', would be
applied when the Roman ford was superseded by the ford at Aldford
Bridge *infra*. This had taken place by Lucian's time (c.1195), when
the usual route from Chester to Aldford seems to have been that
through Boughton and Huntington rather than the Roman road
through Eaton. The spellings suggest that there was a form containing ME *alder*, comparative of *ald*, i.e. 'the older ford', in which
alder was confused with *alor* (*alre-*) and *ellern*.

ALDFORD BRIDGE (109–422594), 1539 Sheaf, *pons de Audeford* 1250
JRC, -Aldeford 1304 *ib, Audford Bridge* 1620 Sheaf, *v.* brycg, cf.
Aldford *supra*.

BLOBB HILL (109–418595), 1842 OS, the site of the remains of a
castle, *castrum de Aldeford* 1276 Cl, 1290, 1311 Ipm, *-Alderford* 1290

ib, -*Aldre*- 1290 Cl. Blobb Hill is the mound of the motte. The bailey
was known as *the Hall Croft* 1819 Orm², cf. *Hall Yard* 1837 *TA*,
from a lost mansion built here (Orm² II 757–8), *v.* castel(l), hall, croft,
geard, hyll. *Blobb*- is ModEdial. *blob* (EDD, NED) 'a bubble, a
rounded lump or blister', from the rounded shape of the castle
mound. Cf Aldford *supra*.

ALDFORD BROOK (R. Dee), *le Aldefordbroke* 1465 *JRC*, *Aldford
Broke* 1520–21 Orm², *Aldford Brook, Lea Brook* 1831 Bry, *v.* brōc,
cf. Lea Newbold 119 *infra*.   ALDFORD HALL, *Aldford Hall,
Monkbeggars Hall* 1668–71 Sheaf, *Mockbeggars*- 1784 ib, *Aldford
Hall, Mockbeggar Hall* 1819 Orm², *Aldford Hall* 1724 NotCestr,
1831 Bry, 'the hall', 'the uncharitable house', from hall and mock-
beggar.   FORD LANE (FM), cf. *Ford Croft, Field & Meadow* 1837
TA, named from a ford at 109–425581.   GLEBE COTTAGES & FM,
v. glebe.   GRANGE FOX COVERT, cf. *Grange Croft & Field* 1837 *ib*,
named from Churton Grange 81 *infra*.   IRON BRIDGE (109–
417600), an iron structure carrying a drive across R. Dee, into the
park of Eaton Hall 148 *infra* on the line of the Roman road from
Chester to Aldford, at the site of *Ettoneforde* 1305 *AddCh*, 'the ford
leading to Eaton', *v.* ford, cf. Aldford, Blobb Hill *supra*.   LEA
FM & MILL, *Lea or New House Farm* 1831 Bry, *New House, Lea
Mill* 1842 OS, cf. *Lea Rake* 1837 *TA*, *v.* myln, rake, cf. Lea Newbold
119 *infra*.   LONG LANE, 1842 OS.   PLOWLEY BROOK (Aldford
Brook *supra*), 1842 OS, probably named from *Plowelowe infra*, *v.*
brōc.   SOURBUTTS COVERT, *Sour Butts Fox Cover* 1831 Bry,
named from *Sour Butts* 81 *infra*.   TOWNFIELD LANDS, cf. *Town
Field* (*Croft*) & -*Meadow* 1837 *TA*, *v.* toun, feld.   WOODHOUSE
FM, adjacent to Blobb Hill *supra*, not near a wood, probably 'house
of wood', *v.* wudu, hūs.

FIELD-NAMES

The undated forms are 1837 *TA* 8. Of the others 1208–29, 1226–8 are
Dieul, 1305 *AddCh*, 1316 Chamb, 1831 Bry, 1842 OS, and the rest Sheaf.

(*a*) Ash Loons (*v.* æsc, land); Big Groves (*v.* grāf); Churton Fd (cf.
Churton 81 *infra*); Clatterbridge Lodge 1831 (at 109–425594, perhaps
'lodge at a noisy bridge', from clæter and brycg, with loge, but this was near
Caterbatch 120 *infra*, with which the name may be connected); The Cockle
Butts (*v.* coccel, butte); Crowton Cottage 1831 (at 109–423595, *v.* crāwe,

tūn); The Dales, Top- & Bottom Dales (v. dæl²); Day Croft (v. dey); Dean (cf. *Holedene* 1208–29, v. hol², denu); Dee Bank (v. banke, cf. R. Dee 1 21); Goose & Gander (v. 336 *infra*); Hales Fd (cf. (*causceya de*) *Hale, le Haledych'* 1305, 'the causeway and ditch at the tongue of land', from halh (dat.sg. hale), with caucie and dīc, alluding to the course of the Roman road across the tongue of land between R. Dee and Aldford Brook at 109–418598, cf. Iron Bridge, Aldford, *supra*); Hoo Rins (v. hōh, rein); Margery Lane Crofts (cf. *Margerys* 1831, at 109–415575, from the fem. pers.n. *Margery*); Mill Fd (cf. *Mill Lane* 1842 at 109–413587 to 416587, and *Windmill House* 1831 at 109–416587, v. myln); Moor Fd (v. mōr¹); Far- & Near New Hays (*the Lower & the Upper New Hayes* 1663, v. (ge)hæg); Quillet (v. quillet(t)); The Radley, Radley Croft & Mdw (*Ridel'* 1316, *Radley Field* 1629, *Radley Meadows* 1831, *Radley* 1842, either 'red glade', or 'cleared wood', from rēad or (ge)ryd(d) and lēah); Rotten Dale (v. roten, dæl²); Round Mdws (*the Round Meadow* 1648, v. rond); Rushmore Style ('(stile leading to) the rush marsh', from risc and mōr¹, with stigel); Weir Moor Mdw (v. wer, mōr¹); Whitefield (v. hwīt, feld). See also 71 *supra*.

(b) *Aldeforde pavement* 1494 (v. pavement); *the Brewers Lownd* 1629 (v. brewere, land); *le Bruchis* 1305 ('the breakings-in of land', v. bryce); *vetus strata de Etton* 1305 (v. 1 42 (Route VIII), cf. *Ettonforde* under Iron Bridge *supra*); *Plowelowe* 1305 ('mound at a ploughland', from plōg 'a plough', in its ME sense 'a plough-land, enough land for a plough' (cf. NED *plough* 3, a), with hlāw, cf. Plowley Brook *supra*); *Wetehull* 1208–29, *-hul* c.1226–8 ('wet hill', v. wēt, hyll. This is placed by Dieul, 105, 106, in *Aldithele* (Audley St), an error for *Aldredele* (Alderley 1 94, cf. Monk's Heath 1 96) but it could well be in Aldford).

2. BUERTON (109–4260) ['bjuːˑətən, 'bjuːˑərtən, 'buːˑətən, 'buːˑərtən]

> Burton c.1220–30 *JRC*, and six examples *ib*, Dieul, Court, with variant spelling *-tona* to 1300–7 *JRC*, (*Buerton alias-*) 1645 Orm²
>
> Borton 1229–32 Dieul
> Berton 1229–32 Dieul
> Beurton (*iuxta Aldeford*) 1287 Court
> Buerton 1286 Court, 1511 Plea *et freq*, (*-iuxta Audford*) 1614 Orm², (*-alias Burton*) 1645 ib, (*-or Burton*) 1778 Sheaf
> Buyrton' 1300–7 *JRC*, 1307 Ch *et freq* to 1536 ChRR, (*-iuxta Salghton*) 1331–3 (16) *JRC*, (*-near Golburn*) 1320 Plea, (*-iuxta Aldeford*) 1353 *Eyre*, 1366 Plea, Buirton 1668–71 Sheaf
> Bwrton 1304 *JRC*
> Byriton 1319 *Chol* (p)
> Bwerton 1592 *JRC*
> Bewerton 1724 NotCestr

'Enclosure belonging to a fortification', v. **byrh-tūn, burh-tūn.**
The township adjoins Aldford 77 *supra* and Saighton 121 *infra*, and
is separated from Golborne David 88 *infra* by Churton Heath 115
infra. The *burh* cannot be identified. The manor-house of Buerton,
mentioned 1429–30 Orm[2] II 761, stood in a moated site at 109–437607.

BOAT LANE (lost, 109–422605 to 436604), 1842 OS, cf. *Boat Meadow
& Moor* 1837 *TA, Le Buyrton More, Dee More* 1430 Sheaf, 'marsh
by the R. Dee', 'meadow and marsh near a ferry', 'lane to a ferry',
v. **bāt, lane, mǣd, mōr**[1]. The name is taken from *Eaton Boat* 150
infra. Also named from the ferry was the lost *Bothill* 1545 Sheaf,
'hill near the boat', v. **hyll,** a place on the Chester-Aldford road.
BUERTON APPROACH, a drive leading to Eaton Hall 148 *infra*, created
by the diversion and closure of Boat Lane *supra*. It is observed by
Orm[2] II 761 that the whole township was imparked and contained
nothing but cottages and plantations and an approach to Eaton.
Similar examples of 'improvement' by Grosvenor of Eaton are to be
observed in Eaton Park 148 *infra*.   CHAPEL LANE, cf. 122 *infra*.
COMMON WOOD, *Aldford Common* 1842 OS, v. **commun,** cf. Aldford
77 *supra*.   CROOK OF DEE COTTAGES, cf. Crook of Dee 118
infra.   HORSE PASTURE, a wood, v. **hors, pasture.**   PENLING-
TON'S WOOD.   SOOTY FIELDS PLANTATION, v. **soti.**

FIELD-NAMES

The undated forms are 1837 *TA* 8. Of the others 1287 is Court, 1300–7,
1304 *JRC*, 1410 *Chol*, 1519 Plea, and the rest Sheaf.

(a) Barton Mdw (v. **bere-tūn**); Big Wd; Binfoot Looms (**loom** 'a broad
selion'); Calves Crofts (*the Calves Crofte* 1663, v. **calf, croft**); Club's Fd
(*Clubs Crofte* 1663); The Grammers Fd ('grandmother's field', supposed
part of the dower-land assigned in 1430 to Joan widow of Sir Thomas
Grosvenor, v. Sheaf[3] 27 (6011)); The Gunmoores 1706 (v. **mōr**[1]); Hassels
Yard (v. **hæsel, geard**); Heath Fd (cf. *brwera de Bwrton* 1304, v. **bruiere,
hǣð**); The Leys (ModE *ley* 'a pasture', cf. **lēah**); Long & Square Pool Fd
(v. **pōl**[1]); Pear Tree Hay; Pike Fd; Rough Fd.

(b) *Adaminsmede* 1287 (probably 'Adamin's meadow', from **mǣd** with a
ME pers.n. *Adamin*, a pet-form or diminutive of *Adam*); *le Bradelake* 1304
('the broad watercourse', v. **brād, lacu**); *le Chirchegrewe* 1304 ('wood at or
belonging to a church', v. **cirice, grǣfe,** probably named from Bruera
chapel 122 *infra*); *le Gorsty Hey* 1430 (v. **gorstig, (ge)hæg**); *le Heye* 1304
(v. **(ge)hæg**); *le Heystowe* 1304 (the first el. may be **(ge)hæg,** but cf. *le
Haystoue* 3 235 ('place with a hedge', v. **hege-stōw**), *le Heystow* 87 *infra*,

v. stōw); *Hontynton Lane* 1593 (cf. 116 *infra*); *le Mere* 1410 (p), *Meyrhowse* 1519, *the Meyre Tenement* 1706 (*v.* mere[1]); *Le Milnefeld* 1430 (*v.* myln, feld); *Le Sevenbuttes* 1430 ('seven selions', *v.* seofon, butte).

3. CHURTON BY ALDFORD (109–420570), cf. *Aldford cum dimidia Churton* 1663 Sheaf, *v.* Churton by Farndon 70 *supra*.

GRANGE FM (109–420573), *Churton Grange* 1831 Bry, 1842 OS, *grangum ipsorum monachorum* 1208–29 Dieul, *grangia* 1251–5 ib, *v.* grange; it belonged to Dieulacres abbey.

CHURCH HOUSE FM. CHURTON LODGE. EDGERLEY LANE, cf. Edgerley *infra*. FORD LANE, *v.* 78 *supra*. HOB LANE, *v.* 71 *supra*. KNOWL LANE, *Knoll-* 1842 OS, *v.* cnoll. LOWER LANE, 1842 ib. SOUR BUTTS (lost, 109–413573), *Sour Butts Farm* 1831 Bry, cf. Sourbutts Covert 78 *supra*, 'sour selions', *v.* sūr, butte. STANNAGE FM, adjoining a sandstone quarry 1842 OS, cf. *Stonage Crofte* 1663 Sheaf, *Stonage Field* 1837 *TA*, *v.* stonage (1618, NED) 'stones collectively', here 'a quarry'.

FIELD-NAMES

The undated forms are 1837 *TA* 8. Of the others 1208–29 is Dieul, 1209–28 (17) Orm[2], 1663 Sheaf. See also 71 *supra*.

(*a*) Banks Moore (*v.* banke, mōr[1]); Barn Fd (cf. *Barne Crofte* 1663); Coppity Gap; Cross Fd (*v.* cros); The Dale (*v.* dæl[1]); The Dean (*v.* denu); Dry Marl Pit Fd (*v.* drȳge, marle-pytt); Goose and Gander (*v.* 336 *infra*); The Howleys; Jack Fd (*v.* jack); Mucklestons Marsh & Mdw (at 109–424568), Mugstone Croft & Mdw ('big stones', *v.* mycel, stān); Palace (*v.* palis); Shaw (*v.* sc(e)aga); Slang (*v.* slang); Tussock Mdw (*the Shorne Tussocke Meadowe* 1663, *v.* tussock); White Marsh (*v.* hwīt, mersc).

(*b*) Heyfurlong 1208–29, -e 1209-28 ('high furlong', *v.* hēah, furlang).

4. EDGERLEY (FM) (109–435570) [ˈedʒərli]

> *Odgerley* 1275 Ipm, *Oggerley'* 1305 AddCh 49886 (Sheaf[3] 37 (8060) reads *Egg-*), *-ley* 1421 ChRR, 1424 Plea, *Ogerley* 1317 ChRR (p)
> *Egerisleg'* 1300–7 JRC (p)
> *Eggerlegh'* 1378 Eyre, 1398 ChRR, *-ley* 1425 Orm[2], 1453 Plea *et freq* with variant spelling *-leght* to 1611 ChRR
> *Edgerley* 1724 NotCestr, 1831 Bry

'Ecghere's wood or clearing', from the OE pers.n. *Ecghere* and lēah, cf. Egerton 33 *supra*. As with the analogous pair Cholmon-

6

deley 21 *supra*, Cholmondeston 3 136, the same person may be involved. The *O*- forms are presumably scribal errors.

FIELD-NAMES

The undated forms are 1837 *TA* 8.

(*a*) Dig Fd (*v.* dīc); Kittles (*v.* keddle-dock); White Fd.

ix. Coddington

Coddington parish contained the townships 1. Aldersey, 2. Chowley, 3. Coddington.

1. ALDERSEY (109–4656) [ˈɔːldərsi]

   Aldrishey 1180–1220 *Chol* (p), *Aldres Heye* 13 *AddCh*, *Aldresheye* 1340, 1344 *Eyre*, *Audrishe* 1272–1307 *StoweCh* (p), *Alderisheye* 1289 *Court*, *Haudershey* 14 *Chol* (p), *Aldreshay* 1366 *Plea*

   Aldrisey 1284 *Ipm*, *Aldresey* 1285 ib *et freq* to 1663 *ChRR*, *Aldersey* 1289 *Plea et freq* with variant spellings *Aldres-*, *Ald(e)ris-*, *Aldirs-*, *Alderes-*, *Aldures-*, *-ay* (1307 *Plea* to 1619 *ChRR*), *-ey(e)*, *-eya*, *-eie*, *-ye*

   Aldrussey l13 *Chol* (p), *Aldressey* 1329 *ib*

   Alderzey, *Aderzey* c.1300 *Chol*, *Aldrezeye* 1304 *Chamb* (p)

   Ald(e)resley 1435 *Chol*, *Aldres-* 1455 (p), 1474 *ChRR* (p), *Alders-* 1457 (p), 1476 ib (p), 1516 *Plea*, *Alderse-* 1476 *ChRR* (p)

   Eddersay 1467 *Cre* (p)

   Aldersen 1472 *ChRR*

   'Ealdhere's fenced-in enclosure', from the OE pers.n. *Ealdhere* and (ge)hæg. The final el. has been confused with lēah.

ALDERSEY GREEN (109–462567), 1842 *OS*, *Great Aldersey or Aldersey Green* 1860 *White*, *Magna Alderisheye* 1289 *Court*, and thereafter with spellings as for Aldersey *supra*, and *Magna-* to 1592 *ChRR*, *Grete-* 1498 *Sheaf*, *Gret-* 1542 *Plea*, *Great-* 1570 *Cre*, 1724 *NotCestr*, *Mikel-* 1503 *ChRR*, *Micle-* 1519 *Chol*, *Mikle-* 1539 *Plea*, 1564 *ChRR*, *Mykle-* 1546 *Orm*[2], *v.* magna, grēat, micel, grēne[2].

ALDERSEY HALL (109–459561), 1724 *NotCestr*, *Medium Aldresey* 1288 *Plea*, and thereafter with spellings as for Aldersey *supra*, and

Media-, Medio- c.1300 *Chol, Med'-* 1331 Plea, *Middel-* 1307 ib *et freq* with variant spellings *Myddel-, Midel(l)-, Myd(d)le-, Myddyl-, Middle-* (1668–71 Sheaf, 1724 NotCestr); *Medel(l)-* 1465 *Chol, Myde-* 1537 Plea, *v.* middel, hall.

CROOK ALDERSEY, THE CROOK (109–455553), *Cruk Aderzey* c.1300 *Chol*, and thereafter with spellings as for Aldersey *supra*, and *Crukke-* c.1300 (15) *Chol, Crucke-* c.1320 *AddCh*, 1331 Plea, *Cruc-* 1329 *Chol, Kroc-* 1307 Plea, *Croke-* 1308 (1565) ChRR, 1422 Plea, 1503 ChRR *et freq* to 1619 ib, *Crooke-* 1421 Orm², 1584, 1609 *Chol, Crook-* 1724 NotCestr, 'the part of Aldersey in the crook', from krókr. Crook Aldersey is the south-east corner of the township, the boundary of which forms a broad 'crook' between Coddington and Clutton township to include the land between Coddington and Aldersey Brooks.

ALDERSEY BROOK (Coddington Brook 86 *infra*), *Coddington Brook* 1831 Bry, *Holywell Brook* 1842 OS, cf. Holywell Brook 1 29, *v.* brōc. PUMP LANE WOOD, *v.* pumpe, lane. SLOBBERCROFTS COVERT, *Aldersey Wood* 1831 Bry, cf. *Big Slobber Croft* 1838 *TA*, 'muddy croft', *v.* slober, croft, cover. SMELLMOOR WOOD, *Smell Moor* 1838 *ib*, probably 'narrow or little marsh', from smæl and mōr¹. YEWTREE FM, *Aldersey Farm* 1831 Bry.

FIELD-NAMES

The undated forms are 1838 *TA* 126. The others are *Chol*.

(a) Carr Fd (*v.* kjarr); Hollin Fd (*v.* holegn); Intake (*v.* inntak); Jacks Croft (*Jackes Croft* 1584, *v.* jack); Meadow Fd (*the Medowe Fielde* 1533, *v.* mǣd); Middle Fd; Mill Mdw; Moor Mdw; New Hay(s) (*v.* (ge)hæg); Outlett (*v.* outlet); Owlery Croft (*v.* alor); Picker (*Pyckoe* 1584, *v.* pichel); Big & Little Plox (*v.* plocc, cf. Plocks 86 *infra*); Rice Mdw (*v.* hrīs); (Far-, Long-, & Near-) Ridding (cf. *le Newe Ruding* c.1300, *v.* nīwe, ryding); Salt Brook Mdw, Salt Grass (*v.* salt, brōc, gærs, cf. Leland v 6, 'Aldresey hath bene a salt pit, but now decayed, as almoste in tyme out of mynde'); Sand Fd; Town Fd; Tween Brooks ('between the brooks', *v.* betwēon, brōc); Wet Mdw; Wool(l)eys.

(b) the *Harowe* 1519 (*v.* erg); *le Merstal* c.1300, -*stall* c.1300 (15) ('a pool of (stagnant) water', *v.* mere-steall, cf. *le Merestal* 2 269, *le Merstal* 3 158); *Mostons Hey* 1584 (from (ge)hæg and either a surname *Moston* or a p.n. 'moss enclosure' from mos and tūn); *le Outlone* c.1300, -*de Medio Aldresey* c.1300 (15) ('outlying lane', *v.* ūt, lane); *le Seven Okys* c.1300, -*akis* c.1300

(15) ('seven oaks', v. seofon, āc); *le Wodefal* c.1300, *-fall* c.1300 (15) ('place where wood is felled', v. wudu, (ge)fall).

2. CHOWLEY (109–4756) ['tʃouli, 'tʃauli]

> *Celelea* 1086 DB
> *Chelleia* 1208–26 Chest (p), *Chelleye* 1290 Ipm
> *Scholley* 1284 Ipm, *Scholleg* 1285 ib, *Sholley* 1443 ChRR (p)
> *Cholleye* 1297 *Dav*, *Cholley* 1272–1307 StoweCh *et freq* with variant spellings *Chollegh, Cholleygh, Cholle* to 1673 Sheaf, *Cholley* or *Chowley* or *Chorley* 1668–71 ib, *Choly* 1695 ib
> *Chollelegh* 1367 Orm²
> *Chowley* 1551 Pat, 1591 Sheaf *et freq*, *Chowley Green* 1671 ib, *Choulley* 1668–71 ib
> *Chorley* 1668–71 Sheaf
> *Thouley, Touley, Towley (Green)* 1690 Sheaf

'Cēola's wood or clearing', from the OE pers.n. *Cēola* and lēah, as in Brooks Mill 3 95, with grēne². The *T-* spellings probably represent a pronunciation [ts-] < [tʃ-], whereas *S(c)h-* represents [ʃ-] < [tʃ-].

CHOWLEY OAK COTTAGES & LANE, *the Okes* 1482 Sheaf, *Nooke* 1668–71 *ib*, *Touley Oke* 1690 ib, *Chowley Oak* 1838 *TA*, '(at the) oak(s)', v. āc, atten. DOG LANE, *Chowley Lane* 1831 Bry, v. dogga, lane. DRAGON FM, 1831 ib. HOLYWELL FIELD (109–474554) 1838 *TA*, cf. *Haly Wall Chapell* 1533 Chol and *Halliwell (House)* 1668–71 Sheaf, both recorded as in Chowley, and Holywell Brook 1 29, v. Holywell Fm 15 *supra*, hālig, wælla, wella. There is no record of the exact site and history of this chapel. SHEEP COTE PLANTATION, v. scēp, cot.

FIELD-NAMES

The undated forms are 1838 *TA* 126. Of the others 1320, 1519, 1533 are *Chol*, 1668–71, 1690 Sheaf.

(a) Acres; Banks; Barrows Croft (v. bearg); Caben Hay Shoot (v. caban, (ge)hæg, scēat); Chowley Hay (*Choulley Hayes* 1668-71, v. (ge)hæg); Eight Damath (v. day-math); Gorsty Fd (v. gorstig); Hay Shoot (v. (ge)hæg, scēat); Hemp Yard (v. hemp-yard); Hob Fd (v. hobbe); Milking Bank (v. milking); Moor Mdw; Old House Fd; Outlett (v. outlet); Pear Tree Fd; Far & Near Pickers (cf. *Picco-sand* 1668–71, *Puk House* 1690. The original f.n. was probably *Pickow's End* 'the end of the *pickow* (i.e. pightle)' or 'the end near a *pickow*', *v.* pichel 'a little plot of ground', ende[1]. An alternative form is either *Pickows* 'the little plots' or an elliptical *Pickow's*, written *Puk House, Pickers*); Red Croft (*v.* rēad); Rishy Fd, Rushy Moor (cf. *the Russhy Croft* 1519, *v.* riscig, croft, mōr[1]); Shoulder of Mutton (*v.* 337 *infra*); Town Fd (cf. *Cholley Felde* 1533); Waintily.

(*b*) *le Maweresridynges* 1320 ('the mower's cleared-lands', from the ME occupational name *mawere* 'mower' (Reaney, from 1225) and ryding).

3. CODDINGTON (109–4455), *Coddington-cum-Beachin* 1721 Sheaf, cf. Coddington, Old Beachin *infra*.

CODDINGTON (BRIDGE, HALL FM, & MILL) [ˈkɔdintən, ˈkɔditn̩]

> *Cotintone* 1086 DB, -*tuna* 1096–1101 (1280) Chest, *Cotituna* 1096–1101 (1150), 1150 ib, *Cotinton* 1188–91 ib, 1349 *AddCh* (p) (Barnes[1] 257), *Cothinton* 1335 *Chol* (p), *Cotynton* 1390 ChRR, *Cottington* 1660 Sheaf
>
> *Codinton* 1157–94, 1194–8, 1250–72 Chest, 13 *AddCh*, 1260 Court *et freq* with variant spellings -*yn*-, -*tun*, -*thon*, -*tona* to 1535 VE, (*Codynton iuxta Barton*) 1422 Orm[2]
>
> *Codington* 1258 Chest, 1278 Ipm *et freq* to 1724 NotCestr, with variant spellings -*yng*- (from 1287 Court), *Codd*- (from 1289 Plea), *Codington Hall* 1724 NotCestr
>
> *Cudington* 1288 Court, *Cudinton* 1311 Ipm
>
> *Codenton* 1291 Tax
>
> *Codunton* c.1415 Sheaf (p)
>
> *Coodington* 1549 Pat

'Cotta's farm', from the OE pers.n. *Cotta* and tūn. The medial -*ing*- is either -ing-[4] or the OE gen.sg. -*an*- replaced by -ing-[4], cf. the form *Codenton*. The -ing-[4] is probably the original form, since *Codenton* is an isolated example. In this township or parish was *le Codyngeheye* 1284–7, *Codyncheheye* 1284, *Codingey* 1296, 1300–7, *Codingeye* c.1300, all *AddCh*, from the same pers.n. and (ge)hæg 'a fenced-in enclosure', in which the medial syllable -*ing*-, ostensibly -ing-[4], shows the assibilated palatal development observed in the Ch '-*ingahām*' p.ns. (*v.* 2 8), perhaps influenced by a survival of the prefix ge- in (ge)hæg.

NEW & OLD BEACHIN FM, BEACHIN LANE (109–445567, 444573)
['biːtʃin]

>Bechene 1258 Chest, c.1300 *Chol* (p), 1311 Plea, 1335 Pat, *Mont*,
>   1351 *Eyre*, *Bechen* 1361 Orm², 1413 ChRR, 1621 Orm²
>*Bechinne* 1278 Ipm, *Bechin* 1412, 1592 ChRR, 1696, 1765 Sheaf,
>   *Old-* & *New-* 1842 OS, *Bechyn* 1498 Sheaf, 1517, 1536 Plea,
>   1522 Orm²
>*Bechon* 1400 Pat (lit. *Bethon*)
>*Bechun* 1435 ChRR
>*Beychyn* 1521, 1540 Plea, *Beichyn* 1536 ChRR
>*Beachen* 1648 Sheaf, (*The*) *Beachin* 1724 NotCestr, (*Old*) *Beachin*
>   1831 Bry, *Beechin* 1708 Cre
>*The Beaching* 1783 Sheaf
>*Old Birchin* 1838 *TA*

'Place growing with beech-trees', from **bēcen**¹, with **ald, nīwe,
lane, riscig**, cf. Beachen 30 *supra*.

BEACHIN WOOD, *Warrington Field Fox Cover* 1831 Bry.   COD-
DINGTON BROOK (Aldford Brook 78 *supra*), 1842 OS, *v.* brōc, cf.
Aldersey Brook 83 *supra*.   EDGERLEY COVERT, cf. *Edgerley Field*
1838 *TA*, named from Edgerley 81 *supra*.   HIGHFIELD FM,
High Fields 1842 OS, (*-Farm*) 1831 Bry, *v.* hēah, feld.   HOLM-
FIELD FM, cf. *Homefield Loons* 1838 *TA*, from home and feld, with
land.   LOWER HOUSES, *Lower House* 1831 Bry, *v.* lower.   MILL
COTTAGES, cf. *Mill Field, Meadow* & *Pool* 1838 *TA, v.* myln, cf.
Coddington Mill *supra*.   SPRING LANE, 1842 OS.   WHITE-
GATE FM.

FIELD-NAMES

The undated forms are 1838 *TA* 126. Of the others, 1913 is Sheaf³ 10
and the rest *AddCh*.

(*a*) Broad Fd; Burley Loams (from burh and lēah, with lām or loom);
Castle Groves; Cumber Breach (*v.* cumber, brēc); Three-, Five Damath,
etc. (*v.* day-math); Grestons Croft & Fd; Hick Stitch (*v.* sticce); Hustley
Fd; Marefield; The Mud-Hill 1913 (a local name for 'the enormous tumulus
of Coddington' (Orm² II 584, 731) at 109–453553, apparently 'mud hill',
from mudde, but perhaps 'hill where a meeting is held', from (ge)mōt and
hyll); Plocks (*le Plockis* 1284, *-es* 1300–7, 1327, *-ys* 1312, cf. *le Plocwey* 13
and Plox 83 *supra*. These forms represent the el. OE *plocc identified
Löfvenberg 154, cf. EDD, NED s.vv. *plack, plock*, and EPN s.v. plek. The

entry *plōc in EPN should be cancelled; Plockwoods YN 72 contains
*plocc. Professor Löfvenberg remarks (but cf. Addenda xvii) that *plock*
in Ch is probably always 'a little plot of ground, a little field' (*plack* NED),
since the sense 'log, lump of wood' appears to be restricted to certain
southern counties (*plock* NED). Le *Plockis* means 'the little plots', and *le
Plocwey* is more likely to mean 'way to a little plot' than 'road made of logs,
a sleeper-track', *v.* weg); Priest Fd; Slang (*v.* slang); Snail Pits (*v.* snægl,
pytt); Stockton Moor (from stocc and tūn, with mōr[1]); Twin Brooks (*v.*
betwīnan, brōc); Warren Dale (*v.* wareine, dæl[1]); Weaver Fd; West Moor
(*Westmere* 13, m14, *Vest-* 13, *Westmerefurlong* 1296, *-merfor-* 1300–7,
'(furlong at) west pool', from west and mere[1] (cf. mōr[1]), with furlang);
Whitefield (*v.* hwīt).

(b) *le Allereneschagh'* 1300–20 ('alder wood', *v.* alren, sc(e)aga); (*le*) *Bothum*
13, c.1295, *-om, -im* 13, *-yn* m14 ('the bottom-land', *v.* bōðm); *le Bradelont*
13 ('broad selion', *v.* brād, land); *le Bradewey, -way* 13 ('the wide road',
v. brād, weg); *les treis Cleifeldes* m14 ('the three clay fields', *v.* clæg, feld);
le Codyngeheye (*v.* Coddington *supra*); *le Crokytlond* 1284, 1300–7 ('crooked
selion', *v.* croked, land); *le Cronkesbuttis* 1298 ('the crane's selions', *v.*
cranuc, butte); *le Crosfeld* 1300–20, c. 1310 (*v.* cros, feld); *le Fengreve* 13
('wood near a marsh', *v.* fenn, græfe); *Fraun(c)keleynisforlong(es)* 1284–7,
c.1300 ('the freeholder's furlong(s)', from ME frankelein (1297, NED) 'a
franklin, a freeholder' and furlang); *Gosegrene* 1296, 1300–7 ('goose green',
v. gōs, grēne[2]); *le Grenewey* 1300–20 ('grassy road', *v.* grēne[1], weg);
Guldenehauedlond 13 ('the golden head-land', *v.* gylden, hēafod-land);
le Harewythingreue 1327 ('hoar willow-wood', from wiðegn and græfe, with
hār[2]); *Hawockes* 1284, *Hauock'* 1300–7, *Hauokes* 1312 (perhaps 'oaks near
a hedge or enclosure', from haga and āc); *Hertesgreue* 1300–20 ('the hart's
wood', *v.* heorot, græfe); Le *Haygreueforlong, Heygreuefurlong* 13, *le Hey-
greue* 1298, 14 ('(furlong at) the fenced-in wood', from (ge)hæg and græfe,
with furlang); *le (parvi) Heystow* 13, *le Heystouwe, Houleheystouwe* m14
('the place with a hedge', from hege-stōw, with lȳtel (Lat. *parvus*), and hulu
'a hovel, a shed'. Cf. *le Heystowe* 80 *supra*); *le Knothadelond'* 1323 ('head-
land near a hill', *v.* cnotta, hēafod-land); *Lechefurlong* 13 ('furlong at a
boggy stream', *v.* lece, furlang); Le *Legwes* 1300–20 (*v.* lēah); *Lendegrene*
1284 (final el. grēne[2] 'a green'); *Litlemers* 13, *le Littille Merhse* 1323, *le
Littilmersh* 1329, *Litlemersh* m14 (*v.* lȳtel, mersc); *Longeforlong, -furlong*
13, 1298, m14, *-forlonges* c.1295 ('long furlongs', *v.* lang, furlang); *le
Mere* 1300–20 (*v.* mere[1]); (*le*) *Middilfurlong* 13, *Medilforlong* 1298 (*v.*
middel, furlang); *Nahtmarefurlong* 1300–20 ('night-mare furlong', *v.*
niht-mare, furlang. The form is ME *naht* from OE neaht, (Anglian) næht.
Presumably this was a difficult field, but the nightmare may have been a
creature capable of haunting a field as well as the bed-room, cf. *Negtmereslond*
70 *supra*); *le Holdefeld* 1284–7, c.1300, *le Oldefeld* 1296 (*v.* ald, feld); *le
Pykedelong* m14 (probably for *-lond*, 'the pointed selion', from piked and
land); *le Portwey* 13 ('the road to a market-town', *v.* port-weg, part of the
Roman road from Aldford to Stretton, *v.* 1 42 (Route VIII); *le Rake sub'
le Heystouwe* m14 ('the narrow path', *v.* rake, cf. *le Heystow supra*); *Sichefeld*

13, (*le*) *Cychefurlong* 13, *le Sycheforlong* 1284–7, *Syche Forlonges* c.1300 (*v.* sīc, feld, furlang); *Le Sourbuttes* 1284 ('sour selions', *v.* sūr, butte); *Sourwyꝫenes* 1300–7 ('sour ground where withins grow', from sūr and wiðegn); *le Stanis* 13, *-es* m14 ('the stones', *v.* stān); *le Stoklondes* m14 ('selions at a dairy-farm', *v.* stoc, land); *Pechmundiscroftes* 1284, *Chedmundis-* c.1300, *Thedmundiscroft* 1300–20, 1303–7, c.1310, *Thedmundescroftes* 1323, *Thedmonescroft* 1329, *Themonescroftes* 1329 ('Theodmund's croft', from the OG pers.n. *Theodmund* (Searle 578, Forssner 230) and croft, *v.* Addenda).

x. Handley

The ecclesiastical parish of Handley contained 1. Golborne David, 2. Handley.

1. GOLBORNE DAVID (109–450600), *Goldeburne Dauid* 1383 CoLegh, thereafter with spellings as for Golborne *infra*, and *-David*, with variants *-Davy* 1430 Eyre, 1462 ChRR, *-Dave* 1541 Orm², 'David's moiety of Golborne', named from David de Golberne E1 StoweCh 171, Orm² II 726, the thirteenth-century grantee of the manor.

GOLBORNE BELLOW & DAVID [ˈgou(l)bɔrn, ˈgou(l)bən-]

Colburne, -borne 1086 DB

Goulborn 1199–1209 (19) Orm² (p), 1724 NotCestr

Golburn 13 Whall (p), *Golborne* 1246 Tab *et freq* with variant spellings *-born* (to 1831 Bry), *-burn(e)* (to 1581 ChRR), *-berne* (E1 StoweCh), *-bourn(e)* (1326 ChRR (p) to 1842 OS), *-born* (1357 Chamb (p) to 1724 NotCestr)

Goldeburm 1259 Court (p), *Goldbur'* 1260 ib, *Goldburn* 1282 ib (p) *et freq* with variant spellings *Golde-* (to 1472 ChRR (p)), *-burn* (to 1465 ChRR), *-bourn(e)* (1290 Ipm to 1472 ChRR), *-bern* (1310 ChRR (p)), *-born(e)* (1461, 1470 ChRR)

Coldbourn 1303 Chamb (p), *-burn* 1307 Eyre (p)

'Marigold stream', *v.* golde, burna. Cf. Golborne David *supra*, Golborne Bellow 95 *infra*. The stream is Golborne Brook 1 26. Here should be noted the lost GOLBORNE HUNDRED, *hundred de Golborne* 1246 Tab, *the hundred court of the lord of Cheshire at Goldeburn* 1290 Ipm II 478, *hundred of Goldebourne* 1290 ib 459, *hundred courts of Golbourne* 1363 BPR III 460, *v.* hundred. To this hundred the manors of Shocklach, Duckington, Pulford, Waverton and Eccleston owed suit, *v.* NRA 3636, No. 276, and Sheaf³ 17

(3938). There seems no reason to suppose a minor hundred here, since Golborne was not the seat of a barony (cf. *Malpas Hundred* 39 *supra, Halton Hundred* 2 2,) and the manors which chance to be on record as owing suit do not fall into a recognizable fee. They are miscellaneous manors of Broxton hundred. The hundred at Golborne was a court of the earldom of Chester, not of a subordinate barony. It seems very likely that the Court which met at Golborne was that of Broxton Hundred, except the manors in peculiar jurisdiction. The meeting-place might have been *Golbournford* at Golborne Bridge *infra*, where at least one Inquisition of Broxton Hundred was taken (1359 *Indict*, printed Sheaf³ 20 (4695)). The meeting at Golborne and not at Broxton 12 *supra* may have been to accommodate the minor hundred jurisdiction at Malpas 39 *supra*, as being a suitable place outside the Malpas barony but still in Broxton hundred. There is no evidence to show whether Golborne was selected for some other reason, perhaps as the site of *Dudestan* hundred in which Golborne would have been central. Cf. Broxton Hundred 1 *supra*.

COLDHARBOUR (a house), *v.* **cald, here-beorg,** cf. Wa xlvii, where W. Fergusson Irvine states that the p.n. was invented in 1903 by a member of his family as the name of a new plantation. DOCTOR'S PLANTATION, cf. Doctors Fd 91 *infra*. GOLBORNE BRIDGE (FM) (109-461592), *Golburneford* 1281 (14), 1281 (17) Chest (lit. *-feld* 1281 (17) ib 11 837), *Goldebourne Ford* 1280 (19) Orm² 11 791, *Golbournford* 1359 *Indict, Golburnesford* 1427, 1429 Sheaf, *Golborne Foorde, -Foworde, Golborn Ford* 1595 ChRR, Sheaf, 1671 ib, *Golborne Bridge* 1690 ib, *Golborn Bridge* 1745 ib, *Golbourn-* 1775 ib, *Bridge House* 1831 Bry, *v.* **ford, brycg,** cf. Golborne, *Golborne Hundred supra.* GOLBORNE OLD HALL, *Old Hall* 1831 Bry, *Golbourne Hall* 1842 OS, *v.* **ald, hall.** GOLBORNE MANOR. GOLBORNE NEWHALL FM, *The Hall* 1831 Bry, *Golbourne Hall* 1842 OS, *v.* **nīwe, hall.** PLATT'S LANE, *Platts Lane* 1831 Bry, 'lane to a foot-bridge', *v.* **plat¹, lane.**

FIELD-NAMES

The undated forms are 1844 *TA* 177. Of the others E2¹ is Orm², E2² *CoLegh*, 1682 *Corp*, 1831 Bry.

(a) Bobs Croft (*Bobbecroft* E2¹, *Bob(b)ecroft* E2², 'Bobba's croft', from the OE pers.n. *Bobba* and croft); Butter Tree Fd; Chitter Pool (*v.* **pōl¹.**

The first el. may refer to some small bird such as the wren or whitethroat, *v.* EDD s.vv. *chitter, chitty*); Heath 1831 (cf. Hatton Heath 100 *infra*); the Hollinheads 1682 (*v.* holegn, hēafod); Ronks Moor; Smooth Wd; Wirrall Fd (*v.* wir, halh).

(b) *Knavenes Grenehull* E2¹, *Knaue(ne)greuehul, Knauenes Greue Hul* E2² ('(hill at) the youths' wood', from cnafa (gen.pl. cnafena) and grǣfe, with hyll); *le Neuueboldisway* E2² ('the way to Newbold', *v.* weg, Lea Newbold 120 *infra*); *Ossebernescroft* E2¹, *Os(se)-* E2² ('Osbern's croft', from the OE pers.n. *Osbern* discussed by Feilitzen 338 (from ON *Ásbiǫrn* or OLG *Osbern*) and croft).

2. HANDLEY (109–4658) [ˈhandli, ˈhanli]

> *Hanlei* 1086 DB, *-leye* 1161–82 Chest *et freq* with variant spellings *-lega, -leg(h), -le(e), -ley, -leyg', -leigh* to 1703 Sheaf
> *Hangley* c.1210 (1724) NotCestr
> *Henleg'* 1237 Cl, *-legh* 1244 *Chol* (p), *-ley* 1414 Orm²
> *Hanneleg'* 1251–5 Dieul, *-legh* 1288 Court (p), *-ley* c.1310 Chest, *Hanelegh* 1350 Plea, 1394 ChRR (p), *-le* 1355 BPR
> *Honlegh* 13 (1525) *Add* 42134A
> *Handlegh* 1360 Orm², 1535 VE *et freq*, *-leye* 1557 Sheaf, *Handeley* 1564 ib, *Haundley* 1572 Orm²
> *Haunley* 1515 Plea
> *Hendele* 1550 *MinAcct*

'The high clearing', *v.* hēah (wk.dat. hēan), lēah.

CLAYLEY HALL, *Cleyley* 1506 (1536) ChRR, 1525 *Add* 42134A, 1558 Orm², 1585 Sheaf, *Cleley* 1506 Orm², 1537, 1648 Sheaf, *Cleby* 1724 NotCestr (for *Cleley*), *Clayley, Cloyley Hall* 1838 *TA* 'clearing on clayey ground', from clǣg and lēah, with hall. *Add* 43134A, f.3r, (date 1525), refers to *Cleyley* as held of Dodleston castle (157 *infra*) by Morgan de Milton (*infra*) in the thirteenth century, and quotes the forms *Cleyhull, Cleyhullesichec* 13 (1525), *v.* clǣg, hyll, sīc. It is not clear what evidence there is for the historical reference, or the suggested identification of the thirteenth-century form with Clayley. The spelling *-sichec* suggests that the final el. sīc appears in a derivative form, perhaps with the suffix -uc.

MILTON GREEN (FM) (109–462588)

> *Milneton* 1257 *AddCh* (p), *-ton* 13 (1525) *Add*
> *Mulneton* 13 *Vern* (p) *et freq* to 1417 Orm², *le Mulneton* 1402 ChRR (p)

Mullington 1289 Court (p)
Multon 1407 (p), 1433 ChRR
Milton 1510, 1515 Plea *et freq* with variant spelling *Mylton* (to
 1607 Orm²); *Milton Green* 1671 Sheaf, 1842 OS, *Green Farm*
 1831 Bry
Melton 1524 Plea

'Mill farm or mill-enclosure', from **myln** and **tūn**, with **grēne**².

ALLEY BANK COTTAGES.   CALVELEY HALL, 1724 NotCestr, cf.
'Lady Calveley who hath built a faire house and chapel upon it
1674', 1674 Sheaf³ 48 (9677), *v.* **hall**.   GOLBORNE BRIDGE, *v.* 89
supra.   HANDLEY COVERT, *-Cover* 1831 Bry, *v.* **cover**.   MILL
HILL, 1831 ib, cf. *Mill (Hill) Ground* 1711 Sheaf, *v.* **myln, hyll**.
PIGEONHOUSE FM, 1831 Bry, *v.* **pigeon-house**.   ROCKY LANE, *v.*
rokky.   STONYFORD (lost, 109–463585), STONYFORD BROOK (109–
463585 to 455578, Coddington Brook 86 *supra*), *Stoneways Ford*
1831 Bry, *Stonyford (Field & Meadow)* 1838 *TA*, 'ford at a stony
road', from **stān** and **weg**, with **ford** and **brōc**. This ford carried the
Chester–Whitchurch road, *regia strata que ducit de Cestr' versus
album monasterium* 1315 AddCh, *regia strata que ducit per mediam
villam de Hanley* c.1315 *ib*, cf. 1 42 (Route VIII, second para.).
WELLHOUSE FM, *Well House* 1831 Bry, *v.* **wella, hūs**.

FIELD-NAMES

The undated forms are 1838 *TA* 187. Of the others 13 (1525) is *Add* 42134A,
E1 *StoweCh*, 1711 Sheaf, 1831 Bry, 1842 OS.

(a) Bay Moor; Broad Field Lane 1831 (*v.* Shawfield *infra*); Cockerill
Fd, Cockern Fd 1711 (*v.* **cocker, hyll**); Coney Grave (*v.* **coningre**); Doctors
Fd; Fetter Falloons, -Fulloons (*Fetterfewlands, Feter Folands* 1711, 'selions
where the feverfew grows', *v.* **fēfer-fuge, land**); Goodmans Hill (cf. Thomas
Godeman of *Mulneton* 1417 Orm² II 727, *v.* **hyll**); Old Handley (*v.* **ald**, cf.
Handley *supra*); Handley Keys (*v.* **cae**); Handley Oak (*v.* **āc**); Hatch Fd
(*v.* **hæc(c)**); Holmes (*v.* **holmr**); Howstock; Lea Mill (*v.* **myln**, cf. Lea
Newbold 119 *infra*); Malkins (*-Field* 1711, *v.* **malkin**); Morgans Mow (from
the Welsh pers.n. *Morgan* and **mūga**, cf. *Morgan* de Mulneton 13 *StoweCh*
171); Peel Croft (*v.* **pēl**); the Pike; Pingot (*v.* **pingot**); Pump Ho 1831 (*v.*
pumpe, hūs); Ravens Croft; Ridding (*v.* **ryding**); The Roan; Shawfield (cf.
Shay Field Gorse, Broad Field Lane 1831, *Shay Field Lane* 1842, at 109–
454586 to 447582 to 433588, *v.* **sc(e)aga, brād, feld, gorst, lane**, cf. Broadfield 120 *infra*); Short Butts (*v.* **sc(e)ort, butte**); White Fd.

(*b*) *Almundshale* 13 (1525) ('Almund's nook', from halh (dat.sg. hale) and the pers.n. *Almund* (from OE *Æðelmund* or *Ealhmund*, *v.* Feilitzen 149)); *Heywode* E1 ('fenced-in wood', *v.* (ge)hæg, wudu).

xi. Harthill

Harthill was a free chapelry. The manor was part of Malpas barony, and the chapelry was originally probably part of Malpas parish.

HARTHILL (109–5055) ['ha:rtil]

> *Hert'* 1208–29 (1580) Sheaf, *Herthil* 1259 Court (p), *Herthul* 1281 AddCh, *Herthull* 1297 Plea *et freq* with variant spellings *Herte-*, *-hulle* to 1517 ChEx, *Herthill* 1357 BPR (p), 1558 Orm², *-hyll* 1402, 1451 ChRR, *Hertyll* 1432 Dav, *Herthell* 1449 ChRR
>
> *Harthil* 1259 Court (p), *-hill* 1325 (1619) Chol (p), E4 (1574), 1589 ChRR, *Hartehull* 1353 Chol
>
> *Hertleye* 1557 Sheaf³ 1 (43)

> 'Hart hill', *v.* heorot, hyll.

BODNICK WOOD (109–507553), *Bodnock Wood* 1831 Bry, *Badnook Wood* 1842 OS, *v.* Bodnick Cottage 94 *infra*.   CHURCH FM. HARTHILL COOMBS, *Comb Wood*, *The Comb* 1831 Bry, *The Coombes* 1842 OS, probably *Harthill Slade* 14 (17) Sheaf, 'the valley', *v.* slæd, cumb, wudu. Cf. Mad Allen's Hole 4 *supra*.   HARTHILL LANE (FM), *Harthill Lane* 1831 Bry.   HARTHILL POOL, *The Pool*, *Pool Field* 1838 TA, cf. *the Poledale* 1305 (1637) Rich, *Harthill Poole Dale* 14 (17) Sheaf, *v.* pōl¹, dæl¹.   MANOR FM.   MICKERDALE COTTAGE, *v.* 94 *infra*.   THE MOSS, MOSS COTTAGE & FM, *Harthill Moss* 1842 OS, *v.* mos.   NEW LANE (FM).   PARK COTTAGE & WOOD, 1831 Bry, *v.* park.   OLD PINFOLD, *v.* pyndfald.   RAW HEAD, *v.* 5 *supra*.   SALTER'S LANE, *Salters Lane* 1842 OS, on the southern boundary of the township, *v.* saltere, lane, cf. 1 48 (Route XXV).   WOODEND FM, *Wood End* 1842 OS, *v.* wudu, ende¹.

FIELD-NAMES

The undated forms are 1838 *TA* 191. Of the others, 1811 is Sheaf, 1483 *Chol*.

(*a*) The Acres; The Billings (probably another instance of the hill-name *Billinge*, *v.* Billinge Hill 1 138); College Bank; Dale (*v.* dæl¹); Edgery Bank

& Hill (v. hecg-rǣw, banke, hyll); Fullers Moor; Gorsty Butt(s) (v. gorstig, butte); Green Loons (v. grēne[1], land); Harthill Heath & Park; The Hill; Hook Loont 1811 (v. hōc, land); Lidgate (v. hlid-geat); Marl Fd; Moor(s); Old Croft (cf. *the Oldecrofte* 1483, v. ald, croft); Pigg; Stockings (v. stoccing).

(b) le Wasshpit Frith Mosses 1483 ('mosses at the wood near the washpit', from wæsce and pytt with (ge)fyrhð and mos).

xii. Bunbury

The rest of Bunbury parish is in Eddisbury Hundred, v. 3 300.

12. BURWARDSLEY (HALL) (109–5156) [ˈbəːwədzli, ˈbəːwəzli] locally [ˈbouəzli, ˈbuːəzli]

    Burwardeslei 1086 DB, *Burewardesleia* 1096–1101 (1150), 1150 Chest, *Burwardesleya* 1186–94 ib, -*ley* 1216–72 Orm[2] *et freq* with variant spellings -*is*-, -*legh*, -*le(g')*, -*leye* to 1819 Orm[2], *Burwardsley* 1653 Cre *et freq*, (-*Hall*) 1831 Bry

    Ber(e)wardesleya 1096–1101 (1280) Chest, *Berewardesleia* 1096–1101 (17) ib, -*legh* 1360 Orm[2]

    Borwardesleye 1249–65 Chest, -*leg* 1290 Ipm, *Boruardesleye* 1295 AddCh, *Borwardesley*, -*legh* 1320 Chol, *Borewardeslegh* 1271 (1580) Sheaf

    Borewardelegh 1289 Court (p)

    Boardslegh 1396 Orm[2]

    Burwaresley 1456 Rich

    Borosley 1499 Eyre, *Borrowsley* 1520 ChEx

    Bursley 1524, 1534 Plea, 1656 Orm[2], (-*alias Burwardsley*) 1668–71 Sheaf, *Burseley* 1530 Chol, (*Burwardesley alias*-) 1580 Orm[2]

    Burwaslegh 1541 Orm[2]

    Borsley 1550 MinAcct, *Bores*- 1560 Sheaf, 1561 Pat

    Bulwardley 1656 Cre

    Burwardley 1702 AddCh

v. lēah 'a wood, a glade', hall, cf. Higher Burwardsley *infra*. In this p.n. and *Burwardestone* 1 *supra*, and Brewer's Hall 336 *infra*, the first el. is probably OE burh-weard, byrh-weard, 'the guardian of a town or stronghold', but the derivative OE pers.n. *Burgweard* is possible. Perhaps at some early date these places owed service in the defence of Chester or some fortification on the Welsh border.

THE BARRACKS, v. barrack. BODNICK COTTAGE (109–508553), *Badnook* 1842 OS, cf. Bodnick Wood 92 *supra*. The house is at the head, and the wood on the shoulder, of a steep-sided valley in the side of Burwardsley Hill. The modern form looks like a 'bad nook', v. badde, nōk, but the original p.n. may be Welsh (or pseudo-Welsh) 'house at a hill', from bod and cnwc. BROAD ROUGH, v. brād, rūh. HIGHER BURWARDSLEY, *Upper Barn* 1831 Bry, *Higher Bardeardsley* 1842 OS, v. bere-ærn. BURWARDSLEY HILL (FM), *Hill Farm* 1831 Bry, *Burwardsley Hill* 1840 *TA*, v. hyll, cf. Rock Fm *infra*, Peckforton Hills 3 312. CAWLEY'S WOOD. CHERRY-TREE FM. CURDLAND FM. DROPPINGSTONE HO & WELL, *the blind will called the droping stonne* 14 (17) Sheaf, *Dropping Stone Well* 1831 Bry, 'spring at a dripping rock', v. dropande, stān, wella. FOWLERS BENCH LANE, *Fowlers Bench* 1831 ib, benc 'a bench', perhaps topographical. This is a place in Peckforton Gap 3 312 on the Peckforton boundary. HILLSIDE FM, LOWERHILL FM, cf. *Lower Hill Field* 1840 *TA*, Burwardsley Hill *supra*, v. hyll, sīde, lower. MANORHOUSE FM. MICKERDALE, 1842 OS, *Mickledale* 1840 *TA*, cf. Mickerdale Cottage 92 *supra*, 'big valley', v. micel, dæl[1]. MILLER'S PLANTATION, cf. *Millers Field* 1840 *ib*. OUT LANE, OUTLANE FM, *Out Lane* 1842 OS, 'outlying lane', v. ūt, lane. THE PAGES, 1840 *TA*. PENNSYLVANIA, cf. Pennsylvania Wood 3 304. QUARRY HO. RIDDING BANK (FM), v. ryding, banke. ROCK FM, ROCKHOUSE FM, cf. *Burwardsley Hill Rock* 1840 *TA*, v. roke, cf. Burwardsley Hill *supra*. SANDHOLE FM. SMITHY-BANK FM, v. smiððe, banke. SPRING HO, 1831 Bry, v. spring 'a well-spring'. WELL HO, *Cherry Tree* 1842 OS. WILLOW HILL (FM), *Willow Hill* 1831 Bry, v. wilig. WOOD COTTAGE, WOODSIDE FM, v. wudu, sīde.

FIELD-NAMES

The undated forms are 1840 *TA* 87. Of the others, 1418, 1662 are Cre, 1476 ChRR.

(a) Allegor; Bache (v. bæce[1]); Bantlings; Birch Croft (*the-* 1662, v. birce); Brook Fd; Broom Hill; Brow Fd (v. brū); Buckley Hill (cf. Bulkeley Hill 18 *supra*); Chapel Croft & Fd; The Close; Cockerhill Fd (v. cocker, hyll); Common Yard (v. geard); Drumbo Fd (dial. *drumble*, v. dumbel); Fold Fd (v. fald); Fox Hill; Glee Blooms ('glebe selions', v. glebe, loom); Gorstage (from gorst and the ME collective suffix -age); Great Fd 1662; The Hays (v. (ge)hæg); Hollins (v. holegn); Hollow Fd; House Fd (cf. *the Croft by the*

House 1662); Kittles (*v.* keddle-dock); Lark Hill (*v.* lǣwerce, hyll); Mans Croft; Marl Fd; Meadow Bank Croft; Milking Bank (*v.* milking); Moor; Ox Hays (*v.* (ge)hæg); Paradise (*v.* paradis); Pied Flatt (*v.* pyed); Pinfold (*v.* pynd-fald); Pingo(t) (*v.* pingot); Red Flatt; Ridding(s) (*v.* ryding); the Rough Croft 1662; Rush Bloom; Salver Fd; The Scar (*v.* sker); Sheep Cote (*v.* scēp, cot); Tongue Shoot (*v.* tunge, scēat); Townfield Croft; Well Croft, Fd & Moor; Welshmans Croft (*v.* Wels(c)hman); Wickett Fd (*v.* wiket); Willows; Withins Croft (*v.* wiðegn).

(*b*) *Caycroft* 1476 (probably 'hedged croft' from cae and croft, but Professor Löfvenberg thinks the first el. could be cǣg 'a stone'); *le Woodhouse* 1418 ('house at a wood', *v.* wudu, hūs).

xiii. Tattenhall

The ecclesiastical parish of Tattenhall contained the townships 1. Golborne Bellow, 2. Newton by Tattenhall, 3. Tattenhall.

1. GOLBORNE BELLOW (109–4759) [ˈgou(l)bɔrn, ˈgou(l)bən-]

Belewgolburn c.1300 *Chol*
Golburne Belewe 1304 Chamb, thereafter with spellings as for
   Golborne 88 *supra* and -*Belew*(*e*) (to 1422 Plea), -*Bellow*(*e*)
   (from 1415 ChRR), with variants -*Bello*(*u*), -*Bellewe* (1415 ChRR,
   1597 Orm[2]), -*Belleau* (1602 Orm[2], 1842 OS)
Golborne Bellows, or Below 1656 Orm[2]

'The moiety of Golborne which belonged to the *Belewe* family', cf. Golborne and Golborne David 88 *supra*. The manorial affix is the surname of Thomas *de Bellew* or *de Bella Aqua* 13 Orm[2] II 721, or his son Robert E1 *StoweCh* 171.

RUSSIA FARM & HALL (109–475589) [ˈruʃə]

?Rushale 1272 Cl 512 (p)
Russhal 1348 *Eyre*, -*hale* 1386 ChRR (p)
Risale 1357 *Eyre*
Ruysshall 1422 Plea
Ruschhaule c.1536 Leland, *Russhall* 1539 ChRR, *Rushall* 1565 ib,
   (-*Hall*) 1819 Orm[2]
Rusha Hall 1724 NotCestr, *Rushia-hall* 1782 Sheaf, *Russia Hall*
   1831 Bry
Rushill or Rushall Hall 1860 White

'Corner of land where rushes grow', from risc and halh, with hall.

FROG LANE, v. 98 infra.   GATES HEATH (COTTAGE, FM & HO),
Gates Heath 1831 Bry, 'heath near, or allotted into, cattle-walks', v.
gata, hǣð.   PRINCE'S FM.   NEW RUSSIA HALL, *New Hall* 1860
White, v. nīwe, hall, cf. Russia Hall *supra*.

FIELD-NAMES

The undated forms are 1838 *TA* 385. The others are Sheaf.

(a) Ankers Fd (v. ancra); Bellows Croft & Hay (*Bollers Hey* 1600, from
the surname *Belewe* as in Golborne Bellow *supra* and croft, (ge)hæg);
Bottoms (v. botm); Butcher's Fd; Common Croft; Big- & Little Copy
(v. copis); The Eleven Demath (v. day-math); The Gib Iron (v. gibbe,
hyrne); Heath Fd; Kiln Fd (v. cyln); Ledge Fd (v. lece); Pike Fd (v. pīc[1]);
Rough Fd; Russia Fd (cf. Russia Hall *supra*); Slacky Fd (v. slakki, -ig[3]);
Sleath Mdw; Sour Fd (v. sūr); Verginals Croft.

(b) the *Leighfield* 1600 ('field at a clearing', v. lēah).

2. NEWTON BY TATTENHALL (109–4960), NEWTON FM, HO &
LANE

Newton iuxta Tatenhall 1298 ChF *et freq* with variant spellings
  Neuton (to 1505 ChRR) and as for Tattenhall 97 *infra*, *-iuxta
  Hatton* 1382 Plea, *-iuxta Sydenall* 1482 Chol
Neubold iuxta Tatenhale 1374 Chol

'New farm', from nīwe, and tūn, bold, cf. Tattenhall, *Siddall*,
Hatton 97, 97, 100 *infra*

BRIDGE COTTAGE, named from a railway bridge.   BROOK HOLE
(COTTAGE), v. 102 *infra*.   CROW'S NEST BRIDGE, *Crows Nest
(Bridge)* 1831 Bry, a hamlet (109–495605) and a bridge over the
Shropshire Union Canal, cf. Crow's Nest Cottage & Gorse 100, 102
infra, v. cräwe, nest.   FORD LANE, 1831 ib, leading to a ford at
109–513599, cf. 98 *infra*.   HIGHER HUXLEY MILL, cf. 101 *infra*.
TATTENHALL RD, cf. 97, 100 *infra*.   WHITEGATE COTTAGES.

FIELD-NAMES

The undated forms are 1838 *TA* 385.
(a) Bottoms (v. botm); Broad Fd; Cock Shoot (v. cocc-scyte); Ellnor
Ridding (v. ryding); Hatch Fd (v. hæc(c)); Hodney Park; The Liverpool;
Long Hay (v. (ge)hæg); Muck Fd; Parsley Wd (cf. *a little wood called Person
Hey* 1482 Chol, 1486, 1488 *MinAcct*, 'parson's enclosure', v. persone,
(ge)hæg); Sincoe Ridding (v. ryding); Three Nooks; Two Foot Acre.

3. TATTENHALL (109–4858), *Tattenhall cum Sydinhall* 1478 ChRR, cf. Tattenhall, *Siddall infra*.

TATTENHALL HALL, LANE, LANES FM, MILL, RD & WOOD FM ['tætnɔːl] older local ['tætnə]

> *Tatenale* 1086 DB, *Tatin-*, *Tatenhala* 1096–1101 (1280), 1150 Chest, *Tatenhale* 1157–94 ib *et freq* to 1487 ChRR (p) with variant spellings *-in-* and *-yn-* (to c.1322 *Dav*), *-hal* (1241 Lib to 1408 ChRR (p)), *Tatenale* (1308 to 1400 ChRR)
> *Tatehale* 1251 Pat, *-hal'* 1251 Cl, 1289 Court
> *Tattenhall* 1289 (17) Court, 1400 Pat (p) *et freq*, *Tatten Hall* 1569, 1655 Sheaf, *Tattenhall Lanes* & *-Woodsyde* 1601 ib, *-Wood* 1656 Orm², *-Hall* 1671 ib, *-Mill* & *-Woods* 1831 Bry
> *Tatenhall* 1298 ChF, 1308, 1414 ChRR *et freq* to 1527 ib, *Tatenall'* 1429 AddCh
> *Tatenhull* 1310 Pap
> *Takenhale* 1370 Orm²
> *Tatnall* 1473 ChRR (p), 1516 *ChEx*, 1551 Pat, 1558 ChRR, 1652 Cre, 1653, 1686 Sheaf, *Tatt-* 1519 *Dav*, 1644, 1729 Sheaf, *Tatna* 1690 ib
> *Tottenhall* 1553 Pat, 1696 Sheaf, *Totnall* 1581 ib
> *Tatton Hall* 1565 Cre, *Tattonhall* 1601, 1604 ib
> *Tettenhall* 1649 Cre

'Tāta's nook', from the OE pers.n. *Tāta* and **halh** (dat.sg. **hale**), with **hall**, **lane**, **myln**, **wudu**, **sīde**. The mill is probably 'a water mill in *Tatenhall*' 1414 ChRR. It gives name to Mill Brook *infra*.

SIDDALL (lost)

> *Sidenhale* c.1280 *Chol*, *Syden-* 1345 (p), 1355, 1378 *Eyre* (p), 1443 ChRR, (*-iuxta Tatenhale*) 1503 Orm², *-hal'* 1348 *Eyre* (p)
> *Sidnall* 1468 *Sotheby*, 1492 Plea, 1563 Orm², *Syd-* 1533 Sheaf, 1538 ChRR, 1558 Orm², 1563 ChRR, 1595 Sheaf, 1664 Cre
> *Sydinhall* 1478 ChRR, *Sydenhall* 1482 *Chol* (*Newton iuxta-*), 1529 Plea, 1588 ChRR, *Siden-* 1486, 1488 *MinAcct* (*Newton iuxta-*), *Syddenhall* 1580, 1655 Cre, *Sidden-* 1613 Orm², 1648 Sheaf, *the Hall of Siddenhall* 1626 AddCh
> *Sidwall* 1485 ChRR, 1580 Sheaf, 1656 Orm²
> *Sydenham* 1541 ChRR
> *Siddall* 1671 Sheaf³ 48 (9795)

'The broad nook or valley', from sīd (wk.dat.sg. sīdan) and halh (dat.sg. hale), with hall. The location has not been found, but it must have been towards Newton 96 *supra*.

BACK LANE, *v.* back, lane.   BARROW FORK PLANTATION, *The Barrow Faugh* 1838 *TA*, from falh (ModEdial. *faugh*) 'fallow ground', with bearu 'a grove' or, perhaps more likely, bearh 'a barrow-pig'. BEBBINGTON TENEMENT, 1673 Cre, *Bebbingtons-* 1702 ib, from the surname *Bebington* (cf. Bebington 245 *infra*) and tenement, cf. John *Bibington*, licensed to enclose his messuage, 1602 Cre 70.   BEE-HIVE FM, 1831 Bry.   BIRDS LANE, 1842 OS.   BOLESWORTH RD, *Isle of Wight Lane* 1831 Bry, *Isle of Want* 1842 OS (109–490573). BROAD OAK, 1831 Bry, *v.* brād, āc.   BROOK COTTAGE & HO, named from Keys Brook 1 30, *v.* brōc.   BROOK FM, *Brook Bank* 1842 OS, *v.* brōc, banke, named from Crimes Brook 3 304.   CAM-BRIDGE FM.   CARRS LANE, *Cars Lane* 1842 ib, *v.* kjarr.   CHE-SHIRE CHEESE.   DAISYBANK FM, *Daisey Bank* 1831 Bry.   DARK LANE, 1842 OS, *v.* deorc, lane.   EDGECROFT HO.   ELM FM. THE FIELDS COTTAGE, *v.* feld.   FORD LANE, cf. *Ford Field* 1838 *TA*, *v.* 96 *supra*.   FROGHALL, FROG LANE, *Frog Lane*, *Frog Moor Lodge* 1831 Bry, 'lodge at frog marsh, frog's lane', *v.* frogga, mōr[1], cf. 96 *supra*.   GOSHEN LODGE & SPINNEY.   GREAVES FM, *The Graves* 1831 ib, *The Greaves* 1842 OS, *v.* græfe.   THE GROVE.   HENHULL COTTAGE.   IRON GATE PLANTATION, named from a park gate of Bolesworth Castle 14 *supra*.   MILLBANK COTTAGES & HO, *Windmill House* 1842 ib, *Mill Bank House* 1860 White, cf. *Windmill Field* 1654 Cre, *v.* myln, wind-mylne, banke. Bryant, 1831, shows a windmill here.   MILL BROOK (> Keys Brook 1 30), *v.* myln, brōc, cf. Tattenhall Mill *supra*.   NEWTON (FM), *v.* Newton 96 *supra*.   NEWTOWN, *v.* nīwe, toun.   OAK-FIELD FM.   OAKSGATE, 1842 OS, *Oakes-Gate-House* 1702 *AddCh*, *Oak Gate Farm* 1831 Bry, 'gateway near oak-trees', *v.* āc, geat. This is on the boundary of Bolesworth 14 *supra*.   OWLER HALL, *v.* alor.   PLATTS LANE, 1831 Bry, from plat[1] 'a footbridge'.   THE RIGHI, a house, perhaps named after the Swiss mountain *Rigi* near Lucerne.   ROCKY LANE, *v.* rokky.   THE ROOKERY, *Bank House* 1842 OS, 1860 White, *v.* banke.   SHARPLINGS HOLE, *Sharplin Old House* 1842 ib. *Hole* (*v.* hol[1]) is here used in its col-loquial sense, 'a miserable dwelling'.   SQUAREHOUSE FM, *v.* squar(e).   WELL BRIDGE.   WHITEHEAD FM.   WHITENING

FM. WINDMILL FM, *Windmill House* 1842 OS. WOOD-
HOUSE FM, *v.* wudu, hūs. WOODLAKE FM, 1831 Bry, 'watercourse at a wood', *v.* wudu, lacu. WOODSFIN LANE, probably
'marsh at a wood', from wudu and fenn, but the origin could be OE
wudu-fīn 'a wood-heap', *v.* fīn. WORLEYBANK, 1842 OS. YEW-
TREE FM, *Yewtree House* 1831 Bry, cf. *Yew Tree Lane* 1831 Bry.

FIELD-NAMES

The undated forms are 1838 *TA* 385. Of the others 1272–1307 is *AddCh*,
1549, 1595, 1633, 1635, 1672, 1751 Sheaf, 1554 ChRR, 1601, 1603, 1607,
1649, 1652, 1654 Cre, 1656 Orm², 1691, 1694 *Corp*, 1831 Bry, 1842 OS.

(*a*) The Acre; Baughs Fd; Birchalls; Broad Fd; Broom Pit Mdw (*v.*
brōm, pytt); China Mdw; Chowley Oak Fd (*v.* 84 *supra*); Church Fd;
Big & Little Close; Cobbers Croft Mdw; Cockerly (*v.* cocker, lēah); The
Commons; Coppies (*v.* copis); Cordy Hill (*the Caudivall Hill* 1691, *Caudwall
Hill* 1694, 'cold-spring hill', from cald and wælla, with hyll); Cow Acre &
Hay (*v.* (ge)hæg); Ditch Fd; Drain Fd (cf. *The Drain* 1831, a watercourse,
v. drain); Drumbo (*v.* drumble); Duns Fd; Filkins Lands; Flack Mdw,
Flacker Fd (*the Middle Flackermeadow* 1649, perhaps from flak 'turf', with
an occupational-name derivative *flakere* 'a turf-cutter', but an alternative
origin is suggested by Professor Löfvenberg, ME *flake* a side-form of *fleke*
'a hurdle', and ME **flakere* 'one who makes *flakes*, i.e. wattle hurdles',
cf. *flekeman, flekewynder* Fransson 172); The Flash 1831 (*v.* flasshe); Flooding
Mdw; Four Lane Ends 1831 (109–512893); Giants Mdw; Goose Acre;
Gravel Hole Fd; Big & Little Groves (*v.* grāf); Gullet Lane (*v.* golet);
Hatch Fd (*v.* hæc(c)); Big & Little Hays (*v.* (ge)hæg); House Fd; How Hill
(*v.* hōh); Intake (*v.* inntak); Big & Little Irons (*v.* hyrne); Kay's-, Keys
Brook Fd (*v.* Keys Brook 1 30); Ladies Croft; Leeches Fd (cf. *Leche Croft*
1554, *v.* lece); Litchfield (*v.* lece); Lithwood; Marl Fd (cf. *the two Old
Marle Fields* 1649, *v.* marle); Marsh Croft; Milking Bank (*v.* milking);
Moat Mdw; Moss Hay (*the Mossehey* 1601, cf. *Mosseley* 1601, 1607, *le
Mosseley* 1652, *v.* mos, (ge)hæg, lēah); Muck Fd; The New Comes; Oak Car
(*v.* āc, kjarr); Old Fd; Ollery (*v.* alor); Penny Croft (*v.* peni(n)g); The
Pickers; Pingo (*v.* pingel); Pool Head ('top end of a pool', *v.* pōl¹, hēafod);
Pringle; Quillet Lane Fd (*v.* quillet(t)); Riddings (*v.* ryding); Roodee
(perhaps named after the well-known Roodee in Chester 337 *infra*, but not
topographically similar, hence more probably a f.n. meaning 'enclosure
at a clearing' from rod¹ and (ge)hæg, influenced by the form of the more
famous Roodee); Rough Hay (*the-* 1601, *the Roghe Hey* 1549, *the Roughey*
1633, *Rowehey* 1652, *v.* rūh, (ge)hæg); Round Hill(s) ((*the*) *Round Hill* 1691,
1694, *v.* rond, hyll); The Scenes; Sheep Coat Fd (*v.* scēp, cot); Long Shoot
(*v.* scēat); Slang (*v.* slang); Stock Ridding (*v.* stocc, ryding); Tattenhall
Nook (*v.* nōk); Town Fd (*Town Fields* 1751); Wall Cross ('cross at a well',
v. wælla, cros); Wet Reans (*v.* rein); Wicket (*v.* wiket); Willmoor Fd
(probably 'wild marsh', from wilde and mōr¹); Woodfires Fd.

(b) *the Cleys* 1656 (*v.* clǽg); *the Holemill Meadow* 1633 ('mill meadow in a hollow', *v.* hol², myln, mǽd); *the Meydow Field* 1595 (*v.* mǽd); *the Common Pound or Pinfold* 1603 (*v.* pund, pynd-fald); *le Redeclowis* 1272–1307 ('the red hollows', *v.* rēad, clōh); *the Ston(er)y Feelds* 1635, *the Stonery Fields* 1672 ('fields where stones are got', *v.* stonery, cf. stanry).

xiv. Waverton

Waverton parish contained the townships 1. Hatton, 2. Huxley, 3. Waverton.

1. HATTON (HALL) (109–4761)

> *Etone* 1086 DB f.267b, *Hetone* 1096–1101 (1280) Chest
> *Hottone* 1096–1101 (1150), 1150 Chest I 3, 56
> *Hettun* 1185 Facs (p)
> *Hatton* 1249–65 Chest *et freq,* (lit. *Hacton* 1300, 1315 Plea) with variant spellings *-tun, -tona; (-iuxta Goldburn)* 1289 Court, *(-Huxlegh)* 1331 Plea, *(-Waverton)* 1539 (1564) ChRR, *Hatton Hall* 1724 NotCestr

'Farm at a heath', from hǣð and tūn, with hall, cf. Hatton Heath *infra*. Hatton adjoins Golborne Bellow *&* David 95, 88 *supra*, Huxley and Waverton 101, 103 *infra*. The identification of the DB form rests on the argument in Tait 205 n.210. On formal grounds Ormerod proposed Eaton 148 *infra*, and Beamont proposed Eaton near Tarporley, 3 289, but the form *Etone* arises from loss of initial *h-* before a vowel, an Anglo-Norman feature (cf. Feilitzen 119), the true form appearing as *Hetone* 1096–1101 (1280) Chest. The form *Hottone* in fourteenth-century copies is almost certainly a misreading of *Hettone*, cf. Facs p. 12.

CROW'S NEST COTTAGE, cf. *Crow Nest Meadow* 1838 *TA*, *v.* Crow's Nest Bridge 96 *supra*.   FISHPOND FM, 1831 Bry.   GOLDEN NOOK (BRIDGE), *Golden Nook Bridge* 1831 ib, *Golden Hook* 1842 OS, *Goulden Nook* 1860 White, cf. *Great & Little Golden Nook* 1838 *TA*, probably 'corner where marigolds grow', *v.* golden, nōk, hōc. HATTON FM, *Billams Heath* 1831 Bry, cf. *Billams Heath Field* 104 *infra*.   HATTON HEATH, *v.* 122 *infra*, cf. Hatton *supra*.   LAKE FM, cf. *Lake Field* 1838 *TA*, *v.* lacu.   LONG LANE, cf. *Long Lane Croft* 1838 ib, *v.* lang, lane.   NIXON'S BRIDGE, *Bebingtons Bridge* 1831 Bry, a bridge on the Shropshire Union Canal.   OAK FM. POPLARHALL FM, *Fishers Farm* 1831 Bry.   RED LANE, *v.* 102 *infra*.   TATTENHALL RD, *v.* 97 *supra*.

FIELD-NAMES

The undated forms are 1838 *TA* 197. Of the others, 1692 is *BW*, 1700 *Chol*, 1743 Sheaf, and 1831 Bry.

(*a*) Bakehouse Croft; Boors Croft (*v.* bār[2] or (ge)būr); Great & Little Bottoms (*Great Bottoms* 1700, *v.* botm); Briny Wd; Burnt Yards (1700, *v.* brende[2], geard); Cassia Fd (cf. Cassia Green **3** 182); Cow Hay, -Hey (*v.* (ge)hæg); Crib (*v.* crib); Cross Fd, Cross Lane Head, Cross Wd (*v.* cros); Dig Lake (*v.* dīc, lacu); Drunken Croft (*v.* 336 *infra*); Farrows Fd; Foot Hill Croft; Hatton's Hey Wd 1743 (*v.* (ge)hæg, wudu); Hoolands Croft; Horse Coppy (*the Horse Coppice* 1692, *v.* copis); Intake (*v.* inntak); Kiln Yards (*v.* cyln, geard); Marl Fd; Milking Bank Fd (*v.* milking); Nandee; Newton Hay (*v.* (ge)hæg, cf. Newton 96 *supra*); Nickers Fd; Old Yards (*v.* geard); One Shilling Croft (*v.* scilling, cf. 337 *infra*); Pale Croft (*v.* pale); Pan Pot Hay & Mdw; Parsons Hay (*v.* persone, (ge)hæg); Reading Fd (*v.* ryding); Rhodes's Croft (*Rodes Croft* 1700, from the surname *Rhodes*); (Big & Little) Robins Wd (*Great & Little Roberts Wood* 1700, from the ME pers.n. *Robert*, diminutive *Robin*, and wudu); Shooting Butt Lane; Swine Pale (1700, *v.* swin[1], pale); Three Nooks (*v.* þrēo, nōk, cf. three-nooked); Toothill Croft 1700 (*v.* tōt-hyll); Great & Little Town Fd (*Great Towne Field* 1700); Way Fd (*v.* weg); White Hay (*v.* hwīt, (ge)hæg); Within Croft & Hay (*v.* wiðegn); Woods Croft, Wood Fd (cf. *Woods Lane* 1831).

2. HUXLEY (BRIDGE, GORSE (FM), GREEN & LANE (FM)), HIGHER & LOWER HUXLEY HALL & MILL (109–5061)

Huslehe 1185 Facs (p), *Huseley* 1489 ChRR (p)

Huxelehe 1202–29 *BW* (p), -*leg*(*h*) 1260 Court (p), 1267 (1285) Ch (p), Chest (p) *et freq* with variant spellings -*l'*, -*ley*(*e*) to 1363 ChRR (p), *Huxileg'* 1329 AD (p)

Huxleg' 1260 Court (p), *Huxley* 1271–4 Chest (p) *et freq* with variant spellings -*legh*, -*leyg*, -*le*(*e*), -*ly*, -*leighe*, -*lay*; -*Greens* 1671 Sheaf, -*Hall* 1724 NotCestr, *Lower Huxley Hall* 1819 Orm[2], *Huxley Gorse, Green & (Lower) Mill, The Lanes* 1831 Bry, *Huxley Lane, Higher & Lower Hall* 1842 OS

Hoxeleg' 1260 Court (p), 1279 Chest (p), 1306 *Chol*, *Hoxel'* 1279 Chest, -*legh* 1279 Orm[2], *Hoxl'* 1265–76 Chest (p), *Hoxlegh* 1313 MidCh (p)

Houxseleyg' 1274 *Chol* (p)

Huxclyve 1281 Court (p)

Huckysley 1284 Ipm (p)

Hukele 1301 (1344) Pat (p)

Hokesley 1485 Orm[2]

The final el. is lēah 'a glade', with **brycg, gorst, grēne**[2], **hall, lane**, and **myln**. Ekwall (DEPN) recognises the unsatisfactory evidence of his material for the first el., and tentatively suggests the OE pers.n. *Hōc* (gen.sg. *-es*). On formal grounds Barnes[1] 285 suggests either an OE pers.n. *Huc*, or *hūc* 'a river bend'. At Huxley the R. Gowy turns northward, but the change of direction is not so sudden as to form a remarkable topographical feature. The first el. is probably an OE pers.n. **Hucc*, cf. **Hucca* in Hucklow Db 131, Hucknall Db 268. However, the spellings indicate that this p.n. could be from OE *husc, hucs, hux* (gen.sg. *-es*, gen.pl. *-a*), ME *hux*, 'insult, ignominy, scorn, mockery, scoffing, a taunt' (BT, BTSuppl, NED). It would be of a kind with p.ns. in **beadu, bismer, (ge)flit, mandrēam, strūt, þrēap** (*v.* EPN, WRY 7 159), in which a human emotional state, activity or response is part of the name. Huxley would mean 'woodland or glade where ignominy is offered or suffered', alluding either to some social activity here, or to some inhospitable feature of the ground which made a mockery of inhabitation or cultivation. Huxley gave name to Southley Brook *infra*.

BROOK FM & Ho, named from Southley Brook *infra*, *v.* **brōc**. BROOK HOLE, *Brockholes* 1831 Bry, *Brook Holes* 1838 *TA*, cf. 96 *supra*, and *Brock Holes Moore* 1692 BW, 'badger holes', *v.* **brocc, hol**[1], **mōr**[1]. CROW'S NEST GORSE, *v.* **gorst**, Crow's Nest Bridge 96 *supra*. DODESTON HO, an antiquarian allusion to the old hundred-name *Dudestan* 1 *supra*. ELMTREE FM. GREEN-FIELD COTTAGE, cf. *Green Field* 1838 *TA*, *v.* **grēne**[1], **feld**. HARGRAVE FM, *Stubs Farm* 1831 Bry, *Hargrave Stubbs* 1842 OS, cf. *Hargreave Field* 1838 *TA* v. Hargrave 105 *infra*. The farm adjoins the site of *The Stubs* 1831 Bry in Hargrave. LEADGATE FM, *Leg Gate Farm* 1831 ib, *Lead Gate* 1842 OS, *v.* **hlid-geat**. LOWER FM. POOLBANK FM, *Pool Bank* 1831 Bry, *v.* **pōl**[1], **banke**. RED LANE, 1831 ib, *v.* **rēad** 'red'. SOUTHLEY BROOK (R. Gowy), 1842 OS, *Huxleghbrok* 1331 Orm[2], *Huxley Brook* 1671 Sheaf, *v.* **brōc**, cf. Huxley *supra*, Southley *infra*. WILLIAMSON'S BRIDGE. WOODLAND COTTAGE.

FIELD-NAMES

The undated forms are 1838 *TA* 216. Of the others, 1330 is Plea, 1476, 1588, 1613 ChRR, 1482 *Chol*, 1486, 1488 *MinAcct*, 1671 Sheaf, 1692 *BW*, 1842 OS.

(a) Barn Hey (v. (ge)hæg); Beancroft 1692; Bickenfield 1692; Biskenwood 1692 (perhaps byxen 'growing with box'); By Flatts 1692 (v. byge[1], flat); Calvers Croft (the Colvercroft 1692, 'calves' croft', v. calf (gen.pl. calfra), croft); The Claugh (v. clōh); Clemley Park (cf. Clemley 3 47); Cockshut (Le Cokeshete 1330, the Cockshoot 1692, v. cocc-scyte); Coppy (v. copis); Crookings (v. krókr, -ing[1]); Dovehouse Fd (v. dove-house); Dracoe 1692; Big- & Little Eddish (the Eddish 1692, v. edisc); Ess Moor; Big-, Middle & Near Filkins; Gate Fd (v. gata); Golden Knowl (v. golden, cnoll); Old Grass Fd (v. gærs); Higgins Hey; Hollinhurst (1692, v. holegn, hyrst); Hob Fd (v. hobbe); Hough Fd 1692 (v. hōh); Jacks Mdw (v. jack); Joans Fd (Johnesfield 1588, cf. John's Medo 1482, Johannis Mede 1486, 1488, 'John's field and meadow', from the ME pers.n. John and mæd, feld); Joy Croft 1692; Big & Little Ladys Heys (the Litle Ladye Hey 1613, v. hlæfdige, (ge)hæg); Lane Stead (v. lane, stede); Lea Wood 1692 (v. lēah); Long Heys (v. (ge)hæg); Long Moor & Shoot (v. mōr[1], scēat); Milking Bank Fd (v. milking); Mill Croft, Fd, Mdw & Moor (cf. the two Mill Meadows 1692, Mill Lane 1842, v. myln); Ollery Mdw (v. alor, mæd); Ox Hey (v. (ge)hæg); Pinfold Yard (v. pynd-fald, geard); Pingle (v. pingel); Pingot (v. pingot); Rough Fd; Running Brook 1671; Big & Little Scotch; Further-, Little- & Near Southley (Little Southley 1692, 'south clearing', v. sūð, lēah, cf. Southley Brook supra); Strong Mdw (v. strang); Town Fd (The Town Field Meadow 1692); White Hey (v. hwīt, (ge)hæg); Wood Fd.

(b) Chayneslond 1476 ('land belonging to the Cheyney family', from the surname Cheyney (cf. Cheney Hall 3 39) and land).

3. WAVERTON (109–4663) ['weivǝrtǝn] older local ['waːrtǝn]

   Wavretone 1086 DB, Waveretone 1096–1101 (1150) Chest, -tona 1150 ib, Wavertone 1096–1101 (1280) ib, -tona 1271–4 ib (p), -tun 1185 Facs, 1248 Chest (p), -ton 1188–91, 1249–65 ib, 1260 Court et freq with variant spelling Wavir-; (-iuxta Stapilford) 1281 Court, (-iuxta Hatton) 1315 Plea (lit. Hacton), 1319 ib et freq
   Weverton 1272–1307 Orm[2]
   Waruerton 1325 Chol (p)
   Warton 1363 ChRR, 1386 Sheaf, 1502 Plea, 1620, 1671, 1690 Sheaf, Wareton 1475 Outl, 1595 ChRR, Wharton 1646 Sheaf, Waverton vulgo Warton 1671 ib

'Farm by a swaying tree', v. wæfre, tūn, cf. Wharton 2 213, with which this p.n. is sometimes confused, e.g. in 1281 'the defendants said there were two Wavertons and claimed to know which was intended', Court 35. It is confused with Weaverham 3 205, in Hatton Church by Waverham 17 (1724) NotCestr, v. ChetOS VIII 362.

AVENUE FM.   BLACK DOG FM, cf. Black Dog 1831 Bry, the public

house nearby. BROOKDALE FM, cf. Guylane Brook *infra*, *v.*
brōc, dæl[1]. CHURCH HO. COMMON FM, cf. *Common Field*
1837 *TA*, *v.* commun. DAVIES' BRIDGE, *Deans Bridge* 1831 Bry,
cf. *Davies's Croft, Deans Headland Fens* 1837 *TA*, from the surnames
Davies and *Dean*, with brycg, croft, hēafod-land, and fenn. EGG
BRIDGE (LANE), *Egg Bridge* 1831 Bry, a bridge over the Shropshire
Union Canal. The origin of *Egg* is unknown. FAULKNER'S
BRIDGE, *Falkners Bridge* 1831 ib. FOXES LANE. GUY LANE
(FM), *Guy Lane* 1831 Bry (109–457643 to 482648), leading to R.
Gowy, 1 xxi, 27, at Ford Bridge 106 *infra*, and probably named from
that river with lane. The form has been confused with ModEdial.
guy 'a guide', cf. foll. and Guy Lake *infra*. GUYLANE BROOK (R.
Gowy, 109–465632 to 481648), *Guy Lane Brook* 1842 OS, *v.* brōc,
cf. prec. LONG LANE (109–462633 to 480617), 1837 *TA*, *v.*
lang, lane. MARTIN'S LANE, *v.* 106 *infra*. MILNER'S HEATH,
Millers Heath 1837 ib, 1842 OS, cf. *the Wynde Mylne in Wareton*
1595 Sheaf, *Waverton Mill, Waverton Wyende Mill Lane* 1671 Sheaf
(lit. *Mylnde Mill*), from wind-milne, myln, lane, hǣð and the occupational name mylnere 'a miller', cf. *Mullenerds Tenement* 1649 Cre,
Milliners- 1654 ib. THE MOUNT, cf. *Mount Oaks* 1837 *TA*, *v.*
munt. QUARRY COTTAGE, cf. *Quarry House* 1831 Bry, *v.* quarriere.
SALMON'S BRIDGE, *Dulton's Bridge* 1831 Bry, a canal bridge.
WAVERTON GORSE, *v.* gorst. WELLHOUSE FM.

FIELD-NAMES

The undated forms are 1837 *TA* 415. Of the others 1270 (1648) is *Sotheby*,
and 1831 Bry.

(a) Arland Fens; Billams Heath Fd (*v.* Hatton Fm 100 *supra*); Bradmoor
(*v.* brād, mōr[1]); Clay Croft & Fd (cf. *le Claforlong* 1270 (1648), *v.* clǣg,
furlang); Cotton Hook Croft & Fd (*v.* hōc, cf. Cotton Abbotts 111 *infra*);
Cow Hay (*v.* (ge)hæg); Cribb (*v.* crib); Crooked Loons (*v.* croked, land);
Green Loon Gorse (-*Loons-* 1831, cf. Greenlooms 106 *infra*); Guy Lake
(*v.* lacu 'a watercourse', cf. Guy Lane *supra*); Hargreave Gate & Mdw
(*v.* gata 'a cow-pasture', cf. Hargrave 105 *infra*); Knowles (*v.* cnoll); Mill
Hay & Such (*v.* (ge)hæg, *sic*); Moulding Hay; Oldfield Croft; Outlet (*v.*
outlet); Ox Croft; Pool Head (*v.* pōl[1], hēafod); Quillet (*v.* quillet(t)); Sand
Dale (*v.* sand, dæl[1]); Townfield; Wall Dale (*v.* wælla, dæl[1]); The Way Fd.

xv. Tarvin

The rest of Tarvin parish, including Bruen Stapleford, was in Eddisbury Hundred *v.* 3 268. In DB, both the Staplefords were included in *Stapleford* in *Dudestan* (Broxton) Hundred, from which it appears that this manor was divided at the re-organization of the Cheshire hundreds, cf. 1 *supra*.

11. FOULK STAPLEFORD (109–4863) ['fouk 'steipəlfəd]

Stapelford iuxta Haregrave 1287 Court
Fouk Stapelford 1288 Court, and thereafter with spellings as for
  Stapleford *infra* and *Fouk-* 1288 Court to 1523 Plea, *-Fuke* 1289
  Court, *-Fulk, Fulk-* 1307 *Eyre*, 1563 ChRR, *Fouky-* 1307 *Eyre*,
  -Fulke, Fulke- 1314 ChRR, 1426 (17) Orm², *Fouke-* 1320 Plea
  et freq to 1538 ChRR, *Fowke-* 1395 ib to 1599 Orm², *-Foulk,*
  Foulk- 1411, 1619 ChRR, *Fork-* 1471 *MinAcct, Fuk-* 1486 *ib*,
  Fuck- 1563 Orm², *Fowk-* 1646 Sheaf, *Feulk-* 1663 ib, *Foulke-*
  1671 ib, 1697 *AddCh, Foul-* or *Foulk-* 1724 NotCestr
Fouk Stapelton 1354 BPR
'Fulco's moiety of Stapleford', from the OG pers.n. *Fulco*, named
after *Fulco* de Orreby (Justice of Chester 1259–60) who held half of
Stapleford in 1243 and 1260, Orm² II 802, Sheaf³ 19 (4514), 20
(4711), Court 18. Cf. Stapleford *infra*, Bruen Stapleford 3 269.

STAPLEFORD, BRUEN- & FOULK-

Stapleford 1086 DB, 1243 (17) Sheaf, 1335 ChRR *et freq, -forde*
  1404 (1581), 1538 ib, *Stappleforde* 1539 Sheaf
Stapelford 1190 Orm², e13 Whall, Dieul, 1219 *BW et freq* with
  variant spellings *-forde, -fort, Stapil-, -ul-, -yl-, -ele-, Stappel-,*
  Stapple- to 1599 Orm²
Stepelford c.1219 *BW*
(*Fouk*)*-Stapelton* 1354 BPR
Stableford 1632, 1646, 1691, 1719, 1783 Sheaf, 1697 *AddCh*

'Ford marked by a pillar', *v.* stapol, ford, cf. Ford Bridge *infra*.
There is one instance of an alternative name 'farmstead by a pillar',
from stapol and tūn.

HARGRAVE (109–485623), HARGRAVE (OLD) HALL, HARGRAVE STUBBS
(lost, 109–487621) & HARGRAVE FM (102 *supra*)

le Haregreve e13 Orm² (p), *Haregreve* 1285 Court (p), *Hargreve*
  l13 Orm² (p) *et freq* with variant spellings *Hare-* (to 1545 Plea),
  -grave (from 1287 Court, 1339 *BW*), *-greave, -greeve, -greaves;*

Heregreue 1304 Chamb, *Hardegrave* 1407 Cl (p), *Hard-* 1646
Sheaf, *Hergreff* 1549 *Surv*
Haregreve Stubbes 1533 Plea, thereafter with spellings as above and
-*Stubb(e)s* to *Hargrave Stubbs* 1842 OS, *The Stubs, Stubs Farm*
1831 Bry
Old Hall 1831 Bry, *Hargrave Hall* 1842 OS

'The hoar wood' or 'the hare-wood' from hār² or hara, and
græfe. This is the location of a parochial chapel of Tarvin parish,
Hargrave Chapel 1831 Bry, *Hargrave Stubbs Chapel* 17 (1724)
NotCestr, *v.* chapel, cf. Sheaf³ 48 (9707). Presumably *capella de
Stapelford* 1222 *BW* refers to a domestic chapel. *The Stubs* is mapped
as woodland in Bryant's map, 'place full of tree stubs', *v.* stubb,
presumably the remains of the 'hoar wood', and gave name to Hargrave Fm 102 *supra. Hargrave Ford* 1671 Sheaf was probably the
ford shown in Bryant's map at 109–492628, *v.* ford. *v.* Addenda.

ABBEYDALE HO.   (UPPER) BRERETON PARK FM, *Brereton Park Farms*
1831 Bry, cf. *Brereton Park* 1815 Sheaf, 1819 Orm², Park Lane
infra, and foll., named from *Stapleforde Park(e)* 1484–5 ChRR,
Orm², held by Sir William Brereton (Orm² II 803), *v.* park.   UPPER
BROOKHOUSE FM, *Brereton Park* 1842 OS, cf. prec. and Brookhouse
Fm 3 270.   CHURCH FM, named from the parochial chapel at
Hargrave *supra.*   COW LANE, *Cow Pad* 1838 *TA,* 'path along
which cows are driven', *v.* cū, pæð (dial. *pad*), lane.   FORD
BRIDGE & FM, *The Ford* 1831 Bry (109–483648), cf. *Ford Meadow*
1838 *TA* 77 (Bruen Stapleford), probably the ford which gave name
to Stapleford *supra.*   GREENLOOMS, 1842 OS, -*Loomes* 1709
Sheaf, *Green Looms Common* 1831 Bry, *Green Loons* 1838 *TA,* cf.
Green Loon Gorse 104 *supra,* 'green selions', *v.* grēne¹, loom, land.
GUY LANE, *v.* 104 *supra.*   MARTIN'S LANE, 1842 OS, *Martin
Lane* 1831 Bry.   MEADOW FM.   PARK LANE, 1842 OS, cf.
Brereton Park *supra.*   STAPLEFORD MILL, 1831 Bry.   WALK
MILL, 1787 *BW,* 'fulling-mill', *v.* walke-milne.   WATERLESS
WOOD, *Burton Covert* 1831 Bry, cf. Burton 3 270, later named from
Waterless Brook² 1 37, itself derived from *Watleys* 1838 *TA* (109–
505635), *Whatelegh* 1362 BPR, -*lee* 1443 ChRR, *Whatlegh* 1426 ib,
-*lee* 1426 (17) Orm², -*ley* 1468 *MinAcct,* 1513 ChRR, 'wheat clear-
ing', *v.* hwǣte, lēah. The brook is not waterless, but *Watleys Brook*
may well have become *Waterless Brook.*

FIELD-NAMES

The undated forms are 1838 *TA* 170. Of the others, 1356 is Plea, 1362 ChRR, and the rest *BW*.

(a) Birchall (*v* birce, halh); Bridge Butts 1704 (*v.* butte); Buckley Park (*v.* park); Burn Wd; Carters Flatt 1704; Chapel Fd; Big Cow Hey (*Great & Little Cow Hay* 1692, *v.* (ge)hæg); The Crigoes 1704; North-, East- & West Crimes (*v.* cryme, cf. *le Crymbe* 2 171); Daisy Bank; Doctors Yard; The Dunstead 1704 (cf. *terra vocata Tunstall* 1219, *v.* tūn-stall, tūn-stede); Flatt Loondes 1704 (*v.* flatr, land); Hemp Yard (*v.* hemp-yard); Hoolfield (*v.* hol², feld); Knowles (*v.* cnoll); Lower Leys 1704 (*v.* ley); Milking Bank (*v.* milking); The Moss 1704; Nook Piece; Ox Fd; Pavement Hey (109–482639) (-*Hay* 1692, *v.* pavement); Peaks Moor (*Peakes Moore* 1692); Pinkers Parks (*v.* park); Red Mdw; Rogerson's Tenement 1787 (*v.* tenement); Round Mdw 1704; Slack Fd (*v.* slakki); Sychfield 1704 (*v.* sīc); Tapley Hill Mdw 1704; Three Week Croft; Tintry Mdw (*v.* tentour); Wall Croft 1704; Watleys (*v.* Waterless Wood *supra*); Willies Park; Wimpole Mdw; Worral Fd.

(b) Berecroft 1202–29 ('barley croft', *v.* bere, croft); *le Dounes* 1318, *Wrennowes Meadows, Wrennowes Ground alias William Molson's house* 1572 ('the hills', *v.* dūn. The later name contains the Welsh pers.n. *G(o)ronwy, Grono*, after *Wronou* de Stapleford c.1300 *BW* whose daughter Agnes owned *le Dounes* in 1318); *Elyasmor & Medewe* 1356 ('Elias's marsh and meadow' from the ME pers.n. *Elias* and mōr¹, mæd); *Linde* 1202–29 ('a lime tree', *v.* lind); *Shattelegh* 1362 ('clearing at a corner of land', *v.* scēata, lēah).

xvi. Christleton

The ecclesiastical parish of Christleton contained the townships 1. Christleton, 2. Cotton Abbotts, 3. Cotton Edmunds, 4. Littleton, 5. Rowton.

1. CHRISTLETON (109–4465) ['krɪsltən] older local ['krɪslɪtn̩]

Cristetone 1086 DB

Cristentune 1096–1101 (1280), 1150 Chest, -*tona* 1121–29 (1150), 1150, c.1311 ib

Cristelton 1157–97 Chest *et freq* with variant spellings C(h)rist-, C(h)rystel-, -il-, -ele-, -yl-, -ul-, -ton(a), -tone, -tun to 1653 Sheaf

Christletona 12 Tab, *Christleton* 1200–50, 1257 (17), 1281 (17) Chest, 1410 ChRR, 1579 Dugd *et freq* with variant spelling *Cristleton* (1280 P to 1584 ChRR)

Cristeuton c.1160 (1400) CASNS XIII

Hamcristilton 1200–50 Chest, 1301–6 *AddCh*, *Hom-* 1290 Ipm,

Hamcristelton' 1296 *Vern,* Home- 1317 Plea, 1318 *AddCh,*
Hom *Cristulton'* 1343 *Vern*
Cristutona 13 *Bun* (p)
Magna Cristulton 13 *Vern,* Great *Cristelton* c.1279 AD, *Magna-*
1324 Plea
Christ' e13 Chest
Cristerton 1251–5 Dieul
Kirkecristelton 1289 Court, and thereafter with spellings as for
Christleton, and *Chirch*(e)- 1298 Plea to 1492 ib, *Church*(e)-
1348 MidCh to 1625 ChRR
Cresteltun 1303 *Port* (p), *-ton* 1472 ChRR, *-il-* 1309 Ipm (p)
Chrisilton c.1480 Sheaf, *Chrisleton* 1570 ChRR, 1646 Sheaf, 1724
NotCestr, *Chrisel-* 1685 Sheaf, *Crissle-* 1721 *BW*
Kysterton 1539 Orm², *Chisterton* 1719 Sheaf
Kerselton alias Christleton 1541 Dugd
Kyrsylton 1549 Sheaf
Kyrstelton alias Cristelton 1553 Pat
Chrislington 1620, 1646, 1723 Sheaf, *Crislington* 1668 ib, *Christ-*
lington 1672 ib, 1750 Orm², 1792 *BW*
Cristlenton 1644 Sheaf
Christliton 1662 Sheaf

'Christian, or the Christians', enclosure or farm', *v.* cristen, tūn.
v. Addenda. Christleton is in three parts, cf. Littleton and
Rowton 113, 114 *infra.* The church-hamlet was distinguished by the
affixes *Church-* (*v.* cirice, kirkja), *Magna-, Great-* (*v.* grēat, magna)
and *Ham-, Hom*(e)-. The latter prefix is from hām, cf. home in the
adjectival sense 'home' to distinguish the 'home' part of the manor
and parish, the main hamlet near the church, from the dependent
hamlets of Littleton or Rowton. Cf. Great Sutton 193 *infra,* Oldfield
2 20.

STAMFORD BRIDGE (109–466673), STAMFORD HEATH (FM), STAM-
FORDHOLLOWS FM & STAMFORD LODGE, also STAMFORD MILL 112
infra.

molendinum de Staneford 1188–91 Chest
pons de Stanford 1190–1211 *Cott* Nero C III, c.1200 Dugd, *Stann-*
ford 1262 *JRC* (p), *Stanforde* 1288 Court (p), *Stanford* 1303
Chamb (p) *et freq* to 1724 NotCestr, (*-iuxta Cristelton*) 1343
Orm², *Stanford*(e)*brugg*(e) 1321 City, 1354 (1379) Ch, 1440

Rental, -Brigge 1355 (15) Sheaf, 1499 Orm[2], *-Bridge* 115 Orm[2],
1643 ib *et freq* to 1842 OS, *Stanforbrugge* 1396 ChRR, *molen-*
dinum aquaticum de Stanford 1398 *Add*, 1440 *Rental, pons de*
Stanfford 1454 ChRR, *Stanford Mill* 1579 Dugd, 1842 OS,
Stanford Heath 1842 ib
Stamfordia, c.1271–79 AD (p), *Stamford* 1376 *Eyre* (p), 1546
Dugd, *-forde* 1553 Pat, *Stamford Bridge* 1558 Sheaf, 1831 Bry,
Stamford Heath 1794 *EnclA*, (*-Farm(s)*) 1831 Bry, *Stamford*
Mill 1794 *EnclA*, 1831 Bry
Staunford 1317 Cl (p), *pons de Staunfford* 1454 ChRR, *Staunforde*
Myll 1593 *Vern*
Stampford Mille 1539 Orm[2], m16 *AOMB* 397
Standford Bridge 1667 *Chol*, 1724 NotCestr

'Stony ford' or 'stone-paved ford', from **stān** or **stǣnen** and
ford, with **myln, brycg, hǣð, holh** and **loge**. The mill is in Cotton
Edmunds. The ford carried 'Watling Street' *infra* over R. Gowy.

ABBOT'S WELL (109–433656), cf. *le Wellefeld* 1296 *Vern, the Abbots*
Walefield 1641 Sheaf, *Well Field* (5x), *Wall Field* 1844 *TA, the*
Well Fields 1878 Sheaf, cf. *Abbot(t)s Wel(d)s Feilds* 1653, 1675
Corp (belonging to Great Boughton), 'the abbot's well', *v.* **abbat,**
wella, wælla. This is named from the abbot of Chester, and is the
'spring of water in the field of Christleton', from which a conduit was
led to the abbey in 1282–3 (*v.* Chest I 340–342, Pat 75, Orm[2] II
778, and Burne[2] 40). It is not apparent whether this is the same
spring as *St Winifred's Well* 1700 Sheaf[3] 3 (497), which may, however, refer to the famous shrine at Holywell Fl. BIRCHBANK FM,
v. **birce, banke.** BIRCH HEATH (LANE), *Birch Heath* 1794 *EnclA*,
(*-Farm*) 1831 Bry, *v.* **birce, hǣð.** BROWN HEATH, 1719 Sheaf, *v.*
brūn[1], hǣð. BUSH FM. CHRISTLETON BANK & HALL, *Christle-*
ton Bank, The Hall 1860 White, *v.* **banke, hall.** FINISFIELD
COTTAGE, cf. *Finish-, Finnis Field* 1844 *TA*, probably 'field full of
fin-grass', *v.* **finn, -isc.** GREEN LANE, *v.* **grēne[1], lane.** HEATH-
FIELD HO. HOLLOW FM, cf. *Stamfordhollows Fm supra, v.* **holh.**
LANESIDE, 1831 Bry, *v.* **lane, sīde.** LITTLE HEATH, 1794 *EnclA*,
v. **lȳtel, hǣð.** MILL LANE, *Stamford Mill Road* 1794 *ib*, cf.
Stamford Mill 112 *infra*. OLD HALL, *Christleton Hall* 1831 Bry.
PLOUGH LANE, 1831 ib, *Hockenhull Platt Road* 1794 *EnclA*, cf.
Hockenhull Platts 3 274. The modern name appears to be from a

public house.   QUARRY BRIDGE, 1831 Bry, *v.* quarriere.   RAKE
LANE, *The Rake* 1844 *TA*, *v.* rake.   ROWTON BRIDGE, a canal
bridge, cf. Rowton 114 *infra*.   STREET WAY (109–436655 to
440652), 1842 OS, *Streetway Hill* 1692 *BW*, *Straight-*, *Streetway
Hill* 1844 *TA*, 'paved road', *v.* strǣt, weg, hyll. This is part of the
Chester-Whitchurch road, *v.* 1 42, 48 (Routes VIII, XXIV).   'WAT-
LING STREET', *v.* 1 40 (Route VII).   WHITE GATE FM.   WOOD-
BANK, *v.* wudu, banke.

FIELD-NAMES

The undated forms are 1844 *TA* 113. Of the others, 13, 1296, 1547, 1625,
1629, 1649 are *Vern*, 1536 Orm², 1613 ChRR, 1641, 1700, 1725, 1749, 1914
Sheaf, 1646, 1664 *Corp*, 1692 *BW*, 1794 *EnclA*, 1831 Bry, 1842 OS.

(a) Angel Fd; Badgeret; Bath Fd (*v.* bæð); Bentheath Fd (*v.* beonet, hǣð);
Boughton Ditch (*v.* dīc, cf. Great Boughton 123 *infra*); Burk; Bythom
(*v.* byðme); Caldeshoot (cf. Caldy Shoots 115 *infra*); Clomley Park (cf.
Clemley 3 47); Common Fd (*v.* commun); Cornhill (*v.* corn¹, hyll); Cotton
Gate 1842 (1831, *the Cotton Yate* 1547, 'gateway to Cotton', on the boundary
of Cotton Edmunds 112 *infra*, *v.* geat); Cowhay (*v.* (ge)hæg); Crib (*The
Cribb* 1692, *v.* crib); Cross Flatt (*v.* cros, flat); Doctors Fd; Big & Little
Edderhill (*Great & Little Edershalls, Eddershall Meadows* 1692, *v.* edder,
sc(e)aga, hyll); Emper Cotton (*Hamper Coton* 1536, *Anper Cotton* 1625,
Amper Cotton 1629, 1649, *Amber Cotton* 1646, 'part of Cotton where dock or
sorrel grows', *v.* ampre, cf. Cotton 111 *infra*); Flook; Gibbet Heath (Road)
1794 (*v.* gibet, hǣð); Gorsty Croft (1692, *v.* gorstig, croft); Greenway Fd
(-*Feild* 1641, *v.* grēne¹, weg); Hackenhull Hay (*v.* (ge)hæg, cf. Hockenhull
3 274); The Ten Hadlands (*v.* hēafod-land); Hamletts Hay; Hargreaves
Hill (*v.* hār² or hara, grǣfe, cf. Hargrave 105 *supra*); How Hay (*v.* hol²,
(ge)hæg); Intake (*v.* inntak); Isles Moor (*Ilesmeare* 1613, perhaps 'leech's
pool', *v.* igil, mere¹); Ketlen Reans (*v.* rein); The Lawn (*v.* launde); Big
& Little Long Loons ((*Lower*) *Longeloundes* 1613, *v.* lang, land); Low, The
Lowe (*Lawefeld* 1296, *v.* hlāw, feld); Marl Fd (*v.* marle); Mill Fd & Hill
(cf. *Mill Hill* (*Lane*) 1914, *v.* myln, hyll); Morris's Fd (*Morris Field* 1692);
New Hays (*Newhey* 1536, *v.* nīwe, (ge)hæg); Nomans Flatt (*v.* nān mann,
flat); Old Womans Croft; Oxen Hay (*Oxen Hayes* 1692, *v.* oxa, (ge(hæg);
(Big & Little) Pearl (*the Pearl Field* 1725, *the Pearl Croft* 1749, *v.* pyrl(e));
Pingo (*v.* pingot); Red Hill; Sandy Loon (cf. *Sandey Croft* 1664, *v.* sandig,
land, croft); Shipping Lot (*v.* hlot); The Sims; The Sitch (*v.* sīc); Spridgemar (*v.* marr, cf. Spridge Moor 112 *infra*); Sutton Lane 1831 (*v.* Wicker
Lane 127 *infra*); Sutton Spott (*v.* spot); (Big & Little) Town Fd (*Town
Fields* 1749); Water Lane Croft; Whelps (*campus qui vocatur le Welpes*
1296, 'the whelp's field', *v.* hwelp); White Fd; Wood Edish (*v.* edisc).

(b) le Crosbuttes 1296 ('lands which abut cross-wise', *v.* cros, butte); *the
Crosyeatt* 1641 ('gateway athwart', *v.* cros, geat); *le Cruftenche* 1296 (*v.*
cryfting 'a small croft'. The -ing is assibilated, cf. Altrincham 2 7); *Feirmy*

Feild 1641 (probably 'ferny field', *v.* fearnig); *Gerardescroft* 13 ('Gerard's croft', from the ME (OG) pers.n. *Gerard* and croft); *the Haston Flat* 1641 (*v.* æsc, tūn, flat); *Little Croft* 1641; *Lymers Greaves* 1641 (*v.* græfe); *the Meadow Flat Feild* 1641 (*v.* mǣd, flat); *Nesterne Flatt* 1692; *Pechersiche* 1296 ('fisherman's stream', from OFr *pecheour* 'a fisherman', perhaps here as a ME surname *Pecher*, and sīc).

2. COTTON ABBOTTS (109–464646)

> *Chota Ordrici* 1096–1101 (1280), 1150 Chest, *Cotha Ordrici* 1188–91 ib, *Ordrychescotes* 1295 Ch, *Ordriches-* 1295 CRC, Chest
> *Cotun* 13 *Vern*
> *Coton* 13, 1228 *Vern et freq* to 1473 *Dav*, (*-besyde Crystelton*) 1470 *ib*, (*-iuxta Cristilton*) 1473 *ib*, *Magna Coton* 1324 Plea, 1435 ChRR, *Abbottescoton'* 1440 *Rental*
> *Cotes* 13 *Vern*, c.1230 AD *et freq* with variant spellings *Kotes*, *Cotis* to 1321 City (p), *le Cotis* 13 *Vern*, *le Cotes* 1266 Dugd, 1402 ChRR, *Magna Cotes* 1249–1323 Chest
> *Coten'* 13 *Vern*, *Cotene* 1287, 1288 Court (p), *Magna Coten*, *Cotene Abbatis*, *Abbots Cotene*, *Abbotescoten* 1288 ib
> *Cotton* 1325 Orm[2], 1503 Plea, 1535 VE, 1581 ChRR, 1719, 1775 Sheaf, (*-neghe Cristylton*) 1547 *Vern*, (*-iuxta C(h)ristleton*) 1584, 1591 ChRR, *Cotton ex parte Abbatis* 1471 *MinAcct*, 1555 Orm[2], (*-iuxta Stanford Brugge*) 1509 ib, *Cotton Abbots* 1508 ChRR, *Abbotts-* 1539–47 Dugd, *Abbottes-* 1547 *MinAcct*, *Abbot-* 1656 Orm[2], *-Abbot* 1739 LRMB 264
> *Abbots Caton* 1546 Dugd
> *Cottyn* 1547 *Vern*
> *Cotton Hook(e)*, (*Cotton Abbot(ts) alias-, -alias Cotton Abbotts*) 1708, 1709 *Dep*, 1739 LRMB 264, (*Cotton Abbots or-*) 1831 Bry, *Cotton Hook* 1819 Orm[2], (mansion called-) 1831 Hem, 1839 *TAMap* 415, 1842 OS

'At the cottages, at the shelters', from cot (dat.pl. cotum, nom.pl. cotu, ME nom.pl. *cotes*, cf. Studies[3] 30). For other forms cf. Cotton Edmunds 112 *infra*, Emper Cotton 110 *supra*. Cotton Abbotts belonged to the abbots of Chester, *v.* abbat. It is first referred to as 'Ordrīc's shelters', or 'Ordrīc's part of Cotton', named from one *Ordricus* (OE *Ordrīc*) who was a serf granted to the abbey together with his home 1096–1101 Chest I 3. It was also distinguished from Cotton Edmunds as 'Great Cotton', *v.* magna. The township is called *Cotton Abbots cum Stanford* 1724 NotCestr, and formerly included Stamford Mill 112 *infra*, as in Bryant's map 1831. The forms without affix are difficult to ascribe, and are all included here though many may refer to Cotton Edmunds. The hall at Cotton Abbotts was named *Cotton Hook*, from its position on a slight elevation, *v.* hōc.

FIELD-NAMES

The undated forms are 1844 *TA* 132. Of the others, 1226–28 is *Vern*, 1288 Court, 1321 Plea.

(*a*) Carnswood; Lousy Hay (*v.* lūs, -ig³, (ge)hæg); Spridge Moor (cf. Spridgemar 110 *supra*, *v.* mōr¹); Witter's Hay; Yoking's Hay (*v.* (ge)hæg).

(*b*) *Coton'lee* 1226–28 (*v.* lēah); *Pilatesia* 1288 ('island where pill-oats grow', *v.* pil-āte, ēg); *Schraytefeld* 1321 ('field at a land-slip', *v.* skreiδ, feld).

3. COTTON EDMUNDS (109–470660)

　　Parua Kotes c.1200 *Vern*, *-Cotis* 1333 *Dav*
　　Parva Coton' 13 *Vern*, 1324, 1342 Plea, *Vern*, (*-iuxta Cristelton*)
　　　1379 *Eyre*
　　Parva Coten 1288 Court, 1292, 1293 Plea
　　Edmunds Cotton 1503 Plea, 1613 ChRR, *Cotton de parte Edmundi*
　　　1504 Orm², *Cotton Edmunds* 1508 ChRR *et freq*, *-Edmonds* 1519
　　　ib, 1724 NotCestr
　　Cotton St Edmund 1537 Plea

Cf. Cotton Abbotts 111 *supra*, *v.* parva. The manorial affix is from *Edmund* de Coton 1344 *Vern*, lord of this moiety, cf. Orm² 11 785. The intrusive 'Saint' is matched by that in Mottram St Andrew 1 202, and Lach Dennis 2 186.

COTTON EDMUNDS FM, COTTON FM, HALL & LANE, *the Hall of Cotton* 1547 *Vern*, *Cotton Hall* 1724 *EnclA*, *Cotton Edmunds Hall* 1842 OS, cf. Cotton Edmunds *supra*, *v.* hall, lane.　HOCKENHULL PLATTS, *v.* 3 274.　MILL LANE, named from Stamford Mill *infra*.　PLOUGH LANE, *v.* 109 *supra*.　STAMFORD MILL, *v.* 108, 112 *supra*.

FIELD-NAMES

The undated forms are 1844 *TA* 133. Of the others, 13, 1376, 1547¹, 1596, 1604 are *Vern*, 1381, 1504 Orm², 1503 Plea, 1547² *MinAcct*, 1560, 1719 Sheaf.

(*a*) Barkers Moor (cf. *the Walkers Moore* 1547¹, *v.* barkere, walcere, mōr¹); Big Wd (cf. *Coton Wode* 1381, *Cottonwode* 1503, *-Wodde* 1504,

-Woddes 1547[2], *-Wood* 1547[1], 1560, *v.* wudu); Broad Ends (*the Brode-endes* 1547[1], *v.* brād, ende[1]); Cockshutt Fd (*v.* cocc-scyte); Cotton Heath 1719; The Flatts; Flax Yards (*v.* fleax, geard); Flays (*v.* flage); Hestag; How Grass Fd (*v.* hol[2], gærs); The Moor (*Cotonsmor'* 1376, *v.* mōr[1]); Penny Croft (*v.* peni(n)g); Ryddyn (cf. *Gorsty- & Wheite Ryddyng* 1547[1], *v.* gorstig, hwīt, ryding); Stub(b) (*v.* stubb); Wandry Fd (*the Waynrope Felde* 1547, *the Wayne Roape Field* 1604, apparently 'field with, or at, or measured with, a cart-rope', from wægn and rāp, perhaps a place where carts had to be hauled, or a piece of ground the length of a piece of rope, cf. *Rapdowl(e)s* 3 266).

(b) *Berkeleymor'* 1376 ('(marsh at) the birch wood', *v.* beorc, lēah, mōr[1]); a close called *Derneford* 1376, *the Dernefylde* 1547[1] ('hidden ford', *v.* derne, ford); *Grendonis Halflond* 13 (a half-selion, *v.* healf-land. *Grendon* may be a surname); *The Hall Springe* 1596 ('young wood near a hall', *v.* hall, spring); *le Heystall* 1547[1] (*v.* hege-steall 'a place with a hedge', cf. hege-stōw); *le Heyweyis Halflond* 13 ('half-selion near a highway', *v.* hēah-weg and healf-land); *le Hollorns* 13 (*v.* hol[2], horn); *Middilforlong, le Middilfurlongislond* 13 (*v.* middel, furlang, land); *the Newe Dyche* 1547[1] (*v.* nīwe, dīc); *le Rake* 13 (*v.* rake); *le Spert* 1376, *the Sperte Felde* 1547[1] (*v.* spyrt); *Sprynke* 1547[1] (*v.* spring 'a young wood'); *Turnyngmedwe* 1376 ('meadow which goes round a bend' or '-at a turning', *v.* turning(e), mǣd).

4. LITTLETON (109–440665)

Parva Cristentona 1121–29 (1150), 1150 Chest, thereafter with spellings as for Christleton 107 *supra* and *Littil-* (1311 Plea), *Lit(t)el(l)-, Little-, Lityll-* to *Parva Cristelton* 1524 ChRR *Litelton* 1435 ChRR, 1529 Plea, *Litle-* 1535 VE, *Lytle-* 1565 ChRR, *Lyttle-* 1558 Orm[2], *Littleton* 1724 NotCestr, *Great Littleton* 1539 Plea, *Magna Lyttleton* 1545 ib, *Litleton neere Christleton* 1599 *Chol*

'The smaller part of Christleton', 'the little hamlet', *v.* lȳtel, parva, tūn, toun, cf. Christleton 107 *supra*. *Great* Littleton was probably a manorial division of this township (*v.* grēat).

LITTLETON-HILL, *Littleton House* 1842 OS. OLD HALL (lost, 109–441663), 1831 Bry, noted in 1724 NotCestr, disappeared by 1845, probably occupying *the scite where the Whytehall stood* 1565 Sheaf, 1589 ChRR, *v.* hwīt, ald, hall. PEARL LANE, 1831 Bry, *v.* pyrl(e). VICAR'S CROSS, 1831 ib, *the Viccars Crosse* 1614 Sheaf, *Vicars Crosse* 1620 ib, a cross in a field at 109–440669, giving name to Cross Fd *infra* and to a hamlet here and in Gt. Boughton, cf. 125, 128 *infra*. 'WATLING STREET', *v.* 110 *supra*.

FIELD-NAMES

The undated forms are 1847 *TA* 242. Of the others, c.1230 is AD, 13 *Vern*, 1599, 1600 *Chol*, 1831 Bry.

(a) Chester Fd; The Crib (*v.* crib); Cross Fd (*v.* cros, cf. Vicar's Cross *supra*); Founders Hey (-(*Lane*) 1831, (*The*) *Founders Heyes* 1599, 1600, *v.* (ge)hæg); Green Yard (*v.* grēne¹, geard); Hales Hey (*v.* halh, (ge)hæg); Big Loons (*v.* land); Long Looms (cf *the Longe Loundes Medowe* 1599, 1600, *v.* land, loom); Marl Fd; Six Butts (*v.* sex, butte); Wall Fd (*v.* wælla); White Fd.

(b) Atefurlong 13 ('oats furlong', *v.* āte, furlang); *Pertrichis Buttis* 13 ('selions frequented by the partridge', *v.* pertriche, butte); *Soddale* c.1230 ('south valley', *v.* sūð, dæl¹).

5. ROWTON (GRANGE, HALL & MOOR) (109–4564) [ˈrautən]

Rowa Christletona 12 Tab, *Ruhcristelton* c.1200 *Vern* and thereafter with spellings as for Christleton 107 *supra* and *Ruh(e)-*, *Ruwe-*, *Rogh(e)-*, *Rou(e)-*, *Row(e)-*, *Ro(e)-*, *Roh-* to *Rowchrisleton alias Rowton* 1570 ChRR, *Roe Christleton* 1606 Orm²

Roweton' 13 *Vern et freq* with variant spellings *Rueton, Routon, Rowton* (from 1417 AD), *Roucton, Rauton, Roueton;* (*Rowton alias Roughe Chrystleton*) 1579 Orm², *Rowton Heath* 17 Sheaf, *Routon More* 1690 ib, *Rowton Hall & Moor* 1831 Bry

'The rough part of Christleton', from rūh and tūn with hall, hǣð, mōr¹, cf. Littleton, Christleton 113, 107 *supra*. Rowton Moor was the site of the battle of Rowton Heath 24 September 1645.

BROOK LODGE, from Caldy Brook 1 17.   CLAYPITS FM, *Clay Pits* 1831 Bry, cf. *Common Lane* 1842 OS, formerly *Acres Lane & Clay Pits Lane* 1831 Bry, *v.* clæg, pytt, lane, commun, æcer.   ELM BANK.   GORSEHALL.   HOLLY BANK.   MOORFIELDS, MOOR LANE, cf. Rowton Moor *supra*.   PROMISED-LAND FM, *v.* 337 *infra*. RIDGES LANE (109–448633 to 435636), 1831 Bry, cf. 123 *infra*, *v.* hrycg, lane, cf. foll. This lane is the boundary of Saighton, Rowton and Huntington.   RIDGEWAY FM (109–448633), at the east end of Ridges Lane, *v.* prec., 'way along a ridge', *v.* hrycg, weg.

FIELD-NAMES

The undated forms are 1844 *TA* 341. Of the others, c.1200, 1296 are *Vern*, 1359 *Chol*.

(a) Acres Lane (v. Claypits *supra*); The Birches (v. birce); Brockstons Gap (v **gappe**. The first el. may be a surname); Bummer; Cald(e)y Shoots (v. **scēat**, cf. *Caldewallemor infra*, Caldy Brook 1 17); Coney Grave (v. coningre); The Crib (v. crib); Crosses (v. cros); Grave Loons (v. **grǣfe**, land); Harty Shoots; Horn Nips (109–444646) (cf. *Horngappes* c.1200, probably 'gaps (in a fence, etc.) at a projecting piece of land', from **horn** and **gappe**); Howey; Leg of Mutton Fd (v. 336 *infra*); Pike Head Land ('pointed head-land', v **pīc**[1], hēafod-land); Further-, Nearer- & Round Snabs (v. rond, snabbe); Stoney Flatt (v. stānig, flat); Swander Loons (v. land); Turnabout (v. 337 *infra*); Wester Loons (v. land); Wheat Hay (v. **hwǣte**, (ge)hæg).

(b) *Alfstanesbrugge* c.1200 ('Ælfstān's bridge or causeway', from the OE pers.n. *Ælfstān* and brycg); *Bradewey, Bradesweys nether ende* c.1200 ('the bottom end of) the broad way', from **brād** and **weg**, with neoðera, ende[1]); *Brunlawefurlang* c.1200 ('(furlong at) the brown hillock', from brūn[1] and hlāw, with furlang); *Caldewallemor* c.1200 ('(marsh at) the cold spring', from cald and wælla, with mōr[1], cf. Cald(e)y Shoots *supra*, Caldy Brook 1 17); *le Cherchewey* 1296 (v. cirice, weg); *Cokkeslawe* c.1200 ('cock's hillock', v. cocc[2], hlāw); *Hedyedland Monialium* c.1200 ('the nuns' head-land', v. hēafod-land, presumably belonging to the nuns of Chester); *Hungerfurlang* c.1200 (v. hungor, furlang); *(Nether ende de) Langefriday* c.1200 ('(the lower end of) Long Friday', v. neoðera, ende[1]. The f.n. *Langefriday* may be 'a long field called *Friday*', from lang and Frīgedæg, meaning either a field in which labour was due to the manorial lord on a Friday, or an unproductive field associated with fasting; but the f.n. also resembles OE *Langa-Frīgedæg*, 'Long Friday', i.e. Good Friday, the rigid fasting-day of Easter, which suggests an association with hunger and poor yield of crops on this land. Professor Sørensen observes that Danish p.ns. containing *Langfredag-* are often names of areas which must have required much time and effort for their cultivation); *Tungesharplond* c.1200 ('selion at a pointed tongue of land', v. tonge-sharp, land, cf. Tongue Sharp Wood 1 162); *Tunstall, Overetunstall* c.1200 ('the (higher) farm-site', v. tūn-stall, uferra); *Wellfurlang* c.1200 (v. wella, furlang).

xvii. Bruera Chapelry

Bruera was a chapelry of St. Oswald's parish, Chester, 337 *infra*, and contained the townships 1. Churton Heath, 2. Huntington, 3. Lea Newbold, 4. Saighton. It became a separate parish in 1868, cf. Orm[2] II 762. The chapel is in Saighton and gives name to Churton Heath.

1. CHURTON HEATH (FM) (109–440600), & BRUERA 122 *infra*
   (*ecclesia* (*sancte Marie*) *de*) Bruera 1141–57, 1188–91, c.1200–20
   Chest, *Bruera* 13 ib (p), 1214–23 ib (chapel of), 1257–94 ib (town of), *et freq*, de *Bruario* 1185 Facs (p), *capella de Bruwario*

1216–23 (17) Chest, *Brewera* (*Chappellrie*) 1620 Sheaf, *Bruera or Church en Heath* 1663, 1696 ib (chapel(ry) of), *Bruera situate in . . . Church in Heath* 1724 NotCestr, *Bruera or Churton Heath* 1831 Bry

Heeth 1157–94 Chest, *le Heth* 1317 ChRR (p) *et freq, le Heath* 1303 (18) Orm² (p)

Churchenheath 1294 Court, *-het'* 1309–12 JRC *et freq* with variant spellings *Chirch*(*e*)-, *Church*(*e*)-, *-en-, -on-, -an-, -yn-, -in-, -het*(*h*), *-he*(*a*)*th*(*e*), *-eathe* to *Church in-, -en Heath* 1724 NotCestr, *Churchen Heath* 1729 Sheaf, *Church on Heath Farme* 1701 ib

Chirch(*e*)*o*(*n*)*theheth* 1311 Plea, 1313, 1325 ChRR (p), 1332 Pat, *þe Church on the Heath* 1646 Sheaf

Churton Heath 1547 Orm², 1609 *Chol et freq, Churtonheath Chappell alias the Chappell of Bruera* 1646 Sheaf, *Churton* 1554 ib, *Churton Heath otherwise Churton on the Heath* 1838 *TA*

Church Heath 1729 Sheaf

'The church on the heath', *v.* cirice, en⁴, in, on, hǣð, bruiere (MedLat *bruer*(*i*)*a, bruerium*). The modern form has been affected by that of Churton 70 *supra*, three miles distant. The site of the chapel is in Saighton and a more ancient site may have been in Buerton, *v.* 122 *infra*.

CHAPEL LANE, *v.* 122 *infra*,   PLATT'S LANE, *v.* 122 *infra*.

FIELD-NAMES

The undated forms are 1839 *TA* 119. The others are Sheaf.

(*a*) The Green; Hatton Heath Fd (cf. Hatton Heath 122 *supra*); Intake (*v.* inntak); Milking Bank Croft (*v.* milking); Newbold Fd (cf. Newbold 120 *infra*); White Fd.

(*b*) Higher & Lower Bothoms 1663 (*v.* boðm); Church Croft 1663 (*v.* cirice, croft); Clarkes Gate 1620 (*v.* geat); The Great Feyld 1663 (*v.* grēat); Poole Field Bridge 1620 (*v.* pōl¹, feld, brycg); Whiclock Such 1620 (*v.* sīc).

2. HUNTINGTON, *Huntington cum Cheveley* 1819 Orm², cf. Huntington, Cheaveley *infra*.

HUNTINGTON HALL (109–427628), HUNTINGTON HALL FM (109–420635), HUNTINGTON LANE (lost, 109–420650 to 422605)

Huntingdun 958 (13) BCS 1041, (14) Chest, *-don* 958 (17) KCD 473, Dugd, 1295 Misc *et freq* with variant spelling *-yng-* to

1607 ChRR, (-*alias Huntington*) 1541 Dugd, *Huntyngdonwode*
1354 (1379) Ch, 1404 ChRR, *Huntingdone Lane* c.1620 Sheaf
Hunditone 1086 DB
Huntinthona 1096–1101 (1280) Chest, -*tona* 1096–1101 (1280) (17)
  ib, -*ton* 1244 CRC, 1357 Chamb (p), 1579 Dugd, -*yn*- 1348
  Eyre, 1410 ChRR, 1535 VE, 1549 Sheaf
Huntindona 1096–1101 Chest, -*don* 1188–91, c.1230, 1244 Chest,
  Ch *et freq* with variant spellings -*dun*, -*yn*- to 1361 ChRR
Huntithona 1096–1101 (17) Dugd, Chest, -*tona* 1150 ib
Huntington 1233–37 (17) Chest, 1553 Pat *et freq*, -*yng*- 1289 Court
  (p), 1311 *JRC* (p), 1514 ChRR, -*tona* c.1310 Chest, *Huntyng-
  tonwodde* 1499 Orm², *Huntyngton Lane* 1359 Sheaf, *Hunting-
  tonhey* 1560 ib, *Huntingtonwood* 1573 ib, 1594 Morris, *the hall
  of Huntington* 1589 Sheaf, *Huntington Hall* 1656 Orm², *Little
  Huntington* 1831 Bry
Huntedon 1281 Court (p)
Huntisdon 1281 Court (p)
Hontindon 1281 Chest, 1296–7 Port (p), *Hontyndon* (*Wod*) 1540
  Morris, 1555 Sheaf
Hunton 1353 BPR (p)
Hontynton (*Lane*) 1539 Sheaf

Probably 'hunting-hill, hill where hunting was done', from
hunting and dūn, with hall, wudu, lane and (ge)hæg, though the
first el. may have been hunta 'a huntsman', perhaps as a pers.n.,
with -ing-⁴, cf. Huntington NRY 12, Huntingdon BdHu 251. The
final el. has been replaced by tūn. In 1831 Bry, Huntington Hall was
Little Huntington, and the Hall Fm was *Huntington Hall*. The latter
is a moated site, probably 'the grange of the abbot of Chester at
Huntynton' 1348 *Eyre*, cf. Grange Fm *infra*. The lane was the main
road from Chester to Aldford, maintained by the city, *v.* Sheaf¹ 2,
³14, 17 & 18, and is referred to as *Chevely-Butter-back lane in Huntington* 1724 NotCestr.

BUTTER BACHE (BRIDGE) (109–420652) [-bætʃ]
Potherbache 1354 (1379) Ch
Botherbache 1355 (15) Sheaf, (16) Morris
Puttesbache 1499 Orm²
Butterbache 1540, 1573, 1594 Morris, (-*Bridge*) 1545, 1555 Sheaf,
  -*bach* (*Bridge*) 1620 ib, *the Butter Bach* (*Hill*) 1660 *Rental*,
  Butter Bach 1842 OS

Butter-back 1724 NotCestr
Butter-beach 1785 Sheaf, *Butter Beach Farm* 1831 Bry

'Valley with a stream, where there was rich pasture producing good butter', from **butere** and **bæce**[1], with **brycg**, cf. Butter Bache 3 301. The bridge carries *Huntington Lane supra* over Caldy Brook 1 17 *supra*, the boundary between Huntington and Great Boughton 123 *infra*.

CHEAVELEY HALL FM (109–420617), CHEAVELEY COTTAGES (109–425615) [ˈtʃiːvli]

Ceofanlea 958 (13) BCS 1041, (14) Chest, Dugd, *Ceosaula* 958 (17) Dugd, KCD 473, *Coesaulea* 958 (16) Chest, *Harl.* 2060
Cavelea 1086 DB
Ceueleia 1096–1101 (1280), 1150 Chest
Cheveleia 1096–1101 (1280) (17) Chest, *Cheueley* 1188–91 ib *et freq* with variant spellings *Cheve-, -ley(e), -l(ee), -ly, -leg(h)* to *Cheveley* 1819 Orm[2]
Cheyle 1178 Whall (p), *Cheyly, Chayly* (*Woods*) 1546 Sheaf, *Chelie* 1620 ib, (*Cheaveley or*) *Chealey* 1831 Bry
Chevale 1396 ChRR (p)
Cheyvelegh 1514 ChRR, *Cheavely* 1656 Sheaf, *-ley* 1831 Bry
Chouefly 1698 Sheaf
Caufley 1699 Sheaf

'Ceofa's wood or clearing', from the OE pers.n. *Ceofa* and **lēah**, with **hall, wudu, mǣd**. The forms *Ceosaula, Coesaulea* are in erroneous copies, with confusion of *o* and *e*, *f* and long *-s*, *n* and *u*.

CHEAVELEY BRIDGE (109–424618), the location of *Henlake* 1842 OS, cf. Henlake Brook 1 28, probably 'watercourse, or pool, frequented by waterhens', from **henn** and **lacu** or **lake**.   CHURTON HEYS FM, *v.* (ge)**hæg**, cf. Churton Heath 115 *supra*.   CROOK OF DEE (109–4261), *Crooked Dee* 1831 Bry, a bend of the river, *v.* **krókr**, R. Dee 1 21.   ECCLESTON FERRY (109–416622), 1842 OS, *Eaton Boat Ferry House* 1831 Bry, *Jemmy's Boat* c.1850, 1879 Sheaf, named after the ferry of Eaton Boat which was moved to this site, and one James Harnett, ferryman, at the end of the eighteenth century, cf. Sheaf[1] 1 (313, 324), *v. Eaton Boat* 150 *infra*.   GRANGE FM, *v.* **grange**. MEADOWHOUSE FM, *Meadow House* 1831 Bry, cf. *Huntington Meadows* 1677 Sheaf, *v.* **mǣd, hūs**.   PORTERSHEATH FM (109–433637), 1831

Bry, *Portall Heath, Porta Yate* n.d. (17) Sheaf[3] 25 (5510), *Harl.*
2063, *v.* hǣð, geat, cf. Porters Heath 123 *infra*. *Porta(ll)* may contain
port 'a market-town' or port-weg 'road to, road at, a market-town',
cf. Porter's Hill 128 *infra*. There seems to have been a medieval
road from Portersheath to Hatton Heath along the north boundary
of Saighton, *v. Blake Streets* at Saighton Lane 122 *infra*. RAKE
& PIKEL (p.h.), *Lane End* 1831 Bry, at the north end of Sandy Lane
122 *infra*.

FIELD-NAMES

Of the forms 1432, 1440, 1660 are *Rental*, and the rest Sheaf.

(*a*) Barkers Fd or Brockley Fd 1742.

(*b*) *Brooke Feilde* 1601 (*v.* brōc); *Cheveley Meadow* 1602 (*v.* mǣd);
Claueraymedowe 1432, 1440 ('clover meadow', *v.* clǣfre, ēg, mǣd); *Crom-
wells Gate & House* 1620 (from geat and hūs, with the surname *Cromwell*);
Gorstey Hey 1601 (*v.* gorstig, (ge)hæg, cf. foll.); *Hulmeffild* 1512 (1530),
1530, (*the*) *Holmefild, -feld* 1546, *Hulme's Field or Gorsty Hayes* 1663 (*v.*
hulm, holmr, feld); *Little Meadow* 1601 (*v.* lȳtel); *þe little Ouer Meadow*
1660 (*v.* uferra); *Owler Hall Ground* 1677 (*v.* alor, hall, grund); *Oxheyes*
1602 (*v.* oxa, (ge)hæg); *the Great(e) Park(e)* 1602, 1655, *þe Parke* 1660 (*v.*
park); *Poole Field* 1601 (*v.* pōl[1], feld); *Rushie Crofts* 1539, 1632 (*v.* riscig,
croft); *Stuardes Meadowes* 1539, 1632 (*v.* stīg-weard, mǣd); *þe Swinlow
Hey* 1660 ('(enclosure at) the swine hill', *v.* swīn[1], hlāw, (ge)hæg).

3. LEA NEWBOLD (109–4359) ['li: 'nju:bould], *Le Lee et Newbold*
1462 Orm[2], *Lea cum Newbold* 1819 ib, 1842 OS, cf. Leahall Fm, Lea
Newbold Fm *infra*.

LEAHALL FM (109–431589), LEE COTTAGES ['li:'ɔ:l, 'li:]

   Lai 1086 DB, *Lay* 1096–1101 (1150), 1150, 1177–82 Chest, (*le-*)
      1150 ib, 1536 ChRR, (*the-*) 1622 Sheaf, *the Lay Hall nere
      Odford* 1698 ib
   Leey 1141–57 Chest, 1528 Chol, 1601 Sheaf, *le Leye* 1294 Court,
      Ley 1536 ChRR, Plea, 1547 Pat, (*le-*) 1536 ChRR, (*the-*) 1646
      Chol
   Lee c.1200–20 Chest, 1275 Ipm *et freq* to 1671 Sheaf, (*la-*) 1275 Cl,
      (*le-*) 1290 Fine, (*the-*) 1433 (19) Orm[2], *Lee Senescalli* l13 Chest,
      Lee near Aldeford 1398 ChRR
   la Legh 1259 Cl (p), *Legh* 1701 Sheaf
   Le c.1536 Leland
   Lea (*Hall, Mill, Wood*) 1620 Sheaf, Orm[2]

'The clearing', from lēah, with hall, myln, wudu, cotage. Lea is near Aldford 77 *supra*. The manorial affix *Senescalli*, from Lat. *senescallus* 'a steward', derives from the interest of the Montalt family, several of whom were Stewards of the Earldom of Chester in the twelfth and thirteenth centuries, *v.* Orm² II 764.

LEA NEWBOLD FM (109-442595) ['li: 'nju:bould]

Newbolt 1287 ChF, 1521 Orm², *Neubolt* 1304 Chamb, *Newe-* 1391 ChRR (p)

Neubold iuxta Buyrton 1300–7 *JRC*, (*-Churchenhet'*) 1309–12 *ib*, (*-Goldeburne*) 1311 Plea, (*-Salghton*) 1315–16 ib, *Neubold* 1314 ib *et freq* to 1462 Orm², *Newbolde* 1413 Plea, *Newbold* 1425 ib, *et freq* to 1831 Bry

Neuuebold E2 *CoLegh*, *Newe-* 1414 ChRR

Newbolds 1523 ChRR

Ley Newbold alias Lea Newbold 1615 *ChCert*, *Lea Newbold* 1724 NotCestr

Newbald 1724 NotCestr

Lea Newball 1729 Sheaf

'The new house', *v.* nīwe, bold. It adjoins Leahall Fm *supra*, also Buerton, Churton Heath, Golborne David 79, 115, 88 *supra*, Saighton 121 *infra*.

BRICKYARD PLANTATION, *v.* brick-yard.   NEWBOLD, *Newbold Lodge* 1831 Bry, *v.* loge.   PLATT'S LANE, cf. 122 *infra*.   WIM BRIDGE, 1831 ib, perhaps 'handy bridge', from brycg with dial. *whim* 'handy, convenient', from ME cweme, queme *v.* *queme*, NED.

FIELD-NAMES

The undated forms and 1839 are 1839 *TA* 233. Of the others, 1285 is Ch, 1622, 1650 Sheaf, 1528 (1536) ChRR, 1739 *LRMB* 264, 1831 Bry, 1842 OS.

(a) Little Broadfield (*Great & Little Broad Field* 1650, cf. Shay Field Lane *infra*, *v.* brād, feld); Butcherfield (*the Butchers Field* 1650, *v.* bocher); (Little) Caterbatch (*the Little Caterbach* 1650, probably from dial. *cater* 'diagonal' and bæce¹, cf. Clatterbridge Lodge 78 *supra*); Halfpenny Fd (*v.* halfpeny); Heathfield (*the Field next the Heath* 1650, *v.* hǣð); Hill Croft (*the Hill Crofts* 1650, *v.* hyll, croft); Hop Yard (*v.* hoppe, geard); (Far & Near) Mill Mdw (*the Great & Little Mill-, -Milne Meadow* 1650, cf. *Lea Mill* 1620 Sheaf, *Newbold Mill* 1739, *Lea Newbold Mill* 1839, *v.* myln, mǣd); Newport Yard (*v.* geard); (Great) Ox Leasow (*the Oxlesowe* 1622, *the Great Oxe Pasture* 1650, *v.* **oxa, lǣs, pasture**); Pingot (*v.* **pingot**); Round Fd (1650, *v.* **rond**); Shay Field Lane 1842 (*Broad Field Lane* 1831, cf. Broadfield *supra*, *v.* **sc(e)aga, Shawfield** 91 *supra*); Springfield; Thistle Fd (1650, *v.* **þistel**).

(*b*) *Bostocke Meadow* 1650 (from the surname from Bostock 2 202); *le Brigge Hill* 1528 (*v.* **brycg, hyll**); *the Caulvescroft* 1622 (*v.* **calf, croft**); *the Deu or Dea Croft* 1650 (perhaps 'dew croft', from **dēaw**, with the alternative form *Dea* representing an unstressed pronunciation); *the Haw Field Meadow* 1650 (*v.* **haga**); *le Hethehouses Croft* 1528 (*v.* **hǣð, hūs**); *the Kilne Field Meadow* 1650 (*v.* **cyln, feld, mǣd**); *Great & Little Lea Rake* 1650 (*v.* **rake**); *Neubold Dike* 1285 (*v.* **dīc**); *the Rough Fields* 1650 (*v.* **rūh**); *the Rushey Moore* 1650 (*v.* **riscig, mōr**[1]); *Shocklach Field* 1650 (either a manorial name from, or a further example of the name-type of, Shocklach 63 *supra*); *the Windmill Field* 1650 (*v.* **wind-mylne**).

4. SAIGHTON (FM, GRANGE & HO) (109–4462) ['seitən]

> *Saltone* 1086 DB, *Saltona* 1096–1101 (14), c.1150 Chest, *Salthona* 1096–1101 (1280) Ch, *Salton* 1244 ib, 1252 *Chol* (p)
>
> *Salhtona* 1096–1101 (1280) Chest, *Salghton* 1188–91, 1244 ib *et freq* with variant spellings *-tona*, *-ten*, *Salhton*, *Salig(h)ton(a)*, *Salgton*, *-tun* to 1696 Sheaf
>
> *Sauton* 1208–26 Facs (p), *Saw(g)thon* 1524 AD, *Sawghton* 1562 Orm[2], 1663 Sheaf, *Shaughton on the Hill* 1564 ib, *Saughton* 1579 Dugd *et freq* to 1749 Sheaf, (*-on the Hill*) 1602 ib, (*-super Montem*) 1620 Orm[2], *Saughton Hall* 1749 Sheaf
>
> *Salw(e)ton* 1281 Court
>
> *Saluhton* 1281 Court, *Saluton* 1281 Chest, *-thon* 1291 Tax
>
> *Salthton* 1290 Court (p)
>
> *Saulghton* 1514 ChRR
>
> *Soughton* 1539 (17) Sheaf, (*-super Montem*) 1554 Pat, (*-(up)on the Hill*) 1588, 1648 Sheaf
>
> *Saighton* 1579 Dugd *et freq*, (*-upon the Hill*) 1598 ChRR, *Sayton* 1648 Orm[2], *Sayhton on the Hill* 1700 Sheaf, *Saighton Grange* 1819 Orm[2], (*-now called Saighton Tower*) 1882 ib, *Saighton Farm & Hall* 1831 Bry
>
> *Seyton* 1648 Hem
>
> *Seathton on the Hill* 1700 Sheaf

'Willow-tree farm, or willow enclosure', from **salh, salig**, and **tūn**, with **hyll, grange, hall** and **tour**. The village is on a hill. The hall, or grange, is the site of a manor house of the abbots of Chester, of which a great stone gatehouse tower remains, whence the later name of the house.

BRUERA (109–437605), *the Chappell* 1620 Sheaf, *Saighton Chapel* 1831 Bry, *Bruera or Church on Heath* 1842 OS, *v.* Churton Heath 115 *supra*. A moated site on the Buerton side of Chapel Lane adjacent to Bruera, may be the original site of the chapel, cf. 'the church of Bruera with the croft adjacent between the garden of the said church and the great road from the house towards the town of Lee' 13 Chest II 501, 836.

CHAPELHOUSE FM, CHAPEL LANE, *Chapel Lane* 1831 Bry, *Chapel House* 1842 OS, named from Bruera chapel *supra*, *v.* chapel, lane, hūs, cf. 116 *supra*.   HATTON HEATH (BRIDGE, FM & LODGE), *Hatton Heath* 1690 Sheaf, *bruera iacens iuxta Hatton et Salhton* 1281 (17) Chest, *v.* hǣð, brycg, ferme, loge, cf. 100 *supra*, Saighton Gorse *infra*. The bridge was 'the newe bridge which separateth the said Chappellrie from Warton parish' 1620 Sheaf, cf. Waverton 103 *supra*.   HEATHCROFT FM, *v.* hǣð, croft, cf. prec.   MANOR HO. MILLFIELD LANE, 1831 Bry, *v.* myln, feld, lane.   PLATT'S LANE & ROUGH, 1831 ib, *Plats Rough* 1842 OS, *v.* plat² 'a plot of land', lane, rūh, cf. 116 *supra*.   POWSEY BROOK (> Henlake Brook 1 28), POWSEYBROOK BRIDGE, *Pulsey Bridge* 1558 Sheaf, '(bridge at) a stream to a pool', *v.* pōl, ēa, brycg. W. F. Irvine, Sheaf³ 20 (4695), reports that this bridge was also called *Pool Bridge*, and was near the site of *le Untidymulnedom* 1359 *Indict* (cf. Morris 125), 'the unsuitable mill-dam', from ME *untidi* 'unseemly, inopportune, untimely, inappropriate', myln and damme.   SAIGHTON GORSE, *Hatton Heath Fox Cover* 1831 Bry, cf. Hatton Heath *supra*.   SAIGHTON LANE (FM) (109–445623 to 448633), 1831 ib, identified in Sheaf³ 24 (5510) with *Blackstreete Lane* c.1539 (17) *Harl.* 2063, cf. *Black Streete Lane End* 1620 Sheaf, *Blake Streets* 1840 *TA*, 'black, perhaps dirty, paved road', from blæc and strǣt, with lane, ende[1]. But the fields called *Blake Street(s)* (109–451630) follow the township boundary, 109–448632 to 450631, extending the line of Ridges Lane 114 *supra*, and the road-name may refer to some lost thoroughfare from Portersheath 109–430637 (cf. 119 *supra*) to Hatton Heath 109–457624. Saighton Lane was probably called *The Rake*, cf. Rake Side *infra*.   SAIGHTON LODGE, *v.* loge.   SANDY LANE, 1842 OS, *v.* sandig.

FIELD-NAMES

The undated forms are 1840 *TA* 345. Of the others 1249–65, 1281 (14), 1281 (17), c.1300 are Chest, 16 (17), 1539 (17), 1620, 1696 Sheaf, 1831 Bry.

(a) Big & Little Anthorns; Ash Dale (*bruera prope Assedale* c.1300, 'ash-tree hollow', *v.* æsc, dæl[1], cf. *Heye-, Hessedale infra*); Bagland; Bank Hay (*v.* banke, (ge)hæg); Big & Poor Beggars Brook (*Beggers Brookes* 1620, cf. *Beggaston* 1539 (17), *v.* beggere 'a beggar', tūn, brōc); Benty Croft (*v.* benty); Black Butts (*v.* blæc, butte); Blake Streets (*v.* Saighton Lane *supra*); Broadstone (*v.* brād, stān); Caldy Fd (*v.* Caldy Brook 1 17, cf. *Caldewelle Diche & Forlong* 1249–65, 'ditch and furlong at cold spring', *v.* cald, wella, dīc, furlang); Clemly Park (cf. Clemley 3 47); Coates 1696 (*v.* cot); Common Piece (*v.* commun, pece); Cromes Bridge; Damage Mdw (*v.* demming); Dead Loons (*v.* dēad, land); Devenport Hay (from the surname *Davenport*, *v.* (ge)hæg); Far Duns; Effings; Hall Lane (1831, *v.* hall, lane); The Hantons; Hebbins; Howays End (cf. *le Holeweylond* 1249–65, *Howell Lane* (109–458617 to 445622) 1831, 'the hollow way', from hol[2] and weg, with land, lane, ende[1]); Howlerly Hall Croft (*v.* alor, hall, croft); Intake (*v.* inntak); London; Marl Fd (*v.* marle); Milking Bank (*v.* milking); Mill Hill (*v.* myln, hyll); Monks Hay (Saighton was a manor of Chester abbey, *v.* munuc, (ge)hæg); New Hay (*v.* (ge)hæg); Nields Old Garden (109–440624, cf. *Nield's Orchard* Sheaf[1] 1 301, thought to be an old cemetery); The Nooks (*v.* nōk); Pavement Crofts (109–446625, *v.* pavement); Porters Heath (109–433635) (cf. Portersheath Fm 118 *supra*); Rake Side (a series of fields along Saighton Lane, 'beside the lane,' *v.* rake, sīde); Ridge Lane (cf. *the Ridges, Ridges Yate* 16 (17), *v.* hrycg, geat, Ridges Lane 114 *supra*); Rushy Reans (*v.* riscig, rein); Sand Flatts (*v.* sand, flat); Sheep Hay (*v.* scēp, (ge)hæg); Three Nook Fd (*v.* þrēo, nōk, cf. three-nooked); Little Waddols, Wadhills (either 'woad hollows' or 'woad hills', from wād and hol[1] or hyll); Washing Pits; Water Dale (*v.* wæter, dæl[1]); White Fd.

(b) *Heyedale* 1281 (14), *Hessedale* 1281 (17) (perhaps forms of Ash Dale *supra*, though the seventeenth-century copy represents the fourteenth-century one, which appears to be 'hollow at an enclosure', *v.* (ge)hæg, dæl[1]); *Lonkediche* 1249–65 ('long ditch', *v.* lang, dīc); *Merich'* 1249–65, *Merexedale* 1281 (14) (final el. dæl[1] 'a valley, a hollow', first el. perhaps merisc 'a marsh' or OE merece 'wild celery', with ON -*k*); *le Wodewey* 1249–65 ('the way to the wood', *v.* wudu, weg).

xviii. St Oswald's

For the rest of this parish *v.* 337 *infra*. This survey follows the old boundary between Gt. Boughton and the city of Chester as shown in Bryant's map, 1831.

2. GREAT BOUGHTON (109–4265), BOUGHTON HALL & HEATH
['boutən]

Bocstone 1086 DB
Bochtunestan 1096–1101 (1280), 1150 Chest, *-ston* 1096–1101 (1280)
  ib, Ch, *Bochton'* 1181–1232 Chest, 1188–91, 1249–65 ib, 1260
  Court, *-tone* c.1240 Sheaf (p)
Bocthon(a) 1096–1101 (1280), 1250–78 Chest, *-tona* 1096–1101
  ib, *Bocton* 1239, 1240 Lib, P, 1257–95 Chest, 1276, 1277 P, 1295
  Chest, *-tone* 1325–77 AD (p)
Boghtona 1096–1101 (1280) (17), c.1310 Chest, *Bogthon* 1281 ib,
  Boghton 1283 ib *et freq* with variant spellings *Boh(g)ton* to 1535
  VE, (*Magna-*) 1512 (1530) Sheaf
Bostona 1150 Chest, *Buston* 1275 P, *Bouston* 1275 P(c)
Boiton 1225 (1724) NotCestr
Bothton 1265–91 Chest (p)
Bouhton 1279, c.1311 Chest, *Boughton* 1285 Orm[2], 1300 Fine
  et freq, (*Great-*) 1621 ChRR, (*-now called Great Boughton*)
  1882 Orm[2], *Boughton Hall* 1819 ib, *-Heath* 1831 Bry
Bouketon 14 AD (p)
Bowtun 1303 Port (p), *-ton* 1313 *ib*, 1485 ChRR
Bouchton 1311 *AddCh*

'Beech-tree farm or enclosure', from bōc[1] and tūn, with stān 'a
stone', hall and hǣð. *Great* (*v.* grēat) distinguishes this from
Boughton 336 *infra*, which must anciently have been part of Gt
Boughton. *Bochtunestan* may have been *the Blewe Stone by Spittle*
336 *infra*, on the Chester city boundary.

DEE BANKS, 1848 *TA*, *mons aque de Dee* 1354 (1379) Ch (translated
the hill by the water of Dee 1499 Orm[2], *the hill of the water of De(e)*
1540, 1573, 1594 Morris 210–218), *lez Dey Banck* 1550 MinAcct, le
Deye Bankes 1553 Pat, *the Dee Banks* 1557 Sheaf, *Dee Banke* 1662 ib,
-Bank 1810 ib, *v.* banke, cf. foll. and R. Dee 1 21. Some forms are
influenced by **dey** 'dairy'.

SANDY LANE, 1707 *Assem*, *the Sandie Lane* 1620 Sheaf, *venella que
vocatur le Holweye* 1348 *Vern*, le *Holghewey* (which runs to *Potherbache subtus montem aque de Dee*) 1354 (1379) Ch, 1357 BPR, *the
Holghe Waye that ledys unto Bolterbache under the water of Dee* 1355
(16) Morris, *the Houlghe Waye* 1540 ib, *the Highe Waie* 1573 ib,
the Highway 1594 ib, 'the sandy lane', 'the road in a hollow', *v.*
sandig, holh, weg, lane, hēah-weg, cf. Butter Bache 117 *supra*.

This road was on the boundary of the city of Chester. It runs under the high bluff on the east bank of R. Dee opposite Earl's Eye, cf. prec.

BACHELOR'S LANE, *Bachelors Lane* 1831 Bry, from a surname. BECKETT'S LANE, cf. *Becketts Croft* 1848 *TA*, from a surname. BROOK HO & LANE, named from Flooker's Brook 1 24, cf. *Brook Field* 1848 *TA, the Brooke Feild* 1660 *Rental, v.* brōc. BUTTER BACHE BRIDGE, *v.* 117 *supra.* CHEMISTRY LANE, cf. *Chemistry* 1831 Bry, a chemical works. CHRISTLETON RD, cf. Christleton 107 *supra.* CROW FM. FILKINS LANE, 1848 *TA*, from lane and the surname *Filkin,* cf. John Filkin leaseholder 1682 Sheaf[3] 23 (5391). GREENFIELD LOCK, (on a canal), cf. *Far & Near Green Field* 1848 *TA, v.* grēne[1], feld. GREEN LANE, 1831 Bry, *v.* grēne[1], lane. HARE LANE, 1831 ib. HEATH LANE, 1848 *TA*, cf. Boughton Heath *supra.* KING'S HO. MANOR HO. PEARL LANE, 1831 Bry, *v.* pyrl(e). PIPER'S ASH, 1848 *TA, v.* 131 *infra.* POORHOUSE LANE, 1831 Bry. The Tarvin Union Workhouse was in Gt. Boughton. RED HO, *the Glass House* 1706 Sheaf, 1831 Bry, 1842 OS, *Glasse-house* 1724 NotCestr, 'house made of glass', *v.* glæs, hūs. STOCKS LANE, *v.* stocc. STREETFIELD HO, cf. *Lower Street Field* 1848 *TA, the Street Hey* 1660 *Rental, v.* strǣt, feld, (ge)hæg. These are beside Tarvin Road *infra.* TARVIN BRIDGE, a canal bridge at the site of *Apstree Toll Bar* 1831 Bry, a turnpike at the old junction of Pearl Lane *supra* with Tarvin Road *infra, v.* toll-bar, cf. foll. TARVIN LOCK, this and prec. seem to allude to the fact that Gt. Boughton was once in the Tarvin poor-law union, cf. Poorhouse Lane *supra,* Tarvin 3 281. TARVIN RD, *Tarvyn Lane* 1574 (18) Sheaf, *Tarvin Lane* 1588 (18) ib, 1707 *Assem,* 1831 Hem, leading to Tarvin 3 281 by Stamford Bridge 108 *supra,* probably a Roman road, cf. Streetfield Ho *supra, v.* 1 40 (Route VII). VICAR'S CROSS, cf. 113 *supra* and *Vicars Cross House* 1831 Bry, *the Viccars Cross Hey* 1660 *Rental, v.* hūs, (ge)hæg. 'WATLING STREET', *v.* 1 40 (Route VII), cf. Tarvin Road, Streetfield Ho *supra.* WOODBANK.

FIELD-NAMES

The undated forms are 1848 *TA* 63. Of the others 1398 is *Add,* 1432, 1660 *Rental,* 1539–47, 1579 Dugd, 1653, 1675 *Corp,* 1831 Bry, and the rest Sheaf.

(*a*) Abbot(t)s Wel(d)s Fields, -Feilds 1653, 1675 (*v.* Abbot's Well 109 *supra*); Adder Hill; (Higher) Almonds (cf. *the Ormands Lake Meadow* 1660, *v.* lacu, mǣd); (Far & Near) Birch Fd, Birch Lane Fd, (Far & Top) Birches (*the Hardins-, Higher-, Little-* & *Lower Birches* 1660, *Birch Lane* 1831, perhaps from birce 'a birch-tree'); Black Walls (*the Little Blackwall* 1660, 'black spring', *v.* blæc, wælla); Brow Green Fd (*the Browgreens* 1660, *v.* brū, grēne[2]); Far & Near Busy Ditch (perhaps 'grassy enclosure', from bēos and edisc); Cat Butt; Cocks Hay (*the Further* & *Nearer Coxhey* 1660, *Cocks Hey* 1749, *v.* cocc[2], (ge)hæg); Crib (*v.* crib); Crow Park (*v.* crāwe, park); Daniel Butts (cf. *The Daniels* 1821); Dow(s) ('doles, allottments', *v.* dāl); Flash Mdw (*v.* flasshe); (Big & Little) Fridays (*v.* Frigedæg); Gammon Fd; Glovers Loon(s) (*Glovers-Loans* 1749, *The Glover's Looms* 1920, *v.* land, loom); Gorsy Fd (cf. *the Gorsty Lownds* 1660, *v.* gorstig, land); The High Hadland 1699 (cf. *the Nearer Hadland* 1660, *v.* hēafodland); Heath Croft & Fd (*the Heath Croft* 1660, cf. Boughton Heath *supra*, *v.* hǣð, croft); Hoole Lane Fd (cf. Hoole 129 *infra*); Leek Fd; Marl Croft (cf. *the Marled Hey* 1660, *v.* marle, marled); Orchard Bank (*v.* orceard, banke); Ox Pasture; Pinfold Lane (*v.* pynd-fald); Pingot (*v.* pingot); Pool Hay (*v.* pōl[1], (ge)hæg); Roundhill Fd (*v.* rond, hyll); Scotch Morgan Mdw; Smithy Hill (*the Smith(y) Hill* 1660, *v.* smið, smiððe, hyll); Spoil Bank; Swinley Hay; Town Mdw; Twirl of Hay Fd; Wall Moor (*the Wallmoore* 1660, *v.* wælla, mōr[1]); Water Reans (*v.* wæter, rein); White Mdw; Withy Croft (*v.* wīðig, croft).

(b) *les Bruch'* 1432, cf. *Heedichebruches, Lokesbruches* 1398 ('the breakings-in' from bryce. In the earlier references, *Heediche-* may be 'ditch in which a stream flows', *v.* ēa, dīc, but *cf. Heedichebruches* 175 *infra*; and *Lokes-* is the ME pers.n. *Lok* from the OE by-name *Locc*, *v.* Tengvik 321, Reaney s.n. *Lock*, Feilitzen s.nn. *Locre, Lokki*); *les Conyngrees iuxta Boughton* 1432, *þe Conygrees* 1649, *Connigree* 1662 (*v.* coningre. This was near Dee Banks *supra*, *v.* Sheaf[1] 1 332); *Cranes House* 1620; *the Flax Waye* 1660 (either 'road along which flax is carried' or 'road to a marsh', from weg with fleax or flask, cf. Flash Mdw *supra*); *the Newfield* 1660; *the Odshead* 1660; *the Rake Hey* 1660 ('enclosure near a path or lane', *v.* rake, (ge)hæg); *Boughton Windmill* 1579 (*v.* wind-myln).

xix. Guilden Sutton

Guilden Sutton was in *Wilaveston* (Wirral) Hundred in DB.

GUILDEN SUTTON (109–4468) ['gildən-]
> *Sudtone* 1086 DB f.263
> *Suttona juxta Cestriam* 1154–60 (1329) Ch, 1190–1211 *Cott.* Nero C III, *Sutton* 13 *Vern*, 1288 Court (p) *et freq*, (*capella de-*) 1352 BPR, (*-iuxta Hole*) 1493 Plea
> *Guldenesutton* c.1200 Orm[2] II 807, 1291 Tax, 1306 Plea, *Guldun-* 1304 Chamb, *Gulden-* 1329 Orm[2], c.1350 AD, 1600 Sheaf
> *Guldesocton* 1291 Tax

le Guldensottone 1309 Sheaf

Guyldenesutton 1316 Plea, 1318 *Eyre, Guylden-* 1317 Orm², 1348 Plea, 1391 ChRR and six examples to 1426 ib, *Guilden-* 1398 ib, 1560, 1600, 1646 Sheaf, 1711 *Chol et freq*

Gueldensutton 1327 Orm²

Gyldensutton 1352 Orm², 1483 *Hesk, Gilden-* 1367 Plea *et freq* with variant spellings *Gildon-, Gyldon-* to 1727 Sheaf

Geldensutton 1535 VE, 1545, 1554, 1587, 1602 Orm², 1646 Sheaf, *Geldon-* 1535 VE, 1623 Orm²

Gyldon et Sutton 1554 *MinAcct*

Golden Sutton 1600 Orm²

Sutton-Gelders 1669 (1724) NotCestr

Guilded Sutton 1691 Sheaf, 1711 *Assem*

Gilen Sutton 1694 Sheaf

'The southern farm', from sūð and tūn, with the affix **gylden** 'golden', meaning 'splendid, wealthy'. The discussion in Wo 125 is irrelevant. This was a manor of the bishop of Chester (Coventry and Lichfield) in 1066 and 1086, cf. Tait 89 n.35a. It is distinguished from Great and Little Sutton 193, 195 *infra*, by reference to Hoole and Chester 129, 336 *infra*. The description 'southern' probably arose from Sutton's position at the southern extremity of the DB Hundred of *Wilaveston*.

OXEN BRIDGE (109–457682), and OXEN LANE (lost, 109–450680 to 457682) 1831 Bry, are associated with *Oxen Lane Croft, Oxen Meadow* 1848 *TA, The Oxens* 1665, 1712 *Corp* and *The Oxen Duncroft* 1711 *Assem, Oxen Dunce Croft* 1713 *Corp* (lit. *Open-*). The latter may be associated with 'the carucate between Sutton & Stamford Bridge' called *Dunnescroft* 1190–1211 *Cott.* Nero C III, Dugd VI 314, cf. *Little Dunscroft Meadow* 1623 *Corp*, 'Dunn's croft', from the OE, ME pers.n. *Dunn* and croft, cf. foll. and Dunsfords Mdw *infra*.

WICKER HO (109–454677), WICKER LANE (109–451680 to 457672), *Sutton Lane, Vicar Lane* 1831 Bry, *Wicker House* 1842 OS, cf. *(the) Wicker Meadow* 1665 *Corp*, 1848 *TA*, the *W(h)icker Meadow & Heys* 1712 *Corp*, (*Far-, Long-*, etc.,) *Wicker (Croft)* 1848 *TA*. In Bryant, *Sutton Lane* extends 109–451680 to 457672 and *Vicar Lane* 109–454677 to 459678. These p.ns. probably go back to *Witeker* 1190–

1211 *Cott.* Nero C III, Dugd IV 314, 'white marsh', *v.* hwīt, kjarr. Cf. prec.

BELLEVUE FM & WD, *Belle Vue* (*Barn* & *Nursery*) 1831 Bry. BYATTS HOUSE FM, *the Byatts* 1848 *TA*. This resembles the name of the brine-spring of Nantwich, *the old Biat*, which was the object of a traditional well-dressing ritual, doubtless in honour of the source of the town's prosperity, *v.* 3 38. The name *Biat* would appear to be ME biȝeate 'profit, acquisition' (NED), cf. OE *begietan* 'to beget, to acquire', and *The Byatts* could well refer to land which was very profitable or a notable acquisition to an estate. But the historical background is not known, and the surname *Byatt* (Reaney) might enter into this p.n.   GOWY GORSE, a wood near R. Gowy, *v.* gorst. GREEN LANE, 1842 OS, *v.* grēne¹, lane.   HARE LANE, 1831 Bry, *v.* hara, lane.   HEATH BANK and HEATHFIELD, *Heath Field* 1848 *TA*, near Hoole Heath 130 *infra*, *v.* hǣð, banke, feld.   THE HOOLE (109–453677), cf. *Hole* c.1350 AD, *the Bootee or Common Hoole* 1712 *Corp*, *Bootie Hoo* 1665 *Corp*, 'the hollow', *v.* hol¹, botye, commun.   PIPER'S ASH, *v.* 131 *infra*.

FIELD-NAMES

The undated forms are 1848 *TA* 182. Of the others c.1350 is AD, 1703, 1711 *Assem*, 1629, 1665, 1712 *Corp*, 1831 Bry.

(a) Blake Loons (*v.* blæc, land); Brines Mdw; Broad Moor (1831); Coat Croft (*v.* cot); Cow Hay (*v.* (ge)hæg); Daw Fd; Big & Little Daymath (*v.* day-math); Dunsfords Mdw 1703 (this was near *Oxen Duncroft*, *v.* Oxen Bridge *supra*, and may be from the same pers.n. with ford); Little Griftings (from the archaic and dial. form of *grafting* 'the splicing of shoots into tree-stocks', *v.* graft NED); The Hemp Yard 1712 (1665, *v.* hempyard); Hickmore Heys; Holm (*v.* holmr); The Hooks (*The Hook* 1712, *v.* hōc); (Big) Horse Croft (*the two House Crofts* 1665, -Houss- 1712, *the little Horse Croft* 1712, 'crofts at a house', *v.* hūs); Long Loons (*the Long Loonds* 1665, 1712, *v.* lang, land); Mill Fd (*the-* 1712); New Fd (*the New Fields* 1711); The Picker; Porter('s) Hill (109–446683, beside the road west out of the village; *the Portway Hill* 1712, 'hill near a road to a market-town', *v.* port-weg, cf. Portersheath 118 *supra*); Sandfarloons, -fur- ('sandy furlongs', *v.* sand, furlang); Seven Butts (*the-* 1712); Short Breach (*Shodbridge Feild* 1629, *the Short Breech* 1665, 1712, *v.* sc(e)ort, brēc); Soakersedge; The Stacks (*v.* stakkr); Suttons Pot Mdw (probably from spot 'a bit of ground'); Town Fd (cf. *Townfield Lane* 1831); Vicars Cross Fd (*v.* Vicar's Cross 113 *supra*); Well Green Fd (*the Well Green Croft* 1712, *v.* wella); White Fd.

(b) *le Ferkes* c.1350 ('the forks, *v.* forca); *Holdicheweyeues* c.1350 (probably '(the edge of a wood, or of land, at) a ditch in a hollow', from hol² and dīc, with weg, efes); *Raggisfeld* c.1350 ('Rag's field', from feld and ME ragge 'a rag' used as a pers. by-name); *le Schertegurstingis* c.1350 ('the short gorse-plots', v. sc(e)ort, gorsting; in view of the -gurst- spelling, the OE form should perhaps be *gyrsting); *Wolstaneshaker* c.1350 ('Wulfstān's arable plot', from the OE pers.n. *Wulfstān* and æcer).

xx. Plemstall

The ecclesiastical parish of Plemstall contained the townships, 1. Hoole (this was partly in St John's parish, Chester, but it is now divided into Hoole Village c.p. and the Hoole district of Chester county borough), 2. Picton, 3. Mickle Trafford (which included Plemstall hamlet).

1. HOOLE (109–4368) [hu:l]

> *Hole* 1119 (1150), 1150 Chest *et freq* with variant spelling *Hola* to 1665 Sheaf, (*le-*) 1354 BPR, (*-juxta Chester*) 1542 Orm², (*Hoole alias-*) 1598 ChRR, (*-alias Hough*) 1665 Sheaf
> *Hull* 1272–1307 (17) Harl. 2115, 2057, 1520 Orm²
> *Hoel* 1309 Sheaf
> *Houle* 1345 Pat, 1347 Cl, BPR, 1646 Sheaf, *Howle* 1646 ib, *Howl* 1690 ib
> *Hoole* 1512 (1531) ChRR, 1522 Plea *et freq*, (*-alias Hool*) 1589 Sheaf, (*-alias Hole*) 1598 ChRR, *Hool* 1589 Sheaf, 1708 *Assem*
> *Holle* 1550 MinAcct, 1552 Pat, 1651 *Dow*
> *Howe* 1598 (18) Sheaf
> *Hooe* 1602 (18) Sheaf, c.1645 Orm², *Hoo* 1724 NotCestr
> (*Hole alias*) *Hough* 1665 Sheaf³ 29 (6518)
> *Hoale* 1699 Sheaf

'At the hollow', from hol¹, holh, dat.sg. hole with lengthening of -*o*-. The place is referred to as *Vallis Demonum* c.1195 Luciani 64, 'the valley of devils', perhaps a haunt of thieves. The form *Hough* appears in *Houghshey* a seventeenth-century copied form of *Hole Hey* (v. Near Hay *infra*) and *Hull* also appears in *Hull Sych infra*.

HOOLE VILLAGE (109–430690), a township formed by the division of the old township of Hoole between Chester and the county. It dates from after 1860 White. The two parts of Hoole may represent a distinction between the manor of Hoole and the ancient avowry of Hoole Heath. The boundaries of the latter are not completely identified, but certainly included that part of Hoole which now lies in Chester.

BISHOPSFIELD (lost, 109–416673), 1867 Sheaf[3] 18 (4488a), the name of a postal district and locality, has been associated with *Bispediche* 1354 (1379) Ch, 1355 (15) Sheaf, (16) Morris, 1499 Orm[2], 1540, 1555, 1573 Morris, Sheaf, 'the bishop's ditch' *v.*, biscop, dīc, a ditch joining Flooker's Brook 1 24 opposite the point where the city boundary left the brook to run south towards Boughton, *v.* Sheaf[1] 1, 189–190.

FLOOKERSBROOK, a hamlet in Newton, cf. 146 *infra,* and partly in Hoole, named from Flooker's Brook 1 24 which also gave name to *Brook Cottage & Lodge* 1831 Bry, the former on Hoole Rd *infra* near Ashby Place, the latter lost under the General Railway Station, Chester, which stands over the old course of the stream.

HOOLE HEATH (lost, 109–4267), *bruerium de Hole* 1267–8 Chest, *Hole Heath* 1294 Court *et freq* with variant spellings as for Hoole *supra* and -Heth(e), -Heath(e) to *Hoo Heath* 1724 NotCestr, cf. *Heath Croft, Field & Piece* (freq) 1838 *TA, Hoole Heath Field* 1552 (17) Sheaf, *v.* hǣð. Hoole Heath, like Rudheath 2 198 and King's Marsh 75 *supra,* was a sanctuary. Its function was 'that in time of war in Wales, all lawful men of the earl of Chester . . . were wont to have refuge and receipt on Hoole Heath with their goods, necessaries, and beasts, for a year and a day' and that the citizens of Chester should have common of pasture here at all times, cf. 1339–40 (17) *Harl.* 2057 f.125 and Orm[2] II 813. On the north-east boundary of Hoole Heath was *Salterway infra,* described as 'the kynges highway ner Chester for our Lord the kynge to leide his hoost in the tyme of warr unto Shotwyk ford' E1 (17) *Harl.* 2115, f.55 and Sheaf[3] 50 (10041), which suggests that the heath, like King's Marsh, was also reserved for military barracks when needed.

HOOLE RD (109–411671 to 437690)

    alta via de Hole vocata le Rake 1309 Sheaf, *Holerake* 1395 *Chol et freq* with variant spellings as for Hoole *supra* and -Rack, -Raike to *Hoole Rake* 1712 Corp

    the rake called Chester Rake nygh Flokersbroke 1339–40 (17) Sheaf

    a yate called Chester Yate nygh Flokersbroke 1339–40 (17) Orm[2]

    a Rake called St Anne's Rake in Hoole Heath 1600 Sheaf, *St Anns Rake* 1708 Assem

'The narrow road', *v.* **rake**, cf. Hoole *supra*, Chester 336 *infra.* The later name alludes to lands hereabouts which belonged to the Fraternity of St Anne, Chester, cf. St Ann's St. 337 *infra*, *Ste Annes Heyes infra*, and *a lake called in olde tyme St Anne's Lake* 1573 Morris, part of Flooker's Brook stream, 1 24.

ALDERSEY HO, cf. *Aldersays Closse* 1620 Sheaf, from the surname from Aldersey 82 *supra* and clos. FIELD HO, 1831 Bry, *v.* feld. GREEN-FIELD COTTAGE. HARE LANE FM, *v.* hara, lane. HOLLY HO. HOOLE BANK, 1842 OS, -*or Hoole Mill* 1831 Bry, *v.* banke, myln. HOOLE COTTAGE, FM, HALL, HO, LANE (FM), LODGE & PARK, *Hoole Hall* 1724 NotCestr, *Hoole House & Lodge* 1819 Orm[2], *Hoole Lane* 1842 OS. Cf. Old Hall *infra.* OAK BANK, OAK LEA, near the Royal Oak p.h., *The Oak* 1831 Bry. OLD HALL (109-433686), *Hall Farm* 1831 ib, the site of the Hoole Hall, *the Hall of Hole* 1645 Hem 1 197, which was burnt down in 1642 during the siege of Chester, cf. Orm[2] II 813, ChetOS VIII 137 n.8. PIPER'S ASH (109-434675), 1838 *TA*, *Piper Ash* 1831 Bry, *v.* æsc, at the boundaries of Hoole, Guilden Sutton and Great Boughton. The first el. is pīpere 'a piper', or the derived surname, cf. 125, 128 *supra.* THE STREET, cf. *Street Field* 1838 *TA*, Pavement Croft *infra*, *v.* 1 40 (Route IV).

FIELD-NAMES

The undated forms are 1838 *TA* 205. Of the others 1272-1307 (17), 1393 (n.d.), 1497 (17), 1507 (17), 1519 (17), 1589, 1653, n.d. (17) are Sheaf, 1339 (17) Orm[2], Sheaf, 1393 (17) Orm[2], 1393 (m15) *Harl.* 2061, 1395, 1414, 1440, 1599, 1600 *Chol*, 1459 (1594) ChRR, 1471 *MinAcct*, 1582, 1670 *Corp*, 17 *Bun*, 1831 Bry.

(a) In St John's parish: Bunburys Hay (cf. *the Great Hay* 17, from (ge)hæg and grēat and the surname *Bunbury*); Shoulder of Mutton (*v.* 337 *infra*).

In Plemstall parish: Barn Croft (cf. *the Barne Hey* 17, *v.* bere-ærn, (ge)hæg); Beavans Hay (cf. *Bavands Croft* 17, from the surname *Bavand* and croft); Bottoms (*v.* botm); Brosters Croft (17, from the surname *Broster* and croft); Clay Pitts; Garners Lane 1831 (on the boundary of Mickle Trafford, cf. 137 *infra*); Golden Grove; Gorsey Hays, -Heys (*the Gorstie Hey* 17, -*Gorstye-* 1582, *v.* gorstig, (ge)hæg); Hovel Fd (*v.* hovel); Main Hay (*the Meyne Hey* 17, *v.* (ge)mǣne); Mill Fd (*the Mill Feild* 17, *v.* myln); Moat Fd (*v.* mote); Ox Hay (*the Oxe Hey* 17, *v.* oxa, (ge)hæg); Park Fd; Pavement Croft (109-426687, on The Street *supra*, *v.* pavement); Pickhay; Pingot Fd (*v.* pingot); Sealands; Shoe Bridge Fd; Shonesfield; Slang (*v.* slang); Sparks Hay (*v.* spearca, (ge)hæg); Town Fd; Welch Loons ('Welsh

selions' probably belonging to a Welshman, v. Welisc, land); Withy Hay
(*The Withenhey* 17, *-within-* 1670, v. wiðigen, (ge)hæg).

(b) *Bryklesfeld* 1395, 1414, 1440 (v. feld); *Cauldacres Hey* 17 ('(enclosure
of) cold ploughlands', from cald and æcer, with (ge)hæg); *the Coxheye* 1589,
Coxhty Cornell 1653 ('(the corner of) the cock's enclosure', v. cocc², (ge)hæg,
corner); *Houghshey* 1339 (17), *Hole He(t)gh* 1393 (m15), *Hole Hey* 1393 (17),
1459 (1594), 1471, cf. *þe Heyes* 1497 (17), 1507 (17), 1519 (17) ('the fenced-in
enclosure(s) at Hoole', v. (ge)hæg; the *Harl.* 2061 form may be due to
confusion with Hoole-Heath *supra*); *Hull Sych* n.d. (17) (v. sīc, cf. Hoole
supra); *the Kill Croft* 17 (v. cyln, croft); *the Marld Hey* 17 (v. marled,
(ge)hæg); *Ste Annes Heyes* 1599, *Saincte Annes Heyes* 1600 (*Harl.* 2061
indicates that these are probably the same as *Hole He(t)gh supra*; 'enclosures belonging to the Fraternity of St Anne, Chester,' v. (ge)hæg, cf.
Hoole Rd *supra*); *Salterway* 1272–1307 (17), n.d. (17), *Saltesway* 1339 (17)
('salter's way', v. saltere, weg, cf. 1 40 (Route V), Salter's Lane 132 *infra*,
Hoole Heath *supra*); *Sasse Diche* 1339 (17), *-dyche* n.d. (17) (perhaps 'ditch
at a willow copse', from salceie and dīc); *Wysnaysich* 1339 (17), *Wismay
Sych* n.d. (17) (from sīc 'a watercourse', perhaps with a stream-name
Wysnay 'marsh-stream', from wise and ēa, cf. Wiswell La 77).

2. Picton (Hall & Lane) (109–4371) ['piktən]

Picheton 1086 DB, *-tone* 1096–1101 (1280), 1150 Chest
Picton c.1200–1250 Chest *et freq* with variant spellings *Pycton,
Pi(c)kton, Py(c)kton; (molendinum de-)* c.1200–50 Chest, 1303
Chamb, *(boscus de-)* 1303 Chamb, *(-Farm)* 1656 Orm², *(-Hall)*
1724 NotCestr
Pyketone c.1276–7 AD, 1309 ChRR (p), *-ton* 1295 Cl, *Piketon*
1287 Court, *(-iuxta Hole)* 1288 ib, *Pycketon* 1295 Ipm
Peketon 1304 Chamb, *Pecton* 1318 (p), 1334 Orm² (p)
Pitton (molendinum de) 1326 Chamb
Petton 1332 Pat
Picken 1692 Sheaf

'Pīca's farm', from an OE pers.n. *Pīca* and tūn, with hall, lane,
myln, wudu. Topography and medial *-e-* are against pīc 'a pointed
hill'. Picton was in *Wilaveston* (Wirral) hundred, DB.

Ash Hay Lane, *Seven Acre Lane* 1831 Bry, v. seofon, æcer, cf. *Ash
Hays* 1838 *TA, the two Ash Hays* 1725 Dow, 'ash-tree enclosures', v.
æsc, (ge)hæg.   Hill Fm, v. hyll.   Manor Fm.   Picton
Gorse, a farm named from a fox-covert *Picton Gorse* 1831 Bry, v.
gorst.   Salter's Lane (109–437697 to 430698), 1831 ib, cf.
Salters Butts 1838 *TA*, from saltere 'a salter', and lane, butte, v. 1
40 (Route V).   The Street, *Street* 1842 OS, v. 1 40 (Route IV).

FIELD-NAMES

The undated forms are 1838 *TA* 321. Of the others 1303 is Chamb, 1339 (17) Orm², Sheaf, 1620, n.d. (17) Sheaf, 1725 *Dow*, 1831 Bry, 1842 OS.

(*a*) Birch Dale (*v.* birce, dæl¹); Bridge Mdw 1725; Common Patch; Crabtree Fd (cf. *the four Crabtree Hays* 1725, *v.* crabbe, trēow); Cross Fd (*v.* cros); Dale Fd (cf. *Pykton Dale* 1339 (17), *Pykton Diche* n.d. (17), bounds of Hoole Heath 130 *supra, v.* dæl¹, dīc); Six Days Math (*the Six Day Math* 1725, *v.* day-math); Dove House Croft (1725); Four Lane Ends; Green Lane 1831; Hall Gates (*the Hall Yates* 1725, *v.* geat); Hall Hay 1725 (*v.* hall, (ge)hæg); Heath Fd (cf. *Picton Heath* 1620, *the Heath Hay, the three Great Heaths* 1725, *Heath Lane* 1831); Hervin Fd (cf. Wervin 137 *infra*); Hoole Fds (cf. Hoole 129 *supra*); Horse Hay (*v.* (ge)hæg); Huntlet (for *Outlet, v.* outlet); Intake (*the Intack* 1725, *v.* inntak); Know Hill (*v.* cnoll); Meach Hill Croft; Mick(a)le Mdw (*v.* mikill, mæd); Milking Bank Fd (*-Feild* 1725 *v.* milking)); Moor Fd (*Pickton Moore* 1725, *v.* mōr¹); Outlet (*v.* outlet); Pewit Moor (*v.* pewit); Pingle (*v.* pingel); The Pockets (*v.* poket); Push Plow Mdw (*v.* push-plough); Rathinick Dale & Fd; Rushy Mdw (*v.* riscig); Sheep Cote Hays (*the Five-* 1725, *v.* scēp, cot, (ge)hæg); Sinders (*the Synders* 1725, from synder, adv. 'asunder, apart', here as a sb., cf. Cinders Wo 84); the Sleak's Fd, the Sleaks Mdw 1725 (from slyke, slicu, adj. 'smooth, glossy', here as a sb.); Upper Stalks; Standleys; Stoke Hays (*v.* (ge)hæg, cf. Stoke 181 *infra*); Within Hay (*v.* wiðigen, (ge)hæg); Wood Lane 1842 (*Old Lane* 1831, cf. 140 *infra*, and *boscus de Picton* 1303, *v.* wudu, lane, ald); Woollams Croft (*the Woollhams Crofts* 1725, from croft with either a surname *Woolham* or a f.n. 'wool meadows' from wull and hamm).

3. MICKLE TRAFFORD (109–4469)

Traford 1086 DB f.263b, 1270–71 (1652) Chest (p), *Trafford* 1287 *Dow* (p) *et freq* with variant spellings *Trafforde, Trafforth* to 1742 NotCestr, (-*Green*) 1671, c. 1820 Sheaf, (-*Brooke*) 1671 ib
Troford 1086 DB f.263b (Wimbolds Trafford 3 260), *Trofford* 1288 Plea (p), 1294 ChFor *et freq* with variant spellings *Trofforde, Troffort* to 1446 ChRR, *Throford* c.1330 Chol (p)
Trosford 1086 DB f.263 (Bridge Trafford 3 261), 1288 Court (p), *Trochford* 1096–1101 (1280), 13 (1332) Chest, -*fort* 1150 ib, *Trocford* 1188–91 ib, 1240 P (once lit. *Croc*-), 1241 Lib (lit. *Trot*-), 13 Tab, 1295 Cre (p), *Trokford* 1240 P, 1291 Cl, *Trocfford* c.1270 Sheaf (p), *Trocforde* e14 ib, *Trohcford* 13 Bun, *Throkford* 1240 P, *Trouchford* 1270–1310 Chol (p)
Trohford 1208–26 Facs (p), c.1215 CoLegh (p), 1267 (1580) Sheaf, 1274 (p), c.1306 Chest (p), *Trhoford* 1240 P

Trogford 1240 Cl, 1288 Court (p) and six times, Plea, ChF, ChRR, Pat, Cl to 1398 ChRR, *-forde* 1489 ib

Trogheford 1254 Pat, *Troghford* c.1272 Ipm *et freq* with variant spelling *-forde*, *-fford* to 1524 ChRR, *Throghford* 1456 Pat (p), *Troughfourde* 113 Sheaf, *-ford* 1304 Chamb, 1354 BPR, 1521 Plea, 1524 ChRR, *-forde* 1531 ib

Trovford 1265–91 Chest (p), *Trouford* 1267–8 Sheaf (p), 13 *Bun*, 1327 Ch, 1328 Pat, *Trowefordia* c.1268–95 Chest (p), *-ford* H3 Orm², 1325 *Chol* (p)

Trahford 1271 BW (p), *Traghford* 1535 VE, 1549 Orm²

Trefford 1288 Plea (p)

Troght(h)ford 1290 Court

Magna Trogthforde 1290 Court *et freq* with variant spellings *-Troghford(e)*, *-Troughford(e)*, *-Trafford* (from 1528 Orm²) and variant forms *Trocforde Magna* (e14 Sheaf), *Troghford Magna* (1454 ChRR) to *Trafford Magna alias Midle Trafford alias Mickle Trafford* 1671 Sheaf

Mekeltroghford 1379 *Eyre*, *Mykull Troghford* 1416 ChRR, *Mickle Trafford* 1616 ib *et freq*, *-Traford* 1690 Sheaf, *Michaell Trafford* 1679 ib

Great Troghford 1398 ChRR, *-Trafford* 1549 Orm², (*-alias Mickle Trafford*) 1616 ChRR, *-Traghford* 1549 Orm²

Midle Trafford (*Trafford Magna alias-*, *-alias Mickle Trafford*) 1671 Sheaf

'The main part of Trafford', *v.* grēat, **magna**, **mikill**, distinguished from Bridge- and Wimbolds Trafford 3 261, 260. Mickle Trafford was in *Wilavestun* (Wirral) hundred DB. *Trafford* is 'trough-ford' from **trog** and **ford**. The *Traf-* spellings are partly due to ME unrounding of *-o-*; but also partly to AN influence by which this p.n. appears to have been interpreted as 'ford on a Roman road' i.e. *Stratford* with loss of initial *s-* and assimilation of *tf* > *ff* as in Trafford La 32, DEPN, *v.* strǣt, ford. A Roman road crossed R. Gowy at Trafford Bridge, *v.* 1 40 (Route IV). The 'trough' is probably an allusion to some characteristic of the ford itself, for the valley of the R. Gowy at the point of crossing (Trafford Bridge *infra*) has not the aspect of a trough (cf. DEPN). There may have been a trough standing near the ford; or the ford may have been deeply worn for the approaches to it along low natural ridges of firm ground across the Gowy marshes were very narrow, which would compel all users to follow the same track at and in the river.

PLEMSTALL (109–456700) [ˈplemstɔːl, ˈplemstou] older local [ˈplim-stʌn, ˈplinstə], PLEMONDESTALL BRIDGE

(ecclesia de) *Pleymundistowe* c.1129–48 (l13) *StRO*, n.d. (14) *Harl.* 3286 p.7, (ecclesia de) *Pleymundestowe* c.1161–82 (l13) *StRO*, 1291 Tax *et freq* with variant spellings *Ple(y)-, Play-, Ply-, -mun(de)-, -mundi-, -mon(de)-, -stow(e), -stou* to 1466 ChRR

Plegemundusham l12 Gerv
ecclesia de Pleimindestowe 1280 (l13) *Shrews*
Playmestowe 1348 *Eyre, Pleymstowe* 1512 ChRR, *Plemistowe* 1656 Orm²
Plemstow(e) 1535 VE, *-stou* (lit. *-ston*) 1546 Dugd, *Plymstou(e)* (lit. *-ston(e)*) 1539–47 Dugd, 1671 Sheaf, *Plimstow(e)* 1579 Dugd, 1620 Orm², 1662 Sheaf, *-stou(e)* (lit. *-ston(e)*) 1670, 1699, 1784 ib, *Plumstow* 1646 ib, *-stoue* (lit. *-stone*) 1677 ib
Plawstowe 1560 Sheaf
Plemonstall 1573 Sheaf, *Plemondstall* 1684 ib, 1724 NotCestr (*-or Plemstow*), 1819 Orm² (*-Bridge*) 1831 Bry
Plimstall 1599 *Chol,* 1691 Sheaf, *Plym-* 1600 *Chol, Plemstall* 1620 Sheaf, 1724 NotCestr, 1842 OS
Ploverstowe c.1662 *Surv*
Blimstone 1670 Sheaf
Plimstine 1686 Sheaf

The date of the original of the form from *Harl.* 3286 is that of a witness, Roger bishop of Chester, probably 1132, cf. Orm² II 171, 172. Plemstall is the name of the ancient church here, dedicated to St. Peter, and is extended to the parish, cf. Wilmslow I 219–20. The p.n. is 'Plegmund's holy place' from stōw and the OE pers.n. *Plegmund.* Nearby, on the opposite bank of R. Gowy, in Little Barrow, was *Seint Pleymondes Well* 1302 Plea, 'the well of the holy man Plegmund', cf. 3 264. The two p.ns. must be associated in the tradition that Plemstall was the hermitage of Plegmund, archbishop of Canterbury 890–914 and a literary associate of King Alfred, *v.* Orm² II 808. The first record of this tradition is Gervase of Canterbury's observation of *Plegemundus . . . qui in Cestria insula quae dicitur ab incolis Plegemundusham, per annos plures heremiticam duxerat vitam*, 'Plegmund who had for several years led the life of a hermit in an island near Chester which is called by the inhabitants *Plegemundusham*', Gerv II 350. The religious and hagiological association of the rather rare pers.n. *Plegmund* with two neighbouring places in Ch, the location of Plemstall in the marshes beside R. Gowy at a site liable even now to isolation by floods (cf. Holme Ho *infra*), and the ancient parochial status of Plemstall church (St. Peter's) suggest that Plemstall is the place to which Gervase alludes. Professor Whitelock suggests that Gervase has mistaken the p.n. form by confusing Plemstall with the Kentish place *Pleguuiningham*, *Plegwingham* BCS 407, 408 (cf. KPN 170–171), written *Plegimundham* in Gerv I 45, which was a possession of Christ Church Canterbury. It is not certain whether the tradition originates with Gervase or is reported by him. On the one hand, he may have known archbishop Plegmund to have been a Mercian and then inferred a biographical connection between him and a Ch p.n. whose form he mistook but in which he observed the same pers.n. On the other, he may be reporting an already accepted tradition relating to some place in Ch with a name unfamiliar to him for which he substitutes the more familiar form of another p.n. appearing to contain the pers.n. *Plegmund*. The independent existence by c.1300 of a local tradition of a holy man Plegmund at Plemstall is indicated by the well-dedication, and this suggests that Gervase is reporting. The tradition may erroneously identify the known Plegmund archbishop with an unknown holy man whose name appears in the Ch p.ns., but in view of its age it would be interesting, perhaps also convenient, to suppose the two holy men identical in fact. There is no reason why they should not be. The garbled p.n. form given by Gervase provides the only ground upon which the tradition can be questioned, and Professor Whitelock's observation offers one answer to that question. Another might well be that Gervase could have had information before him which gave an alternative name for this obscure and lonely place beside the marshes of Gowy, such as 'Plegmund's **hamm**' which would suit the situation, but which, under the influence of the religious association, could well have been superseded in local usage by the *-stow* name.

BACK BROOK, *v.* back, brōc, an old channel of R. Gowy forming a watercourse on the boundary between Bridge Trafford and Eddisbury hundred. BEECH HO, *v.* bēce². GREEN LANE, 1842 OS, *v.* grēne[1], lane.   HOLME HO, *Home House* 1671 Sheaf, *the Holm-house* 1724 NotCestr, *v.* holmr 'an island', hūs. This is near to Plemstall; cf. Gervase's allusion to 'an island' *supra.*   HOOLE RD, cf. 130 *supra.*   MEADOW LEA FM, *v.* mǣd, lēah.   THE STREET, *v.* 1 40 (Route IV).   TRAFFORD BRIDGE, cf. Bridge Trafford 3 261, Mickle Trafford *supra, v.* brycg.   TRAFFORD MILL, *molendinum de Trafford* 1304 Chamb, *Trafford Mylne* 1527 ChRR, cf. *Mill Green* 1831 Bry, perhaps also the site of a hamlet called *Trafford Brooke* 1671 Sheaf, *v.* myln, grēne[2], brōc.   TYRE FM, cf. *Tyre Lane* 1831 Bry.

FIELD-NAMES

The undated forms are 1838 *TA* 264. 1831 is Bry.

(a) Bridge Hurst (*v.* hyrst, cf. Trafford Bridge *supra*); Brows (*v.* brū); Church Hurst (*v.* hyrst; named from St Peter's church at Plemstall *supra*); Cranmers Croft; Hall- & Long Dale (*v.* dǣl[2], hall, lang); Daws Mdw; Garners Lane 1831 (cf. 131 *supra*); Hayes Mdw; Hoole Fd (cf. Hoole 129 *supra*); Hungerhill (*v.* hungor, hyll); King Lane 1831; Lady Mdw (*v.* hlǣfdige); Mickle Moor (*v.* micel, mōr[1]); Pains Moor; Pingo (*v.* pingot); Rake Fd (*v.* rake); Ross Hill; Rye Croft (*v.* ryge).

xxi. St Oswald's

For the rest of this parish *v.* 337 *infra.*

3. WERVIN (109–421719) ['wǝ:vin]

   Wivrevene, Wivevrene 1086 DB
   Weruenam (acc.) 1096–1101 (1280) Chest, *Weuenam* (acc.) 1150 ib, *Werven* 1695 Sheaf
   Weveresham 1096–1101 (17) Dugd, Chest
   Wir, Wyruin, Wirvyn 1157–94, 1214–23, 1233–7 Chest *et freq* with variant spellings *Wi-, Wy-, -ru-, -rv-, -in, -yn* to *Wyrvin* 1724 NotCestr, (lit. *Wyroin* 1291 Court 175, *Joyrvyn* 1362 Orm[2] II 772, *Wyrbyn* 1539–47 Dugd II 393, *Wirum* 1610 Speed)
   Wiruena 1188–91 Chest, *Wyruen* 1286 Eyre (p), *Wirven* 1295 Ch (lit. *Wirnen* 1295 CRC), *Wyrven* 1552 Sheaf
   Wireuen 1216–23 (17) Chest
   Wirvyn 1285 Court (p)
   Wyrwin 1291 Tax, *-wyn* 1348 Pat, 1356 *AddCh, Wirwin* 1509–47 Plea, *-wyn* 1516 *ChEx,* 1593 Orm[2]

Wyrfuyn c.1310 Chest
Wervyn 1351 Chamb, 1409 ChRR (p), 1552 Sheaf, 1579 Dugd,
    -*vin* 1509–47 Plea, 1579 Dugd
Wirvell 1554 Sheaf

The form *Weveresham*, occurring in a late copy (*v.* Dugd II 385,
Chest I 3 n.18), is erroneous, and may be due to a confusion with
Weaverham 3 205. A local dialect form appears in Hervin Fd 133
supra.

Wervin is a difficult p.n., for which a number of tentative etymolo-
gies are available. Dr. Barnes (Barnes[1] 323) suggests 'marsh where
the bog-myrtle grows', from **wīr** and **fenn**, but this does not fit the
spellings. The explanation proposed by Ekwall (DEPN and ES 64,
225) from **fenn** and R. Weaver 1 38, is geographically improbable,
since Wervin is three or four miles from the Mersey estuary, which
he supposes part of R. Weaver, and R. Gowy and several townships
intervene. Wervin lies between the west bank of R. Gowy and the
lost *Wervin Brook* (now the Shropshire Union Canal), *a little
rivolet called Wirwir* c.1642 (17) Sheaf[3] 19 (4601), *Harl.* 2155.
Wirwir is probably a mistake for *Wirvin*. This may be a back-
formation from the p.n., but the watercourse-name Warvin Lake 43
supra in Malpas seems similar, may be analogous, and might suggest
a stream-name proper or some common appellative as the origin of
both. Wervin and Warvin may both be from **fenn** with a common
r.n. identical with that of R. Weaver. Again, the first el. in Wervin
may be OE **hwifer*, 'a beam or the like', which Professor Smith
(PNE s.v. **hwip(pe)*) adduces as the origin of the ME *wiver* 'a long
beam of wood' (cf. NED) in explanation of the OE charter-forms
which Ekwall identifies with Withermarsh Sf, *v. infra*. In this case,
Withermarsh and Wervin were both marshes with 'a long beam'.
Archæologically this would be feasible if the allusion were to some
such structure as the legendary *Kate's Pad*, a floating causeway of
single oak logs laid and fastened end to end, traversing several miles
of peat-bog near Pilling La and recently discovered by excavation,
cf. F. J. Sobee, *A History of Pilling* (1953), 19–21, and *Amounderness,
Report of the Regional Planning Committee for the Fylde Area* (The
Fylde Region Joint Town Planning Advisory Committee, 1937),
17–18.

Professor Ekwall (DEPN and Studies[3] 96–98) derives Withermarsh Green Sf (*æt Hwifersce* (for *æt Hwifermersce*) c.995 BCS 1288,

Wifærmyrsc, to Hwifermirsce, to hwifræmera c.9ç; BCS 1289) from
mersc 'a marsh' and OE ***wifer** adj. 'shaking' (cf. BTSuppl ***hwifer**),
which he relates to ModE dial. *w(h)iver, whither* 'to tremble, to
shake'. He rejects Professor Smith's etymology (*supra*), and the
BTSuppl form, explaining the *Hw-* forms in the OE sources, and the
Wither- forms of later spellings of Withermarsh, as onomatopoeic
modifications or as forms influenced by ON **hviðra* 'to go to and fro
with quick movements, to hover', cf. NED *whither* sb. and vb. From
the spellings, Wervin could be like Ekwall's Withermarsh, 'a
quivering marsh, a quaking bog', with **fenn** for **mersc**. The marsh
could have been beside R. Gowy or the canal, *v. supra*. None of these
explanations can be accepted as certain. They represent efforts to
prove this an English p.n. It may eventually appear that Wervin and
Warvin Lake are like Tarvin 3 281 and Macefen 37 *supra*, not
English but Welsh in origin. However, no analogous Welsh p.ns.
have yet been discovered.

ASH WOOD, ASHWOOD HO, cf. *Big & Little Ashes* 1849 *TA*, *v.* æsc,
wudu. CHAPELHOUSE FM, *the Chapel House* 1875 Sheaf, named
from the ruins of Chester abbey's ancient chapel of Wervin. MILL
BROOK, *v.* Mill Brook[1] 1 32. WERVIN NEW- & -OLD HALL.

FIELD-NAMES

The undated forms are 1849 *TA* 419. Of the others, 1398 is *Add*, 1432,
1440 *Rental*, 1620 Sheaf, 1725 *Dow*, 1831 Bry, 1842 OS.

(a) Boar's Heath; Bottoms (*v.* botm); Bridge Moor; Brook Dale (*v.*
dæl[1], cf. *Wervin Brook* 138 *supra*); Bunbury Mdw (from the surname
Bunbury); Butty Fd (*v.* butty); Chester Fd (probably belonging to Chester
abbey, cf. Chapelhouse *supra*); Coalpit Mdw (*v.* col[1], pytt); Cork's Fd &
Moor; Crofts; Crosshays, Cross's Hay, Crosses Heys (either 'enclosures
near a cross or crosses' or 'enclosures belonging to one Cross', from cros or
a surname *Cross* and (ge)hæg); Croughton Mdw (cf. Croughton 179 *infra*);
Densons Leys (from the *Denson* family of Chapelhouse *supra* 1422–1849
Sheaf[3] 7 (1438), *v.* leāh); East and West (*v.* 336 *infra*); Fishers Croft, Fish's
Croft; Gorse Hill (1725); Gorsty Fd (cf. *Gorsty Crofts* 1725); Long Green
(*v.* grēne[2]); Green Lane (1831, *v.* grēne[1], lane, the boundary between
Wervin and Caughall 140 *infra*); Hall Green, Hall(s) Moor (cf. *Halls
Meadow* 1725, *v.* hall, cf. Old Hall *supra*); Further-, Little-, Near & Top
Heath (cf. *Calves Heath, Little-, Marshes- & Next Heath* 1725, *the Heath
Ground* 1620, *v.* hǣð); Hemp Dale (*v.* hænep, dæl[2]); Hickson's Croft (cf.
Hixsons Meadow 1725, from the surname *Hickson*); Hignett's Croft 1725;
Hooded Moor; the Two Hoordings 1725; Hop Yard (*v.* hoppe, geard);

Horsehills (*v.* hors, l.yll); Kiln Croft; Lakes Croft (1725, *v.* lacu); Long Mdw 1725; Mare Fd; Marled Fd; Midfeathers; Monks Croft (*v.* munuc, cf. Chester Fd *supra*); Further-, Near-, Big- etc., Moor(s), Moor Hay (cf. *Wervin Moor* 1725, *Moor Lane* 1831, 1842, *v.* mōr[1]); Outlet (*v.* outlet); Big & Lt Ox Pasture (*the two Ox Pastures* 1725); Pocket (*the Pockitt Feild* 1725, *v.* poket); Poor Fd; Rushy Mdw (*Rushey Meadow* 1725); Shaking-bridge Mdw (cf. Shaking Bridge 3 260); Short Parts (1725, *v.* sc(e)ort, part); Big & Little Stanlas; Far & Near Swartins (perhaps 'black meadow', from svartr and eng); White Fd (*-Feild* 1725); Withy Hay (*the Withen Hays* 1725, *v.* wiðegn, (ge)hæg); Wood Lane 1842 (*Old Lane* 1831, *v.* 133 *supra*).

(*b*) *Broderenes* 1398, *les Brodereenes* 1432, *-renes* 1440 ('broad strips of land', *v.* brād, rein).

xxii. Backford

For the rest of Backford parish, *v.* 172 *infra*.

1. CAUGHALL (BRIDGE, FM & MANOR) (109–4170) [ˈkɔːgəl]

Cochull 1278 Chest, 1315 *AddCh*, *-hul* 1309 Sheaf (p), 1312–18 *JRC* (p)

Corhull 1278 Whall

Coghull 1278 Orm[2] (p), 1295 ChF (p) *et freq* with variant spellings *-hul(le)* to 1525 ChRR, *Coghall or Coghull* 1819 Orm[2]

Cohghill 1295 Cl (p)

Coghhull 1318 *Eyre* (p)

Goghull' a.1360 (m15) *Harl.* 2061 (p)

Coghill 1386 Fine (p)

Coghowe 1554 Pat

Caughall 1612 Orm[2], 1725 *Dow*, (*-Iron Bridge*) 1831 Bry

Coughall 1620 Sheaf, 1831 Bry

Coghall 1656, 1819 Orm[2] (*or Coghull*), 1845 ChetOS VIII

Coughow 1671 Orm[2]

The final el. is hyll 'a hill', cf. Butter Hill *infra*. The first el. appears in alternative forms *Coc-*, *Cog-*. It may be cocc[2] 'a cock, a woodcock', with voicing *c > g* in the cpd., [kɔkul > kɔgul], giving OE **cocc-hyll* 'hill frequented by (wood-)cocks'. But the alternation of forms would be more easily explained if the first el. were taken to be an alternation of cocc[1] 'a hillock, a heap' and the el. cogg 'a cog of a wheel' in the figurative meaning 'a hill' proposed Löfvenberg 43, DEPN s.n. Cogges O (cf. O 333). Perhaps Caughall represents hyll added to an original hill-name *Cock*, *Cogg*.

BUTTER HILL (109-411706), 'a steep sandy hill in this township, which is a considerable thoroughfare towards Chester, has the name of Butter Hill from a tradition that the Wirral market people deposited their butter and other commodities here, when the plague at Chester forbade their nearer approach to the city', 1819 Orm[2] II 818. The commercial importance of this route, known as *Flag Lane* 1831 Bry in Caughall and Upton 142 *infra*, is apparent in the earliest references to Caughall *supra*, where the bounds of Whitby and Stanney 198, 182 *infra* meet a certain public road which leads from Whitby to Chester passing under Caughall (*subtus Cochull*), which was named *le Portwey*, v. 1 49 (Route XXVIII (i)) and Chest I 309. It is not clear whether the tradition reported by Ormerod is the origin of the name, or whether it is a folk-etymology. Butter Hill may be, in contrast with Hungrel *infra*, a hill of rich pasture, v. butere, hyll. The origin of *Flag Lane* is not obvious; it could have been a reedy lane, from flagge 'a reed, a rush'.

FIELD-NAMES

The undated forms are 1838 *TA* 95. Of the others, 1620 is Sheaf, 1725 *Dow*, 1831 Bry.

(a) Butty Fd (v. butty); Chester Fd; Crabboes Hays (from (ge)hæg and the surname from Crabwall 169 *infra*); Flag Lane 1831 (v. Butter Hill *supra*); Green Lane 1831 (v. 139 *supra*); (Big & Little) Heath (*Coughall Heath* 1620, *Caughall Heath* 1725, v. hǣð); Hungrel ('barren hill', v. hungor, hyll, cf. Butter Hill *supra*); Kiln Croft; New Hay (v. (ge)hæg); Sandy Hay (v. (ge)hæg); Town Fd; Whetstones (v. hwet-stān).

xxiii. St Mary on the Hill

The Chester parish of St Mary contained, in Broxton Hundred, the townships Moston, Upton, Claverton (160 *infra*) and Marlston cum Lache (162 *infra*). For the rest of the parish, v. 337 *infra*. Moston was part of Backford parish 172 *infra* down to 1599 (*Chol* A176, Orm[2] II 362, 818). In 1286 *ChFor* it was within the forest of Wirral, and the Chester cartulary indexes it as in Wirral. Upton was in *Wilaveston* (Wirral) hundred DB, and was *-in Wyrehale* 1416 Orm[2] II 819, perhaps mistaken for Upton 305 *infra*.

1. MOSTON (HALL) (109-4070) ['mɔstən]

    Morsetona 1121-9 (1150), 1150 Chest, *-tuna* 1121-9 (1280) ib,   *-tun* 1208-26 ib, AddCh, c.1225 CASNS x, *Morston* 1121-9,   13 Chest, 1286 ChFor *et freq* with variant spellings *-tona, -tone*

to 1436 Tab, (-*iuxta Bacford*) 1331 Plea, *Moreston* 1295 CRC
(lit. *Meres-* 1295 Ch 460), 1357 *ChQW*, *Magna Morston'* 1461
Outl
Morcetone 1121–9 (1285) Chest
Moston 1286 Court (p) *et freq*, (-*iuxta Cestr'*) 1315 Plea, (-*iuxta
Bacford*) 1331–4 *AddCh*, (*Backforde next-*) 1553 Pat, *Moston
Hall* 1831 Bry
Mostyn 1360 ChRR, 1553 *JRC*, 1724 NotCestr, -*in* 1663 *JRC*
Moson 1655 Sheaf, *Mosson* 1663 ib

Ekwall (DEPN) proposes 'tūn by *Mōrsǣ* (lake by a moor)', from
mōr[1] and sǣ, with tūn. However, the second el. is probably (ge)set
'a place for animals, a stable, a fold, a dwelling'. It is not certain
whether the earliest forms represent an OE compound *mōrset-tūn
or a reduced form of the OE dat.pl. *mōr-setum (> *mōr-setun >,
with metanalysis, *mōrse-tūn). The p.n. Moston is either 'the folds
at the moor' or 'enclosure, farmyard, at the moor-fold', *v.* mōr[1],
(ge)set, tūn.

BACKFORD BRIDGE, *Moston Bridge* 1831 Bry, *v.* **brycg.**   THE DALE,
a nineteenth-century residence near a hollow, cf. *Dale Field* 1838
TA, *v.* dæl[1].

FIELD-NAMES

The undated forms are 1838 *TA* 275. Of the others 1392 is *Add*, 1432, 1440
Rental, 1539 Orm[2], 1564 *AddCh*, 1579, 1626 Sheaf, 1599, 1600 *Chol*,
1831 Bry.

(*a*) Amerys Corner 1831; Brickiln Fd (*v.* bryke-kyl); Corner Fd; Fair
Fd (*v.* fæger); Hovel 1831 (*v.* hovel); Long Fd; Sand Hole Fd; White Fd.

(*b*) le Bothum 1432, le Bythum 1440 (*v.* boðm, byðme); *Longe Medowe*
1539, the- 1564, *Le Longe Medowe* 1579, the *Longe Medowes* 1599, 1600,
Long Meadows 1626 (*v.* lang, mǣd); le *More Medowe* 1432, 1440 ('meadow
at a marsh', *v.* mōr[1], mǣd).

2. UPTON (GRANGE, HALL, HEYES & LANE) (109–4169)

Huptun 958 (13) BCS 1041, (14) Chest, -*ton* 958 (16), (17) ib, KCD
473, Dugd
Optone 1086 DB, -*ton* 1260 Court (p), 1291 Tax, 1308 *Port*, 1387
Eyre
Uppetuna 1096–1101 (1280), 1121–9 (1150), 1150 Chest, -*tona*
1150 ib
Uptuna 1121–29 (1285), 13 Chest (p), -*tun* 1295 ib, -*tona* 1129–53

ib, *Upton* 1260 Court *et freq* with variant spellings *-tone, -tona*;
(*-iuxta-, -near-, -by-, -nigh-, -Chester, -Cestr(e)*, etc.) 1323 Orm[2],
Plea *et freq,* (*-juxta Neuton*) 1328 Orm[2], 1357 *ChQW,* (*-in
Wyrehale*) 1416 Orm[2], (*-in the parysshe of Saynt Marys uppon
the Hille*) 1539 ib, (*-iuxta Bache*) 1579 ib, *Upton Grange & Hall*
1831 Bry

'High(er)-up farm or enclosure', from upp(e) and tūn, with
grange, hall, (ge)hæg and lane. This township was originally in
Wirral, *v.* 141 *supra.* It is distinguished from Upton 305 *infra* as
near Chester, Bache and Newton 336, 144, 145 *infra.* Upton was a
manor of Chester abbey.

BACHE POOL (lost, 109–404682), *le Bachepol* 1354 (1379) Ch, *Bachepull*
1355 Sheaf, (*le*) *Bachepole* 1432 *Rental et freq, passim* with variant
spellings as for Bache 144 *infra* and (*the-*) (from 1555 Sheaf), *-Pole*
(to 1549 Pat), *-Poole* (1540 Sheaf to 1713 *Assem*), *-Pool* (from 17
Sheaf), to *Bache Pool* 1842 OS, *Back Pool* 1860 White, 'the pool at
Bache', a lake filled in c.1875–85, on the boundaries of Upton,
Bache and Chester, on the east side of Liverpool Rd, Chester.

ACRES FM, *Acres* (*Lane*) 1831 Bry, cf. *The Acres* 1588 Sheaf, *The
Great Acres* 1596 ib, *v.* æcer, lane, grēat. Acres Lane is in line with
Salter's Lane 132 *supra, v.* 1 40 (Route V).   THE CROSS, a house
named from a cross shown 1831 Bry at the crossroads 109–409689,
cf. *iii landas terre iuxta crucem* 1398 Add, *Cross Croft & Field* 1839
TA, v. cros.   DAMAGE HALL (lost), 1831 Bry.   FROGHALL,
1831 ib.   THE KNOLLS, cf. *Knowles* (*Field & Meadow*) 1839 *TA,
v.* cnoll.   THE MOUNT.   PLÂS NEWTON, pseudo-Welsh, a
nineteenth-century residence near the Newton boundary, *v.* place.
UPTON HEATH, 1620 Sheaf, *le heth* 1432 *Rental, v.* hǣð.   UPTON
PARK, a residential estate, but perhaps the same place as *the parke of
Upton* 1521 Life, *v.* park.

FIELD-NAMES

The undated forms are 1839 *TA* 407. Of the others, 1348 is *Vern,* 1398 *Add,*
1432, 1440 *Rental,* 1550 (1569), 1576 ChRR, 1560 Pat, 1831 Bry, and the
rest Sheaf.

(*a*) Alder Loons (*v.* alor, land); Back Lane 1831; Black Croft; The
Boosoms (perhaps from boðm but Professor Löfvenberg suggests that the
origin may well be OE *bōsum dat. pl. of bōs (ModEdial *boose*) 'a cow stall');

Broad Hay (*v.* (ge)hæg); Brocks Hay (*v.* brocc, (ge)hæg); Caughall Heath
(*v.* hǣð, cf. Caughall 140 *supra*, *Coghulbruches infra*); Claphatch Mdw (*v.*
clap-hatch); Common Fd (cf. Upton Common 1750); Crab Fd; The Dale
(cf. *Waldale* 1432, 1440, 'hollow at a spring', *v.* wælla, dæl¹); Ditch Croft
& Loons (*v.* dīc, land); Flag Lane 1831 (*v.* Butter Hill 141 *supra*); Flats (*v.*
flat); Fluits Hill; Footway Fd (*v.* fote-waye); Fox Holes; Greets (cf. *Grutte*
1398 Sheaf³ 9 p.80 (though *Add* 36764 m.3 may read *le Brucce*), *le Creete*
1432, *le Creece* 1440, perhaps 'gravelly place', from grēote); Hatch Fd (*v.*
hæc(c)); Hay Fd (cf. *le Haylond*, *-hailondes* 1398, (*le*) *Hey-*, *Haylondes* 1432,
les- 1440, 'hay selions', *v.* hēg, land); Hoole Fd (cf. Hoole 129 *supra*);
Horse Pasture; Kiln Croft; Longfield (*le Longfeld* 1398, 1432, 1440, *v.*
lang, feld); Long Lane 1831; Marl Hays (*v.* marle, (ge)hæg); New Hay (*v.*
(ge)hæg); Newton Fd (cf. Newton 145 *infra*); Peas Hay (*v.* pise); The Peg;
Picton Fd (cf. Picton 132 *supra*); Long Piece; Pingot (*v.* pingot); Pitch Croft
(1681); Port Croft & Fd (*v.* port); Rake Hay (cf. *le Rakefeld* 1398, 1440, *le
Rake* 1432, *v.* rake, (ge)hæg); Riddings (*v.* ryding); Round Bottoms & Hill
(*v.* rond, botm, hyll); Salter(s) Butts (cf. *Salteresway* 1398, *Saltersway* 1432,
1440, from saltere 'a salter', and weg, butte, cf. Salter's Lane 132 *supra*, I 40
(route V)); Server (*v.* server); Long Slang (*v.* slang); Sour Fd; Thorn Hay
(*v.* þorn, (ge)hæg); Wall Hills (*le Wallehull* 1398, (*le*) *Walhull* 1432, 1440,
'hill by a spring', *v.* wælla, hyll); Walnut Fd; Water Pit Croft; Wet Reans
(*v.* wēt, rein); Wheat Fd (*le Whetefeld* 1432, *v.* hwǣte, feld); White Fd (*le
Whitefeld* 1398, *v.* hwīt, feld); Wings (*v.* wing, cf. *Bachewynges* 147 *infra*);
Woodfield.

(b) *Coghulbruches* 1398, *Coghull bruches* 1432, 1440 ('breakings-in of
land near Caughall', *v.* bryce, Caughall 140 *supra*); *le Flaxbuttes* 1398, *les-*
1432, 1440, cf. *les Flaxelond'* 1432 ('selions where flax is grown', *v.* fleax,
butte, land); *Haggefurlong* 1398, *Hagfurlong* 1432, 1440 ('furlong where
haws grow', *v.* hagga, furlang); *Hogg House* 1579; *Longefurlong* 1432 (*v.*
lang, furlang); *Long Meadow* 1576, *le Longe Meadowe* 1579; *Lymmes Hey*
1567 (from (ge)hæg and the surname from Lymm 2 36); *Spencer Heyes*
1653 (from (ge)hæg and the surname *Spencer*); *campus de Vpton* 1348,
Upton Feild 1550 (1569), *-Feildes* 1560 (*v.* feld); *Wiruynacres* 1398 ('arable
fields near Wervin', *v.* æcer, cf. Acres Fm *supra*, Wervin 137 *supra*); *les
Wynbuttes* 1432, 1440 (perhaps 'headlands growing with whin', from hvin
and butte, but the first el. could be winn 'a pasture').

xxiv. St Oswald's

For the rest of this parish *v.* 337 *infra*.

4. BACHE BROOK, COTTAGE, HALL & MILL (lost) (109–4068)
[batʃ]

Bache 1119 (1150) Chest *et freq* with variant spelling *Bach* (1428
ChRR to 1713 *Assem*), *la-* 1240–9 Chest, *le-* 1322 Plea, *the-*

1539–47 Dugd; (*molendinum de-*) 1119 (1280) Chest, (*molendinum aquaticum del Bache*) 1398 *Add*, (*the Bache Mylne*) 1555 Sheaf, (*-Milne*) 1570 Morris, (*Bache Mill*) 1579 Dugd, (*messuagium de Bache*) c.1240 Chest, (*manerium de Bache*) 1584 (1587) ChRR, *Le Bache iuxta Cestr'* 1519 ChRR, *the Bach-hall* 1645 Hem, *Bach by Chester* 1668–71 Sheaf
Beche 1119 (1285) Chest, (*molendinum de-*) 1150 Chest, *la Beche* 1347 BPR, *Bechia* 1121–9 (1150), 1150 Chest, *Bechiana* c.1311 ib
la Bage 1250 *JRC* (p)
Bayche 1540, 1555 Sheaf
the Baits 1656 Orm[2], 18 Sheaf
Beach 1741, 1750 Sheaf

'The valley-stream', from bæce[1], bece[1], with brōc, hall and myln. Cf. *Bache Pool* 143 *supra*, *Bach Meadow(e) infra*, *Bach Dale*, *Beach Flatts* 336, 336 *infra*. Bache Brook becomes Finchett's Gutter 1 23.

FIELD-NAMES

The undated forms are 1844 *TA* 31. Of the others, 1525 is Orm[2], 1555, 1620, 1786 Sheaf, 1660 *Rental*.

(*a*) Crooks Loon 1786 (*v*. krókr, land); Garden Fd; Knowl Fd (*Bach Knowle* 1620, *þe Knowles Hey* 1660, *v*. cnoll, (ge)hæg); Moat Fd (*v*. mote).

(*b*) Bach Meadow(*e*) 1620, 1660 (*v*. mǣd, cf. Bache *supra*); Collys Hey 1555 (from (ge)hæg and a surname *Colly*, cf. *Collys Lands* 336 *infra*); *þe Courtes* 1660 (*v*. court); Douehouse Hey 1660 (*v*. dove-house); Fishers Hey 1660; Glaseors Hey 1620, *þe Glasiers Hey* 1660 (from (ge)hæg and the surname *Glazier*. *v*. Addenda); *þe Grasse Hey* 1660 (*v*. gærs, (ge)hæg); *þe Kilne Hey* 1660 (*v*. cyln, (ge)hæg); Lookers Hey 1620; Rake Hey 1660 (*v*. rake, (ge)hæg).

5. NEWTON BY CHESTER, NEWTON BANK, COTTAGE, HALL & LANE (109–4168)

Newentone 1086 DB
Neutone 1086 DB, *Neutona* 1119 (1280), 1150 Chest, *Neuton* e13 ib *et freq* with variant spellings *-tone*, *-tona* to 1450 *Rental*, 1724 NotCestr, (*-iuxta Cestr'*) 1295 Cl, (*-Upton*) 1318 Orm[2], (*-Hole*) 1450 Plea, (*-le Bache*) 1519 ChRR, *Hole Neuton* 1410 ib
Neton 1295 CRC
Newton 1307 ChRR *et freq*, (*-iuxta Cestr'*) 1329 IpmR, (*-Upton*) 1589 ChRR, *Newton Hall & House* 1831 Bry, *Newton Lane* 1842 OS

'New farm', from nīwe (wk. dat.sg. nīwan) and tūn, with banke, hall and lane. This township adjoins Chester 336 *infra*, Upton, Hoole and Bache 142, 129, 144 *supra*. *Hole Neuton* is a dubious form, perhaps due to bad punctuation in a list of names between Hoole 129 *supra* and Newton, but it may mean 'Newton at the hollow', from hol², cf. Newton Hollow *infra*, or 'Newton near Hoole' with the p.n. Hoole prefixed.

FLOOKERSBROOK (109–411672), now a suburb of Chester, originally a hamlet in Newton and Hoole, cf. 130 *supra*, taking its name from the stream Flooker's Brook 1 24. The hamlet appears as *Flokersbroke, Folkers Broke* 1550 *MinAcct*, and thereafter with spellings as for the stream-name to *Flookers Brook* 1831 Bry, *Flooker Brook* 1842 OS, cf. *Flookersbrooke Crofts* 1615 Orm². There was a hall here, *Flookersbrook Hall* 1664 Sheaf, burnt down 1642, cf. Folly Ho *infra*, *v.* hall, croft.

HEATH HOUSES (lost), 1724 NotCestr, *le Hethous* 1376 *Eyre* (p), (*le*) *Hethehouse, -howsse*, (*-nere Newton*) 1539–47 Dugd, Orm², *MinAcct*, 1553 Pat, m.16 *AOMB* 397, *Heath House* 1579 Dugd, 1681 Sheaf, *the-* 1620, 1696 Sheaf, 'house(s) on the heath', *v.* hǣð, hūs.

BROOKFIELD HO, 1831 Bry, cf. *Brook House* 1831 ib, and foll. BROOK LANE, 1831 ib, *Raymond Lane* 1642 Sheaf, cf. prec., named from Flooker's Brook 1 24. The original of the pers.n. *Raymond* in the older form is unknown. THE CROFTS, *v.* croft. FOLLY HO, 1861 Sheaf, *The Folly* 1644 (1819) Orm², described 1777 Sheaf¹ 3, 46 as 'that strong octagon building formerly built or intended for a Wind Mill' on the site described 1664 ib as 'a capital messuage or scite near *the Brooke*, where *Flookersbrook Hall* formerly stood', cf. Flookersbrook *supra*, *v.* folie. HEYWOOD LODGE, cf. *Little Hay Wood, Hay Wood Field* 1842 *TA*, *the High Heywood* 1620 Sheaf, 'wood in an enclosure', *v.* (ge)hæg, wudu. NEWTON BROOK (> Bache Brook 144 *supra*), *le brocsiche* 1312 *AddCh*, *Newton Bro(o)k(e)* 1540, 1573, 1594 Morris, *v.* brōc, sīc, cf. Flooker's Brook 1 24. NEWTON HOLLOW, *-s* 1842 *TA*, OS, *v.* holh. This lane is on the line of The Street 131, 137 *supra*, 109–416677 to 420678, *v.* 1 40 (Route IV). SPRINGFIELD, *-House* 1831 Bry, probably from spring 'a well-spring'.

FIELD-NAMES

The undated forms are 1842 *TA* 288. Of the others, 1240–9, 1267–8 are Chest, 1273, 1282 Orm[2], 1278, 1560 Pat, 1280, 1291, c.1292, 1312, 1314–17, c.1320, 1342, 1488 *AddCh*, 1280[2], c.1290, 1291[2], 1292[2] CASNS x, 1313, 1318, 1323, 1450, 1620, 17, 1691[2], 1878 Sheaf, 1339 (17) Orm[2] and Sheaf, 1398 *Add*, 1432, 1440 *Rental*, 1550 ChRR, 1691, 1705 *Assem*, 1725 *Dow*, 1749, 1753 *Wil*.

(*a*) Amans Hay; Big Pits (cf. *campus qui vocatur le Puttis* 1291, *the Puttes* 1450, in which were selions called *le Putlondis* 1280, 1291, *-londes* c.1290, c.1292, *le Puttislondis* 1291[2], 'the pits', *v.* pytt, land); The Great- *&* Little Birches (cf. *le Bruches* c.1290, 1398, *Neutonbruches* 1398, 1432, 1440, 'the breakings-in of land', *v.* bryce); Brick Bank (*v.* bryke); Brook Mdw (named from Flooker's Brook 1 24); Channel Croft *&* Fd (*v.* chanel); The Coppice; Folly Fd (cf. Folly Ho *supra*); Grove Fd (*v.* grāf); Heath Piece (cf. Heath Houses *supra*); Hovel Fd (*v.* hovel); Intake (*v.* inntak); Lammas Cote; The Lanclet; the Leverpoole Redding 1749 (*v.* ryding); Mainwaring Heys (from (ge)hæg and the Ch surname *Mainwaring*); Major's Fd; Newton Townfield 1725 (*campus de Neuton* 1240–9, 1267–8, *Newton Felde* 1488, *-Feylds* 1550, *-Feildes* 1560, *Newton Towne Feilds* 1691, *v.* toun, feld); Newton Wd (1831); Great Play Hay; Rake Hay, Rake Lane Fd (*Rakes* 1398, *les-* 1432, *v.* rake, lane, (ge)hæg); Ridding(s) (*les Rydynges* 1432, *v.* ryding); Sandy Lane 1705; St Aganippa's Well (local) 1878 (Sheaf[1] 53, 70, named after the fountain Aganippe at Mount Helicon on account of the purity of its water. Popular error had canonized the name. Cf. *Newtoneswell infra*); Sandhole Fd; Shaw's Fd 1753; Shoulder of Mutton (*v.* 337 *infra*); The Stivers; Strive; Well Croft.

(*b*) *les Bachewynges* 1432 (cf. Wings 144 *supra*, Bache 144 *supra*, *v.* bæce[1], wing); *le Bradelakelondis*, *-es* c.1290, c.1292 ('(selions at) the broad stream' or 'broad selions-by-a-stream', *v.* brād, lacu, land); *le Bradewey* (a road) 1280, *Braddewai Londes* 1450 ('(selions at) the wide road', *v.* brād, weg, land); *le Brocstanlond* 1280, 1290, c.1292, *le Brocstallond* 1314–17, 1318 ('(selion at) the stone near a brook', from brōc and stān, with land); *Caryngfeld* 1398, *Karensfeld* 1432 (perhaps 'Kari's field', from the ODan pers.n. *Kari* with -ing-[4] and feld, cf. Carrington 2 17 *supra*); *le Cleylond(is)* 1280, *-es* c.1290, *le Clayland*, *-londes* c.1292, *the Clelondes yendes*, *-yndes* 1450, cf. *le Cleyhalflond*, *le Cleyheuetlond*, *-heued-*, c.1290, c.1292 ('selion, half-selion and head-land on clay ground', 'the ends of the clay-selions', *v.* clǣg, land, half, hēafod-land, ende[1]); *Newton Common* 1620 (*v.* commun); *le Croftlond* 1314–17 (*v.* croft, land); *the Cuttings* 1691[2] (portions of land cut off from the town field, *v.* cutting); *the old diche* 1339 (17) (*v.* ald, dīc, a boundary ditch); *Edmundislond* c.1290, c.1292 ('Edmund's selion', from the OE pers.n. *Ēadmund* and land); *Fregreue* c.1290, 1291, c.1292, *Frogreue* 1291[2], *le thregreues* 1314–17, *le Thregenes* 1318, *Fregrewes* 1450 ('common wood', *v.* frēo, grǣfe. The forms show confusion of initial *F-* and *Th-* suggesting þrēo, cf. *Figdale* 150 *infra*); Le *Gostland* 1318 ('gorse selion', *v.* gorst, land); *le Grenewey* 1291, *-wegh* 1291[2] (*v.* grēne[1], weg); *Healies Knowle*

1620 (from a surname *Healey* and cnoll); *the old Heys* 1339 (17) (*v.* **ald,** (ge)hæg); *Hoke Hadelond* 1450 ('headland at an oak' or 'at a hook of land', from hēafod-land and āc or hōc); *le Ioustyngheuedlond, le Iusting heuetlond* c.1290, c.1292 ('headland where jousting was held', from justing 'jousting, a tournament' (14, NED) and hēafod-land. Cf. The Justing Croft 336 *infra*); *Le Laynseche* 1314–17 ('watercourse through a tract of arable land', *v.* leyne, sīc); *Le Longheuetlond, -heued-* c.1290, c.1292 (*v.* lang, hēafod-land); *le Longgelond* 1280 (*v.* lang, land); *the Lowe in Seldefeld* 1282 ('the mound', *v.* hlāw); *Lullefurlong(e)* 1432, 1440, *-lond* 1440 ('Lulla's furlong', from the OE pers.n. *Lulla* and furlang); *le Merstallond* 1291, *-land* c.1320, 1323 ('selion at a pool', *v.* mere-steall, land); *Mieldegrene* 1450 (from the plant-name melde and grēne²); *Mollington Meadowes* 17 (*v.* mǣd, cf. Mollington 177 *infra*); *Munkesfeld* 1273 (*v.* munuc, feld); *Newtoneswell* 1278 (*v.* wella, cf. *Wallebuttis infra*. The well was the source from which a conduit was to be led to Chester abbey 1278 Pat 279. On the excellence of the spring-water cf. St Aganippa's Well *supra*); *Parche Croft* 1450; *Seldefeld* 1282 ('field at a dwelling-place', *v.* seld, feld); *le Sondwal(le)lond* 1291, 1291², 1292² ('selion at) the sandy spring or well', *v.* sand, wælla, land); *the Shepe Yate* 1339 (17) ('gateway for sheep' *v.* scēp, geat; an access from Newton to Hoole Heath 130 *supra*); *le Schoterdicheheuetlond, -heued-* c.1290, c.1292 ('(head-land at) the shooter's ditch', from scēotere 'a shooter, an archer' and dīc with hēafod-land); *le Schouelebradlondis* 1280, 1280², *-es, le Shovelebradeslondes* c.1290, c.1292, *le Schouelebradlond* 1312, 1313 ('the shovel's-breadth selions, narrow selions', *v.* scofl-brǣdu, land); *le Sperthe* 1398, *le Spert* 1432, *the Sperthis* 1450 ('the place(s) covered with sheep-muck', *v.* sparð); *le Stiweylandis* 1280, *-londis* 1280², *le Styweylond(es), -is* c.1290, c.1292, *the Styway-* (*Lands*), *the Stiway* 1450 ('(selions at) the path-way', *v.* sty-way, land); *le Twerslondes* 1342 ('selions lying athwart', from ON adv. þvers 'athwart', cf. þverr, and land); *le Wallebuttis* 1291, *-Wale-* 1291² ('butts near a well or spring', *v.* wælla, butte, cf. *Newtoneswell supra*); *le Wetforlongd* 1291 (*v.* wēt, furlang); *Mr Brownes Hey called the White Feild* 1620 (*v.* hwīt, feld. Here (ge)hæg is a living el.); *Withen Hey* 1620 (*v.* wiðegn, (ge)hæg); *Yockinnescrofte* 1398 (from croft and the ME pers.n. *Jokin*, diminutive of *Jok, Juk*, the short form of OBret *Judicael*, cf. Reaney s.n. *Juggins*, Feilitzen 301. Sheaf³ 9, 80 reads *Yockyunestrete*).

xxv. Eccleston

Eccleston parish contained the townships 1. Eaton, 2. Eccleston.

1. EATON (HALL, GREEN (lost) & PARK) (109–4160) ['i:tən]

Eaton iuxta aquam quae dicitur Dee in Cestræ provincia c.1050 KCD 939, Dugd III 191, Orm² II 831, *Eaton* 1313 InqAqd, 1387 Tab, 1551 Pat *et freq*, (township of) *Eaton-boat* 1666 Orm², *Eaton Green* 1671, 1771 Sheaf, *Eaton cum Belgrave* 1724

NotCestr, *Eaton Park* 1837 *TA* 159, *Eaton Hall* 1656 Orm², *Eaton Palace* 1882 Orm²

Etone 1086 DB, 1096–1101 (1150), 1150 Chest, *Etona* 1157–94 ib, *Eton* 1178–90, 1229–33 Whall, 1250 P *et freq* to 1549 Sheaf, (-*Streche*) 14 Whall, (-*iuxta Dee*) 1391 Dugd, *Etun (iuxta Alinton)* 1208–29 Dieul, *the haule of Eton* 1566 Orm²

Etthona, *Etthone* 1096–1101 (1280) Chest, *Ettona* 1180–1216 HarlCh, *Etton* 1305 Sheaf

Ethun 1153–80 (1427) Pat, 1154–60 (1330) Ch, *Ethon* c.1170 (17) Dieul, 1246 Ch, CRC

Heton 1188–91 Chest

Eyton 15, 1709 Sheaf

'Farm by a river', from ēa and tūn, with hall, grēne², and park. Eaton is beside R. Dee 1 21, and is separated from Allington in Denbighshire (NCPN 194) by Poulton and Pulford 153, 155 *infra*. The family *Streche* owned land near *Figdale infra*, cf. Orm² 11 383 n.1. There was a ferry here, *v. Eaton Boat infra*. The extensive park of Eaton Hall extended as far as Chester and across the river into Buerton. It obliterated the hamlets of *Eaton Green supra*, Belgrave, *Figdale infra* and Buerton 79 *supra*. Mr J. E. B. Gover observes that some street-names in the Westminster estate of the Grosvenors of Eaton are taken from places in the family's Ch estate, e.g. Aldford St., Belgrave-, Chester-, Eaton- and Eccleston Square, cf. Mx 175–178.

BELGRAVE (AVENUE, LODGE & MOAT) also BELGRAVE BRIDGE, COTTAGES & FM 151 *infra* (109–390605)

Belgreue c.1290 Chol (p), -*greve* 1309 Orm² *et freq* to 1581 ChRR, (-*in Ecleston*) 1309 Orm², -*greave* 1580 ib, 1618, 1636 Sheaf, 1641 ChRR, *Bellgreave* 1596 ib, 1611 Sheaf

Beligreve 1311 Plea, *Belegreue* 1353, 1355 Indict, Eyre (p), 1357, 1362 BPR (p)

Belgrave 1350 Tab (p) 1362 BPR (p) *et freq*, (-*in the township of Eaton-boat*) 1666 Orm², (*Eaton-*, *Eccleston cum-*) 1724 NotCestr, *Belgrave Farm* 1771 Sheaf, -*Lodge* 1842 OS, -*Moat* 1831 Bry

Bulgreve 1351 Chamb (p)

Bealgrave 1364 BPR (p)

The final el. is græfe 'a grove, a copse, a thicket'. The first el. is bēl¹ 'a fire', probably here 'a beacon' as in Baycliff La 208, notwith-

standing Ekwall's rejection of the element in NoB (1957) 139 and
DEPN. The p.n. might mean 'copse where a beacon stood', but
there would be a fire risk, so the more likely meaning is 'copse for a
beacon, belonging to a beacon' the wood being reserved as fuel.
Belgrave Avenue was *The Avenue* 1842 OS (*v.* **avenue**), the lodge was
'a gothic lodge in the hamlet of Belgrave' 1818 Orm² II 838 (*v.* **loge**).
The moat (109–390605) appears to be the site of the original manor
of Belgrave, cf. Moat Fm *infra*. The hamlet and manor have been
obliterated by Eaton Park.

EATON BOAT (lost, 109–420605), *Etonboot* 1404 ChRR, *le Eton Bote*
1465 Orm², *Eton Bott* 1530 *Dav*, *the Eton Boat* 1549 Sheaf, *Eaton
Bot* 1562 ib, *Eaton-Boat* 1656, 1666 Orm², *Eaton Boat* (*House*) 1671,
1716, 1745, 1771 Sheaf, *Eaton-Boate* 1672 Orm², *Eyton Boat* 1709
Sheaf, *Eaton Boat* 1745 ib, *the Boat House* 1711 ib, *Eytonis Boote*
1415–82 ib, *le Bote* 1430 ib, 'the ferry-boat at Eaton', *v.* **bāt**. This
ferry-boat is mentioned in 1307–27 Orm² II 832 and appears as a
feudal incident of Eaton manor, cf. 'manor of Eaton with the ferry
and free boat there' 1502, 1509, 1543 Orm² II 835. This is an ancient
ferry originally crossing R. Dee from Buerton to Eaton, cf. Boat
Lane 80 *supra*. In the eighteenth century it was removed to Eccleston
Ferry 118 *supra*, 151 *infra*, and the old ferry house, the "Boat
House" inn, was demolished, cf. Sheaf¹ I (313, 324), Sheaf³ 40
(8535, 8545). In 1666 the ferry gave rise to the name *Eaton-boat*
sometimes used as the name of the township.

FIGDALE (lost, about 109–412617)

> *Fikedene* 1296 *Vern*, *Fykedene* 1344 Sheaf, 1353 *Eyre* (p), 1392
> ChRR, 1430 Orm², 1544 (1573) ChRR, *-den* 1392 Orm²,
> *Fikeden* 1439 (1460), 1440 ChRR, *Fykdene* 1460 ib, *Fikden*
> 1460 Orm², 1508, 1519 ChRR, 1537 Plea, 1539 *MinAcct*,
> (*-in Eton*) 1509 Orm², *Fykden* 1544 Plea
> *Thykeden* c.1300 Orm² II 838, n.1.
> *Fygden* 1457 Sheaf, *Figden* 1579 Dugd, 1662, 1671 Sheaf, 1724
> NotCestr, (*Over-*) 1579 Dugd, (*-now called Figdale*) 1816
> Lysons
> *Figdale* 1481 Orm², 1771 Sheaf, 1842 OS, (*-or Figden*) 1739 Sheaf,
> (*Figden now called-*) 1816 Lysons
> *Figdon* (*-within the parisshe of Ekleston*) 1539–47 Dugd, Orm²

'Thicket valley', *v.* þicce[1], denu, dæl[1]. Initial *F-* displaces *Th-*, cf. *Fregreue* 147 *supra*, and the form is influenced by ME *fyke*, *fike* (OE *fīc*) 'a fig-tree', cf. *fike* NED. The site of the hamlet, near Eaton Stud *infra*, is discussed in Sheaf[1] 1, pp. 88, 101.

CROOK OF DEE, *Crooked Dee* 1831 Bry, 1842 OS, cf. 80 *supra*, named from a great elbow of R. Dee here, *v.* krókr, R. Dee 1 21. EATON STUD, *Stud House* 1831 Bry, *v.* stōd. GAS COTTAGES, named from the gas works of Eaton Hall. KENNEL WOOD, named from the kennels at Eaton Hall. MOAT FM, named from Belgrave Moat *supra*, cf. *Moat Croft* 1837 *TA* 159, *v.* mote.

FIELD-NAMES

The *TA* for Eaton township is included with that of the parish of Eccleston in *TA* 159, *v.* 152 *infra*; other minor names listed here are 1307–27 (17) Orm[2], 1358 BPR, 1499 *Chol*, 1549 Sheaf, 1831 Bry, 1842 OS.

(*a*) Brick Fds 1842 (cf. Brick & Tile Works (6″), and Cuckoo's Nest 156 *infra*, *v.* bryke); Greenfield Plantation 1842; New Road 1831 (109–385606 to 395592).

(*b*) *Calvesmore* (*v.* 158 *infra*); *Coltesmore* 1549 Sheaf ('colt's marsh', *v.* colt, mōr[1]); *Eton Weir* 1307–27 (17), *Etonwere* 1358 (*v.* wer); *Hercliffe* 1549 ('higher cliff', *v.* hēarra (Angl. hēr(r)a), clif).

2. ECCLESTON (109–4162) [ˈekↄstən]

Eclestone 1086 DB, Ecclestona c.1188 Tab et freq with variant spellings -ton(e), Ec(c)lis-, (H)Ecles-, Ec(c)kles-, Ekles-, Eck(e)les-, Ecklis-, Ecclus-, Ecculs-; Eccleston ultra Dee 1310 Orm[2], Eccleston cum Belgrave 1724 NotCestr
Heclesenne c.1250 (1353, 1383, 1400) Pat
Egleston, -is- 1506 ChCert

'Farm called *Eccles*', from tūn added to a p.n. from PrWelsh eglẹs 'a church'. The township included part of Belgrave, *v.* foll. It is *ultra Dee* 'beyond Dee' from Chester.

BELGRAVE (BRIDGE, COTTAGES & FM), *v.* 149 *supra*. DEESIDE COTTAGES. EATON RD, *v.* 1 42 (Route VIII). ECCLESTON FERRY, *v.* 118 *supra*, cf. *Eaton Boat* 150 *supra*. ECCLESTON HILL (FM & LODGE), *Eccleston Hill Lodge* 1842 OS, cf. *Hill Wood* 1837 *TA*, *v.* hyll. ECCLESTON KENNELS, LODGE & PADDOCKS, part of the Eaton Hall estate. THE GLEBE (a plantation), *v.* glebe.

THE GULLET, a wood, probably named from a hollow here, *v.* golet.
HALF MOON PLANTATION, from its shape, *v.* 336 *infra.*   JOHNSON'S
ROUGH, 1842 OS.   MILL HILL HO, *Mill Hill & Field* 1837 *TA,*
v. myln, hyll.   MORRIS OAK COTTAGES.   RAKE FM & LANE,
Rake Farm 1771 Sheaf, *Rake (Lane)* 1831 Bry, *v.* rake, lane.
WREXHAM RD, 1837 *TA,* leading to Wrexham, Denbighshire.
WREXHAM ROAD COTTAGES, *v.* 164 *infra.*

FIELD-NAMES

The undated forms are 1837 *TA* 159 which includes Eaton, cf. 151 *supra.*
Of the others 1247, 1270–1307, 1295–6, c.1301, 1342 are *Vern,* 1537, 1549,
1555, 1605, 17, 1613, 1616, 1771 Sheaf, 1540–1 Orm², 1747 *LRMB* 257,
1831 Bry.

(*a*) The Acres; Arm of the Pike; Banbury; Broad Hay (*v.* (ge)hæg);
Butchers Fd & Hay (*the Botchers Hey* 1549, from bocher 'a butcher' and
(ge)hæg); Clem Park (*v.* clǣme, park, cf. Clemley 3 47); Cole Croft (*v.*
col¹); Craven(s) Marsh; Cuckoo's Nest (cf. Cuckoo's Nest 156 *infra*);
Doney Hay; Higher-, Lower- & Middle Dunstan (*Donstanes Gorstes*
1295–6, 'Dunstan's gorsy places' or 'gorse-bushes', from the OE pers.n.
Dunstān and gorst); Bottom Ease (*v.* ēg); Eaton Park Wall Barn 1771
(presumably a barn against the wall of Eaton Park); Eccleston Lane;
Flash Mdw (*v.* flasshe); Founder's Croft; Far- & Near Furlong (*v.* furlang);
The Green Hay (*v.* (ge)hæg); Greets (*The-* 1747, þe *Greetes* 1650, 'the
gravels', *v.* grēot); Intake (*v.* inntak); Lady's Mdw (*v.* hlǣfdige); Landed
Mdw ('meadow divided into strips', *v.* land); Leasowe (*v.* lǣs); Leather
Fd; Marl(ed) Fd; Marsh Croft (1747, *v.* mersc); Mesopotamia Waste
(probably because lying between two streams, a humorous allusion to
the Levant or Eton College, *v.* 337 *infra*); Narrow Lane 1831; Ox Hay
(*v.* (ge)hæg); Paradise Croft (*v.* paradis); The Parson's Heys 1747 (*Parsons
Hay* 1613, *v.* persone, (ge)hæg); The Pavement Croft (at 109–391609, *v.*
pavement, cf. Pavement (Hay) 155 *infra*); Pingo (*v.* pingot); Riddish Hay
(from ryge and edisc, or hrēod and dīc, with (ge)hæg); Sheepcote Hay (*v.*
scēp, cot); Smooth Wd; Sour Croft; Stone Bridge Hay; Stretton (a group of
fields at 109–393614 to 400615; 'enclosure at a Roman road', *v.* strǣt, tūn.
Eccleston is on a Roman road, *v.* 1 42 (Route VIII), but this site is not on
that alignment. Perhaps this f.n., and the f.ns. in *Pavement supra* and 155
infra, indicate some archaeological feature not yet accounted for); Swine
Acres (*v.* swin¹, æcer); Townfield Lane 1831 (*The Great-, -Lesser Townfield,
the Townfield Croft* 1747); White Fd; Wordhead.

(*b*) *Beggersburghe* 17 ('beggar's manor', the sarcastic name of a farm
belonging to one Thomas Wright of Eccleston, cf. Sheaf³ 16 p.65, *Harl.*
2046 f.32, *v.* beggere, burh); *Le Breches* 1295–6 ('the breakings-in of land',
v. brēc); *Cristynch* 1270–1307 ('a croft, an enclosure', *v.* cryfting, cf.
Crystynges WRY 7 176; *le Dale* 1270–1307 (p) (*v.* dæl¹, perhaps from

Figdale 150 *supra*); *le Dinggel* c.1301, *-Dyngull* 1346 ('the ravine', *v.*
dingle); *Eccleston Wood* 1537; *Emby Meadows* 1605; *Hethecocuscroft* 1270–1307
('heath-cock's croft', from croft and an OE **hǣð-cocc* 'heath-cock, grouse',
which lies behind ME *hethe-coc* (recorded here), *hathe-cok* (as a ME nickname 1273–4 Reaney 160, Bardsley 371, s.n. *Heathcock*) and ModE *heath-
cock* (1590 NED). The nickname may also appear in this f.n.); *þe Hyron Yate*
1650 (perhaps 'gate made of iron', but there is no evidence that the reference
is to such a structure, and the form *hyron* suggests 'gateway at a nook or
corner', from hyrne, as in Heronbridge etc., 336 *infra*, *v.* geat); *Kerehull*
1295–6 (from hyll 'a hill', perhaps with kjarr 'brush-wood'); *Ledsoms
Haye* 1605 (from (ge)hæg with the surname from Ledsham 217 *infra*);
(*Le-*, *La-*) *Lee* 1247, 1270–1307, 1295–6 (a wood, *v.* lēah, cf. *Leefeld* 162
infra); *le Longefeld* 1295–6 (*v.* lang, feld); *Pembertons Meadow* 1650 (from
the Chester surname *Pemberton*, cf. Pemberton Croft 161 *infra*); *Quetehull'*
1295–6 ('wheat hill', *v.* hwǣte, hyll); *Saynt Eudlokes Medowe* 1540–41
(Orm² III 195), *Saynt Gudlock's Medowe* 1555, *St Goolock's Meadow* 1616
(Sheaf² I, pp. 121, 124) (named after Saint Gūðlāc, the founder of Croyland
abbey L, c.700. The reason for this dedication is not known); *Sowefeilde*
1650 (perhaps for *Sower-*, from sūr and feld, cf. Sour Croft *supra*, but the
first el. is probably sugu 'a sow'); *le Stremsiche* 1301 ('running watercourse',
v. strēam, sīc); *Wetemor* 1295–6 ('wet marsh', *v.* wēt, mōr¹).

xxvi. Pulford

The ecclesiastical parish of Pulford contained the townships 1. Poulton,
2. Pulford.

1. POULTON (109–3959) ['puːltən]

Pontone 1086 DB f.265
?*Puntona* 1146 *Cott.* Nero C III, f.215
Poutona 1146 Dieul 74, *Pouten* 1699 Sheaf, *Poton* 1557 ib, *Pooton*
    1656 Orm², 1680 Sheaf
Pultun' m12 StRO (abbas de-), *Pulton* 1153 Dugd (*abbatia de-*),
    1153–80 (1427) Pat, 1154–60 (1330) Ch *et freq* with variant
    spellings -*thon*, -*tune*, -*tona* to 1724 NotCestr, *Pulton Green*
    1671 Sheaf
Polton (-*a*, -*e*) c.1180, 1190–94, 13, 1217–29, 1245–50, 1251–5
    Dieul
Poulton c.1208–29 Tab (*abbatia de-*), *Poulton . . . behind the
    Forrest of Delamere* 1543 (1581) Sheaf, *Poulton* 1641 ChRR
Pukton 1277 P
Poolton 1656 Orm², 1724 NotCestr

'Farm by a stream', *v.* pōl[1], pull, tūn. The stream is Pulford Brook 155 *infra*. The DB identification rests upon Tait 143. The spelling of *Cott.* Nero C III f.215, the foundation charter of the abbey at Poulton, is corrupt. Facs 1 and Dugd v 628 read *Puntona*, Dieul 74 reads *Poutona*, but the MS has been altered, either to *Puntonā* from original *Poiltonā*, or to *Puiltonā* from original *Pontonā*. For the date of this document cf. Facs p.2. For the alternation of *-nt-* and *-lt-*, cf. Poltimore D 444. The abbey of Poulton was removed in 1214 and re-established near Leek St as Dieulacres Abbey. Poulton remained a grange of Dieulacres until the dissolution, cf. foll. It lay beyond Delamere Forest from the St house.

BLACK & WHITE COTTAGES (109–407592), *grangia de Pulton'* 1315 StRO, *the Grange of Pulton* 1560 Sheaf, *the Halle of Pulton* 1599 Orm[2], *Pulton Hall* 1671 Sheaf, *Poulton Hall* 1831 Bry, 1842 OS, *v.* grange, hall, cf. Poulton *supra*.   BROAD AVENUE, a ride of Eaton Park, *v.* avenue.   CHAPELHOUSE FM, cf. *capella de Pulton* 1520 ChRR, *the chapell of Poulton* 1543 (1581) Sheaf, *the Chappell Feld & Medowe* 1598 (17) Sheaf, *Chapel Field* 1837 *TA*. The chapel, decayed in 1672, now disappeared, was at 109–403583, cf. Sheaf[3] 35 (7831).   DUCK WOOD, *Meadow Plantation* 1842 OS.   GREEN FM, *Pulton Green* 1671 Sheaf, *v.* grēne[2].   IRON BRIDGE, an iron bridge over R. Dee to Aldford, on a drive of Eaton Park 148 *supra*, *v.* 78 *supra*.   OXLEISURE POOL, an artificial lake made in a meadow called *Ox Leasowe*, *v.* oxa, lǣs, pōl[1].   PEARTREE FM, cf. *Pear Tree Hay* 1837 *TA*.   POULTONHALL FM (109–396597), named after Black & White Cottages *supra*.   POULTON LANE, *v.* lane.   THE SERPENTINE, a lake.   WALLET'S FM, *The Walets*, *Wallet Field* 1837 *TA*, *v.* walet.   WINDMILL HILL, *Mill Hill* 1842 OS.   YEW-TREE FM.

FIELD-NAMES

The undated forms are 1837 *TA* 332. Of the others 1208–29, 1208–10, e13 are Dieul, 1569, 1598 (17) Sheaf, 1831 Bry.

(a) Barns Croft (*the Barne Croft & Pitt* 1598); Boat Mdw (perhaps from bōt, of a meadow where *hay-bote* was used); Butchers Hays (cf. 152 *supra*); Cow Hay (*v.* (ge)hæg); Ell Mdw; Fallow Fd; Gammocks Walks (*v.* walk); Gorsey Hooks (*v.* gorstig, hōc); Hand Hay; Hard Mdw (*v.* heard); Hearnalls Hill; Holywells Croft; Meadow Lane 1831; Mowel Cravens; New Road 1831 (*v.* 151 *supra*); Park Lane 1831 (lost, 109–395592 to 407603, in Eaton Park); Pavement, Pavement Hay (*v.* pavement; the locations are 109–

402594 and 400597 respectively, cf. The Pavement Croft 152 *supra*);
Thorny Doe (*v.* þornig, dāl); Wigmear Fd.

(*b*) *Calvesmore* (*v.* 158 *infra*); *the Deares Orchard* 1598 (*v.*
orceard); *Hartcliff* 1569, *Hardcliffe* 1598 (probably 'hard bluff', *v.*
heard, clif); *the Hemp Butt* 1598 (*v.* hænep, butte); *Hules* 1208–29, 1208–10, e13 ('the
huts', from hulu with a ME plural); *the Poole Mott* 1598 ('embankment or
moat at a pool or stream', from mote and pōl[1], here possibly Pulford Brook
infra); *Priers Meadow* 1569, *the Pryors Meadow* 1598 (probably associated
with the abbey estates, cf. Poulton *supra*, *v.* prior); *Sheep Crofts* 1569.

2. PULFORD (BRIDGE, BROOK & HALL) (109–375588)

Pulford 1086 DB *et freq* with variant spellings *-forth*, *-fort*, *-fordia*,
    -forde; Pulford Brook & Lodge 1831 Bry
Polford l12 (1297) Plea, c.1251–5 Chest (p), Dieul, c.1300 *Chol*
    (p), 1315–18 Sheaf (p)
Puleford e13 Dieul, 1247 P and twelve examples ib, RBE, Cl,
    Pat, Court, Ch, Tax to 1338 Pat, (*passagium de-*) 1278 Pat
Poleford 1254 P, 1255 (p), 1256 Cl, 1295–6, 1315 *Vern* (p)
Polleford 1258 Pat (p)
Pulleford 1260 Court (p)
Bulesford 1277 P
Bulford 1280 P (p)
Poulford 1437 Pat (p), 1645, 1699 Sheaf, *-forde* 1621 Orm[2]
Poford(e) 1557 Sheaf

'Ford on a stream', from pull, pōl[1] and ford, with brycg, brōc,
hall, loge. The ford on Pulford Brook (joining R. Dee), an important
passage on the road from Chester to Wrexham, was guarded by a
castle at Castle Hill *infra*. It was one of the limits of the Welsh
Kingdom of Powys according to a twelfth-century description in the
Mabinogion (*v.* Lloyd I 242 n.76) which records the Welsh form *o
Porford* 'from Pulford' (with assimilation of *l—r > r—r*). For the
context of this Welsh form, see *Breudwyt Ronabwy*, ed. Melville
Richards (Cardiff, 1948) 23–4. Professor Richards points out another
Welsh form, *o bwlffort* 13 (15) *Llawysgrif Hendregadredd* (Cardiff,
1933) 216, in a poem by Llygaid Gŵr to Llywelyn ap Gruffudd,
describing Llywelyn's domain extending *o bwlffort . . . hyd eithaf
kedweli* 'from Pwlffort (Pulford) . . . to the limits of Cedweli (i.e. the
cantref of Kidwelly, Carmarthenshire)'.

BROOKSIDE FM, by Pulford Brook *supra*, *v.* brōc, sīde.   CASTLE
HILL (109–375587, in Pulford village, near the church and the
brook), site of *castrum de Pulford* c.1244 (1580) Sheaf, *-Puleford* 1284

Cl, cf. xviii *supra*, *v.* castel, hyll.   Cuckoo's Nest, *Cuckoo Nest*
1831 Bry, *Cuckoos Nest Cottage* 1837 *TA*, cf. Cuckoo's Nest 152
supra, the name is its own commentary, *v.* cuccu, nest. There was a
brick-works here, *Brick Fields* 1842 *TA*, cf. 151 *supra*. Iron-
house Fm, perhaps 'house at a corner' from hyrne and hūs, cf.
Heronbridge 336 *infra*.   Meadow Ho, 1831 Bry, *v.* mæd, hūs,
cf. the nearby Meadow Nook 158 *infra*.   Moorfield Cottages
& Fm, *Moor Field Barn* 1831 Bry, 1842 OS, cf. *the More* 1598 (17)
Sheaf, *v.* mōr¹.   Oldfields, *le Holdfild* 1472 ChRR, *Old Fields*
(*House*) 1831 Bry, 1842 OS, *v.* ald, feld.   Poulton Lane, *v.* lane,
cf. Poulton 153 *supra*.

FIELD-NAMES

The undated forms are 1837 *TA* 332. Of the others, 1472 is ChRR, 1472² Tab
and the rest Dieul.

(a) The Cindrel (probably 'cinder hill', from sinder, hyll); Cock and
Pinch; Common Piece; Crewel (Professor Löfvenberg thinks this possibly
an instance of creowel 'the fork of a river or road', but the site (at 109–
382599) does not conform to this); Evans Gullet (*v.* golet); Gleaves Hill;
Green Hays (*v.* grēne¹, (ge)hæg); Heale Fd; Ladies Hay (*v.* hlæfdige,
(ge)hæg); Moat Croft (*v.* mote); Ox Pasture; Pig Heath; Pike Hallond (*v.*
pīc¹, hēafod-land); Pillowsyse (*v.* ēg, cf. Pillassey 158 *infra*); The Platt(s)
(*v.* plat²); Pleck (*v.* plek); Poulton Wd (cf. Poulton 153 *supra*); Rough
Wood; Seven Nobles (probably an ancient value (*v.* 337 *infra*), seven nobles,
i.e. three and a half marks, or £2.6s.8d.); Slade Wd (*v.* slæd); Sling (*v.*
sling); Three Corners; Town Fd; Wheat Loons (*v.* hwæte, land); The
Whittles, Whittle Lane Fd (cf. *Wetehul* e13, 'wet hill' *v.* wēt, hyll).

(b) *Blakegreves* 1251–5 ('black woods', *v.* blæc, grǣfe); *le Halfild* 1472,
-feld 1472² ('field at a nook', *v.* halh, feld); *Hendegreve* e13 ('nearer wood',
v. (ge)hende, grǣfe); *Pul(e)nale* 1229–32, 1244–5, *Pul(l)enhale* 13, 1251–55
(perhaps near Burton in Denbighshire; from halh 'a nook, a corner',
probably with an OE pers.n. *Pulla*, cf. OE *pullian* 'to pull'); *Smalsich*
c.1200 ('narrow watercourse', *v.* smæl, sīc).

xxvii. Dodleston

The ecclesiastical parish of Dodleston contained the townships 1. Dodleston,
2. Lower Kinnerton, 3. Higher Kinnerton Fl.

1. Dodleston (Gorse, Hall, House Fm & Lane Fm) (109–3661)
['dɔdɪstən]

   Dodestune 1086 DB
   Dodlest' under Gorstil' 1154–60 (1330) Ch, *Dodleston* 1153 Dugd

et freq with variant spellings *Dodel(i)s-*, *-es-* (l12 Chester to 1488 ChRR), *Do(d)dles-*, *-is-*, *-ton(e)*, *Dodillis-*, *Dod(d)yls-*, *Doddels-*; *Dodleston Hall* 1724 NotCestr
Dudleston 13 (1330) Ch, 1430 ChRR
Dadleston 1208–29 Dieul
Dolliston 1291 Tax
Dodel-, *Dodleson* 1693 Sheaf

'Dod(d)el's farm', from an OE pers.n. *Dod(d)el* and **tūn**, with **gorst, hall, hūs, lane**. The pers.n. is a diminutive form of the OE pers.n. *Dod(d)a*, cf. Feilitzen 223. The hall, or more precisely its predecessor, was the home of Robert *del Hall* 1393 ChRR. Dodleston is near Gorstella 159 *infra*.

BALDERTON (BRIDGE, BROOK, DRIVE & LODGE) (109–3762)

Baldreton 1208–29 Dieul, 1244–5, 1250 ib, 13 (1330) Ch, *Balderton* 13 (1330) ib, 1314 *Chol*, (*Bridge*) 17 Sheaf, 1831 Bry, (*-Lodge*) 1842 OS, *Baldirton* m13 Dieul
Balderston 1294 Orm², 1439 Sheaf
Bordeleston 1363 BPR
Botherton (*Field*) 1842 *TA*

'Bealdhere's farm', from the OE pers.n. *Bealdhere* and **tūn**, with **brycg, brōc** and **loge**. The drive & lodge lead to Eaton Park 148 *supra*. Cf. Greenwalls *infra*. The bridge may be 'the bridge of *Baldert*' 1170 Morris 5. The brook joins R. Dee *v.* Addenda.

GREENWALLS (109–369617)

Grenewall 1323 Tab, 1386 *Vern*, 1392 ChRR (p), 1551 Pat, *-walle* 1323 Orm², *-wal* 1389 ib, *Green Wall* 1360 ib, *Greenwall* 1544 Plea, *Grenwalle* 1468 AddCh, *-wall* 1514 ChRR, 1545 Orm²
Green Walls 1819 Greenwood
Balderton Farm 1777 Burd, 1842 OS

'Green well', *v.* **grēne¹, wælla**. This place is near Balderton *supra*.

BLACK WOOD. BRETTON WOOD, cf. Bretton Fl, NCPN 216. CASTLE (site of) (109–361609), castle of *Dodleston*, *-Dodeliston*, *-Dodeleston* 1277, 1283, 1295 Ipm, 1383 Orm², *v.* **castel**. This is a rectangular moated site with a motte, cf. Orm² II 847. There must

have been a castle here t. Richard I, as Orm[2] II 440 notes a feudal
service of 'two armed men at Dodleston in time of war for forty
days'. MOOR LANE (lost, 109–361607 to 356604), 1831 Bry,
Dodleston More, the moor of Dodleston 1351 BPR, *le More* 1349
(1576) ChRR, *the Moore* 1624 Sheaf, *The Moor(s)*, *Moors Croft*,
Field & Meadow 1842 TA, v. mōr[1]. Dodleston Moor is partly in
Gresford Fl. WINDMILL HILL.

FIELD-NAMES

The undated forms are 1842 *TA* 147. Of the others 1153–81, 1294, 1401,
1623, 1624, 1642 are Orm[2], 1153–80 (1427) Pat, 1154–60 (1330) Ch, c.1170,
1244–5, 1250 Dieul, 1623[2], 1637, 1879 Sheaf, 1831 Bry.

(*a*) Barlands Croft; Bithats Fd; Bridge Fd; Broad Hay (*v.* (ge)hæg);
Brun Yard; Church Croft; Clem Park (*v.* Clemley 3 47); The Clubs Fd;
Coney Grave Hay (*v.* coningre, (ge)hæg); Coppy Trees 1831 (*v.* copis);
County Stone 1831 (on the county boundary against Bretton Fl, *v.* stan);
Cow Hay (*v.* (ge)hæg); Cross Hay (*v.* cros); Big Cynders, Higher Cynder (*v.*
synder 'set apart'); Cyngnes Hay; Eight- & Five Demath (*v.* day-math);
The Flashes (*v.* flasshe); Freckleton (perhaps analogous with Freckleton
La 150, or from the surname from that place); Further- & Long Furlong;
Glades Master; Hatchet (*v.* hæcc-geat); Hill Fd; Horse Stone Hay (prob-
ably 'enclosure at a hoar stone', *v.* hār[2], stān, (ge)hæg); Irish Spring;
Kiln Croft; Lady's Lane (local, *Lady Lane* 1831 (109–368617 to 368623),
cf. *Lauedelondesend* 1250, *v.* hlǣfdige, land, lane, ende[1]); Locken (Hay);
Manna's Green Hay; Meadow Nook 1831 (*v.* nōk, cf. Meadow Ho 156
supra); Moor Well (local 1879, 1642 Orm[2], *Moore Well* 1623, 1624, *v.*
mōr[1], wella, cf. Moor Lane *supra*); Old Yard (*v.* ald, geard); Orchard End;
Ox Hay, Hole, Leasowe & Pasture (*v.* oxa, (ge)hæg, hol[1], lǣs); Palin Tree
Mdw; Parsons Hay (*v.* persone); Pillassey (*v.* ēg, cf. Pillowsyse 156 *supra*.
The first el. may be pill 'a willow' but Professor Löfvenberg suggests ME
*pilates 'pill-oats' (cf. pil-āte)); The Ring, Ringmoor(s) Hay (*v.* hring,
mōr[1]); Salt Dole & Mdw (*v.* salt, dāl); Wallet Croft (*v.* walet); Water-
gate (*v.* wæter, geat); Welshmans Croft & Fd (*v.* Wels(c)hman); The
Wood.

(*b*) *Anneschilderhus* 1250 ('the house of the sons of Agnes', described in
Dieul 61 as 'the messuage in which the sons of Agnes used to dwell', from
the ME fem pers.n. Agnes (*Annes*) and cild (gen.pl. cildra) with hūs. Cf.
Le Childerhus 162 *infra*); *Calvesmore* 1153–81, 1401, *Kalues-* 1154–60,
Kalvemor 1153–80, *Kalvermore* c.1170 (probably in Dodleston, but perhaps
in Poulton or Eaton, cf. 155, 151 *supra*, 'calves' moor', *v.* calf (gen.pl.
calfra), mōr[1]); *Chesterwey* 1250 ('the way to Chester', *v.* weg); (field of)
Edest' 1154–60 (perhaps from an OE pers.n. Ēad with tūn); spring called
Eduardese-, *Edwardeswalle* 1250 ('Ēadweard's or Edward's well', from the
OE pers.n. Ēadweard (ME *Edward*) and wælla); *grangia abbatis et conventus*

1250 ('the barn of the abbot & convent of Dieulacres', *v.* grange); *Hauwurdineswey, via de Hawurdin* 1250 ('the way from Hawarden', *v.* weg, cf. Hawarden Fl, NCPN 215); *acra Hospitalis Cestrie* 1244–5 ('acre belonging to the hospital of Chester', *v.* æcer. This refers either to St John's or to St Giles's hospital, Chester, 337 *infra*); *via de Kinarton* 1250 (*v. Kynerton Lane infra*); *Munkesfeld* (*v.* Lache Hall 336 *infra*); *the New Hey* 1623[2] (*v.* niwe, (ge)hæg); *Reddefeld* 1244–5, *Rudifeld* 1250, *Rudfeld* 1294 ('red field', from rēad, rudig and feld); *Warmessech, Wormessich* 1250 (perhaps originally 'dragon's or serpent's stream', from wyrm and sīc); *Wittefeld* 1244–5 (from feld with an unidentified first el.).

2. LOWER KINNERTON (109–3462), KINNERTON BRIDGE (FM)

Kynarton 1240 Cl *et freq* with variant spellings *Kin(n)-, Kynn-* to 1671 Sheaf, *Nether Kynarton* 1569 Orm[2]
Kynerton 1281 CRV *et freq* with variant spellings *Kynn-, Kinn-* (from 1402 ChRR), *Kin-; Kynerton iuxta Broghton* 1465 Bun, *Lagher Kynerton* 1520 Plea, *Lower Kynnerton* 1534 ib, *-Kinnerton* 1575 ChRR, *Nether-* 1593 Orm[2], *-Inferior* 1636 ib
Kinyrton 1421 Orm[2]
Kinaston 1430 AD (NCPN) 212)
Kenerton 1528 ChRR, 1752 Sheaf

'Cyneheard's farm', from the OE pers.n. *Cyneheard* and tūn, with inferior, neoðera, and brycg. Kinnerton gave name to *Kynerton Lane* 1594 Morris (*via de Kinarton* 1250 Dieul (159 *supra*), *Kynarton Lane* 1540 Morris, *Kynnerton-* 1573 ib, *Kynnarton-* 1573 Sheaf, leading from Chester to Kinnerton, 109–340620 to 380625, *v.* weg, lane), cf. Lache Lane 336 *infra*. Kinnertonbridge Fm was *Kinnerton Hall* 1842 OS, *the Hall* 1671 Sheaf, *Kenerton Hall* 1752 Sheaf. Higher Kinnerton is in Fl (NCPN 212) as also the adjacent Broughton.

GORSTELLA (109–358621) ['gɔrstelə]

Gorstilaua 1153–80 (1427) Pat, 1153–81 Orm[2], (lit. *-lana*)1154–60 (1330) Ch, *Gorstilowe* 1339 Plea *et freq* with variant spelling *Gorsty-* to 1530 Plea, (*la-, le-*) 1391 Orm[2], 1393 ChRR (p)
Gorstillaua c.1170 Dieul 77 (lit. *-anum*), *Gorstillowe* 1375 JRC (p), *Gorsty-* 1416 ChRR (p)
Grostilhowe 13 Dieul
le Gorstelow 1350 Orm[2], *Gorstelowe* 1511 Plea, 1579 Orm[2], *-laue* 1540 MidCh, *-low* 1575, 1692 Sheaf

Gorstelelow 1440 Orm[2]
Gorstella 1831 Bry

'Gorsy mound', from gorstig and hlāw, or 'mound at gorse-hill', from gorst and hyll with hlāw or hōh, (*Gorstill-, Grostilh-*).

BROAD HEY, cf. *Broad Hay* 1842 *TA*, *v.* (ge)hæg.   GELL FM, cf. *Gell Field* (freq) 1842 *ib*, from the Ch dial. form of ModE *deal* 'a share, a portion', cf. EDD *deal* sb[1], *jell*, *v.* dæl[2].   MOOREND FM, cf. *Moor Lane* 1831 Bry, *v.* mōr[1], ende[1].   OAKTREE FM.   YEW-TREEBANK.

FIELD-NAMES

The undated forms are 1842 *TA* 147. Of the others 1154–60 is (1330) Ch, c.1230 Dieul, 1240 Cl, 1483 ChRR, 1671 Sheaf, 1831 Bry.

(a) Acres; Balls Croft; Boots (*v.* bōt); Broughton Fd (named from Broughton Fl); County Stone 1831 (on the county boundary against Bretton Fl); Cribs (*v.* crib); Four Butts (*v.* butte); Golley Croft (cf. *Godeley* 1671 Sheaf[3] 48 (9677), perhaps 'good clearing' or 'Goda's clearing', from lēah and gōd[2] or the OE pers.n. *Goda*); Green Hay (*v.* (ge)hæg); Hatters Croft; Intake (*v.* inntak); Ledgings; Letsomes Fd (from the surname from Ledsham 217 *infra*); Loggerhead Head; Loggreave Hay (probably 'enclosure at long wood', from lang and græfe with (ge)hæg); Seven Loons (*v.* land); Milking Gate ('pasture for milch cows' *v.* milking, gata); Moat Croft (109–348625; perhaps to be associated with *Le Pele de Kynerton* 1483, cf. Orm[2] II 550, a lost fortification, *v.* pēl, mote); Ox Hay (*v.* (ge)hæg); Pavement Hay (109–342623; *v.* pavement, (ge)hæg); Three Pound Croft; Trowspool Drain 1831 (a watercourse on the county boundary against Higher Kinnerton Fl, from pōl[1] with trūs 'brushwood' or trog 'a trough'); Wet Reans (*v.* rein); Windmill Fd.

(b) *Hoga de Kynarton* 1240 ('the mound of Kinnerton', *v.* haugr); *Hulegreves* c.1230 ('owl woods' or 'woods near a hovel', from ūle or hulu and græfe); *Saltpit* 1154–60 (a brine-pit, or a salt-pan, *v.* salt, pytt. Lower Kinnerton would have been on the tidal estuary of R. Dee at this date).

xxviii. St Mary on the Hill

For the rest of this parish, *v.* 337 *infra*.

3. CLAVERTON (109–4063) [ˈklavərtən]

Claventone 1086 DB
Clavertun c.1170 (1400) Pat, *-ton* c.1220 (1400) ib *et freq* with variant spellings *-tona, -tone, -ir-, (-iuxta Chester)* 1288 Court
Clarton 1315 Tab, *Clareton* 1350 ib and ten examples with variant

spellings *Clar(e)-* to 1602 Orm[2], (*-or Claverton*) 1349 ib, (*-alias Claverton*) 1602 ib
Glaverton 1366 Plea
Claierton 1449 Sheaf

'Clover enclosure', *v.* clǽfre, tūn. Almost depopulated by 1957, this was a rich manor in 1086, valued at twelve pence a year, with a salt-wich in Northwich and eight houses in the city of Chester, cf. Duke St. (Chester) 336 *infra. v.* Addenda.

EATON RD, *via que ducit versus le Gretediche* 1278 CASNS x, *via de Clavertone* 1292–3 Sheaf, *Clauerton Waye* 1355 (15) ib, *Clarton' Waye* 1420 *Vern*, *Clauerton High(e) Way(e)*, *-Wey* 1540, 1555, 1573, 1594 Sheaf, Morris, *v.* weg, hēah-weg, cf. 1 42 (route VIII) and Grey Ditch 337 *infra.*

HERONBRIDGE, cf. *Heron Bridge Field* 1838 *TA, v.* 336 *infra.*

FIELD-NAMES

The undated forms are 1838 *TA* 120. Of the others 1259, 1299 are Plea, 1260, 1290 Court, 1278, 1287, 1292 CASNS x, 1285, 1315, 1342 *Vern*, 1285[2] Orm[2], c.1320 *AddCh*, 1366 Plea, 1540, 1573, 1594 Morris, 1590 *Dep*, 1629, 1740 *Corp*, 1725 *Dow*, 1747 *LRMB* 257, 1831 Bry, and the rest Sheaf. Some of the names in (*b*) may belong in St Mary's, Chester, 337 *infra*, but are listed here as belonging to the manor of Claverton.

(*a*) Barn Way 1740 (*Barnes Wey* 1573, *-Way* 1594, 'way to a barn', *v.* bere-ærn, weg, a cart-track on the south boundary of the liberty of Chester. Perhaps the same as *le Lowewey* 337 *infra*); Black Butts (*v.* butte); the further Bottoms 1740 (*v.* botm, cf. Earl's Eye 336 *infra*); Claverton Meadow or Middletons Medow 1629; Claverton Town Fd (*campus de Claverton(e)* c.1242–3, c.1256–7, 1287, 1292–3, 1299, 1308–9, *croftum de Claverton* 1278, *Clauerton Fyldes* 1450, *The Common Fields* 1779, *v.* toun, feld); Dock Fd (*v.* docce); Golden John; Gorsty Croft (*v.* gorstig); Grey Ditch (*v.* 337 *infra*); Gullet (*the-* 1650, 1740, *v.* golet); Haywards Fd (cf. Haywoods Castle 336 *infra*); Long Fd (1740, *the-* 1747, *Longfeld* 1259, 1260, þe *Longfeild* 1650, 1725, *v.* lang, feld); Lower Milstone; Muck Fd (*v.* muk); New Hay (*v.* (ge)hæg); Paradise (*v.* paradis); Pemberton Croft (cf. *Pemberton's Meadow* 1747, *Pembertons Meadow* 153 *supra*, from *Pemberton*, the surname of a prominent Chester family, cf. Pemberton's Parlour 337 *infra*); Poverty Piece (*v.* pouerte, pece, cf. 337 *infra*); Primrose Hill (1831); Red House Croft; Shoulder of Mutton (*v.* 337 *infra*); Swans Nest; Town Fd (*v.* Claverton Town Field *supra*); Wet Reans (1747, *le Waterenes* 1321–2, *Wetrains* 1615, *-reins* 1615, 1672, *-Reanes* 1673, *Whet Raines* 1790, 'wet boundary-strips', *v.* wēt, rein); Wood Head (*the-* 1747, *þe Woodheadcroft* 1650, 'the top end of the wood', *v.* wudu, hēafod, croft).

(b) *Brerifurlong* 1278 ('briary furlong', *v.* brērig, furlang); *Le Childerhous* 1270–3, *Childrehous* 1292 (p) ('the sons' house', from cild and hūs, cf. *Anneschilderhus* 158 *supra*. The 1292 (p) form is the surname of Philip *dil Childrehous*, a landholder in Parson's Lane, Chester, cf. CASNS x 50); *le Cruftinge* 1278 ('the little croft', *v.* cryfting); *Elerinscharde* 1280–1 ('gap or cleft growing with elder-trees', *v.* elren or ellern, sceard); *Emmes Eye* 1568, *Emsey or Claverton Meadow* 1590 (perhaps 'uncle's meadow' from ēam OE, ME 'uncle' and ēg); *Farenhul* 1287, 1316, *-hull* c.1320, *-hulle* 1321 ('fern hill', *v.* fearn, hyll); *Clauertonforde* 1285, *Claverton Ford* 1285[2], *le Fordesway* 1287, 1316, c.1320, 1321, *Claverton Lode* 1354, 1354 (1379) (a lost ford of R. Dee at 109–412640 on the Claverton-Chester boundary, with a lost road leading to it from Eaton Rd *supra*, *v.* ford, weg, (ge)lād); *Le Grenewey* 1259, 1260, *Greneway* 1290 (p) (*v.* grēne[1], weg); *Horderne* c.1256–7 (a selion, 'the store-house', *v.* hord-ærn); *Le Leefeld* 1278 (*v.* lēah, feld, cf. *Lee* 153 *supra* or Netherleigh 337 *infra*); *Longefurlong* 1278, 1280–1, *-e* 1288–9 (*v.* lang, furlang); *Merstanisfurlong, -lond* c.1256–7, *Merstonesfurlong* c.1266–7, field called *Mereston iuxta Eccliston'* 1342 ('(furlong at) the boundary stone', *v.* (ge)mǣre, stān, furlang); *Mersteleye* 1315 (probably '(clearing near) the boundary stone', *v.* lēah, cf. prec.); *Mulnedich* 1259, *Milnedich* 1260 (*v.* myln, dīc); *terra monialium Cestrie* c.1320 ('the land of the Nuns of Chester', cf. *a grene croft, late of the monystorye of the nones of the citie of Chester* 1540 Morris); *Okleston Field* 1278 (CASNS x 33, No. xxxii, wrongly dated 1275–6, probably a misreading of *Ekles-* (for Eccleston 151 *supra*)); *terra prioris hospitalis Sancti Johannis Cestrie* 1292–3 (land belonging to St John's Hospital Chester, cf. *acra Hospitalis Cestrie* 159 *supra*); *Scholebrod* 1273–4, *Scheuelebrade* 1292–3 ('shovel's breadth', *v.* scofl-brǣdu); *Shollelegh in Glaverton* 1366 (DKR xxviii 64, from lēah with an unidentified first el.); *le Stonihulle* 1278 (*v.* stānig, hyll); *Swartingesfeld* 1278, *S. Martyne Felde* 1540, *Swartyne Felde* 1555, *Swartens Filde* 1573, *Swartons Fielde* 1594 ('Swarting's field', from the pers.n. *Svertingr* ON or *Swærting* ODan and feld); *Tweygrenis* c.1256–7 ('the two greens', from grēne[2] and ME *twey* 'two', cf. twēgen, *tway* NED); *Uluesdale* (lit *Ulnes-*) 1278, 1287, 1316, 1321, 1329–30, *Vluesdale* c.1320 ('Ulfr's valley' or 'wolf's valley', from the ON pers.n. *Ulfr*, or wulf or ulfr, and dæl[1] or dalr); *Wetheflosse* c.1242–3, *le Wetflosse* 13, 1294–5, c.1294, 1320–1, *le Waterflossche* 1308–9 ('the wet swamp', *v.* wēt, wæter, flosshe); *le Withines* 1278, *le Wythines* 1280–1 (*v.* wiðegn).

4. MARLSTON CUM LACHE (109–3863), 1724 NotCestr, *Merlestona et Lache* 1285 Ch, *Marleston cum Lach(e)* 1349–50 Orm[2], 1390 ChRR, and thereafter with spellings as for Marlston, Lache *infra*.

LACHE, cf. LACHE HALL 336 *infra*, [ˈlatʃ]
    Leche 1086 DB, *Lech(e)* 1096–1101 (1280), 1150 Chest, *Lech* 1188–91 ib, 1330 Ch, 1791 Sheaf, *Lecche* 13 Dugd

Leech 1096–1101 (17) Chest, (*the*) *Leeche* 1791 Sheaf, (*the*) *Laych*(*e*) 1555 ib, (*the*) *Leach* 1783, 1791, 1883 ib

Lache 1284 (1357) ChFor, 1285 Ch *et freq* with variant spelling *Lach* (1386 MidCh to 1839 *TA* 103), (*-iuxta Marleston*) 1334 Plea, (*-by Chester*) 1671 Sheaf, *le Lache* 1351 ChRR, 1595 Sheaf, *la Lache alias le Lache iuxta Lythee* 1394 Pat, *the Lache* 1573 Sheaf, *Le Lach* 1673 ib

'The boggy stream, the bog', *v.* læc(c), lece. The manor is divided between this township and St Mary's, Chester. It adjoins Marlston *infra*, Chester, and Nether- & Overleigh 337 *infra*.

MARLSTON ['ma:rlstəʌ]

Merlestone 1086 DB, *-ton* c.1220–30 Dieul, 1352 BPR, *-tona* 1285 CRC, Ch

Marleston' 1245 P *et freq* with variant spellings *-tone*, *Marlas-* to 1842 OS, (*Marleston iuxta Lache*) 1355 Plea, *Marlston* 1298 ib, 1740 Sheaf, 1831 Bry

Merston 1270–3 Sheaf, (*-near Eccleston*) 1464 Tab, *-tone* 1280–1 Sheaf

Mershton 1362 BPR, *Merssheton iuxta Cestr'* 1395 (m15) *Harl.* 2061

Marilston 1663 Sheaf

Marston 1727 Sheaf

'Mǣrel's farm', from an OE pers.n. *Mǣrel* and tūn. The pers.n. is not recorded. It would be a diminutive, with an *-el-* suffix, of the OE pers.n. theme *Mǣr-*. It would be comparable with an OE pers.n. *Mǣrla*, an *-ila* derivative of the same theme, suggested for Malborough D 307, Marwell D 283, Marlborough W 297, cognate with OGer *Merila* (Förstemann PN 1102). However, the existence of an OE *Mǣrla deduced from these p.ns. has been challenged. They may be from OE meargealla 'gentian'. The arguments are evenly balanced, cf. W 298, Studies[2] 110, DEPN s.n. *Malborough*, EPN s.v. meargealla. The spellings of Marlston show an *-es* gen.sg. inflexion of the first el. which makes the plant-name formally inadmissible, and the pers.n. is the only probable basis. This strengthens the argument for the existence of a derivative pers.n. in strong and weak form OE *Mǣrel, *Mǣrla, which, furthermore, may well be the first el. of the Anglo-Scand compound pers.n. *Mǣrle-Sveinn* Feilitzen 326, W 298 n.1.

BALDERTON BRIDGE, *v.* 157 *supra.*   DECOY COTTAGES & FM,
Decoy (Farm) 1831 Bry, *Lache* 1842 OS, cf. *the Coy Meadow* 1779
Sheaf, *Coy Field & Meadow* 1843 *TA*, named from 'a Coye' made
1633 (Sheaf³ 40 (8517)), *v.* decoy.   GREEN LANE.   THE
LACHE EYES, 1842 OS, *Lache-eyes* 1671 Sheaf, *Lache Eyes Common*
1831 Bry, cf. 336 *infra*, 'the water-meadows of Lache', *v.* ēg.
Common rights of pasture were held here by the inhabitants of
St Mary's on the Hill, Chester.   MOAT COTTAGES & FM, cf.
Moat Field 1843 *TA*, named from a moat near the farm, perhaps the
site of a manor house of Marlston, *v.* mote.   ONE MILE HO
(109–397637), 1831 Bry, on the Wrexham road one mile from Dee
Bridge, Chester, cf. Two Mile Ho *infra*, and *Mile and Half House*
1778–9 Sheaf³ 32 (7191) probably near Wrexham Road Cottages in
Eccleston, 152 *supra*, on the same road.   ROUGHHILL, *Rough Hill*
1671 Sheaf, *Rough Hill Farm* 1778 ib.   SPARROW HALL alias THE
BARRACKS (local), 1879 Sheaf¹ 1, p.194, *Sparrow Hall* 1831 Bry
(109–385637), *v.* spearwa, hall, barrack.   TWO MILE HO (109–
388623), *Two-mile House* 1671 Sheaf, a house on the Wrexham road
two miles from Dee Bridge, cf. One Mile Ho *supra.*   WREXHAM
RD, *v.* 337 *infra.*

FIELD-NAMES

The undated forms are 1843 *TA* 253. Of the others 1464 is Tab, 1831 Bry,
and the rest Sheaf. Some of the Sheaf material may belong to St Mary on the
Hill parish, Chester, 337 *infra.*

(a) Barn Fd (1778, cf. *Barn Croft* 1764); Belgrave Fd (*v.* Belgrave 149
supra); Birch Hill (1778); Brick-Kiln Fd 1790; Bridge Mdw 1778; Broad
Hey 1779 (-*Hays* 1672, 1673, *v.* (ge)hæg); Brown Croft 1779; Butchers Fd
(*v.* bocher, cf. 152 *supra*); Butter-milk Hall 1778; Chester Fd; Clay Croft
1778; Clover Fd 1790 (1778); Clubs Land; Cow Pasture 1778; Curriers
Croft 1673 (1615, *Coriors Croft* 1615, *Coriers-* 1672, *v.* corier 'a currier',
croft); Digmoth (a meadow, probably a 'day-math', *v.* day-math); Dodleston Mdw (cf. Dodleston 156 *supra*); Goose Neck Fd (from its shape, *v.*
goose-neck, cf. 336 *infra*); Great & Little Gorsty Fd 1778 (1764, *Gorsty
Fields* 1672, 1673, *v.* gorstig); Grass Fd; Green Loons 1778 (-*Loones* 1764,
'green selions', *v.* grēne¹, land); Hales Mdw (*v.* halh); Halterfield; Hanging
Fd; Higher Hayes 1778 (1764, *v.* (ge)hæg); the Homestead 1778–9; Horse
Pasture (1778, cf. *Horse Close* 1779); House Fd (cf. *Croft next the House*
1672); Kiln Croft 1790; Lache Lane Fd (cf. *Lach Lane* 1779, *v.* 336 *infra*),
Ladies Hay (-*Hey* 1779, *v.* hlǣfdige, (ge)hæg); Lamb Orchard 1790 (1764);
Lech Hill 1791 (cf. Lache *supra*); Little Hayes 1778 (*v.* (ge)hæg); Little
Mdw (1672); Long Butts 1778 (1764, *v.* butte); Long Fd 1778; Long Grass
1779 (*v.* gærs); Long Mdw 1778; Marl Fd (cf. *Old Marled Field* 1778, *v.*

marled); the Great Marlston 1779 (cf. Marlston *supra*); Meadow Hay 1778 (1672, *v.* (ge)hæg); Millhouse Closes 1779 (*v.* milne-hous); Nutt Croft 1790 (1764); Old House Fd; Orchard End Fd 1790 (cf. *New- & Old Orchard* 1672, 1673); Other Fd 1778; Ox Croft & Pasture 1673; Pike Hay 1790 (1672); Plumb Tree Croft 1778; Sandy Lane 1831; Seven Acres 1778 (1764); Sheep Coat Crofts & Hey 1779 (*v.* scēp, cot); Smooth Hill 1779 (cf. Roughhill *supra*); Swan Fd; Thistly Fd 1779 (cf. *Thistle Hay* 1672, *v.* (ge)hæg); Three Acre (*the Three Acres* 1778); Tree Fd (1778); Vawdr(e)y Hill 1779 (from the surname *Vawdrey*); Wheat Eddish 1779 (1672, *v.* hwǣte, edisc); Wheat Edgrew 17 (perhaps 'damp hedgerow', from wēt and hecg-rǣw); Whitters Hey 1779 (probably from the surname *Whitt(i)er*, *v.* (ge)hæg).

(*b*) *le Cley Houses* 1464 (either 'houses built of clay' or 'houses at a clay-pit', *v.* clǣg, hūs).

VII. WIRRAL HUNDRED

Wirral Hundred is bounded by the Irish Sea on the north-west, the estuary of R. Mersey on the north-east, Broxton Hundred and the City of Chester on the south-east and south, and the estuary of R. Dee on the south-west. It comprises the peninsula of Wirral. The geological formation is a plateau of Bunter and Keuper sandstones overlaid by boulder clay with occasional pockets of glacial sand and gravel. The sandstone forms a long ridge along the west side of the peninsula, most pronounced at Heswall and Caldy, where an altitude of 300′ is attained. A parallel ridge on the east side of the peninsula forms the hills at Bidston, Storeton and Wallasey. Apart from these ridges, the plateau averages an altitude of between 100′ and 200′. It is broken by the valleys and drainage courses of the feeders of Dibbinsdale Brook and Bromborough Pool and by The Birket and The Fender running into Wallasey Pool. The plateau is cut off from the mainland, as is the peninsula, by a rift or fault, followed by the Ellesmere Canal, running from the north suburbs of Chester to the Gowy valley, past Bache 144 *supra*, Backford and Croughton 172, 179 *infra*. This now forms the boundary of the hundred. The old hundred-boundary was farther south, but this valley must always have been the geographical boundary of the region. At the north end, the sandstone hills fall away sharply to the marshes and blown sands of Great & Little Meols, and the Fender brook basin. Only the hills of Wallasey approach the sea shore to form a promontory, but Bidston Hill and Grange Hill were prominent seamarks standing over the flat dunes and marshes of the coast and the Dee estuary. There has been a progressive erosion of the Irish Sea coast, together with an invasion of blown sand, throughout historic times, and it is obvious that the sea-shore archæology of the Meols district and the existence of drowned forest remains off that shore indicate lost land and settlement areas now covered by the tides. As compensation, the progressive silting, and reclamation, of the Dee estuary has increased the geographical area of Wirral. Effectively, the Dee estuary extends now hardly as far as Parkgate, and that only at spring tides. In the fourteenth century, Chester town was a port, but even then navigation was becoming difficult. Since the eighteenth century, the reclamation of the estuary has thrown the old coastline from Blacon to Parkgate into an inland position. The new land is included in Fl, probably because most of it lay west of the original river-channel.

WIRRAL HUNDRED ['wirəl] older local ['wʌrəl]

> Wilaveston Hundred 1086 DB, hundredum de Wilaston(a) 1278 Ipm, 1353 Dugd, Orm², 1360 BPR, -wylaston 1499 Sheaf
> Wyrhale 1259 Court et freq with spellings as for Wirral 1 7, hundred of- 1309 ChRR et freq

v. hundred. Named after Willaston 232 *infra*, the DB hundred contained the later Wirral Hundred, and also the townships Upton, Wervin, Picton, Guilden Sutton and Mickle Trafford 142, 137, 132, 126, 133 *supra*, now in Broxton Hundred. The DB township of *Edelaue* has been identified with Hadlow 232 *infra* in Willaston. That of *Sumreford*, though listed among manors of *Wilaveston* Hundred in DB f. 267b, and therefore thought to be Tranmere 257 *infra* by Ormerod, is identified with Somerford Booths 1 63 by Tait who supposes the omission of the *Hamestan* (Macclesfield) Hundred rubric, cf. Tait 15, 209, Orm² II 353. The change of the name and boundaries of the hundred cannot be dated precisely. The old name is still in legal use down to 1360. The boundary change appears to have been made between 1086 and 1200. The new name, taken from the regional-name Wirral 1 7, is in regular use from 1259. The process of change may have followed a course parallel to that supposed for Macclesfield Hundred 1 51, the new name arising from the creation of the Forest of Wirral in 1120. It seems probable that after the creation of the forest jurisdiction, the hundred and the forest would be so nearly co-extensive that the regional name would be applied to both, the old hundred-name surviving only in occasional use as the official style of a hundred-court at Willaston.

CALDY HUNDRED (lost)

> *Caldeihundredum* 1182 P, *Caldeie-* 1183 *ib*, *Caldea-* 1185 ib, *Calde-* 1308 IpmR, *Calday Hundred* 1362 Orm²
> *Hundredum de Caldeia* 1184 P *et freq* with variant spellings -*Caldea*, -*Caldey*, -*Kaldeya*, -*Caldeya*, -*Caldeye*, -*Kaldeye*, -*Galdei*, -*Calday*, -*Caldei* to *Hundred' de Calday* 1536 Plea, *the Hundred of Caldey in Wyrehall Hundred* 1428 Orm²
> *curia de Kaldeye* 1238 Ipm

v. hundred, cf. Caldy 282 *infra.* This was a minor hundred having in its jurisdiction the manors of Thornton Hough, Leighton, Gayton, Heswall, Thurstaston, West Kirby, Great & Little Meols, Hoose, Newton cum Larton and Poulton cum Seacombe, but perhaps of greater extent and significance originally, cf. 336 *infra*, Orm[2] II 518, *Saga Book* XIV 303–16, Brownbill 158–163, Sheaf[3] 2 (274), 3 (388), and the discussion of the p.n. Caldy 283–4 *infra.* As a legal entity with manorial rights, the hundred of Caldy survived to about 1860 when its claims to 'wreck of the sea' along the coast from Leighton round to Seacombe, except for the shores of Little Caldy, Wallasey and Liscard, were allowed to the Glegg family of Gayton, holders of the hundred, *v.* Brownbill 163.

A popular local name for that part of Wirral Hundred occupied by the parish of Neston was *Gobbinshire* 1883, 1885 Sheaf[1] 3 pp. 10, 211, 'the land of fools', from dial. *gobbin* 'a fool, an idiot', and scīr[1], cf. Gobbins Butts 295 *infra*, and EENS 24. *v.* Addenda.

UNIDENTIFIED PLACE-NAMES IN WIRRAL. *del Flaskus* 1359 *Eyre* (p) (*v.* flask); *del Helde* 1415 ChRR (p) (*v.* helde); *Knolle muln'* 1356 *Indict* (*v.* cnoll, myln); *Lowheath Greene* c.1666 AddCh (*v.* grēne[2], cf. *the Low Heath* 291 *infra* or *le Loweheth* 191 *infra*); *Reyton'* 1278 *ChFor* ('roe enclosure', *v.* rǣge 'female roe deer', tūn); *Shroulakes* 1357 *ChFor* (p) (*v.* lacu 'a watercourse'); *Stowode* 1335 Pat, *-wodd* 1335 (15) *Mont* (first el. unidentified, perhaps stān 'stone', cf. Stowood O 165, *v.* wudu); *Wcton* 1291 Tax 259 (property of Basingwerk abbey, in Wirral deanery); *Whistonclyf* 1357 *ChFor* (*v.* clif).

i. St Oswald's & Holy Trinity

The township of Blacon cum Crabwall comprised Crabwall in St Oswald's parish (cf. 337 *infra*) and Blacon in Holy Trinity parish (cf. 336 *infra*). Blacon is now included in Chester County Borough, Crabwall is now included in Mollington c.p.

1. BLACON CUM CRABWALL, 1819 Orm[2], *Blaken cum Crabwall* 1385 *ChFor*, cf. Blacon, Crabwall *infra.*

BLACON (109–3868) ['bleikən]
    Blachehol 1086 DB
    Blachenol 1093 Tab

Blachenoth 1096–1101 (1150), 1150 Chest, *Blachenot* 1096–1101 (1280) ib

Blakene c.1200–1250 Chest, 1239 CASNS x, 1259 Plea *et freq* to 1387 Pat, *Blakne* c.1220 (1390) ChRR

Blaken 1262 *JRC* (p), 1289 Sheaf, 1293 Court (p) *et freq* to 1535 VE, 1709 Cre

Blakun 1438 ChRR (p), *Blakon* 1499 Orm², *Blacon* 1536 Cre *et freq*, *Blacon Lordship*(*p*) 1620 Sheaf, 17 (1724) NotCestr

Blacon alias Blakeney alias Blaconhall 1580 Cre

'At the black hill', from blæc (wk.dat. blacan) and cnoll alternating with cnotta, *v.* lordes(c)hip. The township is named from the headland of Blacon Point *infra*, cf. Blacon Hall, Blacon Point (farm) *infra*. A shortened form of the p.n. has prevailed, but the *Blak(e)ne*, *Blakeney* series indicates an intermediate form in the process.

CRABWALL (FM & HALL) (109–3869) ['kræbɔːl, 'kræbwɔːl]
    Crabbewalle c.1200–1250, 1250–78, 1265–78, 1265–81, 1274–78 Chest, 1318 *Eyre*, -*wall* 1346 *StRO*, 1351 ChRR (p)
    Crabbewell 1265 Ch, 1271 *ChFor*, 1278 *JRC*, 1327 ChRR (p)
    Crabwell 1280 *Surv*, 1347 *ChFor*
    Crabwall c.1310 Chest *et freq* with variant spelling -*walle*, *Crabwall Hall* 1842 OS
    Crabho c.1536 Leland, *Crabhall* 1560, 1620 Sheaf, 1656, 1690 Orm², 1724 NotCestr, 1773 *Chol*, 1845 *TAMap*, *Crab-hall* 1752 Sheaf, *Crab Hall* 1831 Bry
    Craball 1547 MinAcct, 1608, 1696, 1727 Sheaf, *Craball* 1563 (17) ib, 1567 Morris, *Crabal* 1709 Cre
    Grabhall 1673 Sheaf

'Cray-fish stream', *v.* crabba, wælla, wella. The final el. has been confused by hall 'a hall'.

BLACON COTTAGES, 1831 Bry.   BLACON HALL, 1831 ib, *Little Blacon* 1818 to 1889 Sheaf³ 39 (8389), cf. Blacon Point (farm) *infra*.
BLACON HOUSE FM.   BLACON POINT (farm, 109–383673), *an olde manor place* (at *Blaken Hedde*) c.1536 Leland, *Blacon alias Blakeney alias Blaconhall* 1580 Cre, *Blacon-Hall* 1621 (1656) Orm², 1645 Hem, *Blacon-Hall Farm* 1751 Sheaf, Cre, *Blacon Hall* 1842 OS, 1847 Sheaf, *Blacon Point Farm* 1749, 1815 Cre, *Point Farm* 1810 ib, *Blacon Point House* 1831 Bry, the site near Blacon Point *infra* of the original hall of Blacon destroyed at the siege of Chester. Blacon

Point Fm continued to be known as *Blacon Hall* down to 1847. The modern Blacon Hall is so named from c.1831. *v.* hall, cf. foll. and Blacon *supra.* BLACON POINT (headland, 109–378670), 1700 *Assem, Blaken Hedde* c.1536 Leland, *the Hill* 1843 *TA*, a promontory formerly on the coast of the Dee estuary, *v.* hēafod, point, hyll, giving name to Blacon and Blacon Point (farm), *supra.* FINCHETT'S GUTTER, *v.* 1 23. MOLLINGTON BRIDGE NO. 1 & NO. 2, *v.* 337 *infra.* MOLLINGTON CAUSEWAY, *Molyngton High Waye* 1540 Morris, *Mollington High(e) Way* 1573, 1594 ib, *Mollington Lane* 1620 Sheaf, *v.* caucie, cf. Parkgate Rd 337 *infra.* RAILWAY COTTAGES. SCOTTS MORRIS BRIDGE, crossing the Shropshire Union Canal. STONE BRIDGE, *v.* 337 *infra.*

FIELD-NAMES

The undated forms are 1843 *TA* 54. Of the others, c.1200–50, 1250–78, 1274–8 are Chest, c.1200 (1390) ChRR, 1316 Misc, 1317 InqAqd, 1347, 1357 *ChFor*, 1539–47 Orm², 1701 *Assem*, 1831 Bry, and the rest Sheaf.

(a) Ash Hey (*v.* æsc, (ge)hæg); Bank Hey & Ridding (*v.* banke, (ge)hæg, ryding); Birches (*The-* 1620, cf. *ii buttis in frussuris de Crabbewalle* c.1200–50, *v.* bryce); Little Blacon Fd, Blacon Green (*v.* grēne²); Blacon Rough 1831; Butchers Hey (*v.* bocher, (ge)hæg); Cob Fd; Crab Wall Nook; Dark Lane 1831; The Dee Cops (embankment along R. Dee, *v.* copp); Right & Slack Hayes (*the greate-* & *-lilte Haigh, Stacke Hay, Wright's Hey* 1620, from (ge)hæg with grēat, lȳtel and slakki and the surname *Wright*); The Hill (1620); Big & Little Hock; Honey Pot; Irish Fd; Leicester Fd (probably named after the *Leicester* family of Tabley); Lords Mdw (*v.* hlāford); Lordy Hey; Lucerne Fd (from the Lucerne grass cropped in it); Marled Hey (*Marled Feild* & *Hey, the ould Marled Hey* 1620, *v.* marled, (ge)hæg); (Bridge-, Further-, Garden-, Middle-, Near-, Point-) Marsh, Marsh under the Hill (cf. *Marsh Bridge* 1621, *Blacon Marsh* 1701, *v.* mersc, brycg, cf. Blacon Point, Blacon *supra*); Milking Bank (*v.* milking); Pigeon House Croft (*the Dove House Yarde* 1620, *v.* dovehouse, geard); Rushy Hey; Sea Fd (*v.* sǣ, this being the sea-coast prior to the draining of the Dee estuary); Sheep Fd; Smooth Wd; Store Fd; Three Nook Fd (cf. three-nooked); Throstles Nest (*v.* þrostle, nest).

(b) *Ball's Feild* 1620; *Becks Feild* 1620; *Blacon Cross* (*v.* Blacon Cross Fd 336 *infra*); *Blake Croft* (*v.* *Stevenecroft infra*); *Blakne Wood* c.1220 (1390), *boscus de Blakene* 1347 (*v.* wudu, Blacon *supra*); *the Blewe Stonne at Blacon* 1671 (*v.* blew 'blue', stān, a boundary mark of the Dee fishing rights of Great Saughall manor from here to 'the style at Woodbank town-field', cf. Gloverstone 336 *infra*); *the Chanell-, -Chenell Shutt* 1563 (17) (a 'flodyard' or fish-trap pound at Crabwall, from chanel 'a channel', and scyte in the sense 'a steep channel of water' as in 'a mill-shoot'); *campus de Crabbewalle* 1200–50 ('Crabwall field', *v.* feld); *vadum de Dee* 1250–78,

1274–8 ('the ford of Dee', *v.* ford, an ancient crossing of the old estuary of Dee); *Gorstie Feild* 1620 (*v.* gorstig); *Hethe Howse* 1560 (*v.* hǣð, hūs); *Hunrage* 1560 ('two closes in-', origin obscure); *the Intacke* 1620 (*v.* inntak); *Iron Bridg in the Feilds on this side Blacon* 1714 (*v.* hyrne, brycg, cf. Heronbridge 336 *infra*); *molendinum ventricitum* 1357 ('the windmill'); (*the*) *Poole Hey(e)s* 1620 (from *Port Pool* 337 *infra*, *v.* pōl¹, (ge)hæg); *Saltgresse* 1620 (saltings, *v.* sealt, gærs); *Stevenecroft* 1316, *croftum Stephani* 1250–78, 1274–8, *Blake croft vocat' Stevencroft* 1317 ('Stephen's croft' and 'dark croft', from croft and the ME pers.n. *Stephen* and blæc. This belonged to St John's Hospital, Chester, and is mentioned c.1200–50 Chest II 858 as 'the croft held by the hospital of St John the Baptist').

ii. St Mary on the Hill

The Chester parish of St Mary on the Hill contained one township in Wirral Hundred, Little Mollington, but cf. Moston and Upton 141, 142 *supra*. For the rest of this parish, cf. 337 *infra*. Little Mollington is now included in Mollington c.p. with Great Mollington 177 *infra*.

5. LITTLE MOLLINGTON (HALL) (109–387693), formerly MOLLING-TON BANASTRE ['banəstər], LOWER MOLLINGTON

> *Molintone* 1086 DB *et freq* with forms as for Great Mollington 177 *infra*, *Molinton prope Cestre* 1278 *JRC*
> *Molynton Banastr'* 1286 *ChFor et freq* with forms *ut supra* and variant spellings *-Banastir, -er, -re, -Ban(n)ester* to *Little Mollington* or *Mollington Banaster* 1743 Sheaf, *-Banastre* 1819 Orm²
> *Parva Molyngton, -Molintone* 1287, 1288 Court, *Little Mollington* 1632 Sheaf, 1831 Bry, (*-Hall*) 1842 OS
> *Molynton Inferior* 1404 Plea, *Mollington Lower* 1727 Sheaf

'The lesser and lower part of Mollington', *v.* lȳtel, inferior, cf. Great Mollington 177 *infra*. The suffix *Banaster* is manorial, from Robert *Banastre*, a Lancashire man to whom the manor was granted by Edward I, Orm² II 573, cf. '*Robert Banastre of Molynton Banastre*' 1368 Orm², and *saliones Domine Clemencie Banastre* l13 *JRC*, 'lady Clemence Banaster's selions' in Little Mollington.

MOLLINGTON BANASTRE, a house near Little Mollington Hall. KNOLLS BRIDGE, MOLLINGTON BRIDGE, crossing the Shropshire Union Canal. MOLLINGTON BRIDGE NO. 2, cf. 170 *supra*.

FIELD-NAMES

The undated forms are 1839 *TA* 270. Of the others, 113 is *JRC*, 1404 Plea.

(*a*) Balls Knowl (*v.* cnoll); Blacon Fd *&* Croft (probably belonging to Blacon manor); Cherry Cows Hay; Chester Mdw; Coney Croft (*v.* coni); Cowaps Croft; Hanging Fd (*v.* hangende); Kiln Croft (*v.* cyln); Moat (*v.* mote); Rushy Mdw; Rye Grass Fd (*v.* rye-grass); Sheep Hay (*v.* (ge)hæg).

(*b*) *Solisdich* 113 ('ditch at a muddy place', *v.* sol¹ (neut. gen.sg. *soles*), dīc); *le Wetewaishote* 1404 ('(the shoot (i.e. a cockshoot) at) the wet road', *v.* wēt, weg, scyte).

iii. Backford

The ecclesiastical parish of Backford contained the townships 1. Caughall (in Broxton Hundred, 140 *supra*), 2. Backford, 3. Chorlton, 4. Lea (now a c.p. including part of Mollington), 5. Great Mollington (now included in Mollington c.p. with Little Mollington 171 *supra*). The township of Moston, now in St Mary on the Hill parish, Broxton Hundred, was originally in Backford Parish, Wirral Hundred, *v.* 141 *supra*.

2. BACKFORD (109–387717) ['bækfəd]

> *Bacfort* 1150 Chest, R1 Orm², *Bacford* 12 Sheaf, 1258 Whall, *Bakford* e 13 Sheaf, *et freq* with variant spellings *Bac-* (to 1663 Sheaf), *Bak-*, *-ford(e)*, *-forda*, *-fort(he)* to 1693 Sheaf
> *Backford* 1186–94 Chest, 1291 Tax, 14 Chest, 1394 ChRR, 1544 Pat *et freq* with variant spelling *-forde*
> *Bakeforde* 13 Orm², 1315 ib, *-ford* 1512 ChRR, 1535 VE, *-forth* 1537 Dugd, *Backeford* 1310 Orm², 1541 Dugd, *-forde* (lit. *Barke-*) 1534–7 Dugd IV 242, Orm² II 462, *Backeford* 1632 Sheaf
> *Bacceford* 1347 ChFor, *Bachforth* c.1554 Whall
> *Bagford* 1535 VE
> *Bakesforde* 1553 Pat

'Ford under a hill', *v.* bæc, ford. The location of a ford which could be so named can hardly have been at Backford Bridge *infra*. The only obvious 'ford under a hill' would have been at 109–396716 where a footpath to Lea crosses Backford Brook at the foot of the 50 ft. hill on which the village stands. The location of *Briggegrene infra* would be useful as an alternative if it were known. The p.n. appears as *Beckford* in a nineteenth-century form for Backfordcross Fm in Great Sutton 194 *infra*.

ACRES FM & WOOD, v. æcer.   AXES FM.   BACKFORD BRIDGE (109–400709), *Moston Bridge* 1831 Bry, named from Moston 141 *supra*, crossing the Shropshire Union Canal, and unlikely to be near the site of the ford from which Backford is named, since there is no adjacent bæc, or ridge. This is not the bridge on the Chorlton boundary at *Briggegrene infra.*   BACKFORD BROOK, v. brōc. BACKFORD CROSS (109–387734), 1842 OS, *ad veterem crucem super bruera de Sutton, -Sotton* 1278 Chest, Whall, *crux sita inter Sotton et Bacford* 1292–1308 Chest, *Fairecrosse* 13 Orm², cf. Backford Cross (Fm) 194 *infra*, v. cros (MedLat *crux*). *Fairecrosse* is 'handsome cross', v. fæger.   BACKFORD HALL, 1831 Bry, *le Old Hall* 1596 Orm², cf. *grangia de Bacforde* 1291 Tax, v. ald, hall, grange. BACKFORDHEATH COTTAGES, cf. Heath Fm *infra.*   CHURCH FM. COALPIT LANE, v. 176 *infra.*   COLLINGE FM & WOOD, cf. *Big- & Little Collinge* 1839 *TA*, perhaps an -ing² formation from coll 'a hill', col¹ 'charcoal' or the OE pers.n. *Col(l)a*, but the material is insufficient.   HEATH FM & WOOD, cf. *Backford Heath* 1842 OS, *bruera* 1294 ChFor, *Heath Acre, -Croft & -Field* 1839 *TA*, Backford-heath Cottages and Backford Cross *supra*, v. hǣð (MedLat bruera).

FIELD-NAMES

The undated forms are 1839 *TA* 30. Of the others 13, 1495, 1548 are Orm², 113 Sheaf, 1357 ChFor, 1553 Pat, 1579 Dugd, 1724 NotCestr, 1831 Bry.

(a) Backside(s) (v. ba(c)ksyde); Benty Part (v. benty, part); Black Loons (v. land); Brow Yard (v. brū, geard); Cannel Croft ('watercourse croft', v. canel); Caughall Fd (cf. Caughall 140 *supra*); Cobler Lane 1831 (109–393735 to 401727); (Little) Dugdale(s); Four Lane End(s) (v. lane, ende¹); Glugg Mdw; Gorstile, Gosthills ('gorse hills', v. gorst, hygel, hyll); Hinterbridge (v. hinder, brycg); Long Mdw (*the Longmedowe* 1553, 1579, v. lang, mǣd); Loonds (v. land); Mill Fd & Croft; New Grounds; Old Man's Yard (v. geard); Ox Pasture; Pingo (v. pingot); Pool Hay (v. pōl¹, (ge)hæg); Priors Hay (v. (ge)hæg, perhaps named from some monastic association, cf. *Routhescroft infra*, since Birkenhead priory, Dieulacres & Chester abbeys all had an interest in Backford parish); Rakes (cf. *le Rake* 1357, v. rake); Three Nook Croft (cf. three-nooked); The Tyth Barn 1724 (v. tēoða); Underyard (v. under, geard); Weat Reans ('wet strips of land', v. wēt, rein); Yockin's Hay.

(b) (the) Briggegrene 1495, *le Brigge Medowe* 1548 (cf. 'two acres in Chorlton *super pontem de Bakeforde*' 13 Orm² II 366, *pons de Bakeforde* 113 Sheaf³ 3, a place on the boundary between Backford and Chorlton 174 *infra*, v. brycg, grēne², mǣd, cf. Backford Bridge *supra*); *campus de Lupus* 13 (perhaps 'Wolf's field', from feld and the pers.n. *Wulf*, Lat. *Lupus*; the grammar of the Latin is incorrect).

3. CHORLTON (109–407707)

> Cherliston 1186–94 Chest
> Cherletunia 1189–99 Orm², Cherletun 12 Sheaf, 1315 Orm², -ton
> 1188–99, m13 ib, 1278 Chest, Whall et freq with variant spellings
> -to(u)ne to 1433 ChRR, (-in Wyrhale) 1294 ChF, JRC
> Cherlton 13 Chest, 1294 ChFor, 1305–23 Chest, 1325 ChRR (p)
> Chorleton 1216–72 Orm², l13 JRC, 1328 ChRR et freq with
> variant spellings -tonne, -tona to 1579 Dugd, (-in Wirhal) l13
> JRC, (-juxta Bacford) 1326 Orm²
> Churliston 1255–62 Orm² (p), 1265–91 Chest (twice, once lit.
> Thurlis-), Churlston (lit. Thurls-) 1265–91 ib
> Chorulton 1262 JRC
> Chorlton 1270–83 Chest, 1288 ChFor et freq, (-in Wirall) 1290–
> 1305 Chest, -tona 1305–23 ib
> Chorletat 1349 Orm² (p)
> Chorton 17 Sheaf
> Chorlton alias Charlton 1613 Orm², Chalton 1724 NotCestr

'The peasant's or peasants' farm', v. ceorl, (gen.sg. ceorles, gen.pl. ceorla), tūn. The township is in Wirral and beside Backford 172 supra. The alternation of sg. and pl. forms in the first el. ceorl indicates that the gen.sg. is used here in a collective sense.

CHORLTON HALL, Chorlton House 1831 Bry, cf. Chorlton Hall 1831 ib now down, on a site near the modern hall.   CHORLTONLODGE FM, v. loge.   THE GROVE, Chorlton Grove 1849 TAMap, v. grāf.   MOUNT COTTAGES & FM, Chorlton Mount 1831 Bry, The Mount 1842 OS, v. munt.   POPLARHALL, Poplar Hall 1842 OS.   STRAWBERRY FM, cf. Strawberry 181 infra.

FIELD-NAMES

The undated forms are 1847 TA 110. Of the others 1340 is ChFor, 1392, 1398 Add, 1432, 1440 Rental, 17 Sheaf, 1637 Chol, 1831 Bry.

(a) Abbotts Hay (probably named from St Werburgh's abbey, Chester, v. abbat, (ge)hæg); Higher & Lower Cleyes (The two Clayes 1637, v. clǣg); Cobler Lane (v. 173 supra); Cross Flatt (v. cros, flat); (Great & Little) Flat(t) (v. flat); Gorsty Fd (cf. the Gorsty Hey 1637, v. gorstig, (ge)hæg); Heath Fd (cf. Chorton Heath 17); In Loons ('inner or nearer selions', v. inn, land); Kiln Croft (v. cyln); Great or Little Long Corn(s) (from lang with corn¹ or horn); Marl Field & Hay (v. marle, (ge)hæg); Mill Hill

(Fd) (cf. *molendinum ventricitum* 1392, also *The Mill Hay* 1637, *v.* myln, (ge)hæg, hyll); Nine Headlands (*v.* hēafod-land); Old Fd (*The Old Feild* 1637); Paddy Pool; Pad Road Fd (a field with a 'pad' or footpath through it, *v.* pæð (ModE dial. *pad*), rād); Ross Croft (*The Roscroft* 1637 *Chol, The Rush Croft* 1819 Orm² II 366, which suggests identity with *Routhescroft* 1246 (14) Orm², 1294 ChFor, E2 *JRC, Roches Croft* m13 (17) Orm², *Rowyscroft* 1279 Whall, *Routhyscroft* 1309 *JRC, -is-* 1312–18 *ib, Routhescroft* 1398 *Add, Rodescrofte* 1432 *Rental,* 1440 *ib,* from the ON pers.n. *Rauðr,* as in Rostherne 2 56, and croft); Roundabout Croft (*v.* 337 *infra*); Rye Croft (*The-* 1637); Stanney Fd & Wd (cf. Little Stanney 180 *infra*); Whitland (*v.* hwīt, land); Wood Lane 1831; Wormy Loons (*Wormlandes* 1637, probably 'selions abounding with worms', *v.* wurm, -ig³, land).

(*b*) Berselehok 1398, *le Bersylhoke* 1432, *le Bersyhoke* 1440 ('hook of land at a fenced-in glade', *v.* berse, lēah, hōc); *le Bruchelond* 1440 ('selion at an intake', *v.* bryce, land, given as in Lea 177 *infra* in 1432 *Rental*); *Chorletonfeld* 1340 (*v.* feld); *The Cuttinges* 1637 ('cuttings', probably allotments cut out of a larger land unit, *v.* cutting); *Heedichebruches* 1398, *Heghdychebruch(e)* 1432, 1440 ('(intake(s) at) the ditch round an enclosure', or '(-at) a high dyke', from bryce with (ge)hæg or hēah and dīc, cf. *Heedichebruches* in Great Boughton 126 *supra*); *the further & the little Hey* 1637 (*v.* (ge)hæg); *the Long Acres* 1637 (*v.* lang, æcer); *le Pyghull* 1432, *le Pyghall* 1440 ('the plot of land', *v.* pighel); *Robinsons Medow* 1637.

4. Lea (Hall) (109–3971) ['li:]

> *Wisdelea* 1086 DB, *Wisdeleth* 1096–1101 (1280) (17) Chest, *-lech* 1096–1101 (14) ib, *Wisdleth* 1096–1101 (17) ib, Dugd, *Vysdeleth* 1096–1101 (1280) Chest, *Vuisdeleth* 1150 ib
>
> *Lee* c.1230 Chest, (*la-, le-*) *Lee* (*-iuxta Bacford*) c.1265–91, 1294 ib, 1300, 1305 Plea, 1348 Orm² *et freq* to *Lee* 1546 Dugd, *Lee vel Ley iuxta Backford* 1579 ib
>
> *Ley* 1505 Orm², 1579 Dugd, c.1720 ChetOS VIII
>
> *Leigh alias Lee* 1560 (1582) ChRR, *Leighe-* 1582 Orm²
>
> *the Lea* 1596 ChRR, 1656 Orm², (*-iuxta Backford*) 1602 Sheaf, *Lea* 1609 ChRR, (*-Hall*) 1831 Bry

The final el. is lēah 'a woodland glade', which stands as a simplex p.n. in the later, shortened, form. The original first el. is difficult to explain unless it be taken as OE *wīsod,* pa. part. of OE (*ge)wīsian,* (*ge)wissian* 'to show (someone) the way (to somewhere or something), to guide, to direct'. The p.n. would mean 'lēah to which the way is shown', or 'lēah which is managed', cf. BT (*ge)wīsian,* (*ge)wissian.* The latter interpretation would arise from the figurative use of the verb, or some lost technical connotation, and might be relevant to the fact that this manor was a demesne of St Werburgh's abbey,

Chester, TRE and DB, and may well have been the subject of early estate-management or forestry.

COALPIT LANE (109–389730 to 370713), *Hook Pit Lane* 1831 Bry, cf. *Coalpit Lane Croft* 1802 Sheaf, Hill Fm 178 *infra* (*Coal Pit House* 1831 Bry), and *Coal Pit Lane* 204 *infra*. It is apparently named from a coal-pit, *v.* col¹, pytt, lane. The pit was 'hook pit', at a hook of land in a corner of the parish, *v.* hōc. It is not apparent whether this was a charcoal or a mining industry.   DEMMAGE FM, *le Demmyng* 1357 ChFor, *the Broad-, the Little Demage Heys* 1698 Sheaf, *the Damage Farm, the two Damages* 1802 ib, *Damage* 1831 Bry, *Demage* 1842 OS, cf. *Damage Lane* 1831 Bry (109– 385715 to 386710), *Damage* 178 *infra*. This is from demming 'a dam', with (ge)hæg and lane.   DUNKIRK (WOOD), *Dunkirk Farm* 1802 Sheaf, *-Nursery* 1831 Bry, *Wood in Dunkirk* 1839 TA. Dunkirk is a hamlet in Lea, Capenhurst and Great Sutton townships, cf. Dunkirk Ho 194 *infra*, Manor Fm *infra*. There is no early record of the place. It is probably named after Dunkirk (Dunkerque) in France (cf. PNK 495 for analogies, also Dunkirk 1 161, 316, 2 196, 276. The name-type is probably an allusion to a faraway place or distant colony or outpost with little permanence or no long history of settlement, but older examples might allude to the French place as a nest of anti-English pirates in Elizabethan times (*v. The Letters & Despatches of Richard Verstegan*, ed. A. G. Petti (Catholic Record Soc., LII, London 1959) 130, 132). Professor Sørensen observes that there are places in Denmark named after Dunkerque in France, e.g. Dynkarken, a st.n. in Århus. He points out that Dunkerque was an important shipping centre in olden days. This kind of mercantile and shipping allusion would be appropriate in ports and seaside towns, but not in lonely inland places. It may just be possible that some of the older examples of *Dunkirk* names in England could be allusions to recusant staging-posts in Elizabethan and Jacobean times. It is altogether most probable, however, that the *Dunkirk* type of p.n. in England often refers to the unfortunate historical associations of the French p.n. with English military and political disaster; in 1558 the English lost Dunkirk to the French, in 1658 the French gave it to the English but Charles II sold the place back to them after the Restoration, and in 1793 it was attacked unsuccessfully and disastrously, with great loss of life, by the Duke of York.   MANOR FM, *Dunkirk Farm* 1802 Sheaf, cf. prec.

Powey Lane, v. I 49 (XXVIII (v)).   Viaduct Wood, v. 178 *infra*.

FIELD-NAMES

The undated forms are 1839 *TA* 231. Of the others 1292–1308 is *Chest*, 1340, 1347, 1357 *ChFor*, 1392 *Add*, 1432 *Rental*, 1539 *Orm²*, 1583 *JRC*, 1698, 1802 *Sheaf*.

(*a*) Backford Quarter (1802, *v.* quarter); Boardens Dale (1802, *Boudingsdale or Bowdens Dale* 1698, *v.* dæl¹); Brook Croft (named from Backford Brook 173 *supra*); Cheers Acre; Chester Croft (probably named from Chester abbey); Church Fd 1802 (*v.* Lea Fd *infra*); Coxtons Hill (*Coxton's Hill* 1802); Crank Fd (*The-* 1802, *v.* cranuc); The Crofts (1698, *v.* croft); Dove House Flat; Great & Little Fidlers Croft (*Big & Little Fiddler's Croft* 1802, probably from the surname *Fiddler*); Gorse Moss; Grandmothers Croft (probably dower-land); The Green Croft 1698; Harvey's Hey 1802; Far & Near Heath Part (cf. *the Lea Heathe* 1583, *brueria inter villam de Lee et Capenhurst* 1292–1308, *v.* hǣð); Hill Fd; Big Knowl Fd, Little Knowl, Knowles Plantation (*Little Knowl* 1802, *v.* cnoll); Lea Fd (*le Leefeld* 1340, *Leafield or Church Field* 1802, *v.* feld, cirice, cf. Lea *supra*); Big & Little Lea Wd (1802, cf. *boscus de (la) Lee* 1347, 1357, *v.* wudu); Long Acre; Long Fd (*the-* 1698); Marled Fd (*v.* marled); Milking Bank (*v.* milking); New Hay (*v.* nīwe (ge)hæg); Seven- & Three Nobles Hay (*The Three and the Seven Noble Heys* 1802, cf. *the Five Nobles Hey* 1698, and Noble Hay 202, 337 *infra*, probably named from an ancient rent or price, *v.* noble); Ouderns Croft (*Aldern's Croft* 1802, probably from a surname, perhaps the Ch name *Arderne*); Outlet (*v.* outlet); Oxpasture; Pool Fd; Round Hill Hay; Sir Harry's Hay (*-Hey* 1698); Stanfords Hill (*Sandford's Hill* 1802); Far & Near Stanley Fd (*Further & Nearer-* 1802); Stanton Fd; Town Fd.

(*b*) *Lez Acreys* 1539 (*v.* æcer, (ge)hæg); *le Bruches* 1392 ('the breakings-in of land', *v.* bryce, cf. foll.); *le Bruchelond* 1432 (*v.* bryce, land, cf. prec., *v.* 175 *supra*); *the Lea Foold* 1583 ('fold at Lea', *v.* fald).

5. Great Mollington (109–3870), formerly Mollington Torold ['tɔroud]

> *Molintone* 1086 DB, *Molinton* e 13 *Chest*, *Molynton* 1278 ib *et freq* with variant spelling *Molin-* to 1581 ChRR, *Mol(l)ingion* 1287 *Court*, 1288 *ChFor et freq* with variant spellings *Moling-* (to 1582 Orm²), *Molyng-* (1295 *Misc* to 1512 *Plea*), *Mollyng-* (1582 ChRR); *Mollinton* 1335 *Mont*, 1632 *Sheaf*
>
> *Magna Molinton* 1271 *ChFor et freq* with spellings *ut supra*, *Great Mollyngton* 1582 ChRR, *Mollington Magna* 1727 *Sheaf*, *Great Mollington* 1819 Orm²
>
> *Molynton Thorot* 1286 *ChFor et freq* with spellings *ut supra* and

variant forms of suffix -*T*(*h*)*orot*, -*Toroth*, -*Torrot*, -*et*, -*Torold*, -*ald*, -*T*(*h*)*orrold*, -*Toroud* (occasionally lit. -*ond*), -*Tor*(*r*)*out* (occ. -*ont*), -*Tyrrald*, -*Tort* or *Torrold*, -*Torrent* to *Mollington Torrant* or *Great Mollington* 1819 Orm² *Mellinton Torout* (lit. -*Toront*) 1335 Pat

'Moll's farm, farm called after Moll', from **tūn**, -**ingtūn**, and the OE pers.n. *Moll* or a wk. form *Molla, cf. Molecomb Sx 78, Mollington O 401, Wa 271. It is distinguished as 'great' from Little Mollington 171 *supra*, *v*. **grēat**. The manorial affix is the surname of a family owning land in Mollington from 1271 *ChFor* to 1354 BPR. Additional forms of the surname are *Toraud*(*e*) 1271 *ChFor*, 1308 Orm², *Thoraud* 1278 *JRC*, *T*(*h*)*orald*, *Thorale* 1337 Cl, cf. ON *Þóraldr*, OSwed *Thorald*.

COALPIT LANE, *v*. 176 *supra*, cf. Hill Fm *infra*.   THE CROSS-LOOMS, CROSSLOOMS FM, cf. *Cross Looms* 1838 *TA*, 'strips of land running athwart', *v*. **cros**, **land**, **loom**.   DAMAGE LANE, 1838 *TA*, 1831 Bry, cf. 176 *supra* and *Higher-*, *Lower-*, *Lees-*, *Marl-*, *Middle- & Nearer Damage* 1838 *TA*, *v*. **demming**, cf. Demmage Fm 176 *supra*.   DODD'S WOOD.   GROVE FM, cf. *boscus vocatus le Groue* 1357 *ChFor*, *nemus Magne Molinton* 1271 ib, *v*. **grāf**.   HILL FM (109–375716), *Coal Pit House* 1831 Bry, *Carters Farm* 1842 OS, cf. Coalpit Lane *supra*, *v*. **col**[1], **pytt**.   HOME FM.   ICEHOUSE PLANTATION.   MOLLINGTON HALL, 1831 Bry.   OVERWOOD LANE, 1831 Bry, cf. *Over Wood*, *Welshman's Overwood* 1838 *TA*, *boscus de Molyngton* 1294 *ChFor*, *v*. **uferra**, **wudu**. The Welshman is not identified.   POWEY LANE, *v*. 177 *supra*.   ROSE FM, cf. *Rose* 1838 *TA*, either 'the rows', *v*. **rāw**, or the surname *Row*(*e*). TARRANT FM, named after the manorial suffix of Great Mollington *supra*.   TOWNFIELD LANE, 1831 Bry, cf. *Town Field* 1838 *TA*, *Mollington Torrald Fyeld* 1583 *JRC*, *v*. **toun**, **feld**.   VIADUCT WOOD, near a railway viaduct over the Shropshire Union Canal. WELL FM, *v*. **wella**.   THE WILLOWS.

FIELD-NAMES

The undated forms are 1838 *TA* 269. Of the others 1278 is Sheaf, 1286, 1347 *ChFor*, 1292 Court, 1404 Plea, 1583 *JRC*, 1831 Bry.

(*a*) Adams Riding (*v*. **ryding**); Austin Lane 1831; Backsides (*v*. **ba(c)k-syde**); The Bran, Big & Little Brans (probably from **brand** 'a place cleared by burning'); Bridge Fd (cf. *Lea Bridge* 1838 *TA*, *v.* brycg, cf. Lea 175 *supra*); Broad Hey (*v.* (ge)hæg); Dingle (*v.* dingle); Ditch Graves (from dīc and græf or grǣfe); Dock Croft (*v.* docce); Early Loons, Five Loons (*v.* land); The Green (cf. *le Grene* 1278, *v.* grēne²); Hanging Ground (*v.* hangende); The Hay Lawn (*v.* hēg, launde); Hen Gorst Fd; Hook (*v.* hōc); Horsestone ('the hoar stone', *v.* hār², stān); Larney Loon(s) (*v.* land); The Lawn (*v.* launde); Light Hooks (*v.* lēoht, hōc); Lilly; Marehay; Marl Fd; Muck Fd (*v.* muk); Nines; Nugwith (perhaps from viðr 'a wood'); Pingo (*v.* pingot); Poor Fd; Saint Bridgets Glebe (cf. St Bridget's, Chester, 338 *infra*, *v.* glebe); Seven Acres; Seven Longs, Seven Loons (*v.* seofon, land); Sour Butts (*v.* sūr, butte); Stoake Glebe (*v.* glebe, cf. Stoke 181 *infra*); Style Croft (*v.* stigel); Wash or Woodcroft (*v.* wæsce, wudu).

(*b*) *Edeuenetisgraue* 1286 (from grǣfe 'a copse', with a ME fem.pers.n. *Edwenet* from the OE fem.pers.n. *Ēadwynn*); *le Heth* 1347 (*v.* hǣð, cf. foll.); *Gruggeworth Heth* 1292 (from hǣð 'a heath' and a p.n. *Gruggeworth* from worð and an unidentified first el.); *le Newfeld* 1404 (*v.* nīwe, feld); *the Ringyord of Mollington Torrald fyeld* 1583 ('circular enclosure', *v.* hring, geard).

iv. St Oswald's

For the rest of this parish, *v.* 337 *infra*.

6. CROUGHTON (BRIDGE & COTTAGE) (109–4172) [ˈkroutən]

    Crostone 1086 DB, *-tona* 1150 Chest

    Croctona 1096–1101 (1280) Chest, *Crocton* 1188–91 ib, 1286 *ChFor*,   *Crochton*(*a*) 1270–1316 Chest

    Croghtona 1096–1101 (1280) (17) Chest, *Croghton* 1361 BPR *et*   *freq* to 1819 Orm²

    Crouhton 1270–1316 Chest

    Croughton 1411 ChRR (p), 1541 Dugd *et freq*, *Chroughton* 1620   Sheaf, *Croughton Cottage* 1831 Bry

'Enclosure or farm where saffron grows', *v.* croh¹, tūn. Ekwall (DEPN) suggests *crōh² 'a nook, a corner', which is a feasible alternative here, cf. The Dungeon *infra*.

BRIDGE FM, cf. Croughton Bridge. THE DUNGEON, *Dungeon* 1849 *TA*, '*a very romantic dingle, called the Dungeons*' 1819 Orm², *v.* dongeon.

FIELD-NAMES

The undated forms are 1849 *TA* 137.

(a) Backsides (*v.* ba(c)ksyde); Cluice (*v.* clūs(e), 'mill-dam; floodgate or sluice'); Damage Hay (*v.* demming, (ge)hæg, cf. Damage Lane, Demmage Fm 178, 176 *supra*); Hatherling; Heath (*Chroughton Heath* 1620 Sheaf); Lanthorns; New Hay (*v.* (ge)hæg); New Ports (perhaps from port, but more likely to be from ModE *part* 'a division of a field', cf. foll.); Old Birds (cf. prec., with which this appears analogous, an alternative corruption of *parts*); Peas Hay (*v.* pise, (ge)hæg); Townsend Hay (*v.* toun, ende[1], (ge)hæg); Twindlers (probably from dial. *twindle* 'a twin' EDD); Wide Yard (*v.* wid, geard).

v. Stoke

The ecclesiastical parish of Stoke contained the townships 1. Little Stanney, 2. Stoke, 3. part of Whitby (cf. 198 *infra*). Part of Ince 3 251 in Eddisbury Hundred, was in Stoke parish, *v.* Holme Ho 3 251.

1. LITTLE STANNEY (109–4174) [ˈstani], 1583 ChRR, *Parua Staneya*, *Paruum Staney(e)*, *Staney(e) superioris*, *villa minoris Staneye*, *minor Staneya* 1278, 1279 Chest, Whall, *Stanney Parva* 1544 Plea, 1724 NotCestr, *Parva Stanney* 1636 Orm[2], *Stanne Parua* 1663 Sheaf, otherwise *Stanney*, with spellings as in Great Stanney 182 *infra*, *v.* lȳtel, parva, minor.

FLINDOW (lost, 109–403745), 1844 *TA*, *Flindale* 1270 (c.1340) Bun, 1278 Whall, *Fliddale* 1278 Chest, (*molendinum de-*, *siketum quod vocatur-*) *Flyndal* 1279 Whall, (*pastura vocata*) *Flyndalles* 1544 Bun, (*close of pasture called*) *Fyndall* c.1544 Whall, *Flindowe* 17 Bun, cf. *Flinder* (ChetNS LXXIX 209) a local name for the watercourse on the boundary of Great and Little Stanney, 'stony valley', *v.* flint, dæl[1].

GOLDWORTH LANE (109–411738 to 395737), 1842 OS, *Gowdearth Lane* 1831 Bry, cf. *Goldworth* 1844 *TA*, probably identical with 'a plot of land called *le Goldhord*' 1270 (13) Bun, cf. 'the old ditch which surrounds a plot of land called *le Goldehord*' 1279 Whall, 'the golden treasure', *v.* gold-hord. No archæology is recorded.

HEATH HOUSES (lost, 109–408735), 1831 Bry, cf. *Heath* 1842 OS, *the Heath Heay* 17 Bun, *v.* hǣð, hūs, (ge)hæg.   HILL FM.   THE

Moors (lost, about 109–430750), 1842 OS, cf. *Moor* 1844 *TA*, a tract of Marsh in Little Stanney and Thornton le Moors, cf. 3 259, the location of *mara de Grundles* 13 Whall, 'the swamp called Bottomless', *v.* grundlēas, mōr[1]. The Old Hall, *aula apud Staney* 1278 ChFor, *Stanny-hall* 1656 Orm[2], *Stanney Hall* 1724 NotCestr, 1831 Bry, *v.* hall. Rake Hall, 1724 Orm[2], *v.* rake, hall. The name appears to have had a jocular origin, being coined at a party on December 15th 1724, cf. Orm[2] II 394, the first el. probably a pun on *rake* 'a dissolute fellow'. Stanney Green (lost, 109–417744), 1831 Bry, 1754 *Bun*, *v.* grēne[2]. Stanney Mill, 1842 OS, *molendinum de Staneya* c.1184 Chest, *the Milles* 17 Bun, *Stanney Water Mill* 1831 Bry, *v.* myln. The mill-lade for this mill is formed by Mill Brook[1] 1 32. Stanney Mill Bridge, *Stanney Bridge* 1831 ib, cf. prec., *v.* brycg. Stanney Wood, 1842 OS, cf. 184 *infra*. Strawberry, 1842 ib, *Strawberry House* 1831 Bry, probably named from the fruit. Wood Fm, *v.* wudu, cf. Stanney Wood *supra*.

FIELD-NAMES

The undated forms are 1844 *TA* 364, 1279 is Whall, 17 *Bun*.

(a) Backsides (*v.* ba(c)ksyde); Butty Hey (*v.* butty, (ge)hæg); Church Fd; Clever Loonds, Clover Loons (*the Clefferlandes* 17, 'the clover selions', *v.* clæfre, land); Coney Greave (*the Cunnygree* 17, *v.* coningre); Cow House Fd (cf. Grange Cow Worth 184 *infra*); Dunstall (*v.* tūn-stall); Hook Moor (*v.* hōc, mōr[1]); Horse Pasture (*the Horse Hey, the Horse Pastures* 17, *v.* hors, pasture, (ge)hæg); Long Cross ('long crosswise field', *v.* lang, cros); Long Loonds (*the long Landes* 17, *v.* lang, land); Longridge (*v.* lang, hrycg); Main Hey (*v.* main, (ge)hæg); Marl Fd, Marled Hay, -Hey (*v.* marle(d), (ge)hæg); Mill Marsh (cf. Stanney Mill *supra*); New Hay (*the Newe Hey* 17, *v.* (ge)hæg); Old Town Fd; Royalty Plantation (*v.* roialte); Rushy Wd; Sheep Cot Hay (*v.* scēp, cot, (ge)hæg); Whitefield (*v.* hwīt, feld); Whitefield Hells (cf. prec., *v.* helde); Wick Butty.

(b) *Brode Hey* 17 (*v.* brād, (ge)hæg); meadow called *Oulton* 17 (perhaps 'old enclosure', from ald and tūn); *Portway* 1279 (*v.* port-weg, 1 49 (XXVIII (i))).

2. Stoke (109–4273) ['stouk] formerly ['stuːək]
  Stok 13 Whall, 1271, 1286 ChFor, 1291 Tax, 1360 BPR (p), (*-in Wirhale*) 1311 Fine
  Stoke 1260 Court (p), 1278 ChFor et freq, passim to 1620 Sheaf, (*-in Wirrall*) 1291 Pap, (*-iuxta Pykton*) 1397 ChRR, *Stoke or Stoak* 1819 Orm[2]

Stokes in Wirhale 1284 ChF, *Stokes* 1289 Court (p), 1319 Pat, 1365 BPR (p), 1582 Orm²
Stooke 1328 Bun, 1462 ChRR
Stoake 1666, 1677 Sheaf, 1766, 1785 *Bun*, 1772 Orm², *Stoak* 1724 NotCestr, 1819, 1882 Orm², *Stoak or Stoke* 1831 Bry

'The dairy farms, the outlying hamlets', *v.* stoc (nom.pl. OE **stocu*, ME *stokes*). The township is in Wirral 1 7, adjacent to Picton 132 *supra*.

DENSION'S BRIDGE, cf. *Denson's Meadow* 1844 *TA*.   HEATH LANE, 1831 Bry, cf. *Stoke Heath* 1620 Sheaf, *Stoake Heath* 1785 *Bun*, *v.* hǣð, lane.   MEADOW LANE (BRIDGE).   MILL BROOK, *v.* Mill Brook¹ 1 32.   MOOR LANE (lost), 1831 Bry, cf. *Stoake Moor(e)* 1766, 1787 *Bun*, *v.* mōr¹, lane.   PICTON LANE BRIDGE, *Stoak Bridge* 1831 Bry, cf. Picton 132 *supra*.   STOKE BRIDGE, *Greenway Bridge* 1831 ib, *v.* grēne¹, weg, cf. prec.   STOKE FM.   STOKE GRANGE, *Stoak Grange* 1831 Bry, *grangia* 1389 ChRR, *v.* graunge.

FIELD-NAMES

The undated forms are 1844 *TA* 372, 1766, 1787 *Bun*.

(a) Backen Butt (*v.* butte); Backside (*v.* ba(c)ksyde); The Cartcroft 1766, 1787; Cats Grave, Catsgrove (*v.* catt, grǣfe, grāf); Clints (*v.* klint); Cow Hey (*v.* (ge)hæg); Flat (*v.* flat); Hay Loonds (*v.* hēg, land); Kings Yard (*v.* geard); Kirk Mdw, Kirkway (*v.* kirkja, mǣd, weg); Longridge (1787, *the Long Ridge* 1766); Lords Mdw (*v.* hlāford); Mackee; Marl Pit Flat (*v.* marle-pytt); Mellor Hey; Mill Hill; Newhey (*v.* (ge)hæg); Nooks (*v.* nōk); Old Hayes (*v.* (ge)hæg); Stanney Fd; Top Ends; Trowse Wds; Wetrains (*v.* wēt, rein); White Fd.

vi. Great Stanney

Great Stanney was an extra-parochial township belonging to Stanlow (later Whalley) Abbey, to which it was granted in 1178. It seems to have included Stanlow originally, and to have been part of Eastham parish 187 *infra*, *v.* Orm² II 397. Bryant's map, 1831 puts it in Stoke parish. It is now included in the c.p. of Ellesmere Port Municipal Borough.

GREAT STANNEY (109–405750) ['stæni]

Stanei 1086 DB, *Staneia* 1096–1101 (1150), 1150 Chest, *Staney* 1163–90 ib *et freq* with variant spellings *Staneie, -eia, -eya, eye* to 1709 *Blun, Stany(e), Stanie* 1547 *MinAcct,* 1554 *Bun,* Whall, 1660 Sheaf

Stanney 1135–54 (17) Orm², *Stanneya* c.1190 *Bun,* e13 Tab, *Stanneye* 1353 BPR, *Stanney* 1351 Chamb, 1459 (1594) ChRR, 1499 *Eyre,* 1544 Plea, 1587 AD, 1594 ChRR, 1600 Sheaf, 1724 NotCestr, *Stanny* 1554 Whall

Stanay 1260 Sheaf, 1347 *ChFor,* BPR, 1361 BPR, 1365 *JRC,* 1384 ChRR (p), 1423 Cre, 1459 Orm², (-*in Wirhale*) 1378 Plea, *Stanaye* 1304 Chamb (p), *Stannay* 1655 Sheaf

Staneya Inferior 1278 Chest, Whall, *inferior villa de Staneye* 1278 Whall

maior (villa de) Staneya 1279 Whall, *magna Staney* 1450 ChRR, *Magna Stanney* 1499 *Eyre, Stany Magna, Magna Stany* 1537 Dugd, 1554 Whall, *Stanney Magna* 1544 Plea, *Greate Stanney* 1577 Sheaf, *Great Stanney* 1600 ib

Stayny 1554 Whall

Great Stanley 1560 Sheaf

Stanhey 1595 AD

Stanwaye 1597 MidCh, -*way* 1727 Sheaf

Stanne Magna 1663 Sheaf

Great Stane 1693 Sheaf

'Rock island', *v.* stān, ēg. The district of Great and Little Stanney comprised the marshland south of the rocky promontory of Stanlow 185 *infra,* between R. Gowy and the Mersey estuary. The stān-ēg would be Stanlow, which would, originally, have been part of Great Stanney. The two parts of Stanney are distinguished as Little-, or Higher- (180 *supra*) and Great-, or Lower-, *v.* grēat, maior, magna, inferior.

THE GRANGE (109–412750) formerly STANNEY GRANGE

grangia de Staneya 1200–11 Whall *et freq* with spellings as for Stanney *supra* to *gra(u)ngia de Stan(n)ey,* -*Stanie* 1544 Plea, *Bun,* c.1554 Whall, *MinAcct*

Staneygraung' 1318 *Eyre,* -*grange* 1347 *ChFor, Stanaygraunge* 1347 BPR, *Stanneygraunge* 1351 Chamb, *Stanney alias Stanney Grange* 1545 Orm², *Great Stanney alias-* 1600 Sheaf, *Stanney Grange* 1831 Bry, *Stany Grange* 1547 *MinAcct, Stany(e)-* c.1554 Whall

'The manor at Stanney', *v.* **grange**, cf. Great Stanney *supra*. This was a grange of Stanlow abbey. Part of the establishment is named *the Grange Court* 17 *Bun*, from court 'a courtyard', and an adjunct was the Cow Worth *infra*.

GRANGE COW WORTH (site of, 109–411753), 1819 Orm², *le Cowe House* (*-Mershe*) 1544 *Bun*, *le Cowe Howse* 1547 *MinAcct*, 1553 Pat, *le Cowhowse* 1554 *MinAcct*, *the Cowhouse* (*Marsh*) c.1554 Whall, 1600 Sheaf, *Higher-* & *Low Cowhouse Field* 1600 ib, *the Cowehouse* (*-Marsh*), *the* (*Higher-* & *Lower-*) *Cowehousefeild* 17 *Bun*, *Cowhouse* 1637 Orm², 'the enclosure belonging to-, the marsh near-, the cow-house of Stanney Grange', *v.* cū, hūs, worð, mersc, feld, cf. Great Stanney, The Grange *supra*, Cow House Fd 181 *supra*, also Plymyard 187 *infra*.

STANNEY WOOD, 1831 Bry, *Stanaygraungewode* 1365 *JRC*, *the ould wood* 17 *Bun*, *The Woodlands* 1785 *ib*, *v.* wudu, ald, cf. The Grange *supra*. Part of this wood is in Little Stanney 181 *supra*.

FOLLY BRIDGE, cf. *The Folly* 1831 Bry, Folly Wood 3 252, *v.* folie. STANLOW BRIDGE, cf. Stanlow 185 *infra*.   GT. STANNEY HALL. UNDERWOOD, *v.* under, wudu, cf. Stanney Wood *supra*.   WEAVER'S BRIDGE (over the Shropshire Union Canal), *Grange Bridge* 1831 Bry, cf. The Grange *supra*.

FIELD-NAMES

Forms dated 1178–90, c.1554 are Whall, ?1178–90 (17) Orm², c.1184 Chest, 1187 Dugd, 1209, 1544, 17 *Bun*, 1271, 1340, 1357 *ChFor*, 1499 *Eyre*, 1508, 1600 Sheaf.

(b) *Barkehouse Croft* 17 ('tannery croft', *v.* bark-howse, croft); *Blanchetts Croft* 17 (*Blancherd's Croft* 1600, from the ME surname *Blanchard* (*v.* Reaney, s.n.) and croft); *the Butchers Feild* 17 (*v.* bocher, feld); *the Calfe Hey* 17 (*v.* calf, (ge)hæg); *Cokes Mershe* 1544, *Cots Marsh* c.1554 ('Coke's marsh', named from William *Coke*, tenant in 1544, and mersc); *the Dalimores Croft* 17; *the Grange Spring* c.1554, *the Spring* 17 (a wood, *v.* spring); *Holmlake* 1209 ('watercourse at a marsh or island', *v.* holmr, lacu, cf. *Holmlache* 186 *infra*); *the Lady Meadowe Feild* 17 (*v.* hlæfdige, mæd, probably named from St Mary, this being monastic land); (*the*) *Great-*, *-Lit(t)le-* & *-King's Marsh* 1600, 17 (cf. *mariscum* c.1184, and *Cokes Mershe* supra, and Grange Cow Worth *supra*, *v.* mersc); *the Higher-* & *-Lower Meadow Field*, *the Little Meadow* 1600 (*v.* mæd); *the Hyer-* & *-Lower Moorefeild* 17 (*v.* mōr¹); *the Newe Hey* 17 (*v.* (ge)hæg); *Oxemoore* 17 ('marsh where oxen pasture', *v.* oxa, mōr¹); *Poole Croft* 1600, 17 (*v.* pōl¹, croft); *Pyde Croft* 17 ('pied-, mottled-, patchy croft', *v.* pyed, croft); *le Rake* 1340, 1357, *the Rake Moorefeild* 17, *the Rakemore Field* 1600 (*v.* rake, mōr[1], feld); *Ritchafeild* 17; *Ryshemersch* c.1178–90, *-marsh* 1187, *Rishy Marsh* ?1178–90 (17), *Russhemersch* 1499 ('rushy marsh', *v.* risc, riscig, mersc); *Sheepcoate Croft* 1600 (*v.* scēp, cot, croft); *campus de Stanney* 1271 (*v.* feld); *the Stanney Hoke Ditch* 1508 ('ditch at a hook of land', *v.* hōc, dīc).

vii. Stanlow

Stanlow was an extra-parochial district, now included in the c.p. of Ellesmore Port Municipal Borough. It was the site of a Cistercian monastery founded in 1178 and removed in 1296 to Whalley La after inundation by the sea. A cell of twelve chaplains was maintained here by the abbots of Whalley until the dissolution. Prior to the foundation of the abbey, Stanlow was probably part of Great Stanney 182 *supra*.

STANLOW ABBEY (site of), STANLOW HOUSE, STANLOW POINT (109–4277) [ˈstanlou]

> (*abbas et conventus de-*) *Stanlawa* 1172–78 *Bun*, Facs, c.1190
> *Bun*, l12 (1347) *ChFor*, *-lawe* 1172–78, 1178, 1178–81 Whall
> *et freq* with variant spellings *-laue*, *-law* to *Stanlaw* (*Monastery*)
> 1819 Orm[2], *sita de Stanlawe* 1499 Sheaf, cf. *abbas de Whalleye*
> *quondam de Stanlawe* 1308 Whall
> *Stanlowe* 1178–89 *Chol*, *Facs et freq* to 1614 Orm[2] with variant
> spelling *-low* from 1260 Court, *Stanllowe* 1299 *Port* (p),
> *Stanlowe in Wirhale* 1289 Cl
> *Stanl'* 1178–82 Whall *et freq* to 1292 ib
> *Stanelawe* 1271 *ChFor* (p), 1283 (1334) Pat
> *Stanhowe* 1283 Pat
> *Stanlagh* 1283 Pat
> *Stanlewe* 1306 Pap
> *Stanley* 1553 Pat
> *Stanlay(e)* c.1554 Whall
> *Standlowe* 1614 Orm[2]

The name of this place is taken from the rocky promontory at Stanlow Point, so named 1831 Bry, the eroded remnant of what must have been a conspicuous headland before the great inundations which caused the evacuation of the abbey. The point is named *Stanlawa que est sedes abatie* ('Stanlow, which is the site of the abbey') 1172–78 *Bun*, cf. '. . . the place called Stanlowa, for the making and building of an abbey there' c.1190 *Bun*, and is named

Steny-hill in 'Stanlow now a farm ... But there was a monastery ... taking the name from *Steny-hill'* 1621 (1656) Orm² II 359. The p.n. is 'stone hill, rock hill', *v.* stān, stǣnig, stǣnen, hlāw, hyll, point. Unless the 1283 Pat form *Stanhowe* is a sport, the second el. is once replaced by hōh. Later forms show confusion with lēah. The name of the abbey itself was *Locus Benedictus* 'the Blessed Place' and *locus Stanlawe qui mutato nomine Benedictus Locus vocari volumus* 'the place Stanlow which we wish to be called by the changed name of Blessed Place' a.1178 Whall, (*ecclesia de-, abbatia de-*) *Locus Benedictus* (*de Stanlawe*) 1178–81, 1178–90, 1186–91 Whall *et freq* with variant spellings as for Stanlow *supra* to *Locus Benedictus de Stanlawe nunc de Whalleye* 1303 Whall. This new name was taken to be a dedication in *abbat(h)ia Sancti Benedicti de Stanlaue, -lawe* 1209 *Bun*, Whall. Stanlow Ho, so named 1831 Bry, the remains of the monastic buildings and the cell maintained there, is *grangia de Stanlowe* 1537 Dugd, *Stanley Grange* 1553 Pat, *Stan(d)lowe alias Stan(d)lowe Grange* 1614 Orm², *Stanlow now a farm* 1621 (1656) Orm², *v.* grange.

MARSH HOUSE (lost, 109–414763), 1831 Bry, cf. *mariscus de Stanlowe* 1279 Chest, *le Stanlowe Mershe* 1547 *MinAcct*, *Stanley Mershe* 1553 Pat, *Stanlow Mershe* (lit. *Meshe*) c.1554 Whall, *v.* mersc, hūs. STANLOW BANKS & POOL, 1842 OS, sandbanks and mud-flats, and a creek, in the Mersey estuary, at the mouth of R. Gowy, *v.* banke, pōl¹.   SWAN POOL (lost, 109–422767), 1831 Bry, a creek of the Mersey estuary, 'pool frequented by swans', *v.* swan¹, pōl¹.

FIELD-NAMES

(b) *pastura que dicitur Biflet* 1241 Whall ('beside the creek', *v.* bī, flēot, cf. Byfleet Sr 104); *le Crynkyll* 1547 *MinAcct*, *le Crynkell* 1553 Pat, *Crymkill* c.1554 Whall (the name of a croft, probably 'the bend, the crinkle', i.e. a plot of ground in the bend of a stream, or of a sinuous shape, *v.* crinkle 1596 NED); *Holmlache, Holumlake* 1209 Chest, Whall ('boggy stream at a marsh', *v.* holmr, lǣc(c), lacu, perhaps the same place as *Holmlake* 184 *supra*); *le Intacke* 1547 *MinAcct*, *le Intak* 1553 Pat, *Intack* c.1554 Whall (*v.* inntak).

viii. Eastham

The ecclesiastical parish of Eastham was created about 1152 as a chapelry of Bromborough parish, *v.* 234, 239 *infra*. It contained the townships 1. Eastham, 2. Hooton, 3. Netherpool, 4. Overpool, 5. Great Sutton, 6. Little Sutton, 7. Childer Thornton, and also (8) part of Whitby 198 *infra*. It would seem that Stanlow and Great Stanney 185, 182 *supra* belonged here originally, Eastham being the mother church of the men of Stanney in 1186–91 Whall (ChetOS XI 533), cf. Orm² II 397. Eastham township with part of Hooton is now included in the c.p. of Bebington Municipal Borough (245 *infra*). The rest of the ancient parish, with Great Stanney and Stanlow, is included in the c.p. of Ellesmore Port Municipal Borough (198 *infra*).

1. EASTHAM (109–3680) [ˈiːstəm]

> *Estham* 1086 DB, 1096–1101 (1150), 1150 Chest, 1100–35 (1285)
>   Ch *et freq* to 1657 *Clif* with variant form *Hestham* 1175 Facs,
>   e13 (17) Chest and variant spellings *Esthama, Estam* (1343
>   Sheaf, 1432 *Rental*), *Esthum* (1549 Sheaf), *Estom* (1599 ib),
>   *Estem* (1671 ib), *Esthim* (1551 ib)
> *Esteham* 1096–1101 (1280), 1178–90 Chest, 1428 Sheaf, *Hesteham*
>   1186–91 Whall
> *Easthamm* 1499 Sheaf, *Eastham* 1539–47 Dugd, 1546 ib *et freq*,
>   *-hame* 1637 Sheaf, *Eastome* 1670 ib, *Eastom* 1715, 1721, 1723 ib
> *Eston(e)* 1687 Sheaf
> *Eastham cum Plymyard* 1724 NotCestr

'Village in the east', *v.* ēast, hām, from its being on the east shore of Wirral.

PLYMYARD, PLYMYARD DALE & PARK [ˈplimjaːd]

> *Plumyerd* 1250 ChFor, *Plumierd* 1280 ib, *Plymyerdheth* 1331 ib,
>   *Plumyard* 1288 ChFor, 1539–47 Dugd, *-yorde* 1407 JRC
> *Plumworth* 1291 Tax
> *Plumʒord* 1378 Eyre
> *Plymyord* 1398 *Add* (p), 1432 *Rental*, *-yorde* 1440 ib, 1555 Sheaf,
>   *-yerde* 1535 VE, *-yerd* 1539–47 Dugd, *-yard* 1556–7 Orm², 1579
>   Dugd, *et freq*
> *Plimyorde* 1412 JRC, *-yard* 1579 Dugd, 1727 Sheaf, 1819 Orm²,
>   1842 OS, (*Hall*) 1845 ChetOS VIII, *-yards* 1831 Bry
> *Plemyerd* 1546 Dugd
> *Plymeyarde* 1553 Pat

'Plum-tree orchard', *v*. plūme, plȳme, geard. In one instance worð replaces geard. As at Grange Cow Worth 184 *supra*, it seems that worð continued as a significant word in Ch down into ME, possibly into ModE. For Plymyard Dale cf. Dale Hey Lane *infra*.

CARLETT COTTAGE & PARK (109–363810) [ˈkærlet], *Carlet Wood* 1831 Bry, 1839 *TA*, *-Park* 1860 White, cf. Eastham Ferry, Eastham Woods *infra*. The origin of *Carlet*(*t*) is unknown. The name has not been observed earlier than 19. It is applied to a district on a hill overlooking the rocky shore of Mersey about 109–363813. If it were an old formation it might be a descriptive name, i.e. 'hill at the rock(s)' or 'rock slope', from carr and hlið[1]. DALE HEY LANE (lost, 109–352795 to 356785), 1831 Bry, cf. *Dale Hey* 1839 *TA* (*freq*) and Plymyard Dale *supra*, which are to be identified with *Esthamdale, Mukeldale* 1305 Chest, *Esthamdale* 1331 *ChFor, Estam Dale* 1432 *Rental*, 'the (great) valley', *v*. dæl[1], micel, (ge)hæg. DAVID'S ROUGH, *Edwards Wood* 1831 Bry, cf. *Davis Rough* 1831 ib at another site, *v*. rūh. EASTHAM FERRY, 1778 Sheaf, *passagium et batillagium de Estham* 1357 *ChFor*, þe *ferrie bote of Esthim* 1551 Sheaf, *passagium de Eastham* 1579 Dugd, *the ferrie boate* 1592 *JRC, Eastom Boat* 1723 Sheaf, *the ferry of Eastham or Carlet Ferry* 1819 Orm[2], *Eastham Ferry House* 1831 Bry, *Eastham Ferry or Carlett* 1842 OS, cf. Carlett *supra*, Job's Ferry *infra*, *v*. ferja, bāt, cf. *Eaton Boat* 150 *supra*. EASTHAM RAKE, 1842 OS, *Rake Lane* 1831 Bry (109–342788 to 360800), cf. *The Rake* 1842 OS, *Rake House* 1831 Bry, a house at 109–364804, *v*. rake 'a lane'. EASTHAM SANDS, 1842 OS, *Eastham Bank* 1831 Bry, a sand-bank in the Mersey estuary. EASTHAM WINDMILL (109–359793), *Eastham Mill* 1831 ib, 1842 OS. EASTHAM WOODS, *boscus de Estham, Estamwode* 1347, 1357 *ChFor, Esthamwode* 1365, 1412 *JRC*, 1432 *Rental, Esthim Woode* 1551 Sheaf, *Carlet Wood, Wood Heath* 1831 Bry, 1839 *TA*, *v*. wudu, cf. Carlett *supra*. THE HEYS, *v*. (ge)hæg. JOB'S FERRY (109–363822), an ancient flight of twelve steps beside the shore of Mersey, supposed the original site of Eastham Ferry *supra*, cf. Sheaf[3] 38 (8281). LOWFIELDS FM. MILL HEY, cf. *Mill Hey* 1839 *TA*, near Eastham Windmill *supra*, *v*. myln, (ge)hæg. PARK COTTAGE & HO. TOWNFIELD LANE (lost, 109–363803 to 363812), 1831 Bry, included in Carlett Park, cf. (*Big*) *Townfield, Town Croft* 1839 *TA*. WADES GATE (lost, 109–365796), 1831 Bry, at the boundary of Eastham and Hooton, cf. 191 *infra*, probably

from geat 'a gateway' and the pers.n. or surname *Wade*. THE
WARRENS, *Warren House* 1831 Bry, *The Warren* 1842 OS, cf. *Eastham
Warren* 1778 Sheaf, *Warrens*, *Warren Croft* 1839 *TA*, *v.* wareine.

FIELD-NAMES

The undated forms are 1839 *TA* 155. Of the others 1398 is *Add*, 1432,
1440 *Rental*, 1831 Bry, 1842 OS.

(*a*) Big & Little Acres; Barkers Hill; Benty Heath (*v.* benty, hǣð);
Birches; Brickleys Cover 1842; Bridgets; Broad Hey (*v.* (ge)hæg); Brom-
boro(ugh) Hey (*v.* (ge)hæg, cf. Bromborough 237 *infra*); Broomy Fds
(*v.* brōmig); Calver(s) Croft & Hey (*v.* calf, calver); Clay Hills; Cock
Lion; Cold Airs (perhaps 'cold shielings' from cald and erg, though ears
or ModE *air* is possible); Coney Hey (*v.* coni, (ge)hæg); Coopers Dale;
Cow Hey (*v.* (ge)hæg); Crabthorns; Cross Hey (*v.* cros, (ge)hæg); Big &
Little Gauley, Gauley Mdw (*v.* gagel, (ge)hæg); Gorse Hill; Green Hey
(*v.* grēne[1], (ge)hæg); Hackrag, (Big & Little) Hackrags; Heath, Heath
Hey (*v.* hǣð, (ge)hæg); Hooton Ends (*v.* ende[1], cf. Hooton 189 *infra*);
Intack (*v.* inntak); Linn Marsh; Liquorice (*v.* 337 *infra*); Loom (*v.* loom,
land); Marsh Lane Croft; New Grounds (*v.* grund); Nook; Ollin Grave
(*v.* holegn, grǣfe); Ox Hey (*v.* (ge)hæg); Porter Hey; Rafflers, Rufflers;
Sheflana Hey; Shew Birds (perhaps from 'shovel-bredes', *v.* scofl-brǣdu);
Shodwele Croft (cf. *Shodwell* 241 *infra*); Short Buts (*v.* sc(e)ort, butte);
Tinkers Dale (*v.* tink(l)ere, dæl[1]); Turfy Croft & Hey (cf. *Turfy Lane*
1831 (109–360795 to 352790), *v.* turf); Under Yards (*v.* under, geard);
Wall Hill (*v.* wælla); Well Fd; Wet Croft; Wheat Reins (from rein with
hwǣte or wēt); Wing (*v.* wing); Within Hey (*v.* wiðegn, (ge)hæg); Wood
Hey (*v.* (ge)hæg).

(*b*) le Bruches 1398, le Bruchelond 1432, -land 1440 ('selion at an intake',
v. bryce, land); *Crokescrofte* 1432, *Croketcroft* 1440 ('crooked croft, croft
with a crook', *v.* krókr, croked, croft); le Gorstilonde 1432, -land 1440
(*v.* gorstig, land); le Grene 1432 (*v.* grēne[2]); *Padocgrove* 1440 ('frog-wood',
v. padduc, grāf); le Shaftefeld 1432, le Shafefeld 1440 (the name of a selion,
'field at a pole', perhaps a boundary mark, *v.* sceaft, feld); *Stanihull* 1398,
Stany- 1432, -hall 1440 (*v.* stānig, hyll).

2. HOOTON (GREEN & HALL) (109–3678) ['huːtən, 'huːtn̩]
  Hotone 1086 DB, *Hotun* 1178 Facs, 13 (1507) ChRR (p), 1274
    Sheaf, Hoton e13 *AddCh et freq* with variant spellings *-tona*,
    Hothon to 1545 ChRR, (*-in Wirall*) e13 (16) Orm[2], (*-Wyrall*)
    1423 Pat, (*-cum Rouakre*) 1385 *ChFor*
  Hutton 1344 (p), 1409 ChRR (p), 1539–47, 1579 Dugd
  Hoghton 1346 BPR (p), *Houghton* 1353 ib (p) *et freq* ib, ChRR all
    (p) with variant spellings *Ho(u)ghton* to 1474 ChRR (p), *Hoghton*
    1361 ib, *Houghton* 1694 ChetOS VIII

Houlton 1369 Bark, 1660 Sheaf, *Hulton* 1553 Pat
Hooton 1459 Pat, 1552 (17) Sheaf, Eliz 1 AD, 1563 ChRR, 1657
    Clif, 1723 Sheaf *et freq*, *Hootton* 1663 Sheaf, *Hooton Hall* 1724
    NotCestr, *Hooton Green* 1831 Bry
Houton 1561 Cre, 1577 ChRR, 1709 *Blun*, *Howton* 1577 ChRR

'Farm at a hill or promontory', from **hōh** and **tūn**, with **hyll**
hall and **grēne**². For *Rouakre*, *v.* Rivacre *infra*.

BOOSTON WOOD (109–385790), *Bolstan* 1340 ChFor, *Bulston* (lit.
Dulston) 1351 BPR III 24, *le champ-*, *le Bonk de Bulston'*, *Bulstonfeld*
1402 *JRC*, *Great & Little Booston Wood* 1831 Bry, from an unidentified first el. (perhaps **bult** 'a heap, a hillock') and **stān** 'a stone,
a rock', with **wudu**, **feld**, **banke**. The name was probably taken from
a rock on the shore of Mersey, cf. Poolehall Rocks *infra*.

RIVACRE WOOD (109–380780) ['rivikər, 'rivəkər, 'riveikə], *Ruacre*
1287 Court, *Rouacre* 1317 Plea, *Rouachre* c.1322 CAS NS VI,
Rouaker 1334 ib, *Olderofacre* 1351 BPR, *Rouakre*, *Rovacre* 1385
ChFor, *le Roveacre* (lit. *Robe-*) 1512 ib, *le Rowacre* 1512 Orm²,
Rivacre Croft 1839 *TA*, *Rivacre House* 1850 *TAMap*, 'the rough
acre or ploughland', *v.* **rūh**, **æcer**, ald. The house became a racing
stables, Hooton Stud Fm.

BANKFIELDS, 1850 *TAMap*, *le Bonk* 1402 *JRC*, *le Bonke* 1432 *Rental*,
le Banke(feld) 1440 ib, *Bankfield House* 1831 Bry, *v.* **banke**, **feld**.
CHURCH WOOD, *Stack Wood* 1831 ib, *v.* **stakkr**.   CLAYHILL
WOOD, cf. *Clay Hill Field & Meadow* 1839 *TA*, *v.* **clæg**, **hyll**.
DAVID'S ROUGH, *Edward's Wood* 1831 Bry, cf. 188 *supra*.   EAST-
HAM SANDS, *v.* 188 *supra*, cf. *Eastham Channel* 1831 ib, in R. Mersey,
v. **chanel**.   HOOTON PARK FM, KENNEL COTTAGES & WOOD,
Kennels Farm 1831 ib.   THE PARK, cf. *New Park* 1831 Bry.
POOLE HALL ROCKS, 192 *infra*, may be referred to in *le skere* (*en
Hoton'*) 1402 *JRC*, 'the rock, the skerry', *v.* **sker**.   ST HELEN'S
WELL (109–385781), *Helen's Well* 1842 OS, 1850 *TAMap*, cf. *St
Helen's Hill Field* 1839 *TA*, *Bath Garden* 1831 Bry and Well Wood
infra, named from a spring, the history of which has not been
discovered, cf. St Helen's Hill 200 *infra*, *v.* **wella**, **bæð**.   SEA
ROUGH (lost, 109–373805), 1842 OS, *Sea Rough Wood* 1831 Bry,
'rough land by the sea', *v.* **sǣ**, **rūh**.   SHOULDER OF MUTTON

PLANTATION, 1839 *TA*, named from its shape, *v.* 337 *infra*.
WADES GATE (lost), *v.* 188 *supra*, cf. *Wade's Gate Fields* 1839 *TA*.
WELL WOOD, *St Helen's Wood* 1831 Bry, cf. St Helen's Well *supra*.

FIELD-NAMES

The undated forms are 1839 *TA* 207. Of the others, 1357 is *ChFor*, 1402 *JRC*, 1803 Sheaf, 1831 Bry, 1842 OS, 1850 *TAMap*.

(*a*) Benty Heath Lane 1831 (*Benty Heath* 1803, cf. 229, 233 *infra*, *v.* benty, hǣð); Chain Mdw; Coneys (*v.* coni); Cross Heys (*v.* cros, (ge)hæg); Gorsy Lea (*v.* lēah); The Lands (*v.* land); Pail Hey 1850 (*v.* pale); Sandy Butt (*v.* sandig, butte); Shires Rothin; Smithy Hay; Square Wd 1842 (*Square Cover* 1831); Wet Reans (*v.* rein).

(*b*) *le Brom* 1357 (*v.* brōm); *Chircheway* 1402 (a road from Eastham to Hooton, 'the way to church', *v.* cirice, weg); *Coulehey(dyche)* (*v. le Nethergap infra*); *Esthamfeld* 1357 (*v.* feld, cf. Eastham 187 *supra*); *le Forgh'* 1402 ('the ditch', *forgh* being a fifteenth-century form of furh 'a furrow, a trench', *v. furrow* NED); (*le*) *Grauntpole, le Grauntpoll* 1402 ('the great pool or stream', running from *le Molyn de Pulle* in Netherpool, 193 *infra*, *v.* grant, pōl¹); (*le*) *Helpole* 1402 (probably identical with *Landpul sive Elpul* 200 *infra*); *le Holghway* 1402 ('the hollow way', either a sunken road or one through a hollow, *v.* holh, weg); *Ketilspoll'* 1402 ('Kettle's creek', from the ON pers.n. *Ketill* and pōl¹); *Longeforlong* 1357 (*v.* lang, furlang); *le Loweheth* 1402 (either 'low heath' or 'heath at a hillock', from hǣð and lágr or hlāw); *le Nethergap de Coulehey(dyche)* 1402 ('the lower gap in (the ditch round) the enclosure at the cow pasture', from neoðera and gappe, and from dīc and (ge)hæg added to a p.n. *Coule* 'cow pasture', from cū and lēah); *passagium et batillagium de Hoton* 1357 ('the toll and ferryboat of Hooton'); *Rastyn* 1357 (the name of a parcel of land, inexplicable); *Thornage* 1357 (the name of a plot of land, 'place where thorns grow', from þorn and the ME, OFr, suffix -age); *boscus de Hoton* 1357, *le grauntboys de Hoton* 1402 ('the (big) wood', *v.* bois, grant).

3. NETHERPOOL (109–3978), *Pulle* e13 Orm², *Nethere-* 1307 Ipm, *ville de Netherpulle en manoir de Pulle* 1402 *JRC*, *Pulle*, called *Nether-Pole* 1539 Orm², *Poole* 1819 ib, otherwise as for Nether- & Overpool *infra*. Netherpool township contained the manor-house of Poole, both house and township bearing the name *Pool(e)*.

NETHER- & OVERPOOL

Pol 1086 DB

Pulla 1157–94 Chest, e13 (16) Orm² (p), *Pulle* e13 ib *et freq* to 1539 Orm², (*Huuer-*, *Uuer-*) e13 Chest, (*Superior-*) 1278 *ChFor*, (*Upper-*) 1361 BPR, (*Nether(e)-*) 1307 Ipm, Plea, 1402 *JRC*,

(*Lower-*) 1361 BPR, (*-called Nether-Pole*) 1539 Orm[2], *le Pulle*
1316 ChRR (p), *Pull* 1208–29 Whall (p), 1284–8 *JRC* (p),
1287 Court (p), 1294 ib *et freq* to 1473 ChRR, (*Nethere-*) 1338
Pat, (*Nether-*) 1357 ChFor, (*Nethir-*) 1511 Plea, (*Ouer-*) 1348
Eyre, (*-called Netherpull*) 1510 Orm[2], *Pul* 1279 Whall (p)
Poole e13 Bark (p), 1294 MidCh (p), 1601 AD, 1624 ChRR,
1660 Sheaf, (*Over-*) 1546 Dugd, (*Nether-*) 1558 ChRR, (*-alias
Nether Poole*) 1615 Orm[2], *Ouer Poolle* 1663 Sheaf (*Over-,
Nether-*) *Pool* 1724 NotCestr
Poull c.1229 Bark (p)
Pole 1364 BPR (p), 1402 Cl (p), 1436 Pat, 1483 ChRR, 1513
    (1585) ib, 1554 Pat, (*-or Pulle*) 1402 Cl (p), (*-alias dict' Neither
    Pole*) 1501 Orm[2], (*Nether-*) 1511 Plea, (*Over-*) 1535 VE
Polle 1403 ChRR (p), *Netherpoll* 1518 Plea
Pele 1436 Pat

'The pool, the creek', *v.* pōl[1], pull, uferra, superior, neoðera, cf.
Netherpool *supra*, Overpool 193 *infra*, Poole Hall *infra*. Poole is
described as a port 1366 Cl 227.

FALLANCE LANE (lost, 109–385775 to 398775), 1831 Bry, into
Overpool 193 *infra*, perhaps 'fallow lands', from falg and land,
with lane, but field-land is possible.   MOUNT MANISTY, an
embankment at the end of the Manchester Ship Canal.   POOLE
HALL (109–392784, demolished c.1919 Sheaf[3] 15), *domus suus
propria de Pulle* 1262 Whall, *le Pullehoux* 1357 ChFor, *capital'
messuagium de Pole* 1499 *Eyre*, Polehouse 1539–47 Orm[2], *Poole
House* 1579 Dugd, *Pool Hall* 1842 OS, otherwise called, simply,
Pool(e), synonymous with Netherpool *supra*, *v.* hall, hūs.   POOL
HALL BANKS & DEEP (lost), 1842 OS, off Netherpool in the Mersey
estuary, *v.* banke, dēope.   POOLE HALL ROCKS, 1831 Bry, cf. 190
supra, *v.* rokke.   POOLES WHARF (lost), 1819 Orm[2] II 12, *Poole
Warth* 1646 Sheaf, *mariscum* 1272 Chest, *Grenewarth(e)* 1499 *Eyre*,
1500 Orm[2], *Le Greneworthe, Greenwarth* 1510 ib, *le Grene Wathe*
1547 *MinAcct*, 1553 Pat, *the Greenworth* c.1554 Whall, 'the green
shore-land', *v.* grēne[1], waroð, a tract of marshland beside the
Mersey estuary, swallowed by erosion, extending from Netherpool
to Great Stanney and Stanlow, along which lay a causeway con-
necting Whitby and the abbey at Stanlow, Orm[2] II 12, 400, 421,
Chest I xix, 198.   STANDING WOOD, 1842 OS.

FIELD-NAMES

Of these forms, 1245–9 is Chest, 1308 IpmR, 1357 *ChFor*, 1365, 1402 *JRC*, 1468 *MinAcct*, c.1538, 1560 Sheaf.

(b) *Ermetescrosse* 1402 ('hermit's cross', *v.* ermite, cros); *passagium et batillagium de Pull* 1357, *passagium de Pull* 1468, *a bot . . . in the passage of Pulpulle* c.1538, *passage' aque de Pulle* 1560 ('the toll and ferryboat of Poole creek', *v.* pull, cf. Netherpool *supra*); *le molyn de Pulle* 1402 (cf. *unum molendinum aquaticum* 1308, *v.* myln); *le Oldefeld* 1357 (*v.* ald, feld); *le Rake* 1357 (*v.* rake); *boscus de Pull(e)* 1245–9, 1357, 1365 (*v.* wudu).

4. OVERPOOL (109–385775), *Pol* 1086 DB, *Pulla* 1157–94 Chest, *(H)Uuerpulle* e13 ib, *Over Poole* 1819 Orm², *Pool* 1831 Bry, *Pooltown or Overpool* 1842 OS, cf. Nether- & Overpool 191 *supra, v.* toun.

BANNERS STYLE (lost, 109–388763), 1831 Bry, -*Stile* 1837 *TA* 427, on the boundary of Whitby, from stigel 'a stile', perhaps with a pers.n. but cf. *Banners Stoope* 2 246. FALLANCE LANE, *v.* 192 *supra.* MILL HO & LANE (lost, 109–385767), 1831 Bry, *v.* myln, cf. 194 *infra.* BIG & LITTLE SHALLACRES (109–389769), two plantations, probably an old f.n., *v.* æcer. SMITHY LANE (lost), *v.* 195 *infra.*

FIELD-NAMES

Of the forms, 1272 is Chest, 1398 *Add*, 1432, 1440 *Rental*.

(b) *Cattesmete* 1398 (*v.* Cat's Meat 196 *infra*); *Daynesfeld* 1432, 1440 ('the Dane's field', from Dene and feld); *Heefeld* 1398, (*le*) *Heghfeld* 1432 ('high field', *v.* hēah, feld); *Hulton'* 1398, *Hylton Feld* 1432, 1440 ('hill farm or enclosure', *v.* hyll, tūn, perhaps identical with Hilton 199 *infra*); *Pullestiwaye* 1398, *Stywaystrete* 1432, 1440 ('the path-way, the road called *Styway'*, *v.* sty-way, strǣt).

5. GREAT SUTTON (109–3775), forms as for Great & Little Sutton *infra*, and *Magna Sutton* 1278 *ChFor, Sutton Magna* 1539–47 Dugd, *Great Sutton* 1361 BPR, 1560 ChRR, 1579 Dugd, *Sutton Maior* 1398 *Add*, 1535 VE, *Much(e) Sutton* 1539–47, 1546 Dugd, *Moche-* 1553 Pat, *Homsutton* 1288 *ChFor, Neerer Sutton* 1669 Sheaf, 'the big(ger) hamlet of Sutton', *v.* grēat, magna, maior, micel. The prefix *Hom-* is ME home (OE hām) 'near home', distinguishing the part of Sutton which contained the major settlement from '*Hall-*' or Little Sutton 195 *infra*, cf. Christleton 107 *supra*, The Grange Wo 297.

GREAT & LITTLE SUTTON
  Sudtone 1086 DB f.263
  Suttona 1096–1101 (1280), 1150 Chest, *Sutthona* 1096–1101
    (1280) (17) ib, Dugd, *Sutton* 1181–1232 Chest, e13 (1300) Pat,
    1260 Court (p), 1286 *ChFor et freq, passim*, (*the bayliwik of-*)
    1539–47 Dugd, (*-in Wyrehalle*) 1539–47 ib
  Sotton 1272, 1278, 1292–1308 Chest

'South farm', *v.* sūð, tūn. Cf. Great Sutton *supra*, Little Sutton
195 *infra*. The Suttons are south of Eastham.

BACKFORD CROSS, cf. foll., *v.* 173 *supra*.   BACKFORDCROSS FM, *The
Beckford Cross Farm* 1843 *TA*, cf. prec.   BRIDGE FM, *Bridge
House* 1831 Bry, *v.* brycg.   CAPENHURST GRANGE & LODGE,
Capenhurst Lodge 1831 ib, *v.* grange, loge, cf. Capenhurst 200 *infra*.
DAMAGE BRIDGE NOS. 1, 2 & 3, *Damage Bridges* 1831 Bry, cf.
Demmage 176 *supra*.   DUNKIRK HO, cf. *Dunkirk Field* 1843 *TA*,
v. 176 *supra*.   HOMEFIELD HO.   IRON COTTAGES, *v.* hyrne.
THE MANOR, cf. foll.   MANOR COTTAGES, *Old Smithy* 1831 Bry,
v. smiðõe, cf. prec.   NEW HEY, cf. *Newhay* 1843 *TA*, *v.* (ge)hæg.
SALTERS LANE (lost, 109–360742 to 375749), 1831 Bry, probably the
remnant of a salt-way along the township boundaries from Shotwick
to Great Sutton, *v.* saltere, lane.   SUTTON GREEN, 1842 OS, cf.
Green Lane 1831 Bry, 'the Green', 'lane leading to the Green',
v. grēne², lane.   WHETSTONE HEY FM, cf. *Whetstone Hay*,
Whitstone 1843 *TA*, either 'white stone' or 'whetstone', *v.* hwīt,
stān, hwet-stān, probably named from a rock or pillar of stone.

FIELD-NAMES

The undated forms are 1843 *TA* 379. Of the others 1272, 1278[2] are Chest,
1278[1] Whall, 1365 *JRC*, 1398 *Add*, 1432, 1440 *Rental*, 1831 Bry.

(a) Acre Hay (*v.* æcer, (ge)hæg); Alder Fd (cf. *Alder Lane* 1831, *v.*
alder); Alley Lane 1831 (109–376757 to 389757, *v.* aley); Benty Croft
(*v.* benty); Birches; Blackelet, Blake Lake (*Blaklake* 1432, *Blaclake* 1440,
'black watercourse', *v.* blæc, lacu); Broadland Hay (*v.* brād, land); Dale
Brow & Hay (*v.* dæl¹); Four Loons (*v.* land); Green Park; The Holme,
Further & Nearer Home (*v.* holmr); Hooton Hay (*v.* (ge)hæg, cf. Hooton
189 *supra*); Hornet Croft; Horse Hay; Howell's Fd (*Howellesfeld* 1398,
Howelsfeld 1432, 1440, from the OWelsh pers.n. *Houel* and feld, cf. *Howelstylth* 196 *infra* in Little Sutton); Intake (*v.* inntak); Kempridge; Liverpool
Hay (from Liverpool La); Main Mdw (*v.* main); The Marl Fd; Mill Lane

1831 (running into Overpool, cf. 193 *supra*); (Gorsy) Organ, Organ Dale (with *Organ Lane* 1831 (109–376755 to 385754), perhaps identical with *Argan* 1432, 1440, 'at the shielings', from erg (dat.pl. *ergum*) and dæl[1]); Quillet (*v.* quillet(t)); Shebsides (*Shepeshed* 1398, 1432, 1440, 'sheep shed', from scēp and OE scead[2], sced 'a shade, a shelter, a shed' BT, cf. *shed, shade* NED and scydd, sceadu); Stanney Hay (*v.* (ge)hæg, cf. Great & Little Stanney 182, 180 *supra*); Street Flat (109–372755; *v.* strǣt); Town Fd; Towns Eng (if not a bad form for Towns End (*v.* ende[1]) this appears to be 'communal meadow' from toun and eng); Washes Lane 1831 (109–380754 to 389745, crossing two fords at 109–382753, *v.* (ge)wæsc); Whissage (cf. *le-, þe Whitesyche* 1432, *-siche* 1440, 'the white stream', *v.* hwīt, sīc).

(*b*) *le Blakacres* 1432, *Blacacres* 1440 (*v.* blæc, æcer); *le Brettelondes* 1398, *Bretlondes* 1432, 1440 ('selions belonging to the Britons', *v.* **Brettas** (gen.pl. Bretta), land); *bruerium de Sotton* 1272, *bruera de Sutton* 1278[1], [2] (*v.* hǣð); *Coscarshull* 1365 (from hyll 'a hill', perhaps with the OIrish pers.n. *Coscrach*); *les Endes* 1432 ('pastures called-', cf. *le Ouerende of the Whitesyche* 1432, *v.* uferra, ende[1], cf. 198 *infra*); *Pull(e)bruches* 1432, 1440 ('the intakes near-, or belonging to-, Pool(e)', *v.* bryce, cf. Nether- & Overpool 191, 193 *supra*); *Stanay Way* 1432, *via de Stanay* 1440 ('the road to Stanney', *v.* weg, cf. Great- & Little Stanney 182, 180 *supra*); *le Walleolers* 1365 ('the alders at a spring', *v.* wælla, alor).

6. LITTLE SUTTON (109–3776), forms as for Great- & Little Sutton 194 *supra*, and *Parua Sutton* 1278 ChFor, *-Parva* 1539–47 Dugd, *Little-* 1539–47 ib, *Litle-* 1553 Pat, *Lytle-* 1585 Cre, *Halle Sotton* 1278 ChFor, *-sutton* 1280, 1288, 1331, 1357 *ib*, 1357 BPR, *alia Sutton* 1286 ChFor, *Sutton in dominicale* 1535 VE, 'the smaller hamlet of Sutton', *v.* lȳtel, **parva**. It is *alia Sutton* 'the other Sutton' as distinct from *Sutton* 1286 ChFor (Great Sutton 193 *supra*). It was in the demesne (*in dominicale*) of the abbot of St Werburgh's, Chester. *Hallesutton* is 'Sutton with a hall, the hamlet of Sutton containing the manor-house', as distinct from the 'home-' or 'village-' hamlet of *Homsutton* i.e. Great Sutton, cf. Sutton Hall *infra*, *v.* hall, and cf. Allostock etc., 2 216–17.

CLAYHILL WOOD, *v.* 190 *supra*. FARRE HO, near *Far Wood* 1831 Bry, on the Childer Thornton boundary, *v.* feor 'far'. GORST-HILL, cf. (*Little*) *Gorse Hill, Gostell Hay, Gostells* 1843 *TA*, *v.* gorst, hyll. GREENFIELDS, *Greenfield Hall* 1831 Bry. HOOTON LODGE, 1842 OS, *v.* loge, cf. Hooton 189 *supra*. LEDSHAM HALL & RD, cf. *Ledsham's Croft* 1843 *TA*, all named from Ledsham 217 *infra*. SMITHY LANE (lost, 109–384770 to 372769), 1831 Bry, *v.* smiððe. SUTTON HALL, 1724 NotCestr, *Sutton-court* 1621 (1656)

Orm², cf. foll. and Little Sutton *supra*, *v.* court, hall.   SUTTONHALL
FM, *New Hall* 1831 Bry.   WOODHEY, 1708 *LRO*, *v.* wudu,
(ge)hæg.   WOODLANDS (part), *v.* 197 *infra*.

FIELD-NAMES

The undated forms are 1843 *TA* 380. Of the others 1398 is *Add*, 1432, 1440
Rental, 1831 Bry.

(a) Ackerleys; Andrew Green (a group of fields at 109–353763); Back
Greaves (*v.* back, græfe); Banishes, Benishes; Bottoms (*v.* botm); Briar(y)
Flatt; Brook Heath; Cat's Meat (*Cattesmete* 1398, (*le-*) 1432, 1440, *-mede*
1432, from mǣd 'a meadow', with catt 'a wild-cat or a pers. by-name
Catt); Crab Tree Fd; Dale Hay (*v.* dæl¹, (ge)hæg); Dan's Croft; Dean's
Mdw; Dunmoor (*Dunnesmore* 1398 'Dunn's marsh', from mōr¹ and the
OE pers.n. *Dunn*, cf. foll.); Dunstill (perhaps from the same pers.n. as
prec., with tilð, cf. *Howelstylth infra*); High Fd (*Heghfeld* 1432, 1440, cf.
Loghfeld, *Lowe-* 1432, *Logh-*, *le Lawfeld* 1440, 'high field, low field', *v.*
hēah, lágr, feld); Hooton Nook (*v.* nōk, cf. Hooton 189 *supra*); Lark Butts
(*v.* lāwerce, butte); Mill Fd; New Hay (*v.* (ge)hæg); Ox Hay (cf. *Ox Hey*
1432, 1440, *v.* oxa, (ge)hæg); Pail Hey & Reans (*v.* pale, (ge)hæg, rein);
(Old) Rake, Rake Croft (cf. *Rake Lane* 1831 (109–359772 to 365774), also
cf. 197 *infra*, *v.* ald, rake, lane); Rough Wd 1831 (the site of Ledsham
railway station); Round Hedge (*v.* rond, hecg); Rylands Mdw (*v.* rye-land);
Shut Butts (*v.* scēat, butte); Sitch (*v.* sīc); Sour Fd; South and North
(*v.* 337 *infra*); Stockport (perhaps named after or analogous with Stockport
1 294); Sweet Fd; Thornton Fd & (Rough) Hay (cf. Childer Thornton
infra); Town Fd; Under Yards (*v.* under, geard); Vineyard; Wash Pit
Hay (*v.* wæsce, pytt, (ge)hæg); Weets; Wind Ways (cf. *le Wayneway* 1398,
'road for carts', *v.* wægn, weg); Wood Fd.

(b) *le Clyntes* 1432, 1440 ('the steep banks, the outcrops', *v.* klint);
Howelstylth 1432, *Howlestylth* 1440 ('Howel's tilth, i.e. arable land', from
the OWelsh pers.n. *Houel* and tilð, cf. foll., Dunstill *supra* and Howell's Fd
194 *supra*); *Magotestilth* 1432 ('Magot's tilth', from the ME fem.pers.n.
Magot, a diminutive of *Margaret*, and tilð, cf. prec. and Maggot Hay 199
infra); *Olderth* 1432, 1440 ('old, or disused, arable', *v.* ald, erð); (*le*)
Tenlandes, *-londes* 1432 ('the ten selions', *v.* tēn, land).

7. CHILDER THORNTON (109–3677) ['tʃildǝr-]

Thorinthun 1200–20 *JRC*, Torinton 1209–29 *AddCh*, Torentune 13
ib (p), Childre Thorinton e14 *JRC*

Thornton 13 *AddCh*, 1331 (p), 1524, 1589 ChRR, Thorneton 1328
ib (p), 1398 *Add*, 1440 *Rental*

Childrethornton 1288 *ChFor et freq* with variant spellings -*Thorinton*
(e14 *JRC*), -*Thorneton* (*freq* to 1602 Sheaf), *Childer-* (from 1305

Chest), *Childern(e)-, Chelther-, Children-, Chilter-, Chiddin-*; *Childerthornton in Wyrhale* 1364 Sheaf

'Thorn-tree farm' or 'thorn enclosure', *v.* þorn, tūn. The affix is ME *childre, children*, pl., from OE cild (gen.pl. cildra), 'the children, the young men, the sons', denoting that this manor was allocated to the upkeep of, or was owned by, young men. Who they were is not recorded, but the manor was a possession of St Werburgh's abbey, and the 'children' may have been junior members of the establishment, cf. Knight's Grange 3 172, Childwick Hrt 91 and EPN 1 93. Professor Cameron adds Ashby Puerorum L, for the upkeep of the choristers of St Mary's, Lincoln.

CROWTHORNS, *Crowthorn', Le Thorne* 1432 *Rental, the Crowthorne* 1704 Sheaf, *Crowthorn* 1839 *TA*, 'the thorn-tree frequented by crows', *v.* crāwe, þorn. HEATH FM, cf. *Heath Lane* 1831 Bry, *Heath Lane & Bridge* 1847 *TAMap, v.* hǣð, lane, brycg, cf. Thornton Heath *infra.* LOWFIELDS, *Lowfield House* 1831 Bry, *v.* lágr, feld. THE OAKLANDS, OAKFIELD, apparently modern. SCHOOL LANE, named from the village school, *School or Branock Lane* 1831 Bry, cf. *Brown Nook* 1839 *TA, v.* brūn[1], nōk. OLD SMITHFIELD. THORNTON HALL, 1831 Bry, *v.* hall. THORNTON HEATH, 1842 OS, cf. *Hathlond* 1432 *Rental, the Three Heathes* 1704 Sheaf, and Heath Fm *supra, v.* hǣð, land. WOODLANDS (part), *v.* 196 *supra.*

FIELD-NAMES

The undated forms are 1839 *TA* 105. Of the others, e13, e14, 1592 are *JRC*, 1305 Chest, 1398 *Add*, 1432, 1440 *Rental*, 1704 Sheaf, 1831 Bry.

(*a*) Acorn-, Acron Hay; Beaches, Lower & Upper Beach (*v.* bece[1]); Bottoms Mdw (cf. *le Bothum* 1398, 1432, 1440, *v.* boðm); Far- & Near Coopers Dale (*the Cowpers Dales* 1704, *v.* deill); Little- & Prices Cow Hay, Cow Hay Mdw (*the Cow Heay (Dale)* 1704, *v.* cū, (ge)hæg, deill); The Crook Croft 1704 (*v.* krókr); Cross Bottoms ('bottom-land selions lying athwart', *v.* cros, botm); The Damage (cf. *Demmyngesfeld* 1432, *v.* demming); Elgrey Butts; Golden Nook; Gold Finder (*v.* 336 *infra*); Goose Pasture (*v.* Rake *infra*); Gorstel (*v.* gorst, hyll); The Hannahs Pitt 1704; The Hemp Yard 1704 (*v.* hemp-yard); Hooton Hay (*v.* (ge)hæg) cf. Hooton 189 *supra*); Lamperloons ('lambs' selions', *v.* lamb (gen.pl. lambra), land); Land Hay ((*Little*) *Land Heay* 1704, *v.* land, (ge)hæg); The Meadow Heay 1704; Further- & Near New Grounds (*the Newe Groundes* 1592, *v.* nīwe, grund); Rake or Goose Pasture, Rake Croft, Rake Part (cf. *the Old Rake* 1704 and *Rake Lane* 196 *supra, v.* rake); the Rough Heas 1704 (*v.* rūh, (ge)hæg); Seven Mens Hay Mdw (*The Seven Mens Heay* 1704, mowing for seven men, *v.* seofon, mann, (ge)hæg); Short Butts (*The-* 1704, *v.* butte); Turf Way Hay (*v.* turf, weg, (ge)hæg, probably a track to a turbary); Under Hill (*v.* under, hyll); Wings Hay (*v.* wing); Within Hay (*v.* wiðegn).

(*b*) *Afnames* e13, e14 ('land cut out', *v.* af-nám); (*le*) *Blakestrete* (*v.* Street Hey 232 *infra*); *Blaklond* 1432, 1440 (*v.* blæc, land); *Bradesiche* 1305 ('the broad stream', *v.* brād, sīc, the stream between Childer Thornton and Willaston 232 *infra*, cf. *le Sych infra*); *le Endes* 1398 (*v.* ende[1], cf. 195 *supra*); *le Seuenacre Vrth', septem acr'* 1440 ('the seven acre enclosure', *v.* seofon, æcer, worð); *le Sych* 1432, *le Seches* 1440 (*v.* sīc, cf. *Bradesiche supra*); *Wallefeld* 1432 (*v.* wælla, feld).

ix. Eastham & Stoke

The township of Whitby lay in Stoke and Eastham parishes, 180, 187 *supra*. It is now included in the c.p. of Ellesmere Port Municipal Borough.

WHITBY (109–3975) ['witbi]

> *Witeberia* 1096–1101 (1150), 1150 Chest
> *Witebia* 1096–1101 (1280) Chest, *Witebi* 1188–91 ib, -*by* 1260 Court, *Plea*, 1272, 1277, 1278 Chest, *Wytebi* 1270–1316 ib, -*by* 1272 ib, 1279 Whall, 1286 ChFor
> *Whiteby* 1241 Whall et freq with variant spellings *Whyte-, Quite-, Qwyte-, Qwite-, -by(e)* to *Whitebye* 1539–47 Dugd
> *Quiteleye* 1291 Tax
> *Whitby* 1402 ChRR (p), 1535 VE *et freq* with variant spellings *Whyt-, Whit-, -bie, -bye, -bey, (-in Wirrall)* 1596 ChRR
> *Whidbie* 1655 Sheaf

'The white manor or village', from hwīt 'white, stone-built', and burh (dat.sg. byrig) 'a manor-house, a fortified place', and býr 'a village, a homestead'. The Scand. el. replaces an original OE el., cf. Greasby 291 *infra*.

ELLESMERE PORT (109–4077), 1819 Orm[2], (-*in Netherpool*) 1831 Hem, (-*or Whitby Locks*) 1842 OS, described in 1819 Orm[2] II 424 as 'a petty port, (named) from the termination of the Dee and Mersey branch of the Ellesmere Canal (i.e. the Shropshire Union), and its connection with the estuary of the latter river, taking place at this point'. It is now a municipal borough, chartered in 1935, and a c.p. including the townships of Gt Stanney, Stanlow, part of Hooton, Netherpool, Overpool, Great-and-Little Sutton, Childer Thornton, Whitby, part of Capenhurst, and Ledsham. *v.* Addenda.

BANNERS STYLE (lost), v. 193 supra. EASTWOOD FM. FLAT
LANE (lost, 109–397760 to 395768), 1831 Bry, cf. The Flatt 1708
LRO, (The) Flat 1837 TA, v. flat, lane. GRANGE FM. HEATH
FM, HEATHFIELD HO, cf. Whitbyheath infra. MARSH LANE (lost,
109–401762 to 412770), 1831 Bry, cf. The Marsh 1708 LRO, Marsh
(Hay) 1837 TA, v. mersc, lane. MEADOW LANE, cf. Great &
Little Meadow, the Meadow Hey 1708 LRO, Meadow Hay 1837 TA,
v. mǣd, lane, (ge)hæg. WHITBY HALL, cf. Whitby Old Hall
infra, v. hall. WHITBY HO, Great House 1831 Bry. WHITBY
OLD HALL, 1831 Bry, the Old House 1708 LRO, Whitby Hall 1842
OS, v. ald, hall, hūs, cf. Whitby Hall supra. WHITBYHEATH,
Whitby Heath 1842 OS, cf. Heath Fm, Heathfield Ho supra, and
magnum bruerium de Witeby et de Pulle 1272 Chest, bruera de Wyteby
1278 ib, -Whiteby 1278 Whall, v. hǣð. WHITBY RD, Whitby
Lane 1842 OS, v. lane.

FIELD-NAMES

The undated forms are 1837 TA 427. Of the others 1245–9, 1272, 1277[1]
are Chest, 1241, 1246, 1262, 1277[2] Whall, 1318, 1499 Eyre, 1398 Add,
1402 JRC, 1432, 1440 Rental, 1708 LRO, 1831 Bry.

(a) Acorn Yard; Great & Little Acre (Acres 1708); Acre Hey (1708,
v. (ge)hæg); Backsides (v. ba(c)ksyde); Bank Fd; Barefoot Loons (v. land);
(Big-, Little-) Birches (cf. the Broad-, the Higher Birches 1708, v. birce);
Bottom Hay (Bothanhey, Little Bothan Hey 1708, v. botm, boðm, (ge)hæg);
Broadlands (v. land); Burnt Tree Fd; By Mans-, Bymans Slacks (v. slakki);
Catchment Hay (-Hey 1708); Colt's Croft; Big & Little Crawley (perhaps
'crow wood', from crāwe, lēah); Crooklands, Crookloons (v. krókr, land);
Cunnery (v. coningre); Danes Coppice; Dales, Dale Fd, Broad Dale,
Dales Lane (v. deill); Dirty Acre; (Big & Little) Ditch Hay(s) (cf. Ditchway
Flatt 1708, v. dīc, (ge)hæg, flat); Ebon Hay; Fallace, Fallace Lane; Fives;
Fold End (v. fald, ende[1]); Broad-, Higher-, Lower-, Little- & Long
Fridays (v. Frīgedæg); Gorsty Hay (cf. Gorsty Field 1708, v. gorstig);
Hall Croft & Mdw; Hal(l)wood(s) Flat(t), Hallwoods Marsh; Hilton(s),
Grass Hilton (cf. Hulton 1398, etc., in Overpool, 193 supra); Hovel Fd
(v. hovel); Intake (the Intack 1708, v. inntak); Lady's Hay (v. hlǣfdige);
Long Butt (v. butte); Maggot Hay (v. (ge)hæg, cf. Magotestilth 196 supra);
Mare Acre; Old Marled Fd; Mill Brow & -Fd, (Big) Mill Hay ((the great-,
the little-) Milne Hey 1708, v. myln, brū, (ge)hæg); Mud Wall; (Old) New
Grounds ((Old) New Ground 1708); New Hay (v. (ge)hæg); Oat Hay (the
Oathey 1708, v. āte, (ge)hæg); Pingot or Long Piece (v. pingot, pece);
Pool Hall (cf. Netherpool 191 supra); Poor Fd (v. pouer(e)); Portlands
(v. port, land); Postern Hay; The Pullingers, Pullingham (the Pullingers
1708, perhaps an old name containing -ing-[4] or -ing[2]); Rake Mdw (v. rake);

Reans (*v.* rein); St. Helen's Hill & Mdw (*v.* St Helen's Well 190 *supra*);
Big Saloon Way, Little Saloon Hay (*v.* land, weg, (ge)hæg); The Sevenbuts
1708 (*v.* seofon, butte); Stanney Hay (*v.* (ge)hæg, cf. Stanney 180, 182
supra); Stokey Loons (*v.* (ge)hæg, land, cf. Stoke 181 *supra*); Sutton Dale
Fd, Big- & Little Sutton Fd (*Suttonfeld* 1398, 1432, 1440, *Great & Little
Suttan Field* 1708, *v.* feld, deill, cf. Sutton 194 *supra*); Three Nook Piece
(*v.* þrēo, nōk, cf. three-nooked, pece); Throlland (5 times, probably 'selion
running through', i.e. from one side of a field to the other without headland,
v. þurh, land); Toll Butt (*v.* toll, butte); (Big-, Higher-, Little-, Long-,
Lower-) Town Fd (cf. *superior campus de Witeby* 1272, *Quitebylond* 1318,
Whitebylond 1398, *v.* toun, feld, land); Walmsgroves, Wangrave (*Warme-
greue* 1398, *le-* 1432, 1440, *Warmes Greave* 1708, 'warm wood', *v.* wearm,
græfe); Winter Thorns (*v.* winter, þorn); Big-, Little Wd, Wood Croft,
Fd & Hay(s) (*The Wood, Woodhey* 1708, *v.* wudu, (ge)hæg); Woodside
Fd; Yew Hay Lane 1831 (109–398758 to 407765, *v.* īw, (ge)hæg, lane).

(*b*) Acrerode 1398, *le-* 1432 ('the acre clearing', *v.* æcer, rod[1]); *Boymere*
1398, *Bymere* 1432, 1440 ('pool at a bend', *v.* byge[1], mere[1]); *Feronhull'*
1398, (*le*) *Fernyhull* 1432, 1440 ('ferny hill', *v.* fearn, fearnig, hyll); *Landpul
sive Elpul* 1241, 1246, *Londepull* 1262, *Lonpul sive Elpul* 1277[1], *Londpul-*
1277[2], (*le*) *Helpole* 1402, *Londpole* 1499 ('creek running up into the land',
'eel creek', *v.* land, pull, pōl[1], ēl[2], cf. other instances of the name at Land
Pool, *Londpull* 322, 337 *infra*); *Mersepull* 1262, *Merspole* 1499 ('marsh
stream', *v.* mersc, pōl[1], pull); *Reynaldesfeld* 1432, *Rawnuesfeld* 1440
('Reynold's field', from feld and the ME pers.n. *Reynald, -old* from OFr
Reinald or ON *Ragnaldr*); *St(h)amladeheth* 1245–9, *Stanladehet'* 1272
('heath at a stone roadway', *v.* stān, (ge)lād, hǣð, alluding to a causeway of
stone built c.1272 (Chest II 695) by the monks of Stanlow); (*le*) *Wagherhoke*
1432, 1440 (final el. hōc 'a hook of land', first el. unidentified); *Whitebypul*
1241, 1246, 1277[2], *Witebipul* 1277[1] ('the creek of Whitby', *v.* pull); le
Wlpul 1272 (probably 'the wool pool', a pool where sheep or fleeces were
washed, from wull and pull).

x. Shotwick

The ecclesiastical parish of Shotwick contained the townships 1. Capenhurst
(part now included in Ellesmere Port c.p.), 2. Great Saughall (now included
with Little Saughall in Saughall c.p.), 3. Little Saughall (cf. prec.), 4.
Shotwick, 5. Woodbank. Shotwick Park 210 *infra* may have been in this
parish originally.

1. CAPENHURST (HALL) (109–368738) [ˈkeipənərst]

   Capeles 1086 DB
   Capenhurst 13 LRO (p), 1278 Whall, Chest, 1288 *ChFor et freq*
     with variant spellings *-hyrst, -hwrst, -hirst,* (*Capenhurst Hall*)
   1831 Bry

Capinhurst c.1235 *Chol*, 1309 Ipm (p), 1322 (p), 1327 Pat (p),
1294 *ChFor*, *Capyn-* 1312–18 *JRC* (p)
Capenthurst 1297 (15) Werb (s.a. 1249) (p)
Capunhurst 1307–27 *JRC* (p), 1313 Chamb (p), 1347 *Eyre* (p)
Capanhurst 1342–53 *ChAttorn* (p)
Caponhurst 1354 Sheaf (p), 1469 Orm², 1478 Plea, 1597 Orm²
Capulhurst 1338 Cl (p), 1343 ib (p), *Capil-* 1339 Cl (p)
Cappenhurst 1655 Sheaf, 1724 NotCestr
Chapenhurst 1663 Sheaf

A difficult p.n. The forms with *Capel-*, *Capul-* are the result of
AN influence, cf. *Boleberie* DB for Bunbury 3 305, *v.* ANInfl 123.
The basic form is *Capenhurst*. The final el. is hyrst 'a wooded hill'.
For the first el. Ekwall (DEPN s.n. *Capton*, *Capenhurst*, but cf.
Capton D 322) and Smith (EPN s.v. **cape*) suggest an OE **cape*
'a look-out place' (OE *capian* 'to look upwards', OHG *kapf* 'look-
out place'). This would give 'wooded hill at a look-out place'.
Capenhurst is in the middle of the Wirral peninsula, on its median
upland which is hereabouts a level undulating plateau. The topography shows no remarkable elevation and does not seem prominent
enough to provide a natural look-out place. Perhaps Capenhurst
was the site of a structure from which watch could be kept across the
peninsula. The best solution might be to suggest that the first el. is a
nomen agentis or pers.n. OE **capa*, **Capa* 'he who looks out', gen.sg.
-an.

BIG WOOD.   BROOK FM, *v.* brōc.   DUNKIRK, 1842 OS, *v.* 176
supra.   THE GREEN (lost), 1831 Bry, at Two Mills *infra*, *v.*
grēne².   HALL LANE (lost), 1831 Bry.   MANOR FM.   MILL
LANE (109–365737 to 360742), 1831 Bry, *v.* myln, lane. There was a
windmill in Capenhurst in 1517 (AD C7347).   NEW HOUSES.
OLD HALL FM, *Old Hall* 1831 Bry, *v.* ald, hall.   PARK FM.
POWEY LANE, POWEYLANE FM, *Povey Lane* 1831 Bry, cf. *Powey
Corner* (*Meadow*) 1840 *TA*, *v.* 177 *supra*.   SALTERS LANE (lost),
v. 194 *supra*.   SIX ACRE LANE (109–359733 to 367722), 1831
Bry, cf. *Gorsey Six Acre*, *Far Six Acres* 1840 *TA*, *v.* sex, æcer.
TWO ACRE WOOD.   TWO MILLS (109–353735), 1831 Bry, *Two
Milnes on the Heath* 1668 Sheaf, *the Two Mills-* 1750, 1763 ib, *-of
the Heath* 1740 ib, cf. Twomills Fm 207 *infra*, Two Mills Fm 216
infra. This is a hamlet in Ledsham, Puddington, Capenhurst and

Shotwick townships supposed to be named from two mills once standing here, v. twā, myln, cf. Sheaf³ 17 (4214), 18 (4241).

FIELD-NAMES

The undated forms are 1840 TA 91. Of the others 1340, 1347, 1357 are ChFor, 1343 Chol, 1517 AD, 1583 JRC, 1831 Bry.

(a) Abbots Fd; Backside (v. ba(c)ksyde); Bause Hay(s) (perhaps dial. boose 'a cow-stall', cf. bōs, v. (ge)hæg); Further Bent (v. beonet); Burloons; Clatterdish Croft, Clatterdishes ('enclosures growing with burdock', v clāte, edisc); Cow Hay (v. cū, (ge)hæg); Horse Wash Croft; Intake (v. inntak); Kitchen Croft; Lark Looms (v. lāwerce, land); Long Ropes ('long ropes', from lang and rāp, apparently referring to the measurement of land by rope as distinct from the rod, cf. Rapdowles 3 226); Mares; Marl Hays (v. marle, (ge)hæg); Mill Fd & Hay; Moss Acre; Noble Hay (cf. 177 supra, 337 infra); Old House Fd; Peely Hays Mdw (perhaps 'enclosures where a fortified house or a palisade stood', from pēl and (ge)hæg. There was a moat at 109–376737); (Big) Pikes (v. pīc¹); Pingo (v. pingot); Rotten-, Rotton Fd; Sandhole Croft; Short Butt Hay; Sluch Croft (v. slutch); Sutton Damage (cf. Damage Bridge 194 supra); Wood End.

(b) le Blakestrete 1343 (probably 109–360740 to 368722; 'the dark road', v. blæc, strǣt, cf. 1 39 (route III)); Capenhurstat' 1357 (probably 'Capenhurst heath', v. hǣð); Capenhurst Heys 1583 (land in Capenhurst belonging to Mollington Torold manor, v. (ge)hæg); le Chirchewaye 1343 (v. cirice, weg; leading 'from Capenhurst next a certain cross to Church Shotwick' Chol T); le Heghedheth 1347 ('heath that has been enclosed by a hedge', v. hǣð. The first el. is probably the pa. part. of the verb hay (NED) 'to enclose, to fence in with a hedge', OE hegian); le Heth 1347 (v. hǣð); le Horeston 1343 ('the old grey stone', v. hār², stān, beside a road which led from Ledsham to Church Shotwick); Ingriessiche 1340 ('Ingrith's stream', from sīc and the ODan pers.n. Ingrith or ON Ingiríðr); Moundesmere 1343 (v. Moon's Mare 209 infra); le Prustesfeld 1343 ('the priest's field', v. prēost, feld).

2. GREAT SAUGHALL (109–3670), Magna Salhale 1278 ChFor et freq with forms as for Great- & Little Saughall infra to Great Saughall 1831 Bry, -Soughall 1842 OS, and variant forms of affix Mucul-, Mikel- 1347 ChFor, Mycul- 1438 ChRR, Graunt- 1353 BPR, Greate- 1539–47 Dugd, v. micel, mikill, grant, grēat.

GREAT- & LITTLE SAUGHALL ['sɔ:gl̩]

Salhare 1086 DB f.263, 1260 Court 13
Salhale 1086 DB f.265 (?), 1096–1101 (1280), 1265–91 Chest, 1259 Plea, 1260 Court, 1278 ChFor, -hala 1096–1101 (1150),

1150 Chest, *-hal'* 1265–81 ib, 1288 Court, 1293 Plea, *-halgh* 1347 *ChFor*

Salchale 1096–1101 (1280), 1150 Chest, 1287 Court (p), *Salkhal* 1260 ib, *Salchal* 1289 ib

Salghale 1096–1101 (17) Chest, 1286 *ChFor et freq* with variant spellings *-hal(a)* to 1516 Plea, *Salghall* 1260 Court, 1354 ChRR *et freq* with variant spellings *-halle*, *Salghall* to 1579 Dugd, *Salgha* 1286 *ChFor* (*apud Parvam Salgham*), *Salghau* 1361 BPR, 1375 *Eyre*, 1382, (lit. *-han*) 1511 Plea, *Salghou* 1535 VE

Saluhale 1189–91, 1249–65 Chest, *Salwchalle* c.1292 CASNS x (p), *Saloughale* 1298 P (p), *Salughall* 1379 IpmR

Salechale c.1220 (1390) ChRR (*Parva-*)

Salighal(e) 1265–81, 1278–81, c.1290 Chest, *Saleghal* 1288 *ChFor*, Court, *-hale* 1297 Pat, 1318 City

Salgthal 1289 Court (p)

Salghill 1296 Plea

Salghagh 1335 Pat, (15) *Mont*

Shalghale 1353, 1359 BPR

Saghau 1358 *Eyre* (p), (lit. *-han*) 1535 VE, *Saghall* 1395 Pat, 1512, 1515 *ChEx*, 1519, 1607 ChRR, *Saghull* 1614 Orm[2]

Saughall 1397 ChRR *et freq*, *Saugha* 1560 (1582) ib, *Saugho* 1615 Sheaf

Sarghale 1414 ChRR, *Sarghall* 1553 Pat

Sauheho c.1536 Leland

Sagthall 1668 Sheaf

Soughall 1842 OS

'Willow nook', or 'corner where willows grow', *v.* salh, halh, cf. Great Saughall *supra*, Little Saughall, Saughall Massie 205, 321 *infra*. The *halh* may have been the valley running down to the old shore of Dee at 109–358697, cf. The Beeches *infra*. The form *Salhale* DB f.265 may belong to Saughall Massie. The identification is uncertain; the case is argued in Tait 147 n.125a, LCHS NS ii 41, VII–VIII 294 for Great Saughall, and Tait 111 n.78, LCHS NS xv 21–25 for Saughall Massie.

ASTBURY COTTAGES, HO, & VILLAS, cf. *Astburys Crofts* 1843 *TA*, from the surname *Astbury* from Astbury 2 286.   THE BEECHES (109–359697), a house and farm at the head of the valley mentioned under Great- & Little Saughall *supra*, cf. f.ns. *Beaches*, *Beach Hay*,

Beech Bottoms, Beeches 1843 *TA*, from bece[1] 'a valley-stream', with
(ge)hæg and botm. BROOKSIDE COTTAGES, named from the
stream which runs down to Crabwall 169 *supra, v.* brōc. COAL
PIT LANE, *Coal Lane* 1831 Bry, cf. 176 *supra*, Hill Fm 178 *supra, v.*
col[1], pytt, lane. THE COTTAGE, *Rowes Farm* 1831 ib, 1842 OS.
Rowe is a surname. THE CROFT, *v.* croft. GIBBET WINDMILL,
Gibbet Mill 1831 Bry, *v.* gibet. This mill was built c.1777, near the
site where two murderers were gibbeted in 1750, *v.* Sheaf[3] 28
(6136), 48 (9600, 9708). GREEN FM, *Rowes Farm* 1842 OS, cf.
The Cottage *supra*. GUARD HOUSE FINGER (lost, 109–353702),
1831 Bry, a finger-post at the east end of a path across the marshes
of Dee, near a building which probably housed a guide who would
look to the safety of passengers fording the Dee estuary, as at the
guide-houses beside Morecambe Bay La. MILL COTTAGES, *v.*
myln. PARKGATE HO, *v.* 211 *infra*. THE PEGG, PEGG COT-
TAGES, cf. *Peg Lane, Bakers Cottage* 1831 Bry, presumably from some
post or stump here, *v.* pegge 'a peg'. PITS FM, *v.* pytt. SAUG-
HALL GREEN, 1831 Bry, -*Greene* 1620 Sheaf, *v.* grēne[2]. SEAHILL
BRIDGE & FM (109–356696), *Johnsons Farm* 1842 OS, named from
the bluff under which they lie, formerly the sea-cliff at the shore of
the Dee estuary, *v.* sǣ, hyll, cf. foll. SEALAND VIEW, named
from the township of Sealand Fl, land reclaimed from the sea in the
ancient estuary of Dee. SHOTWICK PARK, a house named from
Shotwick Park 210 *infra*.

FIELD-NAMES

The undated forms are 1843 *TA* 348. Of the others 1340 is *ChFor*, 1357
MinAcct, 1404, 1614 ChRR, 1432, 1440 *Rental*, 1539–47 Dugd, 1583
JRC, 1650 *ParlSurv*, 1831 Bry, and the rest Sheaf.

(a) Astin('s) Hay, Aston Beach (from the pers. or surname *Austin* with
(ge)hæg and bece[1]); Backside (*v.* ba(c)ksyde); Bank Hay; Blacon Croft
(*the*- 1778, cf. Blacon 168 *supra*); The Bottoms (*v.* botm); The Butt (*v.*
butte); Clover Root (*v.* clæfre, root, cf. *Ryroote* 1 159); Cowaps Fd;
Crabhall Hay (*v.* (ge)hæg, cf. Crabwall 169 *supra*); Cross Hay (*v.* cros,
(ge)hæg); Dale Butts, Dale Ends, Dales ('allotments', *v.* deill, butte, ende[1]);
Damage Hay (*v.* demming); Dingle Fd (*v.* dingle); Dod's Acre (cf. *Dod's
Croft* 1778, from the surname *Dod(d)*); Fidlers Lane 1831; The Gate 1831
(*v.* gata); Guinea Fd; Hay Makers; (New) Heath Hay, Old Heath Fd
(cf. *the old Heath Heys* 1722, 1778, *Salghall-, Saughall Heath(e)* 1563 (17),
1583, 1620, *the Heath Ground* 1677, *the Lower End of the Heath* 1722,
v. hǣð, (ge)hæg); Lings Wd; the Long Croft 1754; Long Lane 1831
(cf. *Long Lane Croft* 1778); Far- & Near Loons (*v.* land); Manger Flatt;

Marlfield, Old Marl Hay; Marsh Piece; Moors Croft (perhaps from the surname *Moor(e)*, but cf. *mora de Salghale* 1340, *v.* mōr¹); Nine Butts (*v.* nigon, butte); Open Marsh (*v.* open); Oulton's Croft ((*the*) *Oulton* 1680, 1778, *v.* ald, tūn, cf. Oulton's Fm 205 *infra*); Pail Hay ('enclosure at a pale', *v.* pale, (ge)hæg); Park Corner; Pear Tree Croft (1745); Pea(s) Hay (*v.* pise); Poor Fd; The Ridings (*v.* ryding); Roadfield (1745); the Rye Grass Fd 1754, 1778 (*v.* rye-grass); Sea Fd (*v.* sǣ, cf. Seahill Fm *supra*); Sour Grass Fd (*v.* sūr); The Stack Hayes 1778 (*the Slack Heys* 1745, probably 'enclosures in a hollow', *v.* slakki, (ge)hæg, the later form being miswritten, *t* for *l*); Stocks Croft (*v.* stocc); (The) Syllaby Butt, Croft & Fd (location, 109–363695) (*the Silly Bub Crofts* (lit. -*Lilly*-) 1680 Sheaf³ 46 (9411), cf. LCHS xcix 22–3, perhaps originally a p.n. in bӯr, changed to ModE *sillabub* by popular etymology, but it is equally likely to have been originally *sillabub*, from the quality of the milk-yield from the pasturage or some other association with this milk-food, reduced to *Syllaby*); Town Fd (1778); Whitby's Acre (cf. *Whitbytylth* 1432, 1440, 'cultivated land belonging to Whitby 198 *supra* or a person so surnamed, *v.* tilð).

(*b*) 'a fishery called *Emole* in the water of Dee' 1357 ('rented water', *v.* ēa, māl¹, perhaps the same as *le King's Channell subtus Magna Saughall* 1614, a channel in the old estuary of R. Dee, *v.* cyning, chanel); *þe New Common nowe called þe Newe Grounde* 1650 (*v.* commun, grund); *le Wall* 1404 (p) ('the well or spring', *v.* wælla).

3. LITTLE SAUGHALL (109–370690), *Parva Salechale* c.1220 (1390) ChRR *et freq* with forms as for Great- & Little Saughall 202 *supra* to *Little Saughall* 1831 Bry, -*Soughall* 1842 OS, and variant spellings of affix *Littel-* 1347 ChFor, *Litel-* 1365 *JRC*, *Letel-* 1379 IpmR, *Lytyl-* 1438 ChRR, *Lytill-* 1563 (17) Sheaf, *v.* lӯtel, lítill, parva.

KINGSWOOD LANE (109–375686 to 373702), *Kingsworth Lane* 1831 Bry, *King's Wood Lane* 1842 OS, cf. *boscus de Parua Saligh'* 1265–81 Chest, *Salghal Wood* 1295 Misc, *Salghalewode* 1331 ChFor, *boscus de Salghale* 1347, 1357 ib, 1353, 1357 BPR, 1390, 1399 ChRR, *boscus et parcum de Salghale* 1387 ib, *Salghalewode* 1440 Orm², 'the prince's wood of *Salghale*' 1353 BPR *et freq* ib, *the Abbottes-*, *the Kinges-*, -*Kynges Wood* 1563 (17) Sheaf, *a place anciently called Kingswood* 1621 (1656) Orm² (in Great and Little Saughall), 'the king's-, the abbot's wood', *v.* abbat, cyning, wudu, lane. The woodland in the two townships of Saughall was divided betweeen the demesnes of the abbots and the earls of Chester.

KIRKLAND HO, cf. *Kirk(s) Field* 1843 *TA*, probably from the surname *Kirk*.   OULTON'S FM, cf. *Little Oulton* 1843 *ib* and Oulton's Croft 205 *supra*, probably 'old enclosure', *v.* ald, tūn.   PARKSTONE, a house at 109–377685, now the name of a district of Blacon in Chester. Neither the house nor the name is ancient, but the name may allude to the nearby Kingswood *supra*, which was a royal park, *boscus et parcum de Salghale* 1387 ChRR, *v.* park. POPLARS FM, *Little Saughall Hall* 1831 Bry, *v.* hall. WASH HALL, 1831 ib, 'hall near a tide-wash', *v.* (ge)wæsc, hall, the site being above the ancient bank of the Dee estuary, overlooking the former sea-marsh and tidal flats..

FIELD-NAMES

The undated forms are 1843 *TA* 349. Of the others, 1265–81, 1265–91 are Chest, 1563 (17) Sheaf.

(*a*) Backside Math (*v.* ba(c)ksyde, mæð); Blacon Fd (cf. Blacon 168 *supra*); Crabwall Fd (cf. Crabwall 169 *supra*); Damage Fd (*v.* demming); Fishermans Croft; Gad Butts (*the Gadbuttes* 1563 (17), *v.* gad 'a gadfly', butte); Managers Flat; Marl Fd; Marsh; (Little) Matthas (probably from the pers.n. *Matthew*); Muck Fd (*v.* muk); Pidgeon-, Pigeons Hey; Sea Fd (*v.* sǣ); Town Fields.

(*b*) The *Ackers* 1563 (17) (*v.* æcer); *The Crowe Butt, the Crobutt Hey* 1563 (17) (*v.* crāwe, butte, (ge)hæg); *The Halle Fyld(e)* 1563 (17) (*v.* hall, feld); *the Heathe* 1563 (17) (*v.* hǣð); *Le Longe Acre* 1265–81 (*v.* lang, æcer); *The Long Closse* 1563 (17) (*v.* lang, clos); *The New Hey* 1563 (17) (*v.* nīwe, (ge)hæg); *Renesfeld* 1265–91 (perhaps 'field at a boundary', *v.* rein, feld); *The (Sand) See Bank(e) Feld* 1563 (17) ('field at the (sandy) sea-bank', *v.* sǣ, banke, sand, on the ancient bank of the Dee estuary); *Weforlong* 1265–91 (*v.* furlang); *Wildemarelode* 1265–81 ('the wild mare's track', *v.* wilde, mere², (ge)lād); *Wodeforlong* 1265–81 ('furlong near a wood', *v.* wudu, furlang, probably at Kingswood *supra*).

4. SHOTWICK (olim CHURCH SHOTWICK) (109–337718) ['ʃɔtwik] locally ['ʃɔtik]

> *Sotowiche* 1086 DB, *Shotowica* 1096–1101 (17) Chest, (*Rowe-*)*sse-
> chotowyk* 13 JRC, *Schotowyk* 1271 ChFor, *Chircheschotowykke*
> 1357 *ib*
> *Sotewica* 1096–1101 (1280), 1150 Chest, *-wic* 1216–23 (17) ib,
> *-wik* 1245, 1250, 1254 P, *Sottewic* 1188–91 Chest, 1242 (lit.
> *Socce-*), 1245, 1254 P, *-wik* 1247 ib, *Schotewic* 1214–23 Chest,
> *-wyc* 1237 P, *Shotewic* 1240 Cl *et freq* with variant spellings
> *Schote-* (to 1407 Chol), *Schotte-* (from 1337 Bark), *-wyc, -wyk(e)*,
> *-wik(e)*, *-uyk*, *-wich* (1241 Cl), *-wych* (lit. *-wyth* 1291 Tax) to
> *Shottewik(e)* c.1536 Leland, *Shotewyk* 1539–47 Dugd,
> *Chircheshotewyk* 1316 Plea, *Church-* 1449 Morris, *Chyrcheschote-*

wyke 1357 ChFor, *Shotewyk in Wyrhale* 1327 Cl, *Shottewike yn Wyral* c.1536 Leland
Sothwica 1096–1101 (1280) Chest, *Suthwic* 1240 P, *Sotwic* 1242 ib
(*Rowhe*)*schetewyk* c.1180 *AddCh*, *Schetewic* 1239 P, (*Rowe*)-
Shetewyke c.1260–70 (14) *AddCh*, *Shetewik* 1280 *Surv*,
(*Row*)*shetwyk* 1463 *Chol*, (*Rogh*)*shetewike* 1511 *ib*
Schetowyca 13 Chest
Schttewic 1237 P
Sochewic 1238 P, *Socwic* 1240 ib, *Scocwicum* 1240 ib
Scotw' 1240 P, *Scotewik* 1247 ib, (*Rowe*)*scotewyke* 1278 *JRC*
S(*c*)*hotwic*, -*wik* 1240, 1242 P, Lib *et freq* with variant spellings
Schot- (to 1403 Pat), *Shot*(*t*)-, -*wic*(*us*), -*wik*(*e*), -*wyk*(*e*), -*wick*
(from 1278 Pat), -*wicke*, -*wycke*, -*wigg*, -*wich* (1398 ChRR),
-*wiche* (1646 Sheaf), *Churcheshotwich* 1398 ChRR, *Shotwyke
Kyrke* 1454 (17) Sheaf
Stokewic 1247 P, -*wik* 1250 ib
Stottewic 1247 P
S(*ch*)*oteswik* 1254 P, *Scoteswich* 1291 Tax
(*Rowe*)*chotewik* 1272–80, 1317 *JRC*, (*Row*-) 1328 CASNS vi
(*Row*)*chokwyke* 1329 (1580) (17) Sheaf
Shitwyke 1437 Pat
Shokwik 1535 VE, *Shockwik* 1687 Sheaf, -*whick* 1693 ib
Shatwicke 1680 Sheaf, *Shattwick* 1698 ib

'Hamlet at a steep promontory', from wīc and a hill-name OE
Scēot-hōh from scēot[3] 'a steep slope', and hōh 'a promontory,
a spur', cf. DEPN, and Studies[2] 147. The affix *Church-* ('with a
church', *v.* cirice) distinguishes this township from Woodbank and
Shotwick Park 208, 210 *infra*.

SHOTWICK BRIDGE, BROOK, DALE, HALL & LANE, *Shottwick Bridge*
1621 Sheaf, *Shotwick Hall* 1724 NotCestr, *Shotwick Dale* 1831 Bry
(cf. *le Ouerdepedale* 1357 ChFor, *the Dale Meadow* 1585 Sheaf, *v.*
dæl[1], dēop, *uferra*). TWO MILLS, TWOMILLS FM, *Two Mills
Farm* 1831 Bry, a farm built c.1763, Sheaf[3] 18, named from the
hamlet Two Mills, *v.* 201 *supra*.

FIELD-NAMES

The undated forms are 1843 *TA* 354. Of the others 1294, 1340, 1357 are
ChFor, 1353 BPR, 1357 *MinAcct*, 1455 (17) Sheaf, 1831 Bry.

(*a*) Argue Loons (*v.* land); The Bog; Brook Loons (*v.* land, cf.
Shotwick Brook *supra*); Brow Fd (*v.* brū); Butts (*v.* butte); Cinders (*v.* sinder, cf.
Cinders Wo 84); The Cliffs (*v.* clif); Daw Butts (probably 'dole butts',
v. dāl, butte); Fredish Hay; Inglefields; Longland Hay (*v.* lang, land,
(ge)hæg); Marled Fd; Mill Post Hay; Moat Nursery (*v.* mote); Moon's
Mere (*v.* Moon's Mare 209 *infra*); Parkside (*v.* side, cf. Shotwick Park 210
infra); Primrose Hill; Queens Hay (*v.* (ge)hæg); Rail Fd (*v.* rail(e));
Reliance Fd; Seafield (*v.* sǣ); Slutch Croft (*v.* slutch); Sun Burnt Fd;
Town Field (cf. *Townfield Lane* 1831); Tudors Croft; Wol Hill.

(*b*) le *Hayfeld* 1353, le *Hey feld* 1357 ('the hay-field', *v.* hēg, feld);
Littlewode 1294, le *Littlewode* 1350, *Libbwood* 1455 (17) (*v.* lȳtel, wudu);
mora de Shotwik 1340 (*v.* mōr¹); le *Oldfeld* 1357 (*v.* ald, feld).

5. WOODBANK (*olim* ROUGH SHOTWICK) (109–345722), WOODBANK
FM, HALL & LANE

Rowheschetewyk c.1180 *AddCh*, *Rowessechotowyk* 13 *JRC*, *Rowe
Shetewyke* H3 (14) *AddCh*, -*chotewik* 1272–80 *JRC*, -*scotewyke*
1278 *ib*, -*schotewik* 1284–8 *ib et freq* with variant spellings as for
Shotwick 206 *supra* and *Row*(*e*)-, *Rouue*-, *Ro*(*u*)-, *Rogh*-, *Rugh*-,
Roth- to *Rowe Shotwick* 1583 Orm², *Rough Shotwick or Wood-
bank* 1819 ib

le *bonk in Rowessechotowyk* 13 *JRC* 1792 (Sheaf³ 50 (9981) dates
1330)

Wodebonc 1260 Court (p), -*bonk* 1280 *Surv*, 1327 ChRR, 1347
ChFor, (*le-*) 1353 *Indict*, le *Wodebong* e14 *AddCh*, -*bonck* 1340
Eyre, *Wodebanke* 1272–80 *JRC*, 1304 Chamb, 1307–27 (p),
(*le-*) 1284–8 *JRC* (p), -*bank* 1335 Pat, 1349 *JRC*, 1423 Pat,
(*the-*) 1499 Sheaf, *the Woodbank* 1499 Orm², *the Woddebanke*
1512 ChRR, *Woodbanke* 1553 Orm², 1579 *Chol et freq* with
variant spellings *Wo*(*o*)*d*-, -*banck*(*e*), -*bank* (from 1597 Orm²),
Woodbanke in Rogh Shotwick 1614 Orm², *Woodbank* (*Toll Bar*)
1831 Bry, *Woodbank Lane* 1831 Hem

'The rough, uncultivated, part of Shotwick', later, 'the hillside,
the wooded hillside', *v.* rūh, banke, wudu, cf. Shotwick 206 *supra*,
Shotwick Park 210 *infra*, from which the affix *Rough*- distinguishes
this township. *The Woodbank* was originally the name of a place in
Rough Shotwick. It is first mentioned in a grant of 'two selions upon

le bonk in Rough Shotwick' 13 *JRC* 1792. Later contexts are 'the field of *le Wodebong*' e14 *AddCh* 66255, 'the township of *Wodebank*' 1335 (15) *Mont*, 'seven acres of land . . . upon our park of Shotwick, called *Wodebank*' 1399 *JRC* 1309, 'two messuages and eighty acres of land in Rough Shotwick called *the Woddebanke*' 1512 ChRR. Some of these suggest that Woodbank and Shotwick Park 210 *infra* were originally together as *Rough Shotwick*.

PLUMHOUSES, 1831 Bry, *Plumbs Houses* 1843 *TA*, perhaps 'houses at a plum-tree', from plūme and hūs.   SHOTWICK LANE, *v.* 207 *supra*.   YACHT INN, '*a new erected house . . . the Sign of the Yacht*' 1763 Sheaf.

FIELD-NAMES

The undated forms are 1843 *TA* 444. Of these, e14 is *AddCh*, 1343, 1463 *Chol*, 1369 Orm² II 558 and Sheaf³ 37 (8115), 1671 Sheaf, 13 *JRC* 1792 dated 1330 by Sheaf³ 50 (9981), and the rest *JRC*.

(a) Backsides (*v.* ba(c)ksyde); Brick Kiln Fd (*v.* bryke-kyl); Great & Little Clay Hill(s) (*v.* clǣg, hyll); Dale Fd (*v.* dæl¹); Marsh; Moon's Mare (*Moundesmere* 1343 (in Capenhurst 202 *supra*), *Moundesmere* (lit. *Moundesinere*) 1369, *Moon's Mere* 1843 *TA* 354 (in Shotwick 208 *supra*), a locality about 109–356732 at the boundaries of Woodbank, Shotwick and Capenhurst. The final el. is probably (ge)mǣre 'a boundary'. The first el. appears to be ME mounde (OFr monde) 'the world' (NED s.v. *mound* sb¹). A name such as 'the world's end' for a remote spot out on a boundary is not improbable. ModE mound 'a hedge, a fence, a boundary', also 'a mound', is not recorded earlier than 1515 NED, otherwise this name could be interpreted as 'a boundary marked by a fence'. Also, cf. EPN s.v. mund); Sea Fd (*v.* sǣ); Slack Croft (*v.* slakki); Steel Fd (*v.* stigel); Sunburnt Fd; Woodbank Fd ('the field of *le Wodebong*' e14, *Woodbank Townfields* 1671, cf. Woodbank *supra*).

(b) *le Appultr'* 13 (*v.* æppel-trēow); *le Brodmed* 13 (*v.* brād, mǣd); *Brokynlitlebach, -litel-* 13 (*v.* Litlebach *infra*); *Calforlong* 13, 1463 (either 'cold furlong' or 'calf-furlong', from cald or calf and furlang); *le Foxholl* 13 (*v.* fox-hol); *Grymisgreue* e14 ('Grim's wood', from grǣfe with either OE Grīm, ON Grímr, a by-name of Woden, Odin, the god, or the common ON pers.n. Grímr); *Litlebach, Litelbach* ('the little valley', *v.* lȳtel, bæce¹), appears in a stream-name *Brokynlitlebach*, also *le sych in fine de brokynlitelbach*, 13 *JRC* 1792 ('(the watercourse at the end of) the-brook-in-Litlebach', *v.* sīc, brōc); (*le*) *Lond(e)lake* 1307–27 ('stream running near the land', *v.* land, lacu, a fishery, probably in the Dee estuary off Rough Shotwick); *le Longe Halflond* 1284–8 ('the long half-selion', *v.* lang, half, land); *le Rydyng* 13, *le Ruding land* 1278, 1284–8 ('(selion at) the clearedland', *v.* ryding, land); *le Storgreves* 13 ('the big woods', *v.* stórr¹, grǣfe); *le Walsemanesland* 1278, *-mannes-* 1284–8 ('the Welshman's selion', *v.* Wels(c)h-man, land, held by Adam *le Waleys* of Hooton 1284–8 *JRC* 1287).

xi. Shotwick Park

Shotwick Park was an extra-parochial liberty, a demesne of the earldom of Chester, later of the crown, the park of the manor of Shotwick Castle *infra*. It was probably within Shotwick parish originally. It is now a c.p., part of it is included in Saughall c.p.

SHOTWICK PARK (109–3571)

> *Burnelleswode* 1327 Cl, *parcum de Burnilhaye* 1327 Chamb, *parcum de Burnhull'* 1331 ChFor, *parcum de Burnelwode* 1335 ChRR, *boscus de Burnhull* 1340 ChFor, *Burnehulwode, Burnelwodehed, -held, parcum vocatum Burnylwod* 1347 *ib*, 'the park of *Shotewyke* lately called *Burnewell Wodes*' 1437 Pat
>
> *parcum de Shotwyk* 1328 Cl *et freq* with variant spellings as for Shotwick 206 *supra* and *parcum de-*, *(le) park de-*, to *Shotwicke Parke* 1615 Sheaf, *Shotwick Park* 1656 Orm[2]

The surname *de Bornell* 13(?) NRA 0406 No. 3 (witness to a deed of Neston, Brimstage and Eastham), *de Burnhull* 1286 ChFor (appearing at Ledsham), 1288 Court 94, may be derived from this place. The p.n. is 'wood of-, park and enclosure at-, *Burnhull*, i.e. hill by a stream or spring', from burna and hyll, with wudu, park, (ge)hæg. *Burnelwodehed, -held* are 'the top end of-, the hill-side or declivity at-, the wood of *Burnhull*', v. hēafod, helde. The district was included in the park of Shotwick Castle *infra* in 1327 Cl 170. In 1335 ChRR (DKR xxxvi 407) the parks of Shotwick and of *Burnilwode* are named separately as if then still distinct. Woodbank 208 *supra* may formerly have been part of the castle park.

SHOTWICK CASTLE (site of, 109–349704), *castrum de Schotwico* 1240 P, *castellum de Shotwic* 1240 Lib *et freq* with variant spellings as for Shotwick 208 *supra* to *Shottewik Castelle* c.1536 Leland, *Shotwick Castle* 1656 Orm[2], v. castrum, castellum, castel, cf. *campus castelli* 1278 ChFor ('the castle field'), the surname *del Castel (de Shotewyk)* 1350, 1354 Eyre, *le Castellake* 1357 MinAcct (a fishery, 'the stream by the castle', v. lacu), *Castle Bridge* 1621 Sheaf ('bridge at, or to, the castle', v. brycg), *Castle Hill* 1831 Bry (the castle mound at the site, v. hyll). The castle was 'the ruins of a fair castle that stands upon the brink of Dee' in 1621 (1656) Orm[2] II 361. It guarded a ford of the old Dee estuary, cf. LCHS LXIV 130 and Shotwick Ford *infra*.

DINGLE WOOD, *v.* dingle. PARKGATE HO, *Parkgate Manor House* 1831 Bry, on the Great Saughall boundary, probably at an old entrance to Shotwick Park. PARK HO (lost), 1831 ib, *Shotwick Park Farm* 1787 Sheaf, probably *Shotwick Parkeside* 1592 *JRC*, *v.* park, side. Only a barn is shown by 1842 OS, at 109–353725. POOL GARDEN WOOD. SHOTWICK FORD (lost), *Shotwyk Ford* E1 (17) Sheaf, 1340 (17) Orm² II 813, *passagium et batillagium de Shotewyk* 1357 ChFor, *Shotwigg Ford* 1707 Sheaf, a crossing of the Dee estuary, guarded by Shotwick Castle *supra*, cf. *Guard House Finger* 204 *supra*, *v.* ford. SHOTWICKLODGE FM, *the Parker's Howse* 1554 Orm², *-House* 1680 Sheaf, *the Lodge in Shotwicke Parke* 1629 ib, *Shotwick Lodge* 1671 ib, 1842 OS, *v.* parkere, hūs, loge. WOOD-BANK LANE, *v.* 208 *supra*.

FIELD-NAMES

Of the forms, 13 is *JRC* 1792 dated 1330 by Sheaf³ 50 (9981), 1357, 1507 *MinAcct*, 1373 *JRC*, 1386, 1485 ChRR.

(*b*) *le Flodʒate* 13, *piscaria del Flodyordes* 1357, *le Flodyord* 1373, *Floddeyord* 1386, *le Flodeyardez* 1485, *lez Flodeyatis* 1507 (a fishery in R. Dee belonging to Shotwick manor and held 'by the tenants of Little Saughall in Great Saughall' 1507 *MinAcct*, so it may have been at Great Saughall 202 *supra*. The name is 'the flood-gate', 'the flood-enclosure(s)', i.e. tidal fish-traps, *v.* flōd, geard, flōd-yate).

xii. Burton

The ecclesiastical parish of Burton contained 1. Burton, 2. Puddington.

1. BURTON (109–3174), BURTON MANOR

> *Burton* 1152 MRA, 1238 Orm², 1278 *ChFor et freq*, *-in Wir(e)hale*
> c.1234 MRA *et freq* with spellings as for Wirral 1 7, *Burton Hall* 1831 Bry
> *Borton* c.1240 (1293) (17) Sheaf³ 17, 1291 Tax, 1349 Pap, *-in Wirral* 1566 Sheaf
> *Bertone* 1310 Pap
> *Bourton* 1363 Pap
> *Bwerton* 1592 *JRC*
> *Barton* 1646 Sheaf

'Farm or enclosure at a fortification', from burh-tūn, byrh-tūn, with hall, maner; named from the earthworks at Burton Point *infra*.

Burton in Wirral was a prebendal church of Lichfield Cathedral, until c.1234 when the prebend was transferred to Tarvin, MRA 718 p.343, Orm² II 555. The bishop of Lichfield held Burton in Eddisbury Hundred 3 270. *Burtone* DB f.263 is entered as Burton in Eddisbury Hundred, but it has been argued that the DB hundred-rubric is wrong, and that the entry refers to Burton in Wirral, *v.* 3 271.

BURTON POINT (109–303736), NESSET (lost, 109–303744), BURTON-HEAD (109–304742)

> *Nesshede* 1450 ChRR, *Nesshead*, *Nessehede* 1450 Orm², *Nessehede* 1468 *MinAcct*, *Nesshed* 1471 *ib*, *Nessehed* 1525 ChRR, *Nesset* (*Lane*) 1817 *EnclA*, *Nesset Barn* 1831 Bry, *Nesset* (*Common & Hay*) 1843 *TA*, 1847 *TAMap*
> *Burton Hedde* c.1536 Leland, -*Head* 1599 Morris, 1621 (1656) Orm², *Burton Head* (*Farm*) 1831 Bry, 1842 OS
> *Burton Hill* 1615 Sheaf
> *Burton Point* 1819 Orm²

'The promontory of Ness, -called Ness, -at Ness' and 'the promontory at Burton', from **ness** or the p.n. Ness 220 *infra*, and the p.n. Burton *supra*, and **hēafod**, point, **hyll**, with **lane**, **bere-ærn**, **commun**, **(ge)hæg**. This headland, giving a name to Ness and Neston 220, 222 *infra*, is described by Webb in 1621, Orm² II 361, as 'a great brow of a promontory reaching into the sea, they call it Burtonhead' and it is the site of an iron-age promontory fort, *v.* Sheaf³ 48 (9694, 9704), from which the p.n. Burton is derived, cf. *Burton Ditch, Castle Field* 1843 *TA*, *v.* **dīc**, **castel**.

BANK HO.   BATH WOOD, *Rookery* 1831 Bry, *v.* **bæð**.   BENT-HEATH COVERT, *v.* **beonet**, **hǣð**.   THE BIRCHES, *Birch Plantation* 1831 Bry.   BURTON BARN, 1831 ib, cf. *Barn Lane* 1831 ib. DUNSTAN FM (109–321752), *Dunston Hall* 1842 OS, *Dunstone* 1847 *TAMap*, cf. foll. and *Dunston Hay* 1843 *TA*, perhaps from the surname *Dunstan, Donston, Dunstance* common in *ParReg* at Bebington 1560–76, Heswall 1714–20, cf. Sheaf³ 37 (8114), but this and Fiddleston and Hampston *infra*, Craxton 215 *infra*, may be p.ns. in **tūn** or **stān** for which no early forms have appeared. Dunstan Fm is on top of a hill, and might be 'rock on a hill', from **dūn** and **stān**. DUNSTAN LANE, *Dunston Lane* 1831 Bry, *Eastham Road*, *The Acre Lane* 1817 *EnclA*, cf. prec., *v.* **æcer**, **lane**, cf. Eastham 187 *supra*. ELTHORNS (109–305750), *Hell Thorn* 1831 Bry, *Hallthorn* (*Hay*),

Hillthorn Piece 1843 *TA*, cf. Health Hornes 222 *infra* at 109–306753, 'thorn-tree(s) on a hill-side', from helde, hyll, hallr, and þorn. FIDDLESTON PLANTATION (109–326747), *Fiddleston* 1817 *EnclA*, *Fiddleston Common Plantation* 1843 *TA*, *Fiddlestone* 1847 *TAMap*, perhaps an old p.n. in stān or tūn, cf. Dunstan *supra*. The first el. could be the ON pers by-name *Fiðill* 'the fiddle-player', *v.* commun, (ge)hæg. HADDON WOOD, cf. *the Hadden Heys* 1817 *EnclA*, *Haddon Field & Lane* 1843 *TA*, *Hadon Lane* 1847 *TAMap*, cf. 221 *infra*. HAMPSTON WELL (109–309743), 1831 Bry, *Hampson's Well* 1950 Sheaf³ 45, *v.* wella 'a well, a spring'. *Hampston* may be an old p.n. in tūn or stān, cf. Dunstan, Fiddleston *supra*, but here the origin might also be *hump-stone*, 'humped-stone', *v.* hump, stān, or *hemp-stone* 'a stone on which hemp is beaten', *v.* hænep, hemp. HEATH FM, cf. *The Heath* 1817 *EnclA*. MARSH COVERT. THE MERE, *v.* mere¹. MILL FM & WOOD, *Mill House* 1831 Bry, named from *Burton Mill* 1842 OS, *molendinum ventricitum* 1357 *ChFor*. MUDHOUSE LANE (modern name), *Mare Hey Lane* 1817 *EnclA*, *Mare Lane* 1831 Bry, cf. *Mare Hay* 1843 *TA*, perhaps 'mare's enclosure', from mere² and (ge)hæg, but this lane leads to the Puddington boundary at Mudhouse Wood *infra*, and the first el. could be (ge)mære 'a boundary', cf. foll. MUDHOUSE WOOD (109–332749), *Mud Hall Nursery* 1831 Bry, named from *Mud House* 1842 OS, *Mud Hall* 1817 *EnclA*, 1831 Bry (109–327747), either a derogatory name or an allusion to daub building, *v.* mudde. PRIESTSWAY (modern name, 1906), *Oceans Lane* 1831 Bry (109–321745 to 324743), cf. (*Great-, Little-*) *Ortion(s)*, *Ortion Priestway*, *Meadow Ortion*, *Priestway* (*Bottoms*) 1843 *TA*, 'priest's way' from prēost and weg, with botm 'bottom-land', and an inexplicable f.n. *Ortion(s)*, *Oceans*.

FIELD-NAMES

The undated forms are 1843 *TA* 85. Of the others, 1286 is *ChFor*, 1592 *JRC*, 1817 *EnclA*, 1831 Bry, 1847 *TAMap* 85.

(a) Bithum (perhaps byðme 'the head of a valley'); Black Butts (*v.* blæc, butte); Brow Fd (*v.* brū); Burden; The Church Rake 1817 (*v.* rake); Common Fd; Copgraves, Cop Graves (109–323745) (*v.* copp, grǣfe, cf. Cross Graves *infra*); Crooked Flat; (Big & Little) Cross Graves (a group of fields about 109–319739; 'fields or lands called *Graves*, which lie athwart', *v.* cros, grǣfe, distinguished from Copgraves *supra*, which were at a 'copp' or hill. These f.ns. may represent a vestige of *Greves* in Puddington 215 *infra*, cf. Copgrave 216 *infra*); The Dale, (The) Dales, Little- & Long Dale, Dale Hey (cf. *Long Dales* 1817, *v.* deill 'an allotment'); Denhall Fd & Hay (cf. *Denna Lane* 1831, named from Denhall 220 *infra*, the old site of which extended into Burton township); Dunshil Croft; Friday Foot ('the bottom end of a *Friday* field', *v.* Frīgedæg, fōt); Holland Side (*Hulland Side* 1817, perhaps 'hill-land', from hyll and land, with sīde); Hollyway (*v.* holh, weg); Lack Lake (*v.* lacu); The Lawn (*v.* launde); Low Field Brow (1831, *v.* brū); (The) Mares; Marl Hay (cf. *the old Marled Hey* 1817, *v.* marled, (ge)hæg); Moore Flat(t) (*the Moor Flat* 1817, cf. *Burton Moore* 1592, *v.* mōr¹, flat); The Old Hay(s) (*v.* (ge)hæg); Pillow(s) Croft; Pingle (*the-* 1592, *v.* pingel); Rake, Rake Croft (*the Rake Hey* 1817, *v.* rake, (ge)hæg); Roundabout (*v.* 337 *infra*); Ryeland Hay (*v.* rye-land, (ge)hæg); Sand Fd; School Fd (*The Burton School Croft* 1817, *School Land* 1831, land dedicated to the upkeep of a school at Burton); Short Butts (*v.* sceort, butte); Shot Butts (unless a mistake for prec., this is 'butts at a corner', *v.* scēat, butte); Slack Lake ('slow watercourse', from *slack* 'slow, sluggish', cf. slakki, and lacu); Studfold (*v.* stōd-fald); Summerlane Croft ('lane used in summer', *v.* sumor, lane); Three Nooks (cf. three-nooked); Tile Kiln 1831; Town Fd; Well Fd; White Hay (*v.* hwīt, (ge)hæg); Wings (*v.* wing); Withyn Way ('willow path', *v.* wīðegn or wīðigen, weg).

(*b*) *Banfelong* 1592 ('bean furlong', *v.* bēan, furlang); *Boate Hill* 1592 (probably a hill where some sort of privilege was used, *v.* bōt, hyll); *Burton Meadowe* 1592 (*v.* mǣd); *Buscheia* 1286 ('bushy enclosure', *v.* busc, (ge)hæg); *Edgrewe* 1592 (*v.* hecg-rǣw); *Granowes Fielde* 1592 (probably 'Gronw's field', from the Welsh pers.n. *Gronw*); *Heades Fielde* 1592 ('field at the headland', *v.* hēafod, cf. Burton Point *supra*); *the Powfielde* 1592 (perhaps 'hill-top field', from polle, or 'pool field', from pōl¹).

2. PUDDINGTON (109–3273)

Potitone 1086 DB, *Potyton* 1397 Pat, *Potintona* 12 (c.1311) Chest, -*ton* 1260 Court, e14, 1330 *JRC*, 1579 Orm², *Potynton* e13 *JRC* (p), 1386 Plea, 1387 *Eyre*, 1397, 1406, 1408 ChRR, 1411 AD, 1421 Orm² (p), *Potington* 1554 Pat, 1656 Orm²

Pudington c.1100 Orm² II 446, 1302 Plea, 1394 (p), 1397 ChRR, 1660 Sheaf, *Pudyngton* 1289 Court, *Pudinton* 1304 Chamb (p) *Pudynton* 1326 ChRR, *Puddyngton* 1353 BPR, *Puddington* 1388 ChRR *et freq*, *Puddingetone* 1615 Sheaf

Puditan c.1150 (1347) *ChFor*, 1128–53 (1580) (17) Sheaf

Podinton(a) 1260 Court, *Plea*, *Podinton* 1278 *ChFor*, 1317 AD (p), *Podynton* 1305 ChF *et freq* to 1535 VE, *Podington* 1287 Court (p), 1294 *ChFor*, 1302 Plea (p), 1537 Sheaf, 1561 Orm², 1601 Sheaf, (-*alias Potington alias Podyngton*) 1554 Pat, -*thone* 1309 ChRR, *Podyngton* 1353 BPR *et freq* to 1589 ChRR, *Poddington in Wirrall* 1547 MinAcct

Putington 1278 Whall (p), *Putyngton* 1289 Court (p), *Puttington*
1588 ChRR
Putkan 1361 BPR III 430, *Pu'ckan* 1362 Orm² II 355
'Farm called after Put(t)a', from the OE pers.n. *Put(t)a* and
-ingtūn, cf. Puddington D 389.

GREVES (lost), *Greues* c.1235 *Chol* (p), 1288 *ChFor*, *Greves* 1284 Ipm
(p) *et freq* with variant spellings (*le(s)*-, *la*-), *Greues*, *Greves*, *Grevhes*,
Greuys, *Greyves* to 1380 *Eyre*, (*-iuxta Shotewyk*) 1333 Plea, (*-in
Wirhale*) 1333 *Blun*, (*-in Podyngton*) 1356 BPR, *boscus del Greues*
1347, 1357 *ChFor*, *foresta de Greues* 1358 ChRR, *le Greue iuxta le
bonk* 1359 *ChFor*, *le Greue* (lit. *Grene*) 1386 Plea, 1438 ChRR (p),
'the groves', *v.* grǣfe. It seems to have been a district of Puddington,
and it gives rise to the surname *de(l) Greves* of a family living at
Greves in Puddington 1356 BPR III 226. *le Greue iuxta le bonk*, 'the
wood next to the bank' (*v.* banke) may be connected with the f.n.
Copgrave *infra*, Copgraves 213 *supra* (*v.* copp).

SALTERS HOUGH (lost), 1727 Sheaf³ 3 (461), *Salteres Halek* n.d. AD
IV 104, 'salters nook', *v.* saltere, halh, halc, must have been near
Puddington. In this township is *Salters Croft* (109–318731) 1839
TA, 1817 *EnclA*, and in the Burton *EnclA*, 1817, is *Salters Gutter
on the north side of the old channel of the River Dee* which is probably
a rode in Dee caullid Salthouse (two miles downstream from Shotwick,
one mile above Burton, opposite) *a salt house cottage* c.1536 Leland
III 91, cf. *Salthowse* 1535 VE 202 (belonging to the Collegiate
Church of St John Baptist, Chester), *v.* salt-hūs, goter, croft, rād.
The 'road' was an anchorage for ships in Dee.

BADGERSRAKE FM, *Badger Rake* 1831 Bry, *Badgers Rake* 1842 OS,
Bagers Rake 1847 *TAMap* 380 (Little Sutton), a hamlet in Puddington, Willaston and Ledsham townships, cf. Badgers Rake, Badgersrake Covert 233, 217 *infra*, probably 'hawker's lane', a road used by
peddlers, *v.* baggere, rake, cf. *badger* NED.   BENTY HEYS WOOD,
Benty Hey Cover 1831 Bry, 'grassy enclosure', *v.* benty, (ge)hæg.
CHAPELHOUSE FM, *Priests House* 1842 OS.   THE CRAXTON (a
wood, 109–345745), *Crackstone Wood* 1831 Bry, *Caxton* 1839 *TA*,
cf. Dunstan 212 *supra*, *v.* tūn, dūn or stān.   CROSS PLANTATION.
HEYBRIDGE HO.   NEWHOUSE FM, *New House* 1842 OS.   OLD

HALL, 1831 Bry, *Puddington Halle* 1615 Sheaf, *v.* hall. This house was superseded by *The Hall* 1831 Bry, 1842 OS, and that in turn by PUDDINGTON HALL.   TWO MILLS FM, *Gardners Farm* 1842 ib, cf. Two Mills 201 *supra.*

FIELD-NAMES

The undated forms are 1839 *TA* 331. Of the others n.d. is AD iv 104, 12 (c.1311) Chest, 1347, 1357 *ChFor*, 1359 BPR, 1369, 1492, 1656 Orm², 1491 ChRR, 1543 Sheaf, 1817 *EnclA*, 1831 Bry.

(*a*) Acorns; Great Bottoms (*v.* botm); Brook Loons (*v.* land); Chesterway Side ('at the side of the way to Chester', *v.* weg, sīde); Copgrave (109–333741; also Copgraves 213 *supra* in Burton, cf. *Greves supra*); Copy (*v.* copis); Cow Hey (*v.* (ge)hæg); Cross Hey (near the Ledsham boundary at 109–345745, the probable site of *Ledeshamcrosse* 1369 Orm² II 558, cf. Sheaf³ 37 (8115), *v.* cros, (ge)hæg, cf. Ledsham 217 *infra*); Crow Holt (*v.* crāwe, holt); Dale Hey & Mdw (*Dale Field, Meadow & Lane* 1817, cf. *Depedale* 1369 Orm² II 558, 'deep valley', *v.* dēop, dæl¹, cf. also Shotwick Dale 207 *supra*); Dam Hey (cf. *The Dam Fields* (modern name), the site of a water-mill dam in 1369, Sheaf³ 37 (8115, 8124); Flash Croft (*v.* flasshe); Flats (*v.* flat); Gorstil (*v.* gorst, hyll); Gorsy Park (*v.* gorstig, park); Green Rake (*v.* rake); Heath Hey (cf. *Heath Lane* 1831, *le Heth* 1347, *v.* hǣð); High Fd (1831); Hugger Hey (perhaps *Hulgreve Hey* 1491, *Hulgrevehey* 1492, 'owl-wood' or 'wood near a hovel' from grǣfe with ūle or hulu, and (ge)hæg); Marl'd Clods (*v.* marlede, clod(de)); Marled Fd; Old Hey; Old Park; Owler Hey (*v.* alor, (ge)hæg); Ox Pasture; Peg (*v.* pegg); Pipers Lane Croft (cf. *Pipers Lane* 1831 (109–329735 to 335745), perhaps from the surname *Piper*, possibly 'piper's lane' from pīpere, cf. Pepper Street 337 *infra*); Provin Allens; Rakeside (*v.* rake, sīde); Sea Lane 1831 (109–326733 to 323727, *v.* sǣ); Smellage (*Smallats* 1491, *Smalleche* 1492, 'narrow watercourse', *v.* smæl, lece, læc(c)); Stanny Hooks (*v.* stānig, hōc); Stone Paddock; Town's End (*The-* 1817, *v.* toun, ende¹); Westmoor (*v.* west, mōr¹); Wings (*v.* wing); Wood Park (cf. *boscus de-, boscus vocatus Podyngton* 1347 *ChFor*, 1359 BPR, *v.* wudu, park).

(*b*) le Bernelont n.d. ('selion near a barn', *v.* bere-ærn, land. This was at *Salters Hough supra*); le bonk 1357 (*v.* banke); *Flodgeard* 12 (c.1311) ('the tide pound', a fish-trap, *v.* flōd, geard); *Motherless Heath* 1543, 1656 (a heath between Puddington and Ledsham, *v.* hǣð. The origin of *Motherless* is not obvious); *Westanesfeld* 1357 ('Wǣrstān's field', from the OE pers.n. *Wǣrstān* and feld).

xiii. Neston

The ecclesiastical parish of Neston contained the townships 1. Ledsham (part now included in Ellesmere Port Municipal Borough, the rest a c.p.), 2. Leighton (now included in Neston cum Parkgate c.p.), 3. Ness, 4. Great Neston (now included in Neston cum Parkgate c.p.), 5. Little Neston cum

Hargrave (Little Neston is now included in Neston cum Parkgate c.p., and the detached parts, Hargrave and Blakeley Brow, surrounded by Raby township, are included with Raby), 6. Raby (now a c.p., included, with Hargrave & Blakeley Brow from Little Neston *supra*, in Bebington Municipal Borough), 7. Thornton Hough (now a c.p. in Bebington Municipal Borough), 8. Willaston.

1. LEDSHAM (109–357744) [ˈledʃəm, ˈledsəm]

> *Levetesham* 1086 DB, *Leuedesham* 1096–1101 (1280) Chest, (lit. *Lenedes-*) 1309 ChRR (p)
>
> *Ledesham* 1287 Court (p), 1294 *ChFor et freq* to 1524 ChRR, with variant spellings *Ledessam*, *Leddesham* (1476 ChRR to (-*in Wyrehalle*) 1539–47 Dugd)
>
> *Letisham* 1318 *Eyre*, *Letesham* 1354 Sheaf (p)
>
> *Lodesham* 1337 Cl (p), 1362 Bark 1400 Pat
>
> *Redesham* 1369 Bark (p)
>
> *Ledsham* 1387 *Eyre*, 1560 ChRR *et freq*, *Ledsam* 1654 Sheaf, 1848 *TAMap* 432, *Ledsom* 1697 Sheaf, *Leadsham* 1663 ib

'Lēofede's homestead or village', from the OE pers.n. *Lēofede* and hām. The same pers.n. was borne by *Luuede* a tenant of Prenton 272 *infra* in 1066 DB, cf. Feilitzen 322.

BADGERSRAKE COVERT, 1831 Bry, *Dean Wood* 1831 ib, *Deans Wood* 1842 OS, 1849 *TA*, cf. Badgersrake Fm 215 *supra*.   SALTERS LANE (lost), *v.* 194 *supra*.

FIELD-NAMES

The undated forms are 1849 *TA* 234. Of the others 1286, 1340, 1347 are *ChFor*, 1369 Orm², 1539–47 Dugd, 1831 Bry, 1842 OS.

(*a*) Acres; Backside (*v.* ba(c)ksyde); Barley Corners (*v.* bærlic, corner); Birch Hey (*v.* (ge)hæg); Bridge Mere (*Briddesmere* 1340, 'pool where young birds haunt', *v.* bridd, mere¹); Calf Hey (*v.* (ge)hæg); Coombs (*v.* cumb); Cow Hey (cf. *Cow Hay Lane* 1842, *v.* (ge)hæg); Crook Loons ('crooked selions', *v.* krókr, land); Dunmore Croft & Mdw (perhaps 'dun moor', *v.* dunn, mōr¹); Flat Hey (*v.* flatr); Fox Holes (*v.* fox-hol); Greets (*v.* grēot); Harbour Croft (from either here-beorg or ModE arbour); The Heath, Heath Croft, Heath Hey, Heath Lane Croft (cf. *Heathy Lane* 1831, *v.* hǣð, (ge)hæg); Hook Hey (*v.* hōc, (ge)hæg); Intack (*v.* inntak); Ketch Fd; Knowy Croft & Hey (cf. *Knowl Hey Lane* 1831, *v.* cnoll, (ge)-hæg); Land Fd (*v.* land); Leys (*v.* lēah); Little Delight; Long Rope Hey (*v.* rāp, (ge)hæg, cf. Rapdowles 3 226); Four- & Long Loons (*v.* land); Lydiate Hey (*v.* hlid-geat, (ge)hæg); Old Marled Hey (*v.* marlede, (ge)hæg);

Meadow Plat & Spot (*v.* plat², spot); Mean Hey (*v.* (ge)mǣne); Newart Hey; Old Hey (*v.* (ge)hæg); Ox Hey Mdw (*v.* (ge)hæg); Pikes (*v.* pīc¹); Pingot (*v.* pingot); Roughland Hey (*v.* rūh, land, (ge)hæg); Six-, Stampy- & Stanny Looned Hey (from sex 'six', and stānig 'stony', and land (ME, ModEdial *lond, loon(d)*) 'a selion', with (ge)hæg. On *Stampy* Professor Löfvenberg observes, 'This may be a derivative of the OE word *stamp* 'tree-stump' discussed by Sundby, *The Dialect & Provenance of the ME Poem "The Owl and The Nightingale"* 194ff. *Stampy* would mean 'stumpy, abounding in tree-stumps'); Slade Hey (*v.* slæd); Swinemans Heath Hey (*v.* hǣð, (ge)hæg. The first el. appears to be an occupational surname *Swineman* 'swine-herd, pig-keeper'); Tapin Yard; Tister Hey & Mdw; Tuit Acre (probably 'peewit's acre', from ModEdial. *tewit* 'a peewit'); Wet Reins (*v.* rein); Within Hey (*v.* wiðegn, (ge)hæg).

(*b*) *fossatum abbatis Cestr'* 1347 ('the abbot of Chester's ditch', *v.* dīc); *the berne of Leddesham* 1539–47 (a tithe-barn, *v.* bere-ærn); *Burnhull* 1286 (p) (a surname which may derive from Shotwick Park, *v.* 210 *supra*); *Ledeshamcrosse* 1369 (Orm² II 558, Sheaf³ 37 (8115), cf. Cross Hey 216 *supra*, *v.* cros).

2. LEIGHTON (HALL) (109–286794) [ˈlɛːtən, ˈleitən]

Lestone 1086 DB
Lechton e13 Bark (p), 1260 Court (p), c.1300 *AddCh* (p), 1307 Sheaf (p), 1309 *JRC*
Lecton 13 Bark, c.1235 *Chol* (p), 1268 Bark (p), 1278 *ChFor*, 1280 *Most*, 1300–7 *JRC* (p), *-tone* 1287 Court (p)
Lehton e13 *AddCh* (p)
Leychtona 1240–9 Chest
Leighton 1240–9 (17) Chest, 1513 (1585), 1523 (1571), 1573 ChRR *et freq*, (*-Hall*) 1831 Bry
Latthon 1249–65 Chest (p)
Leghton 1287 Court (p), 1304 Chamb *et freq* to 1523 ChRR, (*-iuxta Neston*) 1307 Plea, (*-in Wyrhale*) 1350 VR, (*-iuxta Berneston*) 1421 Orm², *Legthton* 1289 Court (p)
Leihton (*in Wirhall*) 1335 Pat

'The herb-garden, the vegetable garden', *v.* lēac-tūn. It is near Neston and Barnston 222, 263 *infra*, and is thus distinguished from Leighton 3 28.

BACKWOOD HALL (109–277796), *Backwood Lodge* 1831 Bry, *the Woodward's house at the upper end of Leighton Wood* 1569 Sheaf, cf. *Woodwards heye* 1619 *Most*, 'the back end of the wood', *v.* back, wudu, loge, and 'the wood-keeper's house', *v.* wodeward. For the other end of the wood cf. foll.

Wood Ho (lost, 109–284786), 1831 Bry, *the Woodhouse at the lower end of Leighton Wood* 1569 Sheaf, cf. *Wodehousse in Wyrhall* 1378 *Eyre*, 'house at a wood', *v.* wudu, hūs, cf. prec. and *boscus de Leghton* 1357 ChFor, *Leighton Wood alias the Greenes* 1578 Most, *The Wood, Wood Field & Hay, Wood Hey Meadow* 1848 *TA*. Wood Lane 224 *infra* leads to the site of Wood Ho.

Boathouse Lane, leading to *Flint and Bagillt Ferry House* 1831 Bry, *Ferry House* 1842 OS, *Boat House* 1847 *TAMap, Park Gate Ferry House* 1848 *TA*, from bāt 'a ferry-boat', and ferja, hūs, cf. Parkgate 223 *infra*. The Dungeon (local, 1923 Sheaf), *Backwood Dungeon* 1831 Bry, *Dept dale* 1569 Sheaf[3] 20, 'the dingle', 'the deep valley', *v.* dongeon, dēop, dæl[1]. Leighton (a house), *Leighton Cottage* 1831 Bry. Leighton Banastre, 1860 White, a residence with no history, probably a name of pretension, after Mollington Banastre 171 *supra*. Leighton Ho, *Leighton Lodge* 1831 Bry, *v.* loge. Leighton Cottages. Longhouse (lost, 109–272293), 1831 Bry, 1842 OS, *v.* lang, cf. Shorthouse *infra*. Mostyn Place, 1831 Bry, named after the place and family of Mostyn Fl, across the Dee estuary, *v.* place. Shorthouse (lost, 109–273791), 1831 Bry, 1842 OS, cf. Longhouse *supra*, *v.* sc(e)ort, hūs.

FIELD-NAMES

The undated forms are 1848 *TA* 240. Of the others c.1280, 1688 are *Most*, 1569 Sheaf, 1831 Bry.

(a) Backsides (*v.* ba(c)ksyde); Banacres (*v.* bēan, æcer); Bennetts Fd (cf. *Bennetts Cottage* 1831); Bran Fd (*v.* brand 'place cleared by burning'); Common Fd; Cow Pasture; Cross Hey (*The Crosse Hey* 1688, *v.* cros, (ge)hæg); Dam Hedges (perhaps the re-duplicated plural of a f.n. *Damheads*, 'the top ends of a dam', *v.* damme, hēafod, but *Damage* an assibilated form of demming 'a dam', might be the origin. These fields are at 100–282798 above Fish Pond *infra*); Dock Fd (*v.* docce); Fish Pond (a group of fields at 100–277793, probably the site of a fish-pond fed by a spring in Dam Hedges *supra*); Flat; Galloway Hay; Groat; Hollands (-Hay, -Hey) (*v.* hēafod-land, (ge)hæg); Homes Hays (*v.* holmr, (ge)hæg); Five Horns (*v.* horna); Kitchen Croft; Limits Cross (a field adjoining Leighton Hall to the south, perhaps the site of a boundary cross); Loom, Nine Looms, The Loonis (*v.* loom, land); Rough, The Roughs; Sich Mdw (*v.* sīc); Slang (*v.* slang); Wall Hey(s) (*v.* wælla, (ge)hæg).

(b) *Helgreue* 1569 (*v.* grǣfe, first el. obscure); *Petyfurlong* c.1280 ('little furlong', *v.* pety, furlang); *Raby Yate* 1569 (on the boundary of Leighton and Thornton Hough, 'gate leading into Raby', *v.* geat, cf. Raby 228 *infra*); *le Rake* c.1280 ('the lane', *v.* rake).

3. NESS (109–302760)

> *Nesse* 1086 DB, *Nessa* 1096–1101 (1280), 1150 Chest, *Nesse* 1228–40, c.1230 ib, 1253 Pat *et freq, passim* to 1656 Orm², (*-in Wirehale*) 1381 ChRR, (*-iuxta Burton in Wyrehale*) 1393 (1474) ib, *Ness* 1392 IpmR, 1646 Sheaf
>
> *Nasse* 1322 Cl (p)

'At the promontory', *v.* ness, næss. The name is taken from the promontory at Burton Point 212 *supra*. Part of the township is called *Littell Nesse* 1670 Sheaf³ 3, *v.* lȳtel.

DENHALL (109–300748) [ˈdenɔːl] older local [ˈdenə], DENHALL HO (109–297750), DENHALL QUAY (109–289759), DENNA LANE (lost, 109–301748 to 307753)

> *Danewell* 1184 P (lit. *Baue-*), *hospital' de Danewell in Cestresira juxta litus maris* 1238 Orm², (*hospital of (St Andrew)*) *Danewall* 1302 ib, 1333 Fine, *-walle* 1349 Pap, *Danewell(e)* 1310, 1318, 1343 ib
>
> *Denewell* c.1240 (1293) (17) Sheaf, c.1268 (1400) CASNS XIII, (*portus de-*) 1308 Fine, (*the hall of-*) *Denewelle* 1293 (17) Sheaf, *Denewelle* 1311 Fine, *hospital de Denewale* 1288–90 Sheaf, *-walle* 1343 Cl, 1349 Pap, *-wall* 1353 ib, 1369 ChRR
>
> *Denhale* 1293 (17) Sheaf, 1353 *Eyre* (p)
>
> *Dennewalle* l13 Orm² (p)
>
> *Davenell* 1318 Pap
>
> the hospital of *Danwell* 1320 MRA, *Danwall Hospitall* 16 Harl. 2061
>
> *Donewell* 1322, 1323, 1327 Fine, (port of-) 1328 Cl
>
> (*hospital (Sancti Andree) de*) *Denwall* 1345 Pap, 1376 *Eyre*, l14 (m15) Harl. 2061, 1540 Sheaf, *Denwall* 1399 ChRR *et freq* to 1819 Orm², (port of-) 1405 Pat, (*-House*) 1650 Sheaf, (*hospital Sancti Andree*) *Denwhall* 1499 ib, *Denwaulle village & Haul*, *Denwale Rode* c.1536 Leland
>
> *Denna Lane* 1817 EnclA, *Denna* (*House & Lane*) 1831 Bry, *Dennah House, -Hey & -Meadow* 1839 TA, *Denhall* (*House*) 1842 OS

'The Danes' spring', from **Dene**, **Danir** and **wella**, **wælla**, with hūs, hall, lane, (ge)hæg, mæd. The form *hospital de Newalle* 1349 Pap III 293 is a metanalysis. *Denwale Rode* (*v.* rād) was an anchorage for ships in the port of Chester, cf. Denhall Gutter, Old Quay 223, 225 *infra*. The hospital, for the use of poor travellers from Ireland and other poor or shipwrecked men is first mentioned c.1234 MRA 718 p.343 as 'the hospital of Burton in Wirehall', cf. Orm² II 543, 556, but some foundation was here in 1184 (LCRS XCII 15 n.1 and Addenda 186, under the erroneous form *Bauewell*'). The hamlet of Denhall was in Ness township, it gives name to Denhall Gutter in Great Neston and to Wirral Colliery 226 *infra* in Little Neston. The hospital was closely associated with Burton parish by appropriation c.1234 MRA *loc. cit.* (or 1238 Sheaf¹ 3, p.176); the site of its chapel is in Burton township at 109-302747; and the hamlet was reckoned a part of Burton parish in *Danwell in the parish of Barton* 1646 Sheaf³ 1.

BROOK WELL.   FRIENDS HALL FM, *Friends Hall* 1831 Bry. HADDON HALL FM (109-315757), HADDON WOOD, *common or waste in Ness called Haddon* 1817 *EnclA*, *Hadden Hall* 1831 Bry, 1842 OS, *Hadden Hill Plantation* 1831 Bry, probably 'heath hill', *v.* hǣð, dūn. This district extends into Burton township, cf. 213 *supra*. Dunstan and Fiddleston 212, 213 *supra* are on the same hill.   HEATHFIELD, cf. *Heath* 1839 *TA*, *v.* hǣð.   MARSH COTTAGES.   MICKWELL BROW, (*Cover*) 1831 Bry, *Mickwell*, *Great Mickwell*, *Mickwell Covert* 1839 *TA*, 'big well or spring', *v.* micel, mikill, wella, brū. NESSHOLT, *Ness Out* 1842 OS, cf. *Holt Hey* 1839 *TA*, *le Houtrake* 1228-40 Chest, and Holt 227 *infra*, 'the wood', *v.* holt, rake. NESS WOOD, *Ness Cover*(*t*) 1831 Bry, 1839 *TA*.   NEW HOUSES, 1831 Bry.   SNAB WOOD, cf. *Snab Pits & Lane* 1831 Bry, (*Great*) *Snab*, *Snab Plantation* 1839 *TA*, 'the hill', *v.* snabbe.

FIELD-NAMES

The undated forms are 1839 *TA* 282. Of the others, 1626, 1711 are Sheaf, 1817 *EnclA*, 1831 Bry.

(*a*) Black Hey (*v.* blæc, (ge)hæg); Blackwell (*v.* blæc, wella); Brook Green (*v.* brōc, grēne²); Brotherin; Camberloons (this might contain either land 'a selion', or furlang 'a furlong', cf. Lamper Loons 243 *infra*); Cate Gree; Clammer Hey (cf. dial. *clame* 'to bedaub'); Clane, Clanes (probably from clǣg 'clay', with an -en adj. suffix); Colliery Green (cf.

Wirral Colliery 226 *infra*); Corn Hill Gap (*v.* corn[1], hyll, gap); Cross Green
& Heath (*v.* cros); Cumbo, Cumboes; Great & Little Dale (Hey) (*v.* deill);
Flashes Lane 1831 (*v.* flasshe); Furrocks; Health Hornes (*v.* Elthorns 212
supra); Hollin Grave Hey (*the Hollen Green Hey* 1626, *the Hollingreave Hey*
1711, 'enclosure at a holly wood' *v.* holegn, grǣfe, (ge)hæg. *Green* is pro-
bably a reading of *grene* by mistake for *greue*); Hook Hey (*v.* hōc, (ge)hæg);
Lampits (*v.* lām, pytt); Lightfoots Green & Mdw (from the surname
Lightfoot which also appears in *Lightfotes Poole* 1547 *v.* Old Quay 225 *infra*);
Little Stile (*v.* stigel); Long Ditch; Loonons (perhaps loning 'a lane, a
right-of-way'); Mare Hey & Mdw, Mares (*v.* mere[1] or (ge)mǣre or mere[2]);
Marled Hey(s) (*v.* (ge)hæg); Mill Hill, Millen Heys (cf. *Mill Lane* 1831,
v. myln, lane, hyll, (ge) hæg); (Long) Moor; Moor Hey (*v.* mōr[1], (ge)hæg);
Neathert; Palace Hey ('palisaded enclosure', *v.* palis, (ge)hæg); Pingo
(*v.* pingel); Pit Dale 1831 (*v.* pytt, deill); Preestons Fd (perhaps from a
surname, but as this field is not far from Denhall Ho *supra*, it may be a
late formation from prēost and tūn, toun); (Middle & Nearer) Sich Hey
(*the Sitch Heys* 1817, *v.* sīc, (ge)hæg); Souns Croft (probably from ME
sond(e) 'sand', *v.* sand); Stablin Hey; Stone Drill; Stripe (*v.* strīp); Stud
Fold (*v.* stōd-fald); Townsend (*v.* toun, ende[1]); Wood Head (*v.* hēafod).

4. GREAT NESTON (109–2977), as for Great- & Little Neston *infra*,
distinguished as *Magna-* 1300–7 *JRC et freq, Mikel-*, 1318 *AddCh
et freq* with variant spelling *Mukel-, Mykul-* to *Mykulneston* 1426
Orm[2], *Grett-* 1521 Sheaf, *Great-* 1553 Pat, *Neston Village* c.1536
Leland, *Neston Market* 1750 Sheaf, 'the greater or more important
part of Neston', i.e., the hamlet with the church, *v.* magna, micel,
mikill, grēat, village, market.

GREAT & LITTLE NESTON [ˈnestən, ˈnessn̩]

> *Nestone* 1086 DB, *Nestuna* 1096–1101 (1150), 1150 Chest, *Nestona*
> 1096–1101 (1280) ib *et freq* ib to c.1310, *Neston* 1096–1101 (17)
> ib, 1130–50 (1285) ib, Ch *et freq*, (*-in Wyrhal*) 1258 Chest,
> (*-infra portum civitatem Cestrie*) 1477 Morris, *Nesston* 1348
> Sheaf, 1581 Cre, 1663 Sheaf
>
> *Neeston* 1338 (1357) *ChFor*
>
> *Naston* 1351 BPR (p)
>
> *Newston* 1560 Sheaf
>
> *Nesson* 1596 AD, 1671 Sheaf *et freq* ib with variant spellings
> *Nes(s)on, Nesen* to 1723
>
> *Neason* 1674 Sheaf, 1677 Hem

'Farm or enclosure at the Ness', or 'farm belonging to the village
of Ness', from tūn and ness, næss (cf. Burton Point 212 *supra*) or

tūn prefixed by the p.n. Ness 220 *supra*. Cf. Little Neston 225 *infra*. Some of the forms suggest also OE nesu (neosu), ME nese (neose) 'the nose', figuratively 'a headland, a promontory'.

ASHFIELD COTTAGES, HALL, HOUSE & LODGE (109–2979), 1831 Bry, *Asshefeld* 1342 ChRR (p), *-felde* 1353 ChFor, *Ashefield* 1569 Sheaf, *Ashfield* 1661 ib, 'open land near ash-trees', v. æsc, feld.

HINDERTON (BROW, HALL & RD) (109–305780), *Hinder-town* 1621 (1656) Sheaf, *Hinderton* 1831 Bry, cf. Hinderton Lodge 226 *infra*. The form *Hynderton* 1336 Plea (DKR XXVIII 31) appears to be an error for *Kynderton*, Kinderton 2 236. The p.n. means 'the part of the village which lies more to the back, the hinder part of the town', from hinder (cf. ON *hindri* adj) and toun, with (ge)hæg, feld, brū, hall. Hinderton Rd, in this and Little Neston townships, was *Chester Lane* 1831 Bry, named from Chester 336 *infra*. There were other Hindertons at 258, 302 *infra*.

PARKGATE (109–2778), 1707 Sheaf *et freq*, the name of a settlement which grew up to cater for the passenger traffic to Ireland (as also, no doubt, did the local girl Emma who became Lady Hamilton), and the eighteenth-century novelty of sea-bathing. Gastrell notes 'some houses upon the Water-side in Great Neston are called *Park Gates*' 1724 NotCestr. The name was taken from (*the*) *Parkgate* 1610 DepEx, 1690 Sheaf, an entrance to NESTON PARK (lost), *parcum de Neston(a)* c.1258 Chest, 1350 Chamb, *the Parke of Grett Neston* 1521 Sheaf, *Neston Park* 1569 ib, cf. f.ns. *Park, Park Head, Parkers Hey, Parks* 1854 *TA*, *The Parks* 1878 Sheaf, a group of thirteen fields about 109–285785, v. park, geat, hēafod, (ge)hæg.

THE BIRCHES (a wood), 1845 *TA*. BROADLAKE, *Broad Lake Cottage* 1831 Bry, 'broad watercourse', v. brād, lacu. CHERRY FM, cf. *Cherry Lane* 229 *infra*. CLAYHILL COTTAGES, cf. *Clay Hill Croft & Field* 1845 *TA*, v. clæg, hyll. DENHALL GUTTER, *Parkgate Deep* 1842 OS, a channel in the Dee estuary, now silted up, formerly *Denwale Rode* c.1536 Leland, an anchorage of the port of Chester off Denhall 220 *supra* and Parkgate *supra*, v. dēope, goter, rād. FIVE LANE ENDS, *Five Lanes End* 1831 Bry. THE HERMITAGE, 1831 ib. HIGHFIELD HO. KEMNAY COTTAGE. LEIGHTON COURT, cf. Leighton 218 *supra*. LIVERPOOL RD

leading towards Birkenhead 313 *infra*, for Liverpool La.   MANOR
HO, 1831 Bry.   MOORSIDE, *Moor Side* (*Nook*) 1831 ib, *v.* mōr[1],
sīde, nōk.   MOSTYN HO, named from Mostyn Fl.   NEW FM.
OVERDALE, cf. (*Little*) *Overdale* 1845 *TA*, 'the higher allotment', *v.*
uferra, deill.   PARK VIEW, cf. Parkgate *supra*.   THE QUAY (at
Parkgate), 1831 Bry, *Neston Key* 1690 Sheaf, *v.* key, cf. Old Quay
225 *infra*.   RABY PARK, *v.* park, cf. Raby 228 *infra*.   RABY RD,
Raby Rake 1845 *TA*, 'lane leading to Raby', *v.* rake, cf. prec.
UPLANDHOUSE, 1842 OS, *School Lane End* 1831 Bry.   WINDLE
HILL (109–3177), 1831 ib, a district in Great & Little Neston
townships, *v.* 225 *infra*.   WOOD LANE, 1831 ib, cf. 219 *supra*.

FIELD-NAMES

The undated forms are 1845 *TA* 283. Of the others, 1347 is *ChFor* (p),
1610 *DepEx*, 1677 Hem, 1724 NotCestr, 1831 Bry, and the rest Sheaf.

(*a*) Alder Graves ('alder woods', *v.* alor, grǣfe, cf. Eldergraves *infra*);
Backsides (*v.* ba(c)ksyde); Blacky Lane 1831; Bloody Hill Fd; Bowling
Green Croft; Brandlooms ('burnt selions', *v.* brende[2], land); Brewhouse
Croft, Brew House Mdw (cf. 'the deep water below *the Brewhouse*' 1677
Hem II 306, an anchorage of the port of Chester near Neston, *v.* brew-hous);
Brick Kiln Fd; Brow Fd (*v.* brū); Charrington Moor; Church Fd (cf.
Churchlands 1724, *v.* cirice, land); (The) Common (Fd) (cf. *Common Lane*
1831); Crooked Heys (*v.* croked, (ge)hæg); Dirty Lane 1831; Douglas
Hurst (a group of fields, 100–301797, *Dogleshurst* 1569 Sheaf[3] 20, *v.* hyrst,
first el. obscure); Drury Lane Fd (perhaps 'love lane', a courting place,
v. druerie, but this is at Parkgate and may be a fashionable borrowing from
the London st.n.); Eldergraves, Elder Greaves ('elder woods', *v.* ellern,
grǣfe, cf. Alder Graves *supra*); The Field; Flag Fd (*v.* flagge); Folly Fd
(*v.* folie); Four Lane Ends; Headless Cross (three fields at 109–288789,
near the boundary of Leighton township, perhaps an old boundary cross,
v. hēafod-lēas, cros); Higher Well; Holmes Heys (from (ge)hæg and either
holmr or the surname *Holme*); Hook Hey (*v.* hōc, (ge)hæg); The Intack,
-Intake (*v.* inntak); Leighton Fd (cf. Leighton 218 *supra*); Lidgate (*v.* hlid-
geat); Marl Fd; Marled Hey; Marsh Fd; Mill Brow, Croft, Fd, Hay, Hill
& Mdw (cf. *Neston Mills* 1831, *Wind Mill* 1847 *TAMap*, *Old Windmill* 6″
OS); (The) Moor; New Hay(s) (*v.* nīwe, (ge)hæg); Nook (*v.* nōk); Old
Mill Brow (*v.* ald, myln, brū); Ouler Mdw (*v.* alor); The Pykes ('the sharp-
cornered field(s)', *v.* pīc[1], cf. Pykes Weint (st.n.) 1899 Sheaf[3] 3, from
(ge)wind[2], dial. *wint* 'a winding path or alley'); (The) Quillet (*v.* quillet(t));
Raby Fd (cf. Raby 228 *infra*); Rope Walk Fd; Rylands Fds (*v.* rye-land);
(The) School Fd (*v.* scōl); Shoemakers Croft; Sich Mdw, Sitch Croft
(*v.* sīc); Smithy Hays (*v.* (ge)hæg); Sniglane Mdw (*v.* snygge, lane); Sour
Flatt (*v.* sūr, flat); Spring Fd (cf. *Spring Field House* 1845, *v.* spring 'a well-
spring'); Stoney Hill; Stub(b)s Hey (perhaps from stubb); Three Nooks

(cf. three-nooked); Tinkers Croft (*v.* tink(l)ere); Town Fd (*the-* 1724); Water Rains, Wet Rains (*v.* wæter, wēt, rein); Willaston Hay (*v.* (ge)hæg, cf. Willaston 232 *infra*).

(*b*) *Cokshots* 1522 (*v.* cocc-scyte); *the Customs House* 1610 (the customs post of the port of Chester at Denhall roads); *Neston Bridge* 1621 (*v.* brycg); *Radecliff* 1347 (p) ('red cliff', *v.* rēad, clif, perhaps from 'The Red Bank' in Thurstaston 281 *infra*).

5. LITTLE NESTON CUM HARGRAVE, *Parva Neston et Haregrave in Wyrhale* 1353 Plea *et freq* with variant spellings as for Little Neston *infra*, Hargrave *infra* to *Little Neston cum Hargr(e)ave* 1819 Orm².

i. LITTLE NESTON (109–2976), as for Great *&* Little Neston 222 *supra*, and *Parua-* 1278 ChFor *et freq*, (*-in Wirrall*) 1397 ChRR, *Littel-* 1347 ChFor *et freq* with variant spellings *Li(t)te(l)l-*, *Lytle-*, *Lytel-*, *-yl-*, *-ul-*, *Lityl-*, *Littill-*, *Little-*, 'the smaller part of Neston', *v.* lȳtel, lítill, parua, cf. Great Neston 222 *supra*.

THE LYDIATE (109–318783), *le Lydegate* 1350 *Eyre*, *le Lydeyate* 1354 *ib*, *Lydiate House & Lane* 1831 Bry, *Lydiate* 1842 OS (a hamlet here and in Willaston township), cf. (*Big & Little*) *Lidget(s)* 1845 *TA*, *the Great-* *& -Little Liddiat* 1711 Sheaf, 'the swing-gate', *v.* hlid-geat, cf. 233 *infra*.

OLD QUAY (109–286767), 1831 Bry, cf. *Old Key Meadow, Old Quay Croft & Garden* 1845 *TA*, the site of *a newe haven at Lightfotes Poole* 1547 Morris 460, *a new key in Wirrall upon the River Dee* 1551 ib, *the new(e) haven (of Chester water)* 1567, 1576, 1588 ib, *the New Key* 1569 (1656) Orm², 1572 Sheaf, 1608 Morris, 1656 Orm², *New Key (in Worrall)* 1586 Morris 87, c.1590 Sheaf, *New Kay* 1690 Sheaf, which was superseded by the quay at Parkgate 223 *supra*, as R. Dee silted up, *v.* ald, nīwe, key. The silting of the Dee estuary made navigation to Chester itself so difficult by 1574 that it was necessary to provide port facilities at the roads off Denhall and Neston (*Denwale Rode, Neston Rode* c.1536 Leland) cf. Hem II 303, Morris 460. At Old Quay was *the Key House* 1711, 1750 Sheaf, *v.* key, hūs. *Lightfotes Poole* would be a creek or channel in the estuary, *v.* pōl¹, named after some person with the surname *Lightfoot*, as in Lightfoots Green 222 *supra* in Ness, the adjacent township.

WINDLE HILL (109–313775), 1728 Sheaf, *Windhul* 1259 Court (p), *Wyndhull* 1286 ChFor (p), *Wyndhull* 1318 *Eyre* (p), *Wyndell* 1400

ChRR (p), 1612 Sheaf³ 7 (1441), 'windy hill', v. wind, hyll, cf. 224 supra. It was the Wind Milne Hill 1626 Sheaf, site of molendinum de Parua Neston 1340 ChFor, v. wind-mylne, hyll.

BANKHEY (HO), cf. Bank Heys 1845 TA, -Hayes 1626 Sheaf, the Great- & Little Bank Hey 1711 ib, 'enclosures at a bank', v. banke, (ge)hæg, cf. Wirrall Colliery infra.   THE FLAXYARD, cf. Flax Yards 1845 TA, the Flax Yard 1626 Sheaf, 'enclosure where flax is grown', v. fleax, geard, cf. Mason's Yard infra.   GORSTONS, on Gorsey Lane 1831 Bry, cf. Gorsty Hey, Gorston (freq) 1845 TA, 'gorsey enclosure', v. gorst, tūn, gorstig.   HALLFIELD, cf. (Little) Hall Field 1845 TA, the Little Hall Field 1626 Sheaf, the Little Half Field, the two Half Fields, the Longhall Field 1711 ib, probably named from a mease place called the hall of Lytyll Neston 1523 Orm², v. hall, feld.   HANNS HALL (COTTAGES), Hands Hall 1831 Bry, cf. Hands Hey 1845 TA.   Perhaps named from a finger-post at the crossroads near Lydiate.   HINDERTON (LODGE & RD), Hinderton Lodge, Chester Lane 1831 Bry, cf. Hinderton Meadow 1845 TA, v. 223 supra.   SOD HALL (lost, 109–313782), 1842 OS, probably a house built with turf nogging, v. sodde.   STAPLANDS. STONYCROFT.   UNDERHILLS (a house), cf. Underhill(s) infra, v. under, hyll.   WEATHERSTONES (a house), cf. Weathertons infra. WIRRAL COLLIERY, Denna Coal Works 1831 Bry, Denna Colliery 1842 OS, cf. Denhall 220 supra, and '. . . a share of the farm of coal to be raised out of the closes called the Bank Heys' 1768 Sheaf³ 27 (6077), cf. Bankhey supra.   WOODPARK.

FIELD-NAMES

The undated forms are 1845 TA 284. Of the others 1347, 1357 are ChFor, 1831 Bry, and the rest Sheaf.

(a) Acres; Backside (v. ba(c)ksyde); Badger But(t); Brunshing Heath (cf. Brunchion Heath Lane 1831 Bry, 109–321792 to 327787); Clayley Hey(s) (v. clǣg, lēah, (ge)hæg); Coppy (v. copis); Crickett Flatt (the Lower Cricketts Flatts, the old Crickett's Flatt Hey 1626, the Cricketts Flats 1683, v. flat. The first el. is either cricket 'a cricket', or cricket 'the game of cricket'); Cross Lane Croft (cf. Cross Lane 1831 (109–293764 to 293768), 'lane running across', v. cros); Cuckoo Hey (v. cuccu, (ge)hæg, cf. Cuckoo Lane 1831, also Padmans Way infra); Dam Head Lane 1831 (on the Willaston boundary, cf. 233 infra); Ditchey Hey (cf. lane called The Ditch Way 1626, 'road beside a ditch', v. dīc, weg); Eldergreave ('elder wood', v. ellern, grǣfe); The Fernice Pitt 1711 (v. forneis, pytt); Flatt Heath (v. flatr);

Flint Mdw (*the-* 1626, 1711, *v.* flint); Fluke; Greenow, Grina Hey (probably 'green hill', from grēne¹ and hōh); Guinea Croft; Heath Heys (*the-* 1626, 1711, *v.* hǣð, (ge)hæg); Holt (*the-* 1683, *v.* holt, cf. Nessholt 221 *supra*); Hooks (*v.* hōc); Horse Pool; Killhoons ('kiln loons', *v.* cyln, land); Knife and Fork Fd; the Knowy Wood 1711 (*the Knowle Wood* 1683, *v.* cnoll, -ig³, wudu); Mallocks, Mallock(s) Croft; Masons Yard, Mason Yard Croft (*a little hemp yard called Mason's Croft* 1626, from geard and the surname *Mason*); Mere Loons & Mdw, (Gorsty & Ness) Meres (*the Meare Meadow* 1683, *the Mere Meadow, Great & Little Meares* 1711, *v.* (ge)mǣre); Milky Hey (*the Milcoe Hey* 1683); Mill Fd, Hey & Hill (cf. *Mill Lane* 1831, *v.* myln); the Mickle Moor Mdw 1711 (cf. *the Moor Heys* 1626, *v.* mikill, mōr¹, mǣd, (ge)hæg); Nessfield, Ness Heath Common (*v.* hǣð, cf. Ness 220 *supra*); the Oat Part 1711 (*v.* āte, part); Oval Croft; Ox Pasture; Oxton Garden (cf. Oxton 269 *infra*); Paddock Pools (*v.* padduc, pōl¹); Padmans Way Fd (cf. *Padmans Way* 1831 (109–313775 to 310773), also *Cuckoo Lane* 1831, cf. Cuckoo Hey *supra*, *v.* weg. The first el. may be the surname *Patman*, but a *padman* would have been 'one who uses footpaths' possibly 'a footpad'); Pike Heyes (*v.* pīc¹, (ge)hæg); Rake Ends (*v.* rake, ende¹); Rye Croft & Hey (*v.* ryge, croft, (ge)hæg); Sand Fd (*the-* 1711); Sich Fd (*v.* sīc); Sour Milk Mdw; Stone Stupes (*the Stone Stoope* 1711, 'stone post or pillar', *v.* stān, stolpi); Town Fd; Underhill (near Windle Hill *supra*, giving name to a house, *v.* under, hyll); Vicars Hey (*the Vicar's Hey* 1626); Wastefield (*v.* waste); Weathertons (*Whetherstone* 1683, *the Whetherton* 1711, a group of fields about 109–318773 and giving name to a house, probably the same as *Wethredoun* 1309 Sheaf³ 25 in Willaston 234 *infra*. The p.n. would be 'wether's hill, hill where wethers graze', *v.* weðer, dūn); The Welsbys Mdw 1711 (*Wellsbyes Croft* held by Robert *Wellesbye* 1626 Sheaf³ 27); Woefy (a group of fields about 109–310770; *the great-, higher-* & *Lower Woolfeall-, -Woolfeale Hey* 1626, *the Great Woefall Hey* 1683, *the Great-, Little Wofall* 1711, *Woefy Lane* 1831, apparently 'wolf corner', from wulf and halh (dat.sg. hale)); Wood Croft, Wood Part Common (cf. *boscus de Parua Neston* 1347 *a close called the Wood* 1626, *the Great-* & *Little Wood, the Wood Meadow* 1711, *Wood Lane* 1831, *v.* wudu).

(b) le Bruche 1357 (an assart, *v.* bryce); *Loon(e)s Wood* 1626 ('wood at the selions', *v.* land, wudu, probably old arable afforested).

ii. BLAKELEY BROW & HARGREAVE 1845 *TA* 55, two detached parts of Little Neston township, in Raby township, collectively called *Neston-Raby* 1459 ChRR (DKR xxxvii 676), i.e. 'part of Raby belonging to Neston', *v.* foll., Hargrave 228 *infra*.

BLAKELEY BROW (109–335808) [ˈbleikli], (-*Farm*) 1845 *TA*, *Blakely* 1831 Bry, *Bleaky Brow* 1842 OS, *Brow Lane* 1831 Bry, 'hill-side at a dark clearing', *v.* blæc, lēah, brū. cf. Blakeley *infra*, Raby Hall Rd 229 *infra*.

HARGRAVE (HALL & LANE) (109–328796)

> *Haregrave* 1086 DB, 1305 Chest, (-*in Wirral*) 1330 Pat, *Haregreue*
> 13 *AddCh* (p), -*greve* 1313 Plea (p) *et freq* to 1521 ib, (-*in
> Wirhale*) 1315 Adl, (*Parva Neston et-*) 1353 Plea
> *Hargreue* 1304 Chamb (p) *et freq* with variant spelling -*greve* to
> 1602 Orm², (*Litel-Neston et-*) 1431 ChRR, *Hargreave* (*in
> Wyrhal*) 1316 ib, *Hargreave* 1724 NotCestr, (*Little Neston cum-*)
> 1819 Orm², *Hargrave* 1432 ChRR (*Litelneston et-*), 1724
> NotCestr, 1819 Orm², (-*Hall & Lane*) 1831 Bry
> *Harregreve* (*Little Neston cum-*) 1499 ChRR, 1507 Orm²
> *Hergreave* 1620 Orm²

'The hoar wood', from hār² and grǣfe, with hall and lane.
Hargrave was a manor in the same hands as Little Neston, TRE
and 1086. hār is probably used here in the sense 'boundary', hence
'the boundary wood', cf. Raby 229 *infra*. Boundary marks and
territory would tend to be left undisturbed for fear of trespass, and
an unbroken wood or an untouched boundary stone would grow
mossy, venerable and 'hoary' with age. Cf. Hargrave Cottages, etc.
229 *infra*. *v.* Addenda.

FIELD-NAMES

The forms are from 1845 *TA* 55. Fields of Blakeley Brow are marked by
an asterisk.

(a) Backside* (*v.* ba(c)ksyde); Blakeley (*v.* Blakeley Brow *supra*); Lower,
Middle & Top Branna (cf. Branner(s) 229 *infra*); Fowl Parts (*v.* fūl, part);
Heath Grounds (*v.* hǣð); Leechs (*v.* lece); Orrids Hay (from (ge)hæg
and the surname *Orred*); Outlet* (*v.* outlet); Ox Pasture; Piladall (*v.*
Pellerdale 229 *infra*. Professor Sørensen would claim *Piladall* as a Danish
f.n.); Poulton Mdw (cf. Poulton 250 *infra*); Second Gate*, Third Gat
Field* (*v.* gata 'a pasture-gate').

6. RABY, RABY HALL (FM), -HOUSE (FM) & -MILL (109–310798)
[reibi]

> *Rabie* 1086 DB, *Raby* 1096–1101 (1280) Chest *et freq* with variant
> spellings *Rabi(e)*, *Raby in Wyrhale* 1377 Plea, *Raby Mill* 1831
> Bry, -*Watermill* 1842 OS
> *Rabbi* 1150 Chest
> *Robi* 1208–11 Chest (p), *Roby* 1321 City (p)
> *Reaby* 1663 Sheaf

'Village at a boundary', from rá and býr, Meer Hey *infra* and cf. Roby La 113, Raby Cu 292, NbDu 161. This p.n. suggests the confines of a Scandinavian enclave in Wirral, *v.* Thingwall 273 *infra*, cf. Hargrave 228 *supra*. For the form *Neston-Raby* 1459 ChRR, cf. Blakeley Brow & Hargreave 227 *supra*.

BANK COTTAGE. BENTY HEATH LANE (109–335794 to 345782), 1831 Bry, cf. *vastum de Raby* 1340 ChFor, *v.* benty, hǣð, cf. 191 *supra*, 233 *infra*. BROMBOROUGH NEW BRIDGE, *New Bridge* 1831 Bry, *Bromborrow Bridge* 1843 *TA*, on the boundary of Bromborough 237 *infra*. FOUR LANES END, *Four Lane Ends* 1831 Bry. HARGRAVE COTTAGES, HARGRAVEHOUSE FM, *Hargrave (House Farm)* 1831 Bry, *v.* dæl[1], Hargrave 228 *supra*, cf. foll. PLYMYARD DALE, *Hargrave Dale* 1843 *TA*, the boundary with Eastham township, *v.* prec., and Plymyard (Dale) 187 *supra*. RABY HALL RD, *Brow Lane* 1831 Bry, leading to Blakeley Brow 227 *supra*. RABY MERE, *Mill Dam* 1843 *TA*, *v.* damme, mere[1], cf. foll. and Raby Mill *supra*. RABY MERE RD, *Water Mill Lane* 1831 Bry, cf. prec., *v.* water-milne. WILLOWBROW FM, *Willow Brow* 1831 ib, *v.* wilig, brū.

FIELD-NAMES

The undated forms are 1843 *TA* 333; 1831 is Bry.

(a) Blakeley Brow (*v.* 227 *supra*); Bramfield Hey (*v.* brōm, feld, (ge)hæg); Branner(s) (cf. Branna 228 *supra*, Brandhurst 247 *infra*); Brunchion Heath Lane 1831 (*v.* Brunshing Heath 226 *supra*); Burton Hey (cf. *Burton Lane* 1831, cf. Burton 211 *supra*); Cherry Lane 1831 (cf. Cherry Fm 223 *supra*); Cinder Hey (*v.* sinder, (ge)hæg); Cock Fd; Common Lane 1831; Cutfield Hey; Dale Hey (*v.* deill); Dam Fd; (*v.* damme); Dirty Land 1831; Dolly Wells Lane 1831 (*v.* 231 *infra*); Flatt Hey (*v.* flat or flatr, (ge)hæg); Follies; Grass Ground (-s 1831); Kirkett Hey (on the road to Great Neston, 'enclosure near a church-way', from kirkja and gata, with (ge)hæg); Ladies Garden; Laking; Long Shoot (*v.* scēat); Meer Hey (109–313793, 'enclosure at a boundary', *v.* (ge)mǣre, (ge)hæg); Mill Hill; Musk Fd; Neston Mdw (cf. Little Neston 225 *supra*); Old Heads (*v.* hēafod); Pellerdale (Sheaf[3] 25 (5753) connects this with *Piledale* 1309 loc. cit., a place in the boundary of Willaston and Little Neston, cf. Piladall 228 *supra*. The name is probably 'willow valley', from ON píll and dalr); Pingles (*v.* pingel); Rake Hey (*v.* rake, (ge)hæg); Rye Hey (*v.* ryge, (ge)hæg); Rye Shed; Sandy Hole Lane 1831; Short Parts (*v.* part); Slackey Fd (*v.* slakki, (ge)hæg); Stack Hey (*v.* stakkr, (ge)hæg); Thornton Dale (1831, *v.* dæl[1], cf. Thornton Hough, Dale Hey 230, 231 *infra*); Three Lane Ends 1831; Twizzle Hey (*v.* twisla, (ge)hæg).

7. THORNTON HOUGH (109–3080) [ˈþɔrntən ˈʌf]

Torintone 1086 DB, *Torinton* e13 Bark, *Torrinton* e14 *JRC* (p),
Thorinton c.1235 *Chol* (p), 1254 P (p), 1268 Bark (p), 1277 P (p),
-tone 1252 RBE (p), *Thorrinton* c.1280 Sheaf (p), *T(h)orenton*
1276 P, 1287 Court (p), *Thurhinton* 1290–1327 *AddCh* (p)

Thornton 1260 Court (p) *et freq* with variant spelling *Thorne-*
(1288 Court (p) to 1624 ChRR), *Thornton in Wyrhale* 1301
Chamb[1]

Matheue Thornton 1287 Court, *Thorneton Maheu* 1307 Plea *et freq*
with variant spellings *Thorn(e)ton-*, *Matheu-* (1360 BPR),
-Maheu (1329 Plea, 1357 *ChFor*), *-Mayeu* (1347 *ChFor*), *-Mayo*
(1385 *ChFor*, 1418 Orm[2], 1513 Plea, 1624 ChRR), *-Mayow*
(1397 ChRR, 1483, 1656 Orm[2]), *-Mayowe* (1409 ChRR, 1421
Orm[2], 1437, 1483 ChRR, 1507 *MinAcct*), *-May* (1579 *Dep*),
-Mayes (1831 Bry), *Thornton Mayowe in Wyrehale* 1409 ChRR

Thorneton Graunge 1415 ChRR, 1422 Orm[2], *grangia de
Thornton in Wirehale* 1465 *AddCh*, *Thornton Grange* 1579 *Dep*
(*Thornton May alias-*), 1585 Orm[2] *et freq*, *Thorneton Grange*
1620 ib

Thorneton Hough 1624 ChRR (*Thorneton Mayo alias-*), *Thornton
Hough or Thornton Mayes* 1831 Bry, *Thornton Hough* 1842 OS

'Thorn-tree farm', v. þorn, þyrne, tūn. Basingwerk abbey Fl,
had a grange here until 1465 *AddCh* 6278, cf. Thornton Grange and
Little Grange *infra*. The manorial affixes are the Christian name
of *Mathew* (OFr *Mahieu*, v. *Mayowse* 3 29) de Thornton tenant here
c.1252 and the surname *Hough* (cf. Hough 3 64) of the family of
Richard *del Hogh* c.1329 Orm[2] II 549.

BRIDGES HO, 1831 Bry, v. brycg. BROOK FM. CLATTER
BRIDGE, CLATTERBRIDGE FM, *Clatter Bridge* 1831 Bry, *Claterbrugge*
1396 *Most* (a bridge), cf. (*Great*) *Clatterbridge* 1843 *TA*, and Clatterbridge Workhouse (252 *infra*) 1842 OS. Bryant's map 1831 shows
Clatter Bridge, a bridge, and *Clatter Bridge*, a hamlet, at the boundary
of Thornton Hough and Poulton cum Spital, cf. 252 *infra*. The p.n.
is probably 'noisy bridge', from ME *clater* 'clatter, noise', but it
could mean 'causeway of loose stones or rubble', from clæter, v.
brycg. COPLEY HO, cf. *Copley Hills* 1843 *TA*, probably '(mounds
at) a clearing with mounds or embankments', from copp and lēah,
with hyll. CROFTS BANK, v. croft. THE FOXES. LITTLE

GRANGE (lost, 109–313819), 1842 OS, *Grange Head* 1831 Bry, *Grange Head House* 1843 *TA*, 'the top end of-, the lesser part of Thornton Grange', *v.* grange, hēafod, lȳtel, cf. Thornton Grange *infra*. HESKETH GRANGE, no early forms observed, perhaps from the La surname *Hesketh*, cf. Hesketh 265 *infra*. LODGE FM, *v.* loge. MANOR HO & WOOD. MERE BROOK HO, 'house at a boundary brook', *v.* (ge)mǣre, brōc. NEW HALL, 1831 Bry. PARK COTTAGES. RABY VALE, cf. Raby 228 *supra*. STAN-ACRES, 1843 *TA*, 'stony fields', *v.* stān, æcer. THORNTON COMMON RD, (*High*) *Heath Lane, Thornton Heath* 1831 Bry, *Higher Heath, Heath Croft & Ground* 1843 *TA*, *v.* hǣð, commun. THORNTON COTTAGE, HALL & HO, cf. Thornton Hough *supra*. THORNTON GRANGE, 1831 Bry, cf. *Thorneton Graunge* 1415 ChRR, Little Grange *supra*, and (*Big*) *Grange, Grange Hay* 1843 *TA*, *v.* grange, (ge)hæg, cf. Thornton Hough *supra*. THORNTON LODGE, 1831 Bry, *v.* loge. WILLOW FM. WIRRAL MANOR HO.

FIELD-NAMES

The undated forms are 1843 *TA* 392. Of the others 1398 is *Add*, 1831 Bry, 1842 OS.

(*a*) Acre Hey, Acres (*The Acres* 1831, cf. *Acre Brook* 1831 joining Dibbinsdale Brook 251 *infra*, *v.* æcer); Backside (*v.* ba(c)ksyde); Barley Lane; Barn Hey (*v.* (ge)hæg); Berriers Hey; Black Acre; Blind Pit Heys (*v.* blind, pytt); Bloens; Brick Kiln Fd; Brook Fd & Mdw; Calves Hey (*v.* (ge)hæg); Cel Yard; Cockbutt Fd (*v.* butte, cf. foll.); Cocklow ('hillock', *v.* cocc¹, hlāw, cf. prec.); Coney Grue (*v.* coningre); Corner Fd; The Croft; Crofty Nook (*v.* croft, -ig³); Cross Lane 1831 (*v.* cros); Dale Hey, Mdw & Quarters (cf. *Thornton Dale* 1831, and 229 *supra*); Dolly Wells Lane 1831 (109–305807 to 303798, cf. 229 *supra*); Drakelows ('dragon mounds', *v.* draca, hlāw, cf. *Dracclowelegh* 250 *infra*, Drakelow 2 198); Gostill(s), -ylls ('gorse hills', *v.* gorst, hyll); Horse Stiles (cf. *Hall Style Lane* 1831, *v.* hall, stigel); Intack (cf. *Intake Lane* 1831, *v.* inntak); Ladies Hey (*v.* hlǣfdige (ge)hæg); Lands (*v.* land); Long Hip; Long Looms (*v.* land); Long Part (*v.* part); Mare Lane 1831; Marsh Mdw; Mere Hey; Milking Bank (*v.* milking); Mill Brow & Hay, -Hey (cf. foll., *v.* myln, brū, (ge)hæg); Mill House Lane 1831 (cf. prec.); Moat Mdw (*v.* mote); Money Pits (*v.* manig, pytt); Mutlow (a group of four fields, about 109–297813, cf. Mutler 236 *infra*, *v.* (ge)mōt, hlāw); Neston Hay, -Hey (*v.* (ge)hæg, cf. Neston 222 *supra*); Nook Hey; Paviours Hay (near an old quarry); Peel Hey (*v.* pēl); Pike Hey (*v.* pīc¹); Raby Side (*v.* sīde, cf. Raby 228 *supra*); Rake Hey (*v.* rake, (ge)hæg); Rough; Rough Hey & Pools (*v.* rūh, (ge)hæg, pōl); Rue Ditch (from rūh and dīc or edisc); Ruloe Hay, -Hey ('enclosure at a rough hillock', *v.* rūh, hlāw, (ge)hæg); Towns(h)end ('the end of the village', *v.* toun, ende¹, cf. *the Endes infra*); Wall Fd (*v.* wælla); West Fd; Whiskitt Hull; Yolk of the Egg (*v.* 337 *infra*).

(*b*) *the Endes* 1398 ('the end pieces of land', *v.* ende¹, cf. Towns(h)end *supra*).

8. WILLASTON (GRANGE & HO) (109–329775) [ˈwiləstən]

Wylaveston 1230 (1580) Sheaf
Wilaston 1286 *ChFor et freq* with variant spellings *Wy-*, *Wilaston*(*a*) to *Wilaston* 1512 Plea, (*-iuxta Parva Neston*) 1313 ib, *Willaston* 1481 Pat *et freq*, (*Wollaston alias-*) 1580 Cre, (*in Wirrall*) 1640 ChRR, *Wyllaston* 1484 Pat, *Williston* 1663 Sheaf
Wiliaston 1341 ChRR
Welaston 1344 *ChGaol*, *Wellaston* 1539–47 Dugd
Walaston 1500 Orm², 1507 *MinAcct*
Wollaston 1546 Dugd *et freq* with variant spellings *Wollos-*, *Wolles-*, *Woolas-*, *Woollaston* to 1860 White, (*-alias Willaston*) 1580 Cre, (*Willaston alias-*) 1652 Sheaf, (*Willaston or*) *Wollaston* 1860 White
Wyllysan 1560 (1582) ChRR

'Wīglāf's farm', from tūn and the OE pers.n. *Wīglāf*. The place is first mentioned in 1230, but it gave name to the DB hundred of *Wilaveston*, *v.* Wirral Hundred 167 *supra*, cf. foll. It adjoins Little Neston 225 *supra*. The affix *-in Wirral* distinguishes it from Willaston 3 78.

HADLOW RD (109–326763 to 330775), HADLOW WOOD (109–327767), [ˈhadlou] older local [ˈadlə], *the three Adlowes* 1688 Sheaf, *The Alders* 1789 ib, *Hadlow Lane* 1831 Bry, 1842 OS, (*The*) *Adler* 1843 *TA* (*freq*), a group of fields and a road which probably carry the p.n. *Edelaue* 1086 DB f.263b, cf. Tait 113 and xiii. The identification was made by W. Fergusson Irvine in 1893, who suggested this was the meeting-place of *Wilaveston* hundred, cf. prec. and Wirral Hundred 167 *supra*. *Edelaue* is 'Ēada's mound', from hlāw and the OE pers.n. *Ēada*, a pet-form for one of the OE pers.ns. in *Ēad-*.

STREET HEY (109–338785), *the Straitway Hey Meadow* 1688 Sheaf, *Streety Hey Lane* 1831 Bry, *Street Hay* 1843 *TA*, 'enclosure on the street-way', from strǣt and weg, with (ge)hæg, on the line of (*le*)*Blakestret*(*e*) 198 *supra* and 1 39 (Route III), 330.

WILLASTON MILL (109–327784), 1831 Bry, cf. *Mill Croft, Field &*
Hey 1843 *TA, the Milne Hey* 1688 Sheaf, *Mill Croft* 1789 ib, *v.*
myln, (ge)hæg, croft. Hereabouts was a place *Midlethrinlowe* 1309
Sheaf[3] 25, (a mill built at) *Trymelowe* 1321 ib 18, 'at (the middle one
of) the three mounds', *v.* middel, þrēo (dat. þrim), hlāw. In Sheaf[3]
26 (5762) *Midlethrinlowe* is located about two hundred yards north
of Willaston Mill, which may be the mill mentioned in 1321.

BADGER'S RAKE, 1842 OS, *Badger Rake* 1831 Bry, *v.* 215 *supra.*
BENTY HEATH LANE, 1831 ib, cf. 191, 229 *supra* and *Benty Heath
Field, Bentley-* 1843 *TA*, 'grassy heath', *v.* beonet, benty, hǣð.
CHESTER RD, cf. *Chester Road Field*, etc., 1843 *TA*, the Chester-West
Kirby road, cf. foll., and *Porteswaye infra.*   DAM HEAD LANE
(lost, 109–319770 to 320780), 1831 Bry, cf. (*Little*) *Dam Head Field*
1843 *TA*, 'the source of a mill-stream', *v.* damme, hēafod. This
lane is the boundary of Willaston and Little Neston townships. It
joins Chester Rd at 109–319770, 'the ancient burial place in the
Porteswaye of a man who was beheaded, being the place where the
bounds of Willaston, Ness and Little Neston join' 1309 *Plea*,
Sheaf[3] 25 (5753), cf. ib[3] 26 (5762), and *le Crosseveye, Portesweye
infra.*   FERN BANK, cf. *Fearn Heath Lane* 1831 Bry.   HALL
WOOD (COTTAGES), *Hall Wood or Hullets Hall* 1831 Bry, *Hall Wood*
1842 OS, 'wood at or belonging to a hall', *v.* hall, wudu. The
alternative, derogatory, name is 'owlet's hall', *v.* howlet.   HEATH
HEY, cf. *Heathy Lane* 1831 Bry, *Heath Hay, -Hey* 1843 *TA*, 'heath
enclosure', *v.* hǣð, (ge)hæg.   JACK'S WOOD.   LYDIATE (lost,
109–324783), 1842 OS, a hamlet near The Lydiate 225 *supra*, cf.
Lidget Croft & Field 1843 *TA*, *v.* hlid-geat.   MILL LANE, cf.
Willaston Mill *supra.*   OLD HALL, 1842 OS, *Willaston Hall* 1831
Bry.   SEIDLOOM HO, cf. *Seed Looms* 1843 *TA*, 'wide selions', *v.*
sīd, land, loom.

FIELD-NAMES

The undated forms are 1843 *TA* 432. Of the others 1305 (14) is Chest,
1309 *Plea* and Sheaf[3] 25, 1831 Bry, and the rest Sheaf.

(*a*) The Accors (*the Ackers* 1688, *v.* æcer); Adfalent (perhaps 'top
furlong', from hēafod, furlang); Asp Hey; Badger Butt (*v.* butte); Bridge
Fd; Calf Croft; Cawmore Hey (cf. *Cawmer Heath* 1688, *the Columber Heath*
1652, probably 'lumpy or rocky heath', from hǣð and dial. *clumber*, cf.
clympre, and *clumper* EDD); Change; Damage (*v.* demming); Edwardes
Fd, The Edwardses, Further-, Little-, Long Edwardses (*the two Edwards's*
1688, *The Edwards'* 1789, from the pers.n. *Edward*); The Ellams; Ferny

Heise (*v.* (ge)hæg or hǣs); Flash(es) Mdw (*v.* flasshe); Fox Holes (cf. *Fox Holes Lane* 1831, *v.* fox-hol); Goose Pasture; Hollin Greave (*v.* holegn, grǣfe); Hurt Hey; Intake (*v.* inntak); (Big & Little) Knowl (*the Cnow* 1688, cf. *Knowl Pits* 1831, *v.* cnoll); Ladies Hay, -Hey (*v.* hlǣfdige); The Lands (*v.* land); Marled Hey; Ness Acre (cf. Ness 220 *supra*); New Hey, -Hay (*the New Hey* 1688, *v.* (ge)hæg, cf. foll.); Newel Lane Croft (cf. *New Hey Lane* 1831, *v.* prec.); Outlet (*v.* outlet); Ox Hey (*v.* (ge)hæg); Pasture Hay (*v.* (ge)hæg); Pavement Fd (109–335774; *v.* pavement); Porter Hay (cf. *le Port(es)waye infra*, Portersheath 119 *supra*, *v.* port-weg, (ge)hæg); Rake End & Hey (*v.* rake, ende¹, (ge)hæg); Scotchman's Fd; Skins; Smith Fd (cf. *Smithy Lane* 1831); Stan(s)field (*v.* stān, feld); Stanleys Dale (*v.* deill); Stockage Fd (from stocc 'a tree-stock', and the ME collective suffix -age as in *Thornage* 191 *supra*); Three Nooks (cf. three-nooked, *v.* 337 *infra*); Tied Looms; Town Field (*The-* 1789); Turnpike Croft & Fd (*v.* turnepike, cf. *Willaston Toll Bar* 1831 Bry); Two Tails; Wall Croft (*the-* 1688, *v.* wælla); Widow Dale, Widows, Widow's (Hey) (*the Widdow Dales, the Widness Hey* 1688, 'the widow's allotments', probably dower land, *v.* widuwe, deill); Wood Fd.

(b) *le Crosseveye* 1309 ('road running athwart', *v.* cros, weg, a road crossing *le Port(es)waye infra*, on the boundary of Willaston and Little Neston, perhaps Dam Head Lane *supra*); *le Harestane* 1309 ('the hoar stone', *v.* hār², stān, a boundary stone between Willaston and Little Neston); *ducta de Lecherichewalledale* 1309 (a watercourse, 'the valley of the spring at the mound', from cruc¹ (PrWelsh *crŭg > OE *cric), and wælla, with dæl¹, with the def.art. le-); *Mickeldale* 1309 ('big valley', *v.* micel, mikill, dæl¹, dalr); *Piledale* 1309 (*v.* pill, dæl¹, dalr, cf. Pellerdale 229 *supra*); *(le) Port(es)waye* 1309 (*v.* port-weg, cf. 1 39 (Route II), Chester Rd, Dam Head Lane *supra*); *Richardston le Reve* 1309 ('Richard the Reeve's stone', a boundary stone between Willaston and Little Neston, *v.* stān); *(le) Stokuuelsiche* 1305 (14) (('watercourse at) the stock-well', *v.* stocc-welle, sīc); *Uilkynstane* 1309 ('Wilkin's stone', a boundary stone between Willaston and Little Neston, from stān and the ME pers.n. *Wilkin*, dimin. of *William*); *Wethredoun* 1309 (*v.* weðer, dūn, cf. Weathertons 227 *supra*)

xiv. Bromborough

The parish of Bromborough anciently included Eastham parish, *v.* 187 *supra*, and Bromborough 237 *infra*. After about 1152, when Eastham chapelry was created, the parish of Bromborough consisted of 1. Brimstage, 2. Bromborough, both now included in Bebington Municipal Borough (*v.* 245 *infra*).

1. BRIMSTAGE (HALL) (109–3082) [ˈbrimstidʒ]

Brunestaþe 13 AddCh, *Brunstath* 1260 Court (p) *et freq* with variant spellings -*stath(e)*, -*stat* to 1819 Orm², (-*in Wyral*) 13

Whall, (*-stathe alias Brynston*) 1555 Orm[2], (*-stath alias Brunston*)
1579 *Dep*, (*-stath or-*, *-commonly called Brimstage*) 1819 Orm[2],
the hall of Brunstath 1819 ib
Brimstache 1275 Ipm (IpmR reads *Brenefathe*), 1278 ib (*Brunstahe*
IpmR)
Bronstathe l13 Bark, *-stath* 1348 *ChGaol*, *Bronestath* 1343 Bark
Brunstach 1326 ChRR (p), *-statch* 1340 *ChFor*
Bromstache 1335 Pat, (15) *Mont*
Bromstah 1335 (15) *Mont*
Brounstat' 1343 *AddCh*
Brimstath 1351 BPR, 1396 *Most*, 1521 Plea
Brynstat c.1387 (l15) Sheaf[3] 36 (p), *-stath* 1395 (p), 1408 ChRR
(p), l15 Orm[2], 1521 Plea, 1524 ChRR, *Brinstath* 1459, 1592
Orm[2]
Burnstache 1400 ChRR
Brynstaph 1511 ChRR
Brunstaph 1511 ChRR
Brymstath 1549 Orm[2]
Brymstaghe 1616 ChRR, *Brimstage* 1647 Sheaf, 1724 NotCestr,
(*Brunstath commonly called-*) 1819 Orm[2], *Brimstage Hall* 1831
Bry
Brinstage 1637 *Dep*
Brimsage (*Hall*) 1742 NotCestr

This must be OE (*æt*) *Brūnan stæþe* 'Brūna's river-bank', from
stæþ 'frontage along a stream, land along the bank of a stream',with
the same OE pers.n., Brūna, as in Bromborough 237 *infra*, cf.
Brimston infra. In fact, the same person may be involved, giving
his name to a settlement at Bromborough and to part of his estate
three miles away at Brimstage, a detached part of the same parish.
The meaning of *stæþ* 'a landing-place' is improbable here for the
smallness of the water at Brimstage, which is inland, cf. DEPN s.n.
The normal development of the first el. is represented by *Brun(e)-*,
Bron(e)-, *Brom(e)-*, cf. Bromborough loc. cit., the other forms being
due to the influence of the cognate OE pers.n. *Brȳni*, to scribal
confusions of *Brun-* and *Brim-*, or to the occasional change *u > i* as in
Dinnington YW 7 88, cf. Dutton 2 112. The normal development of
the final el. is represented by *-stath(e)*, *-stat*, *-staph*, and *-stah*, the
others being spelling pronunciations from scribal confusions of *-c-*
and *-t-* in *-stath(e)*, *-stach(e)*.

BRIMSTON (lost)

Brynston 1534–47 Dugd, 1535 VE, 1537 Orm², m16 *AOMB* 397,
    1555 Orm² (*Brunstathe alias-*), *-stone* 1547 *MinAcct, Bryneston*
    1554 ib, *Brinston* 1566, 1567, 1579, 1595, 1673 Sheaf, (*-and*
    Brinston Parke) 1579 ib, *-stone* 1621 (1656) Orm²
Burneston 1539–47 Orm² 1 275 (lit. *-sto'*)
Bronston 1564 Sheaf
Brunston (*park of Brunstath alias-*) 1579 *Dep, Brunstoe* 1646
    Sheaf³ 50 (? for *-stone*)
Brimston 1739 *LRMB* 264

This was used as an alternative name for Brimstage *supra*. It is
probably the origin of the surname *Brunston* 1291–1323 Chest, 1398,
1407 ChRR, *Brunstan* 1418 ib, *Brynston* 1410 ib. It is 'Brūna's
stone', from stān and the same OE pers.n. *Brūna* as in Brimstage
supra, Bromborough 236 *infra*. No doubt the same man is involved,
the *stæþ* and the *stān* at Brimstage may have been the limits of his
territory. The park was about Brimstage Green *infra*, at 109–305819
adjacent to the boundary of Thornton Hough 230 *supra*.

BRIMSTAGE BRIDGE & LANE.   NEW FM.   PEARTREE HO, 1831
Bry.   WHITEHOUSE LANE, *White House Lane* 1831 ib, cf. Whitehouse 263 *infra*.

FIELD-NAMES

The undated forms are 1840 *TA* 72. Of the others, 1278, 1357 are *ChFor*,
1343 *AddCh*, 1398 *Add*, 1831 Bry.

(a) The Acres (cf. *Acre Lane* 1831, *v.* æcer); Back Side (*v.* ba(c)ksyde);
Brimstage Green (*The Green* 1831, 109–305819, approximate location of
the park of *Brimston supra*, *v.* grēne²); Church Ground; Clay Pit Hey;
Commock Croft; (Little) Common; Coppies, Coppy, Copy Rough (*v.*
copis); Dale Hey; Diglakes (*v.* dīc, lacu); The Flat; Gilberts Ends (*v.* ende¹);
Gorsty Hey (*v.* gorstig, (ge)hæg); Grey Thorn(s); (Lower) Heath, Heath Fd
(cf. *la brouere de Brounstat'* 1343, *vastum de Brunstath* 1357, *v.* hǣð);
Hook(e)s (*v.* hōc); Leave Lands; Meads (*v.* mǣd); Mill Hey, Mill Way
(cf. *Mill House or Thatched Hall* 1831 (109–300818) and *unum molendinum*
1278, *v.* myln, (ge)hæg, weg, hūs); Mutler (sixteen fields about 109–302822,
probably associated with Mutlow 231 *supra*, in the adjacent township of
Thornton Hough, and probably with *Motelowe* 1398 (p) the surname of a
person appearing at Bromborough, 'moot-hill', *v.* (ge)mōt, hlāw, cf. 338
infra); Old Orchard; Ox Pasture; Paddock Hey & Moor (*v.* pearroc,
(ge)hæg); Corn-, Gibbons-, Peas-, Wilkinsons Park (*v.* park, cf. *Brimston*

supra); Pikes (*v.* pīc[1]); Rake Ends, Rake Shute (*Rake Ends* 1831, *v.* rake, ende[1], scēat); Roundsill(s) (*The Rondsills* 1831, a group of fields at 109–295833, cf. the adjacent Ransel 256 *infra*); Silly Pit Croft; The Sitch (*v.* sīc); Slacket Hey; Storeton, Storeton-, Stourton Fd (cf. Storeton 253 *infra*); Thirst, Thrust; Thornton Fd (cf. Thornton Hough 230 *supra*); Town Fd; Way Butt ('head-land bearing a right-of-way', *v.* weg, butte); White Leys (*v.* lēah); Upper Yards (*v.* geard).

2. BROMBOROUGH (109–3482) [ˈbrɔmbərə] locally [ˈbrumbərə]

> *Brunburg* 1100–35 (1285) Ch, 1155 (1285) Chest, 1278 Sheaf, *-burch* e13 *JRC*, (17) Chest, 13 (p), e14 *JRC* (p), *-burh* 1214–22 Chest, 1217–30 *JRC*, *-burgh* 13 Orm[2], 1330 *Vern* (p) *et freq* to 1421 Bark (p), *Brunnburh* 1356 *Eyre*
>
> *Bruneburgh* 1153 (1285) Chest, *-bur'* 1291 Court (p)
>
> *Brumburg'* 1153 (1280) Chest, (1300) Pat *et freq* with variant spellings *-burg*, *-burgh(e)*, *-bur(h)*, *-brugh* to *Brumburgh* 1535 VE, *Brumburth in Wiral* 1297 (15) Werb (s.a. 1284)
>
> *Brombur'* 1153–9 Chest *et freq* ib to 1305–23, *-burth* 1221 (17) ib, 1347 *ChGaol*, *-burg* c.1232 (1307) *Eyre et freq* with variant spellings *-b'*, *-buru*, *-burgh* (1308 Pat to 1474 ChRR), *-burogh*, *-burg(e)* to *Brumburgh* 1474 ChRR, *-burough* 1558–79 ChancP
>
> *Brumboreh* c.1200 Bark (p), *-brough* 1237 (17) Chest, 1610 Sheaf, 1656 Orm[2], *-brogh* 14 Chest, c.1538 *JRC*, *-borgh* c.1310 Chest, *-boro* 1504 ChRR (p), *-borowe* 1552 Sheaf (p), 1615 Orm[2], *-borrow* 1664 *JRC*, *-brow* 1579 Dugd, 1694 Sheaf, *-bro* 1579 Dugd, 1692 Sheaf
>
> *Brunbrock* 1214–22 (17) Chest
>
> *Broneburgh'* 1260 Court (p), *Bronburgh* 1657 *Clif*
>
> *Brumbergh* 1277 Sheaf, *-ber* 1286 *ChFor*
>
> *Bromborough* 1277 Cl, Pat, Fine, 1415 ChRR, 1558–79 ChancP *et freq* with variant spellings *-boroughe* to *Bromborough* 1831 Bry, *Bromborw*, *-borth* 1291 Tax, 1348 *ChGaol*, *-borht* 1297 *Port* (p), *-borogh* 1534–47 Dugd, *-borow(e)* 1539–47, 1541 Dugd *et freq* to *Bromborow* 1840 *TAMap* 75, *Brombroe* 1549 Sheaf, *-bro* 1579 Dugd, *-broghet* 1549 Sheaf, *-brough(e)* 1560 ChRR *et freq* with variant spelling *-brugh* to *Brombrough* 1724 NotCestr, *-brow(e)* 1565, 1619 Cre, 1579 Dugd, *-brorow(e)* 1579 ib
>
> *Brounburg'* (lit. *Bromiburg*) 1297 *Port* (p), *Brounburgh* 1398 *Add*, *Brownborowe* 1550 Pat
>
> *Braumburgh* 1315 Plea (p), *Brambrowe* 1610 Sheaf
>
> *Brunnburh* 1356 *Eyre*

Bromeburgh 1367 *JRC*, *-borrow* 1541 Dugd
Bumbrough 1658 Sheaf
Brumbara 1676 Sheaf

'Bruna's stronghold', from the OE pers.n. *Brūna* and **burh**, cf.
Burton 3 270, Brimstage, *Brimston* 234, 236 *supra*. The *burh* may
have been at Court Ho *infra*. The etymology in DEPN, '*burh* where
broom grows', from **brōm**, will not do on the evidence of the forms,
cf. Brimstage loc. cit. Bromborough is probably the *Brunanburh*
near which Athelstān defeated a great invasion of Norsemen and
Scots in 937 at the battle celebrated in heroic verse in ASC, *v.*
LMS 1 i 56, Sagabook XIV 303, Sheaf[3] 32 (7227), Campbell *Brunanburh* 57–80. The place-names *Brunanburh* and Bromborough are
identical. The places may not be. The best arguments for the
identity of the two places are presented in LMS and Sagabook, *loc.
cit.* Against their identity, one circumstance is that the battlefield is
referred to by many names, not all synonymous with *Brunanburh* nor
otherwise recorded as p.ns. in the Bromborough district, cf. LMS 1 i
56 n.2, Campbell *loc. cit.*, E & P II 141. The names of the battlefield in ASC are (*ymbe*) *Brun(n)anburh* (A), (*ymbe*) *Brunanburh* (D),
(*embe*) *Brunnanburh* (C), (*to*) *Brunanbyrig* (E), (*to, in*) *Brunan byri*
(F), and this tradition is followed by *in loco qui dicitur Brunanburh*
FW (c.1118), SD (c.1130), and the *Brunebirih* of *Flores Historiarum*
(cf. LMS *loc. cit.*). These forms suit Bromborough. SD 1 76 names
the battlefield *apud Weondune quod alio nomine Etbrunnanwerc vel
Brunnanbyrig appelatur*. The forms *Etbrunnanwerc* (OE *æt Brūnan
(ge)weorce*, 'at Brūna's fortification') and *Bruneswerce* 12 Gaimar have
suggested Burnswark in Dumfriesshire, the only other proposed
site for which a strong case can be made out on the basis of p.n.
forms. However, the *-werc(e)* forms are no more than a paraphase of
Brunanburh (**burh** replaced by the almost synonymous (**ge**)**weorc**)
and they would suit Bromborough as well as Burnswark. In the
p.ns. of the Bromborough district there is no trace of the alternative
names of the battlefield, *Weondune* c.1130 SD ('holy hill', *v.* **wēoh**[2],
wēoh DEPN, **dūn**), *Brunandune* 975–998 Æthelweard ('Brūna's
hill', *v.* **dūn**), *Brunefeld* 12 WM ('Brūna's tract of country', *v.* **feld**,
cf. *Bruningafeld* BCS 713, 727 (*v.* **-ingas**), also *Brunfort* Liber de
Hyda, which may be a form of *Brunfeld*, if not 'Brūna's ford', from
ford). The forms quoted in LMS *loc. cit.*, from Welsh chronicles,
Brune (c.1100, c.1460), *Brun* (c.1380), *Brunawc* (c.1380), *Brynner*

(c.1470), arise from the first el. of *Brunanburh* treated as a simplex p.n. (cf. **bryn** 'a hill'). The ON name *Vinheiði við Vinuskóga* in *Egils Saga Skallagrimssonar* is shown by Campbell to be irrelevant to geography. The non-appearance of certain alternative names for *Brunanburh* in the Wirral area does not disqualify Bromborough from identification with the battlefield. There is evidence which suggests that before 1086 Bromborough was the capital of an extensive tract of country, cf. Brimstage, *Brimston* 234, 236 *supra*. The parish of Bromborough anciently included Eastham parish, *v.* 187 *supra*, and perhaps also Bidston parish 307 *infra*. The ecclesiastical parish of Eastham, created as a chapelry of Bromborough c.1152, coincides with and represents a division of the earl of Chester's great DB manor of Eastham (held by Earl Edwin TRE). The DB manor of Eastham would seem to have included the territory of Whitby, Brimstage, Oxton, Tranmere, Bidston, Birkenhead, Claughton, Moreton, Saughall Massie, Great Stanney, Stanlow, Eastham, Bromborough, Childer Thornton (probably) and perhaps also Higher Bebington and Netherpool, *v.* Orm[2] ii 407, 405, 430, Tait iii, LCHS NS xv 21–5. As late as 1291, Orm[2] *loc. cit.* and Tax, Eastham was a chapel of Bromborough, 'ecclesia de Bromboro' cum capella de Eastham', cf. Chest i 129–130. Although Bromborough is not named in DB, it is to be supposed that it was the seat of the priest supported by the DB comital manor of Eastham, of whose later divisions Bromborough parish church long continued to be the mother church and Bromborough Court the manor house. As Bromborough was originally the parish church of the DB manor of Eastham, and as the ecclesiastical and manorial organisations correspond so clearly in their division as to suggest original identity, it might plausibly be inferred that Bromborough's parish ought to have been co-extensive with the manorial territory and to have included also the territory of Bidston parish. It is quite possible that the battle was named either after several localities in one large district, or after a district which had several names, or after a place whose name was repeatedly paraphased, and it should be noted that although the alternative names *Brunandune*, *Brunefeld* and *Brunfort*, which have as first element the OE pers.n. *Brūna*, do not appear among Wirral p.ns., analogous ones do, at Brimstage and *Brimston*, in Bromborough parish itself.

Another circumstance arguing against the identification of Bromborough and the battlefield is that Florence of Worcester places the invasion, defeated at *Brunanburh*, as a landing in Humber, cf. Saga-book XIV 314, but this may well be irrelevant, *op. cit.* 315 and n.48, as the point of re-embarkation need not be near that of landing.

A third argument against Bromborough is that there is no evidence about the identity of *Dingesmere* ASC (A, C, variant spellings *Dinnesmere*, *Dyngesmere*, *Dynigesmere*) the water over which the defeated Norsemen fled from *Brunanburh* to Dublin. If it were dis-covered that this was a name for the Irish Sea, then Bromborough's claim could be emphasised further. As it happens, the sea-name *Dingesmere*, a poetical nonce-word, analyzes into **mere**[1] 'a lake, a mere' and here, in a poetic text, 'the sea', with the gen.sg. of a proper name **Ding*. An attempt was made in LCHS CXIX 2 n.11 to explain this as a sg. *-ing* formation from the r.n. Dee 1 21, OE **Dē-ing* contracted to **Ding*, meaning 'that which is called after Dee, the Dee water, the sea into which the Dee flows' (*v.* **-ing**[2]). However, OE **Dē-ing* would contract to **Deng* rather than **Ding*, and the poem-text is too early for the late OE, eME change *-eng* > *-ing*, so this attempt cannot be maintained.

The identification of Bromborough with *Bremesburh* 909 ASC (D), 910 ASC (C), probably Bromesberrow (near Ledbury) He or Bromsberrow Gl, is discounted, and with it the tradition of Æþelflæd's foundation c.915 of a monastery at Bromborough, *v.* Sheaf[3] 19 (4582), Orm[2] II 427, Dugd VI 1616, Gl 3 166.

ALLPORT LANE & RD, THE ALLPORTS, cf. *Hawput Common* 1831 Bry, *Allport* (*freq*), (*Little*) *Allport Croft* 1839 *TA*. The meaning of this p.n. is uncertain. It may be 'old market', *v.* **ald**, **port**, alluding to some market or route to a market, along *le-, la Brodeway* 1407 *JRC*, 'the broad way', *v.* **brād**, **weg**, described as leading from Brom-borough to Plymyard 187 *supra*, i.e. Allport Lane.

BROMBOROUGH MILLS, 1831 Bry, *Brombrogh Milnes* 1536 Sheaf, *molendinum de Bromburgh* 1313 Chest, *-Brounburgh* 1398 *Add*, probably 'the mill or mills built or to be built in lands in Poulton and Bebington beyond *le Pul* in *Pultondale*' 1291–1323 Chest II 689 n.1, *v.* **myln**, cf. Bromborough Pool *infra*, Poulton cum Spital 250 *infra*. These mills give name to *le Mulneway* 1412 *JRC*, 'the way to the mill', *v.* **weg**, cf. *The Mylne Haye* 1610 Sheaf, *Mill Hay, -Marsh & -Pool*, (*Big & Little*) *Mill Field* 1839 *TA*, *v.* (ge)**hæg**, **mersc**, **pōl**[1], **feld**.

BROMBOROUGH POOL (109–3484), 1842 OS, cf. *le Pul* 1274–80, 1291–1323 Chest, *le Pull* 1313 ib, referring to Dibbinsdale Brook *infra* at Poulton Bridge 252 *infra* and Bromborough Mills *supra*, and to Bromborough Pool at Bromborough Pool Bridge *infra*, 'the creek', *v.* pull.

COURT HO (109–345842), *The-* 1842 OS, *Court Hall* 1831 Bry, *the manor called Bromborowe Corte* 1539–47 Dugd, *Bromborough Court* (lit. *Crom-*) 1583 Orm[2] ii 521, *Brambrowe-, Brumbrough Courte* 1610 Sheaf, *Brumborowe or Brombroughe Courte* 1615 Orm[2], cf. Cart Lane (*le Courteway* 1412) *infra*, 'the court-house', *v.* court. This is the moated site of the manor house of the abbots of St Werburgh, Chester, the capital of their manors of Bromborough and Eastham, cf. 239 *supra*. It is described in 1819 as 'occupying an extremely strong position at the neck of land, accessible only from the south, to the east it is defended by the estuary, on the other sides by precipitous banks descending to an inlet which forms a channel between this parish and Bebington' Orm[2] ii 428. There was an earthwork about this site enclosing nine acres which could well be the burh from which Bromborough *supra* is named.

RICE WOOD (109–353838), 1831 Bry, *Welondriȝ* 1347 ChFor, (*boscus de*) *Welondrys* 1357 *ib*, *Welandrys* 1432 Rental, *Wellandryse* 1440 *ib*, *The Wyllenrice or William Drife* 1615 Orm[2] ii 428, cf. Sheaf[3] 29 (6463), *The Rice* (*Wood*) 1839 *TA*, from hrīs 'brushwood'. The first el. appears to be the OG pers.n. *Weland* (Feilitzen 411, Forssner 250), but OE *Wēland* is possible, perhaps after the mythological Wayland Smith, son of Wade (OE *Wada*).

SHODWELL (lost, 109–362825), 1842 OS, *Shod Well* 1831 Bry, a fishing hamlet beside R. Mersey of which only a ruined cottage and a limekiln remained in 1924 (letter to Allen Mawer from R. Stewart Brown), apparently from the p.n. *Shotehale* recorded in *le Holghshotehale* and *le Shot vocat' le Holghshotehalefeld* 1412 *JRC*. *Shotehale* is 'corner of land in a nook or hollow', from scēata and halh, and the *shot* would be a scēat(a) (ME, ModEdial. *shot*) 'a division of a field, a piece of ground', called 'the low-lying part-, the low-lying field-, of *Shotehale*', *v.* holh.

WARGRAVES (109–357831), 1877 Orm² ii 427n., *Wergreaves* 1839
TA, a field supposed the site of the battle of *Brunanburh*. The anti-
quity of the name is not known. The Rev. Mr Green, incumbent at
Bromborough, who informed Helsby (Orm²), obviously supposed
it an old f.n., from ME *werre* 'war', and **græf** 'a grave, a digging'.
There is another example of this f.n., *Wargreaves* 1838 *TA* 404 in
Tushingham cum Grindley 49 *supra*. The final el. is **græfe** 'a wood'.
The first el. is probably ME **werre** (ModEdial. *war*, cf. ON *verri*)
adj., 'worse, the less valuable'. Professor Sørensen points out a
Danish parallel in the common Funen p.n. *Elved* (ON *illviði*) 'bad
wood, wood of no value'. The name is not evidence for a battlefield.

WOOD LANE (lost, 109–350824 to 355827), 1831 Bry, cf. *le Wodforlong*
1412 *JRC* and *Wood Clints, -End & -Hay, Woods Meadow* 1839 *TA*,
named from *boscus de Brumburgh(e)* 1347, 1357 *ChFor, Brumburgh
Wode* 1348 Sheaf, *Bromborough Woode* 1551 ib, *v.* **wudu, furlang,
klint.**

BROMBOROUGH HALL (lost), 1724 NotCestr, also called *Manor Farm*
1941 Sheaf³ 36 (7915), demolished in 1930, cf. Sheaf *loc. cit.*
BROMBOROUGH NEW BRIDGE, *v.* 229 *supra*, cf. foll.   BROMBOROUGH
POOL BRIDGE, *Brumbrough Bridge* 1621 Sheaf, *Bromborough Bridge*
1819 Orm², *v.* **brycg**, cf. Bromborough Pool *supra*.   CART LANE
(lost, 109–345841 to 350825), 1831 Bry, *via vocata la Courteway*
1412 *JRC*, cf. *Cartway Croft & Field, Cartways* 1839 *TA*, 'the way
to the Court', *v.* **court, weg**, cf. Court Ho *supra*. This old road was
superseded by New Chester Rd *infra*.   NEW & OLD CHESTER RD,
the road to Chester, the latter a modern turnpike, cf. prec.   COW-
PASTURE WOOD, cf. *Cow Pasture* 1839 *TA*.   DEVIL'S BANK, a bank
in the Mersey estuary.   DIBBINSDALE BROOK, LODGE & RD, cf.
Dibbinsdale Rough 1839 *TA*, Poulton Bridge *infra*, *v.* 251 *infra*.
EASTHAM SANDS, a sand-bank in the Mersey estuary, *v.* Eastham 187
supra.   THE GREEN, *v.* **grēne²**.   LITTLE HEY, cf. *Little Hay* 1839
TA, *v.* **(ge)hæg**.   THE MARFORDS, cf. *The Marford, Marford
Wood, Gleggs Marford* 1839 *TA*, *v.* Mareford 253 *infra*. *Glegg* is a
notable surname in Wirral.   MARK RAKE, a road, *v.* **rake** 'a
narrow lane'.   MEADOWHOUSE, 1831 Bry.   OAKLEIGH, appa-
rently a modern house-name not connected with Richard son of
John *de Okelegh* 1353 (1378) Ch (*v.* **āc, lēah**) who gave land in
Bromborough to St Werburgh's abbey, Chester.   OAK WOOD,

Oaks Wood 1831 Bry.   POULTON BRIDGE, *Dibinsdale Bridge* 1842
OS, *v.* 252 *infra*, cf. Dibbinsdale *supra*.   THE RAKE, RAKEHOUSE,
(The) Rake House 1831 Bry, 1842 OS, 'the lane', *v.* **rake**, cf. Mark
Rake *supra*.   ST PATRICK'S WELL (109–346829), associated with a
local legend that St Patrick visited this district, *v.* Sheaf[3] 27 (6023).
SHORE WOOD, 'wood by the sea-shore', *v.* **scor(a)**.   SLACK WOOD,
'wood at a hollow', *v.* **slakki**.   STANHOPE HO, 1944 Sheaf[3] 39
(8450). 'Since c.1900 this is the name of what was formerly *Spann's*
Tenement, a seventeenth-century building' Sheaf *loc. cit.*, *the*
Spanne property 1882 Orm[2] II 429, named from the *Spann* family,
landholders here from the fifteenth to nineteenth centuries, *v.*
tenement.   TILE YARD COTTAGE, *v.* **tile-yard**.   WETCROFT
LANE, cf. *Whatecroft* 1412 *JRC*, *Wet Croft* 1839 *TA*, 'wheat croft',
v. **hwǣte, croft**.   WOODLANDS, *Lime Grove* 1831 Bry.

FIELD-NAMES

The undated forms are 1839 *TA* 75. Of the others, 1265–91 is Chest, 1357
ChFor, 1398 *Add*, 1407, 1412 *JRC*, 1432, 1440 *Rental*, 1610, 1789 Sheaf,
1831 Bry.

(*a*) (The) Acre; Acre Lane Croft (cf. *Acre Lane* 1831, *v.* **æcer, lane**);
Acre Slack Wd (*Acre Slack* 1831, *v.* **æcer, slakki**); Balls Rough; Bank Fd,
Bank ((*le*) *Bonkefeld* 1432, 1440, cf. *le Bonkefurlong* 1432, *v.* **banke, feld,
furlang**); Bean Acre; Bradmoor (*v.* **brād, mōr**[1]); Bromborrow Mdw (cf.
le Medewcrofte 1398, *le Medowefeld* 1432, *the little meadowe, the longe meadowe*
1610, *v.* **mǣd, croft, feld**); The Brows (*v.* **brū**); The Butteries; Church Fd
(cf. (*le*) *Chirchecroft* 1265–91, 1432, -*crofte* 1440, *v.* **cirice, croft**); Clay Hills;
The Clints (cf. Wood Lane *supra*, 'the rocky banks', *v.* **klint**); Corn Hill
(*v.* **corn**[1]); Cuckoo Hay; The Cunney Grove (*The Conegree* 1610, *v.*
coningre); The Cupboard; Dale Cross Hay (-*Hey* 1789, 'enclosure lying
athwart, at a valley', *v.* **dæl**[1], **cros, (ge)hæg**, cf. foll.); Dale Hill Mdw *&*
Rough (cf. *Dale Hills* 1831, 'slopes at a valley', *v.* **dæl**[1], **hyll**, cf. Dibbinsdale
supra); Does Acre (*v.* **dāl**); Flash Fd *v.* **flasshe**); Flatts (*v.* **flat**); Gorsty Hay
(*v.* **gorstig, (ge)hæg**); Goss Hills (*v.* **gorst**); Green Hay (*The Greene Haye*
1610, *v.* **grēne**[1], **(ge)hæg**); The Hale(s) (*v.* **halh**); Hearth Stones (*v.* **herth-
ston**); Far-, Higher-, Lower Heath (cf. *le heth* 1412, *the Heath Close* 1610,
v. **hǣð, clos**); Intake (*v.* **inntak**); Johnsons Hay (*Joynsons Haye* 1610, *v.*
(ge)hæg); Big- *&* Little Lady Hay (*the twoo Ladye Hayes* 1610, *v.* **hlǣfdige,
(ge)hæg**); Lamper Loons (from **lang** or **lām** with **furlang**, or from **lamb**
with **furlang** or **land**, cf. Lamperloon 253 *infra*); Lawn Park (*v.* **launde,
park**); (The) Leeches (*v.* **lece**); Lime Fd (*v.* **lim**); Lodge Park; Marl Hayes
(*v.* **(ge)hæg**); Morrow Fd (*Moraldefeld, le Morewallefeld* 1412, cf. *Morwey*
1432, '(field at) the marsh spring', 'way to a marsh', *v.* **mōr**[1], **wælla, weg,
feld**); New Fd (cf. *le New(e)feld* 1412, 1432, *v.* **feld**); New Hay, Little New
Hayfield (cf. *the Great & Little Newe Hay(e)* 1610, *v.* **(ge)hæg**); Normans

Hay (from Norðmann, nān mann or the pers.n. *Norman*); North and South Fd (*v.* 337 *infra*); Ollerheads Croft (perhaps from a surname, but a p.n. 'alder head or hill' is possible, from alor and hēafod); Ox Pasture (formerly *The Knowle* 1610 Sheaf³ 29 (6463), *v.* cnoll); Plimyard Croft (cf. Plymyard 187 *supra*); Poolton Lane End, Poolton Mdw (*Poolton Meadow* 1789, cf. Poulton cum Spital 250 *infra*); Round Orchard; The Saighs (*v.* sǣge (EPN, more correctly sǣg ERN 284) 'a swamp, a marsh', or cf. foll.); Big Sea Fd, Little Sea Hay (*the Great-, the Little Say Hay* 1610, *v.* sǣ, (ge)hǣg, or cf. prec.); Shows Dows (final el. dāl, dole); Shearns (*v.* scearn); Shepherds Hay (cf. *the Great- & the Little Shep(h)eards Feilde* 1610, *v.* scēap-hirde); Shooters Moor (*Shitterresmore* 1412, *Shotersmore alias dict' Morefeld* 1432, 1440, cf. *Shotersfeld* 1432, 'shooter's marsh otherwise marsh field', and 'shooter's field', *v.* scēotere, mōr¹, feld); Short Butt Hay (cf *Shortebuttes* 1412, *v.* sc(e)ort, butte); Stores Croft; Town End, Townsend; Town Field Crofts; Tunster Hay (perhaps from tūn-stall 'site of a farmyard'); Tuthills (*v.* tōt-hyll); The Warrens (*v.* wareine); White Fd.

(b) *Bemfurlong* 1398, *le Beneforlong* 1412, *Benfurlong* 1440 ('furlong where beans are grown', *v.* bēan, furlang); *Blackhurstcroft* 1610 ('(croft at) the dark wood or hill', *v.* blæc, hyrst, croft); *Blackepole Croft* 1610 ('(croft at) the dark pool', *v.* blæc, pōl¹, croft); (*le Ouer-, le Nether-*) *Crowethorn* 1412, *Crowethorne* 1432 ('crow's thorn-tree', from crāwe and þorn, with uferra and neoðera); *le Daynegreuesway* 1412 ('the way to *Daynegreue* ('the dairymaids' copse'), *v.* dǣge (gen.pl. dǣgena), grǣfe, weg); *le Ellengreuehallond* 1412 (a selion in *le Newefeld infra*, '(the head-land at) the elder grove', *v.* ellen, grǣfe, hēafod-land); *le Fyssheyordeway* 1412 ('(the road to) the fish trap', *v.* fisc-geard, weg); *Fysshwalhull* 1357 ('(hill near) the fish pool', *v.* fisc, wælla, hyll); *les Gorstybuttes* 1432 ('gorsey selions', *v.* gorstig, butte); *le Heghlefeld* 1412 ('(field at) the high clearing', *v.* hēah, lēah, feld); *Hondeponnesfeld* 1412 (*v. Lylleponne infra*); *Kermynchamhadlond* 1412 (from hēafod-land and the surname of its tenant John *Kermyncham*, cf. Kermincham 2 281); *Lathegestfeld* 1412 (an unusual f.n., apparently 'unwelcome visitor's field', from OE lāð, ON leiðr 'unpleasant, hateful', and OE gest, ON gestr 'a stranger, a traveller, a visitor', with feld. Professor Sørensen suggests that *Lathegest* may represent an ON pers.n. *Leiðgestr* ('the unwelcome visitor') analogous with the ON pers.n. *Leiðulfr* ('the unwelcome wolf')); *Loselowe* 1407 (the name of 'a certain little hillock', probably 'mound at a pig-sty', from hlōse and hlāw, analogous with Lowsay Cu 279, from haugr, and Lose Hill Db 121 from hyll); *le Lylleponne* 1412 ('the little pan', *v.* lȳtel, panne. With this should be taken *Hondeponnesfeld supra*, 'the field (at-, of-, called-) *Hondeponne*' i.e. '*Honde's pan*', where the first el. is a ME pers.n. *Honde*. What the 'pan' could be is uncertain); *le Mallard acr* 1412 ('mallard field', from mallard and æcer); *Manislawe feld' de Bromb'* 1265–91, *Monylowes* 1412 ('Man's mound', from hlāw and the OE pers.n. *Mann*, confused with manig 'many')); *le Newefeld* (*v.* New Fd *supra*); *Northemerenes* 1398, *Northmere Renes* 1440 ('boundary strips at the north boundary', *v.* norð, (ge)mǣre, rein, cf. *Southemere infra*); *passagium et batillagium de Brumburgh* 1357 (a toll and ferry at Bromborough); *le Ouer*

Forlong, le Ouershotte 1412 ('the higher furlong', 'the higher field', *v.* uferra, furlang, scēat); *Ranesfeld* 1265–91, *Raunesfeld* 1398, *Rauenesfeld* 1407, *Rawnesfeld* 1432, 1440 ('Raven's field', from the pers.n. ON *Hrafn* or OE *Hraefn*, or OE hræfn 'a raven', and feld); *le Sechers* 1412 (*v.* sīc); *le Shepyorde* 1432 ('the sheep-pen', *v.* scēp, geard); *le Skereyorde* 1412 (a fish-trap, 'the fish-trap at the skerry', *v.* sker, geard); *Southemere* 1407 ('south boundary', *v.* sūð, (ge)mǣre, cf. *Northemerenes supra*); *Suchacresendes* 1265–91 (cf. *le Syches* 1432, 'the end-pieces of the ploughlands at the watercourse', 'the watercourse fields', *v.* sīc, æcer, ende[1]); *Symes Hay* 1610 ('Simon's enclosure', from *Sime*, a ME pet-form of *Simon*, and (ge)hæg); *le Turfway versus Estam Dale* 1432 ('the way to the turf-moss, leading towards Eastham Dale', *v.* turf, weg, cf. Dale Hay (*Eastham Dale*) 188 *supra*).

xv. Bebington

The ecclesiastical parish of Bebington contained the townships 1. Higher Bebington, 2. Lower Bebington, 3. Poulton cum Spital, 4. Storeton, 5. Tranmere (now included in the County Borough of Birkenhead). All these townships except Tranmere are now included in Bebington Municipal Borough (chartered 1937) which comprises the c.ps. of Bebington cum Bromborough, Brimstage, Eastham, Poulton cum Spital, Raby, Storeton and Thornton Hough. The boundaries followed in this survey are those of Bryant's map, 1831. The age of the parish is not certainly known. Bebington is not mentioned in DB, but there was a priest maintained in the manor of Poulton (Poulton cum Spital 250 *infra*) who was probably the parish priest for Bebington, and perhaps the original parish church was at Poulton. Bebington church existed as a chapel, *capella de Bebinton*, in or before 1093, and it was a parish church by 1291 Tax.

1. HIGHER BEBINGTON (109–315845), as for Bebington *infra* and distinguished as *Parua Bebinton* 1260–80 *JRC, Little Bebynton* 1491 ChRR, *Superior Bebinton* 1278 *ChFor, Bebington Superior* 1819 Orm[2], *Overbebynton* 1342 (1438) ChRR, *Ouuerbebynton* 1347 *ChFor et freq* with spellings as for Bebington and variant prefix *Over-* to 1656 Orm[2], *Upper-* 1361 BPR, *Higher Bebington* 1724 NotCestr, *-Bebbington* 1842 OS, 'the smaller-, the higher-, part of Bebington', *v.* parva, lӯtel, superior, uferra, higher, upper.

HIGHER- & LOWER BEBINGTON [ˈbebiŋtən]

Bedintone 1096–1101 (1150) Chest, (?) *Beditona* 1175 Facs 3 *Bebinton* 1096–1101 (1280) Chest *et freq* with variant spellings *Bebyn-, -t(one), -tona, -thon* to *Bebynton* 1535 VE, (*-in Wyrhale*) 1386 Pat, *Bebbynton* 1549 Sheaf *Bebington* H2 (1666) Orm[2], 1270–83 Chest *et freq* with variant

spellings -*yng*- (1283 Ipm to 1569 AD), -*ton*(*e*), -*thone*, *Bebbington* (1583 Sheaf to 1880 Orm²)
Byuinton 1324 Orm² (p)
Bulyngton 1351 BPR (p) (III 13)
Bibynton 1403 Fine (p)
Bevyngton 1534–47 Dugd, -*ing* 1686 Sheaf, *Beventon* 1695 ib
Bobynton 1535 VE
Beabington 1646 Sheaf

'Farm called after Bebba', from the OE pers.n. *Bebba* and -*ing*-[4], tūn. Cf. Higher-, Lower Bebington 245 *supra*, 248 *infra*.

ROCK FERRY (109–335868), a district in Tranmere 257 *infra* and Higher Bebington, including ROCK LANE & PARK (cf. Rock Fm 258 *infra*). The various names are recorded as *del Fere* 1350 Sheaf (p), *passagium et batillagium de Bebynton* 1357 ChFor ('the toll and ferryboat of Bebington'), *house called the Rocke* 1644 Sheaf, *Rocke house land and ferryboate* 1646 ib, *the Rock Ferry* 1757 ib, 1819 Orm², *the Royal Rock Ferry* 1805 Sheaf, *Rock Ferry House, Rock Cottage* 1831 Bry, *Rock Park* 1843 *TA*, 'ferry at the Rock', from **rokke** and **ferja**, with **park, lane**. Rock Lane leads to Rock Ferry, and gave name to *Rock Lane Cottage* 1842 OS, *Firbob Hall* 1831 Bry. The rock was an outcrop on the Wirral shore of Mersey. Cf. *Tranmere Ferry* 258 *infra*.

BENTY HEY, 'grassy enclosure', *v.* **benty, (ge)hæg**. BRACKEN LANE, BRACKENWOOD, *v.* **braken**. BUNKER'S HILL, *v.* 336 *infra*. DACRE HILL, HOUSE & MOUNT, presumably after Dacre Cu, now giving name to Dacre, a district. THE DELL, *v.* **dell**. DERBY Ho, 1621 (1656) Orm², *Darbye Howse* 1646 Sheaf, *v.* **hūs**, probably named after the earls of Derby by the Stanley family. GORSEY HEY, cf. *Gorsey Hay* 1843 *TA*, *v.* **gorstig, (ge)hæg**. HIGHER BEBINGTON HALL, cf. Old Hall *infra*. HEATH RD, cf. (*Lower*) *Heath, Heath Field & Hay* 1843 *TA*, *v.* **hǣð**. THE HURSTS, cf. *The Hurst* 1644 Sheaf, 'the wooded hill', *v.* **hyrst**. INGLEFIELD COTTAGE, *Winterton Cottage* 1831 Bry. Both names are probably from surnames, cf. foll. KING'S BROW, LANE, FM (lost) & RD, probably from the surname *King*. King's Rd was *Broad Lane* 1831 Bry, cf. *Broad Lane Field* 1843 *TA*, *v.* **brād, lane**. King's Fm, built c.1520, demolished 1932, was the home of the *Inglefield* family, cf. prec., *v.* Sheaf³ 31 (6911). King's Brow is an ascent, *v.* **brū**. MILL

BROW, MILLBUTT HO, MILL TERRACE, cf. *Mill Common* 1831 Bry, *Mill Butts, Field & Hay* 1843 *TA*, named from a windmill 109–316845, *Storeton Hill Mill* 1842 OS, *molendinum versus Stortona* c.1260–80 *JRC*, cf. Storeton Hill 253 *infra*. MOUNT RD, cf. 255 *infra*, named from Mount Wood 272 *infra*. NEEDWOOD FM, *Needless Inn* 1831 Bry, 1842 OS. OLD CHESTER RD, the former main road to Chester. OLD HALL, *Hall* 1831 Bry, cf. Higher Bebington Hall *supra*. SCHOOL LANE. TEEHEY LANE. TOWN LANE, v. 249 *infra*. VILLAGE RD, the old village street of Higher Bebington hamlet. WOODHEY (RD), a district in Higher & Lower Bebington, cf. *Wood Hay* 1843 *TA*, 'enclosure at a wood', v. wudu, (ge)hæg.

FIELD-NAMES

The undated forms are 1843 *TA* 43. Of the others 1250–1300, 1260–80, l13, 1337, 1592 are *JRC*, 1278, 1357 *ChFor*, 1558–1603, 1560, 1569, 1576, 1594 AD, 1644, 1646, 1777 Sheaf, 1831 Bry.

(a) Acres; Backside (v. ba(c)ksyde); Blakeland Hay (v. blæc, land, (ge)hæg); Bone Dust Fd (v. bone-dust); Bottoms (v. botm); Brandhurst Hay (cf. *the Brandarse* 1777, 'burnt stubble', v. brende², ersc. This may be the original form of Branner(s), Branna 229, 228 *supra*, which show *Branners* leading to an analogical sg. form *Branner, Branna* when the land called *Branners* is split up into several lots); Brandy Hay Mdw (*the Brend Hey* 1569, -*Breinde*- 1594, 'burnt enclosure', v. brende², (ge)hæg); Broom Fd (v. brōm); Caddy Croft; Clogg Hall; Cock Pit (v. cockpit); Common Piece; Cow Pasture; The Croft; Far-, Middle- & Near Croftens (v. cryfting); Cross Hay (v. cros, (ge)hæg); Cumber Croft (v. cumber); Dock Mdw (v. docce); The Ends; Hunstable Dale & Hay (*Anstable Dale* 1558–1603, 1592, *Anstuble Damm* 1644, perhaps '(hollow at) the lonely pillar or post', from āna and stapol with dæl¹, though the significance is obscure); Marsdale Hay ('(enclosure at) the marshy hollow', from marr or mersc, and dæl¹, with (ge)hæg); Moor Fd (cf. *le Morefeld* 1357, v. mōr¹, feld); Norrige Hay (perhaps *Northgate Hey* 1645–6 Sheaf³ 50, the former '(enclosure at) the north ridge', from norð and hrycg, the latter '(enclosure at) the north pasture', from gata, with (ge)hæg); Park, Park Fd; Patents Hay; Rake Hay (v. rake, (ge)hæg); Rough Hay (v. rūh, (ge)hæg); Sea Hay (v. sǣ); Short Butts (v. sc(e)ort, butte); Slade (v. slæd); Higher & Lower Spangs (*the Longe Spange* 1576, *The Spangs* 1645–6, v. spang); Springs (v. spring, 'a well-spring'); Thorny Rean (v. þornig, rein); Threat Mdw; Treble Ho; Well Fd.

(b) *Bebyngton Wood* 1560, *Bebington*- 1594, *boscus de Bebington* 1278 (v. wudu); *Brodegreue* 1250–1300, *Bradegreue* 1260–80 ('broad wood', v. brād, grǣfe); *le Bruches* 1250–1300 ('the intakes', v. bryce, cf. Birches 249 *infra*); *campus ecclesie* 1250–1300 (v. cirice, feld, cf. Church Field 249 *infra*); *Koksote Land* 1260–80 (cf. *unus voley'*-, *unus volatus*-, *-in Bradegreue* 1260–80, *v.* cocc-scyte); *Colders* 1337 (the name of a watercourse, probably taken from a locality in which it flowed, i.e. 'cold shielings' from cald and erg, or 'cold arse' (a hill-name) from ears, cf. *Caldy* 282 *infra*); *Duphyard* 1260–80 (a fish-trap, i.e. a fisc-geard or flōd-geard, 'the deep fish-trap', *v.* dēop, djúpr, geard, cf. *le Depeyhard* 250 *infra*); *Estmundesdiche* 1260–80 ('Ēastmund's ditch', from the OE pers.n. *Ēastmund* and dīc); *le Heyegreue* 1250–1300 ('wood at an enclosure', *v.* (ge)hæg, grǣfe); *Holdhaly* l13 (the name of a cockshoot, from ald or hald[1] or hald[2], with halh or hǽli); *Horstord* 1337 (the name of a watercourse, 'horse-turd', *v.* hors, tord, probably a filthy drain, foul with horse droppings); *Lilleburne* 1250–1300 ('little stream', *v.* lȳtel or lítill, burna or brunnr); *le Longegreue* 1250–1300 (*v.* lang, grǣfe); *Medlestehyard* 1260–80 (a fishery, 'the middlemost fish-trap', *v.* midlest, geard, cf. fisc-geard); *Northgate Hey* 1646 (*v.* Norrige Hey *supra*); *Pikedelond* 1250–1300 ('selion running to a point', *v.* piked, land); *Risewalleheth* 1357 ('(heath at) the spring in the brushwood', from hrīs and wælla, with hǣð); *le Schamforlong* 1250–1300 ('the short furlong', *v.* skammr, furlang); *Woriythlond* 1250–1300, *Wuride land* 1260–80 ('selion at a crooked stream', from wōh and rīð, with land).

2. LOWER BEBINGTON (109–3384), as for Bebington 245 *supra*, and distinguished as *Inferior Bebinton* 1250–1300 *JRC*, 1278 *ChFor*, *-tona* 1309–12 *JRC*, *Bebinton Inferior* c.1280 Chest, 1286 *ChFor*, *Bebington Inferior* 1294 *ib*, 1594 ChRR, *Bebyntone Subteriore* c.1275 Sheaf[3] 48, *Netherbebinton* 1249–1323 Chest *et freq* with spellings as for Bebington and variant prefix (*le*) *Neȝer*-, *Nethir*- to *Nether Bebington* 1819 Orm[2], (*Lower or*-) 1882 ib, *Lowerbebynton* 1439 Orm[2], *Bebynton Lower* 1450 ChRR, *Lower Bebington* 1594 ib, 1724 NotCestr, 1831 Bry, and as *Chirchebebyngton*, *-ing-* 1289 Court, *-bebynton* 1346 BPR, *Kirke Bebynton* 1429 Sheaf, *Church Bebingtone* 1613 ChRR, 'the lower part of Bebington, the part with a church', *v.* inferior (also MedLat *subterior*), neoðera, lower, cirice, kirkja.

ELLEN'S LANE, RD & ROCKS, *Ellen's Lane* 1842 OS, *Helen Lane* 1831 Bry, cf. *Hellelond* 1250–1300 *JRC*, l13 *ib*, the name of a selion and a cock-shoot, 'grove at a flat rock', from hella (gen.sg. hellu) and lundr, with rokke and lane.

HOWLEY MARSH (lost, 109–335848 between Lower Rd and Windy Bank), with *Howley Lane Toll Bar* 1831 Bry (at 109–334849 on Bebington Rd) probably associated with *le Holouwey*, *le Hollewey* 1250–1300 *JRC*, 'road in a hollow, sunken road', *v.* hol[2], holh, weg.

NEW FERRY (109–3485), 1831 Bry, *the New Ferry* 1777 Sheaf, *The New Ferry-house* 1810 ib, a district named from a Mersey ferry founded here in the eighteenth century, *v.* nīwe, ferja.

ABBOT'S GRANGE, named after the abbot of Chester's grange of Bebington, cf. *Graunge* 1468 *MinAcct, v.* grange.   THE ACRES, ACRES RD, cf. *les Acres iuxta le Rake* 1357 *ChFor, The Acres* 1777 Sheaf, 'the plough-lands', *v.* æcer.   BEBINGTON HALL, 1831 Bry. BROMBOROUGH POOL (BRIDGE), BROMBOROUGH RD, cf. Bromborough 237 *supra.*   OLD CHESTER RD, the former main road to Chester. CHURCH FM & RD, *v.* cirice, cf. Kirket Lane *infra.*   CROSS LANE, *v.* cros 'a cross'.   GREEN LANE.   HEATHFIELD, a house beside *Spittle Heath infra.*   HEATH RD, cf. prec.   HULME HALL. KIRKET LANE, the old name of Church Rd *supra*, cf. *Kirkett Heys* 1646 Sheaf, from a road-name *Kirkgate, v.* kirkja, gata.   OLD MARGERY'S (lost, 109–329854), 1831 Bry, a cottage at Woodhey. PORT SUNLIGHT (109–3484), a model village and soap factory of international repute, named after a brand of soap.   SPITTLE HEATH (lost, 109–325832 to 329832), 1831 Bry, *le Spitelheth* 1406 *JRC*, cf. Heathfield *supra*, Heath Fm, Spital 252, 251 *infra, v.* spitel, hǣð.   STANTON (RD).   TOWN LANE, the township boundary, cf. 247 *supra.*   TOWNFIELD LANE, 1831 Bry.   TRAFALGAR, a district named after *Trafalgar Place* 1844 *TAMap*, no doubt called after the naval battle.   THE VILLAGE, the old village-street of Lower Bebington, *v.* village.   THE WIEND, *v.* (ge)wind.   WOOD-HEAD FM, 1831 Bry, 'the top end of a wood', *v.* wudu, heafod. WOODHEY, cf. 247 *supra.*

FIELD-NAMES

The undated forms are 1843 *TA* 44. Of the others, 1270–83 is Chest, 1288, 1294, 1347, 1357 *ChFor*, 1777 Sheaf, 1831 Bry, and the rest *JRC*.

(a) Backside (*v.* ba(c)ksyde); Birches (cf. *le Bruches* 1250–1300, 247 *supra*, and *le Bruche infra*); Brick Dale Fd (*The Brickdale* 1777, 'the clay-pit', *v.* bryke, dæl[1]); Church Fd (*le Chirchefeld* 1306, -*Chyrche-* 1357, cf. *campus ecclesie* 1250–1300, 247 *supra, v.* cirice, feld); Cupboard; Damage (*v.* demming); Forward Head; Goose Holes (probably 'gorse hollows', *v.* gorst, hol[1] but the first el. may be gōs 'a goose'); The Greenlooms 1777 (*v.* grēne, land, loom); Hats; Heath Fd (*The-* 1777, cf. *bruera de Bebington* 1288, *bruerium* 1307–22, *v.* hǣð); Hogshead (perhaps from hafoc-scerde, cf. *The Hawkesyord* 1 166); Howey Hill ('enclosure at a hill', from hōh and (ge)hæg, with hyll); Intake (*v.* inntak); The Marled Hey 1777 (cf. *les*

Marlputtis 1306, *v.* marle, marled, (ge)hæg, marle-pytt); The Newhey 1777 (*v.* (ge)hæg); The Ouduck 1777; Pasture Fd (*The Pastures* 1777, cf. *Pastures* 1831); Rain Fd (cf. *le Renis* 1272–1307, *v.* rein); Ridings (*v.* ryding); Rock Fd, Mdw & Hill (*v.* rokke); Sea Brows & Hey (*v.* sǣ, brū, (ge)hæg); Slang (*v.* slang); Stones; Three Corners (*v.* 337 *infra*); Wall Fd (Sheaf³ 49 (9929) suggests association with *Walleslade infra*, *v.* wælla); Waterns Wood Hey; Wirrall Looms (from land with the region- and Hundred-name Wirral 167 *supra* or an identical formation from wir and halh).

(*b*) *les Botilerisbuttis* 1306 ('butts belonging to the butler', from butte and the ME occupational surname *Botiler*, ModE *Butler*); *le Bruche* 1270–83, 1272 (cf. Birches *supra*, 'land broken-in for cultivation', *v.* bryce); *volatus Henrici Carettarii* l13 ('Henry the Carter's cock-shoot', cf. coccscyte, MedLat *volatus*); *le Depeyhard* 1250–1300 ('the deep fish-trap', the name of a fishery in Mersey, cf. *Duphyard* 248 *supra* probably the same fishery, *v.* dēop, geard, cf. fisc-geard); *Dracclowelegh* 1347, *fossatum de Drakeloweleyes* 1357 ('(clearing(s) at) *Drakelow* ('the dragon's mound')', *v.* draca, hlāw, lēah, cf. Drakelows 231 *supra*, Drakelow **2** 198); *Fleckeriscroft* l13 ('Fletcher's croft', from croft and flecher or the ME occupational name *Flecher*, with -*ck*- from Scand. influence); *Fulfos* 1260–80, *le Foulflossh* 1357² ('foul swamp', *v.* fūl, flosshe); *le Heye* 1294 ('the fenced-in enclosure', *v.* (ge)hæg); *Longediche* l13, *le Longedich* 1307–22 ('the long ditch', *v.* lang, dīc, cf. *quoddam vetus fossatum* 1270–83 Chest II 691); *le Oldfyshyordstedes* 1337 ('the former sites of the fish-traps', *v.* ald, fiscgeard, stede); *le Rake* 1307–22, 1357 ('the narrow lane', *v.* rake); *Ruycroft* 1309–12 (*v.* ryge, croft); *Stortoneyord* 1337 (a watercourse, probably named from a fish-pond, *v.* geard, cf. fisc-geard and Storeton 253 *infra*); *Walleslade* 1300–20, 1307–9 ('valley with a spring', *v.* wælla, slæd, cf. Wall Fd *supra*); *Withynwalle* l13 ('spring growing with withies', *v.* wiðigen, wælla); *Wluedalehoc* l13, -*hok* 1309–12 ('(hook of land at) the wolves' dale', from wulf (gen.pl. wulfa) and dæl¹, with hōc); *Wlstan* 1250–1300, c.1330 (a fishery in Mersey, named from a rock, *v.* stān. The first el. is not identified. It might be wulf 'a wolf', perhaps as a pers.n.).

3. POULTON CUM SPITAL, *Pulton cum le Spitell* 1385 Chest, *Pulton and Spittelle* 1592 *JRC*, *Powton cum Spyttle* 1614 Orm² *et freq* with variant spellings as for Poulton, Spital *infra*, *Poulton cum Spittell or Poulton Lancelyn* 1819 Orm², *Poulton Lancelyn cum Spittle* 1831 Bry, *v.* Poulton *infra*, Spital *infra*.

POULTON (formerly POULTON LANCELYN), POULTON HALL (109–335816), HEY (335823), RD, & ROYD (327828) ['poultən, 'puːltən]
    Pontone 1086 DB
    Pulton 1154–89 (1666) Orm², l12 (1331) Plea, e13 Chest *et freq*
        with variant spellings -*tun*, -*tona*, -*tone* to 1592 *JRC*, -*Launcelin*
        E1 *AddCh et freq* with variant spellings -*Launcelyn*, -*Lancel(yn)*,

-*Launselin* to 1539–47 Dugd, -*Law(n)son* 1522 Sheaf, -*Lancelett*
1626 ib
Poultona 1260–80 *JRC*, *Poulton* 1624 ChRR, (-*Hall*) 1819 Orm²,
Poulton Launcelin 1315 Plea, -*Lawncellame* 1534 *Chol*, -*Launcelyn*
1624 ChRR, -*Lancelyn* 1831 Bry
Poltona 1270–83 Chest, *Polton* c.1280, c.1283 ib
Pulleton 1340–41 Orm²
Powton Launcelott 1547 *MinAcct*, -*Launcelett* 1560 Sheaf, *Powton*
1577 ChRR, 1614 Orm²
Pooton, or Poolton, . . . distinguished by the name of Lancelot 1621
(1656) Orm²
Poolton 1621 (1656) Orm², 1840 *TAMap* 75, (-*Hall*) 1842 OS

'Farm by a pool or creek', *v.* pōl¹, pull, tūn, cf. Bromborough
Pool 241 *supra*, Dibbinsdale Brook *infra*. The manorial suffix is the
surname, occasionally confused with the ME (OFr) pers.n. *Lancelot*,
of the *Lancelyn* family, lords of this manor 12th to 16th centuries,
whose castle was at Poulton Hall, *v.* Orm² II 440. Poulton Hey and
Royd (*v.* (ge)hæg, rod¹) appear to be modern names; the latter is
certainly not a local dialect form. *v.* Addenda.

SPITAL, SPITAL (OLD) HALL (109–340830) ['spitɬ, 'spitəl], *le Spitel(l)*
1347, 1357, 1385 *ChFor et freq* with variant spellings (*le-*), *Spytell,*
-yll, Spetyll, Spitill, Spittell(e), Spyttle, Spittle to *Spittell* 1819
Orm², *Spittle* 1842 OS, *Spittale* 1840 *TAMap* 75, *Spittle in Wirral*
1597 Orm², 'the hospital', *v.* spitel. This was a lazar-house, (*versus*)
domos leprosorum 1270–83 Chest, *domus leprosorum de Bebynton*
1283 Dugd, 1286 *ChFor*, (*a*) *domibus quondam leprosorum de Bebinton*
1300–20 *JRC*. It appears to have been associated with the older
foundation, St Thomas the Martyr's chapel, cf. Chapel Dale *infra*.
The hospital was at Spital Old Hall (*v.* ald, hall), cf. *Spittle Green &*
Hay 1843 *TA*, *v.* grēne², (ge)hæg.

CHAPEL DALE FM (109–337830), *Chapel Dale* 1843 *TA*, named from
capella Thome Martyris in Wirrall' 1174–84 Chest I 91 (cf. *op. cit.*
126, n.), founded shortly after Becket's death (1170) and probably
the basis of the hospital foundation at Spital *supra*, cf. Orm² II 443,
v. chapel, dæl¹.

DIBBINSDALE (BROOK), *Pultundale* 1278–80 Chest, *Pultondale*
1291–1323 ib, *Pulton Dale* 1462 Orm², cf. Dibbinsdale Brook,

Lodge & Rd 242 *supra*, Poulton Bridge *infra*. The modern name of this valley, which runs down to Bromborough Pool, appears as *Dibbinsdale* 1839 *TA* 75 (Bromborough), *Dibinsdale* (*Brook*) 1842 OS. It is hard to see what its origin is, unless it be from dēoping 'a deep place' and dæl[1]. The older name was 'Poulton valley', from dæl[1] and Poulton *supra*.

POULTON BRIDGE, *pons de Pulton* 1291–1323 Chest, *Poulton Bridge* 1621 Sheaf, *Dibinsdale Bridge* 1842 OS, first mentioned as 'a certain bridge to be built in Poulton across *le Pul* in *Pultundale* between Bromborough and Bebington' 1274–80 Chest ii 688, *v.* brycg, cf. Poulton, Dibbinsdale *supra*.

SPITAL HILL, *Spittle Lane* 1842 OS, 'a certain green-way called *Pulton Mulneway*' 1270–83 Chest, *via que ducit ab hospitali* 113 *JRC*, a certain way from the abbot's mill of Bromborough ascending to a certain old ditch' 1313 Chest, *le Rake* 1357 *ChFor*, 1398 *JRC*, *le Mulneway* 1406 *ib*, 'the lane at Spital', 'the narrow lane', 'the way to the mill', *v.* spitel, lane, myln, weg, rake, cf. Spital *supra*, Bromborough Mills 240 *supra*.

CLAREMONT COTTAGE, *New Building* 1831 Bry.   CLATTER BRIDGE, CLATTERBRIDGE (WORKHOUSE), 1842 OS, *Clatter Bridge* (*Toll Bar*) 1831 Bry, *v.* 230 *supra*.   HALF WAY HO (lost, 109–327830), 1831 Bry, *v.* half-way.   HEATH FM (109–330831), cf. *bruera vocata le Spitelheth* 1406 *JRC*, *Heath Field* 1843 *TA*, and Heathfield, *Spittle Heath* 249 *supra*, *v.* hǣð.   LANCELYN FM, a modern name, borrowed from the manorial suffix of Poulton *supra*.   NESTON CROSS (lost, 109–325823), 1831 Bry, the name of a cottage.   NEW RD, *Broad Lane* 1831 ib.   THE VINEYARD FM.   WINDY HARBOUR, *Windy Arbour* 1842 OS, 'windy shelter', *v.* windig, herebeorg.   WOODHEYS, cf. *Wood Heys* 1843 *TA*, 'wood enclosures', *v.* wudu, (ge)hæg.

FIELD-NAMES

The undated forms are 1843 *TA* 325. Of the others, 1270–1283, 1313 are Chest, 1287 Court, 1334 Sheaf, 1357 *ChFor*, 1396 *Most*, 1819 Orm[2], 1831 Bry, and the rest *JRC*.

(a) Alleloons (*le Alleuenelondes* 1307–22, 'the eleven selions', *v.* endleofan, land); Backsides (*v.* ba(c)ksyde); Barm Hay; Bent (*v.* beonet); Cabin

Croft (*v.* cabin); Cake; The Chace 1831 (a wood, *v.* chace); Cock's Head (*v.* cocc-scyte); Crowsdale (*Crosdale* 1313, 'valley with a cross', *v.* cros, dæl¹ or dalr); Crows Hill Brow (*v.* brū); Cockoos Wd; Flat; Heavy Hook, Heavy Oak Fd; Lamperloon(s) (cf. Lamper Loons 243 *supra*); (Far- & New-) Mareford (*the Marfords* 1819, cf. The Marfords 242 *supra*, cf. also *Mareford-way*, *vallis de Merefordale* 1406, '(valley of-, way to-) the boundary ford', *v.* (ge)mære, ford, dæl¹, weg); (Old) Marled Hay (*v.* marled(e), (ge)hæg); Marsh Hay (*v.* mersc, (ge)hæg); Mill Fd (*le Mulnefeld* 1343, 1357, *The Mille Fielde* 1592, *v.* myln, feld); Moss Hay (*v.* (ge)hæg); New Fd; New Hay (*le Neuhey* 1398, *v.* nīwe, (ge)hæg); New Shoot (*v.* scēat); Patrick Wd 1831 (cf. St Patrick's Well 243 *supra*); Quillet (*v.* quillet(t)); Raby Croft (cf. Raby 228 *supra*); Stapple Hay (*Staple Hayes* 1592, probably named from *le Stopples* 1314, -*Stoples* 1357, *la Stopelrake* 1406, 'the steps' or 'the stepping-stones', *v.* stōpel, rake, cf. Stoop Lane WRY 6 187. There were stepping-stones in the stream at Raby Mill on the Poulton boundary at 109–332812. *la Stopelrake* would be a path leading to the stepping-stones, or a stepped path); Swinesty Hay (*v.* swīn¹, stigu, (ge)hæg); Tungrave (*T(h)urngreue feld* 1357, 'field at a thorn wood', *v.* þyrne, græfe, feld); Vicars Hay (*v.* vikere, (ge)hæg); Yard End (*v.* geard); Yolk of Egg.

(*b*) *Baldauteresfeld* 1357 (*v.* feld. The first el. is obscure. It looks like a pers.n.); *le Blakelondes* 1398 ('dark selions', *v.* blæc, land); *le Chyrcheway* 1357, -*Schyrche-* 1398, -*Chirche-* 1406 (*v.* cirice, weg); *le Crokede Feld* 1357 ('crooked field', *v.* croked, feld); *Emmotesgape* 1334 ('Emmot's gap', from gappe and the ME fem. pers.n. *Emmot*, dimin. of *Emma*); *le Nether-*, *le Ouereharstonfeld* 1406 ('(the lower and higher fields) at the hoar stone', *v.* neoðera, uferra, feld, hār², stān); *le Hertesflore* 1357 ('the hart's floor', from heorot and flōr. The significance is unknown. It may be archæological, since OE flōr may be 'a pavement'); *Litlewodefeld* 1287, *Litelwodefeld* 1406 ('Little-wood field' or 'little Wood-field', *v.* lȳtel, wudu, feld); *le Lym Put* 1270–83 (*v.* lim, pytt); *le Mersstale* 1307–22 (probably 'fishing place at a marsh', from mersc and stæll, stall); *le Mosseway* 1396 (*v.* mos, weg); *le Mulneheth* 1343 ('heath at a mill', *v.* hǣð, myln); *le Park Haistowe* 1406 ('park enclosure', *v.* park, hege-stōw); *le Stopples* (*v.* Stapple Hey *supra*); *le Throleghfeld* 1357 ('glade at a trough', from þrūh and lēah, with feld. OE þrūh means 'water-pipe, conduit, coffin', and it appears in other p.ns. with lēah, i.e. Throwleigh D 453, Throwley K (PNK 298), St (DEPN and D 453), for which DEPN suggests a figurative meaning, 'deep valley', cf. PNK *loc. cit.*); *le Torfmos* 1315, *le Turfheth* 1343, *Turfsefeld* 1357 ('peat-moss', 'peat-heath', 'field where turf is cut', *v.* turf, mos, hǣð, feld); field called (*le*) *Wynterthorn(a)* c.1260–80, 1307–22, *Winterthornfeld* 1315 (perhaps 'winter-thorn', i.e. thorn-tree which flowers in winter', from winter¹ and þorn, with feld, alluding to some specimen like the Glastonbury Thorn, an early-flowering hawthorn supposed to bud on Christmas Day); *le Wytesiche* 1307–22 (*v.* Sitch Cottages 254 *infra*).

4. STORETON (109–3084), GREAT & LITTLE STORETON, STORETON GRANGE, HALL, HILL, LODGE & QUARRIES ['stortən]

Stortone 1086 DB, 1154–81 Chest, *-tuna* 1096–1101 (1150),
 1150 ib, *-tona* 1096–1101 (1280) ib, *-ton* 1202–29 *AddCh et freq*
 with variant spelling *-ton*(*a*) to 1427 Plea, 1490 ChRR, 1619
 Sheaf, *Maior-, Minor-, Magna-, Parva Storton*(*a*) 13 *AddCh*,
 1216–30 *JRC, Storton Maior* 13 *AddCh, Mikulstorton* 1290–
 1327 *ib, Litul-* 1367 *JRC, Stortona et alia Stortona* 1240–9
 Chest
Storeton 1070–1101 (19) Orm², 1305 ChF, 1306 *AddCh* (*-in
 Wyrhale*), 1415, 1491 ChRR, 1529 Plea, *Parva-* 1325 ib, *Magna-*
 1428 Sheaf, *Great-, Little-* 1428, 1512 ChRR, 1724 NotCestr,
 1819 Orm², 1831 Bry, *Storeton Hall* 1831 ib, *-Hill & Cottages*
 1842 OS
Stort' 1175 Facs
Magna Stortton, minor villa de Stortton 13 *AddCh*
Parva Sturton 13 (17) Orm², *Sturton*(*e*) 1341 ib, *-ton* H7, 1614 ib,
 Great-, Little Sturton 1645 ib, 1657 *Clif* (lit. *Slur-*), 1743 Sheaf
Storthon 1323 *AddCh*, 1334 *JRC, Magna-* 1333 *AddCh, Parva-*
 1334 *JRC*
Stourton 1334 (17) Sheaf, 1362 (1387) Orm², c.1536 Leland, 1579
 Sheaf, 1842 *TAMap* 72, *Magna-, Parva-* 1426 ChRR, *AddCh*,
 Stourton Parva, -Magna 1592 *JRC*
Stoorton 1656 Orm²
Stoarton 1727 Sheaf

'The great farmstead', from **stórr**[1] and ON **tún** or OE **tūn**,
with **grange, hall, hyll, loge, quarriere** and various affixes. Storeton
Lodge was *Storeton Cottage* 1842 OS. Storeton Hall, an ancient
house, is mentioned c.1536 Leland v 225 as 'the Lorde Stourton's
howse in Stourton'. The form *Stortton* appears to contain as first
el. ON **storð** 'a young wood, a plantation, land growing with brushwood'. There is no evidence which would identify *una bovata terre
in Stortone quam Wlfricus tenebat* 1154–81 Chest, 'one bovate of
land in Storeton which Wulfrīc used to hold', with the land *on
Wirhalum* 'in Wirral' mentioned in the will of Wulfrīc Spot 1002
ASWills 46. Wulfrīc is not an uncommon pers.n., cf. *terra Wlfrici
prepositi foris portam de North* 1119 (1280), 1150 Chest 'Wulfrīc
the reeve's land outside Northgate (Chester)'.

SITCH COTTAGES (109–319828), named from a watercourse at the
boundary of Poulton cum Spital cf. 253 *supra, le Wyte seche* 13

AddCh, album sychum 1300–27 *ib, le Wytesiche* 1307–27 *JRC, album citum* 1318 *ib, le Witesiche, album sichum* 1323 *AddCh*, 'the white stream', *v.* hwīt, sīc.

UMBERSTONE COVERT (109–317833), *Storeton Fox Cover* 1831 Bry, named from *Umberstone* 1839 *TA, Homilston'* 13 *AddCh, campus de Homelstones* 1300–27 *ib, -Hunbulston* 1318 *JRC, -Homelston* 1323 *AddCh*, 'two acres of waste in *Homelston'* next to the heath of Brimstage' 1343 *AddCh* 66279. This f.n. was quoted as *Umlisons* 1896 Sheaf[3] 1 (117), with the hint of a Celtic etymology on account of flints found in a mound of sand. The true etymology is 'mutilated stone or rock', from hamol and stān. This could refer either to a natural outcrop of the local rock (which is quarried at Storeton), or to some lost megalithic archæological feature.

BEBINGTON RD, *Kirkup Lane* 1896 Sheaf, probably a corruption of *Kirket-*, i.e. 'road to church', from kirkja and gata. BRIMSTAGE LANE & PLANTATION, cf. *Brimstage Hey* 1839 *TA*, named from Brimstage 234 *supra*. BROOK COTTAGE, cf. Brook Croft *infra*. COW HEY COVERT, cf. *Cow Hey* 1839 *TA, v.* (ge)hæg. HILLSIDE COTTAGES, *Hill Side* 1831 Bry, cf. foll. and Storeton Hill *supra*. HILLSIDE FM, *Wanton Dale* 1839 *TA*, erroneously *Danton Dale* 1831 Bry. *Wanton Dale* occurs as a f.n. in Landican, Pensby and Gayton 268, 272, 276 *infra*. It may be either dæl[1] 'a valley, a hollow', or deill 'an allotment, a plot of ground', with ME *wantowen*, ModE *wanton*, in the sense 'wild, uncultivated, out of hand'. LEY FM, *v.* lēah. LOWER HEATH WOOD. MARSH HEY, 1839 *TA, v.* (ge)hæg. MARSH LANE, 1831 Bry. MOUNT RD, *v.* 272 *infra*. NEW HEY COVERT, cf. *New Hey* 1839 *TA* and *le Newefeld* 1318 *JRC, le Newe-, le Neufeld* 1323 *AddCh, v.* nīwe, (ge)hæg, feld. RAKE HEY (109–303838), 1839 *TA*, cf. *Rake Ditch* 1839 *ib, Rake Lane* 1831 Bry (109–303838 to 305842), *v.* rake, (ge)hæg, lane, dīc. RED HILL (RD). REST HILL, probably a tiring ascent where a rest was needed. STANLEY WOOD, *Stanley Gorse* 1831 Bry. The *Stanley* family were lords of Storeton. WOODEND COTTAGE, *v.* wudu, ende[1].

FIELD-NAMES

The undated forms are 1839 *TA* 373. Of the others 1216–30, 1300, 1318, 1334, 1340, 1367 are *JRC*, c.1265, l13 (17), 1896 Sheaf, 1331, 1347 *ChFor*, and the rest *AddCh*.

(a) Backside (v. ba(c)ksyde); Brook Croft & Fd, Brookfield (cf. le Brokdiche 1347, and campus de le Brocwaye 1216–30, 13, c.1265, cf. Sheaf³ 44 (9137), 'the ditch at a brook, the way near or to a brook', v. brōc, dīc, weg); Calver Hey (v. calf (gen.pl. calfra), (ge)hæg); Copsti(d)ge ('plot of ground at a bank', v. copp, stycce); Crusy Croft; Doubloons (probably 'Double Loons', double-sized selions, v. duble, land); Faugh Hey ('fallow enclosure', from falh (ModEdial. faugh) and (ge)hæg); Flat (v. flat); Flatbutts (v. flatr, butte); Galleons; Gorsy Hey (v. (ge)hæg); Greets (v. grēot); Hasty Hey; Hell Hole; Hippingstone Mdw (from hipping-stone 'a stepping-stone'); Intack (v. inntak); Leather Sitch (v. sīc 'a watercourse'); Main Hey (v. main, (ge)hæg); Mill Hey (cf. molendinum de Storton 13; there were a windmill and a watermill in Storeton in 1284 Ipm, v. myln, (ge)hæg); Old Hey (cf. vetus campus minoris ville c.1300, le Oldefeld c.1306, le Oldefeld de Parva Storthon 1334, Holde Feld 1343, le Oldeffeld 1347, v. ald, feld); Oxendough, Oxendow (v. oxa, dāl); Ox Pasture; Pingle (v. pingel); Ransel (Rauncele Rake 1318, Rauncelrake 1323, cf. the adjacent Roundsill(s) 237 supra, 'hut by a rowan-tree', from raun and sel, with rake 'a narrow lane'); Rye Wd; Sour Flats (v. sūr, flat); Thirty Acre 1896 (consisting of 30 strips, traceable in 1896, v. þrittig, æcer, cf. Sheaf³ 1 117); Town Fd, Town Yard (cf. Town Lane 1896 Sheaf³ 1, v. toun, lane); Well Lane; Welsh Graves (v. Welisc, græfe, probably belonging to some Welshman); Wet Reins (cf. le Wetelandis 1330, 'wet selions', v. wēt, land, rein).

(b) le Bradlond 1340 (v. brād, land); le Brichis 1330 (v. bryce); le Caplesfeld 1331 ('the horse's field', v. capel², kapall, feld); Cappis feld 13 (cf. Capesthorne 1 73, which appears analogous with this, the first el. being either an OE pers.n. Capp, Cæpp or ON kapp 'a contest' (although the gen.sg. -is might be unusual with kapp), v. feld); crux de Storthon 1344 ('Storeton cross', v. cros); le Dedemonnes Greue 1323 ('dead man's wood', v. dede-man, græfe); le Falles 1347 ('the fellings, places where wood has been felled and cleared,' v. (ge)fall. Turbary upon le Falles in the forest of Wirral was a perquisite of the manors of Storeton, Bidston, Caldy, Thurstaston and Oldfield 308, 282, 279, 277 infra); le Goldifeld 13, -fyld 1300 ('field where marigolds grow', from OE *goldig (v. golde, -ig³) and feld); le Gremotehalland 1330 (v. hēafod-land. The first component may be OE *grið-(ge)mōt or ON *griða-mót 'a meeting under truce, a meeting at which a truce is arranged', v. grið, (ge)mōt, mót); Henri pull' 13, Harriespole 1318, Hanriespole 1323 ('Henry's pool', from pull, pōl¹ and the ME (OFr) pers.n. Henri, Harry); le Heye 1367 (v. (ge)hæg); Hullesichemedwe 1306, le Hulsichemedue, -medewe 1323 ('(meadow at) the stream on a hill', v. hyll, sīc, mæd); le Leyt Yate 13 ('gate on a road', v. leið, geat); Pulton' feld 13 (v. feld, cf. Poulton 250 supra); via turbarea 13, 1300–27, -turbaria 1318 ('turf-way', a road to a turbary, v. turf, weg, cf. le Turfway 245 supra); selionis Vmfray 13 ('Umfrey's selion', from the ME pers.n. Umfrey (OG Um-, Unfred) cf. Forssner 236); Waringsdale 113 (17) (a doubtful form, perhaps 'Warin's valley', from dæl¹ and the ME (OFr) pers.n. Warin, but OE wæring, 'a weir' is feasible); le Witeston' 1323 ('the white stone or rock', v. hwīt, stān. The Storeton quarries produce a white freestone); le Wytelandis 1330 (v. hwīt, land).

5. TRANMERE (109–3287) now ['trænmiə], formerly and dial.
['tranmə]

Tranemul l12 Mainw, 1202–10 Sheaf and fourteen examples
(seven in 13) with variant spellings Trane- (to 15 AD), Tran-
(from 1250–55 Orm²), -mul, -mull(e) to 1594 ChRR, (Tranmull
in Wyrall) 1423 AD, (Tranmul alias Tranmore) 1594 ChRR,
Tramull 1587 Orm², (-alias Tranmore) 1594 ib
Tranemol e13 AddCh et freq with variant spellings Trane- (to
1417 Orm²), Tran- (from 1266 ib), -mol(e), -moll(e) to Tranmoll
1716 ib, (Tranmore alias Tranmoll) 1598 ChRR, (Tranmoll
alias Tranmore) 1595 AD, 1716 Orm², (Tranmole alias Tranmore) 1613 ib, Thranmolle 1534–47 Dugd, Trammole alias
Trammore 1545 Pat
Tranemor 1260 Court (p) et freq with variant spellings Trane-
(to 1560 Sheaf), Tran- (freq from 1352 Plea), -mor(a), -more to
Tranmore 1843 TAMap, (Tranmore in Wyrehale) 1439 ChRR,
(Tranmor in Worall) 1564 Sheaf, (Tranmoll alias Tranmor(e))
1587, 1595 AD, (Tranmore alias Tranmoll) 1598 ChRR, Tran-
moore 1569, 1714 Sheaf
Tranemel 1290 Ipm, Tranmell, Trammell 1537 Sheaf
Traunmoll 1307–27, 1554 Orm²
Tranemoels 1318–99 ChRR, 1398 Orm² (p)
Tranmer' 1393 Orm², -mere 1587 J.E.A., 1716 Orm², 1724 Not-
Cestr, 1819 Orm² et freq
Tranmur 1396 JRC
Tranmour 1398 Add
Tranemoele 1398 ChRR (p)
Trannenoll 1510 Sheaf
Tramnol 1524 ChRR
Trandmor 1576 AD
Trenmole alias Trenvile 1600 Orm²
Tranmols 1605 Plea
Trawmore 1621 (1656) Orm²
Tronmere 1655 Sheaf
Tramour 1660 CroR

'Cranes' sandbank', v. trani (gen.pl. trana), melr. This derivation
appears in DEPN. In correspondence with the Society, October
1937, Mr J. E. Allison objected to Ekwall's derivation that whereas
the modern village and town centres upon the lost hamlet of Hinder-

ton (*Lower Tranmere* 19) *infra*, the ancient nucleus of the township was upland (*Higher Tranmere* 19) and would hardly be a sandbank. This circumstance probably inspired Helsby's derivation, Welsh *Tre-yn-Moel* 'hill-village' (not Welsh, makes no sense and does not fit the spellings). The development of the final el. here presents difficulties, however. Professor Sørensen hazards that, in view of the many old spellings in -*mul*, -*mol*, the second el. might be ON mǫl (~ melr) 'mound of pebbles, especially along the shore', which is probably the first el. in the name of the Danish peninsula Mols. But the development of melr in Tranmere reflects that noted under Meols, *v.* 297 *infra*, with the further complication of an assimilation of *r—l* > *l—l*, whence *Tran(e)mel* > -*mer* and *Tran(e)mol*, -*mul* > -*mor*. Tranmere township is named from a feature of its Mersey coastline, not from the location of its late-medieval nucleus. An interesting reversal of orientation is apparent, between the name of the township taken from a coastline feature, and the name of the shore-side hamlet *Hinderton* which is relative to the upland settlement. Mr Allison also objected that since the whole Mersey shore of Wirral would have been rock and sand there would have been no reason for the cranes to single out this particular part of it. The p.n. proves that they did and that is rather a problem of oecology than of toponymy. Orm[2] II 450–451 supposes Tranmere is to be identified with *Sumreford* DB f.267b, but cf. Somerford Booths I 63.

HINDERTON (lost, 109–325878), HINDERTON RD, *Hinderton* 1624 J.E.A., *Ainderton* 1724 NotCestr, *Hinderton* Lane 1719–1812 J.E.A., *Inderton Lane* 1820 Sheaf, *Hinderton Lane Croft* 1843 *TA*, *Hinderton* 1842 OS, 'the hinder part of the township', *v.* hinder, toun, lane. In 1724 Tranmere contained the two hamlets *Hinderton* and *Saugh Lane*, cf. Woodchurch Rd *infra*, Hinderton 223 *supra*, 302 *infra*.

ROCK FM (lost, 109–332868), 1831 Bry, 1842 OS, þe *Rock House* 1689, 1750 Sheaf, cf. *Rock Hole* 1831 Bry a deep place in R. Mersey, Rock Ferry 246 *supra*, and foll., *v.* rokke, hūs, hol[1].

TRANMERE FERRY (lost, 109–327880), 1843 *TAMap*, *Tranmere Ferry House* 1831 Bry, *passagium et batillagium de Tranemoll* 1357 ChFor, 'passage of *Tranmoll alias Tranmor*' 1587 AD, 'a passage of water in *Tranmore*' 1739 LRMB 264. Cf. Rock Ferry 246 *supra*. In Sheaf[3] 4 (9874) it is stated that Rock Ferry was called Tranmere

Ferry until the Tranmere Slip on the south side of Tranmere Pool was built in the eighteenth century and the ferry at this slip became *Tranmere Ferry*, the old one becoming *Rock Ferry*.

TRANMERE HALL (lost, 109–317869), 1831 Bry, *Tranmere Hall or Tranmere House* 1716 Orm². In 1663, Sheaf³ 32 (7221), there were two mansions, *the old hall* and *the new hall*. The *Old Hall* to which the 1716 forms refer, was pulled down in 1863, the site being occupied by the street Tower Hill, cf. Sheaf³ 26 (5913), (5931). The *New Hall*, so called down to 1863, to which the 1831 form refers, survived as *the Old Hall* until 1937, adjoining Greenway Rd, cf. Sheaf³ 35 (7825), *v.* ald, nīwe, hall.

TRANMERE POOL (lost, 109–330882 to 322885), 1842 OS, *The Pool* 1831 Bry, 1842 OS, *Birkett Pole* 1552 Sheaf, -*Poole* 1659 ib, *Berkit-pool* 1757 ib, *Birket Pool* 1818 ib, *Birkenhead Pool* 1824 Lawton, 'the creek or pool at Birkenhead or Tranmere', a creek of Mersey, *v.* pōl¹, cf. Birkenhead 313 *infra*, The Birket (r.n.) 1 15. Hereabouts would be *Raynildes Pool* 1330 Sheaf³ 43 (9082), 'Ragnhild's pool', from the ON fem.pers.n. *Ragnhildr* and pōl¹. About 109–330872 was another creek of Mersey, *Gonell's-*, *Gonelly Pool* 1885 Sheaf (*Gonnille Pool* (lit. *Gomulle-*) 1529 (17) Orm², *Gonell's-*, *Gonall's Pool* 1552 Sheaf, *Gunnel Pool* 1800 ib), 'Gunnil's pool', from the ON fem.pers.n. *Gunnhildr* and pōl¹, cf. Orm² II 548, Sheaf³ 49 (9874). Tranmere Pool is now lost in the docks which were built in it; the stream above it is drained, its valley gives name to Dingle Rd *infra* and The Valley Lodge in Devonshire Park.

NEW & OLD CHESTER RD, leading to Chester.   CHURCH RD, *Church Lane* 1783–1827 J.E.A., 1831 Bry, leading to the parish church in Lower Bebington, *v.* cirice, lane, cf. Kirket(t) Hay *infra*. DINGLE RD, in the valley of *Tranmere Pool supra*, *v.* dingle.   GREEN BANKS (lost), 1831 Bry, *v.* grēne¹, banke.   GREEN LANE, *v.* grēne¹, lane.   HOLT HILL, (*Common*) 1831 Bry, *Holte Hill* 1584 J.E.A., *Hoult-* 1558–1701 ib, *the Hoult Hill* 1818 Sheaf, cf. (*Higher & Lower*) *Holt, Holt Croft, Holt Hill* (*Field*) 1843 TA, 'copse hill', *v.* holt, hyll, commun, croft. At Holt Hill was a windmill, *The Mill* 1831 Bry, 1842 OS, on a site at Mill St and Church Rd.   MOSS GROVE & LANE, near the lost *Moss Hall* 1831 Bry, cf. *Moss Hall Field* 1843 TA, 'hall at a bog', *v.* mos, hall, lane.   MOUNT RD,

Mount Lane, Back Lane 1824 Sheaf, *Mount Lane* 1831 Bry, *v.* mont,
cf. 272 *infra*. OXTON RD, *Grange Road* 1842 OS, *Grange Way*
1843 *TA*, named from Grange 316 *infra*, Oxton 269 *infra*, *v.* weg.
PRENTON RD, cf. Prenton 272 *infra*. THE SLOYNE (109–335875)
1842 OS, *Tranmere Slyne* c.1580 J.E.A., *the Sleyne* 1693 ib, *Slyne*,
Sline 1776, 1777 ib, from slinu 'a slope'; the river bed shelves down-
wards steeply here. This is the best known and safest Mersey
anchorage, with depths up to 55 feet and a bottom of sand and mud
with good holding ground (J.E.A.). THE VALLEY LODGE, in
Devonshire Park, *v. Tranmere Pool supra*. WATCH HEATH (lost),
1843 *TA*, 1682 J.E.A., *Watte Heath* 1621 ib, *Watts Heath* 1630 ib,
The- 1645 Sheaf, *Watsheath* 1647 J.E.A., *Watcheath* 1691 ib,
probably from the ME pers.n. *Wat* (*Walter*) and hǣð. Cf. Woodchurch Rd *infra*, Watch Hay 319 *infra*. WELL LANE, 1824 Sheaf,
v. wella, lane. WHETSTONE LANE, *v.* Whetstone Meadow 319
infra. WOODCHURCH LANE, cf. foll. and Woodchurch 274 *supra*,
v. lane. WOODCHURCH RD, *Saugh Lane* 1724 NotCestr, *Slush-*,
Snush-, *Slough Lane* 1719–1812 J.E.A., *Slush Lane* (*Cottage*) 1831
Bry, *Slough Lane Croft & Field* 1843 *TA*, 'muddy lane', *v.* sogh,
slōh, slush, lane, cf. *Watch Heath, Hinderton supra*. J.E.A. points
out that *Watch Heath* seems to have been superseded, about 1700, by
Slush Lane as the name of this hamlet.

FIELD-NAMES

The undated forms are 1843 *TA* 403 and 1843, 1857 *TAMap* 403. Of the
others, 1270–80, 1300–7, 1309 are *JRC*, 1646, 1663 Sheaf, 1347, 1357
ChFor, 1354 Orm², 1407 ChRR, 1582 *Clif*, 1831 Bry, 1842 OS.

(a) Asker Dale (perhaps an old name, from ON askr (pl. *askar*, gen.pl.
aska) and dalr 'a valley, a hollow', but the first el. could be ModEdial.
asker 'a lizard', and the second el. dæl¹, or deill 'an allotment'); Backside
(*v.* ba(c)ksyde); Bassage Mdw; Blacket Hay; Brad(d)ow Hay (*v.* brād, dāl);
Brow Fd (*v.* brū); Bucknal(l) (*Bokenhull* 1357, 'hill growing with beech-
trees', *v.* bōcen, hyll); Canester Holt; Cheap Side (near the site of the
nineteenth-century Wakes fairs, J.E.A., *v.* cēap, sīde); Dam Hay(s) (*v.*
damme); Dunkirk Fd (cf. 176 *supra*); Folly Croft; Gall Butts (*v.* butte);
Greedy Butts (*v.* grǣdig); Greens (*v.* grēne²); Headland Hay (*v.* hēafod-
land, (ge)hæg); Heath Fd (cf. *le Hethfeld* 1357, *v.* hǣð); Hollins Ditch
(*v.* holegn, dīc); The Hurst (*v.* hyrst); Intake (*v.* inntak); Iron Hay (*v.*
hyrne, (ge)hæg); Kirket(t) Hay (*Kirkett Heys* 1646, adjoining Church Rd
supra, one of them now Egerton Park, '(enclosures near) the road to the
church', from (ge)hæg and ME *kirk-gate* from kirkja and gata); Knobbs
End (*v.* knob, ende¹); Lawn (*v.* launde); Lime Kiln Fd & Lane (cf. *Lime*

Kiln Cottage 1842, *v.* limkilne); Marl Croft; Marled Hay; Marsh; Mill Hill (J.E.A. observes that there is no evidence of a mill here); Newhay (cf. *le Newefeld* 1357, *v.* nīwe, feld); North and South; (Big) Old Fd (cf. *le Nethyrholdefeld* 1309, *le Oldfeld* 1347, *v.* neoðera, ald, feld); Old Lads Croft; Outlet (*v.* outlet); Oxton Hay (cf. Oxton 269 *infra*); Park (a group of seven fields, *v.* park); Pasture Hay(s) (*v.* (ge)hæg); Pike Looms (*v.* pīc¹, land); Pinfold (*v.* pynd-fald); Rake Hay (cf. *le Rake* 1300–7, 1357, *v.* rake, (ge)hæg); Rye Croft; Sea Hay (*v.* sǣ, (ge)hæg); Slack Fd (*v.* slakki); Storeton Fd (cf. Storeton 253 *supra*); Strand (the shore of R. Mersey, *v.* strand); Town Fd; Triangle (*v.* 337 *infra*); Vexation (*v.* 337 *infra*); Wall Butts (*v.* wælla, butte); Wood Butts (*le Wodbuttes* 1357, 'selions near a wood', *v.* wudu, butte); Wood Hay (*v.* (ge)hæg); Yolk of Egg (Lane) (a complimentary name, *v.* 337 *infra*).

(*b*) *Holme House* 1663 (Sheaf³ 32 (7221), cf. John de *Hulme* 1407, Richard de *Houlme* 1582, a manorial name, *v.* hūs); *le Leʒe* 1357 (*boscus de Tranemul* 1270–80, *-mol(l)* 1347, 1357, *Tranemollegh* 1347, 'wood of *Tranmole*' 1354, 'the glade', *v.* lēah); *Netherridyng, le Ouerrydyng* 1357 ('the lower and the upper cleared-land', *v.* neoðera, uferra, ryding).

xvi. Woodchurch

The ancient parish of Woodchurch contained the townships 1. Arrowe, 2. Barnston, 3. Irby, 4. Landican, 5. Noctorum, 6. Oxton, 7. Pensby, 8. Prenton, 9. Thingwall, 10. Woodchurch. Of these, all except Barnston, Irby and Pensby are now included in Birkenhead County Borough. Part of Irby belonged to Thurstaston parish 279 *infra*, and to Woodchurch parish belonged part of Claughton cum Grange township, cf. 316 *infra*. The origin of Woodchurch parish is discussed 267 *infra*.

1. ARROWE (109–2786) [ˈarou]

    Arwe 1240–9 Chest 1307 *Eyre* (p) *et freq* to 1497 ChRR, (*-in Wyrehale*) 1420 Plea

    Haree 1278 *ChFor*, *Haregh* 1305 (1344) Pat

    Harugh l13 AD

    Harghee l13 Tab

    Harettee l13 Tab

    Harough l13 (18) Sheaf

    Argh' 1296 Court (p), (*-in Wyrhale*) 1312 InqAqd, *Arghe* 1307, 1347 *Eyre*, *Arhe* 1347 *ChFor*

    Areghe in Wir-, *-Wyrhale* 1311 Fine

    Arwey 1347 *ChFor*

    Erwe 1348 *Indict*, 1433 ChRR

    Arewe 1351 *MinAcct*, (*-in Wirhale*) 1351 Chamb

Arowe 1397 ChRR, 1400 *Mainw*, 1428 Orm², *Arrowe* 15 ib *et freq*
with variant spellings *Arowe* (to 1499 Plea), *Arrow*
Harrow 1727 Sheaf

'At the shieling', from ON erg, or in this case probably directly
from MIr airge. In this township appear the f.ns. *Bennetts-, Bithels-,
Broad-, Browns-, Gills-, Harrisons-, Linacres-, Smiths-, Whartons-,
Widness-,* and *Youds Arrowe* 1846 *TA*, cf. *Ball's, Bennet's-, Broad-,
Leene's-, Old-, Walls-, Young's-,* and *Samuel Yonges Arrow* 1688
Sheaf³ 46 (9386). In these, *Arrowe* means 'a part, an allotment, of the
township of Arrowe', rather than 'shieling, *erg*'. Arrowe was enclosed c.1574, cf. Sheaf³ 22 (5232) and Arrowe Park *infra*, and these
are the apportionments of the enclosure. The el. erg may also appear
in Ashton Brook 1 14, Ark Wood 3 245, Bickerton Fm and Harrow
Flan 4, 3 *supra*. Orm² II 527 notes a church at Arrowe in the
fifteenth century, a chapel of ease to Woodchurch, but there is no
trace of it.

ARROWE BROOK (The Birket), *Arrow Brook* 1831 Bry, *v.* brōc, cf. foll.
ARROWEBROOK FM, *Lower Arrow House* 1831 ib, *Arrowbrook Farm*
1842 OS, cf. prec. and foll.   ARROWHOUSE FM, *Arrow House* 1831
Bry, *v.* hūs, cf. prec. This and Arrowe Hill 306 *infra* are *Arrow
Houses* 1842 OS.   CARD PLANTATION.   THE COTTAGE, *Cherry
Cottage* 1831 Bry, 1842 OS.   IVY FM.   LIMBO LANE, 1831 Bry,
Limber Lane 1846 *TA*, probably named from its being along the
edge of the township on the Irby boundary, cf. 265 *infra*, *v.* limbo.
NEILSON'S PLANTATION.   NICHOLSON'S PLANTATION.   RAKE
LANE, *v.* 306 *infra*.   ROBINSON'S PLANTATION.   TOPHOUSE
FM, *Arrow Top* 1831 Bry, *Arrow* 1842 OS, *v.* topp.

FIELD-NAMES

The undated forms are 1846 *TA* 19. Of the others, 1329 is *JRC*, 1347, 1357
ChFor, 1688 Sheaf.

(a) Arrowe Hill (cf. Arrowe Hill 306 *infra*); Banks Hey (*v.* banke,
(ge)hæg); Outlet (*v.* outlet); Pinfold Fd (*v.* pynd-fald); Race Fd & Mdw
(*v.* ras); Tart Fd; Wall Gutter (*v.* wælla, goter).

(b) *Arwegreue* 1357 ('grove at Arrowe', *v.* græfe); *Arweymulne* 1347
('mill at Arrowe', *v.* myln); *Gwynnes Hayes* 1688 (from (ge)hæg and the
surname *Gwynne*); *Leenes Land* 1688 (from land and the surname *Leen(e)*);
Leonards Heys 1688 (from (ge)hæg and the pers.n. or surname *Leonard*);
Merehills 1688 (probably 'boundary hills, hills at a boundary', *v.* (ge)mǣre,

hyll); *the Quarryes alias the Quarrells* 1688 (*v.* quarrelle); *Wermesgreue* 1329 (the final el. is grǣfe 'a wood'. The first el. appears to be a pers.n., either OE *Wǣrhelm* or an OE **Wermi* as in Warmsworth WRY 1 62).

2. BARNSTON (109–2883)

Bernestone 1086 DB, *Berneston* 1208–29 Whall (p), e13 *AddCh* (p),
  et freq with variant spellings *Bernis-* (1259 Court to 1497 ChRR),
  -ton(e) to 1524 ChRR, *Bernuston* 1348 *Eyre, Bernston* 1289
  Court (p), 1293 (p), 1354 Orm², 1490 ChRR (p)
Berles-, Berlistona in Wirhale 1096–1101 (1280) Chest, *Berlestona*
  1150 ib *et freq* with variant spellings *Berlis-, -t(on), -tona, -tone*
  to 1308, 1309 Ipm, *Berluston* 1309 *JRC* (p)
Beruleston 1199–1216 *AddCh* (p)
Bernolweston 13 Whall (p)
Borneston c.1250 Bark (p)
Binston 13 Chest (p)
Burneston 1539–47 Dugd
Barneston 1579 Dugd, *Barnston* 1659 Sheaf

'Beornwulf's farm', from the OE pers.n. *Beornwulf* and tūn.

CARNSDALE HO (109–282828), *Carnesdale* 1439 Bark, 1459 Orm²,
1503 ChRR *et freq, Kernesdall* 1588 Bun, *Karnsdale House* 1736
Blun, 'valley at a cairn', *v.* carn, dæl¹. This place adjoins Haby *infra*.

THE ACRES, cf. *Bottom-, Middle- & Top Acre(s)* 1846 *TA, v.* æcer.
BARNSTON COMMON, 1831 Bry, *v.* commun. BARNSTON HALL
(lost), *Barnston Hall now ruinous* 1724 NotCestr. BORDER FM,
near the township boundary. DALE HOUSE (RD), *Dale House* 1831
Bry, *Deal House* 1842 OS, named from *The Dale* 1831 Bry, 'house at
a dale', *v.* dæl¹, hūs, brū, wudu, (ge)hæg. GILLS LANE. LOWER
FM. MANOR FM & HO. MEADOW HO. NEWTOWN.
OAKLANDS. PENSBY HO & RD, cf. *Pensby Lane* 1831 Bry, 1842
OS, named from Pensby 271 *infra*. THE PRINGLES (a house),
perhaps from pingel 'a little enclosure'. SLACK RD, *v.* slakki.
SMITHY LANE, *v.* smiðõe. STREEVE, (a house). WHITEHOUSE
(LANE), 1831 Bry, *v.* hwīt, hūs, lane. WHITFIELD LANE, cf.
Whitfield(s) 1846 *TA, v.* hwīt, feld.

FIELD-NAMES

The undated forms are 1846 *TA* 35. Of the others, 1347, 1357 are *ChFor*,
1736 *Dep*.

(a) Affghan Mdw; Back Grave (v. back, græfe); Backside (v. ba(c)ksyde); Barley Hey (v. (ge)hæg); The Barton (v. bere-tūn); Bennetts-, Bannetts Wd (named from the *Bennet* family, landowners here); Bentley Brow (v. beonet, leāh, brū); Clatter Bridge (v. clæter, brycg); Corn Fd; Deans Hey; Dirty Lane 1831; The Eliza; The Folly (v. folie); Grassy Ends (v. ende[1]); Griffins Head; Haby Ho & Kiln (109–280827, two fields adjoining Carnsdale *supra*, perhaps from an old p.n. in bȳr, but no evidence is available); Hare and Hounds Land (v. land); The Harrick (cf. Harrock, etc. 265 *infra*); Heath Fd (1736); Intake (v. inntak); Kant Much Hey; Kitchen Croft; Marl Hey (v. marle, (ge)hæg); Mens Hey; Naps Fd; New Grounds (-*Ground* 1736); New Hey (cf. *New Hay Copy* 1736, v. (ge)hæg, copis); Oat Hey (v. (ge)hæg); Out Fd (v. ūte); Pingle (v. pingel); Pipers Fd & Hey; Ramsdale (probably 'raven's valley' from hræfn and dæl[1], though the first el. may be hramsa 'wild garlic' or ramm 'a ram'); Sand Fd; Sheepcote Heys (v. scēp, cot, (ge)hæg); Short But(t)s (v. butte); Small Flat (v. smæl, flat); Town Croft, Townsend; Wash Heys (v. wæsce); White Hey; Withins (v. wiðegn); Wood Croft, Further- & Middle Wd (*boscus de Berneston* 1357, *Lower Wood, Woodcroft* 1736, v. wudu, croft); Woody Knot (v. knottr, cnotta); Little Yard (v. geard).

(b) via Cestr' 1347 ('the Chester road, *via Cestrensis*'); le Rake 1347 ('the narrow lane', v. rake).

3. IRBY (109–2584), IRBY FM, HALL, HEATH, HILL (FM) [ˈə:rbi]

Erberia 1096–1101 (1280), c.1150, (lit. *Erbeia*) 1096–1101 (1280) (17) Chest

Irreby 1096–1101 (1280), 1181–1232, 1188–91, 1249–1323 Chest, 1271 *ChFor*, 1297 CRV, 1307–23 Chest, 1347 *ChFor*, 1440 *Rental*, 1455 ChRR (p), 1535 VE, 1579 Dugd, *Yrreby* 1271 *ChFor*

Ireby 1181–1232 (1300) Pat, 1288 *ChFor*, 1318 Cl (p), 1538 *JRC*, 1541, 1546 Dugd, 1565 Cre, 1566, 1596, 1660 Sheaf

Iireby c.1232 (1307) *Eyre*

Hirby 1278 ChFor, Hyrby 1361 BPR

Yrby 1278 ChFor, 1291 Tax, c.1310 Chest, 1340 *Eyre*, Irby 1288 *ChFor*, 1361 BPR, 1539–47 Dugd, 1552 (17) Sheaf, 1579 Dugd, 1724 NotCestr, *Irbi* c.1293 AD, *Irbye* 1539–47 Dugd, *Irbie* 1553 Pat, *Irby Hall* 1724 NotCestr, *Irby Hill* 1842 OS

Herby 1515 ChEx

Erby 1646, 1726 Sheaf, *Erbye* 1648 ib

'Farm of the Irishmen', from Íri (gen. Íra) and bȳr, with hall, hǣð and hyll, cf. Irbymill Hill *infra*. The early forms show confusion between bȳr and burh, cf. Greasby 291 *infra*. Irby Hall was *Manor*

Farm 1831 Bry (cf. The Rookery *infra*), and at Irby Heath was *Heath Houses* 1831 Bry.

HEATHFIELD (109–254863, in Greasby 6″ OS, in Irby 1831 Bry). IRBYMILL HILL, *Irby Millhill* 1724 NotCestr, cf. *oon wyndemylne called Ireby Mylne* 1538 *JRC*, *Irby Mill* 1552 (17) Sheaf, *Irby Milne* 1660 ib, and *Mill Lane* 1831 Bry, *v.* myln, hyll, lane. This hill lay in Thurstaston parish. Cf. foll. IRBYMILLHILL FM (109–252860, in Greasby 6″ OS, in Irby 1831 Bry), *Irby Hill Farm* 1842 OS, cf. prec. LIMBO LANE, 1831 Bry, cf. 262 *supra* and *Big- & Little Limbers* 1846 *TA*, *v.* limbo. MILL COTTAGE (109–253861, in Greasby 6″ OS, in Irby 1831 Bry). REDSTONES FM, cf. *Redstones* 1846 *TA*, from the red sandstone rocks here, *v.* rēad, stān. THE ROOKERY, *Old Hall* 1831 Bry, cf. Irby Hall *supra*.

FIELD-NAMES

The undated forms are 1846 *TA* 218 (Irby in Woodchurch parish). Of the others, 1307–23 is Chest, 1329 *JRC*, 1440 *Rental*, 1831 Bry, 1847 *TA* 393 (Irby in Thurstaston parish) and the rest Sheaf.

(a) Asp Tree Croft (*v.* æspe); The Autons (six times, twice lit. *Antons*, identical with 'a close called *Antherm*' 1592, *The Autornes* 1648, probably 'the hawthorns', from hagu-þorn); Backside (1847, *v.* ba(c)ksyde); Common (1847); Cow Hay (*v.* (ge)hæg); Crowders 1847; Fitter Hay; Higher & Lower Flatt(s), Flatt Hay (cf. *Flats Lane* 1831, *v.* flat, (ge)hæg); Little Great Hay 1847, Big Great Hay (*v.* (ge)hæg); Green Hays (*the Green Hey* 1639, *v.* grēne[1], (ge)hæg, cf. *the Ditch Stead infra*); The Greets Pits 1847, The Greets (*the Greetes* 1639, *v.* grēote); Gutter Leys 1847 (*v.* goter, lēah); (Great) Harrock, Little Horrock (cf. Harrick 264 *supra*); Hesketh('s) (*Heskeths* 1847, *Heskitts* 1639, either from hesta-skeið 'a horse-race track' or the La surname *Hesketh*, cf. Hesketh Grange 231 *supra*); High Fd 1847; Little Horrock (*v.* Harrock *supra*); Horse Pasture 1847; Intake (*v.* inntak); Kiln Croft 1847 (cf. *Kill Hey* 1639, *v.* cyln, (ge)hæg); Lane Croft; Long Loons (1639, *v.* land); Marled Hay (*v.* marled, (ge)hæg); Marsh Hay (Brow) 1847; Michansedge, Mickansedge (*Meckansedge* 1847, *the Mekonsuch* 1639, *v.* sīc 'a watercourse'. The first el. may be the same as in Micker Brook 1 32, *v.* Mecca Brook 290 *infra*); Millers Hay (1847, cf. *Millo Flat*, *Millo Hey* 1639, *The Millway Hey* 1648, '(enclosure at) the road to the mill', *v.* myln, weg, (ge)hæg); Old Hay (1847, *v.* (ge)hæg); Pan Mdw; Porto Hay (*The Porto Hey* 1639, probably originally *Portway Hay*, '(enclosure at) the road to the market-town', *v.* port-weg, (ge)hæg); Rake Hey (cf. *the short Rake Hey* 1639, *the Rake End* 1685, *v.* rake, (ge)hæg, ende[1]); Rye Hay 1847; Smores (*Old- & New-* 1847, 'the butter pastures', *v.* smjǫr); Sour Loons (1847, *the Sower Lands* 1648, *v.* sūr, land); Stack Yard

(v. stak-ȝard); Town Fd (The- 1648, v. toun, feld); Wall Hay (The- 1648, v. wælla, (ge)hæg); Wet Reans (cf. the Reanes, the Broade Riene 1639, v. wēt, rein); Whitegreaves, v. hwīt, grǣfe).

(b) the blind pit 1639 (a dry, empty, or overgrown pit, v. blind, pytt); the Ditch Stead 1639 ('the site of a ditch', v. dīc, stede. This was in Green Hays supra, and may be named from 'a certain old ditch where a leper-house formerly stood' (ad caput cuiusdam veteris fossati ubi domus leprosorum quondam fuit sita) in the boundary of Irby and Thurstaston 1307–23 Chest II 696); the Dooe Stone 1639 (v. stān. The first el. may be dāl 'an allotment', cf. Dawstone 278 infra); the Greenway 1639 (v. grēne[1], weg); Knukyn 1307–23 (quidam monticulus qui vocatur-, 'the hillock', v. cnycyn, cf. Kne(c)kyn 286 infra); Londymere 1307–23 (the name of 'a certain fountain walled about with big stones', meaning 'the land boundary', from land-(ge)mǣre, marking the boundary between Irby and Thurstaston, cf. Chest II 696); the Long Pitts 1639; the Penisack 1639 (part of Green Hays supra, with the Ditch Stead supra. The origin of the f.n. is not known); pons de Irby 1329 ('the bridge at Irby', v. brycg); le Pyledhoke 1440 ('the stripped oak', from āc and ME pilede 'stripped, peeled'); the Upper Shoot 1639 (v. scēat); the Wall Gatts Hey 1648 ('(enclosure at) the pasture plot at the spring', v. wælla, gata, (ge)hæg).

4. LANDICAN (109–283856) [ˈlandikən]

Landechene 1086 DB
Landekan 1240–9 Chest, Landecan 1265–90 ib, 1278 ChFor et freq
   with variant spelling Landekan to 1469 Cre, (Lanian or-) 1621
   (1656) Orm[2], Landecon (lit. -ton) 1332 Ipm (Landetan IpmR),
   Landecan (lit. -tan) 1338 Cre, Landeca 1346 CampbCh, Landecan
   in Wyrhale 1390 Orm[2]
Landican 1342 (1438) ChRR, 1391 Pat (p), 1535 VE, 1724 Not-
   Cestr, (Lankhorne alias-) 1671 AddCh
Lankekan 1347 ChFor
Ludecan 1536 Dugd, 1538 AOMB 399, 1560 Sheaf
Lancan 1539 Plea
Ludcame 1547 MinAcct
Lancon 1566, 1570 Sheaf
Lancan 1569 Sheaf
Lancame 1629 Sheaf
Lanian or Landecan 1621 (1656) Orm[2]
Lankhorne alias Landican 1671 AddCh

'Tegan's church', from lann and the OWelsh pers.n. Tecan. MWelsh Tegan. Professor Richards observes that there is no known Welsh saint Tegan (cf. DEPN). He draws attention to Capel Degan and *Llandegan* in the parish of Llanwnda, Pembrokeshire, supposed to be named after one *Degan* identified by Baring-Gould and Fisher, *Lives of the British Saints* II 279–285, with OIrish *Dagan*, i.e. St. Dagan of Inverdaile (Ennereilly, co. Wicklow, *v.* Hogan 457) bishop c.600, died 640, cf. Sheaf[3] 45 (9369), 49 (9885–8). He demonstrates that *llan* + *Degan* would have led to a p.n. form *Llanddean whereas *Llandegan* supposes *llan* + *Tegan*. (*Capel Degan* could be a formation based upon the p.n. *Llandegan* < *llan* + *Tegan*, so it need not infer a pers.n. *Degan*.) There may well have been an unrecorded Welsh saint *Tegan*. Professor Richards & Professor Jackson remark that there are several instances of the pers.n. as the second el. in Welsh p.n. compounds, where it might appear to be merely a common pers.n., but after *Llann*- a pers.n. is usually taken to be that of the person revered as a saint at that place. Cf. Sheaf[3] 45 (9369), 49 (9885–8). It has been remarked in Sheaf *loc. cit.* and Orm[2] II 520, 525, that Woodchurch 274 *infra* is not mentioned in DB, whereas Landican (and its priest) is, that Woodchurch is not distinctly named until 1093 as a separate township, and that the advowson of Woodchurch was vested in the manor of Landican down to the time of Henry VIII (cf. 'the manor of *Wodechirche* which is a member of the manor of *Thingewall*' 13 Bark 21, cf. Thingwall 273 *infra*). These circumstances suggest that Woodchurch is the later name for Tegan's church at Landican, and that the township called Woodchurch was originally included in that called Landican. Sheaf[3] 49 *loc. cit.* notes that Woodchurch had a typical Celtic circular churchyard, perhaps the original *lann* a sacred precinct.

ELLISON'S FM (lost), 1831 Bry, from the Wirral surname *Ellison*. LANDICAN LANE, *Heath Lane* 1831 ib, cf. *Heath Field* 1846 *TA* and *Landican Lane End* 1831 Bry, *v.* hǣð, lane, ende[1]. PRENTON BRIDGE, cf. Prenton 272 *infra*. WOODCHURCH LANE, cf. Woodchurch 274 *infra*.

FIELD-NAMES

The undated forms are 1846 *TA* 230. Of the others, 1357 is *ChFor*, 1440 *Rental*, 1831 Bry.

(*a*) Acres; Backside (*v.* ba(c)ksyde); Broad Hey (*v.* (ge)hæg); Carr Bridge Fd & Mdw (cf. *Carremedowe* 1440, *v.* kjarr, mǣd); Cuckoo's Fd (*v.* cuccu); Dale Hey (*v.* dæl[1], (ge)hæg); Dig Meat; Honey Fd (*v.* hunig); Honey Suckle; Hooks (*v.* hōc); Kily Hill; Long Acres; Mill Fd; New Hay, -Hey (*v.* (ge)hæg); Nostage; Prenton Dale 1831 (cf. Prenton Dell 272 *infra*); Rake Shoots, Rakes (*v.* rake, scēat); Rough Shoots (*v.* scēat); Sandy Hey (*v.* (ge)hæg); Sour Mdw; Storeton Fold Hey (*v.* fald, (ge)hæg cf. Storeton 253 *supra*); Swangs (*v.* swang); Three Nooks (*v.* þrēo, nōk, cf. three-nooked); Town Mdw; Wanton Dale (cf. Hillside Fm 255 *supra*); Wilful Mdw (*v.* 337 *infra*); Wood Hey (*v.* (ge)hæg).

(*b*) *le Bothom* 1357 ('the valley bottom', *v.* boðm); *placea terre iuxta cruces* 1357 ('a plot of land next to the crosses', perhaps standing crosses such as that of which the Overchurch rune-stone formed part); *Landekangreue* 1357 ('grove at Landican', *v.* grǣfe).

5. NOCTORUM (109–290877) ['nɔk'tourəm]

   Chenoterie 1086 DB
   Cnoctyrum 1119 (1150), 1150 Chest, *Cnoctirum* 1119 (1280) ib, *Knoctyrum* 1240–9 ib *et freq* with variant spellings *Knoctirum*, *-tyrum*, *-tyrom*, *-tirom*, *Knocttyrum*, *Conctirum*, *Knoghtirum*, *-tyrum*, *-tiroum*, *Knocktyrom* to *Knoctyrom* 1535 VE
   Cenoctirum 1119 (1285) Ch
   Knoutyrom 1286 ChFor, *Knothirom* 1294 *ib*, *Knottyrum* 1357 *ib*
   Kugghtyrum 1357 ChFor
   Knettyrom 1377 Plea (Orm² II 526 reads *Knectyrom*)
   Knoctrout 1539–47 Dugd
   Knocktor 1546 Dugd
   Knocktoram 1553 Pat, *Knoctorum* 1566 Sheaf *et freq* with variant spellings *Knocktorum*, *Knoctorun*, *-torom* to *Knocktorum* 1845 ChetOS VIII, *Knoctorum* 1831 Bry, 1882 Orm², (*Knocktorum within Worrall*, *-Woirel*) 1709, 1735 Blun, *Noctorum* 1708 Sheaf, (*-till of late years called Knoctorum*) 1882 Orm²
   Knockram 1583 Sheaf
   Knocketerne 1589 Sheaf
   Knocturme 1604 Sheaf
   Knoctorn 1623 Sheaf
   Knoctorine 1628 Sheaf

'Dry hill', *v.* cnocc¹, tírim. This etymology, making Noctorum a pure OIr p.n., was proposed in Sagabook XIV 306, cf. Dinnseanchas I i 24, and was tentatively adopted by Ekwall in DEPN (4th edition), who long ago identified the first el., cnocc. Professor Jackson contributes an interesting observation on the spellings. Whilst the OIr form *tírim* with long *í* is old and must be regarded as original, nevertheless there is also a form *tĭrim* with short *ĭ*, and this must be old since it is the Scottish Gaelic and Manx form. It might then be argued that the ME -*tyr*-, -*tir*- spellings could represent the alternative forms *tírim* and *tĭrim*. But the result would be the same in either case, [ˈ(k)nɔkˈti:rəm] or [-ˈtirəm] > [ˈ(k)nɔktirəm] > [ˈ(k)nɔktərəm] spelt *noctorum* whence under Lat influence [ˈnɔkˈtourəm]. Professor Ekwall in correspondence made the reservation about the proposed etymology of Noctorum, that the compound *cnocc-tírim* does not appear elsewhere. Dr Liam Price, on the other hand, observed that although the compound is not found in p.ns. in Ireland, it is perfectly feasible and would be analogous with the township-name Tullyhirm, cos. Armagh and Monaghan, OIr *tulach thirm* 'dry hill', from *tírim* and OIr *tulach* 'a hill' (Joyce II 413). The topography of Noctorum makes the derivation fairly certain, for in 1819 (Orm² II 526) the hamlet consisted of two or three farmhouses on an elevation opposite Woodchurch over the marshy land beside the stream The Fender.

THE FARM, *Coventry(e)s House* 1709 *Blun*, named from the *Coventry* family, tenants here, cf. Rake Hey *infra*.

FIELD-NAMES

The undated forms are 1844 *TA* 295. Of the others 1294, 1347 are *ChFor*, 1709 *Blun*, 1831 Bry.

(a) Calf Croft; Deep Reens (*v.* dēop, rein); The Dell (*v.* dell); Field under the Hill (cf. *the Little Field under the Hill* 1709); Flat (*v.* flat); Grave (*v.* grǣfe); the Hempyard 1709 (*v.* hemp-yard); The Hill (1709); Kessie Hey (*the Kelshaw-, Killshaw Heys* 1709, 'copse at a kiln', *v.* cyln, sceaga, (ge)hæg); Leys (*v.* lēah); Lillaper Hey (*the three Lilly Poole Heys* 1709, *v.* lilie, pōl¹) the Lower End 1709 (*v.* ende¹); Marled Field (*The Marle Field* 1709); the New Close & Heys 1709; Nine Fd; Outlet (*v.* outlet); Ox Hey (cf. *the three Halkes Heys* 1709, *v.* halc, (ge)hæg); Rake Hey (cf. *Coventryes Rake Hey* 1709, *v.* rake, (ge)hæg; cf. The Farm *supra*); Sand Fd; Steel Wd (*the Steel Woods* 1709, *v.* stigel, wudu); Wallows (*the (two) Wollamsides, -sies* 1709, *Wollans Brow* 1831, probably '(the sides of-, the hillside at-,) the crooked selions', from wōh and land with sīde and brū).

(b) *boscus de Bradegreue* 1294 ('broad wood', *v.* brād, grǣfe); *boscus de Knoghtyrum* 1347 ('Noctorum wood', *v.* wudu).

6. OXTON (109-2987) [ˈɔkstən, ˈɔkssn̩]

> *Oxton* 13 (1605) ChRR, 1275 Cl *et freq*, (-*alias Oxon*) 1616 ChRR,
> *Oxtone* 1275 Ipm
> *Oxeton* 1278 Ipm

Oxon 1549 Orm², 1566, 1611, 1652 Sheaf, 1724 NotCestr, 1818 Sheaf, (*Oxton alias-*) 1616 ChRR, (*-alias Oxton*) 1620 Orm² 'Farm, or enclosure, where oxen are kept', *v.* **oxa, tūn.**

ARNO HILL, *Arnehowe* 1331 *ChFor*, (subtus) *Arnowe* 1357 *ib*, cf. *Arno(s)*, *Little Arno* 1795 *Bainb* (f.ns.), (*The*) *Arno* 1846 *TA*, 'Arni's hill or mound', from the ON pers.n. *Arni* and **haugr.**

LINGDALE (HO & QUARRY), *Lyngedale* 13 (1605), E1 (1577) ChRR, *Ling Dale Hill* 1831 Bry, 'heather valley', *v.* **lyng, dalr,** cf. Lingdale Hill 318 *infra*.

HEATH HEYS, cf. Heath Heys *infra*.   HOLM LANE, NEW HOME FM, *Home Lane, Home(s), Home Croft(s), Home Hey* 1795 *Bainb*, *Holme Lane* 1831 Bry, 'the marsh', *v.* **holmr.**   MERE FARM RD, commemorating a pool here 1795 *Bainb, v.* **mere¹.**   MILL HILL, cf. Mill Heys *infra*.   OXTON HALL, 1831 Bry.   OXTON HEATH, 1842 OS, *Oxton Common* 1795 *Bainb*.   OXTON HILL, 1831 Bry, *South Oxton* 1842 OS, *v.* **sūð.**   TOWNFIELD LANE, 1795 *Bainb*, passing *Town Field Crofts* 1795 *ib*.   VILLAGE RD.   WOOD-CHURCH RD, *Slush Lane* 1831 Bry, *v.* 260 *supra*.

FIELD-NAMES

The undated forms are 1846 *TA* 313. Of the others 13 (1605), l13 (1577) are ChRR, 1272 Sheaf, 1282 Court, 1357 *ChFor*, 1795 *Bainb*.

(a) Backside (1795, *v.* ba(c)ksyde); Carr Bridge Croft (- & *Meadow* 1795, *v.* brycg, cf. foll.); Carr Field Hey (*-Heys* 1795, *v.* kjarr, cf. prec.); Crook Loon (1795, *v.* krókr, land); Dale Bank (1795, *v.* dæl¹); Higher & Lower Flatts (cf. *Flat* 1795, *v.* flat); Fotherings (1795, cf. *Fothers* 1795, probably from ModEdial. *fother* 'fodder', cf. *foddering* EDD); Head Butts (1795, cf. *Hauedlon* 1272 Sheaf³ 34 a selion in *Culnegreuefeld* (cf. Kiln Hey *infra*), *v.* hēafod-land, heved-butte); Heath Heys (1795, *v.* (ge)hæg); Kiln Hey (1795, cf. *Culnegreuefeld* 1272, *v.* cyln, grǣfe, feld, (ge)hæg); The Knowles, Knowles Hey (cf. *Knows* (*Hey*) 1795, *v.* cnoll, (ge)hæg); Land Pit; Lilly Wd (*-s* 1795, probably 'little wood', *v.* lȳtel, wudu); Mill Heys (1795, cf. *molendinum ventricitum* 1357, *v.* mlyn, (ge)hæg); New Hey (*-s* 1795, *v.* nīwe, (ge)hæg); Old Fd(s) (1795); Penny Pot Hey 1795; Rabby Loon 1795; Rake Hey 1795 (*v.* rake); Sand Heys (1795); Short Shoots (*v.* scēat); Slate Brick (*Slate Prick(s)* 1795); Spath (1795, *v.* sparð); Stye Fd 1795 (*v.* stigu); Thurstons (1795); Town Croft (*Town Field Crofts* 1795); Water Furrow (*-s* 1795); Well Fd 1795; Weybutt Hey 1795 ('(enclosure at) the head-land with a right of way', from weg and butte, with (ge)hæg); Youlands Hey (1795).

(b) *Bottislowe* 13 (1605), *Bottes-* l13 (1577) ('Bott's mound', from **hlāw** and a pers.n., either an OE *Bott*, a strong form of the OE pers.n. *Bot(t)a* (Redin 45), or an OE *Bōtic* discussed by Feilitzen 207); *Knavenebrec* 13 (1605), l13 (1577) ('the young men's hill', v. **cnafa**, (gen.pl. **cnafena**), **brekka**, probably a place on Oxton Hill which young men frequented); *Lewynesfeld* 1357 ('Lēofwine's field', from **feld** and the OE pers.n. *Lēofwine*); *Oxtonewey* 1282 ('the Oxton road', v. **weg**. Sheaf³ 34 (7603) suggests Christchurch Rd, Oxton); *Portestrete* 1282 ('road to a market-town', v. **port²**, **strǣt**. Sheaf³ 34 (7603) suggests Upton Rd, Oxton); *le Raggedestoan* 13 (1605), l13 (1577) (from **stān** and ME ragged, 'ragged, shaggy', either 'the rough-, the chipped stone' or 'the mossy stone'); *Swalewelowe* 13 (1605), *Swalewclewe* l13 (1577) (the first el. **swalwe¹** 'a swallow', the second probably **hlāw** 'a hill, a mound', the name would be 'hill frequented by swallows').

7. PENSBY, LOWER & MIDDLE PENSBY, PENSBY HALL, LANE (lost) & WOOD (109–2683) [ˈpenzbi]

> *Penisby* c.1229 Bark (p), 13 *JRC* (p), 1278 *ChFor*, 1329 *JRC*, *-bi*
> 1346 Bark, *Penesby* 1261–3 Chest (p)
> *Pennisby* 1270–80 *JRC*, *Pennesby* 1286 *ChFor et freq* with variant
> spellings *-bi*, *-bye*, (lit. *Pennesley* 1438 ChRR) to 1535 VE, (*-in Wirhale*) 1316 Misc, *Pennysbye* 1566 Sheaf
> *Peneiby* 1272–1307 *JRC* (p)
> *Penlisby* 1307 Sheaf (p)
> *Pynnesby* 1522 Sheaf
> *Pemmesby* 1523 (1571) ChRR
> *Pensby* c.1574 Sheaf, (*Lower*) *Pensby* 1831 Bry, (*Higher-*, *Lower-*)
> *Pensby* 1846 *TA*, *Pensby Lane* 1831 Bry, *Pensby Gorse* 1831 Bry

'Farm at a hill called *Penn*', from **penn¹**, and **býr**, with **hall**, **lane**, **wudu**, **gorst**. Pensby is under the north-east slopes of Heswall Hill, a prominent elevation, which would seem to have borne the name **Penn*, i.e. PrWelsh penn 'top, end' treated as a *name* by the English, cf. DEPN. Mr. J. Brownbill in correspondence with Allen Mawer, in 1925, reported forms *Penelsbury* and *Penlesby* n.d. Sheaf (no volume quoted, and not traced). These, and *Penlisby* 1307 Sheaf *supra*, suggest not only that the final el. **býr** may have alternated with **burh**, as in Greasby 291 *infra*, Irby 264 *supra*, but also that the hill-name *Penn* may have been compounded with **hyll** to give an alternative first component *Pen-hyll* as in Pendle, Pendlebury and Pendleton La 68, 42, 41. As with Arrowe 261 *supra* and the f.n. *Arrowe* there, the inclosure of Pensby c.1574 (Sheaf³ 22) produced allotments called after the township, cf. *one pasture called Pensby*

1592 *JRC*. Dr Barnes notes *Pennesbyes* 1628 *JRC*, *Peansbyes* 1664 *JRC*.

THE CROFT, *v.* croft.   ELMS FM.   HIGHFIELD HO.   OAK-
LAND.   THE ORCHARD.   THISTLEFIELD, cf. *Thistly Field* 1846
TA, *v.* þistel.

FIELD-NAMES

The undated forms are 1846 *TA* 316. Of these, fields in Higher Pensby
are marked with an asterisk.

(a) Backsides* (*v.* ba(c)ksyde); Benty Hay (*v.* benty, (ge)hæg); Dale Fd*
(*v.* dæl[1]); Intake* (*v.* inntak); Kitchen Croft; Oat Hay; Old Mdw* & Wd*;
Outlet* (*v.* outlet); Ox Hay* (*v.* (ge)hæg); Rushy Fd*; Sand Fd; Wanton
Dale (cf. Hillside Fm 255 *supra*).

(b) *Pennesbygreues* 1353 *Indict*, *groua de Pennesby* 1357 *ChFor* ('the
wood(s) at Pensby', *v.* græfe, grāf).

8. PRENTON (HALL) (109–3085)

Prestune 1086 DB, *Prestona* 1096–1101 (1280), 1150 Chest
Premptona 13 *AddCh* (p), *Prempton* c.1620 Sheaf (p)
Prenton 1260 Court *et freq* with variant spellings *-tona*, *-tone*,
   -thon, *-toune; Prenton Hall* 1724 NotCestr
Printon 113 (17), c.1642 (17) Sheaf

'Pren's farm', from tūn and the rare OE pers.n. *Præn*, discussed
in Redin 34, borne as a surname by Eadberht *Præn*, king of Kent
796–798, (ASC A). DEPN proposes this pers.n. for Prenton Ch,
Prendwick Nb, and Princethorpe Wa, cf. NbDu 160, Wa 141–2.
The DB and Chest forms record 'priest's farm', from prēost, but this
is probably an error for a form *Prenes-tun* in which the pers.n.
appeared in the gen.sg.

LOWER FM.   MOUNT HO, RD & WOOD, *Mount House* 1818 Sheaf,
Prenton Common Plantation 1831 Bry, *Mount Pleasant* 1842 OS,
1845 *TA*, *v.* mont.   PRENTON BRIDGE, 1831 Bry, crossing Prenton
Brook on the Landican boundary.   PRENTON BROOK (> The
Fender 1 23).   PRENTON DELL, *Prenton Dale* 1831 Bry, cf. *The
Dale, Dale Hay & Wood* 1845 *TA v.* dell, dæl[1], (ge)hæg, wudu.
PRENTON LANE, *v.* lane.   STORETON RD, cf. Storeton 253 *supra*.
WOODCHURCH RD, cf. Woodchurch 274 *infra*.

FIELD-NAMES

The undated forms are 1845 *TA* 328.

(*a*) Ashes (*v.* æsc); Backside (*v.* ba(c)ksyde); Brickkiln Croft (*v.* bryke-kyl); Calver Hay (*v.* calf, (ge)hæg); Cunney Burrow (*v.* coni, borow); Ecland Hay; The Harner; The Haughton; The Holme, Holme Bridge, Lower-, Top- and Five Acre Holme (*le Holm* 1340 *ChFor*, 'the marsh', *v.* holmr); Kirk Hay ('church field', *v.* kirkja); Old Hay; Park Stile (*v.* park, stigel); Rake Hay (*v.* rake); Sheep Fd; Shop Croft; Slang (*v.* slang); Swallow Soon Hay; Town Fd; Triangle; Wall Field Wd (*v.* wælla); White Loons (*v.* land); Wood Hay (*v.* (ge)hæg).

(*b*) *Prentonwode* 1340, *nemus de Prentone* 1294, *boscus de Prenton* 1357 (*v.* wudu).

9. THINGWALL (109–2784), HIGHER THINGWALL ['þiŋwɔ:l]

Tinguelle (lit. *Tuig-*) 1086 DB, *Tingewella* 1249–65 (p), 1250–90, 1265–91 (p), *-welle* 1265–91 Chest (p), *Thyngwelle* 13 Bark, *-well* 1303 Chamb, *Thingwelle* 1278 *ChFor*, *-well* 1325 Orm² (p), 1657 *Clif*, 1727 Sheaf, *Thingwell* 1848 *TAMap*
Finghwalle c.1180 *AddCh*
Thinghwalle 12 (17) Chol, *Thynghwall* 1426 *JRC*
Tingewalle 13 Chest (p), *Tyngwall* 1522 Sheaf, *Thyngwall* 13 Orm², *Thingwall* c.1235 *Chol* (p) *et freq* with variant spellings *Thyng-* (to 1524 ChRR), *Thinge-*, *Thynge-*, *-wal(l)*, *-walle*
Thingale c.1250 Bark (p)
Thyngwale 1339 Pat
Thryngwall 1519 Earw

'Field where an assembly meets', *v.* þing-vǫllr. This would be the meeting-place of the *Thing* for the Scandinavian community in Wirral, cf. Raby 228 *supra*. There is another Thingwall, near Liverpool, on the opposite side of R. Mersey, which would represent the centre for a Norse community in south-west Lancashire, *v.* La 112.

CROSS HILL (109–282842), 1831 Bry, *le Hull* 1340 *ChFor*, *v.* cros 'a cross', hyll. This is associated in local antiquarian tradition with the meeting-place of the *Thing* at Thingwall, *v.* Sheaf³ 50 (10063). THE FIDDLER'S FOLLY (lost, 109–282841), 1848 *TAMap*, *The Folly* 1831 Bry, *v.* folie. The fiddler, or *Fiddler*, is not known. HEATH-FIELD, cf. *Heath Field* 1846 *TA*. MANOR HO (lost, 109–280847),

1831 Bry.   POOL COTTAGE.   THINGWALL COMMON, 1831 Bry,
Thingwell- 1848 *TAMap.*   THINGWALL HALL   THINGWALL
MILL (lost, 109–275850), *Thingwell Mill* 1848 *TAMap*, *Thingwall
Mill* 1722 Sheaf, 1842 OS, *Windmill* 1846 *TA*, *v.* myln.

FIELD-NAMES

The undated forms are 1846 *TA* 390.

(*a*) Backside Mdw (*v.* ba(c)ksyde); Bleak Looms (*v.* bleak, land); Breach
Hay (*v.* brēc, (ge)hæg); Cart Gap (*v.* cræt, gappe); Cross Hay (*v.* cros,
(ge)hæg); Dale Hay, -Heaps, -Shoot (cf. *le Dale* 1347 *ChFor, v.* dæl¹,
(ge)hæg, scēat, hēap); Folly (*v.* folie); Gala Pits; Intake (*v.* inntak); Marl(ed)
Hay; The Mistake; Money Pits (*v.* manig, pytt); Old Road Track; Out
Gates ('outlying pastures', *v.* ūt, gata); Priest Park ('priest's paddock',
v. prēost, park); Sand(y) Hay; Shocking Dale (*v.* deill); Sitch (*v.* sīc);
Stony Wall; Swans; Two Loaves; Whelpers; Wood Croft.

10. WOODCHURCH (GREEN), HOLY CROSS CHURCH (109–2786)

Odecerce 1096–1101 (1150), 1150 Chest
Wodechirche 1096–1101 (1280) Chest *et freq* with variant spellings
    -chyrch(e), *-chirch(e)* to 1530 Plea, *-cherch(e)* 1271 *ChFor*, 1281
    Court, 1322 *JRC*, *-church* 1288 *ChFor* and twelve examples with
    variant spelling *-churche* to 1539–47 Dugd
Wdekirche c.1200 Bark, *Wodekirke* c.1250 ib
Hwodekerk c.1240 (17) Sheaf
Wudechurch 1241 Cl (p)
Wodchurche 14 Chest, 1511 Plea, 1549 Sheaf, *-chirche* 1365 *JRC*,
    1418 ChRR, 1428 Orm², 1433 Plea, *-chirch* 1440 ChRR
Woodchurch 1396, 1512 ChRR *et freq* with variant spellings
    -church(e), *-chourch*, *Woodchurch Green* 1842 OS
Wodenchurch 1499 Sheaf
Woodechurch 1499 Orm²
Woddechirche 1503 ChRR, *-churche* 1522 Plea
Wadchurche 1535 VE
Wudchurche 1535 VE

'Church in a wood', also 'wooden church' *v.* wudu, cirice. One
form has ModE *wooden* adj (1538 NED). The final el. shows Scand
influence, cf. kirkja. The name refers to the predecessor of Holy
Cross Church, which stands in a circular churchyard, probably the
religious precinct which gave name to Landican, *v.* 267 *supra.*

FLEET COTTAGE.   HOME FM.

FIELD-NAMES

The undated forms are 1846 *TA* 445. Of the others, 1347, 1357 are *ChFor*, 1440 *Rental*, 1831 Bry.

(*a*) Accars, Ackers (*v.* æcer); Ash Alland (*v.* æsc, hēafod-land); Corn Wd; The Greaves (*v.* grǣfe); Green (*v.* grēne²); Hoole (from OE *hōle*, dat.sg. of holh 'a hollow'); Landican Mdw (cf. Landican 266 *supra*); Park (*v.* park); Pigeon Croft; Pool Wd; Salacre Lane 1831 (*v.* Salacres 306 *infra*); Sand Fd; Sherry Brow (*v.* brū); Swine Croft (*le Swynecroft* 1440, *v.* swīn¹, croft); Town Fd; Whitefield Croft & Mdw (*v.* hwīt, feld); (Higher & Lower) Wood (cf. *boscus de Wodechirch(e)* 1347, 1357, *v.* wudu).

xvii. Heswall

The ecclesiastical parish of Heswall contained two townships, 1. Gayton 2. Heswall cum Oldfield.

1. GAYTON (COMMON, COTTAGE, FM, GRANGE & RD) (109–2780) ['geitn̩, 'geitən]

> *Gaitone* 1086 DB, *Gaiton* 1238 P, *Gayton* 1237 ib *et freq* with variant spelling *-tone*, (*-in Wyrhale*) 1277 (1350) VR, *Gayton Common* 1849 *TA*, *-Cottage* 1842 OS
> *Geytona* 1238 P, *Geython* 1239 Lib, *Geyton* 1240 P *et freq* ib, Lib, Pat, *ChFor*, Tax, Plea, *Eyre* to 1377 ib, 1658 Sheaf, (*-in Wyrhale*) 1313 Plea, *Geiton* 1280 CRC, 1569 Orm² 1658 Sheaf
> *Geyerthona* 1238 P
> *Geyiton* 1240 P
> *Geaton* 1615, 1649, 1727 Sheaf, 1724 NotCestr, *Geaten* 1649 Sheaf
> *Gaton* 1669 (1724) NotCestr

'Goat farm', from geit and tún, with commun, cottage.

BOUNDARY LANE, adjoining Heswall. BOWLING GREEN FM, 1831 Bry. DAWSTONE RD, *v.* 278 *infra*. DENHALL GUTTER, *v.* 223 *supra*. GAYTON HALL, 1831 Bry, *Geaton* 1724 NotCestr, *v.* hall. GAYTON SANDS, *Gayton Bank or Big Ben* 1842 OS, a sandbank in the Dee estuary, *v.* banke. *Big Ben* may commemorate the Westminster Palace bell. GAYTON WINDMILL, *Gayton Mill* 1831 Bry, cf. *Mill Croft & Hay* 1849 *TA*, *v.* myln, croft, (ge)hæg. LIGHTFOOT'S LANE, probably from the surname *Lightfoot* as in Lightfoots Green, Old Quay 222, 225 *supra*. OAKLANDS.

PROSPECT FM.   SLACK RD, cf. 278 *infra*.   WELL LANE, named from a well at 109–275807, cf. *Far Well* 1849 *TA* (f.n.), *v.* wella, lane.

FIELD-NAMES

The undated forms are 1849 *TA* 202. Of the others, 13 is Chest, 1294, 1347, 1357 *ChFor*, 1348 Chamb, 1569, c.1725 Sheaf, 1831 Bry, 1831[2] Hem.

(*a*) Annuity (presumably the endowment of a pension); Backsides (*v.* ba(c)ksyde); Bank Hay, Banks (*v.* banke, (ge)hæg); Benty Brow (*v.* benty, brū); Brotherings; Carpet Hay; Coachmans Fd; Cow Cross; Cow Hay (*v.* (ge)hæg); Cradle Brow (*v.* brū); Damage (*v.* demming); Eddish Croft (*v.* edisc); Fish Pond Fd; Higher-, Lower- & Town Flatt (*The Flatts* c.1725, *v.* flat); Foxholes (cf. *Gayton Fox Cover* 1831, *v.* fox-hol); Garden Fd; Gayton Wd 1831 (*boscus de Geyton* 1294, *-Gayton* 1347, 1357, *v.* wudu); Gayton Lane End 1831[2] (an anchorage in the Dee estuary, *v.* lane, ende[1]); Gayton Toll Bar 1831; Hamlets Hay (*Hamnett's Hey* c.1725, from the pers.n. *Hamnet*); Heath Hay; Hollins Grove Hay, Hollins Head (*v.* holegn, grāf, hēafod); the Horseheyes c.1725 (*v.* hors, (ge)hæg); Lilly Fd; Long House Fd; Morris Fd; Little Nook c.1725; Norris Croft (cf. *Norris House* 1831); Outlet (*v.* outlet); Old Fd; Paddle Pit; Pale Hey (cf. *parcum de Gayton* 1348, *v.* pale); Pit Water Fd; Pludge Ditch; Rake Ditch (*v.* rake); Runnock Hill; Sea Fd (*The-* c.1725, *v.* sǣ); The four Sharp Seas c.1725; Thornton Hay (cf. Thornton Hough 230 *supra*); Town Field Butt (*v.* butte); Town Hay (*v.* (ge)hæg); (Little) Wanton Dale (*v.* Hillside Fm 255 *supra*); Wishing Well 1831.

(*b*) Carrowe 13 (a fishery in R. Dee, perhaps named after a shore-line feature. The name may be 'rocky point' from carr and hōh); *Geyton Meyre* 1569 ('boundary-mark of Gayton', *v.* (ge)mǣre, at 109–285805 where Leighton, Gayton and Thornton Hough meet).

2. HESWALL CUM OLDFIELD, 1831 Bry, *Heswall-* 1727 Sheaf, cf. Heswall, Oldfield *infra*.

HESWALL (109–2681) ['hezwɔːl, 'hezwəl], dial. ['hesəl]

Eswelle 1086 DB

Haselwell 1190–1200 Facs (p), (1285) Ch (p) and forty-one examples with variant spellings *Hasel-*, *-il-*, *-wel(l)*, *-well(e)* to *Hasilwelle* 1535 VE, *Haseleuelle* 1244–5 Dieul, *-welle* 1252 RBE (p), *Hasselwell* (*Heswall alias Heswell alias-*) 1682 Sheaf

Heselwall c.1200 Bark (p), 13 ib (p), 1270 Sheaf, 1272 (17) Chest (p), 1278 Dugd (p), (*Heswall alias-*) 1612 Orm[2], *Hesil-* E1 *JRC* (p), *Heselewall* 1288 ChF (p), *Hesselwall* (*Heswall or-*) 1621 (1656) Orm[2]

Heselwell 13 Bark (p) and nine examples with variant spellings *Hesel-, -il-, Hesle-, -well(e)* to *Heslewelle* c.1330 *Blun* (p), *Heselewelle* 1250–70 Tab (p), 1280 ChF (p), 1283–8 *AddCh* (p), *-well* 1288 ChF (p), *Hes(s)elwelle* 1291 Tax

Haselwall c.1220 (1390) ChRR and ninety-two examples with variant spellings *Hasel-, Hasil-, -yl-, -ul-, -wall(e), -walla, -wal'* to 1819 Orm[2], (*-alias Hesewall*) 1586 ChRR, *Haselewalle* c.1290 *Chol, Hasselwalle* 15 ChRR, *-wall* (*alias Hesewall*) 1626 Orm[2], *Hassellwall* (*alias Hasewall*) 1627 *AddCh, Hassulwall* 1441 *ib*, 1523 Orm[2], *Hashulwall* 1478 AD, *Hassilwall* 1513 *ChEx*

Hazelwalle 13 *AddCh* (p)

Hesewell 1247 P (p), *-wall* 1299 (17) Chest (p), 1558 *AddCh*, (*Haselwall alias-*) 1586 ChRR, *Hessewall* 1636 Sheaf

Hasewell 1254 P (p), 1281 CRV (p), 1286 *ChFor*, 1301 (1344) Pat (p), 1307 Ipm (p), Fine (p), *-wall* 1288 Court (p), *ChFor* (p), 1387 *Eyre*, (*Heswall or-*) 1882 Orm[2], *-walle* 1435 VR (p), *Hasiwalle* 1307–23 Chest (p)

Haseleswalle 1276 *Chol* (p)

Hateshale 1291 Tax

Hosewall 1398 (17) Orm[2]

Weswall 1418 ChRR (p)

Heswall 1520 AD *et freq*, (*-alias Heselwall*) 1612 Orm[2], (*-or Hesselwall*) 1621 (1656) ib, (*-alias Eastwall*) c.1662 *Surv*, (*-alias Heswell alias Hasselwell*) 1682 Sheaf, *Eswall* 1537 Orm[2], *Hes(s)wall* 1724 NotCestr, *Heswell* 1682 Sheaf (*Heswall alias-*, *-alias Hasselwell*), 1727 ib, 1842 OS

Estewall 1534–47 Dugd, *Estwalle* 1547 *MinAcct*, *Eastwall* (*Heswall alias-*) c.1662 *Surv*, *Eastwell* 1739 *LRMB* 264

Hewall 1546 Dugd, 1547 *MinAcct*, *Hevall* 1560 Sheaf

Haswell 1739 *LRMB* 264

'Hazel spring', *v.* hæsel (cf. Merc. hesel, ON hesli), wella (cf. Merc. wælla). Popular tradition associated the p.n. with a well by the roadside in Heswall village, called *the Hessle Well*, cf. Sheaf[3] 1 (89).

OLDFIELD (Rd) (109–255828), *Aldefeld* 1278 *ChFor, Oldefeld* 1347 *ib*, *-field* 1569 Orm[2], *Oldfyld* 1504 ChRR, (*-in Wyrehall*) 1534 Plea, *-feld* 1618 Orm[2] (a chief messuage called-), 'the old field', *v.* ald, feld.

BACK LANE, v. back, lane.   BANKS RD, v. banke.   BOUNDARY
LANE, adjoining Gayton.   BROW LANE, v. brū, lane.   BUG
SPIT, a bank in the Dee estuary, v. spit.   DAWPOOL BANK, a bank
in the Dee estuary, cf. Dawpool 280 infra, v. banke.   DAWSTONE
(RD), Dowstone Cottage 1831 Bry, cf. the Dooe Stone 266 supra.
These names may derive from some ancient boundary stone, v. stān,
perhaps marking out 'doles' or allotments of land, v. dāl.   DELA-
VOR HO & RD, cf. Dellover 1849 TA, 'hillside near a valley' v. dell,
ofer². Sheaf³ 48 (9679) takes the group of fields called Dellover and
speaks of them as 'Dale-overs' alluding to Dale Hay, Hall Dale,
infra, cf. Sheaf³ 7 (8371).   THE DUNGEON, Depedall c.1293 AD,
'deep valley', v. dēop, dell (Merc. dæll, cf. dalr), dongeon.   FARR-
HALL, Far Hall 1831 Bry, Heswall Hall 1842 OS, cf. Far Hall
Meadow 1849 TA, v. feor, hall.   FEATHER LANE.   GAYTON
HOLE, a channel in the Dee estuary, Parkgate Deep 1842 OS, v.
hol¹, cf. Gayton, Parkgate, Denhall Gutter 275, 223, 223 supra.
GAYTON RD, leading to Gayton 275 supra.   HESWALL HILL, 1831
Bry, Heswall on the Hill 1954 Sheaf, v. hyll, cf. Village Rd infra. A
local name for Heswall Hill was Telegraph Hill, cf. Telegraph Rd
infra. Cf. also the p.n. Pensby 271 supra.   HESWALL POINT (lost,
109–247819), 1842 OS, Heswell- 1831 Bry, a lost feature on the shore
of the Dee estuary, v. point.   IRBY RD, leading to Irby 264 supra.
LYDIATE RD (109–266810), v. hlid-geat 'a swing-gate', cf. Lediate
Hay, Lidiate Gutter 1849 TA (109–260812), v. (ge)hæg, goter. In
1930, Sheaf³ 27 (6086) mentions a stream 'anciently called Scarbrook
or Lidiate Gutter', from Heswall Common to R. Dee at 109–253813,
'recently called Bloody Brook or Bloody Gutter from the red colour
of the sand carried down in spate' and suggests this as the origin
of a local name Bloody Dyke. Scarbrook would be 'brook at a bluff or
scar', v. scar, sker, brōc. The name appears in the f.n. Scarbrook
1849 TA, (109–258817).   MANNERS LANE, 1831 Bry.   MERE
LANE.   PENSBY RD, cf. Pensby 271 supra.   PINNACLE HILL.
PIPER'S LANE, PIPER WELL, Piper Lane 1831 Bry (109–255821 to
251828), v. pīpere, lane, wella, cf. Pepper St. (Chester) 337 infra.
PUDDY DALE.   QUARRY ROAD, named from Smallwood's Quarry
(6″).   SANDFIELD, cf. Sand Field 1849 TA, v. sand.   SANDY
LANE, v. sandig.   THE SLACK, SLACK RD, 'the hollow' v. slakki.
TELEGRAPH RD, named from a nineteenth-century telegraph on
Heswall Hill, v. Sheaf³ 49 (9920), cf. Village Rd infra.   THUR-
STASTON RD, cf. Thurstaston 279 infra.   VILLAGE RD, The Lower

Green 1954 Sheaf³ 49 (9920), the old centre of the township. The later centre is at *Heswall on the Hill* Sheaf *loc. cit.*, established after the inclosure of the commons on Telegraph Hill. WALL RAKE, 'lane at or to a well', *v.* wælla, rake. WITTERING LANE, cf. *Whitering(s)*, *Whiterings Hay* 1849 *TA*, 'the witherings', from dial. withering 'a hurdle of dead brushwood'.

FIELD-NAMES

The undated forms are 1849 *TA* 202. Of the others, c.1293 is AD, 1303 Chamb, 1347 *ChFor*, 1540 Morris, 1831 Bry.

(*a*) Backside (*v.* ba(c)ksyde); Bank Hay; Beggars Flat (*v.* beggere); Broad Lane 1831 (109–249819 to 257816); Church Hay; Coney Graves, Coney Grove Hay (*v.* coningre); Coppy (*v.* copis); Cowhay (*v.* (ge)hæg); Cross Looms ('selions lying athwart', *v.* cros, land); Dale Hay, Hall Dale (cf. *The Dales* 1943 Sheaf³ 37 (8371), *v.* deill); Dove Coat Hay (*v.* dovecote); Flays (*v.* flage); Goodmans Hay (*v.* gōd-man, cf. 1 xxi, 243); Higher Gorse; Harrow Hay ('a field called *Harrowe*' c.1293, perhaps 'the higher hill', from hērra and hōh or hærri and haugr); Kings Butts (*v.* butte); Land Hay (*v.* land); Lonsdale; Marl Fd; Marsh Hay; New Ditch; Oldfield Common, Oldfield Hay (cf. Oldfield *supra*); Old Road Croft; Pike Hay (*v.* pīc¹); Pingle (*v.* pingel); Pissoc Hay; Quillet (*v.* quillet(t)); Rye Croft (*freq*); Scout Hay & Mdw; Sea Bank, Looms & Mdw (*v.* sǣ, banke, land, mǣd); Stive Longs (from stīf with furlang or land); Strothers Hay; Townsend (near to the township boundary, *v.* ende¹); Little Vineyard; Warmby Lane 1831 (109–253819 to 248823, perhaps from a lost *Warmby*, 'warm farmstead', *v.* varmr, bȳr); Windlass (*v.* windels); Woodside; Yellow Bank (*v.* geolu).

(*b*) le Falles 1347 (a turbary, 'the fellings', *v.* (ge)fall); *Flodeyordes* 1347 ('tide-pounds', *v.* flōd-geard. These were fish-traps in Dee); *parcum iuxta Haselwell* 1303 (*v.* park); *the roode of Heswall* 1540 ('the anchorage off Heswall', *v.* rād); *le Wythies* 1347 (a wood, 'the willows', *v.* wīðig).

xviii. Thurstaston

The ecclesiastical parish of Thurstaston contained the township of Thurstaston, and parts of Irby (264 *supra* in Woodchurch parish) and of Greasby (291 *infra* in West Kirby parish).

1. THURSTASTON (HALL) (100–2484) ['þə:stæstən]

Turstanetone 1086 DB, *Thurstantona* 1119–28 (p), 14 Chest, *Thurstanton* 1119–28 ib, e13 (1315) Plea (p), 1250–78 Chest and sixteen examples with variant spelling *-tone* to *Thurstanton* 1621

(1656) Orm², (-*in Wyrhale*) 1392 Cl, *Thurstonton* (*Firstonton or*-) 1569 Sheaf

Turtaniston 1119–28 (1154–89) (18) Orm² II 503

Turstaniston 1120 (1724) NotCestr, *Thurstaneston* 1121–9 Chest *et freq* with variant spellings *T*(*h*)*urstanes*-, *Thurstan*(*y*)*s*-, -*tun*, -*ton*(*e*), -*tona* to *Thurstanston* 1579 Dugd, 1819 Orm², *Thrustanston* 1351 BPR

Tursteineston(*e*) (lit. -*temes*-) 1121–9 (1280) Ch, Chest, *Tursteineston* 1202–29 *AddCh* (p), c.1220 Sheaf (p)

Thorstanton 1202–16 (16) Orm² (p)

Thorstanistona 1216–30 *JRC* 1808 (p) (dated c.1265 in Sheaf³ 44 (9137)), *Thorstanston* 1281 (18) Sheaf, *Thorstoniston* 1278 ChFor

Tursteinton 1223 ClR

Thrustington c.1536 Leland, *Thurstinton* 1615 Sheaf, *Thurstington* 1621 (1656) Orm², 1670, 1673, 1727 Sheaf

Thirstynton 1539–47 Dugd

Thursaston (lit. *Ch*-) 1546 Dugd

Thurstestan 1549 Sheaf

Thurstaston 1553 Orm², 1579 Dugd, 1646 Sheaf *et freq*, -*Hall* 1724 NotCestr

Firstonton or Thurstonton 1569 Sheaf

'Þorsteinn's farmstead', from **tún** or **tūn** and the ON pers.n. *Þorsteinn* (anglicized *Thurstan*). The argument about the etymology 'Thor's-stone-ton', deriving from an outcrop of sandstone on Thurstaston Common, belongs to pseudo-folklore. That etymology is incorrect, cf. Orm² II 511, Sheaf³ 3 (467 and 475), 16 (3893 and p.31), N & Q 5th ser., VIII 364, 6th ser., III 30.

DAWPOOL COTTAGES (109–236835), DAWPOOL BANK (109–230830, *Dawpool Deep* 1842 OS, a sandbank covering a silted-up channel in Dee, *v*. **dēope, banke**), DAWPOOL (109–246842, a nineteenth-century mansion) and DAWPOOL SCHOOL (109–246847), with DAWPOOL COTTAGES (109–243847) 284 *infra*, are named after the lost hamlet of DAWPOOL (109–233838 according to Bry). The name appears in *Dalpole Dale & -Medo*(*w*) 1454 Sheaf, 286 *infra*, and as *Dawpoole* 1707 ib, (-*or Dalpoole*) 1819 Orm², -*pool* 1724 NotCestr, 1831 Hem, *Dalpoole* 1752 Sheaf, 1819 Orm², *site of Dalpool Town* 1831 Bry, cf. *Dalpool Lane* 1831 ib (109–233838 to 245839), *Dawpool Meadow*

1847 *TA*, 'pool or creek at a valley', *v.* dæl[1], dalr, pōl[1], the site lying at the mouth of a 'steep, rocky valley' opening through the cliffs on the shore of Dee, cf. Orm[2] II 489.

REDBANK (lost), (*le-*, *la-*) *Redebank(e)* 1320 Chamb, 1360 ib, 1396, 1465 ChRR, 1470 *MinAcct*, (*le-*) *Redebonk(e)* 1357 ChFor, Chamb, 1388 *MinAcct*, 1403 ChRR, *Redbank* 1320 Chamb, 1402 ChRR, *the Red Bank* 1358 (17) (19) Morris 433, 1621 (1656) Orm[2], *the Redde Bank* c.1536 Leland, *the redd bank* 1540 Sherriffs, *le Reed(e)-bonk* 1354, 1358 Chamb, 'the red bank', *v.* rēad, banke, named from the red sandstone cliffs along the shore of the Dee estuary at Thurstaston and Caldy, overlooking the site of an ancient anchorage of the port of Chester, *portus del Reedbonk* 1354 Chamb, *portus apud le Redebonk* 1358 ib, *the roode of the redd bank* 1540 Sheriffs, 'the harbour and roadstead of the Red Bank', from rād in the sense 'a roadstead, an anchorage'.

BENTY FM, cf. *Bent(y) Hay* 1847 *TA*, *v.* benty, (ge)hæg.   HILL FM, HILLSIDE FM, cf. Thurstaston Hill *infra*.   HOME FM. LIMEKILN, 1831 Bry, *v.* limkilne.   THURSTASTON COMMON, 1831 ib, cf. *Common Rocks* 1831 ib, *v.* commun, rokke, cf. Thurstaston *supra*.   THURSTASTON HILL, 1842 OS, *-Hills* 1848 *TAMap*.

FIELD-NAMES

The undated forms are 1847 *TA* 393. Of the others 1298 is Plea, 1347 *ChFor*, 1454 Sheaf, 1831 Bry.

(*a*) Backside (*v.* ba(c)ksyde); The Banks; Brink Hay (*v.* brink); Chalk Fd; Cinders (*v.* sinder or synder, cf. 208 *supra*); Cottor Fd; Crook Corner (*v.* krókr, corner); Crowlands; The Dee Lands (*v.* dey, land); Dry Pit Fd; Flock Loons (*v.* land); Fox Holes; Gorsty Fd, Gorsy Hay (*v.* gorstig, feld, (ge)hæg); Guinea Fd; Heath Fd; Lower Hays (*-Heys* 1831, *v.* (ge)hæg); Malt Hay; Marled Hay; Mearland Hay (*v.* (ge)mǣre, land, (ge)hæg); Meland Dee (perhaps (ge)hæg and the f.n. *Mellon* as in Croft Mellon 285 *infra*); The Nooks; Oak Lands; Ox Hay; Pike Fd (*v.* pīc[1]); Pringle; Rough; Smithy Bank; Steep Bank (*v.* stēap); Stromby Hay (perhaps an old p.n. from ON straumr 'a stream' and býr, with (ge)hæg, cf. Stromford 2 5; the field adjoined the south side of Tinkers Dale, at 109-240829); Tinkers Dale (109-240829 to 241831, probably identical with *Steyncolesdale infra*, cf. prec., *v.* tink(l)ere, dæl[1]); Town Hay (*v.* (ge)hæg); Well Green; Whitfield Hay (*v.* hwīt, feld); The Yawnsley.

(*b*) *le Falles* 1347 (the name of a turbary, 'the fellings', *v.* (ge)fall);

Steyncolesdale 1298 ('Steinkell's valley', from dalr and the ON pers.n. *Steinkell*, probably identical with Tinkers Dale *supra*, cf. Stromby Hay *supra*); *Thurstanton Fylde* 1454 (*v.* feld).

xix. West Kirby

The ancient parish of West Kirby contained the townships 1. Caldy (formerly Little Caldy), 2. Frankby, 3. Grange (formerly Great Caldy or Caldy Grange, now a c.p. including Newton cum Larton *infra*), 4. Greasby (part of which lay in Thurstaston parish, cf. 279 *supra*); 5. Hoose (now included in Hoylake cum West Kirby c.p.), 6. West Kirby (now in Hoylake cum West Kirby c.p., which includes Hoose and Great & Little Meols), 7, 8, Great & Little Meols (cf. prec. In 1882, Orm² II 501, the old c.p. of Little Meols included the extra-parochial liberty of Hilbre 302 *infra*), 9. Newton cum Larton (now included in Grange c.p.). All these townships are now within the Urban District of Hoylake. Hilbre 302 *infra* was originally part of West Kirby parish, cf. Little Meols *supra*.

1. CALDY (olim LITTLE CALDY) (100–2285), *Calders* 1086 DB f.264b, thereafter as for Great- & Little Caldy *infra* and distinguished as *Parva Caldey* 1280 ChF *et freq* with variant spellings *-Caldey(e)*, *-Caldey(a)*, *-Calday*, *(-in Wirall(e)*, *-Wirallia)* 1281 Tab, 1288 ChF, 1289 *ChFine*, *le Parva Calday* 1281 (18) Sheaf, *Calday* 1518 AD, *Little Calday* 1552 ib, *Calday Parva* 1629 ChetOS VIII, *Little Caldy* 1621 (1656) Orm², *-now called Caldy* 1882 ib, *Caldey* 1722 NotCestr, *Caldy* 1842 OS, *v.* parva, lȳtel, cf. Grange 288 *infra*.

GREAT- & LITTLE CALDY, CALDY HUNDRED (cf. Caldy *supra*, Grange 288 *infra*, Caldy Hundred 167 *supra*) [ˈkɔːldi]

   Calders 1086 DB (twice), 1096–1101 (1280) Chest, 13 Dugd, 1348 *ChFor*, (*-in Wyrehale*) 1287 Court, *Kalders* c.1350 Brownbill 175

   Caldelrs 1136–53 (1357) *ChFor*

   Caldhers 1152 Brownbill 312

   Caldei 1182, 1283 P, *Caldeie* 1183 ib, 1283 Misc, *Caldeia* 1184 P, *Caldey* 1237 ib and fifty-one examples with variant spelling *Kaldey* and various affixes to 1724 NotCestr, *Kaldeya* 1239, 1240, 1247 P, *Caldeya* 1240 ib, 1289 *ChFine*, *Caldeye* 1245 P and ten examples with variant spelling *Kaldeye* and various affixes to 1351 BPR

   Caldea 1185, 1186 P

   utraque Caldera 1240–9 Chest II 489

Galdei 1275 P
Calday 1276 P and forty examples to 1629 ChetOS VIII, *Caldaye* 1466 Orm[2]
Calde 1308 IpmR, 1547 *MinAcct*
Caldye 1454 Sheaf, *Caldy* 1553 ib, 1819 Orm[2], *Caldeie* 1766 Sheaf
Caulday 1553 Orm[2], *Cawldaye* 1604 Sheaf, *Cauldye* 1632 ib
Cawedy 1606 Brownbill 32
Chaldee 1646 Sheaf
Calder 1724 NotCestr
Caldley 1727 Sheaf

The form *Calders* with its variants represents OE *cald-ears* 'cold arse', a hill-name, *v.* cald, ears, cf. Calders, Colders WRY 6 266, 2 283. It would allude to the prominent hill on which lie Grange and Caldy, the two manors of Great & Little Caldy, cf. Mawer in Brownbill 312–13. The forms *Caldei (-e, -a)*, *Caldey (-a, -e)*, *Cald(a)y*, and the form *Calder(a)* represent respectively OE *cald-ēge* and ON *kald-eyjar* 'the cold islands', *v.* cald, kaldr, ēg, ey, cf. Ekwall DEPN. For a comparable substitution of ēg and ey, cf. WRY 7 119–120 and *Arnold's Eye* 300 *infra*.

Mawer and Ekwall find the relationship of the various forms difficult. Mawer (*loc. cit.*) supposes a prudery about ears 'arse' at rather too early a date for such an attitude, and the spellings now available do not bear out his suggestion ersc 'stubble, arable'. Ekwall's explanation (DEPN) infers that *Caldei(e, -a)*, *Calder(a)* is the original material and that *Calders* is a plural of *Calder* (itself a Scand pl. *Kald-eyiar* 'the (two) Caldys'), i.e. 'the two places called *Calder*'. But the form *Calders* is used of the individual manors of Great & Little Caldy. There is no evidence that the two manors mentioned as *utraque Caldera* 'each of the two places called *Calder*' were collectively known as 'the (two) *Calders*'. It seems likely that *utraque Caldera* means 'each of the two parts of *Calder*'. Also, another relationship is possible, where an original form *Calders* might have been mistaken for a plural 'the two places called *Calder*', and the new singular, *Calder*, could have been interpreted as ON *kald-eyjar*, anglicized OE *cald-ēge*, thus *Caldei (-e, -a)*. Either way, there would be some doubt about how to prove which form is the starting point.

It would be simpler, but no more certain, to argue that the forms represent two distinct p.ns., one in -ears, one in -ēg, -ey, neither of which derives from the other, one of which replaces the other. To justify an etymology 'cold islands', since this does not fit the topography of Grange and Caldy townships, it would be necessary to suppose that the p.n. *Caldei* (*-e*, *-a*), *Calder*(*a*) denoted a district including the Hilbre islands off the shore of West Kirby. West Kirby and Hilbre appear to have been included in one or other of the manors of Caldy in DB (Tait 46). A church on Hilbre was granted, as an appurtenance, with the manor and church of West Kirby, to the abbey of St. Évroul in the bishopric of Lisieux, by Robert de Rhuddlan before 1081, *v*. Ord III 26, France 223. St Peter's Church (Chester) was part of the same donation. If account be taken of the common manorial disposition of Hilbre and West Kirby and the two Caldys in a.1081 and in 1086 and of the suggestion in Brownbill 158 and Sagabook XIV 310 that this group of Robert de Rhuddlan's manors was the nucleus of the hundred of Caldy, then it is possible to suppose that *Caldei* (*-e*, *-a*), *Calder*(*a*) would mean 'the district at the cold islands', denoting a territory including the islands of Hilbre and the opposing high ground on the Wirral mainland occupied by Grange, Caldy and West Kirby townships. A parallel case of a mainland village named after a coastline or offshore feature occurs at Tranmere 257 *supra*. Within such a district, *Calders* would be the name of the mainland hill and the settlements upon it. After the separation of Hilbre and West Kirby from the original territory, Caldy would in fact consist only of the *Calders* part (i.e. the hill of Grange and Caldy), there would be no need to distinguish the part from the whole, and the p.n. *Calders* would fall into disuse.

This would explain the alternative forms of the p.n. It would also reveal another name, 'cold islands', for Hilbre 302 *infra*.

CALDY HILL, 1842 OS, *Caldy Common* 1831 Bry, *v*. hyll, commun. This and Grange Hill 290 *infra* form the prominent elevation from which Caldy and Grange were probably named, *v*. prec.

BOUNDARY COTTAGES, adjoining West Kirby.   CALDECOTT, a house, probably not original.   LOWER CALDY.   CALDY BLACKS, a reef and bank in the Dee estuary, *v*. blæc.   DAWPOOL COTTAGES (109–242848), *v*. 280 *supra*.   HIGHWOOD.   MANOR HO, *Caldy Manor* 1844 *TAMap*.   SHORE COTTAGE, *Lime Kiln* 1842 OS, the seaward end of *Rake Lane*, cf. Rake Hay *infra*, *v*. limkilne, scora.

FIELD-NAMES

The undated forms are 1844 *TA* 89. Of the others 1454 is Sheaf³ 5, 1639 Sheaf³ 23, 1831 Bry, 1907 Sheaf³ 23 (5307).

(*a*) The Banks, Long Bank Lane (cf. *the Bonke* (*-Hey, -Londe*) 1454, *Bonck Hey* 1639, *v.* banke, (ge)hæg, land); Butter Hay (*v.* butere); Caldy Hay (*Cald(a)y Hay, -Hey* 1454, *v.* (ge)hæg); Callots (*the Cale Yortes, the Calezartes* (lit. *Calezarter*), *the Caleyort Hadelonde* 1454, *The Callatts* 1639, 'the vegetable-, or cabbage-, plots', *v.* cāl, geard, hēafod-land); Camloons (WFI in Sheaf³ 5 (825) identified this with *the Camben, Camben Had(e)londe, the Cambause* 1454, which may contain camb in its topographical sense 'ridge, crest of a hill', though *Camloons* may well be the true name, 'crooked selions', from cam and land, the 1454 readings being unreliable); Common Piece; Corner; Croft Mellon, (Croft) Mill Looms (*Croft(e) Melayne* 1454, *Towne Crock Mellin* 1639, and cf. the adjacent Mellons, Croft Mellon (*Crockmellin* 1639) 296 *infra* in West Kirby, an unusual name (for a group of small fields 109–222850 to 219853) which may also be found in Maloons 2 19, Mellins 2 12, Meland Dee 281 *supra*. There is no mill here. *Mill Loons* appears to be a rationalization of *Mellons*. *Mellon(s)* is probably 'narrow strips of land', from mjór 'narrow', and leyne, land. The el. croft is prefixed as an adj., meaning 'thrown into a croft', to describe the grouping of a number of small selions into a more conveniently worked little field. The spelling *crock* represents eModE croght, a form of croft. *Towne* (*v.* toun) indicates communal land. There seems to be no need for the etymology offered in Sheaf³ 23 (5312), "Celtic *Croch melin*, 'yellow hollow'"); (Croft) Mill Looms (*v.* prec.); Day Looms ((*the*) *Dale Londe(s), the Dale Hadelonde* 1454, *v.* deill, land, hēafod-land); Dolphin Lane 1831 (109–227850 to 228845); Fleck Lane 1907 (109–228853 to 226859); Frankum Pit; Goldstone (*Goldson's Hey* 1639, probably from a surname); Gorslooms (*the Goslonde(s), the Gorst(e) Buttes, -Bottes* 1454, *Goslan Hey* 1639, 'gorse selions', *v.* gorst, land, butte); Gorsy Moor; Greedy Butt Hay (*the Gred(e)y Bottes* 1454, *v.* grǣdig, butte); Green Way (*the Grene-, -Green Way* 1454, on *Hoole Lane*, *v.* grēne¹, weg); Hal(l)wall (*the Halle Walle* 1454, perhaps 'spring belonging to a hall', from hall and wælla); Haywood Hay (*the Haywo(o)de, Haywode Grene* 1454, the *Heywood* (*Hey*) 1639, 'enclosed wood', *v.* (ge)hæg, wudu, with grēne², (ge)hæg); Heath (cf. *Lower Heath* 1831); Hill Hay; Hindolons Hay ('hinder-lands', *v.* hinder, land, cf. *Bake Bredes infra*); Big Hoole, Hoole Hay (109–236845; *Hooe Hey* 1639, cf. *Hoole Lane* 1831 (109–230853 to 235845), *v.* holh (dat.sg. hōle), (ge)hæg, lane); Hungry Hay (*v.* hungrig); Intake (*v.* inntak); Lamp Loons (*the Lamb Loon(e)s* 1639, *v.* lamb, land); Mare Hay (*the Mere Fylde, the Mere Way* 1454, (*The*) *Mere Hey* 1639, 'field and enclosure at a pool', 'way to a pool', *v.* mere¹, feld, weg, (ge)hæg); Marled Hay; Meadow Hay, The Meadow (*Meadow Hay* 1639, *v.* mǣd); Meadow Sheets (*the Medo(w) Sych(e), -Seche* 1454, 'watercourse in a meadow', *v.* mǣd, sīc); (Little-, New-) Mill Hay (*the Mylne Way* 1454, *Myl-hey, the Millway* 1639, *v.* myln, (ge)hæg); Mill Looms (*v.* Croft Mellon *supra*); Narrow Lane 1831; New Hay (*-Hey* 1639, *v.* (ge)hæg); Officer's Croft; Old Hey (1639, *v.*

(ge)hæg); The Pikes (v. pīc¹); Rake Hay (-*Hey* 1639, cf. *Rake Lane* 1831 (109–225852 to 222848), *The Rake* 1454, v. rake, (ge)hæg, lane, cf. Shore Cottage *supra*); River Cliff (v. clif. Named from the R. Dee); Sequan New Hay; Town Fd & Mdw; South Wirloons (*the Werle Londes, the Werne Londes* 1454, v. land. For the first el. Dr Barnes suggests Brit *verno-, Welsh gwern 'alders'); Yew Hay (*the Yew Way, the Yeuway* 1639, 'enclosure at a yew-tree', v. īw, (ge)hæg); Yew Mill Hay (v. īw, myln, (ge)hæg).

(b) *Ascow* 1454 ('ash wood', v. askr, skógr); *the Assan Syche, the Astansyche* 1454 (perhaps 'Hēahstān's watercourse' from the OE pers.n. *Hēahstān* and sīc); *the Bake Bredes, the Bake Brede Londe, the Bake Brede Hadelonde* 1454 ('the back strips', v. bæc, brǣdu, land, hēafod-land, cf. Hindolons *supra*); *the Blake Hadelonde* 1454 (v. blæc, hēafod-land); *the Boke Greues, the Boke Grene, the Boke Grene Hallandes, the Boke Grenys, -Grenes, the Bukke Greuys* 1454 ('beech woods', v. bōc¹, grǣfe, hēafod-land. The forms indicate confused reading of -*n*- and -*u*-); *the Bowrys Ende* 1454 ('the end of the bower or of the storehouse', v. būr¹, ², ende¹); *the Brankers Pytte* 1454 ('(pit at) the burnt-off marsh', v. brende², kjarr, pytt); *the Brode Rene* 1454 ('the broad boundary-strip', v. brād, rein); *the Bryche Hallandes* 1454 ('head-lands at the broken-in land', v. bryce, hēafod-land); *the Copyt Greue* 1454 ('the pollarded wood', v. coppod, grǣfe); *Crossbutts* 1639 ('crosswise head-lands', v. cros, butte); *Dalpole Dale & Medo(w)* 1454 ('valley and meadow at Dawpool', v. dæl¹, mǣd, cf. Dawpool 280 *supra*); *the Dyche Hallandes* 1454 (v. dīc, hēafod-land); *Dofokys Fylde* 1454 (v. feld); *the Elbowys* 1454 (probably crooked selions, v. elbowe); *Emokes Hallandes, Emmokes londe, Emmots londe* 1454 ('Emmot's selion(s)', from hēafod-land, land and the ME fem.pers.n. *Emmote*, dimin. of *Emma*); (*the*) *Fluccobutts* 1639 (v. butte); *Foculle Medow* 1454; (*the*) *Gorst Hey(e)* 1454 (v. gorst, (ge)hæg); *the Harde Londe* 1454 (v. heard, land, cf. *the Hoordlands infra*); *the Hennys* 1454; *the Hoordlands* 1639 (either a later form for *the Harde Londe supra*, or connected with foll.); *the Hordeways Endys* 1454 ('the selion-ends along the *Hordeway*', v. ende¹. *Hordeway* is 'way to a treasure', probably from some ancient treasure-trove here, cf. prec., v. hord, weg); *The Horne Dyche Londe* 1454 ('(selion at) the ditch at a projecting place', v. horn, dīc, land); *Johnson's Hallond* 1639 (from hēafod-land and the surname *Johnson*, cf. Johnson Mdw, Johnsons Hey, v. Addenda xix); *the Kyn(g)ge Londe* 1454 ('the king's selion' or 'selion belonging to one *King*', from land and either cyning or the ME surname *King*); *the Kyrke Crosse* 1454 ('the church cross', v. kirkja, cros. This may have been in W. Kirby 294 *infra*); *the Knooe* 1639 (v. cnoll, cf. Knowls 302 *infra*); *Kne(c)kyn, (the) Knekyn* 1454 ('the little hill', v. cnycyn, cf. *Knukyn* 266 *supra*); *Ledeȝatys* (lit. -ȝatys) 1454 ('the swing-gates', v. hlid-geat); *Little Hey* 1639 (v. lȳtel, (ge)hæg); *the Longe Furlong* 1454, *Longfor Loone Hey* 1639 (v. lang, furlang, (ge)hæg); *The Longe Londe(s)* 1454 (v. lang, land); (*the*) *Mabel(y)s Fylde* 1454 ('Mabel's field', from feld and the ME fem. pers.n. *Mabel*); *the Medylfylde* 1454 (v. middel, meðal, feld); *Padocke Mere* 1454 ('frog pool', v. padduc, mere¹); *the Portway Bottes, -Butt* 1454 ('head-land(s) near the road to the market-town', v. port-weg, butte, cf. Porter Butt Hay

288 *infra*); *the Sandy Butts* 1639 (*v.* sandig, butte); *The Schote Londe* 1454 (*v.* scēat, land); *the Se Bonke* 1454 (*v.* sǣ, banke); *the Souter(y)s Londe, the Sowters Londe, -Land* 1454 ('the cobbler's selion', *v.* sūtere, sútari (perhaps here a pers. by-name), land); *The Stifefield, the Sty Fylde* 1454, *the Stife Way, the Stifeway* 1639 ('the stiff, or clayey, enclosure', *v.* stīf, stif, feld, weg); *the Syre Hallandes* 1454 (*v.* hēafod-land); *Taralayne, Tarlara(y)ne, Tarlarone* 1454 (from leyne or rein and an unidentified first el., cf. foll.); *Tarleton's Hey* 1639 (from (ge)hæg and the surname *Tarleton*. There is no evidence to support Sheaf[3] 23 (5307) which suggests connection with prec.); *Thurstanton Way* 1454 (*v.* weg, cf. Thurstaston 279 *supra*); *the Townys Ende* 1454 (*v.* toun, ende[1]); *Wakyr Fede* 1454; *the Wall* 1639 ('the well or spring', *v.* wælla); *the Walle Sprynge* 1454 ('well-spring', *v.* wælla, spring, cf. prec.); *the Wett(e) Haves* 1454 (perhaps 'damp hillocks' from wēt and haugr, cf. *Wyt Haves infra*); *the Wet(t) Reynys, the Wete Reynes, the Wette Reynes Fylde* 1454 (*v.* wēt, rein); *Whitfield Hey* 1639, (*the*) *Fyr(re)-, (the) Hedyr-, -Hydder-, -Nerre-, -Whitfelde, -W(h)ytt(e)fyld(e), -Whit(e)fylde, -Wittefylde, The Whytefylde Hade Londe* 1454 ('the white field', *v.* hwīt, feld, hēafod-land, (ge)hæg, cf. Whitfields Hay Mdw, Whitfield Hay 293 *infra*); *the Wyt-, the White Haves* 1454 (*v.* hwīt, haugr, cf. *Wett(e) Haves supra*); *the Wranglandes, -Wrangolondes* 1454 ('crooked selions', *v.* wrang, vrangr, land); *the Wro* 1454 ('the corner', *v.* vrá); *Wymbulys Dyche* 1454 ('Win(e)bald's ditch', from dīc and the gen.sg. of the same pers.n. as appears in Wimbold's Trafford 3 260, OE *Winebald* (rare), *Wynbald*, or OG *Winebald*).

2. FRANKBY (HALL) (100–2486) [ˈfræŋkbi]

Frankeby 1230 (17), 1244 (17) Sheaf, 1278 *ChFor*, 1304 ChF, 1387 ChRR (p), (*-in Wirhal*) 1315 Plea, (*-Wyrehall*) 1526 Orm[2], *-bie* 1553 Pat, *Franceby* 1629 ChetOS VIII

Fraunkbi 1346 BPR

Fraunckeby 1347 *Eyre, Fraunkebi* 1347 BPR, *-by* 1355 *Eyre,* 1357 ChRR (p), 1359, 1362, 1364 BPR, 1434 Plea

Fraunkeley in Wyrall 1421 Plea

Frankley 1523 Plea, *Franckley* 1612 ChRR

Frankbye 1539–47 Dugd, *-by* 1546, 1579 ib *et freq* with variant spelling *-bie*

'Frenchman's farm', from ME *by* (ON býr) 'a farmstead' and ME *Franke* (OE Franca) 'a Frenchman, a Frank'. DEPN and Mawer in Brownbill 313 adduce the ODan pers.n. *Franki*, which would be remarkable in a Norse–Irish district like this. The cognate ON *Frakki* does not fit the forms, although if the p.n. were formed early in the tenth century, it might possibly contain the unassimilated OWScand form **Franki*. The ME derivation follows upon Brown-

bill 171 and 218, Tait 135, where it is observed that in Robert of
Rhuddlan's DB manor of Little Caldy (Caldy 282 *supra*), *unus
Francigena cum i serviente habet ii carucas*, 'one Frenchman with one
serf has two ploughs' (DB f.264b, Tait 135). His home would be
known as *Frank-by*. It was obviously a part included within the
manor of *Calders* (Caldy), not a distinct manor, so it was not named
in DB. Cf. Sagabook XIV 308 n.23. This p.n. may be evidence of the
use of -*by* in a post-conquest formation.

FORTON HEY.   HILLBARK (FM), HILLBARK COTTAGE, *Hill Bark*,
Frankby Cottage 1831 Bry, 'cliff in a hill', from **hyll** and **bjarg**,
alluding to a quarry-face here.   LARTON HEY, cf. Larton 300
infra.   MANOR HO, *Manor Farm* 1831 Bry.   THE MERE,
Frankby Mire 1842 OS, *v.* mere[1], cf. **mýrr** 'a bog, a mire'.
RHOODEE MERE, *Rhodee Mere* 1844 *TA*, *v.* mere[1].

FIELD-NAMES

The undated forms are 1844 *TA* 171. Of the others, 17, 1639, 1641 are
Sheaf, 1831 Bry, 1842 OS.

(a) Birch Hay *freq* (*Frankby-*, -*bie Berch Hays*, -*Heys* 1639, 17, *v.* **birce**,
(ge)hæg, though the first el. could be **brēc**); Brook Looms (*v.* **land**); Church
Lane 1831; Frankby Heath 1842; Hill Barn 1831, 1842; Hulls Ditch (*v.*
hyll, **dīc**); Kiln Fd; Lilly Heath (probably 'little heath', *v.* **lỹtel**, **lítill**, **hǣ̆ð**);
New Hay (*the New Heay* 1641, *v.* **(ge)hæg**); Peel Hay (*v.* **pēl**, **(ge)hæg**,
cf. Peel Hay 292 *infra*); Porter Butt Hay (cf. *Portway Butt* 286 *supra*);
Rake Hay, Rake Hay Brow (*v.* **rake**, **(ge)hæg**, **brū**); Reave Acre Hay
(perhaps an old f.n. 'rough acre', from **rūh** and **æcer**, following the same
development as Rivacre 190 *supra*); Sandfield; Scorry; Stone Bridge Hay
(*v.* **stān**, **brycg**); Tottie Fd; Wall Fd (*v.* **wælla**); Wheat Butts (*v.* **butte**);
Wirral Looms (*v.* **land**, cf. Wirral 167 *supra*, 1 7. Presumably these selions
lay in the hundred of Wirral rather than of Caldy, or belonged to some
estate which lay outside Wirral, cf. Grange 289 *infra*); Within Hay (*v.*
wiðegn, **(ge)hæg**).

(b) *Holckroft Heay* 1641 (*v.* foll.); *Norcroft alias Holcroft* 17, 1639,
Holckroft Heay 1641 ('the north croft', 'croft in a hollow', *v.* **norð**, **hol**[2],
croft, **(ge)hæg**).

3. GRANGE (*olim* GREAT CALDY or CALDY GRANGE) (100–2286),
GRANGE HALL (100–223867)

    Calders 1086 DB f. 266 b, 1096–1101 (1280) Chest, *Kalders* c.1350
    Brownbill 175

Magna Caldeye 1281 Court, *-Calday* 1385 *ChFor*, 1518 AD,
Plea, *Great Caldey* 1552 (17) Sheaf, 1621 (1656) Orm², 17
Sheaf, 1629 ChetOS VIII, 1639 Sheaf, *Calday Magna* 1629
ChetOS VIII, *Magna Caldey* 1641 Orm², *Magna Cawedy* 1606
Brownbill 32

Caldaygrange 1341 Sheaf, *Caldey-* 1347 *ChFor*, *Caldegraunge*
1547 *MinAcct*, *Caldygrange* 1553 Sheaf, *Cald(e)y Grange* 17 ib,
1629 ChetOS VIII, 1639 Sheaf, *Caldey-, Cauldye Grange* 1632 ib,
Caldey Grange 1641 Orm², *Caldie-* 1766 Sheaf, *Caldy Grange*
1882 Orm²

Graunge 1519 ChRR, (*The-*) 1621 (1656) Orm², *Grange* 1656
Sheaf *et freq*, (*The-*) 1670 ib, 1724 NotCestr

graunge vocat' le Hall in Westkirkeby, Grangia de Hall 1547
*MinAcct, grangia vocat' le Hall, the grange of Hall alias Hall
Grange* 1553 Pat, *Grange Hall* 1724 NotCestr

grangia de Wyrrall 1547 *MinAcct, Wirrall in parochia de Westekyrk-
bie* 1554 *ib*

Great-, Magna Caldey alias Cald(e)y Grange 17 Sheaf, 1629
ChetOS VIII, 1639 Sheaf, 1641 Orm²

Kirby Grange 1724 NotCestr

Grange otherwise Caldie Grange 1766 Sheaf

Great Caldy, commonly called Grange 1819 Orm², (*-or Caldy
Grange*) 1882 ib

'The greater part of Caldy', *v.* magna, grēat, cf. Caldy, Great- &
Little Caldy, 282 *supra*. This manor was a grange of Basingwerk
Abbey Fl, *v.* grange, and took its later name from the old hall,
demolished by 1819 (Orm² II 491), replaced by the later Grange
Hall, cf. *the New Hall, the Old Hall* 1774 Sheaf, *Old Hall* 1831 Bry, *v.*
hall. The grange was also named after Wirral 167 *supra*, 1 7, and
West Kirby 294 *infra*, the hundred and parish in which its estates lay.

NEW HO (100–240882), *Neubolt* 1291 Tax, 1385 *ChFor*, *-bold* 1357
ChFor (p), *Newbold* 1552 (17), 1660 Sheaf, *-bald* 1639 ib, *Newbott*
1546 Brownbill 186, *Newe House* 1578 ib, *the New House* 1579 Sheaf,
1676 Orm², *Newhouse* 1613 ib, 'new house', *v.* nīwe, bold, hūs. In
1385 *ChFor*, *Newbold*, Newton and Larton are all included in Great
Caldy (i.e. Grange). In 1676 Orm² II 488, Newhouse is said to be in
Newton. The *TA* boundaries place it in Grange township. The later
form of the name probably arose from a rebuilding.

GRANGE HILL (100–2187), 1842 OS, cf. Caldy Hill 284 *supra*, and Great- & Little Caldy 282 *supra*.   HERON RD, *The Footway* 1639 Sheaf³ 23 (5313), *Long Rake Lane* 1831 Bry, *v.* lang, rake, fote-waye, cf. *Herring Ho* 322 *infra*.   RAKE HO (lost, 100–233877), 1847 *TAMap* 289, *Rackhowse* 1534 (1560) Sheaf³ 19 (4645), *the Rake House* 1535, 1608 Brownbill 177, 187, 'house by a lane', *v.* rake, hūs. It adjoined Long Rake Fm 301 *infra*.

FIELD-NAMES

Some of the f.ns. listed under Newton, 302 *infra*, may belong here. The undated forms are 1844 *TA* 180. Of the others, 17, 1639, c.1780 are Sheaf, 1819 Orm².

(a) The Browns (*the Browne alias Underweet* 1639, 17, *Further-, Middle-, Nearer- & Potter's Brown* c.1780, 'the brows', *v.* brún²); Carr (*The Carr* 1819, *Carr Hay* 1639, *-Hey* 17, c.1780, *the Car Meadow* 17, cf. *Newton Car* 301 *infra*, *v.* kjarr, (ge)hæg, mǣd); Colley Hey c.1780 (*v.* colig); Coventry Hay, Coventrys Fd (from the Wirral surname *Coventry*); Cross Hay (*Cross Hey Meadow* 1639, *Crosse Hay-* 17, *Cross Hey* c.1780, *v.* cros 'a cross', (ge)hæg); Daulby's Hay (*Dawbyes Hay* 1639, 17, from a surname *Dalby*); Fornall Mdw (cf. Fornall Bridge 301 *infra*); Garden Hey c.1780 (*-Hay* 1639, *v.* gardin, (ge)hæg); Grass Hay (1639, *the Grasse Hay* 17, *v.* gærs, (ge)hæg); Broad- & Gorsey Lang Hey c.1780 (*Longe Hayes* 17, *Langhays* 1639, *v.* lang, (ge)hæg); (Near-) Larton Hay (*Further-, (the) Toune-, Towne Larton Hay* 17, 1639, *v.* toun, cf. Larton Hey 288 *supra*, Larton 300 *infra*); Mecca Brook (c.1780, cf. Micker Brook 1 32, Michansedge 265 *supra*. It may be that these three stream-names are identical in origin, i.e. 'gentle stream', from ON mjúkr (late OE mēoc, ME meke) 'meek, smooth, gentle, soft' and á, with brōc, sīc); Mill Hay (*Mile Hay* 1639, 17, *v.* myln); Mistresses Mdw c.1780; Mulses Hey c.1780; New Hay (*the Great- & Little-* 1639, 17, *v.* nīwe, (ge)hæg); New Mdw c.1780; Pigeon Croft (*the Pigeon House Croft* 17, 1639); Pike o'th' Lang c.1780; Pingle (1639, 17, *v.* pingel); Rainsford Fds c.1780; Rake Fd (cf. *Upper Rake Hay, the (two) Rake Hayes* 1639, 17, *Further, Little & Middle Rake Hey, Rake Hey Meadow* c.1780, *v.* rake, (ge)hæg); Sandy Hay ((*the*) *Sound(e)y Hay* 1639, 17, *v.* sandig, (ge)hæg); Saugham Fd ((*the*) *Sawghon Flat(t)* 1639, 17, *v.* flat, cf. Saughall Massie 321 *infra*); Scamblants (*Scanllones Meadow, Little Scanllones* 1639, *Little Scablons Meadow* 17, *Seamblants* c.1780, 'short selions', *v.* skammr, land); Six Loons (*Six(e) Loon(e)s* 1639, 17, *v.* six, land); Stokenham Hay (*Ston' Hay Meadow* 1639, *Stocs Hay Meadow* 17, *Stokeham Hey* c.1780); Thistle Hay (1639, *the-* 17, *v.* þistel).

(b) *Abbotts Yards* 1639, 17 ('the abbots enclosures', *v.* abbat, geard, probably named after the abbots of Basingwerk); *Calvercroft* 1639, 17 ('calves' croft', *v.* calf, croft); *Cow Pasture* 1639 (*v.* cū, pasture); *the Cross Sute* 1639 (*v.* cros 'across', scēat); *Fulemon Field* 1639, *Falemouse Field*

17 (probably from a pers.n.); *Gale Lowns* 1639 (*v.* gagel, land); *Green Yard* 1639, *the Greene Yard* 17 (*v.* grēne[1], geard); *the Long-*, *the Short Hay* 17 (*v.* (ge)hæg); *Hill Hay* 1639, 17 (*v.* hyll, (ge)hæg); *Hunger Croft* 1639, 17 (*v.* hunger, croft); *Linikers Barne & Yards* 17 (from bere-ærn and geard with the surname, *Linacre*, of an ancient family in this parish); *the Low Heath* 17 (*v.* hǣð); *Rye Hay* 17, 1639 (*v.* ryge, (ge)hæg); *the Such Meadow* 1639, 17 (*v.* sīc, mǣd); *Tupyards* 17, 1639 ('yards where a ram stands', *v.* tup, geard); *Vicarstall* 1639 ('the vicar's standing', *v.* vikere, stall); *Wyhon Flatt* 17 (*v.* flat; the first el. is obscure. Professor Löfvenberg suggests the surname *Wyon* (Reaney 364)).

4. GREASBY (100–2587) [ˈgriːzbi]

Part of this township near Irby 264 *supra*, was in Thurstaston parish.

Gravesberie 1086 DB, *Grauesbyri* 1096–1101 (1150), 1150 Chest, *-biri* 1096–1101 (1280) ib, *-beri* 1096–1101 (1280) ib, Ch

Grauisby 1096–1101 (1280), 1153–60 (1280) Chest, *Graues-*, *Gravesbi(a)* 1153–60 (1285) Ch, Chest, (*-in Wirhale*) 1283 Chest, *-by* 1153–81, 1188–91, 1285, c.1310 ib, *-beia* 1153–60 (17) ib

Greuesby 1249–1323 Chest, 1347, 1357 *ChFor*, 1432 *Rental*, *Greves-* 15 Orm[2], 1552 (17) Sheaf

Greseby 1271 *ChFor*, 1341 *Eyre*, 1360 *Tourn*, 1374 *ChCal* (p), *-bie* 1553 Pat, *Gresby* 1271 *ChFor* and eleven examples with variant spellings *-bye*, *-bie* to *Gresby* 1639 Sheaf

Griseby 1280 Cl

Groseby 1329 Plea (p)

Greauesbury (lit. *Greanes-*) 1352 Morris 125

Grasby 1513 *ChEx*

Grebesey 1535 VE

Gruesby 1538 Orm[2]

Greaseby 1579 Dugd, 1819 Orm[2], *Greasby* 1621 (1656) ib, 1724 NotCestr *et freq*

Graysby 1610 Speed

Graisby 1648, 1668, 1727 Sheaf

Graceby 1724 NotCestr

'Stronghold at a wood', *v.* grǣfe, burh (dat.sg. byrig). The final el. is replaced by ON býr, and OE grāf alternates with grǣfe. Other interchanges of burh and býr occur in Whitby 198 *supra*, Irby 264 *supra*. Brownbill's derivation (Sheaf[3] 2 (299) and correspondence with Allen Mawer 30 August 1925) from OE (ge)rēfa, 'reeve, officer', is to be discounted. DEPN suggests an alternative first el. grǣf 'a digging, a grave, a pit, a trench', but it seems unnecessary to suppose this, and the form *Groseby* requires **grāf** unless *-o-* is a scribal error for *-e-*. Bryant's map, 1831, shows *Greasby Hall*, (also 1849 *TAMap* 181) and *Old Hall*, *v.* ald, hall.

GREASBY BRIDGE & COPSE.   GREASBY BROOK (Arrowe Brook 262 *supra*), 1842 OS, cf. *Saughau Brook Hey* (lit. *Saughan*) 1639 Sheaf, *v.* brōc, cf. Saughall Massie 321 *infra*.   GREENHOUSE FM, *Green House* 1831 Bry.   IRBYMILLHILL FM, *Irby Hill Farm* 1842 OS, 1848 *TA* 393, named from Irbymill Hill 265 *supra*. This was part of Irby township 264 *supra* in 1831 Bry.   MILL COTTAGE & LANE, named from a windmill on Irbymill Hill 265 *supra*, cf. *Windmill* 1847, 1849 *TA* 181, 393 and *Mylway Pikes*, *Mylway Such* 1639 Sheaf, *v.* myln, weg, pīc[1], sīc, cf. *The Pikes infra*. The cottage is in part of Irby township 264 *supra* in 1831 Bry.   THE THORNS, cf. *The Thornes* 1639 Sheaf, *Thorns* 1847 *TA* 393, 'the thorn-trees', *v.* þorn.   WOOD LANE, 1831 Bry, *boscus de Gre(ue)sby* 1347, 1357 *ChFor*, *v.* wudu.

FIELD-NAMES

The undated forms are 1844 *TA* 181, 1849 *TAMap* 181 (Greasby in West Kirby parish) and, marked *, 1847 *TA* 393 (in Thurstaston parish). Of the others, 1432, 1440 are *Rental*, 1639 Sheaf, 1831 Bry.

(a) *Backside (*v.* ba(c)ksyde); Bank Loons (*Boncklands, Boncklond Hey* 1639, *v.* banke, land, (ge)hæg); Blakelond Fd (*Blakeloone Hey(es)* 1639, *v.* blæc, land, (ge)hæg); Brook Hay; Cabin Hay (*The Cabin Heyes* 1639, 'enclosures with a cabin in them, or at a cabin', *v.* cabin, (ge)hæg); Clover Root (*v.* root); *Coppy (*v.* copis); Bithells Cower; Crankloons (perhaps from cranuc 'a crane'); Ebby Leens (*v.* leyne); Broad-, Little- & Long Flatt (cf. *The Flatt* 1639, *v.* flat); Frankby Fd & Mdw (cf. Frankby 287 *supra*); Gooseberry Hay & Mdw (*the Gosbuts Hey* 1639, 'enclosure at gorsey butts', *v.* gorst, butte, (ge)hæg); Gorsty Hay (*v.* gorstig, (ge)hæg); Greasby Common (1831); Greasby Fd & Mdw (probably town-fields, *v.* Towne Field *infra*); Great Loons (*v.* land); *Heath Mdw; Hill Hay (*the Hill Hey* 1639, *v.* hyll, (ge)hæg); Hooks (*Hookes Medow* 1639, *v.* hōc); *Horse Pasture; Kirk & Loons, Kirka Loons (adjoining the road between Greasby & Frankby, 100–255873 to 245867, cf. *the Kirkeway* 1639, 'the way to church', *v.* kirkja, weg); *Limbo Lane Croft (*v.* Limbo Lane 262 *supra*); Locker Hay; Marl Clods (*v.* marle, clodd); Marled Fd; *New Hay Mdw; *Oat Field Hay (*v.* āte); Peel Hay (109–248870; *the Peele Hey* 1639, cf. *the Peele Hadlows* 1639, and the adjacent Peel Hay 288 *supra*, 'enclosure-, head-lands-, at a palisade or stockade', *v.* pēl, (ge)hæg, hēafod-land); Pingle (*v.* pingel); Reylonds Hay (*v.* rye-land, (ge)hæg); Far- & Near Riders Hay (*les Rydyngs* 1432, *le Rudyng* 1440, *Ridings Hey(e)s* 1639, *v.* ryding, (ge)hæg); Rye Grass (*v.* rye-grass); Saughall Fd & Way (*v.* feld, (ge)hæg), cf. Saughall Massie

321 *infra*); Senses; Shepherds Hay (cf. *Sheperified Hey* 1639 (!)); Smithy Fd (*Smithfield, alias Smithfield Hey* 1639, *v.* smið, feld, (ge)hæg); Starkey Loons & Mdw, *Starkey's Way Mdw (cf. *Starkey Way* 1639, 'stiff, hard field', from stearc and (ge)hæg, with weg, land, mæd); Sugars Mdw; Swine Loons (*v.* swin[1], land); Top of the Hill; Upton Mdw (cf. Upton 305 *infra*); Westage (*v.* weste); Whitelands Mdw (*v.* hwīt, land); Whitfield Hay, *Whitfields Hay Mdw (cf. *Whitfield Hey* 287 *supra*, *v.* hwīt, feld, (ge)hæg); Wimbricks (*the Wimbreck* 1639, 'gorse bank', *v.* hvin, brekka); Big- & Little Wirral (*the Worell* 1639, cf. Wirral 167 *supra*, 1 7, Wirral Looms 288 *supra*); Withen Field Hay (*Within-, Withynfield Hey* 1639, *v.* wiðegn, feld, (ge)hæg).

(*b*) *Faugh Hey* 1639 (*v.* falh, (ge)hæg); *Field Hey* 1639; *le Hallorchard* 1440 (*v.* hall, orceard); *Heynes Medow* 1639 (*v.* hegn); *Kill Croft* 1639 (*v.* cyln); *Madocks Hey* 1639 (from (ge)hæg and the Wirral surname *Maddock*, from Welsh *Madog*); *Medow Hey* 1639 (*v.* mæd); *the Parish Medow* 1639 (*v.* *Towne Field infra*); *the Pikes* 1639 (cf. Mill Lane *supra*, 'pointed lands', *v.* pīc[1]); *the Ricky loones* 1639; *Seint Marybuttes* 1432, 1440 ('St Mary's head-lands', *v.* butte); *Sandy Hey* 1639 (*v.* sandig, (ge)hæg); *Saughau* (lit. *Saughan*) *Brook Hey* 1639 (*v.* (ge)hæg, cf. Saughall Massie 321 *infra*, Greasby Brook *supra*); *Short Shoote* 1639 (*v.* sc(e)ort, scēat); *Tensteed* 1639 (perhaps tūn-stede 'site of an enclosure or farm', as Sheaf[3] 23 (5328A) suggests); *the Towne Field & Medowes* 1639, cf. *the Parish Medow supra* (land belonging in common to the township and the parish, probably identical with Greasby Fd & Mdw *supra*, *v.* toun, paroche, feld, mæd); *the Twelcoss Butts alias Hadlows* 1639 Sheaf[3] 23 (5328A) (probably 'the twelve cross-butts or head-lands', *v.* twelf, cros, butte, hēafod-land).

5. HOOSE (lost, 100–219895) [¹(h)u:s], described as an extra-parochial township in Orm[2] II 500. Now swallowed by Hoylake, Hoose comprised the district between Lake Place and Deneshey Rd, from the shore inland to The Fender.

> *Holes* 13 Dugd, 1288 *ChFor*, 1375 Bark (p), *le Holes* 1418 ChRR (p)
> *Hose* 1270 Bark (p)
> *Howes, Howos* 1346 *JRC*
> *Hulles* 1378 (p), *Huls* 1421 Bark (p), *Hulse* 1535 Brownbill
> *le Holles* 1420 *Dav* (p)
> *Hooles* 1539 Plea
> *Hoose* 1629 ChetOS VIII, 1812 Sheaf, *the-* 1819 Orm[2], 1844 *TA* 262
> *Hoes* 1636, 1735 Brownbill
> *Hoose or Oulse* c.1850 Brownbill, *Hoose or-, -usually called Hoylake* 1860 White

'The hollows', v. hol¹, cf. Hulse 2 185. Some of the forms suggest a confusion of hol¹ with hyll and hōh, perhaps due to the sand-dunes along this coast. Grants of land in Great Meols 296 *infra*, in 1346 and 1348 *JRC* 1280, 1284, 1712, specify appurtenant rights in woods, clearings, roads etc., marshes, waters, arable and non-arable lands, and in *howes, -os*, i.e. 'in the Hoose'. Cf. the f.n. *Far- & Near Water Hooses* 1844 *TA*, *The Water Hoose* 1812 Sheaf, 'the *Hoose* which floods', v. wæter. For Hoylake, originally a hamlet in Little Meols and Hoose townships, v. 299 *infra*.

THE DALE, *Hoose Hotel* 1831 Bry, *Hoose Cottage* 1842 OS.

FIELD-NAMES

The undated forms are 1844 *TA* 206. 1812 is Sheaf.

(a) The Big Fd; East Fd; House Fd; Middle Fd 1812; Parsonage Croft; Poor Fd; Water Mdw; West Fd.

6. WEST KIRBY, formerly KIRKBY IN WIRRAL, (100–2186) [ˈkəːbi]

    Cherchebia 1081 (12) Ord III 26, (1672) Orm² I 56, 1121–9 (n.d.) France, *Cerchebia* 1081 (17) Orm² II 485, *Chercabia* 12 Ord III 281, n.d. ib v 187, France

    Ki-, Kyrkeby (in Wyrhale) 1137–40 (1271), (14) Chest, *Kircheby* 1153–81 France *et freq* with variant spellings *Kyrke-, Kirke-, Kirche-, -bi* to 1535 VE, *West-, (-in Wirhale)* 1285 ChFine *et freq* with variant spellings *West(e)-, -Kyrke-, -by(e)* to 1632 Sheaf

    Kirkby 1237 (17) Chest, *West-* 1287 Court *et freq* with variant spellings *Kyrk-, Kirk-, -be, -bie, -bye, Weast-* to 1657 Clif, *Kirkby(e) alias West Kirkby* 1629 ChetOS VIII, 1633 Sheaf, *West Kirkby alias Kirbye* 1633 ib

    Westkyrby, -kirby, (-in Wyrhal(e)) 1287 Court, (17) Chest, 1508, ChRR, 1546 Dugd, 1621 (1656), 1646 Orm², 1724 NotCestr, *West Kirbe* 1539 Morris, *-kirbie* 1592 *JRC*, *Kirby(e), (West Kirkby alias-)* 1633 Sheaf

    Westkerkeby 1330 Ipm, *Kerkeby West* 1347 ChGaol, *Kerkeby* 1355 Eyre, *West Kerkbye* 1553 Sheaf, *Westkerkby* 1632 Sheaf

    West kerbie 1621 *JRC*, *-Kerby* 1632 Sheaf (*-alias West Kerkby*), 1652 *JRC*, *Weskerby* 1668 Sheaf, *Wescerbye* 1670 ib, *-bey* 1697 ib

    Westenkebye 1553 Sheaf

'Village with a church', v. kirkju-býr. It is distinguished as 'west', v. west, and as '-in Wirral', from the other *Kirkby* in Wallasey 332 *infra* at the east side of the Wirral peninsula. For the historical and literary associations of the p.n. West Kirby, v. Sagabook XIV 307, EENS 23.

BANKS RD, cf. (*The*) *Banks* 1844 *TA, The Bon(c)k(e)s* 1639 Sheaf, sand-hills etc., v. banke. BEACON HILL, 1842 OS, named from *Grange Beacon* 1882 Orm[2], a stone column erected in 1841 as a beacon for Mersey navigators, giving name to Column Rd and replacing Grange Mill, the old landmark blown down in a storm in 1839, cf. Brownbill 64. BIRKETT RD, named after The Birket (r.n.) 1 15. CALDY HILL, 1842 OS, cf. Grange Hill *infra*, v. 284 *supra*. CALDY RD, cf. Caldy 282 *supra*. DARMOND'S GREEN, cf. *Darmons* 1844 *TA* and Richard *Dormond* 1674 Brownbill 201, v. grēne[2]. DEE LANE, site of *Dee Inn* 1842 OS, named from R. Dee, v. lane. GRANGE HILL, 1842 ib, cf. Caldy Hill *supra*. GRANGE MILL (lost), 1831 Bry, 1842 OS, cf. Beacon Hill *supra*, cf. Grange 288 *supra*. GRANGE RD, cf. Grange 288 *supra*. GREEN HO (lost), 1842 OS. GROVE HILL (lost), 1831 Bry, 1842 OS. HILBRE HOUSE, *Victoria's Bank* 1842 ib. HILL VIEW, *the Red House* 1774 Sheaf, *Red House* 1831 Bry, *Hill Houses* 1842 OS, v. rēad, hyll, hūs. KIRBYMOUNT, 1831 Bry, *Mount Kirby* 1842 OS, a house on Caldy Hill, v. mont. LANG LANE, cf. (*Lower-, Top-*) *Lang* 1844 *TA*, and *Lang House* 1761 Brownbill 339, from lang[2] 'a long strip of land'. MILL COTTAGE, named from Grange Mill *supra*. SANDY LANE, 1844 *TAMap*, v. sandig, lane. TOWNFIELD RD, cf. (*the*) *Town Field* 1639 Sheaf, 1844 *TA*, v. toun, feld. THE OLD VILLAGE, VILLAGE RD, the ancient hamlet of West Kirby, v. village. WETSTONE LANE, probably named from some sandstone outcrop here, v. hwet-stān.

FIELD-NAMES

The undated forms are 1844 *TA* 225. Of the others, 1325, 1639 are Sheaf, 1547 *MinAcct*, 1553 Pat, 1831 Bry. v. Addenda.

(a) Back Fd (v. back); Bawk (v. balc); Brow; Butchers Bank; Common Allotment (cf. *Kirby Common* 1831); Cowhay (*The Cow Hey* 1639, v. (ge)hæg); Croft Mellon (v. Mellons *infra*); Flat; Gobbins Butts (v. butte. The first el. may be a surname, cf. Ellen *Gobbin* beneficiary in the will of Robert Wigan clerk of Hilbre 1550 Sheaf[3] 18 (4404), cf. also *Gobbinshire* 168 *supra*); Grass Hay, -Hey (*The Grass Hey* 1639, v. gærs, (ge)hæg);

Hoo Headlands (*v.* hōh, hēafod-land); Kiln Hay; Little Hay, -Hey (cf. *the Parsons Little Hey* 1639, *v.* lȳtel, (ge)hæg); Longtonn Fd (cf. *the feld under the ton* 1325 Sheaf³ 18 p. 105, *v.* lang, tūn); Lower-, Middle-, Higher-, Brown- & Linacres Loohon (*v.* land); Marl Hay (cf. *the new Marled Hey* 1639, *v.* marle, marled, (ge)hæg); Mellons, Croft Mellon (*Crockmellin* 1639 Sheaf³ 23 (5321), *v.* Croft Mellon 285 *supra*); Mill Ditch (*v.* myln, dic); Mutch Hay; Nottrills; The Rugs (*v.* hryggr); Little Salver (*the Sarvor, -Sarver* 1639, *v.* server); Sandhills; Slack (*v.* slakki); The Stones, Lower Stones (*v.* stān); Swithens Green; Town Fd (*the Town Field* 1639).

(b) *le Conyngre* 1547, *le Conygre* 1553 (*v.* coningre).

7. GREAT MEOLS (100–232900), *Melas* 1086 DB f.264b, thereafter as for Great- & Little Meols *infra* and distinguished as *Magna-* c.1274–81 (1580) Sheaf, 1288 *ChFor et freq*, *Mangna-* 1287 Court, *-Magna* 1629 ChetOS VIII, *-Maior* 1346 *JRC*, *Mikel-* 1358 Plea, *Mukel-* 1359 Orm², *Mikul-* 1374 *JRC*, *Mykel-* 1410 Sheaf, *Mykull-* 1417 Orm², *Great-* 1552 (17) Sheaf *et freq*, *villa de Melus Maioris* 1346 *JRC*, 'the larger part of Meols', cf. Great & Little Meols *infra*, *v.* magna, mikill, micel, maior.

GREAT- & LITTLE MEOLS [ˈmels]

Melas 1086 DB (twice), 1353 Orm², *Meles* 13 Whall (p), 1229–33 Orm² (p), 1229 (1580) Sheaf, 1249–65 Chest (p), Whall (p) and twenty-seven examples with variant spellings *Melis, -ys, -us* to 1427 Plea, (*Parua-*) 1270–83 Chest, (*Magna-*) c.1274–81 (1580) Sheaf, 1280–1320 Chest, (*Lytel-*) 1358 Orm², (*Mikul-*) 1374 *JRC*, (*Mykel-*) 1410 Sheaf, (*-Maioris*) 1346 *JRC*, *le Meles* 1348 *Eyre* (p), 1387 *ib*, 1400 ChRR (p), 1410 Sheaf (p)

Molis 1195–1205 Facs, *JRC* and eleven examples with variant spelling *Moles* to 1338 Pat (p), (*Litle-*) 1283 Ipm, (*Great-*) 1295 ib, *le Molis* 1216–30 *JRC*

Moeles 1228–37 Facs and twenty-seven examples with variant spelling *Moelis* to 1432 Orm², (*Parva-*) e13 Chest, (*Magna-*) 1288 *ChFor*, (*Mikel-*) 1358 Plea, (*Mukel-*) 1359 Orm², (*Great-*) 1365 ChRR, (*Mykull-*) 1417 Orm², *le Moelis* 13 *AddCh* (p), *le Moeles* 1314 *JRC*, 1350 Orm² (p), 1361 BPR (p), 1400 ChRR (p), 1406 AD (p)

Meoles 1274–82 Orm² and thirty-seven times with variant spellings *Meolez, Meolas* to 1819 Orm², (*Magna-*) 1295 Cl (p), (*-Magna*) 1629 ChetOS VIII, (*Mykull-*) 1417 Sheaf, (*Great-*) 1527 ChRR, (*Littel-*) 1347 *ChFor*, (*Litel-*) 1383 Orm², (*Little-*) 1724 Not-

Cestr, (*Parva-*) 1584 ChRR, (*-Parva*) 1629 ChetOS VIII, *le Meoles* 1347 *ChFor* and fifteen times with variant spelling *Meolys* to 1438 ChRR (p)

Meeles 1278 Whall (p), 1286 *ChFor* (p) and eight examples with variant spelling *Meelys* to 1581 ChRR, (*Lytle-*) 1315 Plea, (*Little-*) 1361 BPR, (*Magna-*) 1346 *JRC*, (*Great-*) 1361 BPR, *le Meeles* 1378 *Eyre* (p)

Mell' 1278 Dugd (p), c.1280 *JRC* (p), *Melle* 1278 Orm² (p), *Melles* 1287 Court (p), *the Melles* 1423 AD (p)

Molles 1287 Court (*Mangna-*)

Meales 1287 Court (p), 1592 *JRC*, 1621 (1656) Orm², (*Great-*, *Little-*) 1724 NotCestr

Moelles 1289 Court (p), 1317 City (p), *Moell'* 1290, 1291 Court (p)

Mekes 1295 Tab (*Parva-*)

Meules 1303 Chamb (p), 1310, 1311 ChRR (p)

(*Little-*) *Meolse* 1498 Sheaf, (*Great-*) 1844 *TA* 261, (*Great-*, *Little-*) 1882 Orm²

(*Great*) *Melse* 1594 Orm², (*Great-*, *Parva*) c.1642 (17) Sheaf, *The Melts* 1898 Sheaf

(*Great-*) *Mooles* 1621 (1656) Orm²

Great-, *Little Meols* 1831 Bry, 1842 OS

'The sandhills', *v.* melr, cf. Great Meols *supra*, Little Meols 299 *infra*, and North Meols, Ravensmeols and *Argarmeles* La 125. The pronunciation of the Ch p.n., [mels], is now different from that of the La names, [mi:lz], but there appears to have been some common form in the past. The spellings for the el. **melr** in these Ch and La places, and in Ingoldmells L (DEPN) and Meaux YE 43, show that the *e* in the English pl. form of **melr** was rounded in pronunciation. In contrast, the English sg. form for **melr** preserves simple [mel], as in Cartmel La 195, Rathmell YW 6 148. Tranmere 257 *supra* appears to be an instance of sg. **melr** in which the *e* has been rounded to *o*, but there is a further complication in that name. The spellings of **melr** in its English pl. form (*melas*, *-es*, etc.) are *-m(e)ol-*, *-mo(e)l-*, *-meul-*, *-muel-*, etc. Here, the *u* and *o* characteristics indicate something like *œ* [ø] or even a diphthong. Presumably the *l* was partly vocalised before the [s] > [z] of the plural inflection, sufficiently to affect the *e* but not sufficiently to cause loss of *l*. Such a feature would have encouraged the vocalisation of *l* to the point of disappearance under AN influence in Meaux [mius] YE 43. A different account of the matter is given by Ekwall in La 125, but it does not take into account all the evidence. *v.* Addenda.

THE BERCHES, cf. *Little Birches* 1844 *TA*, 'lands broken in for cultivation', *v.* brēc. BIRKENHEAD RD, leading to Birkenhead 313 *infra*. DOVE POINT, 1831 Bry, site of DOVE LIGHT, a light-house, sea-marks on the Irish Sea coast, perhaps named after John *Dove*, landowner here in 1555 Sheaf³ 15, *v.* point. FORNALL BRIDGE, FORNALLS GREEN, *v.* 301 *infra*. LEASOWE LIGHTHOUSE, 1842 OS, one of two lights for the Mersey, *the Mockbeggar Light-houses* 1761 Orm² II 497, *the Upper Lighthouse* 1764 ib, *the Lingham Lighthouse* 1815 Sheaf³ 34, *Leazou Light-house* 1819 Orm², *Mock-beggar or Leasowes Light* 1831 Bry, cf. Leasowe, Lingham, Mockbeggar Hall 332, 319, 333 *infra*. LOWER GREEN, *v.* grēne². PARKFIELD HO, PARKFIELDS, cf. (*The*) *Park* 1844 *TA*. RYCROFT RD, cf. *Rye Croft* 1844 *ib*. SANDHEY, *v.* sand, (ge)hæg. SEABANK COTTAGES, *v.* sǣ, banke. WALLASEY EMBANKMENT, *Leasowe Embankment* 1842 OS, *v.* 333 *infra*.

FIELD-NAMES

The undated forms are 1844 *TA* 261. Of the others, 1280–1320 is Chest, 1340, 1347 *ChFor*, 1350, 1555², 1720 Orm², 1555, 1639, 1775 Sheaf, 1831 Bry, 1842 OS.

(*a*) Caldey Hay (*v.* (ge)hæg, cf. Caldy 282 *supra*); Carr Side Fd (cf. *le car* 1347, *Newton Car* 301 *infra*, *v.* kjarr, sīde); The Clarrell 1775 (*Clauerhill* 1340, *the Clare Hyll*, *Clarehill* 1555, 1555², 'clover hill', *v.* clǣfre, hyll); Common; Cow Hay (*v.* (ge)hæg); The Dean; Green Park; High Fd(s) (cf. *Highfeld Medowe* 1555, *v.* hēah, feld); The Hook (*v.* hōc); Big- & Little Hoose Fd (cf. Hoose 293 *supra*); Horney Marsh; Intake (*v.* inntak); The Meoles Stocks 1720 (tree-stocks of a submerged forest on the foreshore at Meols, *v.* stocc); Marl Yard (*v.* geard); Moreton Pasture 1775 (cf. Moreton 319 *infra*); New Fd; The Nook; Old Garden; Old Yard(s) (*v.* geard); The Paddock, Paddock Park (*v.* pearroc); Rabbit Burrow 1842 (cf. *Warren House* 1831); Rye Fd; Settle Yard (*v.* geard); Summer Hay (*v.* sumor, (ge)hæg); Town Fd & Park (*v.* toun, park); Water Hay (*v.* wæter); The Yard, Yard Fd (*v.* geard).

(*b*) *Crystoresse Hey* 1555 (probably 'Christopher's enclosure', from (ge)-hæg and the ME pers.n. *Christopher*); *Herrottffeld* 1555 ('heriot field', land upon which a heriot was due, *v.* heriot); *Hogekynse Hey* 1555 (from (ge)hæg and the ME pers.n. or surname *Hodgkin*); *le Lytle Holt* 1555 (*v.* lȳtel, holt); *Iagowesmedwe* 1280–1320 ('Iago's meadow', from mǣd and the Welsh pers.n. *Iago* (James), cf. James's Mdw 307 *infra*); *the Parson's Loones* 1639 (*v.* persone, land).

8. LITTLE MEOLS (lost, 100–2188), *Melas* 1086 DB f.264b, and as for Great- & Little Meols 296 *supra*, distinguished as *Parua-* 1200–45 Chest *et freq*, *-Parva* 1629 ChetOS VIII, *Litle-* 1283 Ipm, *Lytle-* 1315 Plea, *Littel-* 1347 ChFor, *Lytel-* 1358 Orm[2], *Litel-* 1383 ib, *Little-* 1361 BPR, 1498 Sheaf, 1724 NotCestr *et freq*, 'the smaller part of Meols', cf. Great- & Little Meols 296 *supra*, v. parva, lȳtel, lítill.

HOYLAKE (100–2189) [ˈhɔileik]

> *Hyle Lake* 1687 Brownbill 315, 1690 Sheaf, 1809 Brownbill 61, *the Hyle-Lake* 1751 Sheaf, *Hylelake* 1762 ib, *Hilelake* 1690 Assem
>
> *High Lake* 1689 Sheaf, 1698 Fiennes 180 *et freq* to 1793 Brownbill 58, *Highlake harbour* 1689 Sheaf
>
> *Hylake* 1709 Sheaf
>
> *Hoyle Lake* 1796 Brownbill 58, 1808 ib 61
>
> *Hoylake* 1813 Brownbill 62

This was the name of a roadstead, now silted up, off the north-west coast of Wirral, east of Hilbre, inside the Hoyle Bank (*Hyle Sand* 1687 Brownbill 315, *Hoyle Sand* 1757 Sheaf, 1808 Brownbill 61, *The-* 1796 ib 57, *Hoyle Sands* 1813 ib 62, *Hoyle Bank* 1806 Sheaf, 1831 Bry, v. sand, banke). It gave name to a hamlet, *Highlake* 1766 Orm[2] II 498, *High Lake* 1794 Brownbill 58, *Hoylake* 1806 Hem II 259, which grew up around an hotel built here for sea-bathers in 1792 (cf. Royal Hotel *infra*). This hamlet, in Little Meols and Hoose townships, expanded in the nineteenth century until by 1882 (Orm[2] II 498) it included those townships and Great Meols. It is now joined in the c.p. of Hoylake and West Kirby. The p.n. and that of the sandbank derive from hygel 'a hillock', ME *huyle*, ModEdial. *hile*. No doubt the sandbank was named 'the Hile', i.e. 'the hill of sand', and the tide-lake inshore of it would be 'the lake at the Hile', v. lake. Metanalysis of *Hile-lake* would produce *High-Lake*. It is merely co-incident geography that this anchorage is probably *lacum de Hildeburghey que vocatur le Heypol* 13 (14) Chest, 'the lake of Hilbre which is called the High-pool', i.e. 'the deep pool', v. hēah, pōl[1].

HILBRE POINT, RED STONES (100–200887), 1842 OS, *the Red Stones near Hoyle Lake* 1819 Orm[2] I 205, *Red Stone (Hill)* 1831 Bry, a reef and promontory at the extreme NW tip of Wirral, *v.* point, rēad, stān, cf. Red Noses 327 *infra*. These rocks marked the seaward limit of the jurisdiction of the port of Chester, cf. Orm² I 205. In 1705, Hem II 321 reports the city sergeant patrolling as far as Hilbre. Although Orm² I 205, 373, II 832 puts it near Chester, it appears very probable (as Morris 529n.) that the Red Stones is the location of the medieval seaward limit, ARNOLD'S EYE (lost) 1819 Orm² *loc. cit.*, (*Arnoldsheyre* E2 (17) Orm², *Arnadesyr'* 1354 (1379) Ch, *Arnaldesire* 1358 BPR, *Arnoldeshere* 1416 Orm², *Arnoldesheir* 1499 Chol, *Arnalds-, Arnoldsheire* 1499 Sheaf, *Arnoldesheire, -hiere* 1499 Orm², *Arnaldesherre* 1506 Morris, 1563 Pat, *Arnoldesheire* 1506 (1507) MinAcct, *Arnalds Eije* 1543 Orm², *Arnoldsheir* 1704 Hem, 'Arnald's islands', from ey (nom.pl. eyjar), ēg, and the OG pers.n. *Arnald*). *v.* Addenda.

CARR LANE, cf. *Carr, Carr Lane Field*, 1844 *TA* and Carr Side 298 *supra, v.* kjarr, lane.   FLATMAN'S GUTTER, a channel in Liverpool Bay off the east Hoyle Bank, *v.* goter.   THE GAP, a way down to the beach, *v.* gappe, cf. foll.   THE KING'S GAP, c.1728 Sheaf, cf. prec., named from the occasion of William of Orange's embarking here for his Irish campaign, *v.* gappe.   LIGHTHOUSE RD, site of *Hoylake Lighthouse* 1831 Bry, *the brick lighthouse . . . at Highlake* 1766 Orm² II 489. There was another, *the low wooden lighthouse* 1766 Orm² loc. cit., *Low Light* 1831 Bry, *Lower Lighthouse* 1842 OS. NEW HALL.   ROYAL HOTEL, 1831 Bry, *The hotel lately erected by Sir John Stanley* 1796 Brownbill 57, *v.* Hoylake *supra*.

FIELD-NAMES

The undated forms are 1844 *TA* 262.

(*a*) Brick Fd; Common; Cornet Hay; Dogs Yard; Green; Horse Hay; Marsh; Paddock (*v.* pearroc); Park; Rotton Hay; Stones Hay; Yord (*v.* geard).

9. NEWTON CUM LARTON, 1650 Sheaf, *Neuton cum Layrton* 1385 *ChFor, Larton cum Newton* 1646 Sheaf, *Newton alias Newton cum Larton* 1847 *TAMap*, cf. Larton, Newton *infra*.

LARTON (100–237871) ['lærtən, 'lɑːrtən]

Layrton 1291 Tax, 1347 *ChFor*, 1349, 1354 *Eyre*, 1385 *ChFor*, *Lairton* 1345 *Eyre* (p), 1516 Plea, 1533 ChRR

Leyrton 1295 Tab, *Leirton* 1584 ChRR
Lareton 1459, 1523 (1571) ChRR
Larton 1517 AD, 1527 (1592) ChRR, 1553 Pat, 1646 Sheaf *et freq*
Laverton 1552 (17) Sheaf
Layton 1557 Sheaf
Park Farm 1831 Bry

'Farm at a clayey place', from leirr and ON tún or OE tūn.

NEWTON (HALL) (100–233877)

> *Neuton* 1278 ChFor, 1281 Court *et freq* to 1724 NotCestr, (*-iuxta
> Upton*) 1317 Plea, *-in Wyrhale* 1345 ib *et freq* with variant
> spellings as for Wirral 1 7 to 1514 ChRR, *le Neuton* 1347 ChFor
> *Neweton* 1291 Tax, 1595 AD (p)
> *Newton* 1295 Tab, 1516 Plea *et freq, -in Wirrall* 1367 (1582) ChRR
> *et freq* with variant spellings *ut supra* to c.1561 ib
> *Nuton* 1695 Sheaf

'New farm', *v.* nīwe, tūn. This was a new settlement early in the
fourteenth century. In 1347 *ChFor* it was reported that Lord Warin
Trussell (*floruit* 10 E 2 (1317–18), Orm² III 229) had made a certain
vill called *le Neuton* within the bounds of the forest of Wirral without
licence and had dug a hundred pits there. His name persists in
Trussels Hay *infra*. The pits would probably be clay-pits, cf.
Larton *supra*.

CHINA FM, so named on account of a circular plate of Liverpool
china ware let into the wall of the house, built c.1748, cf. Brownbill
214.   FORNALL BRIDGE, FORNALLS GREEN (LANE), cf. Fornall(s)
Bridge & Green 298 *supra*, Fornall Mdw 290 *supra*. The bridge
(100–235895) is *Stone Bridge* 1831 Bry, *Fornall Bridge* 1842 OS,
v. stān, brycg. Fornalls Green was a piece of waste on the Great
Meols boundary 100–232892, *v.* grēne². The p.n. appears in a f.n.,
(*the*) *Farno, the Great Fornoe* 1639 Sheaf, perhaps 'old mound', from
forn and haugr, but the material is insufficient for certainty.
LONG RAKE FM, beside *Newton Rake* 1639 Sheaf, *v.* lang, rake, cf.
Rake Ho 290 *supra*.   NEWTON BRIDGE, 1831 Bry, *v.* brycg.
NEWTON CAR (lost, 100–225881), 1842 OS, *Newton Carr* 1552 Orm²,
cf. *Car Meadow* 1639 Sheaf, *Carr Lane* 1831 Bry, 1847 *TAMap*, cf.
also Carr, Carr Lane, Carr Side 290, 300, 298 *supra*, 'the marsh',

v. **kjarr.** This ancient common was about to be enclosed in 1819, Orm² II 491.   OLD FIELDS, a farm, cf. Old Fd *infra.*

FIELD-NAMES

The undated forms are 1844 *TA* 289. Of the others, 1552, 1724, 1814 are Orm², 1552 (17), 1609, 17, 1639, c.1780 Sheaf, 1831 Bry, 1842 OS.

(*a*) Arkee Butts (*The Arcenbutts, two Arkabutts* 1639, *v.* butte); Backside (*v.* ba(c)ksyde); Banakers ('bean acres', *v.* bēan, æcer); Bennetts Yard (1724, *v.* geard); Bradlands Barn (*v.* brād, land, bere-ærn); Brook Hay (1639, *the Brooke Hay* 17, cf. *the Brooke, the Brookefield Hey* 1639, *v.* brōc, feld, (ge)hæg); Coventry Fd (1814, from the surname *Coventry*); The Croft; Cross Lane 1831 (*v.* cros 'a cross'); Little Cubbert (dial. for -*Cupboard*); Dirty Fd; (Far- & Near-) Flatt (cf. *the Great Flat* 1639, *v.* flat); Hassams; The Heath (*Newton Heath* 1842); Heath End (cf. *the Low Heath Ende* 1609, *v.* hǣð, ende¹); Hindertons Hay (*Hinderton* (*Hay*), *Hinderton alias Smith's Plocke* 1639, 'the hindermost enclosure', *v.* hinder, tūn, plocc, cf. Hinderton 223, 258 *supra*); Long Holl; Holmesides (*Holme* 1639, *North-, South Holme* c.1780, cf. *the Home Hadlows* 1639, *v.* holmr, sīde, hēafod-land); Kent Hay; Knave Loons (*v.* cnafa, land); Knowls (*v.* cnoll); The Lays, -Leys (*v.* lēah); Big- & Little Lilly Heath (cf. *two Lilymore Meadows* 1639, *North-* & *South Lillymore Meadow* c.1780, *v.* lítill or lilie, mōr¹, hǣð); Marl Ground (cf. *the Marled Hey* 1639, *v.* marle, marled, (ge)hæg); Mill Hay (*the Mile Hay* 1639, *v.* myln, (ge)hæg); Moreton Hay (cf. Moreton 319 *infra*); Newton Common; Old Fd (cf. Old Fields *supra*, also *Neerer-, Nearer Old Hay, the Old Hays, -Heyes* 1639, 17, cf. also *the Old Hay Brooke* 1639, 17, *v.* ald, (ge)hæg, brōc, feld); Park (*v.* park); Quillet (*v.* quillet(t)); Rags; Sally Carr Lane 1831 ('lane at willow-marsh', *v.* selja, (or late OE salig 'willow', Löfvenberg 176–7), kjarr, cf. Salacres 306 *infra*); Sour Loons (*v.* sūr, land); Town Fd; Towns End, Townsend, (*v.* toun, ende¹); Trussels, Trussels Hay (*v.* (ge)hæg, cf. Newton *supra*); Wet Reans (*v.* wēt, rein). *v.* Addenda.

(*b*) *The Bollones land, William Warrington's* (*two*) *Bollon(s), the two Bollows* 1639, 17 (unexplained, cf. Bollands 311 *infra*); (*the*) *Cowcroft, Cowcrofts Ditch* 17, 1639 (*v.* cū, croft); (*the*) *Hill Field, the Hill Hay* 1639, 17; *Newton Meadows* & *Well* 1639, 17; *the Wall Hay* 1639, 17 ('well field' *v.* wælla, (ge)hæg).

xx. St Oswald's

For the rest of this parish cf. 337 *infra.*

7. HILBRE (100–1987). This township consists of Hilbre Island and Little Eye *infra.* It was a detached part of St Oswald's parish because it was transferred to St Werburgh's abbey Chester from its previous

owners, the abbey of St Évroul (cf. Great- & Little Caldy 282 *supra*) to whom Robert de Rhuddlan had granted it as part of West Kirby manor (and, therefore, parish). In 1882 it was described in Orm² II 501 as an extra-parochial liberty of the parish of St Oswald, following the sale of Hilbre by the Dean and Chapter of Chester in 1856 to the Mersey Docks and Harbour Board. The archipelago may have given rise to the p.n. Caldy, *v.* 283–4 *supra*.

HILBRE ISLAND (100–185885) [ˈhilbri(ː)]

> *Hildeburgheye* 12 Chest *et freq* with variant spellings *Hylde-*,
> *-bur(g)h-*, *-burg(h)-*, *-ey(e)*, *-e(ie)*, *-eghe*, *-aye* to *Hildeburghee*
> 1388 MinAcct, *Hildeburweye* c.1280–1320 Chest, *Hildeburgheye*
> 1545 Sheaf, *Heildeburg- sua Hilbre Island* 1724 NotCestr
> *Hilburghee* 1521 Life
> *Hil(le)-*, *Hylbyri*, *Hilbery* c.1536 Leland
> *Hilbree* 1538 *JRC et freq* with variant spellings *Ilbree, Hillbree*,
> *Hilbry* to 1819 Orm², *Hilbree Island* 1695 Sheaf, *Ilbree Island*
> 1724 NotCestr, *the island of Hilbree* 1819 Orm²
> *Hilbre* 1550, 1552 (17) Sheaf, *Hilbre* (*Island*) 1842 OS, 1882
> Orm²
> (*the Iland of*) *Helbrie* 1575 Sheaf, 1593 Morris, *Helbry* 1584, 1593
> Morris, *-bree* c.1590 Sheaf, 1602 Morris, *Helbree-island* 1656
> Orm², 1724 NotCestr, *Helbrey* 1660 Sheaf, *Helbre Island* 1831
> Bry
> *Elborough* 1891 Sheaf³ 4 (563)

'Hildeburg's island', from the OE fem. pers.n. *Hildeburg* and ēg. The pers.n. may be that of some Anglo-Saxon holy woman, for there was a church on Hilbre from early times. This church was granted to St Évroul by Robert of Rhuddlan before 1081, subsequently becoming a cell of St Werburgh's Chester. The church, its community, and the island are mentioned as *alia* (ecclesia) *prope illum manerium* (West Kirby 294 *supra*) *in insula maris* 'the other church near that manor on an island in the sea' 1081 (12) Ord III 26, *ecclesia de Insula* 12 ib III 281, a.1081 (n.d.) ib v 187, France 221, *monachi de Insula* 1275 P, *quadam Insula prope Wyrhale* 1277 ib, *the Ileland in the parish of Westkirbie* 1592 *JRC* and also as *capella de Hildeburgheye* 12 Chest, *insula de Hildeburghey cum sua capella* c.1287 ib, *prior(atus) de Hyldeburheye* 1280 P, *capella* (*de*) *Beate Marie de Hildeburgheye* 1302 Chamb, 1356 MinAcct, *Hildburghey heremitagium* 1328 Dugd,

a celle of monks of Chester and a pilgrimage of our lady of Hillbyri
c.1536 Orm² II 501, Leland v 55, *a Meace or Celle called the house
of Hilbree and the Ile there* 1538 *JRC*, *the cell of Hillbree* 1819 Orm².
The pilgrimage is probably to be associated with the miracle of the
Constable's Sands, *infra*. There are references to a light in Hilbre
chapel, *luminaria Sancte Marie* 1232–7 Chest, *luminaris in capella
de Hildeburg'* 1277 P, *luminar' Beate Marie in eodem prioratu* 1280 ib,
*elemosina pro luminari inueniendo in cappela beate Marie de Hilde-
burgheye* 1356 *MinAcct*. It may have served as a lighthouse.

CHESTER BAR, *Chester Barre* c.1536 Leland, 1540 Sheaf, *the Barre
of Chester* 1597 ib, the bar across the mouth of the Dee estuary, *v.*
barre.   CONSTABLE'S SANDS (lost), *the constable sondes* 1521 Life.
Bradshaw (EETS LXXXVIII 179–81) reports that William fitz Nigel,
constable of Chester, crossed the Dee Estuary with his army by a
ford created at Hilbre by a miracle of St Werburgh, to rescue Richard
earl of Chester (1109–1119) who was ambushed by the Welsh at
Holywell Fl, and that the place of this miraculous crossing was
known 'to this day' (i.e. 1521) as 'the constable sondes'. In 1842 OS
a shoal off Chester Bar, lying off Rhyl and Colwyn Bay in N. Wales,
is named *Constable Bank*, (*v.* **banke**), which probably preserves the
local tradition. It must be remembered that the sands of Dee are
notorious for their shifting. The historical importance of the Constable's Sands is discussed in Brownbill 29–30, 137, and the possible
relevance of their legend to *Sir Gawain and the Green Knight* in
EENS 19–25.   DEE ESTUARY, *aqua Cestr'* 1320 *MinAcct*, *Dee-
mouth* 1621 (1656) Orm² II 359, *v.* **mūða**. This body of water, and the
sea into which it opens, may be the *Dingesmere* named in *The Battle
of Brunanburh*, *v.* 240 *supra*.   EMESLAKE (lost), 1529 Brownbill
33, Sheaf³ 10, a channel between Hilbre and West Kirby, *v.* **lacu** or
lake, cf. Hoylake *infra*.   HILBRE SWASH, *Helbre-* 1831 Bry, *the
Swash* 1819 Orm² II 498, *v.* **swash** 'a channel across a shoal, a rush
of water', here alluding to the rush of the tide over the Hoyle sands.
HOYLAKE. The Hoylake anciently extended to Hilbre Island, and
was *lacum de Hildeburghey que vocatur le Heypol* 1254–83 (14) Chest,
v. 299 *supra*, cf. *Emeslake supra*.   LITTLE HILBRE ISLAND, *-Helbre-*
1831 Bry, *Middle Island* 1842 OS, 1882 Orm², *v.* **lȳtel**, **middel**.
LITTLE EYE, 1842 OS, *Eye* 1831 Bry, *The Eye vulgo 'ee'* 1882 Orm²,
v. **lȳtel**, **ēg**.   LIME WHARF, 1842 OS, a sandbank off Hilbre, *v.*
waroð.   There were lime-kilns along Dee shore in Caldy and

Thurstaston, *v.* lim.   SALISBURY BANK, a sandbank in the Dee estuary, *v.* banke.   TANSKEY ROCKS, a reef extending south from Little Hilbre Island, perhaps the same as *Old Skey Rocks* 1813 Brownbill 62, probably 'toothed skerry' from ON tǫnn 'a tooth' and sker, with rokke. The other name is 'old reef', *v.* ald, sker. WELSHMAN'S GUT, *Welchman's-* 1842 OS, *v.* Wels(c)hman, gote, a channel in the Dee estuary.

xxi. Overchurch

The ancient parish of Overchurch contained one township, Upton (now included in Birkenhead County Borough).

1. UPTON (BRIDGE, HALL & MANOR) (100–2788)

> *Optone* 1086 DB, *Hopton' in Wyrale* c.1300 *JRC, Opton* 1318 *Eyre,*
> 1347 *ChFor,* 1361 BPR, (*-in Vyrale*) 1321 *JRC*
> *Upton* 1265–91 Chest (p) *et freq* with variant spellings *Hup-,*
> *Upp-, -tone, -ton(a),* (*-iuxta Wodechirche*) 1307 Plea, (*-in*
> *Wyrhale*) 1307 Ipm *et freq* with spellings as for Wirral 1 7 to
> 1567 Orm², (*-iuxta Morton*) 1315 Plea, (*-alias Overchurch*) 1645
> Sheaf, *the Hall of Upton* 1614 Orm²
> *Ouptone* c.1328 CASNS VI

'Farm on a hill', *v.* upp, tūn, hall, cf. Woodchurch 274 *supra*, Moreton 319 *infra*.

KILN WALBY (f.n., 100–281877), 1837 *TA, Gildewalleby* 1321 Plea (PRO, Chester 29, 32 m.7d, a dispute about the pathway leading to it), Sheaf 3 24 (5515), may be 'the house and croft lying beside the spring (*iuxta fontem*)' mentioned 1300–7 *JRC* 1523, and may further be associated with the surname *Gildewelle* of the rector of Woodchurch 274 *supra* in 1288 *ChFor* (PRO, Chester 33, 1 m.12, called *Caldewell* in 1286, ib 2 m.2). The p.n. is 'guildsman's spring', from (ge)gilda (influenced by gildi) and wella, wælla, to which býr has been suffixed. Cf. *Gildwell* n.d. Wo 125. Kiln Walby is beside The Fender. *Gildewalleby* would mean 'farm at *Gildewalle*', or 'farm belonging to one *Gildewelle*'. In either case, the p.n. presents further evidence of the use of *-by* to a late date, cf. Frankby 287–8 *supra*. For the modern form of the name, cf. *Kill Flatt infra*.

OVERCHURCH (HILL) (100–263889), site of the ancient parish church and its circular churchyard, *Ouerchirche* 1345 *Eyre*, *church of Upton in Wirhale* 1354 BPR, *ecclesia de Overchirche juxta Upton* 1370 Orm², *Overchurch(e)* 1535 VE, *Over Churche* 1549 Sheaf, *Overchurch* 1621 (1656) Orm², 1724 NotCestr, (*Upton alias-*) 1645 Sheaf, (*-in Upton*) 1724 NotCestr, *Church upon Upton* 1722 ib, *Church Yard* 1722 ib, 1831 Bry, *Old Church Yard* 1842 OS, *Overchurch or Upton, Overkirk Hill* 1837 *TA*, 'church on a hill', *v.* ofer², cirice, hyll. The Overchurch runic stone in the Grosvenor Museum, Chester, came from this site.

SALACRES (100–273879), a house adjacent to a field *Salacre* 1837 *TA*, on *Salacre Lane* 1831 Bry (100–276870 to 273879), cf. 275 *supra*. The f.n. appears as *Selaker* 1275 Sheaf, *Selakur* 1370, 1411 *JRC* (where it is a *londa*, *v.* land), 'willow acre' from selja and akr, æcer, cf. Sally Carr Lane 302 *supra*.

ARROWE HILL, *Arrow Houses* 1842 OS, cf. *Arrowe Hill* 1846 *TA* 19 also Arrowhouse Fm 262 *supra*.   BRIDGEHEY FM, adjoining *Bridge Meadow* 1837 *TA* on the road to Ford Bridge *infra v.* brycg, (ge)hæg.   BROOKFIELD COTTAGE, named from Arrowe Brook 262 *supra*.   FORD BRIDGE, FORD RD, cf. *Ford Meadow* 1726 Sheaf, 1837 *TA*, *v.* Ford 309 *infra*.   GREENBANK.   HOME FM. LANACRE, 1837 *TA*.   MANOR SIDE.   RAKE LANE (109–271881 to 272870), *v.* rake.   SANDBROOK LANE.   WOOD LANE, 1831 Bry, *v.* wudu.

FIELD-NAMES

The undated forms are 1837 *TA* 311. Of the others 1286, 1294, 1357 are *ChFor*, c.1300, 1307–27, 1370, 1402, 1411 *JRC*, 1364 BPR, 1398, 1726 Sheaf, 1629, c.1666 *AddCh*, 1831 Bry.

(a) Backside (*v.* ba(c)ksyde); Bidstow Mdw (cf. Bidston 308 *infra*); Birda Fd; Blakelands Hay (*v.* blæc, land); Bog Mdw (*v.* bog); Brook Hills; Two Butts (*v.* butte); Chequer (*v.* cheker); Church Hay (*Little Church Hey* 1726, *v.* cirice, (ge)hæg); Corfes Fd (cf. *Colverscroft* 1726, *v.* calver, croft); The Crofts (cf. *The Great Croftes, The Little Croft* c.1666, *v.* croft); Ditch Fd (*Ditch Fields* 1726, *v.* dīc); Drag Hay (cf. *The Gorsye- & The Greate Draggehey* c.1666, from ME dragge 'a harrow' and (ge)hæg); Flatts, Greasby Flatt (*v.* flat, cf. Greasby 291 *supra*); Great Hey 1726; Green Lane 1831; Hall Hill (1726, *The Hallhillfeild* c.1666, *v.* hall, hyll); Hatcha Croft (*the Satchow Croft* c.1666); Heath 1726 (*v.* hǣð); Hop Fd (*v.* hoppe); Hough Holmes (*v.* hōh, holmr); James's Mdw (pratum vocatum *Iames-*

medowe 1402 *JRC*, from mǣd and the ME pers.n. *James*, cf. *Iagowesmedwe* 298 *supra*); Kinga Fd; Marsh, Marsh Mdw (*le Mersh* 1370, *le Merchemedue* 1307–27, *the Marsh Meddow* c.1666, *Marsh Meadow* 1726, *v.* mersc, mǣd, cf. *le Kar infra*); Mill Hay (cf. *Mill Flatt* c.1666, *v.* myln, (ge)hæg, flat); Mill Moat (*Mill Moote* 1726, *v.* mote); Moreton Hay (*-Hey* 1726, *v.* (ge)hæg, cf. Moreton 319 *infra*); New Hay (*Great -& Little Newhey* c.1666, cf. *the Newfeild Meddow* c.1666, *v.* nīwe, (ge)hæg, feld); North and South; Hungry Oxton (*v.* hungrig, cf. Oxton 269 *supra*); Great- & Little Quarters (*v.* quarter); Saughan Fd (cf. Saughall Massie 321 *infra*); School Fd; Town Fd; Vineyard; Warwick Hay (*the Warwicke Hey* c.1666, *v.* (ge)hæg, cf. Margery *de Warrewik* holding land in Upton in 1364 BPR); White Hay; Whitelands Hay (*White Loons* 1726, *v.* hwīt, land, cf. Blakelands Hay *supra*); Wood Hay (*The Wood Hey* c.1666, *v.* wudu).

(*b*) *Barker Hey* c.1666 ('tanner's enclosure', *v.* barkere, (ge)hæg); *the Barley Hey* 1629 (*v.* bærlic, (ge)hæg); *Bulgreuefeld* (?*-grene-*) 1370, 1411 ('(field at) the bull's wood or green', *v.* bula, grǣfe or grēne², feld); *le Kar* 1294, *le Carmedowe* 1370 ('the marsh', *v.* kjarr, mǣd, cf. Marsh *supra*); *The Crosse Tree Flatt* c.1666 ('flat plot with a rood tree in it', perhaps associated with a standing cross like that shown 1831 Bry near Saughall Massie Bridge, *v.* cros, trēow, flat); *The Gorsye Croft* c.1666 (*v.* gorstig, croft); *Hok* 1370, 1411 ('the hook', *v.* hōc. This was a piece of meadow lying in The Marsh, probably a promontory of dry ground, cf. *Saulhoke infra*); *Kill Flatt* c.1666 (*v.* cyln, flat. There were two fields so called, *the Higher-* and *the Lower-*. It is possible they are the same as *the Top-* and *the Lower Kiln Walby* fields (Kiln Walby, *supra*) and this would explain the modern form of Kiln Walby); *la Lee* 1286 (*v.* lēah); *the New Marled Flatt* c.1666 (*v.* marled, flat); *the Marrows Meddow*, c.1666; *le Regges* 1357 ('the ridges', *v.* hrycg); *Saulhoke* c.1300 ('hook of land growing with willows, or at a willow', *v.* salh, hōc, cf. foll. and *Hok, Salacres supra*); *Welynfeld* 1370, 1411 ('field at the willows, or growing with willows, *v.* wiligen, feld); *Vluyngreuefeld* (?*-grene-*) 1370, 1411 (probably '(field near) the she-wolf's wood', possibly '-near the she-wolf's green', *v.* wylfen, grǣfe or grēne², feld); *the Lower Yard* c.1666 (*v.* geard).

xxii. Bidston

The ecclesiastical parish of Bidston contained the townships 1. Bidston cum Ford (now included in Birkenhead *infra*), 2. Birkenhead (an extra-parochial liberty created out of Claughton township to contain the demesne of Birkenhead Priory, chartered as a County Borough in 1877, including Arrowe, Landican, Noctorum, Prenton, Thingwall and Woodchurch from Woodchurch parish 261 *supra*, Upton from Overchurch parish 305 *supra*, Bidston cum Ford and Claughton cum Grange from Bidston parish, and Tranmere from Bebington parish 245 *supra*), 3. Claughton cum Grange (part was in Woodchurch parish, all now included in Birkenhead *supra*), 4. Moreton cum Lingham (now included, with Saughall Massie, in Wallasey County Borough 323 *infra*), 5. Saughall Massie (cf. prec.).

1. BIDSTON CUM FORD, 1724 NotCestr, *Budeston cum le Forde* 1385 *ChFor et freq* with forms as for Bidston, Ford *infra*.

BIDSTON (100–2890)

Bideston 13 Chest, 1272 (1580) Sheaf, 1287 *ChFor* (p) (Barnes[1]), 1407 ChRR (ib), 1459 ChRR, *Bydeston* 1534–47 Dugd, 1545 Pat, *Bidsto . . .* 14 Chest, *Bidston* 1397 ChRR (Barnes[1]), 1430 Orm[2], 1508 *JRC* (Barnes[1]), 1535 VE *et freq*, *Bydston* 1482 ChRR, 1485 Orm[2], 1523 (1571) ChRR, 1660 Sheaf, *Biddeston* 1507 ChRR, *ChCert*, 1523 (1571) ChRR, *Byddeston* 1522, 1549 Sheaf, 1534–47 Dugd

Bediston 1260 Court, *Bedeston* 1291 Tax, 1303 *MinAcct* (Barnes[1]), 1338 Plea, 1342 ChRR (p), 1350 *Eyre*, 1353 *MinAcct*, 1507 *ChCert*, *Beduston* 1343 Sheaf, *Bedston* c.1490 *Surv*, *Bedson* 1646 Sheaf

Bodestan' 1260 Court

Budeston 1260 Court and nineteen examples with variant spelling *Budestona* to *Budeston* 1572 ChRR, *Buddeston* c.1295 (17) Sheaf, 1344 ChRR (p), 1347 *ChFor*, 1354 Orm[2], 1359 ChRR, 1361 BPR, 1624 ChRR, *Budston* 1351 BPR, 1382 Plea, 1385 Pat, 1407 ChRR, 1554 Sheaf

Budestan 1286, 1340, 1347, 1357 *ChFor*, 1345 Plea, 1353 *MinAcct*, 1376 *Eyre*, 1506 ChRR, *Budstane* 1305 Sheaf, *Budstan* 1321 Plea

Bidestan 1288 *ChFor*

Bidelston' 1294 *ChFor*

Bedestan 1309 InqAqd, 1347 *ChFor*, 1348 *MinAcct* (Barnes[1]), 1361 Fine

Boudistan a.1342 Tab (Barnes[1])

Bethestan 1347 *ChFor* (twice)

Boduston 1347 *ChFor*, *Bodeston* 1351 BPR

Bidstone 1521 Sheaf, 1546 Dugd, 1724 *NotCestr*

Beedston c.1642 (17) Sheaf

Bidstowne 1665 *Map* (W.F.I.)

Ekwall (DEPN) proposes 'Byddi's farm' from tūn and an OE pers.n. *Byddi*, a derivative of the OE pers.n. *Budda*. The early *-stan* forms prove that the final el. is stān 'a rock, a stone'. For the first el., the forms *Bidelston'*, *Bethestan* are important, for they rule out the pers.n. derivation. Rather, they suggest that the first el. is (ge)bytle, byðle 'a building, a dwelling', cf. DEPN s.nn. Biddlesden

Bk, Biddlestone Nb, cf. also bōōl, *bylde. The original form of the
p.n. Bidston would be *(ge)byðle-stān or the like, in which -ðles- >
-thels-, and > -dles- > -dels- with subsequent loss of -l-.

Bidston then means 'rock with a dwelling or building near it, on it,
or in it'. This may allude to a cave. There was a cave at Bidston, at
100–285904, cf. Cave Plantation *infra*, but whether this was a natural
feature or an artificial grotto is not clear. The allusion may be to a
house or building upon or against a rock, and the p.n. may be an OE
equivalent of Liscard 324 *infra*. At this point, the forms *Buddeston-
kar(k)* 1347 ChFor, *Bedestoncarre* 1303 MinAcct, etc., under Bidston
Moss *infra*, should be noted, where kjarr 'a marsh' may have been
confused with carr and carrec 'a rock', pointing to the same feature
as the stān in *Bidston*. Finally, it should be noted that Bidston stands
at the north end of a prominent steep, rocky, sandstone hill, Bidston
Hill, a steep slope, with outcrops and cliffs at 100–287903.

Upon considering the draft of this entry, Dr von Feilitzen com-
mented that there were hardly enough forms in *t*, *th* and *l* to support
an etymology in bytle or byðle, only *Bethestan* 1347 and *Bidelston*
1294. He suggests that the origin of Bidston may have been OE
Byden-stān, from byden 'a vessel, a tub' figuratively 'a hollow, a
depression, a valley' (*v.* EPN I 72). He thinks this would suit the
majority of the forms recorded, with normal early loss of -n- or
dissimilation *n—n* > *l—n* leading to *Bideston* and *Bidelston*. This is
a valuable contribution to a difficult problem. It does not explain the
form *Bethestan*, but that is very rare and might be an accident.
However, this alternative solution creates a problem of interpretation, for it is not clear what the el. byden would refer to at Bidston.
If the reference were to some feature of Bidston Hill, the p.n. might
mean 'rock shaped like a tub' or 'rock with a hollow in it'; otherwise the allusion may have been to some stone or rock near a hollow
or tub. I still think that the first etymology is more likely, especially
as it associates Bidston with the adjacent p.n. Liscard, and it accom-
modates the form *Bethestan*.

FORD (BRIDGE) (100–279883), *le Forde* 1353 Eyre, 1357, 1385 ChFor,
1407 ChRR, *the Forde* 1430 Orm², *le Forth* 1522 Sheaf, *the Foord-
bridge* 1621 ib, *the Ford* 1633 ib, *the Foord* 1647 ib, *Forde* 1667 ib,
Ford 1724 NotCestr *et freq*, cf. *Ford Field* 1665 Map (W.F.I.), 1838
TA, *Ford Hill Common* 1838 TA, and also Ford Bridge & Rd
306 *supra*, *v.* ford, brycg, hyll, commun. This ford carried the old

main road from West Kirby to Birkenhead over The Fender. *Ford Hill* was the southern end of Bidston Hill *infra*.

BIDSTON MOSS (100–2891), *mossa de Bideston* 13 Chest, *Bedestoncarre* 1303 *MinAcct* (Barnes[1]), *le Car de Boduston, -Bethestan, -Bedestan, Buddestonkar(k), mosseta de Budestan* 1347 *ChFor, MinAcct* (Barnes[1]), *vastum de Budestan scilicet Budeston' keer, le Car de Budeston, mossetum extendens versus Kyrkeby, le mor* 1357 *ChFor, Bidstone Mosse* 1521 Sheaf, *Mosset, Le Mosse* 1522 ib, *Bidston Moss* 1838 *TA, -or Salt Marshes* 1831 Bry, cf. Leyhall *infra*, and *Moss Hay* 1838 *TA, Moss Hey* 1665 *Map* (W.F.I.), *v.* mos, mōr[1], kjarr. On the forms *Buddestonkar(k), Bedestoncarre*, etc., cf. Bidston *supra*, Bidston Hill *infra*.

WOOTON (lost, 100–292903)

> *Wolueton* 1286 *ChFor* (lit. *Wolne-*), (*boscus de*) *Wolueton* 1347, 1357 *ib, Woluetonwode* 1347 *ib* (lit. *Wolne-*)
> *Welleton* 1286 *ChFor*
> *Wlfeton* 1294 *ChFor*
> *Wolvetone Wode* 1346 Sheaf
> *boscus de Woluerton'* 1347 *ChFor*
> *boscus de Wolleton* 1357 *ChFor, Woltonwod(de)* 1522 Sheaf, (*manor of*) *Wolton* 1537 Orm[2], 1534–47 Dugd IV 242 (lit. *Bolton*), 1545 Sheaf, m16 *AOMB* 397
> (*manor of*) *Wolton alias Wotton* 1572, 1615, 1624 ChRR
> (*manor of*) *Walton* 1624 ChRR
> *Far- & Neere Wooton Hey* 1665 *Map* (W.F.I.), *Far- & Near Wootton Hay* 1838 *TA, Wooton Heys* 1902 Sheaf[3] 4 (589)

'Wulfa's farm', from tūn and an OE pers.n. *Wulfa* (Feilitzen 418), probably a short form for OE *Wulfhere* which lies behind *Woluerton'*, with wudu. The fields, which survived down to c.1902, were the vestiges of a manor of the prior of Birkenhead, *v.* (ge)hæg.

BIDSTON HALL (100–285902), *Bidston, a goodly house* 1621 (1656) Orm[2]. BIDSTON HILL, 1842 OS, *Bidstowne Common, The Towne Common* 1665 *Map* (W.F.I.), *Bidston Common* 1831 Bry, *Ford Hill Common* 1838 *TA, v.* toun, commun, hyll, cf. Ford *supra*. This hill's rocky north end may be given name to Bidston *supra*, and may be the object of the form -*kar(k)* (*v.* carr, carrec 'a rock') among the forms of Bidston Moss *supra*. BIDSTON LIGHTHOUSE, 1831 Bry. FENDER BRIDGE, FENDER LANE (FM), *Fender Wa* 1665 Sheaf, *Fender Lane* 1842 OS, *v.* weg, lane, brycg, cf. The Fender 1 23. FLAYBRICK COTTAGE, *Nut Grove* 1831 Bry, cf. Flaybrick 317 *infra*. LEASOWE RD, LEASOWE SIDE, *Leasowe Side* 1831 ib, *v.* sīde, cf. Leasowe 332 *infra*. LEYHALL, *Moss Cottage* 1831 Bry, *Moss House* 1842 OS, cf. Bidston Moss *supra*. THE PARK (lost, 100–280890 to 280900), *Park Field, Further & North Park* 1838 *TA*, *the Parke of Bidston* 1521 Sheaf, *parcum de Biddeston, le Park* 1522 ib, *parke and grounde at Bidston* 1583 ib, *the upper Parke, Bidston Park, the North Parke* 1644, 1646 ib, *Bidston Park* 1649 ib, *the Deere Parke, Corne Park* 1665 *Map* (W.F.I.), *v.* park. This park had disappeared by 1882, Orm² II 468, except for the remains of a summer-house, cf. *Summer House Hill* 1838 *TA, the summer-house at Bidston* 1683 Orm², *v.* somer-hous. UPTON RD, leading from Birkenhead to Upton 305 *supra*. WALLASEY BRIDGE RD, cf. Wallasey Pool Bridge *infra*. WALLASEY POOL, *v.* 333 *infra*. WALLASEY POOL BRIDGE, cf. prec. WARRINGTONS BRIDGE (lost, 100–295914), *v.* 334 *infra*.

FIELD-NAMES

The undated forms are 1838 *TA* 49. Of the others 1260 is Court, 1288 Orm², c.1295 (17), 1521, 1522, 1644, 1646, 1665² Sheaf, 1347, 1357 *ChFor*, 1353 *MinAcct*, 1354 BPR, 1365 *JRC*, 1665 *Map* (W.F.I.), 1842 *TAMap*.

(*a*) Acre or Springs (cf. *First & Second Acre* 1665, *v.* æcer, spring); Half Acre (1665); Backside (1665, *v.* ba(c)ksyde); Between Banks (cf. *Double Dyke* 1522, a levée near the confluence of The Birket and The Fender, 100–285916, *v.* betwēonan, banke, dīc); Birket Lot (*v.* hlot 'an allotment', cf. The Birket 1 15); Black Mdw (*Blakemede* 1353, (*the*) *Black(e) Meadow* 1644, 1646, *v.* blæc, mæd); Bog Lot (*v.* bog, hlot); Bollands (*Balance* lit. *Valance*) 1522, (*the*) *Bollandes* 1644, 1646, identified by W.F.I., Sheaf³ 4 (589) with ground let to a man named *Bolland* in 1522, but perhaps another instance of *Bollones* 302 *supra*); Brook Hey 1665 (*v.* brōc, (ge)hæg); Brow (*v.* brū); Calf Hay (*Calfehey* 1665, *v.* calf, (ge)hæg); Cave Plantation (a cave is shown in the *Hall Paddock* in Bidston village in 1665 *Map* (W.F.I.), cf. Bidston *supra*); Clay Fd (1665); Corn Hay (cf. *Sandy or Corne Hey* 1665, *v.* sandig, corn¹); Corner Hay (*v.* corner, cf. Kinnerclough *infra*); Deans Mdw (*Deanes Meadow, Dean's Yard* 1665); Field Hay ((*Little*) *Fieldhey* 1665, 'an enclosure in a field', *v.* feld, (ge)hæg); Friz ((*the*) *Frize* 1665); Furze Fd (Dean's-) (*Deanes Furzie Field* 1665, *v.* fyrs); Gregory Hey 1665; Hall Paddock 1665 (cf. Cave Plantation, Bidston (Hall) *supra*); Big Hesby (109–283890 *campus qui vocatur Eskeby* 1357, 'farmstead at a place growing with ash-trees', *v.* eski, bȳr); Hill Hay (*Hillheys* 1665, *v.*

hyll, (ge)hæg); Hoolerake (*Hoolerake Hey & Lane* 1665, 'lane to a hollow, or sunken lane', *v.* hol¹, rake, (ge)hæg, lane. The lane is at 100–287903 to 287905); Horton's Hay (*Hootorns Hey* 1665, probably 'hawthorns enclosure', *v.* hagu-þorn, (ge)hæg); Grass- & Little Hoveacre (*Gresse Ovaker, Little Ovaker, Great Ovaker or Gresse o'bucker* 1665, perhaps 'marsh by the bank of a stream', from ōfer¹ and kjarr; these fields at 100–277893 are beside The Fender); Intake Mdw (*The Intake* 1646, *the Intacke* 1644, *v.* inntak); Kill Calf (*Kilcalfe* 1665); Killhey 1665 (*v.* cyln, (ge)hæg); Kinnerclough (*Corner Hey alias Killins Clough* 1665, *v.* clōh); Lady Mdw (*The-* 1646, *-Ladie-* 1644, *v.* hlǣfdige); Ley Fd (*Layfield or Great Hey* 1665, *v.* lēah); Ley Hook (*le Hoke* 1521, 1522, *Great-, Middle- & Meadow Lee Hooke* 1644, *The Hookes, The Middle Hooks, Great- & Meadow Lee Hookes* 1646, *Middle Ley Hooks* 1665², *v.* hōc, lēah); Little Hay (*Pasture or Little Hey* 1665, *v.* (ge)hæg); Lone End (*Lane End* 1665, *v.* lane, ende¹); Lower Hay (*-Hey* 1665); Marled Hay (*-Hey, -Hay* 1665, *v.* marlede, (ge)hæg); Marsh Lane 1842); New Mdw (*le Newemedewe* 1357, *the New Medow* 1521, *the New Meadow(e)* 1644, 1646, *v.* nīwe, mǣd); Old Wd (*boscus de Bodestan* 1260, *Bidston Wood* 1288 (17), *Bedestanwode* 1347, *boscus de Buddeston* 1347, *Budestonwode* 1354, *Budestanoldewode* 1357, *boscus de Budeston* 1357, 1365, *v.* ald, wudu, cf. Bidston *supra*); Oxholme (*The Oxholme* 1646, *the Oxe Holme* 1644, 'marsh where oxen pasture', *v.* oxa, holmr); Pike Mdw (1644, 1646, *Pykedmede* 1353, *Pykemedewe* 1357, *-Medow* 1521, *le-, -medew* 1522, 'pointed meadow', *v.* pīced, pīc¹, mǣd); Pingle (*The-* 1644, 1646, *v.* pingel); Rie Croft 1665 (*v.* ryge, croft); Rushy Mdw (cf. *The Rushes* 1646, 1644, cf. marsh called *Rysshoke* 1522, *v.* risc, riscuc); Rushy Paddock (cf. *(the) Great- & Little Paddock* 1644, 1646, *v.* pearroc); Sandy Hay (*-Hey* 1665, *v.* sandig, (ge)hæg); School Fd; Sherlock; Short Fd 1665; Springs (cf. *The Spronge* 1665, *v.* spring, 'a well-spring'); Suppers Fd (*Sweperfeld* 1522); Thwaite Lane, The Cornhill-, The Great-, Marled-, Meadow-, Salt-, Spencer's-, Tasseys-, & Whinney Thwaite (*le Thwayt iuxta le Newemedewe* 1357 (an assart made c.1337), *le Thwaytes* 1357, *Oldetwayt* 1357 (assarted c.1337), *Inderthwaite, Utterthwaite* 1522, *the Cornell Thweat(e), the Great Thweat, the Little Thweate, -Thwaite, the (Little) Marled Thweate, the Meadow Thweate, the Salt Thweate, -Thwaite, Tassyes Thweate, the Whinney Thweat(e), The Twaite* 1644, 1646, 'the clearings, *v.* þveit, (cf. Addenda), with ald, grēat, lȳtel, marled, mǣd, salt, whinny and lane. *Cornhill-* is 'corn-hill', *v.* corn¹, hyll. *Tassey* is a surname. *Inder-, Utter-* are 'inner, outer', from ON innar, ūtarr); Town Moss (*Towne Mosse* 1665, *v.* toun, mos); Vorick Hay; Warren (*v.* wareine); Wilcox Mdw 1665.

(b) Calmount, *-monnt* 1347 ('bare hill', *v.* calu, munt); Chestregreue (lit. *Thefte-*) 1353, *le Chestergrenemedewe* 1357 (there is no evidence for a *ceaster* at Bidston so this must be 'meadow at a wood belonging to Chester', *v.* grǣfe, mǣd, cf. Chester 336 *infra*. The place is perhaps associated with the abbot of Chester's unidentified wood in the Forest of Wirral, *boscus de Grescow, -Gresowe, -Groscow* 1357 ChFor, from ON skógr 'a wood', with an unidentified first el. for which Professor Löfvenberg suggests OE grēosn 'gravel' or OE grēot 'gravel' or perhaps rather ON grjót 'gravel, stones'); *le Falles* 1347 ('the fellings', v. (ge)fall); *Grene* 1522 ('the green', v. grēne², the name of a plot of marsh); *le Houndemedow* 1522 ('hounds' meadow', v. hund, mǣd); *Lambrokmede* 1353 ('('meadow at) the lamb brook', probably near a sheep-wash, v. lamb, brōc, mǣd); *le Holdefeld* 1357 (v. ald, feld); *Olurkar, -car* 1347, *Olrecar* 1357 ('alder marsh', v. alor, kjarr); *Patishullcroft* c.1295 (17) (land belonging to Richard de *Patishull*, Sheaf³ 17 p.108, v. croft); *Penny-a-day Dike* n.d. (Sheaf³ 45 (9276), 48 (9686, 9696), a wall round the lost Deer Park at Bidston (Bidston Park *supra*), probably a park pale dug at the stated contract-rate, v. dīc); *le Perotte* 1522 (v. pearroc); *le Pool, Pulsiche* 1353 ('the pool, stream to a pool', v. pōl¹, pull, sīc); *Nethershyte, Ouershite* 1353 ('lower and upper slope', v. neoðera, uferra, scyte '(steep) slope' (Löfvenberg 186–7)).

2. BIRKENHEAD (100–3288) [bə:kən¹ed, ¹bərkən¹ed]

Bircheveth 1190–1216 *AddCh*, *Bircheuet* 1260 Court, *Byrcheved* 1277 Pat, c.1282 (1605) Sheaf, 1291 Tax, 1305 Plea, *Byrcheued* 1318 *Eyre*

Birheuet c.1200 Bark, *Birhefde* 1272–1307 *JRC*

Byrkeheveht 1259 Court, *Birkheued* 1260 Plea *et freq* with variant spellings *Birk(e)-, Byrk(e)-, -heued(e), -heved, -heuid, -hevet, -hefd, -heud* to *Birkheved* 1579 AD, *Birkeved* 1318 Pat, 1361 BPR, *Birkeued* 1356 *Eyre*

Byrkehed 1259 (1286) *ChFor*, 1417, 1553 Sheaf, 1557 Pat, *Birk(e)hed* 1347 *ChFor*, 1353 Dugd, 1364 Orm², 1522 Sheaf, 1527 ChRR, 1535 VE, *Byrkhed* 1512 (1551) ChRR, *Birked* 1558 Sheaf

Berkeheved 1275 Pat

Byrchenid 1277 Sheaf (p), *Birchened* 1325, 1342 ChRR

Birkhened c.1278 (18) Sheaf, Orm² *et freq* with variant spellings *Birk(e)-, Byrk(e)-, -hened, -henid* to *Birkhened* 1615 ChRR

Birkenhed 1278 Dugd, 1462 Orm² and seventeen examples with variant spellings *Birkyn-, Byrken-, -hed(e), -hedd(e)* to 1666 ib, *Birkeenhed* 1400 ChRR, *Birkenheade* 1552 Sheaf, -*head* 1594 ib, 1724 NotCestr *et freq*, *Byrkenhead* 1624 ChRR

Birkened 1278 Dugd, Orm², 1285 (18) Sheaf, 1317 City (p), 1510 AD (p), 1612 Cre (p)

Berkened c.1280 (18) Sheaf

Birchinheuid 1294 *ChFor*

Birhed 1346 Sheaf

Birchumhened 1478 ChRR (p)

Birchynhed 1478 ChRR (p), *Byrchen-* c.1565 (p), 1581 AD (p),

Burchin- 1573 ib (p), *Burchen-* 1574 ib (p), *Byrchinhead* 1574
AD (p)
Birkynhened 1505 ChRR
Byrlehedde 1505 Sheaf
Byrket, Briket c.1536 Leland, *Birket* 1552 Sheaf and six examples
   with variant spelling *-ett* to 1666 Orm[2]
Berkhed 1538 Sheaf
Berkhened 1639 Sheaf
Berked 1649 Sheaf
Berkenhead 1673 Sheaf, 1724 NotCestr
Birket Head 1818 Sheaf

'Headland, promontory, growing with birch-trees', from **birce**
and **bircen**[2] with **hēafod**, influenced by **birki** and **hǫfuð**. The alternative forms of the p.n. are represented by *Bircheveth* (> *Birket*)
and *Birchinheuid* (> *Birkenhead*). The numerous spellings *-hened*,
-henid in the *Birkhened* series, all from printed sources or calendars,
and occasionally matched by unmistakable *-heued, -heved* spellings,
are suspect. They should probably be taken as *-heued, -heuid*. Like-
wise *Birchumhened* is probably for *Birchinnheued*, *Birkynhened* for
Birkynheued, and *Byrlehedde* for *Byrkehedde*. However, in the
many instances where the MSS. have been checked, it has been
found that the *-n-, -u-* form is ambiguous, and the possibility of a
genuine MS. reading *-hened* cannot be dismissed. Such a form
could arise from scribal error or from a popular confusion of the two
original forms of the p.n. such as would account for the ambiguous
Byrchenid, Birchened, Birkened. It may be observed that the form
Birkened is recorded from 1278, not c.1150 as in DEPN.

STREET-NAMES: ABBEY ST., CHURCH ST., PRIORY ST., 1824 *Lawton*, with
OLD PRIORY and ST MARY'S GATE, commemorating Birkenhead Priory
infra; OLD BIDSTON RD, formerly the main road to Bidston 308 *supra*, *v.*
ald; BRIDGE ST., cf. *Bridge End* 317 *infra*; CHESTER ST., 1824 *Lawton*,
the beginning of the road from Woodside Ferry to Chester, called Chester
Old Road in various parts of its course; OLIVER ST., *New Road* 1831 Bry.

BIRKENHEAD POOL (lost), 1824 *Lawton*, *v.* Tranmere Pool 259 *supra*.

BIRKENHEAD PRIORY (100–328885), *Priory* 1831 Bry, *Ruins* and
Church Yard 1824 *Lawton*. This was a priory of sixteen Benedictine
monks, dedicated to St James, founded c.1150 by Hamo de Massey,

third baron of Dunham Massey 2 19 (cf. Saughall Massie 321 *infra*). It is mentioned, with variant spellings as for Birkenhead *supra*, in *the prior of Bircheuet* from 1260 Court, *domus Sancti Jacobi de Birkeheued* from c.1267 CASNS x, *prior ecclesie Sancti Jacobi de Birkeheved* from 1284 *ChFine*, and as *monasterium sive prioratus de Birkhed* 1535 VE, *Byrket a late priory of a xvi monkes* c.1536 Leland, *priorie of Birket* 1552 Sheaf, *Byrkenhead nuper prioratus* 1660 *CroR*, *the priory of Birkenhed in Wirral commonly called Birket-Abby* 1666 Orm², *Birket Head Abby* 1818 Sheaf, cf. *the abbot of Birkheved* 1294 Pat, *-Birkheved* 1333 Cl.

BIRKENHEAD FERRY (lost, 100–330885), 1842 OS, *Ferry House* 1831 Bry, founded in 1819 (J.E.A.), *v.* ferja, hūs. This ferry was defunct by 1882 (Orm² II 464) and *Monk's Ferry infra* was about to close down. BIRKENHEAD HALL (lost, 100–327885, west side of Priory St.), 1824 *Lawton*, 1714 Sheaf, *v.* hall. IVY ROCK (lost), 1824 *Lawton*, a property beside Mersey, south of Woodside, cf. Ivy St. MONK'S FERRY (lost, 100–331887), *The-* 1882 Orm² II 464, established 1838 (J.E.A.), cf. *Birkenhead Ferry supra*. WALLASEY POOL, *v.* 333 *infra*. WIRRAL HO (lost, 100–326889, approximately Duncan St., Brandon St. & Chester St.), 1831 Bry. WOODSIDE FERRY (100–329892), 1842 OS, *the fery house on Wyrale shore* c.1536 Leland, *ferry from Liverpool to Birket Wood* 1628 Sheaf, *the Woodside Boats* 1714 ib, *the Woodside House* 1757 ib, *the Woodside Ferry (House)* 1806 ib, 1824 *Lawton*, *v.* ferja, hūs, bāt, named from the locality *Woodsyde* 1621 ChCert, *the Woodside* 1707 Sheaf, *Woodside* 1818 ib *et freq*, 'beside the wood, the side of the wood', *v.* wudu, sīde, in turn named from the old wood of Birkenhead, *boscus de Birkeheued*, *Birkehedwod* 1347 ChFor, *Berket-wood* 1621 (1656) Orm², 1628 Sheaf, *Birkett Woodd* 1645 ib, cf. (*Lytle*) *Oldwoode Coppes* 1545 ib, *Ouldwoode* 1645 ib, (*Little*) *Wood* 1824 *Lawton*, *v.* wudu, ald, copis. Presumably this was the birch-wood which gave Birkenhead its name. The priory of Birkenhead worked a ferry over Mersey under letters patent dated 1311 (Orm² II 458, 463, cf. 1318 Pat 108, 1330 ib 505) requiring the provision of a lodging-house for passengers.

FIELD-NAMES

The undated forms are 1824 *Lawton*.

(*a*) Bridge Fd (cf. Bridge St. *supra*, *v*. *Bridge End* 317 *infra*); Lancelot Mdw (probably from the surname of the *Lancelyn* family, cf. Poulton *Lancelyn* 250 *supra*); Pea Fd; Robinson's Croft.

(*b*) *Birkeheved fyssheyordys* 1510 Sheaf (*v*. fisc-geard); *James att Pooles Coppes* 1545 Pat, Sheaf ('coppice belonging to James *att Poole*', *v*. copis. The surname is from Wallasey Pool *supra*).

3. CLAUGHTON CUM GRANGE, 1882 Orm², -*come*- 1775 J.E.A., *Claughton cum le Grange* 1453 Orm², cf. Claughton, Grange *infra*.

CLAUGHTON (100–305887) ['klɔ:tən]

Clahton 1260, 1282 Court

Claghton 1272–1307 (1577), (1607) ChRR, 1286 *ChFor*, 1345 Plea, 1353 Dugd, 1361 BPR, 1365 *JRC*, 1378 Pat, 1385 Sheaf, 1455 ChRR, 1510 Sheaf, 1535 VE, 1710 J.E.A.

Clauhton 1282 Court, *Clauton* 1286, 1288 *ChFor*, *Claughton* 1345 Plea, 1353, 1534–47 Dugd, 1545, 1552 Sheaf, 1572, 1615, 1624 ChRR

Clatton c.1282 (1605) Sheaf

Clocton 1291 Tax, ?1335 Pat 129

Clayton (*grange*) 1303, 1348 *MinAcct* (Barnes¹)

Clachton 1346 *ChGaol*

Coton in Wirehall 1519 Orm²

Caughton 1621 (1656) Orm²

Claighton c.1642 (17) Sheaf, 1724 NotCestr

'Farm on a hillock', from klakkr and tūn or tún, cf. DEPN, and Claughton La 162, 178. The manor house of Claughton (*Claughton Farm* 1824 *Lawton*, *Claughton Farm House* 1831 Bry, *Claughton* 1842 OS) stood at approximately 100–305887 at the junction of Park Rd West and Park Rd South. Part of the land belonging to this farm adjoining the Oxton boundary was in Woodchurch parish, *v*. 307 *supra*. *Claytongrange* is Grange *infra*.

GRANGE (lost, 100–310884 at Alfred Rd, cf. st.ns. Grange Rd, Grange Mount), *Claytongrange* 1303, 1348 *MinAcct* (Barnes¹), *grangia in foresta de Wyrhale* 1305 Plea, *le Grange* 1453 Orm², 1739 *LRMB* 264, *The*- 1725 to 1747 etc. J.E.A., *Birket Graunge* 1535 VE, *Graunge* 1705 J.E.A.(p), *the Grange Barne* 1645 Sheaf, *Grange* 1794

ib, *Grange House Farm* 1824 *Lawton, Grange House* 1831 *Bry,*
Grange Farm 1842 OS, part of the demesne of Birkenhead Priory,
v. grange, bere-ærn.

BRIDGE END (lost, 100–320895, at Bridge St., Freeman St. & Marcus
St.), 1776 J.E.A., 1824 *Lawton,* cf. *Bridge Meadow* 1824 *ib, Bridge
End Terrace* (st.n.) 1939 J.E.A., *v.* brycg, ende[1], mæd. *Bridge End
Brook* 1850 J.E.A. was a stream (100–315892 to 323889 to 321895)
falling into Wallasey Pool about the site of Egerton Dock. At Bridge
End it was crossed by the road from Birkenhead Priory and Woodside
to Bidston, now called Bridge St.

FLAYBRICK HILL (lost), UPPER FLAYBRICK RD (100–295895), *the
Flabrick Heays* 1645 Sheaf, *Flay-brick, Further-* & *Lower Flaybrick, Flaybrick Hill Common* 1824 *Lawton, Flaybrick Hill* 1831
Bry, 1842 OS, from brekka 'a hill, a slope' and either flaga
'a slab of stone, a flagstone', or, perhaps more likely, flag 'a turf,
a sod', with (ge)hæg, hyll, commun. The dialect forms *flay, flee*
appear also in the f.ns. *Fleas, Fly's* 322, 320 *infra.*

GILL BROOK BASIN (100–305902), an inlet in the docks, at the mouth
of a lost stream shown 1824 *Lawton* running in a valley 100–298896
to 305902, from near Toad Hole Fm under Flaybrick Hill down to
Wallasey Pool, cf. *the Gill Field* 1645 Sheaf, *Gill Field* 1838 *TA,* and
Gill Brook Plantation, Big & *Little Gill Field, Gill Field Meadow* &
-Moss 1824 *Lawton,* 'brook & field at a dell', *v.* gil, brōc, feld, mos.
Gill Brook is now the name of a housing estate (J.E.A.).

SHARPS HOUSE FM (lost, 100–302893 in Birkenhead Park), 1824
Lawton, cf. *(Higher) Sharp's Meadow* 1824 *Lawton,* 1838 *TA,* from
the surname *Sharp,* found in Bidston parish c.1680 (J.E.A.).

SLATEY RD, *Slatey Lane* 1842 *TAMap,* cf. *the Slate Hey* 1645 Sheaf,
Big & *Little Slate Hay* 1824 *Lawton,* 'sheep pasture', *v.* slæget,
(ge)hæg, lane.

THE TASKAR (lost), 1646 *Harl., Tollescowe* 1259 (1286) *ChFor,
Tollestou* E1 (1347) *ib, Tolscowe* 1286 *ib, Taskelowegreue* 1357 *ib,*
'wood on which a toll or tax is levied', *v.* toll, tollr, skógr, græfe, cf.
Toad Hole *infra. Taskelowe-* is '*Tolscowe*-hill', *v.* hlāw.

TOAD HOLE (lost, 100–297895, on Bidston Ave., opposite Alderney
Ave.), 1746 ParReg, 1842 OS, *TAMap, Toad Hole Farm, Common* &
Field 1824 *Lawton, Toad Hole Field* 1838 *TA,* probably 'fox-hole',

v. **tod-hole,** but a derogatory sense 'toad's hole' is possible, *v.* **tāde.**
R.S.B. judged this to be the site of *The Taskar supra.*

BOUNDARY RD, adjoining Bidston boundary.   LINGDALE HILL, cf.
Lingdale 270 *supra.*   NORTH BIRKENHEAD (lost), 1831 Bry.
OAKFIELD (lost), 1842 OS, *Hookfield House* 1831 Bry, *v.* hōc.
OXTON RD, cf. Oxton 269 *supra.*

FIELD-NAMES

The undated forms are 1838 *TA* 49. Of the others, 1331, 1340, 1347, 1357
are *ChFor*, E1 (1577) ChRR, 1330, 1545, 1645 Sheaf, 1605 J.E.A., 1824
Lawton. Fields of Claughton Fm which were tithed in Woodchurch parish
are marked *.

(*a*) Higher & Lower Backside (1824, *v.* ba(c)ksyde); Barn Hay (1824);
Big Fd (1824); Blackbutts (*-buts* 1824, *v.* butte); Big-, Little- & Long
Broom, Broomfield 1824 (*v.* brōm); Clover Bridge 1824 (*v.* brēc); Common
Croft 1824; Cook's Croft 1824 (*the Cooke's Croft* 1645, *v.* cōc); The Cop
1824 (*v.* copp); Cow Hay 1824 (*the Cow Hey* 1645, *v.* (ge)hæg); Flat Cow
Mdw (*Fat-cow Meadow* 1824, *v.* flatr, cū, mǣd); Cow Pasture (1824);
Cowslip Fd (1824); *Crooked Loons 1824 (*v.* land); Doakers (*Doukers*
1824); Eccles's Fd 1824; *Flook-hay 1824; Four Acres 1824; Gorsty Fd
(*Gorse Field* 1824, *v.* gorstig); Green Fd 1824; Green Hay Brow, Big-,
Grass- & Little Green Hay 1824 (*the Green Hey* 1645, *v.* grēne[1], (ge)hæg,
brū); Grenshes Croft 1824; Hallfield 1824; Lower Heath (1824, *the Low
Heath* 1645, *v.* lágr, hǣð, cf. foll); Heath Fd (1824, cf. *Claghtonheth* 1340,
v. hǣð, cf. prec.); *Heath Hay 1824 (*v.* hǣð, (ge)hæg); *(Big) Hill Top
1824; Hilse Fd 1824 (cf. *Hillefelde Coppes* 1545, *v.* hyll, feld, copis); Further
& Near Holmes Wd 1824 (*v.* holmr, wudu); Holywell Fd 1824 (*v.* hālig,
wella); Horse Pasture 1824; Intake 1824 (cf. *the Intacke Coppes* 1545, *v.*
inntak, copis); Kiln Fd 1824 (cf. *the Kiln Hill* 1645, *v.* cyln, hyll); Lasses
Hays 1824 (100–308900, at Cavendish St. & Wharf; *Lassellesfeld* 1357, *Lassels
Hey* 1646, *Lasles Hey* 1689, from (ge)hæg and feld with the surname of
John *de Lascel(le)s* 1357 ChFor, whose family owned in 1397 a ferry from
Poulton in Wallasey 329 *infra* which landed here); Middle Lay, Big Lays,
Further-, Little- & Near Lays Marsh 1824 (*the Leas* 1645, *v.* lēah); Long
Croft; Long Fd (1824); Long Hay 1824 (*v.* (ge)hæg); Lower Flat (1824);
Low Fields Lane 1842 *TAMap* (a line north from Claughton Fm house,
now lost in Birkenhead Park); Marsh 1824; Meadow Brow 1824; Moat
Croft 1824 (a moat at 100–312895 approximately the corner of Arthur St.
and Price St.; *quoddam peele in Claghton* 'a certain stockade in Claughton'
1347, *the Peele Meadow, the Little Peele Heays* 1645, *Pelehay* (lit. *Pole-*)
1739, *v.* pēl, mote, mǣd, (ge)hæg); Moss, (Little) Moss Hay, Moss Mdw
1824; New Fd (*Higher-* & *Lower-* 1824); New Heath Fd 1824; New Leys
Mdw (*v.* ley); Newby's Mdw 1824 (cf. Henry *Newby* of Woodside, 1681,

1683 J.E.A.); Oat Fd 1824; Owen's Green 1824 (*v.* grēne²); *Oxon Hay
1824 (*v.* (ge)hæg, cf. Oxton 269 *supra*); Parsons Hays 1824 (*v.* persone,
(ge)hæg); Pool Fd 1824; Roscoe's Mdw 1824 (from the surname *Roscoe*);
Rye Grass Fd 1824 (*v.* rye-grass); Sand Croft 1824 (*the Sandcroft* 1645,
v. sand, croft); Sand Mdw 1824; Seals 1824 (*the Sale* 1645, *v.* salh, selja
'a willow'); Seven Acres (Marsh) 1824; Long- & Lower Shoot 1824 (*v.*
scēat); Short Fd (1824); Shrubs 1824 (*v.* scrubb); Slang 1824 (*v.* slang);
Slutch Fd 1824 (*v.* slicche); Smithy Mdw (1824); Soughton (1824, 'boggy
enclosure', *v.* sogh, tūn); Square Mdw 1824; Big Suck Fd (*Big- & Little
Suckfield* 1824, *v.* sugga); Tabins 1824; Top Flat (1824); *Townfield 1824;
Town Pits (1824); Trowster (*Troyter* 1824); Twenty Acres 1824; Higher
& Lower Watch Hay (*the Watts Heath* 1645, *v.* Watch Heath 260 *supra*);
Well Croft 1824; Whetstone Mdw 1824 (between Cook St. and Whetstone
Lane, cf. 260 *supra*, *v.* hwet-stān).

(*b*) *le Blakestrete* 1331, 1347, 1357, *vicus qui ducit versus Cestr'* 1357
('the black paved-road', *v.* blæc, strǣt); *the Blew Morise, Blewmorris Croft*
1645 (*Beaumores Coppes alias Bawmares Coppes* 1545, from copis 'a coppice'
and the p.n. *Beaumaris*, probably a surname); *Bottislowe* (*v.* 271 *supra*);
the Grene 1605 (*v.* grēne²); *the Two Hagges* 1645 (*The Hagge Coppes* 1545,
perhaps 'copse where haws grow', *v.* hagga, copis); *the Hilley Wood* 1645
(*v.* hyll, wudu); *the Hoult* 1645 (*v.* holt); *le Mulne How* 1330 ('mill hill',
v. myln, hōh); *le Raggedestoan* (*v.* 271 *supra*); *Swalewelowe* (*v.* 271 *supra*);
Vlfeldesgrene (?-*greue*) 1340 ('Ulfeld's green or wood', from grēne² or
grǣfe with the gen.sg. of a ME pers.n. form *Ulfeld* from the ON pers. by-
name *Ulfaldi*, or the OE fem.pers.n. *Wulfhild*, cf. Newgate (Chester) 337
infra).

4. MORETON CUM LINGHAM, 1860 White, cf. Moreton, Lingham
infra.

LINGHAM (100–252910) ['lingəm, 'liŋəm], *Langholme Farm & Lane*
1831 Bry, *Lingham* 1842 *TAMap*, 'long marsh', *v.* lang, holmr, cf.
Holme Hay *infra*.

MORETON (100–2689) ['mortən]
    Mortona E1 *JRC*, *Mortone* 1287 Court (p), *Morton* 1272 (17)
      Chest (p), 1291 Tax *et freq* with variant spelling -*tun* to 1534–47
      Dugd, (-*juxta Salghale*) 1322 Orm², (-*Budeston*) 1354 *Eyre*, (-*in
      Wirrall*) 1385 ChRR, *Mortonemassy* c.1328 CASNS VI
    Moreton 1278 Whall, 1310, 1329 Plea, 1325, 1398, 1415, 1512
      ChRR, 1403 Pat, 1408 AD, 1542 ChRR *et freq*, (-*in Wyrhale*)
      E2 *JRC*, (-*in Wirhale*) 1310 Plea, (-*in Worall*) 1601 AD
    Murton 1321 Plea
    Moorton 1377 *Eyre*, 1511 Plea, -*in Woorrall* 1580 Sheaf, *Mooreton
      in Wirrhall* 1589 ChRR, *Mooreton* 1597, 1605 AD

'Farm at a marsh', v. mōr[1], tūn, cf. Saughall Massie 321 *infra*, Bidston, Wirral 308, 167 *supra*. *Mortonemassy* contains the manorial suffix -*Massy*, the *Massey* family of Saughall Massie were also lords of Moreton in the thirteenth century.

BANKFIELD.   BRIDGE HO, cf. Moreton Bridge *infra*.   CHAPEL HILL, *Morton Hill or Chapel Hill* 1831 Bry, site of *Moreton Chapell* 1549 Sheaf, *Morton Chappell* 1645 ib, *Moreton, a chapel in Bidston parish* 1724 NotCestr, an ancient chapel of Bidston parish demolished c.1680–90 (ChetOS VIII 156), v. chapel, hyll, cf. *Motelawe infra*. DANGER LANE, *New Lane* 1842 OS, cf. Sheaf[3] 45 (9262), 49 (9852), LCHSNS VII 279, quoting a local form *Dangkers (or Dankers) Lane*, and counterparts in North Meols and Formby La, suggesting that the final el. is kjarr 'a marsh', v. nīwe, lane.   FENDERLANE FM, cf. The Fender I 23.   GORSE LANE, 1842 OS *Green Lane* 1831 Bry, cf. *The Gorse* 1789 Sheaf, v. grēne[1], gorst.   LEASOWEBANK, LEASOWE RD, cf. Leasowe 332 *infra*.   MORETON BRIDGE, 1842 *TAMap*.   NEW FM, *Pasture Side* 1831 Bry, cf. foll., v. sīde. PASTURE FM & RD, cf. prec. and *The New Pasture, Pasture Part* 1789 Sheaf, *Pasture Lane Bridge* 1831 Bry, v. pasture.   REEDS BRIDGE, FM & LANE, *þe Reedbridge* 1621 Sheaf, *The Reade alias Morton Reade* 1644 ib, *the Reede* 1646 ib, *the Reed's Lane* 1815 ib, 'the reed-bed', from hrēod, with brycg and lane. Reeds Fm is *Long Acre* 1831 Bry, v. lang, æcer.   SANDBROOK LANE, cf. *Sand Brook Field, Sand Brooks* 1838 *TA*, v. sand, brōc.   SEABANK, cf. Wallasey Embankment 333 *infra*.

FIELD-NAMES

The undated forms are 1838 *TA* 49. Of the others, 1286 is ChFor, 1338 Plea, 1359 Orm[2], 1471, 1554 MinAcct, 1789 Sheaf, 1831 Bry.

(a) Backside (v. ba(c)ksyde); Big Gorse; Big Yard (v. geard); Black Looms (v. land); Bottom o' th' Carrs (v. botm, kjarr); Braddow Fd (*the Braddo Field* 1789, probably 'broad allotment', from brād and dāl); Brick Kiln Fd; Broad Hay (v. (ge)hæg); Brook Hay; Brow Fd (v. brū); Bull Dow in town ('allotment where a bull stands, in the village', v. bula, dāl, toun); West Car (Hay) (*the Big West Car* 1789, v. west, kjarr); Chief; Cloddy Butts (v. clodd, -ig[3], butte); Cow Pasture; Craver Hay; Crocket Pasture (*the Cocket* 1789); Cross Lane 1831 ('lane running across', v. cros); Dial Post; Ditch Fd (v. dīc); Dovehouse Yard (v. dove-house, geard); Drake Hooks (v. hōc); Fallins (v. fælling); Flaggs (v. flagge); Flax Hill (v. fleax); The Fly's 1789 (cf. Flaybrick 317 *supra*); Foddering ('muckings', v. dial. *foddering* EDD); Goglands Yard; Goose Green (v. gōs, grēne[2]);

Grayhooks 1789; Over Green (*v.* uferra, grēne²); Great & Little Halthorn, Great Halthorn Mdw (*Hawthorn Hey* 1789, *v.* hagu-þorn, (ge)hæg); Holme Hay, Intake & Itch (*the Holme* 1789, cf. Lingham *supra*, *v.* holmr, (ge)hæg, inntak, hiche); Hop Fd; In Brook; Intake (*v.* inntak); Lackway Hay; Lay Green (*v.* lēah, grēne²); Lingham Daubuttes (*le Dobuttes* 1338, probably 'allocated head-lands', from dāl and butte); Mad Dog Lane; Little Marl Heaps (cf. *the Marled Hey* 1789, *v.* marled, (ge)hæg, marle, hēap); Mill Hay & Moat (*v.* myln, (ge)hæg, mote); (Lower) Morgans (*Higher-* & *Lower Morgan* 1789); Nangrave; Old Fd; Old Mans Hay; Oult Fd (perhaps from holt); Outlet (*v.* outlet); Pocket Hay (-*Hey* 1789, *v.* poket); Press Fd (1789); Prior's Fd (*Priors Heye* 1554 *MinAcct* (PRO, SC6, P & M 45) belonging to Birkenhead Priory, not to St John of Jerusalem as W.F.I. in Sheaf³ 4 (627), *v.* prior, (ge)hæg); Rake Hey (*v.* rake, (ge)hæg); The Roundabout (*v.* 337 *infra*); Sherlock's Fd (cf. Sherlock Lane 330 *infra*); Shrub Fd (*v.* scrubb); Smarl Hay; Stanford(s) Croft; Tail Ends, Tail End(s) Meadow (Lane) (*v.* tægl, ende¹, mæd, lane); Thorney Butts (*v.* þornig, butte); Thornton Butts ('head-lands at thorn-tree enclosure', from þorn and tūn, with butte); Thrush Butts; Town Gorse & Mdw (*The Town Meadow* 1789, cf. *Town Meadow Lane* 1831, *v.* toun, gorst, mæd, lane); Tows (*The Towse* 1789); Triangle (*The-* 1789); Upton Fd (cf. Upton 305 *supra*); West Carr Mdw (*v.* west, kjarr); Wheat Loons (*v.* hwæte, land); Wheel Butts (*v.* hwēol, butte); Wings Hay (*v.* wing); Witharts Hay; Withy Fd (*v.* wiðig); Yord (*v.* geard).

(b) *le Hole* 1338 ('the hollow', *v.* hol¹); *Motelawe* 1471 ('the moot-hill', *v.* (ge)mōt, hlāw. This would probably be near Chapelhill *supra*. It was the name of a house with four carucates of land).

5. SAUGHALL MASSIE (100–2588) [ˈsɔːgəl]

Saham in Wirhallia 1202–29 *JRC*

Saligh' 1249–1323 Chest

Sallechale iuxta Morton' E2 *JRC*, *Salechale iuxta Moreton in Wyrhale* E2 *ib*

Salghale 1309 InqAqd, 1321 Plea, 1365 *JRC*, 1378 Pat, (-*Mascy*) 1322 Plea, *Salghall* 1354, 1401 Orm², 1579 Dugd, (-*Massy*) 1567 Orm², *Salghal Mascy* 1383 ib, *Shalghall Mascy* 1386 ChRR

Salghau 1353 MinAcct, 1357 ChFor, -*Mascy* 1407, 1459 ChRR

Salgham 1385 Pat, 1522 Sheaf, 1534–7 Dugd, Orm², m16 *AOMB* 397, 1553 Sheaf, (lit. *Salgllam*) 1547 *MinAcct*, *Salgham-Massey* 1522 Sheaf

Massey-Soughall 1459 ChRR

Salghton' Massy c.1490 *Surv*, 1523 (1571) ChRR

Saughoughe 1546 Dugd, 1547, 1554 *MinAcct*

Saughall Mascie 1600 AD, -*Massie* 1621 (1656), 1819 Orm², 1831 Bry, -*Massey* 1667 Sheaf, *Saughall* 1724 NotCestr

Saugham Massie 1618 Sheaf, *Saugham* 1647 ib
Saughen Massey 1659 Sheaf, *-Massie* 1662 ib, *Saughan Massey*
1844 *TAMap* 180
Saughaw Massey 1844 *TAMap* 261

'Willow nook', *v.* salh, halh, cf. Saughall 202 *supra.* The manor
was held by Hamo *de Mascy* (*Massey*, *Massie*) in 1309, and earlier.
Many spellings in *-an* appear in transcriptions for *-au*, but *-am* and
its reductions to *-an*, *-en* appears to be unmistakable. This form
derives from either a mistaken interpretation of a Latin acc. *Saham*
(< *Saha*) as a p.n. in ham(m) or from the alternation of final el.
between halh and hamm, or from the manorial affix. The p.n.
enters into Greasby Brook 292 *supra*, cf. Brook Loons *infra.*

BRIDGE COTTAGE, cf. Fornall Bridge *infra.* CARR FM & HO,
CARR LANE (FM), CARR HOUSES, *mossa de Saligh'* 1249–1323 Chest,
Salgham Carr 1522 Sheaf, *Carr House(s)* 1831 Bry, 'the marsh', *v.*
mos, kjarr, hūs. FORNALL BRIDGE, 1842 ib, OS, *v.* 301 *supra.*
GARDEN HEY TERRACE, cf. *Round Garden Hay* 1838 *TA*, *v.* gardin,
(ge)hæg. HERON RD, *Long Rake Lane* 1831 Bry, site of *Herring
House* 1831 ib, *v.* lang, rake, lane. *Herring House* seems to be named
from the fish, but the reason is not known. THE HEYES, *v.*
(ge)hæg. MILL HO, 1831 ib, cf. *The Mill* 1831 ib, *Saughau
Windmill* 1838 *TA*, *Saughall Mill* 1842 OS, *v.* myln, hūs. PUDDLE
HALL (lost), 1838 *TA*, 1831 Bry, cf. *Mud Hall* 1842 *TAMap*, *v.*
puddel. SAUGHALL MASSIE BRIDGE, *Saughall Bridge* 1621 Sheaf,
v. brycg. THREE LANES END, 1842 OS, *v.* lane, ende[1].

FIELD-NAMES

The undated forms are 1838 *TA* 49. Of the others, 1353 is *MinAcct*, 1522,
1560 Sheaf, 1831 Bry.

(*a*) Allbutt Hay; Backside (*v.* ba(c)ksyde); Banakers ('bean fields', *v.*
bēan, æcer); Bar Croft Hay; Black Loons (*v.* blæc, land); Bottom Hay
(*v.* botm, (ge)hæg); Brick Hay; Broad Mdw; Brook Loons (*v.* land, cf.
Greasby Brook 292 *supra*); Bull Dow (*v.* bula, dāl); Cally Shoot (*v.* scēat);
Clay Fd; Corn Hay (*v.* corn[1]); Coup Hay; (The) Duan(s), Broad Duan,
Duan Back, Fd & Mdw ('the dunes', *v.* dūn); Fleas (*v.* Flaybrick 317
supra); Land Pool (*v.* land, pōl[1], cf. *Landpul* 200 *supra*); Leay Fd(s), Ley
Fd (*le Leefeld* 1522, *v.* lēah, feld); Little Close Hay (*v.* clos, (ge)hæg);
Great Marled Hay (*v.* marled, (ge)hæg); May Green; Near & Far
Mestils; Moory Flaggs (*v.* mōr[1], -ig[3], flagge); New Lane 1831; Old Carr

Mdw (*v.* kjarr); Outground (*v.* ūte, grund); Outlet (*v.* outlet); Oven Hay (*v.* ofen, (ge)hæg); Pellitan Hay; Quillet (*v.* quillet(t)); Rush Mdw; Sandland Hay (*v.* sand, land); Sandy Hay; Saughall Fd & Mdw (cf. Town Fd *infra*); Six Hay; Sour Butt (*v.* sūr, butte); Thistle Hay; Town Field Lane, Town Mdw (cf. *Town Field* 1831, cf. Saughall Field *supra*, *v.* toun); Ufilys Brow, Lower Ufilys; Werritt Hay & Mdw; Whitelands Hay (*v.* hwīt, land); Wimbricks (adjoining Wimbricks 293 *supra*, *v.* hvin, brekka); Withinhay (*v.* wiðegn, (ge)hæg); Yard Hay (*v.* geard, (ge)hæg).

(*b*) *Prykefeld* 1353 ('prickle field', *v.* pricca, feld, presumably growing with briars or thistles).

xxiii. Wallasey

The ecclesiastical parish of Wallasey contained the townships 1. Liscard, 2. Poulton cum Seacombe, 3. Wallasey. It is now included, with Moreton cum Lingham and Saughall Massie from Bidston parish 307 *supra*, in the County Borough of Wallasey, chartered 1910.

WALLASEY (parish, cf. Wallasey (township) 332 *infra*)

Walea 1086 DB

Waleie 1096–1101 (1150), 1150 Chest, *Waleia* 1175 Facs, *Waley* 1096–1101 (1280) Chest *et freq* with variant spellings -*eya*, -*eye*, -*e*(*y*), -*ej*, -*ay* to 1555 Orm², *Waleh* 1199–1216 *AddCh* (p), *Valeye* 1294 ChF

Wallea 13 *AddCh*

Walleye 1259 Court (p), 1262 Whall (p), c.1280 Sheaf, 1374 (p), 1351 BPR, *Walleya* 1312 Tab, *Walley* 1421 ChRR, 1428 Sheaf, 1439, 1594 Orm², Sheaf, 1621 (1656) Orm², -*alias Walleyseye* 1639 Sheaf

Weyeleye 1284 Ipm, *Welee* 1429 Orm²

Walessy 14 Chest, *Walesse* 1507 ChRR

Waleyesegh 1351 BPR, *Walayesegh* 1363 Orm², *Waleysegh'* 1364 Chol, *Waleysee* 1391 ChRR

Waylayesegh 1363 Orm²

Waleseye 1377 *Eyre*, *Walesegh* 1416 Sheaf, *Walesee* 1429 ib, 1439, 1459, 1460 ChRR, 1659 Sheaf, *Walesey* 1523 (1571) ChRR, 1579 Dugd, *Walesy* 1531 Sheaf, *Walese* 1512 Orm², 1562 Sheaf

Wallasegh 1418 ChRR, *Wallasay* 1514 *ChEx*, *Wallase* 1522 Sheaf, *Wallasey* 1545, 1646, 1659 ib, *Wallaseye* 1614 Orm²

Walsey c.1490 *Surv*, 1621 (1656) Orm²

Wallese 1507 ChRR, 1546 Dugd, 1553 Pat, 1579 Dugd, 1819 Orm², *Walleseye* 1614 ib, *Wallesey* 1657 *Clif*
Wallessey 1507 ChRR
Walase 1522 Sheaf
Walezey 1534–47 Dugd, 1557 Sheaf, 1592 *JRC*, *Walezy* 1537 Orm², *Walezeys* 1549 Sheaf
Wallezey 1534–47 Dugd, 1554 *MinAcct*, 1572 ChRR, 1593 Morris, 1724 NotCestr, (*Kirkebie Walley alias-*) 1598, 1600, 1604 AD, *Wallezie* 1594, 1608 Sheaf, *Walleze* 1550 *MinAcct*
Walize 1535 VE
(parish of) *Kyrkbye Walley* 1539–47 Dugd, *Kyrkeby-*, *Kirkeby-*, *Kirkebie Walley alias Wallezey*, *-Wallazey* 1598, 1600, 1604 AD
Wallesl(e)y 1558 Pat
Wallazey (*Kirkeby Walley alias-*) 1604 AD, *Wallazie* 1663 Sheaf
Wallizey 1624 ChRR
Walleyseye (*Walley alias-*) 1639 Sheaf
Wallisey 1684 Sheaf
Wallowsy 1721 Sheaf, *Wallosy* 1727 ib

'The island of *Waley(e)*', from ēg and the gen. (*v.* -es²) of the p.n. *Waley(e)* 'Welshmen's-, or Britons' island', from walh (gen. pl. wala) and ēg. In former times, at high tide and in time of flood the *Waleye* would be connected to Wirral only by the sand-hills along Leasowe, when the Wallasey Pool and the marshes along The Fender would form an arm of the Mersey estuary. The p.n. Wallasey properly denotes the geographical region contained by R. Mersey, The Fender and the Irish Sea. The village called Wallasey 332 *infra*, takes its name from the region which was co-terminous with the parish.

1. LISCARD (100–3092) ['liska:rd], LISCARD HALL, HO & LODGE (lost)

Lisnekarke 13 *AddCh*, *-carke* c.1260 Sheaf, *-caryc*, *-caric* E1 *AddCh* 51436 (Sheaf³ 46 (9384) reads *-carte*), *Lysnechark in Waley* m13 *AddCh*, *Lisenecark* 1260 Court, *Lysene-* 1307 Plea
Liscerke 13 (17) Sheaf³ 17
Liscak 1260 Court
Liscark 1260 Court (p) (lit. *Listark*), E1 *JRC*, 1347 *ChFor*, 1358, 1372 Plea, 1385 *ChFor*, 1425, 1462 Plea, *Lisscarke* 1271 *ChFor* (p), *Lyskark* 1307 Plea, *Lyscark* 1307 Ipm, c.1320 *Chol*, 1347 *ChFor*, 1348 *AddCh*, 1354 Orm² (lit. *Lystark*), 1359 ib, 1361

BPR, (*-in Wyrrall*) 1388 ChRR, *Liskarke* 1329 IpmR, 1468 Plea, *Liskark* 1355 BPR, *Lyscarc* 1417 Sheaf

Lisecark 1260 Court, 1288 ChFor, *-carck* E1 *AddCh*, *-kark'* 1347 *ib*, *Lysecark* 1349 *Eyre*

Lisecair c.1277 AD, *Lisecare* n.d. ib (A193)

Lymskarke 1294 ChF, 1302, 1305 Orm²

Lysenker 1295 Lacy, 1306 *MinAcct*

Lesynker 1305 Lacy, 1307 *MinAcct*

Liskard in Waleye 1350 Orm², *Liskard* 1439 ib, 1511 Plea and sixteen times with variant spelling *Li-*, *Lyskard(e)*, *Lyscard*, *Liscard* (from 1558 Pat) to *Liscard House & Lodge* 1831 Bry, *Liscard Hall* (*Farm*) 1841 *TAMap*, 1842 OS

Luscard 15 Orm², *-card(e)* 1529 ChRR

Lyscart 1417 Orm², *-e* 1555 Sheaf, *Liskarte* 1437 ChRR, (*-in Walesee*) 1439 ib, *Liscarte in Walesee* 1439 Orm², *Liscarte* 1555 Sheaf, Orm², *Liscart* 1440 (1460), 1460 ChRR, 1594, 1663 Sheaf

Luscark 1425 Plea, *Luskark(e)* 1493 Orm², *Luskark* 1530 Plea

Lyscar 1455 ChRR, *-carre* 1455, 1527 ib, *Liscar* 1459, 1523 (1571) ib, (*-in Walesee*) 1460 ib

Lyscer c.1490 *Surv*

Luscart 1516 Plea, 1533 ChRR

Lycard 1558 Orm²

Liscert 1602 *AddCh*

Liskatt 1604 AD, *Liskett* 1614 Sheaf

Liscarie 1629 Orm², *Lyscarye alias Lyscard* 1639 Sheaf, *Lyscurye alias Lyscard, -Liscard, Lyscarye* 1639 Orm²

Liscarth 1663 Sheaf

Lister 1727 Sheaf

'Hall at the rock', PrWelsh **lis ən garreg, v. *lisso-* (*llys* Welsh), **en* [ən] def.art. (an early form parallel to Cumbric **en*, MCorn and MBret *en* (**sindos* Brit, but *ir* OWelsh), cf. Jackson 657 and 10 (also 10 n.2)), carrec (*carreg* Welsh). The p.n. is discussed by Ekwall DEPN and ES 64 ii 322, cf. also IPN 1 30. On the type of p.n. compound and the form of the first el. (a vowel represented by OE *-i-*, *-y-*) see Jackson 226 n.2, 285. The site of Liscard Hall, 100–312914, is now in Central Park. The original manor house was probably elsewhere, cf. Old Manor *infra*. The rock in the p.n. may have been one of the reefs at Black Rock or Red Noses, or

Yellow Noses *infra*, but it could well have been an outcrop, or the whole, of the rocky hill on which Liscard lies, cf. Stoneby Drive *infra*.

BLACK ROCK or PERCH ROCK (local, Sheaf³ 48) (100–308947), ROCK CHANNEL & LIGHTHOUSE (in Liverpool Bay), *the Rock Channel* 1762 Sheaf, *Rock Perch Battery & Lighthouse* 1831 Bry, *Black Rock Lighthouse* 1842 OS. Orm² 11 480 reports that about 1828 a new fort of considerable strength was built on the rock near what was formerly known as *the Rock Perch*, v. perche. The perch was a navigation-mark. The reef which gives name to the lighthouse, the fort and the sea-channel, and perhaps even to Liscard *supra*, is called *The Black Rock* 1683 Sheaf³ 48 (9807), formerly *le skere* 1274–81, 1278–81 *JRC*, *Swarteskere* 1300–7 *ib*, 1308 Misc, *Squartesclure* 1309 ib, *Swerdeskere* 1351 BPR, 'the black skerry', v. svartr, sker, blæc, rokke. The colour must be due to seaweed growths, for the stone ought to be red or yellow, cf. Red Noses *infra*. It was the limit of the port of Frodsham, v. 1308 Misc 46, 1309 Misc 53, 1351 BPR III 7, cf. *le Wormehole infra*. In the Rock Channel, beside the reef, was a fishery called *Hoysterlak* 1274–81 *JRC*, *Hostirlach* 1275 (18) Sheaf, *Hoysterlake* 1278–81 *JRC*, *Hosterlake* c.1280 (18), c.1285 (18) Sheaf, 'the oyster stream or pool', from ME (h)oystre (NED from 1357, cf. OE ōstre BTSuppl) and lacu or lake. Another, called *Pulyord sub Swarteskere* 1300–7 *JRC* ('fish-trap in a creek', v. pull, geard, cf. fisc-geard), was an appurtenant of Tranmere manor. In Sheaf³ 49 (9189, 9842) it is noted that 'Fishyards'—basket traps—used by Wirral fishermen had blocked the navigation of Rock Channel in 1762, and that they were dredging oysters in Rock Channel in the eighteenth century, at Hoylake in 1754, and taking oysters in Mersey in 1773.

HOSE SIDE RD, OARSIDE DAIRY FM (lost, 100–303929), and HOSESIDE 333 *infra*, *le Houe* E1 AddCh, *the Hose* 1809 Sheaf, also *How Side* 1831 Bry (Mount Pleasant Rd), 'the (side of the) hill or ridge', v. hōh, sīde.

BRECK HEY, 'enclosure on a hillside', v. brekka, (ge)hæg. BRIDGECROFT RD, *Bridge Croft* 1841 *TA*, *the Brysse Croft* 1536 (17) Sheaf, *le Bruches* E1 AddCh, 'the intakes', v. bryce, croft.   BURBO BANK, in Liverpool Bay, *Burboe* 1762 Sheaf, *Burbo Banks, Burbo Sand* 1831 Bry.   CAPTAIN'S PIT, 1841 *TA*, v. pytt, cf. *le Merebut infra*.   CHURCH LANE & ST., *Church Street* 1841 *TAMap*, from St John's church, v. cirice.   THE CLIFF, v. clif, a steep bank over

The Red Noses *infra*. EGREMONT (FERRY & PROMENADE), *Egremont* 1831 Bry, *(Ferry)* 1841 *TAMap*, *North Egremont* 1842 OS (cf. Egremont 330 *infra*), a nineteenth-century development, perhaps named after Egremont Cu. GREEN LANE, 1841 *TAMap*, *v.* grēne[1]. LISCARD VILLAGE, the old village-street, *v.* village. MAGAZINE BROW & LANE, MAGAZINES PROMENADE, the site of *Powder Magazine* 1831 Bry, *Magazines* 1841 *TA*, 1842 OS. MANOR LANE & RD, named from Liscard Hall, *v.* maner. MILL LANE, cf. 330 *infra*. MOUNT FM (lost, Rake Lane and Earlston Rd), 1831 Bry. MOUNT RD, cf. *Mount House* 1831 ib, *Mount Pleasant* 1842 OS and Mount Pleasant Rd (*v.* Oarside). NEW BRIGHTON, 1841 *TAMap*, *New Brighton Ferry* 1842 OS, a seaside resort developed in the nineteenth century and named after Brighton Sx. A *Ferry House* is shown in 1831 Bry, 1841 *TAMap*, near Vale Park. THE OLD MANOR (100–305390, Earlston Rd, site subsequently Earlston Library), cf. Liscard Hall *supra*, *v.* ald, maner. RAKE LANE, 1841 *TAMap*, cf. *Rakehey* 1841 *TA*, *v.* rake, lane, (ge)hæg. RED NOSES (100–298940), 1831 Bry, *the Red Stones* 1660 Sheaf, rocks on the old shore of the Irish Sea, cf. Liscard *supra*, *v.* rēad, stān, nōs(e), cf. Yellow Noses *infra*, Red Stones 299 *supra*. The colours are those of the mottled Bunter Sandstones and Pebble Beds also exposed at Hilbre and Black Rock, which are bedded in red and yellow layers. RICEHEY RD, RICE LANE, *Rice Hey* 1563 (17) Sheaf, *close called The Rise* 1654 *ParlSurv*, 'the brushwood', *v.* hrīs, (ge)hæg, lane. SANDFIELD RD, *Sand Field* 1841 *TA*, *Sandye Feild* 1654 *ParlSurv*, *v.* sand, sandig, cf. foll. SANDHEYS (RD), 1841 *TAMap*, near to *Sand Field* 1841 *TA*, cf. prec., *v.* sand, (ge)hæg. SEABANK RD, *Sea Bank* 1804 Orm[2], *Seal Bank* 1831 Bry, *v.* sǣ, banke. STONEBY DRIVE, *Stonebank Hill* 1831 Bry, *Stonebark, Stone Bark* 1841 *TA*, *TAMap*, *v.* stān, banke, berg, bjarg, hyll, cf. Liscard *supra*, which may have its name from this rocky hill. STRINGHEY RD, cf. *le Strynge* 1398 *AddCh*, *Stryng lond* 1563 (17) Sheaf, from strengr 'a watercourse'. VALE PARK & DRIVE, *Liscard Vale* 1831 Bry, a dell opening upon the bank of Mersey, *v.* val. WITHENS LANE, *Withan Lane* 1841 *TAMap*, *Withins* 1841 *TA*, 'the withies', *v.* wīðegn, wīðigen, lane. YELLOW NOSES (100–301942), rocks on the old shore of the Irish Sea, *v.* geolu, nōs(e) cf. Red Noses *supra*. ZIGZAG RD, cf. 'site of Zig Zag Hall' 1841 *TAMap*, 1842 OS, origin not ascertained, perhaps from some pattern of decoration on the house.

FIELD-NAMES

The undated forms are 1841 *TA* 241. Of the others E1, 1398 are *AddCh*, 1413, 1563 (17) Sheaf, 1654 *ParlSurv*, 1831 Bry.

(*a*) Bank Hey (*v.* (ge)hæg); Bridge Yard (*v.* brēc, geard); Cambrick Hay (perhaps from kambr 'a ridge', brekka 'a hill-side, a brow'); Dunland Hey (*the Dunland* 1563 (17), either 'selion on a hill' or 'brown selion', from dūn or dunn and land, with (ge)hæg); Flagg Fd (*v.* flagge); Golacre (*le Goliacr'* 1398, 'cheerful acre', from æcer, akr, and ON góligr (cf. ME *gollī, golike*) 'gay, joyful, beautiful, fine'); Hat-, Hotacre Hey; Knot Croft (*le Knot* E1, a selion, 'the hill', *v.* knǫttr, cnotta); Longland Hey (*v.* lang, land); Loons (*v.* land); Mill Fd (cf. *Liscard Mill* 1831 (100–306933, Mount Pleasant Rd and Sandrock Rd) *v.* myln); Moor Hay, -Hey (*the Moore* 1654, *v.* mōr[1]); Peartree Butts (*v.* butte); Pinfold (*v.* pynd-fald); Ransacre Hay, -Hey; Rowlands Croft (cf. *ii landes and iii hollandes called Rowlandes and Rowlandes Hollandes* 1563 (17), 'the rough selions, the head-lands at the *Row-lands*', *v.* rūh, land, hēafod-land); Sand Hills; Slip Acre; Ton Acre; Town Fd & Hey; Wallacre ('well acre', *v.* wælla, æcer); Warm Grove Hey (*the Warmegreve Hey* 1563 (17), 'warm wood, sheltered wood', *v.* wearm, grǣfe, (ge)hæg); Big-, Little Yard, etc. (*v.* geard).

(*b*) the (*Bothome*) *Brode Lau(n)d* 1563 (17) (*v.* botm, brād, land); *Camacre Hollandes* 1563 (17) ('head-lands at *Camacre*', from hēafod-land and a f.n., 'acre at a ridge', *v.* camb, æcer); *the Croft* 1654 (*v.* croft); *Crosse Acres Land* 1563 (17) (*v.* cros, æcer, land); *the Flaxe Croft* 1563 (17) (*v.* fleax, croft); *le Gatebut* E1 ('selion near a road', *v.* gata, butte); *Heiefeld* (*v.* 331 *infra*); *the Hill* 1563 (17) (*v.* hyll); *Melse Land* 1654 ('sand-hill selion', *v.* melr, land); *le Merebut* E1 (either 'selion at a pool', from mere[1], or '-at a boundary', from (ge)mǣre, *v.* butte. Sheaf[3] 46 (9384) suggests that the *mere* was Captain's Pit *supra*); *Poulton Field & Lane* 1654 (cf. Poulton (Fd) 329, 331 *infra*); *Richards Feild(es)* 1654; *Sexacres* 1563 (17) (*v.* sex, æcer); *The Shambrook(e)s* 1654 '(narrow brook-fields', *v.* skammr, brōc); *le Sheuelebrod'* E1 (Sheaf[3] 46 (9384) reads *Scheuelbrod*; probably 'the shovel's-breadth selion', with *e* for *o* by scribal error, *v.* scofl-brǣdu); *Sucyker Holland* 1563 (17) (perhaps 'head-land at *Sixacres*', *v.* hēafod-land, cf. *Sexacres supra*); *Wourmebuttes* 1563 (17) (perhaps 'selions full of worms', *v.* wurm, butte, but the name may be older, cf. foll.); *le Wormehole* 1413 ('the serpent's, the dragon's hole', *v.* wurm, hol[1]. This was a limit of the port of Frodsham, cf. Sheaf[3] 28 (6234), 29 (6375), therefore probably near Black Rock *supra* or on the Irish Sea shore, perhaps a cave). *v.* Addenda.

2. POULTON CUM SEACOMBE, *Pulton and Secum* 1361 BPR, *Pulton cum Secum* 1385 *ChFor et freq* with spellings as for Poulton, Seacombe *infra*, *Pulton et Seacum in Walley* 1421 ChRR, -*waley* 1483 Orm[2], *Puton Secam* 1563 (17) Sheaf, *Pulton Secum* 1574 Orm[2], *Poulton Seacombe* 1659 Sheaf.

PoULTON (100–3091) ['poultən] formerly ['puːtən, 'puːltən]

> *Pulton* 1260 Court *et freq* with variant spelling *-tone* to 1637 Orm², *-in Walay* E1 *JRC, -in Waley* 13, c.1277 AD *et freq* with spellings as for Wallasey 323 *supra* to 1483 ChRR, *-in Waleysee* 1391 ib *et freq* with spellings as for Wallasey, *-iuxta Secum* 1425 Plea, *-in Wyrehall* 1561 ChRR, *that other Pulton called by the name of Seacombe* 1621 (1656) Orm²
>
> *Pulton' Walay* 1278 ChFor, *Pulton' Waley* 1307 Plea, *Pulton Waley* 1387 *Eyre*
>
> *Poulton in Waley* 1307 Plea, *-in Wallesly* 1558 Pat, *Poulton* 1637 Orm², 1639, 1659 Sheaf *et freq*
>
> *Polton* 1347 *ChFor*, 1354 (17) Orm², 1582 ChRR
>
> *Poton* 1558 Orm², c.1642 (17) Sheaf
>
> *Puton* 1563 (17) Sheaf
>
> *Poolton* 1718 (1724) NotCestr, 1831 Bry, 1842 OS

'Farm by a creek', *v.* pull, tūn, named from its being beside Wallasey Pool 333 *infra*, formerly a great tidal inlet from Mersey.

SEACOMBE (100–3290) ['siːkum]

> *Secumbe* 13, c.1277 AD, *-in Waleye* 1301 Chamb[1], *Secoumbe in Waleye* 1302 Chamb, *Secoumbe* 1356 *MinAcct*
>
> *Secom* 1303 Chamb (p), 1347 *ChFor*, 1354 BPR, 1438 Orm², 1523 (1571) ChRR, 1537 Orm², (*-in Walesee*) 1441 ib, *Secome* 1304 Chamb, 1459, 1523 (1571) ChRR, 1534–47 Dugd, (*-in Walesee*) 1460 ChRR
>
> *Secum in Waleye* 1304, 1306 Chamb, *-in Wallesie* 1460 Orm², *Secum* 1354 (17) ib, 1356 *Eyre*, 1361 BPR, 1385 *ChFor*, 1425, 1462, 1516 Plea, 1533 ChRR, 1558, 1574, 1637 Orm², 1639 Sheaf
>
> *Seacum* 1421, 1455 ChRR, 1468 *MinAcct*, 1483 Orm², 1659, 1663 Sheaf, *-in Walley* 1421 Orm², *-in Walesee* 1439 ChRR, *-in Waley* 1483 ib
>
> *Seacom* 1505 ChRR
>
> *Seacoum* 1515 *MinAcct*
>
> *Seykym* 1538 Orm²
>
> *Secam* 1563 (17) Sheaf
>
> *Seycom* 1558 Pat
>
> *Seycon* 1560 Sheaf

Seacombe 1659 Sheaf, 1724 NotCestr, (*Higher-*) 1831 Bry, *Seacomb* 1673 Sheaf
Sacom c.1724 Sheaf
'Valley by the sea', *v.* sǣ, cumb. The cumb was probably the dale at Oakdale *infra*.

SEACOMBE FERRY (100–325907), 1842 OS, 'the ferry of *Secom* across the river *Mersee*' 1354 BPR, *passagium de Seacum* 1468 *MinAcct*, -*Seacom* 1505 ChRR, -*Seacoum* 1515 *MinAcct*, -*Secum* 1516 Plea, 1533 ChRR, -*Seycon* 1560 Sheaf, *v.* ferja.

BRECK PLACE, *Breck Hey* 1839 *TA*, cf. Breck Road 333 *infra*, *v.* brekka, (ge)hæg.   CINDER LANE, probably metalled with cinders, *v.* sinder.   CREEK HO, CREEK SIDE, named from a lost creek off Wallasey Pool, *v.* ModE *creek*.   EGREMONT, 1842 OS, *v.* 327 *supra*.   EAST-, WEST & GREAT FLOAT, parts of the docks in Wallasey Pool, *v. float* 'a dock or place where vessels may float', NED 1840.   GORSEY LANE, *v.* gorstig.   GUINEA GAP (100–323913), a valley opening upon the shore of Mersey through a gap in the cliff, *v.* gappe, cf. King's Gap 300 *supra*. The origin of the first el. is not known. Unless there is some topical allusion, it may be ginnel, 'a narrow passage'.   LIMEKILN LANE, *v.* limkilne. LITHERLAND COTTAGE (lost) 1831 Bry, probably named after Litherland La.   LOVE LANE, a courting-place name, *v.* lufu, lane. MANOR FM.   MILL LANE, cf. *Mill Hey* 1839 *TA*, *Poulton Wind Mill* 1663 Sheaf, also *le Rake Mylne*, *infra*, *v.* myln, wind-mylne, (ge)hæg.   OAKDALE (RD) (100–316908), *the Dale* 1563 (17) Sheaf, *Dale Hey* 1839 *TA*, cf. *Oak Cottage* 1842 OS, 'the valley', *v.* dæl¹, (ge)hæg, cf. Seacombe *supra*.   ORREL COTTAGE (lost), 1831 Bry, probably named from Orrell, La.   POOL COTTAGE (lost, Poulton Rd and Adelaide St.), *Greenfield Cottage* 1831 Bry.   POULTON HALL, *Manor House* 1831 Bry.   POULTON LODGE OR HEATH COTTAGE (lost, Oxton Road, Claughton Drive and Poulton Rd), *v.* loge, hǣð.   SHERLOCK LANE, probably from a surname, cf. Sherlock's Field 321 *supra*.   SMITHY LANE, cf. *Smithy Hey & Butt* 1839 *TA*, *v.* smiððe, (ge)hæg, butte.   WALLASEY POOL, *v.* 333 *infra*.   WHEATLAND LANE, *Whiteling Lane* 1815 Sheaf, cf. *Whiteland Hey* 1839 *TA*, *Wheatland Place* 1831 Bry, either 'white land' or 'white heath', from hwīt and lyng or land.   WILLOW LODGE (lost, Victoria Rd and Church Rd), 1831 Bry.   WINTERHEY AVENUE,

Winter's Hey 1839 *TA, the Winter Hey* n.d. Orm[2] II 477, 'enclosure used in winter', *v.* winter[1], (ge)hæg.

FIELD-NAMES

The undated forms are 1839 *TA* 324. Of the others 1260 is Court, E1 *JRC*, 1842 OS, c.1260 and the rest Sheaf.

(*a*) Apple Ditch Hay (*Apodyche Holland* 1563 (17)); Backside (*v.* ba(c)ksyde); Bank Hay (*Bank Hey* 1650, *v.* banke, (ge)hæg); Black Butt Hay (*v.* blæc, butte, (ge)hæg); Brier Ridge (*le Brereacher* E1, *the Brerege* 1563 (17), 'brier acre', *v.* brēr, æcer. This form shows the same assibilated palatalisation in æcer as Alsager 3 2); Butlands Hay (*v.* butte, land); Cockbutt; Crook Hay (*v.* krókr); Cross Looms (*v.* cros, land); Cuff Hay (*the Caffe Hey* 1650, 'calf enclosure', *v.* calf, (ge)hæg); Duckfield Hay; Farland Hay (*le Fairrehallond* E1, 'the fairer head-land', *v.* fǣger, hēafodland); Fatan Hay; Flook Hay; Gorsty Hay (*v.* gorstig); Gravelland Hay (*v.* gravel, land); Greedy Butt Hay (*v.* grǣdig, butte); Hook Hey, The Hooks (*The Hooks* 1842, *v.* hōc); Money Part; Pikey Loons (*v.* pīc[1]); Platkin Hay; Poolton Fd (cf. Poulton *supra*, Town Fd *infra*); Renwell Hay (*Randolf Hey* 1650, from (ge)hæg with the ME pers.n. *Randolf, Randle*); Shebsters Mdw; Sitch (*v.* sīc); Slang (*v.* slang); Still Land Hay; Sunderland Hay (cf. *Sundridnedland super Pultonling* c.1260, 'the separated head-land', from OE *ge-syndrod*, pa.part. of *ge-syndrian*, 'to separate' and hēafod-land, the *-n-* representing an old wk. inflection. *Pultonling* is 'Poulton heath', *v.* lyng. Cf. sundor-land); Town Fd; Twistle Hay (from twisla 'a fork'); Yards End (*v.* geard, ende[1]).

(*b*) Bottynbrydge Pykes 1563 (17) ('pointed selions at the bottom intake', or '-at the bottom bridge', or 'the bottom pointed-selions-', from botn and brēc or brycg, with pīc[1]); *the Brade Butt at the Dale* 1563 (17) (*v.* brād, butte, cf. Oakdale *supra*); *Lower Broad Hey* 1650 (*v.* brād, (ge)hæg); *the Ferry of Pulton* 1565 (Sheaf[3] 43 (9085)) suggests this was a crossing of Wallasey Pool, cf. *Tokesford* 335 *infra*); *Harde Buttes* 1563 (17) (*v.* heard, butte); *Heiefeld* 1260 (Court 29, 217, a field held to be in Liscard but found to be in Poulton, 'hedged- or fenced-field', *v.* hege, feld); *Pultonling* c.1260 (*v.* Sunderland *supra*); *le Rake Mylne* 1555, -*Milne* 1594 ('mill by a lane', *v.* rake, myln, cf. Mill Lane *supra*); *Redd Londes* 1563 (17) (*v.* rēad, land, cf. Red Lound Hey 334 *infra*); *le Schortefeld* E1 (*v.* sc(e)ort, feld); *Stokkeland* 1563 (17) ('land, or a selion, full of stocks', *v.* stocc, land); *the Stywey Croft* 1563 (17) ('croft near a path-way', *v.* sty-way, (cf. stīg, weg), croft); *the Swellyng Londes* 1563 (17) ('the swelling lands', *v.* swelling, land, probably selions which broadened or rose higher towards one end. OE swelgend is hardly applicable here); *Tottyes grounde* 1563 (17) (from the surname *Totty, v.* grund); *Wrynkilsiche* E1 ('watercourse with a twist in its course', from sīc and ME wrinkel 'a wrinkle, a winding', (NED c.1420), cf. OE *gewrinclod(e)* pa.part., 'winding' BT, 'serrated' BTSupp, and *wrinkled* NED); *Wychehard* E1 ('enclosure at a dairy-farm or a manufactory', *v.* wīc, geard).

3. WALLASEY (township, cf. Wallasey (parish) 323 *supra*) (100–2992) ['wɔləsi]

> *Kirkeby in Waleya* c.1180–1245 Chest *et freq* with variant spellings *Kirk(e)-*, *Kyrk(e)-*, *-bi(e)*, *-by(e)* and *Waley(a)*, *-ey(e)*, *-ay*, *Walley* to *Kyrkbye in Waley in the parisshe of Walezey* 1534–47 Dugd, m16 *AOMB* 397
>
> *Kirkeby* 1254 Cl, 1352 BPR (p), 1523 (1571) ChRR, *Kyrkeby* c.1320 *Chol, Kirkby* 1354 Orm², *-bye* 1539–47 Dugd
>
> *Kyrkeby Waley* E1 Orm², *Kirkeby-* 1398 *Add et freq* with variant spellings *Kirk(e)-*, *Kyrk(e)-*, *-by(e)*, *-bi(e)*, and *-Wal(l)ey* to *Kirkby Walley alias Wallesey* 1657 *Clif*
>
> *Kyrby-Walley* 1439 ChRR, 1513 Plea, (1585) ChRR, *Kirbie-* 1553 Pat, *Kyrby-Waley* 1439 Orm²
>
> *Kirkeby in Walesee* 1459 ChRR, *-Walesey* 1523 (1571) ib, *Kyrkby in Walsey* c.1490 *Surv*
>
> *Kyrkeby-Walesee* 1459 Orm², *Kirkeby-Wallasey* 1545 Sheaf, *Kirkby Walase* 1522 Sheaf, *-Walleseye* 1614 Orm²
>
> *Kyrkewalese* 1512 Orm², *Kirkewalesee* 1512 ChRR
>
> *Walesey village* c.1536 Leland, *Walesey in the parysshe of Kirkby Walley* 1539–47 Dugd, *Wallasey* 1545 Sheaf, 1831 Bry, *Wallezie* 1579 Sheaf, *Wallezey* 1598 AD, Sheaf, 1600, 1604 AD, 1624 Orm², 1649 (1724) NotCestr, *Wallazey* 1604 AD, *Walsey* 1621 (1656) Orm², *Walleyseye* 1639 Sheaf, *Wallesey* 1657 *Clif*
>
> *Kerkebie Walley* 1594 Sheaf, *Kerkby Walley* 1629 Orm²
>
> *Kirby in Walley or Walsey* 1621 (1656) Orm²
>
> *Walley's Kirk* 1718 (1724) NotCestr

'Church-village in Wallasey', from kirkju-býr and the district-name Wallasey 323 *supra*, which distinguishes this place from West Kirby 294 *supra*. Orm² II 472 notes that *Kirkeby in Waleia* or *Kyrkeby Waley* is the 'uniform designation' in the Lichfield episcopal registers down to 1487 when it is written *Walesey*. Obviously, the village of *Kirkby*, in which the parish church of Wallasey stood, has gradually taken the name of the parish.

LEASOWE (RD) (100–280920) ['li:zou], *Wallezy Leasow* 1703 *Chol*, *Wallasey Leasowe* 1831 Bry, *the Leasowes* 1812 Sheaf, *the Leasowe* 1815 ib, 1819 Orm², 'the meadows', v. lǽs (dat.sg. lǽswe), cf. The Hooks, Wallasey Pastures *infra*. Here, along the sea-shore, were

Leasowe Sand Banks 1842 OS, *the Sand Hills* 1815 Sheaf, 1841 *TA,*
Sand Hill Cottage 1831 Bry, *v.* sand, banke, hyll.

LEASOWE CASTLE, MOCKBEGGAR HALL (109–264918), *Mock Beggar*
Hall 1690 Orm², *the New Hall by Wallasey Race* 17 Sheaf, *the New*
Hall 1770 Orm², *Leasowe Castle* 1802 ib, *a manor house formerly*
called New Hall, afterwards Mock Beggar, and now Leasowe Castle
1819 ib, a sporting lodge with an octagonal tower (*v.* castel(1)),
built in 1593 at the earl of Derby's race-course here (*the horse-races*
at Wallasey in Wirral 1683 Orm², whence the famous Derby
Stakes, now run at Epsom Sr, *v.* ras) *v.* mock-beggar, nīwe, hall, cf.
Leasowe *supra.* Orm² II 474 ascribes the name *Mock-Beggar* to its
lonely delapidation after the Civil War.

WALLASEY POOL, *le Pull* c.1280 (18) Sheaf, *le Pulle* 1357 *ChFor,*
Walypole 1347 *ib, Walaypull* 1357 *ib, Wallesey Pool* 1819 Orm², 'the
creek', an inlet from the Mersey estuary, *v.* pull, cf. Wallasey 323
supra.

BRAZIL BANK, 1831 Bry, a sandbank in Liverpool Bay off Wallasey
and Liscard, *v.* banke.   BRECK RD, *le Brecfeld* c.1280 (18) Sheaf,
le Brekkes 1331 *ChFor, Wallasey-breck* 1815 Sheaf, (*The*) *Breck* 1841
TA, 'the hillside', *v.* brekka, feld, (ge)hæg, geard.   CHURCH HILL,
cf. *Kirkway* 1718 (1724) NotCestr, a disused approach to a lost church
called *Lee's Kirk* (ib), *v.* cirice, hyll, weg.   FOLLY GUT & LANE,
v. folie, gote 'a drain, a gutter', lane.   GREEN LANE, 1841 *TA.*
HEATHBANK, 1842 OS, *v.* hǣð, banke.   THE HOSESIDE, HOSE SIDE
RD, *How Side Farm* 1831 Bry, *Hose Side Field* 1841 *TA, Oarsides*
1842 OS, *v.* 326 *supra.*   MILL LANE, cf. *Mill Hey* 1841 *TA, v.* 330
supra.   MOCKBEGGAR WHARF, 1757 Sheaf, a sandbank off the
Wallasey shore, named after Mockbeggar Hall *supra, v.* waroð.
SANDIWAYS RD, SANDY LANE, cf. *Sandy Hey, Sandfield* 1841 *TA.*
also *Sandfield Hall* 1842 OS, *v.* sand, sandig, feld, (ge)hæg, lane,
SLOPES, *Poolton Field or Slopes* 1841 *TA, v.* slope.   SPRING HALL
(lost), 1831 Bry.   STONE HOUSE (RD), *v.* stān, hūs.   TOWNFIELD
LANE, cf. *Townfield Ground* 1714 Sheaf, *Town Field* 1841 *TA, v.*
toun, feld.   WALLACRE RD, *Wallacre* 1841 *TA,* a tract of marshland
beside the old course of The Fender, probably 'Waleye-carr', i.e.
'Wallasey marsh', from kjarr and the p.n. *Waleye* (Wallasey).
WALLASEY EMBANKMENT, *Leasowe Embankment* 1842 OS, a sea-

defence protecting Leasowe *supra* and Bidston Moss and the Wallasey Pool basin, against tidal inundation. WALLASEY HALL (lost, Church Hill), 1831 Bry, *the hall of Wallasey* 1659 Sheaf, *v.* hall. WALLASEY MILL (lost, near St Hilary Brow), 1831 Bry, 1842 OS, *v.* myln. WALLASEY PASTURES (lost, 100–275915), 1831 Bry, *Wallasey Pasture, Pasture Gates* 1794 Sheaf, *Pasture* 1841 *TA*, allotments of pasture-land in Leasowe *supra*, *v.* pasture, gata. From *TA* 409 it seems the *Leasowes* were north of Leasowe Rd, the *Pastures* south of it. WALLS HOLE (lost, 100–297939), 1831 Bry, an inlet on the old sea-shore near the Red Noses rocks 327 *supra*, perhaps the same as *le Wormehole* 328 *supra*. WARRINGTON'S BRIDGE (lost, 100–295914), 1842 OS, said to be the site of *pons desuper Pulton*, 'the bridge above Poulton', c.1280 (18) Sheaf³ 44 (9156). *Warrington* is a surname.

FIELD-NAMES

The undated forms are 1841 *TA* 409. Of the others 1272–81, 1278–81, l13 are *JRC*, 1306 *AddCh*, 16 *AOMB* 408, 1718 (1724) NotCestr, 1629, 1724 Orm² and the rest Sheaf.

(a) Black Butts (*v.* butte); Braddy Fd, Brady Field Hey; Cop Fd (*v.* copp, cf. foll.); Cope Grave (from grǣfe 'a wood', with copp 'a bank' or coppod 'pollarded'); Crook Hey (*the Near-, the Turn Crook Hey* 1724, *the Nar-, the Tum Crook Hey* 1718 (1724), *v.* krókr, (ge)hæg, trun); C(r)ushes Mdw; Delph Hey (*v.* (ge)delf, (ge)hæg); Ditch Hay, -Hey; Endridge (*v.* ende¹, hrycg); Fearney Flat (*v.* fearnig, flat); Flook Hey; Foss's Hey; Gorse Lane; Hand Staff; The Hooks (*Lesswehock* c.1280 (18), 'leasowe hook', *v.* lǣs, hōc, cf. Leasowe *supra*); Intake (*v.* inntak); Kettle Well Garden (*v.* ketill, wella. Presumably there was a spring or well here which swirled like a kettle of water, or which filled a kettle); Lawn (*v.* launde); Liscard Hey (*v.* (ge)hæg, cf. Liscard 324 *supra*); Locker Hey (*v.* loca); Lumpy; Marl(ed) Hey; Marsh; Meadow Spot (*v.* spot); Moor Hey; Old Fd (*le Aldfyld* c.1285 (18), *v.* ald, feld); Old Hay (*v.* (ge)hæg); Poolton Fd (*Pulton Feld* 1555, *Pulton Feild* 1594, *Poulton Feild* 1639, *Poulton Feilde in Walley* 1629, *v.* feld, cf. Poulton (Fd) 329, 331 *supra*); Poplady; Quillet (*v.* quillet(t)); Red Lound Hey (*le Redelond* l13, cf. *Redd Londes* 1563 (17) 331 *supra*, *v.* rēad, land); Rush Hey (cf. *le Crok Rishmedes, infra*, *v.* risc, (ge)hæg); Salt Croft, Salt Hay, -Hey, Saltway Mdw, Salty Fd (*v.* salt, saltig, croft, (ge)hæg, mǣd, referring to tide-washed land up Wallasey Pool); Sparrow Croft; Stanish or Lower Hay; Stock up Butt Hey; Stone Bark (*v.* stān, berg, bjarg); Stony Rake (*v.* stānig, rake); Three Nook Cake; Vineyard; Wardsmeer; Widmu(s)s; Wynny Hey (*v.* hvin, -ig³, (ge)hæg).

(b) *le Blodgreueland* 1278–81 ('(selion at) the bloody wood', from blōd and grǣfe, with land, though the meaning is not apparent); *the Clynsse* 1642 (the plural of dial. *clint* 'a projecting rock', cf. klint); *le Crocishind* c.1280 (18) (perhaps 'the end-' or 'the head of the crook', from krókr with ende[1] or hēafod); *le Croc Rishmedis de Kirkeby* c.1280 (18) ('the crooked rush-meadows' or 'rush-meadows at a crook', v. krókr, risc, mǣd, cf. prec. and Rush Hay *TA supra*); *le Foule Pul* c.1285 (18) ('foul pool', v. fūl, pull); *Havenanhishacker* c.1280 (18) (perhaps originally æcer with a pers.n.); *Holesiche* 1278–81 ('stream in a hollow', v. hol[1], sīc); *Neteli Croft* c.1285 (18) ('nettly croft', v. netelig (not recorded before *nettly* 1825 NED), croft); *le Rake* 1278–81 ('narrow lane', v. rake); *Routheholm* 1306, *le Rugh' hollome* 16 ('red marsh or island', from rauðr and holmr); *Seurydas alfland* 1272–81 ('Sigríðr's half-selion', from the ON fem.pers.n. *Sigríðr* and half-land); *le Scheperake* 1278–81 ('the sheep lane', v. scēp, rake. Sheaf[3] 32 (7128) reports forms *Shipwrack, Shipwreck* 17, 18, in unspecified documents); *Tokesford* 1397 ('Tóki's ford', from the ON pers.n. *Tóki* and ford. This was a crossing of Wallasey Pool, v. Sheaf[3] 43 (9085), 44 (9111), cf. Toxteth La 115).

INDEX OF CROSS-REFERENCES

References in Part IV of *The Place Names of Cheshire*, to names and topics contained in Part V. Township- and parish-names are cited simply; other names are followed by the name of the township or parish in which they lie.

INDEX OF PARISHES AND TOWNSHIPS
IN PART IV